# THE TIMES
# GOOD UNIVERSITY
# GUIDE 2003

### in association with

# PRICEWATERHOUSECOOPERS 🄿🄦

# THE  TIMES
# GOOD UNIVERSITY
# GUIDE 2003

in association with

PRICEWATERHOUSECOOPERS 🔲

Edited by
John O'Leary

with
Andrew Hindmarsh
Bernard Kingston

## TIMES BOOKS

Published in 2002 by Times Books
HarperCollins Publishers
77–85 Fulham Palace Road
Hammersmith
London W6 8JB

This edition has been produced in association with PricewaterhouseCoopers.
To find out more about undergraduate opportunities with PricewaterhouseCoopers,
please visit their website: www.pwcglobal.com/uk/sidp/

The HarperCollins website address is www.**fire**and**water**.com/GUG
Copies of this book can be ordered through this website.

First published in 1993 by Times Books
Tenth edition 2002

ISBN 0–00–712648–4

**Acknowledgments**
We wish to offer our personal thanks to the many individuals who have helped
with this edition of *The Times Good University Guide*. To Nicola Bright who, once
again, has lent her very considerable statistical expertise to the rigour of the
Tables, to our colleague, Alison Patterson for her assiduous research, to Ana
Kingston for sharing professional insights, to Jonathan Waller for his technical
advice, to Christopher Riches for his editorial and publishing expertise, and to
Kim Bridges of PricewaterhouseCoopers, our sponsors, for her generous interest
and support.

Please see pages 15–16 for a full explanation of the sources of data used in the
League Table. The data providers do not necessarily agree with the data aggregations or manipulations appearing in this book and are also not responsible for
any inference or conclusions thereby derived.

Printed and bound in Great Britain by
Clays Ltd, St Ives plc

# Contents

## About the Authors

John O'Leary is the Education Editor of *The Times*, having joined the paper in 1990 as Higher Education Correspondent and assumed responsibility for the whole range of education coverage in 1992. Previously the deputy editor of *The Times Higher Education Supplement*, he has been writing on higher education for more than fifteen years. He has a degree in politics from the university of Sheffield.

Andrew Hindmarsh is Planning Officer at the University of Nottingham, where his responsibilities include providing management information and statistical returns to official bodies. Until 1998 he was head of the Undergraduate Admission Office at the University of Sheffield, where for ten years he worked closely with admissions tutors and UCAS. He has degrees in zoology and animal behaviour from the university of Oxford.

Bernard Kingston is now a university consultant, having been Director of the Careers Advisory Service and latterly Director of International Affairs at the University of Sheffield. He is a past president of the Association of Graduate Careers Advisory Services and has advised governments and universities in Asia, Africa, Australia and the UK. He has degrees in chemistry from the universities of Leicester and Sussex.

Andrew Hindmarsh and Bernard Kingston are Partners in Mayfield University Consultants, who have compiled the main University League Table and the individual subject tables, as well as contributing six chapters.

# How to Use
# This Book

*T*he *Times Good University Guide 2003* provides a wealth of information to help you select the courses and universities of your choice and to guide you through the whole process of applying to study at university.

### Which are the best universities?
The place to start is the main *Times League Table* on pages 23–29. This ranks the universities by assessing their performance not just in their teaching and research but also through another seven factors, including the student–staff ratio and the spending on student facilities. This table gives an indication of the overall performance of each university. Each measure used in making the assessment is described in the pages that precede the table.

It is also important to read *Chapter 2*, which provides an invaluable introduction to the many aspects of selecting an appropriate university for you.

### Which are the best universities for particular subjects?
*Chapter 3* provides guidance on how to start selecting courses that you are interested in. It is a good introduction to *Chapter 4*, which gives detailed information on 62 different subject areas, where universities appear in ranked tables, with our assessment of the top universities for each subject. Background information is given about the subject, along with the latest data on what graduates did on completion of the courses. The notes on pages 46–8 explain the data that is included within these tables.

By using both the subject tables and the main university league table, you can begin to narrow down your search for appropriate universities.

### What is each university like?
*Chapter 9* devotes two pages to each university, giving a general overview of the institution as well as data on student numbers, how to contact the university, the accommodation provided by the university, and the quality of teaching. There are also profiles of the main university towns in *Chapter 10*, complete with travel information and websites for further information.

### As an international student, how do I choose?

In addition to using all the data on universities and subjects, *Chapter 7* is devoted to the needs of international students. As well as providing practical advice for students coming to the United Kingdom, this chapter gives details of the most popular subjects and the most popular universities attended by international students, so helping further in the selection of a university.

### How do I apply?

*Chapter 5* outlines the application procedure for university entry. It starts by advising you on how to complete the UCAS Application Form, and then takes you step-by-step through the process that we hope will lead to your university place for Autumn 2003.

### How much will it cost?

*Chapter 6* provides advice on the costs of studying at university (including the payment of fees) as well as sources of funds (including student loans). Additionally, the range of charges for accommodation are given in each university profile in *Chapter 9*.

### How do I find out more?

In each university profile (pages 201–411) contact details are given (including e-mail addresses and websites), so you can obtain more information on any university you are interested in. More help is provided in the *Glossary and Websites* section (pages 438–41) which lists many appropriate websites for students, while a further listing (pages 433–7) provides contact details for Higher Education Colleges which are not covered within the book.

We hope you find the information presented in the book useful in planning for your university career. If you have any suggestions for further information you would like to see, please send them to: *The Times Good University Guide*, Reference Department, HarperCollins Publishers, Westerhill Road, Bishopbriggs, Glasgow G64 2QT or contact us through our website, www.fireandwater.com.

# Introduction

Every year since *The Times Good University Guide* first appeared, in 1993, changes have been made to reflect developments in higher education, the availability of more relevant statistics or constructive criticism from readers. But all the previous modifications pale beside those in the current edition.

Not only are four more universities included in the new guide but, for the first time, rankings cover all 62 subject areas in British higher education. In addition, a more sophisticated method has been used to compare institutions. Like the comparisons published by Government advisers, the main League Table takes account of the different mix of subjects in universities. By allowing for the higher proportion of first-class degrees in the sciences, for example, the system is better able to compare like with like.

Other developments, such as the results of the 2001 Research Assessment Exercise, disguise the effects of the new methodology. But there can be no clearer illustration of its impact than the first change of leadership in the overall ranking of universities. Albeit by the slimmest of margins – one that would not be regarded by experts as statistically significant – Oxford takes pride of place for the first time.

The first *Times* League Table effectively produced a dead heat between Oxford and Cambridge, with the light blues a fraction ahead. Now roles are reversed: only three points out of 1,000 separate the ancient rivals. Cambridge has the better record in teaching and research assessments, which are the most heavily weighted elements in our rankings, but extra spending on computing and student facilities combines with the 'benchmarking' system to give Oxford the lead.

For most readers, the scramble over a handful of points at the top of the overall ranking of universities will be literally academic. The key information is contained in the subject tables, which, for the first time, cover every area of higher education. Only in the past year has the Quality Assurance Agency completed teaching assessments in the nine subjects which have produced a full set. Here at last is the ranking for economics, which has been in such demand, not to mention politics, classics and the growing area of sport and tourism.

Ironically, however, the belated completion of that first round of assessments also marks the end of the process in universities. Only those departments which registered poor scores previously will be inspected in future. While reports will still be compiled for the moment in Scotland, students looking for objective information on English universities will have to rely on much more general audit reports. Only further education colleges will continue to undergo teaching quality assessments of the type that has been the norm over the past decade. And even they will switch to a lighter touch eventually if their grades are consistently good.

University vice-chancellors succeeded in persuading ministers that the assessment arrangements were wastefully bureaucratic and expensive without pointing up significant differences in quality. Grades had drifted inexorably upwards as academics learnt what was required to satisfy the system. Instead of devising a better method of external assessment of individual courses, the vice-chancellors and the national bodies responsible for quality and funding in higher education decided that universities should be responsible for their own quality assurance. The audit system, which will begin in February 2003, will ensure that internal arrangements are reliable, but will only 'drill down' to a sample of subjects.

To compensate for the absence of detailed reports, universities will have to publish particular statistics – some of which are already available nationally – as well as surveys of student opinion and summaries of external examiners' reports. The statistics will cover areas such as drop-out rates and the destinations of students, but some of the information will refer to whole universities rather than to individual subjects. The switch has been overwhelmingly popular among academics, who resented the previous system, but the new system is unlikely to be as effective at pointing up the gems (or duds) in unexpected places.

One of the strengths of this guide and others like it has been to highlight the quality of hitherto underestimated universities such as York, and to celebrate the achievements of centres of excellence such as the social sciences at Essex. But, far from seeing the end of league tables, as the critics of subject assessments intended, the likely impact will be to make them more influential. The vice-chancellors' own research shows that half of all applicants use newspaper guides and, as the one round of teaching quality reports becomes increasingly dated, more students will look for alternative sources of comparison. University rankings existed before teaching assessments were published and they will continue under the new system.

Any doubt that students would become more selective about the courses they chose has evaporated in recent years. As tuition fees and the withdrawal of maintenance grants have added to the financial pressures on students and their families, the winds of change have turned into a gale for some universities. Amid the government's expansion plans, academics by the score have been made redundant in some institutions, and we have seen the first campus closures.

The lure of a degree remains strong in some subjects and some universities, but by no means all. Successive studies confirm the financial advantages conferred by a university education, but the customers in the new higher education market know that some degrees are worth more than others, financially and intellectually. Although the prospect of higher fees has receded for the remainder of this Parliament, the cost of higher education is still considerable. Who knows how long it will be before American-style charges are back on the agenda?

The need for comparative information to help guide prospective students is greater than ever, for the divisions are far from simple. The institutional casualties have been mainly in the new universities, but some are thriving while some of the older foundations are in the doldrums. Even within universities, different departments have been experiencing contrasting fortunes. The demand for places on new universities' vocational degrees is often buoyant, for example, while applicants are looking elsewhere for traditional academic subjects.

Higher education has been changing rapidly over recent years, with successive governments creating incentives to extend access to more of the population, but allocating research funds more selectively. The result is a gradual return to the hierarchical system that seemed to have been abandoned when the polytechnics acquired university status; only this time there are more than two tiers.

At the top, in terms of funding and prestige, is a group of fewer than 20 universities, which attract 90 per cent of the resources available for research and also take the lion's share of money for teaching, partly because they offer expensive subjects such as medicine and engineering. A middle group, composed mainly of traditional universities, has been taking more undergraduates while trying to compete on research. The remainder are having to survive mainly by expanding, or at least maintaining, student numbers.

Universities in the last group are feeling the squeeze all the more because extra places have been allocated to those at the top of the tree, as part of the effort to expand higher education. As universities become free once more to recruit as many students as they can, those with the necessary qualifications will migrate towards the more prestigious institutions.

The picture will continue to develop over the next few years, as the new two-year foundation courses establish themselves and other changes, such as the increase in medical courses, filter down through the system. An extra 1,000 places a year are being created in new and existing medical schools, reducing the number of disappointed applicants and making it easier to win places in related subjects.

Changes at sixth-form level are complicating matters further for those hoping to begin a course in 2003. Teenagers and mature applicants would do well to examine the small print in universities' prospectuses and on their websites to gauge their approach to 'Curriculum 2000'. The demand for more than the conventional three A levels and the attitude towards Key Skills, AS levels and vocational qualifications still vary enormously from university to university.

Whatever the changes the next year may bring, competition for places at the leading universities is not going to slacken, and every grade may help in the race for selection. The right choice of course is almost equally important, however. This book should help in that process for, unlike other guides, its emphasis is on the quality of education. As well as the original university rankings, which now have a variety of imitators, the book contains advice for both home and overseas students on how to choose a suitable course, and there are extended profiles of all the universities in our tables.

Mindful of the competition for graduate jobs, applicants are looking as never before for quality and are also gravitating towards the more vocational subjects. The pattern established in Australia, which began charging for higher education more than a decade ago, is being repeated in Britain. Business courses, computing and certain vocational subjects are seeing a significant rise in applications, while some traditional academic subjects are struggling. There will be a place somewhere in higher education for most of those hoping to start a course in 2003, but competition for the top degrees will be as fierce as ever. To give yourself the best possible chance of coming out ahead of the field requires careful consideration of the options, as well as hard academic work.

This book offers a starting point in the increasingly complex search for the right course. No guide can cater for individual tastes, but a wealth of information is available to narrow the possibilities. *The Times Good University Guide* distils some of this information into a more manageable form, with profiles of each institution, rankings and advice on the applications process.

## The University Explosion

At first sight, choosing a university appears to have become simpler over the past decade. The distinction between universities and polytechnics was swept away in 1992 and the number of places expanded to the point where far more young (and not so young) people could benefit from higher education. A consensus has grown among politicians and business leaders that, quite apart from the benefits to the individual, a modern economy needs mass higher education. Countries such as the United States and Japan reached the same conclusion long ago but a combination of factors – not all of them planned – has seen Britain making up for lost time at a rate that has prompted concerns about the quality of some courses.

Almost a third of 18-year-olds are now going on to higher education, compared with one in seven in 1980, while at least twice that proportion will take a higher education course at some point in their life. The Labour Government has promised to raise that number still further. Yet, paradoxically, by ridding Britain of its elite university system, the last government sowed the seeds of a different form of elitism. The very process of opening up higher education ensured the creation of a new hierarchy of institutions. The old myth that all degrees were equal could not survive in a nation of almost 100 diverse universities and a growing number of degree-providing colleges.

## The New Hierarchy

There always was a pecking order of sorts. Oxford and Cambridge were world leaders long before most British universities were established, and parts of London University have always enjoyed a high status in particular fields. But few could discriminate between Aberdeen and Exeter, for example. Employers, careers advisers, even academics, had their own ideas of which were the leading universities, but there was little hard evidence to back their conclusions. Often they were based on outdated, inaccurate impressions of distant institutions.

The expanded higher education system has made such judgements more scientific as well as more necessary. Prospective employers want to know not only what a graduate studied, but where. Those who are committing their money to student sponsorship or funding research are comparing institutions department by department. This has become possible because of a new transparency in what a former higher-education minister described as the 'secret garden of academe'. Official demands for more and more published information may have taxed the patience of university administrators, but they have also given outsiders the opportunity to make more meaningful comparisons.

Many see the beginnings of a British Ivy League in the competitive culture that has ensued. Even before the recent upheavals, the lion's share of research cash went to fewer than 20 traditional universities, enabling them to upgrade their facilities and attract many of the top academics. As student numbers have gone through the roof, however, general higher education budgets have been squeezed and the funding gap has widened. Beneath the veneer of a unified higher education system, three types of university are emerging: the research-based elite; a large group dedicated primarily to teaching; and an indeterminate number of mixed-economy institutions in the middle struggling to maintain a research base.

Whatever the intentions of ministers following the publication in summer 1997 of Lord Dearing's review of higher education, it is hard to imagine that pattern changing in the short or medium term. There is no need for formalised divisions because the market is already taking the university system in the direction that both main political parties probably favour.

## Why University?

Doubtless some will be tempted, once the cost of living has been added to the new fees burden and the attractions of university life balanced against loss of potential earnings, to write off higher education. There are plenty of self-made millionaires who still swear by the University of Life as the only training ground for success. Yet even by narrow financial criteria it would be rash to dismiss higher education. The graduate labour market is still recovering from the recession and with so many more competing for jobs, a degree will never again be an automatic passport to a fast-track career. But graduates' financial prospects still compare favourably with school leavers'. Even for those who cannot or do not wish to afford three or more years of full-time education after leaving school, university remains a possibility. The modular courses adopted by most universities enable students to work through a degree at their own pace, dropping out for a time if necessary, or switching to part-time attendance. Distance learning is another option, and advances in information technology now mean that some nominally full-time courses are delivered mainly via computers.

For many – perhaps most – students, therefore, the university experience is not what it was in their parents' day. There is more assessment, more crowding, more pressure to get the best possible degree while also finding gainful employment for at least part of the year. The proportion of students achieving first-class degrees has risen significantly, while an upper second (rather than the ubiquitous 2:2) has become the norm. Research shows that the classification has a real impact in the labour market: a quarter of those taking a third-class degree in 1992 were unemployed six months later, compared with a mere 4.5 per cent of those with a first.

## Toward the Future

There will be no slackening in the pace of change. In the future it is likely that more students will begin their degrees at further education colleges, more will opt initially for two-year courses and the range both of subjects and teaching methods will grow still further. Some predict the rise of the 'virtual university' or the demise of the conventional higher education institution, as companies customise their own courses. However, universities have demonstrated enduring popularity and show every sign of weathering the current turbulence.

The demand for degree places this year will follow a familiar pattern. Especially in traditional universities, arts and social science degrees remain oversubscribed and some science subjects also have high entrance requirements. Places will again be plentiful, however, in engineering, technology and the 'hard' sciences, such as physics, for those with the right qualifications.

# 1

# University Rankings

The *Times* first published a University League Table in October 1992 as a distinctive way of measuring the quality of British universities. Every year since then the Tables have been the subject of vigorous debate among academics. Subsequently, too, a number of other broadsheet newspapers have got in on the act with not dissimilar university tables and this has inevitably led to a certain amount of confusion. Nonetheless, *The Times* Table retains its position as the respected and authoritative guide to the quality of UK universities and is frequently used and quoted overseas. Indeed, it has been incorporated into recent attempts by some to produce global comparisons among universities across the English-speaking world.

Given that analyses of this type within higher education and elsewhere – in schools, health, etc. – have come to be seen as legitimate aids, it is perhaps surprising that many universities remain implacably opposed to the very notion of comparing one with another, and yet that is what applicants have to do all the time. They claim in defence that each is unique, has a distinct mission and serves a different student community. Be that as it may, universities have been known to quote favourable League Table rankings when these assist their cause. Nor will you find tables of the type reproduced in this book in any material published by UCAS or The British Council and yet we remain convinced that comparisons are valid and helpful to students and their mentors when it comes to choosing a university.

Interestingly, the Higher Education Funding Council for England (HEFCE) has itself published sets of performance indicators for each UK university. We have chosen to use one of them, the so-called Efficiency measure, in *The Times* League Table. This set of 'official' performance indicators covers access, non-completion rates, teaching and learning outcomes, research output and employment. It is in many ways a commentary on how well each university is doing at delivering government policy and, as such, has a different purpose to the measures of quality used in *The Times* League Table.

The raw data for the League Table and other tables in later chapters all come from sources in the public domain. The Higher Education Statistics Agency (HESA) provided data for entry standards, student–staff ratios, library and computer spending, facilities spending, firsts and upper seconds, graduate destinations and overseas student enrolments. HESA is the official agency for the collection, analysis and dissemination of quantitative information about the universities.

The HEFCE, along with the Scottish Higher Education Funding Council (SHEFC) and the Higher Education Funding Council for Wales (HEFCW), are the funding councils whose remit it is to develop policy and allocate public funds to the universities. The 2001 Research Assessment Exercise, conducted by the funding councils, provides the data for the research measure used in the tables. The funding councils also have a statutory responsibility to assess the quality of learning and teaching in the UK universities they fund. In England, Wales, Northern Ireland and, latterly in Scotland, too, this duty is discharged through the Quality Assurance Agency for Higher Education (QAA) and we use their programme of Subject Reviews as a measure of teaching quality.

In a few cases the source data were not available and were obtained directly from the individual universities.

All universities were provided with complete sets of their own HESA data well in advance of publication. In addition, where anomalous figures were identified in the 1999–2000 HESA data, institutions were given a further opportunity to check for and notify any errors. Similarly, we consulted the universities on methodology; in particular in respect of the Subject Tables in Chapter 4. Once a year, a Review Group with university representatives meets to discuss the methodology and how it can be improved. Thus, every effort has been made to ensure accuracy, but no responsibility can be taken for errors or omissions. The data providers do not necessarily agree with data aggregations or manipulations appearing in this book and are also not responsible for any inferences or conclusions thereby derived.

A particular feature of *The Times* tables is the way the various measures are combined to create a total score. In many other tables each institution's score, for each measure, is expressed as a percentage of the maximum score. Where there is little variation in the scores these percentages are often scaled to spread the variation out and so ensure that the measure contributes something to the overall score in the table. The percentages are then summed to form an overall score.

This approach has the advantage that it is possible to see how a particular institution is performing relative to the best performing institution for a particular measure. The main disadvantage is that year-on-year comparisons are not possible. For example, an institution which scored 86 one year (ie had a score that was 86 per cent of the top score) might perform better the next year but still have a lower score if the top institution happened to perform even better still.

In *The Times* tables the scores have undergone a Z-transformation. This is a statistical way of ensuring that each measure contributes the same amount to the overall score and so avoids the need for any scaling. (For the statistically minded, it involves subtracting the mean score from each individual score and then dividing by the standard deviation of the scores.)

Given the various changes and the continuing refinement of the process over the years, it is not possible to compare positions in the League Table from year to year. This year four institutions have been added to the table: the University of Gloucestershire (formerly Cheltenham and Gloucester College of Higher Education), the University of Surrey Roehampton, the University of Wales College, Newport and the University of Wales Institute, Cardiff. The Open University and the privately funded Buckingham University, and universities like Cranfield with mainly postgraduate students are not included.

Apart from noting the overall position of any one university of interest, you can home in on a particular measure of importance to you like entry standards or graduate destinations. But bear in mind that this composite table says nothing about specific subjects at a university and so should be scrutinised in conjunction with the other tables and university profiles in later chapters.

## How the Table Works

The table measures nine key aspects of university activity using the most recent data available at the time of going to press. A statistical technique called the Z-transformation was applied to each measure to create a score for that measure. The Z-scores on each measure were than weighted by 2.5 for teaching, 1.5 for research and 1.0 for the rest and summed to give a total score for the university. Finally, these total scores were transformed to a scale where the top score was set at 1000 with the remainder being a proportion of the top score. This scaling does not affect the overall ranking but it avoids giving any university a negative overall score. A new feature of this year's table is that some measures (Entry Standard, Firsts and Upper Seconds, and Graduate Destinations) have been adjusted to take account of the subject mix at the institution. The details of how the measures were compiled, together with some advice about their interpretation, is given below.

### Teaching Assessment

*What is it?* A measure of the average teaching quality of the university.

*Where does it come from?* The QAA sends teams of assessors to university departments and publishes the outcomes.

*How does it work?* The results of assessments of teaching quality are averaged for each university. In the early stages of the assessments the outcomes were

Excellent, Satisfactory, and (in Scotland) Highly Satisfactory. The later scores are out of a maximum of 24 and the original categories have been converted to numerical scores on this scale in order to calculate an average.

**What should you look out for?** The very first results (1993–94) are now quite old and a lot may have happened in a department since then. The earlier assessments, leading to the Excellent or Satisfactory outcomes, were also undertaken on a rather different methodology to the later ones with numerical outcomes. In particular, the early assessments were an assessment of actual quality while later ones were an assessment of whether the teaching contributed to the department's objectives. This means that two universities with different objectives and standards could nevertheless achieve the same score – both would be equally good at achieving what they set out to achieve, but they set out to achieve rather different things. The later results are thus more difficult to interpret.

### Research Assessment

**What is it?** A measure of the average quality of the research undertaken in the university.

**Where does it come from?** The 2001 Research Assessment Exercise undertaken by the funding councils.

**How does it work?** Each university department entered in the assessment exercise was given a rating of 5* (top), 5, 4, 3a, 3b, 2 or 1 (bottom). These grades were converted to a numerical scale and an average was calculated, weighted according to the number of staff in the department getting each rating.

**What should you look out for?** The rating of 5*, 5, etc., is accompanied by a letter which indicates the proportion of staff included in the assessment. Thus a 5A indicates that most staff were of 5 standard but a 5F indicates that most staff were not included in the return (and so unlikely to be active at that level).

### Entry Standards

**What is it?** The average A-level score of new students under the age of 21.

**Where does it come from?** HESA data for 1999–2000.

**How does it work?** Each student's best three A level or AS grades are converted to a numerical score (A level A=10, B=8 ... E=2; AS A=5, B=4 ... E=1) and added up to give a score out of 30. HESA then calculates an average for all students at the university. The results were then adjusted to take account of the subject mix at the university. The new UCAS tariff (a scoring system covering a wider variety of qualifications) was introduced in 2002–03 and so was not available to be used this year.

**What should you look out for?** A-level scores are used for Scottish as well as other UK universities because experience has shown that the usual scoring system for Scottish Highers gives slightly lower results for Scottish universities. At present there is no widely accepted way of converting scores from other qualifications, eg BTEC awards, GNVQ, International Baccalaureate or Access courses, and so these are not included. This will not matter for some universities, where the majority of the intake has A levels, but for others the score will represent a smaller proportion of the intake. Universities which have a specific policy of accepting students with low grades as part of an access policy will tend to have their average score depressed.

## Student–Staff Ratio

**What is it?** A measure of the average staffing level in the university.

**Where does it come from?** HESA data for 1999–2000.

**How does it work?** HESA has calculated a student–staff ratio, ie the number of students divided by the number of staff, in a way designed to take account of different patterns of staff employment in different universities.

**What should you look out for?** A low SSR, ie a small number of students for each member of staff, doesn't guarantee good quality of teaching or good access to staff. Universities with a medical school will tend to score better.

## Library and Computer Spending

**What is it?** The expenditure per student on library and computing facilities.

**Where does it come from?** HESA data for 1997–98, 1998–99 and 1999–2000.

**How does it work?** A university's expenditure on library and computing facilities (books, journals, staff, computer hardware and software, but not buildings) is divided by the number of full-time-equivalent students. Expenditure over three years is averaged to allow for uneven expenditure (for example, a major upgrade of a computer network might cause expenditure to rise sharply in one year but fall back the next). Libraries and information technology are becoming increasingly integrated (many universities have a single Department of Information

Services encompassing both) and so the two areas of expenditure have been taken together.

*What should you look out for?* Some universities are the location for major national facilities, such as the Bodleian Library in Oxford and national computing facilities in Bath and Manchester. The local and national expenditure is very difficult to separate and so these universities will tend to score more highly on this measure.

### Facilities Spending

*What is it?* The expenditure per student on student facilities.

*Where does it come from?* HESA data for 1997–98, 1998–99 and 1999–2000.

*How does it work?* A university's expenditure on student facilities (sports, recreation, health, counselling, etc.) is divided by the number of full-time-equivalent students. Expenditure over three years is averaged to allow for uneven expenditure.

*What should you look out for?* This measure tends to disadvantage Oxford and Cambridge (and possibly some other universities with a form of collegiate structure) as it mostly includes central university expenditure. In Oxford and Cambridge, a significant amount of facilities expenditure is by the colleges but it has not yet been possible to extract comparable data from the college accounts.

### Firsts and Upper Seconds

*What is it?* The percentage of graduates achieving a first or upper second class degree

*Where does it come from?* HESA data for 1999–2000.

*How does it work?* The number of graduates with first or upper second class degrees is divided by the total number of graduates with classified degrees. Enhanced first degrees, eg an MEng awarded after a four-year engineering course, are treated as equivalent to a first or upper second for this purpose, while Scottish Ordinary degrees (awarded after three years rather than the usual four in Scotland) are excluded altogether. The results were then adjusted to take account of the subject mix at the university.

*What should you look out for?* Degree classifications are controlled by the universities themselves, though with some moderation by the external examiner system. It can be argued, therefore, that they are not a very objective measure of quality. However, degree class is the primary measure of individual success in British higher education and will have an impact elsewhere, such as employment prospects.

## Graduate Destinations

*What is it?* A measure of the employability of a university's graduates.

*Where does it come from?* HESA data for 1999–2000.

*How does it work?* The number of graduates who take up employment or further study divided by the total number of graduates with a known destination expressed as a percentage. The results were then adjusted to take account of the subject mix at the university.

*What should you look out for?* The outcome is influenced by how good the university is at collecting the data: a high proportion of 'not knowns' (who are excluded from the calculation) will tend to improve the outcome because research shows that the 'not knowns' tend to include a disproportionate number of unemployed graduates. A new measure of the employability of graduates has been developed by HEFCE but this is only available at institution level. The HESA data was used so that a subject-mix adjustment could be made.

## Efficiency

*What is it?* A measure of the efficiency of study at the university.

*Where does it come from?* HEFCE performance indicators, based on data for 1998–99 and earlier years.

*How does it work?* The HEFCE calculated the length of time students studied at each university compared with the length of time they would be expected to study if they completed the course normally. The main reasons for reduced efficiency are students who fail to complete their course or who repeat a year. The figures in the table show the percentage of students who complete their courses in the specified time.

*What should you look out for?* The efficiency of a university is a projection based upon a shapshot of data. It is therefore vulnerable to statistical fluctuations.

## Conclusions

Universities' positions in *The Times* table inevitably reflect more than their performance over a single year. Many of those at the top have built their reputations and developed their expertise over many decades or even centuries, while some of those at the bottom are still carving out a niche in the unified higher education system. Perhaps the least surprising conclusions to be drawn from the table are that Oxbridge and the University of London remain the dominant forces in British higher education and that, on the measures adopted here, the new universities still have ground to make up on the old. The former polytechnics have different priorities from those of any of their more established counterparts, however, and can demonstrate strengths in other areas.

Even on the traditional measures adopted here, the table belies the system's reputation for rigidity. For example, a former polytechnic (Oxford Brookes) continues to outperform a number of long-established universities. No doubt others will follow before long. The remarkable rise of universities such as Warwick and York, both founded less that 40 years ago, shows what can be achieved in a relatively short space of time.

In an exercise such as this, some distortions are inevitable and the main ones have been identified in the *'What should you look out for?'* sections, above. The use of a variety of indicators is intended to diminish such effects, but they should be borne in mind when making comparisons.

| | Teaching assessment | Research assessment | Entry standards | Student–staff ratio | Library/computing spending | Facilities spending | Firsts and upper seconds | Graduate destinations | Efficiency | TOTAL |
|---|---|---|---|---|---|---|---|---|---|---|
| Maximum possible score | 24.0 | 7.0 | 30.0 | N/a | N/a | N/a | 100.0 | 100.0 | 100.0 | 1000 |
| 1 Oxford | 22.3 | 6.5 | 29.5 | 12.2 | 1417 | 184 | 84.9 | 95.2 | 96.0 | 1000 |
| 2 Cambridge | 22.7 | 6.6 | 29.7 | 11.9 | 959 | 150 | 93.4 | 98.5 | 98.0 | 997 |
| 3 Imperial College | 22.0 | 6.4 | 27.9 | 8.1 | 933 | 369 | 93.1 | 97.7 | 89.0 | 987 |
| 4 Bath | 21.4 | 5.7 | 25.4 | 14.0 | 789 | 403 | 70.1 | 96.2 | 95.0 | 934 |
| 5 London School of Economics | 21.9 | 6.4 | 28.2 | 14.6 | 1058 | 146 | 70.3 | 95.3 | 93.0 | 931 |
| 6 Warwick | 22.5 | 6.0 | 26.3 | 15.7 | 657 | 171 | 72.1 | 94.6 | 96.0 | 920 |
| 7 Bristol | 21.6 | 5.7 | 26.5* | 12.8 | 559 | 352 | 88.1 | 95.9 | 94.0 | 917 |
| 8 York | 22.6 | 5.8 | 25.5 | 13.0 | 520 | 152 | 68.5 | 96.3 | 94.0 | 911 |
| 9 Nottingham | 21.7 | 5.3 | 26.2 | 14.1* | 740 | 218 | 80.1 | 96.6 | 95.0 | 903 |
| 10 St Andrews | 22.0 | 5.7 | 24.7 | 9.8 | 668 | 221 | 83.3 | 95.6 | 92.0 | 902 |
| 11 University College London | 21.9 | 6.0 | 25.8 | 6.7 | 837 | 191 | 82.4 | 93.4 | 92.0 | 899 |
| 12 Manchester | 21.9 | 5.7 | 23.5 | 14.1 | 678 | 205 | 78.0 | 96.3 | 93.0 | 884 |
| 13 Durham | 21.9 | 5.7 | 25.4 | 14.4 | 575 | 269 | 63.4 | 94.0 | 94.0 | 881 |
| 14 Loughborough | 22.0 | 5.1 | 22.0 | 16.3 | 583 | 277 | 59.8 | 97.2 | 90.0 | 879 |

| | Teaching assessment | Research assessment | Entry standards | Student–staff ratio | Library/computing spending | Facilities spending | Firsts and upper seconds | Graduate destinations | Efficiency | TOTAL |
|---|---|---|---|---|---|---|---|---|---|---|
| Maximum possible score | 24.0 | 7.0 | 30.0 | N/a | N/a | N/a | 100.0 | 100.0 | 100.0 | 1000 |
| 15 Edinburgh | 21.5 | 5.6 | 26.5 | 13.8 | 742 | 234 | 86.6 | 95.9 | 86.0 | 870 |
| 16 Newcastle | 21.6 | 5.2 | 23.0 | 13.3 | 845 | 263 | 70.2 | 94.3 | 89.0 | 863 |
| 17 Birmingham | 21.7 | 5.3 | 23.7 | 13.5 | 560 | 223 | 72.9 | 95.6 | 90.0 | 852 |
| 18 Sheffield | 22.0 | 5.5 | 25.4 | 15.8 | 470 | 185 | 73.8 | 95.1 | 90.0 | 847 |
| 19 Aberdeen | 21.3 | 4.7 | 19.7 | 11.0 | 712 | 290 | 72.4 | 97.0 | 84.0 | 834 |
| 20 King's College London | 21.7 | 5.5 | 24.1 | 11.0 | 609 | 174 | 84.5 | 93.6 | 91.0 | 833 |
| 21 Lancaster | 21.6 | 5.8 | 22.1 | 18.3 | 544 | 258 | 61.7 | 93.0 | 92.0 | 831 |
| 22 Royal Holloway | 21.2 | 5.7 | 22.1 | 15.1 | 491 | 316 | 60.2 | 94.4 | 91.0 | 829 |
| 23 Queens, Belfast | 21.5 | 4.9 | 24.2 | 15.6 | 471 | 287 | 62.8 | 95.8 | 90.1 | 828 |
| 24 Southampton | 21.6 | 5.8 | 23.0 | 15.8 | 567 | 189 | 57.8 | 94.8 | 90.0 | 824 |
| 25 Essex | 21.7 | 5.6 | 18.3 | 15.5 | 618 | 270 | 53.1 | 95.0 | 83.0 | 816 |
| 26 Leicester | 21.7 | 5.0 | 21.9 | 15.3 | 491 | 188 | 60.4 | 95.1 | 92.0 | 815 |
| 27 SOAS | 21.5 | 5.5 | 22.7 | 12.8 | 1077 | 100 | 72.2 | 89.1 | 83.0 | 813 |
| 28 Glasgow | 21.7 | 5.2 | 24.2 | 13.9 | 573 | 166 | 80.5 | 93.5 | 85.0 | 809 |

| | | | | | | | | | | | |
|---|---|---|---|---|---|---|---|---|---|---|---|
| 29 | Leeds | 21.3 | 5.3 | 23.8 | 15.2 | 578 | 137 | 65.9 | 96.2 | 91.0 | 808 |
| 30 | Reading | 21.3 | 5.3 | 20.9 | 13.5 | 530 | 189 | 60.3 | 95.8 | 88.0 | 807 |
| 31 | UMIST | 20.6 | 5.5 | 22.7 | 9.4 | 521 | 209 | 58.2 | 95.1 | 88.0 | 804 |
| =32 | Surrey | 20.5 | 5.4 | 19.6 | 12.9 | 531 | 249 | 55.3 | 99.0 | 90.0 | 803 |
| =32 | Stirling | 21.4 | 4.8 | 19.1* | 16.7 | 564 | 186 | 62.2 | 95.7 | 90.0 | 803 |
| 34 | Cardiff | 21.1 | 5.7 | 22.8 | 17.2 | 487 | 216 | 62.7 | 94.4 | 89.0 | 795 |
| 35 | Exeter | 21.4 | 5.2 | 23.0 | 18.2 | 440 | 133 | 66.2 | 94.0 | 94.0 | 791 |
| 36 | Aston | 21.1 | 5.0 | 22.0 | 19.4 | 433 | 236 | 61.3 | 96.3 | 85.0 | 781 |
| 37 | Dundee | 21.0 | 5.1 | 19.8 | 10.9 | 528 | 181 | 79.1 | 95.9 | 84.0 | 776 |
| 38 | Liverpool | 21.4 | 5.2 | 20.7 | 15.2 | 412 | 139 | 67.3 | 95.5 | 88.0 | 772 |
| 39 | Queen Mary | 21.3 | 5.0 | 18.9 | 10.8 | 629 | 200 | 70.7 | 92.8 | 85.0 | 771 |
| 40 | East Anglia | 21.0 | 5.4 | 21.1 | 19.0 | 482 | 187 | 64.4 | 93.3 | 91.0 | 770 |
| 41 | Strathclyde | 21.5 | 4.7 | 20.4* | 17.5 | 421 | 172 | 60.9 | 95.3 | 82.0 | 767 |
| 42 | Kent | 21.0 | 4.8 | 20.2 | 17.9 | 534 | 151 | 55.8 | 97.9 | 88.0 | 766 |
| 43 | Hull | 21.3 | 4.3 | 19.5 | 17.0 | 482 | 93 | 58.5 | 97.0 | 93.0 | 765 |
| 44 | Sussex | 20.7 | 5.5 | 22.6 | 15.4 | 593 | 190 | 61.5 | 91.9 | 86.0 | 758 |
| 45 | Swansea | 21.1 | 4.6 | 19.7 | 15.6 | 419 | 183 | 54.2 | 95.0 | 87.0 | 751 |
| 46 | Keele | 21.2 | 4.6 | 18.9 | 17.6 | 272 | 139 | 64.1* | 95.2* | 92.0 | 748 |
| 47 | City | 20.7 | 4.4 | 20.5 | 13.6 | 481 | 178 | 55.8 | 95.9 | 83.0 | 747 |

| | Teaching assessment | Research assessment | Entry standards | Student–staff ratio | Library/ computing spending | Facilities spending | Firsts and upper seconds | Graduate destinations | Efficiency | TOTAL |
|---|---|---|---|---|---|---|---|---|---|---|
| Maximum possible score | 24.0 | 7.0 | 30.0 | N/a | N/a | N/a | 100.0 | 100.0 | 100.0 | 1000 |
| 48 Heriot-Watt | 20.6 | 4.7 | 19.3 | 14.3 | 640 | 219 | 45.2 | 94.5 | 86.0 | 743 |
| 49 Aberystwyth | 20.9 | 4.5 | 18.7 | 19.0 | 507 | 246 | 57.9 | 91.3 | 90.0 | 741 |
| 50 Brunel | 21.2 | 4.3 | 18.3 | 20.2 | 440 | 161 | 52.4 | 97.2 | 84.0 | 736 |
| 51 Oxford Brookes | 21.4 | 2.8 | 16.2 | 14.4 | 383 | 247 | 53.9 | 94.7 | 82.0 | 733 |
| 52 Ulster | 20.7 | 3.8 | 18.9 | 16.9 | 360 | 132 | 63.4 | 93.6 | 89.8 | 717 |
| 53 Plymouth | 20.8 | 3.2 | 15.1 | 13.3 | 589 | 142 | 49.1 | 92.9 | 88.0 | 704 |
| 54 Bradford | 20.2 | 4.4 | 17.8 | 15.8 | 461 | 243 | 48.7 | 95.8 | 85.0 | 703 |
| 55 Nottingham Trent | 20.4 | 2.8 | 17.3 | 17.4 | 419 | 212 | 48.6 | 97.8 | 87.0 | 700 |
| =56 Northumbria | 21.4 | 2.3 | 16.4 | 18.1 | 380 | 152 | 49.5 | 92.9 | 89.0 | 695 |
| =56 Bangor | 20.9 | 4.7 | 16.3 | 18.4 | 530 | 147 | 50.2 | 91.5 | 88.0 | 695 |
| 58 West of England | 21.4 | 2.8 | 16.9 | 19.2 | 412 | 145 | 41.9 | 95.3 | 81.0 | 680 |
| =59 Hertfordshire | 21.1 | 2.5 | 15.1 | 17.2 | 483 | 124 | 50.4 | 93.3 | 83.0 | 675 |
| =59 Robert Gordon | 20.6 | 1.9 | 14.2 | 16.9 | 447 | 132 | 59.9 | 98.1 | 82.0 | 675 |
| 61 Sheffield Hallam | 21.0 | 3.0 | 15.9 | 21.4 | 382 | 186 | 49.0 | 93.5 | 86.0 | 674 |

| Rank | University | | | | | | | | | |
|---|---|---|---|---|---|---|---|---|---|---|
| 62 | Portsmouth | 20.6 | 3.2 | 15.8 | 18.4 | 409 | 111 | 48.1 | 96.3 | 85.0 | 668 |
| 63 | Goldsmiths College | 20.1 | 5.3 | 19.1 | 16.8 | 405 | 109 | 54.5 | 92.4 | 85.0 | 666 |
| 64 | Abertay Dundee | 20.2 | 2.0 | 11.8 | 17.1 | 1016 | 152 | 50.2 | 92.6 | 88.0 | 665 |
| 65 | UWIC, Cardiff | 21.1 | 2.7 | 15.8 | 15.2 | 333 | 91 | 49.8 | 91.5 | 88.0 | 664 |
| 66 | Napier | 20.2 | 2.3 | 11.8 | 17.7 | 426 | 143 | 58.6 | 96.9 | 87.0 | 654 |
| 67 | Coventry | 20.7 | 2.1 | 13.5 | 16.7 | 441 | 194 | 44.4 | 95.1 | 82.0 | 652 |
| 68 | Brighton | 20.7 | 2.9 | 13.6 | 21.3 | 425 | 140 | 48.5 | 95.5 | 83.0 | 647 |
| 69 | Westminster | 20.5 | 2.8 | 13.6 | 11.2 | 428 | 132 | 56.0 | 91.7 | 74.0 | 640 |
| 70 | Lampeter | 20.6 | 4.7 | 13.4 | 18.5 | 502 | 162 | 49.6 | 87.3 | 89.0 | 635 |
| 71 | Sunderland | 20.7 | 2.8 | 12.7 | 18.5 | 331 | 185 | 47.9 | 94.4 | 79.0 | 634 |
| =72 | Luton | 20.9 | 1.8 | 10.6* | 15.4 | 408 | 165 | 47.6 | 99.4 | 74.9 | 632 |
| =72 | Kingston | 21.2 | 2.7 | 14.2 | 22.7 | 393 | 132 | 49.2 | 94.0 | 75.0 | 632 |
| 74 | Salford | 20.5 | 4.3 | 14.9 | 18.4 | 340 | 154 | 45.5 | 90.6 | 80.0 | 626 |
| 75 | Manchester Metropolitan | 20.8 | 2.9 | 15.4 | 19.6 | 384 | 81 | 44.1 | 92.0 | 83.0 | 623 |
| 76 | Surrey Roehampton | 20.1 | 3.2 | 12.8 | 20.5 | 295 | 157 | 48.4 | 95.2 | 85.0 | 612 |
| 77 | Glasgow Caledonian | 20.7 | 2.5 | 17.1 | 16.6 | 220 | 63 | 51.7 | 93.0 | 76.0 | 610 |
| =78 | Central Lancashire | 20.5 | 2.2 | 14.5* | 20.1 | 346 | 146 | 45.9 | 92.0 | 77.4 | 605 |
| =78 | Leeds Metropolitan | 20.1 | 2.2 | 15.4 | 19.0 | 502 | 124 | 50.0 | 91.4 | 83.0 | 605 |
| 80 | Bournemouth | 19.6 | 1.9 | 17.6 | 16.2 | 393 | 45 | 51.5 | 93.0 | 89.0 | 602 |

| | Teaching assessment | Research assessment | Entry standards | Student-staff ratio | Library/computing spending | Facilities spending | Firsts and upper seconds | Graduate destinations | Efficiency | TOTAL |
|---|---|---|---|---|---|---|---|---|---|---|
| Maximum possible score | 24.0 | 7.0 | 30.0 | N/a | N/a | N/a | 100.0 | 100.0 | 100.0 | 1000 |
| =81 Staffordshire | 20.2 | 2.2 | 12.7 | 21.6 | 450 | 157 | 42.5 | 92.4 | 87.2 | 595 |
| =81 Glamorgan | 20.4 | 2.4 | 13.1 | 16.6 | 389 | 165 | 47.6 | 90.3 | 77.0 | 595 |
| =81 Gloucestershire | 20.1 | 3.0 | 13.4 | 22.9 | 371 | 101 | 44.9 | 95.5 | 84.0 | 595 |
| 84 Wolverhampton | 20.4 | 2.0 | 12.8 | 17.9 | 359 | 195 | 51.4 | 89.3 | 79.0 | 594 |
| 85 Liverpool John Moores | 20.2 | 2.6 | 15.4 | 17.9 | 396 | 100 | 48.6 | 90.4 | 83.0 | 593 |
| 86 De Montfort | 20.0 | 3.1 | 13.5 | 19.1 | 399* | 52 | 56.4 | 93.6 | 78.0 | 591 |
| 87 Central England | 19.9 | 2.2 | 14.1 | 22.5 | 354 | 145 | 52.4 | 93.9 | 81.0 | 585 |
| 88 Middlesex | 20.4 | 2.7 | 12.3 | 19.2 | 496 | 51 | 51.9 | 91.6 | 77.0 | 584 |
| 89 Huddersfield | 20.5 | 2.4 | 13.6 | 19.7 | 317 | 120 | 47.0 | 91.1 | 77.0 | 579 |
| 90 Greenwich | 20.2 | 2.5 | 11.5 | 20.5 | 495 | 157 | 40.8 | 93.1 | 77.0 | 570 |
| 91 Lincoln | 19.5 | 1.7 | 13.7 | 19.7 | 464 | 80 | 44.8 | 92.2 | 85.0 | 552 |
| =92 Paisley | 20.4 | 1.6 | 12.1 | 18.5 | 450 | 114 | 41.1 | 87.6 | 80.4 | 551 |
| =92 Teesside | 19.9 | 1.9 | 12.2 | 16.4 | 382 | 129 | 39.8 | 91.2 | 82.0 | 551 |
| =92 Anglia | 20.2 | 1.5 | 13.6 | 20.3 | 295 | 100 | 47.7 | 93.6 | 76.0 | 551 |

| | | | | | | | | | | |
|---|---|---|---|---|---|---|---|---|---|---|
| 95 | South Bank | 20.0 | 2.9 | 17.6* | 16.1 | 318 | 144 | 37.8 | 87.1 | 73.0 | 540 |
| 96 | UWCN, Newport | 19.5 | 3.0 | 12.6 | 28.5 | 331 | 84 | 50.5 | 92.2 | 80.0 | 522 |
| 97 | North London | 19.9 | 2.3 | 11.3 | 22.8 | 384 | 167 | 42.3 | 92.9 | 69.0 | 521 |
| 98 | Derby | 19.7 | 1.5 | 12.4 | 30.8 | 333 | 111 | 45.6 | 92.2 | 85.0 | 504 |
| 99 | East London | 19.2 | 2.5 | 12.5 | 18.7 | 385 | 131 | 47.0 | 86.4 | 75.0 | 489 |
| 100 | London Guildhall | 20.0 | 1.9 | 11.8 | 20.5 | 424 | 99 | 32.0 | 87.1 | 70.0 | 468 |
| 101 | Thames Valley | 19.1 | 0.5 | 10.3 | 35.7 | 387 | 44 | 30.0 | 88.9 | 82.0 | 360 |
| | | | | | | | | | | | |
| | median | 21.0 | 4.4 | 18.3 | 16.7 | 470 | 161 | 55.3 | 94.4 | 86.0 | 733 |
| | maximum | 22.7 | 6.6 | 29.7 | 35.7 | 1417 | 403 | 93.4 | 99.4 | 98.0 | 1000 |
| | minimum | 19.1 | 0.5 | 10.3 | 6.7 | 220 | 44 | 30.0 | 86.4 | 69.0 | 360 |

Note: data marked * have been supplied directly by the university concerned.

# Choosing a University

Choosing a university is a big decision, one which will have an enormous impact on your future life. It will affect the place you live, the friends you make, and quite possibly your future career. It is also a very difficult decision: with a hundred universities to choose from (nearer 150 if you include higher education colleges), all of which have their own distinctive character, it can be difficult to know where to start, let alone which to choose.

For some, the choice of course will narrow the possibilities down to few. If you want to study veterinary science, there are only six places you can go. If you want to study paper science, only one. For many though, particularly if you are interested in one of the major subjects such as English, chemistry, law or mechanical engineering, there may be 20 or more similar courses. Choosing a course will be looked at in more detail in the next chapter, but for now we will assume there are plenty of suitable courses.

So how do you go about choosing a university? There are no easy answers, but it is possible to list a range of factors which need to be looked at. Different people will attach different levels of importance to each one, but most will need at least to think about them all. HERO (www.hero.ac.uk), the national website for higher education in the UK may help you to do this.

## Location
Where do you want to go? Do you really like your parents or do you want to get as far away as possible? Do you want to visit your boyfriend or girlfriend every weekend (or, perhaps, want an excuse not to)? Do you want to find the cheapest way of going to university? One way or another, location is likely to be an important factor. If you want to live at home, the decision might be straightforward, though if you live in London there could easily be half a dozen local universities. If you want to go away from home, then distance or travel time will probably be a factor. Incidentally, if you can go away from home it may be to your longer-term advantage to do so. Some recent research has shown that students who move away

from home have better job prospects. This is probably because those who stay at home tend to end up with narrower horizons and have less self-confidence in new situations.

If a particular town or city is acceptable, you will need to look at the location of the university itself in relation to that town or city. Is it in the city-centre or several miles outside? The former will be handy for shops and transport but may be noisy and less than picturesque. The latter may be a beautiful setting, but if you have to live off-campus there could be high travel costs. Another factor might be security: is the university in a well-lit suburban area or in a less desirable and possibly less safe part of town?

---

**English Speaking Aternatives to British Universities**

While UK universities have a world-wide reputation, the UK is not the only country with good universities. You may dream of doing your first degree in the USA or a Commonwealth country and every year such dreams become a reality for some students. For example, the latest figures show almost 5,000 UK undergraduates were enrolled at US universities. Many more go overseas for further study or employment once they have graduated.

The world of university education is shrinking and the idea of going abroad to study is becoming more common. Advice and information are at hand if this features in your plans. First ports of call are the Fulbright Commission (USA) and the Association of Commomwealth Universities: both have London offices and useful websites at www.fulbright.co.uk and www.acu.ac.uk. Every year, usually in September or October, there is a 'College Day' in London when around 100 US universities come to extol the virtues of an American university education.

There are university ranking tables, similar to those found in *The Times Good University Guide*, for each of the major English-speaking country. Among the more respected are:

| | |
|---|---|
| Australia | *The Good Universities Guide* (www.thegoodguides.com.au) |
| Canada | *The Maclean's Guide to Canadian Universities* (www.macleans.ca) |
| USA | *US News & World Report* (www.usnews.com) |

---

The facilities of the town or city may be important for you, too. Whether you like to dance the night away, follow the Premier League or take the theatre seriously, you will want to ensure you can do it. Indeed, your time at university will be a time when you can pursue your interests in a way you may never be able to again. Access to many things, such as sports facilities, will be very cheap and you will have the time to take them seriously. So if you want to do it, make sure you can.

Prospectuses frequently boast about the attractive surrounding countryside, so much so that it seems that *every* university is situated in the most picturesque region of the country. However, unless you have a particular interest that takes you there, such as climbing or fell walking, it is doubtful if you will spend much time taking in the sights.

Then, of course, there is cost. Generally, the south of England and London are more expensive places to live than the rest of the country, so if cost is significant for you, you will want to take this into account.

## Type of University

Universities are not all the same, and nor is it easy to put them into simple categories. At one extreme is an ancient collegiate university, a world leader in terms of research, offering traditional academic courses, having most students with

---

**Ten Things You Didn't Know About Universities**

- The oldest university in the country, Oxford, was probably founded in 1096, but no one knows precisely. It was there in 1187, but must have been founded before that
- There are over 50,000 courses to choose from
- Fancy a degree in Brewing and Distilling? Go to Heriot-Watt
- The total income of universities in 1999-2000 was nearly £13 billion, which is more than that of some countries
- Women outnumbered men among first-year students in 1996-97 for the first time
- In his Will, the philosopher Jeremy Bentham instructed that his skeleton and head be preserved, clothed and mounted in a seated position. He has sat like that in University College London since 1850
- There are about 200,000 overseas students from over 180 countries in the UK
- At some Scottish universities the Rector is elected by the staff and students. This has sometimes resulted in the election of celebrities rather than distinguished academics
- The student population in the UK has increased to over 2 million from just 200,000 in the 1960s
- 'University' is a legally controlled title in the UK – only institutions with a Royal Charter or some other legal authority can call themselves a university

---

AAA at A level, and with large numbers of postgraduates, many from overseas. At the other extreme is a very locally orientated university which does little research, offers more vocational courses to largely local students, many of whom are mature and do not have A levels. Both universities may be very good at what they do, but what they do is very different and they will feel very different to attend as a student.

Generally, older universities (pre-1970) will do more research, recruit a higher proportion of school leavers and offer more traditional academic courses, while newer universities will be more locally and vocationally orientated and recruit more mature and part-time students.

Universities also vary greatly in size, from fewer than 2,000 students to well over 20,000. A small university will be more personal and cosier but have fewer facilities and non-academic activities; a big university will be busier and more impersonal (lectures may be to hundreds at a time) but there will be a lot more going on. Student numbers are a guide to where a university lies on this spectrum, but it is not the whole story. Some large universities are divided into colleges, which helps to create a small university feel within a big university context, while others are on several sites, each of which may be relatively small.

## Quality and Reputation

Most people want to go to a good university if they can, and this is where *The Times* League Table is helpful. By bringing together a variety of measures it tries to give a reasonable basis for deciding how good a university really is. Differences of a few places in the table are insignificant, but a university in the top ten is doing a lot better than one in the bottom ten or even in the middle.

| Top Ten for Teaching Quality | Top Ten for Average A-Level Score |
|---|---|
| 1 Cambridge | 1 Cambridge |
| 2 York | 2 Oxford |
| 3 Warwick | 3 London School of Economics |
| 4 Oxford | 4 Imperial College |
| 5 Imperial College | 5 Edinburgh |
| 6 Loughborough | 6 Bristol |
| 7 St Andrews | 7 Warwick |
| 8 Sheffield | 8 Nottingham |
| 9 London School of Economics | 9 University College London |
| 10 Durham | 10 York |
| **Bottom Ten for Teaching Quality** | **Bottom Ten for Average A-Level Score** |
| 92 South Bank | 92 Middlesex |
| 93 North London | 93 Teesside |
| 94 Central England | 94 Paisley |
| 95 Teesside | 95 Napier |
| 96 Derby | 96 Abertay Dundee |
| 97 Bournemouth | 97 London Guildhall |
| 98 Lincoln | 98 Greenwich |
| 99 UWCN, Newport | 99 North London |
| 100 East London | 100 Luton |
| 101 Thames Valley | 101 Thames Valley |

When you look at the subject tables, it is clear that even the best universities vary in quality across subjects. Some universities perform consistently well and appear in the top 20 of many subject tables, while others come low down in the main table but have one or two very good departments that do well in the subject tables. So it is important to look at the main table alongside the subject tables.

As ever, quality has to be paid for. A Mercedes costs more than a Ford, and Cambridge 'costs' more than other universities, though in this case the currency is examination results rather than cash. Look at the entry standards column in the main table and you will see that it follows the main ranking fairly closely. In other words, universities high up the table will, in general, ask for higher grades in whatever qualification you are offering than those lower down the table. You will need to make a judgement about how well you are going to do in your school or college examinations and choose universities where you have a realistic chance of meeting the entry requirements. If you are taking A levels and are going to get AAA, there is no problem, but in many subjects CCC will exclude most of the universities near the top of the table.

## Facilities

The facilities offered by universities are fairly similar in general terms. All will have a library, sports halls, a health service, a careers service and so on. But there will be differences and if something is particularly important for you it is worth checking out. Sometimes this will be hard to do – all universities will claim to have a really good careers service, but it is difficult to find out how true those claims are. In other cases, however, it is more straightforward.

| Top Ten for Student Facilities Spending | Top Ten for Library/Computing Spending |
|---|---|
| 1 Bath | 1 Oxford |
| 2 Imperial College | 2 SOAS |
| 3 Bristol | 3 London School of Economics |
| 4 Royal Holloway | 4 Abertay Dundee |
| 5 Aberdeen | 5 Cambridge |
| 6 Queen's, Belfast | 6 Imperial College |
| 7 Loughborough | 7 Newcastle |
| 8 Essex | 8 University College London |
| 9 Durham | 9 Bath |
| 10 Newcastle | 10 Edinburgh |
| | |
| **Bottom Ten for Student Facilities Spending** | **Bottom Ten for Library/Computing Spending** |
| 92 Hull | 92 UWIC, Cardiff |
| 93 UWIC, Cardiff | 93 Derby |
| 94 UWCN, Newport | 94 Sunderland |
| 95 Manchester Metropolitan | 95 UWCN, Newport |
| 96 Lincoln | 96 South Bank |
| 97 Glasgow Caledonian | 97 Huddersfield |
| 98 De Montfort | 98 Anglia |
| 99 Middlesex | 99 Surrey Roehampton |
| 100 Bournemouth | 100 Keele |
| 101 Thames Valley | 101 Glasgow Caledonian |

Accommodation will be important if you are going away from home. Is there an accommodation guarantee for first years? What about later years? If you are a computer geek who spends the early hours on the internet, you will want to know if the rooms are wired up. If you are often out late (and how many students are not?) you may want to know where the accommodation is, how you can get back to it late at night and whether you will feel safe doing so. If you can't live in university accommodation for the whole of your course, where is the private accommodation? Is it all in a city five miles down the road (which could be good for access to shops, night-clubs and maybe the beach, but will probably be bad for travel costs), or in the grotty end of town, or in a leafy suburb by the university?

If you have a particular minority interest you want to follow while at university, then this could be a factor. Most universities will have football pitches and a Liberal Democratic Society, but a climbing wall and a deep-sea fishing group may be harder to find. The students' union will be able to tell you.

In fact students' unions are an increasingly important aspect of student life and have come a long way from the traditional image of providers of cheap beer and student protests. The modern entrepreneurial union will have a wide range of services from food and stationery outlets through to comprehensive advice services. Increasingly they are providers of part-time employment for students and are becoming involved in personal skills development. Inevitably, some are more active and innovative than others, so they are worth looking at.

---

### Tricks of the Prospectus Trade

The claims made by universities are rarely untrue, but they do need to be read carefully and critically. Here are a few cases where *The Times* League Tables can help you to interpret what the prospectuses and websites are saying. All the quotations were taken from university websites in December 2001.

"Our procedures for ensuring our courses are carefully designed, well taught, relevant to employment and backed up by research, are nationally recognised as being of the highest standard and quality." *Read the sentence carefully: it is the procedures that they claim to be of the highest standard and quality, not the courses themselves. The claim about procedures may well be true, but you are probably more interested to know that this university failed to make the top 60 for teaching quality in the 2002 League Table.*

"The University is well known for its strong track-record for graduate employment - consistently among the highest in the country." *This is a big claim, but the university did not make the top 60 for graduate destinations in the 2002 League Table.*

"[The University] is one of the UK's leading research universities with a reputation nationally and internationally for high quality teaching and research." *The research record is impressive, but in the 2003 Table over 30 other universities were more impressive. And while the quality of teaching may have an international reputation, in the 2003 Table over 30 universities scored higher.*

"Alongside teaching, research of the highest level is carried out in [our] six academic faculties and additional research centres." *In the 2001 Research Assessment Exercise none of this university's research was given the top rating of 5\* and only two out of 23 submissions were given the next to top rating of 5. Over 50 universitites scored higher in the 2003 table.*

---

As the financial position of students has worsened, universities have responded by setting up employment agencies. These are generally based in careers services or students' unions and use their contacts with employers to identify employment opportunities and their contacts with students to identify suitable employees. The agency will also ensure that rates of pay and hours of work are reasonable. If you think you may be short of cash, a good agency of this type could be vital.

Finally, if you have any particular needs, you will want to know that they can be catered for. Support for students with disabilities has improved greatly in recent years but some universities are particularly good at supporting some kinds of disability, while others have old buildings that make wheelchair access difficult.

**Making the Decision**

For some, location will be critical and this will immediately narrow down the choice. Others may be keen to go to as prestigious a university as possible and then the key question will be whether they can meet the entry requirements. Others may be particularly keen to carry on with an obscure martial art and so will want to go to one of the two or three places where they can do this. But for most, a combination of factors such as these will result in the elimination of most universities so that a manageable list of perhaps five or ten emerges. Then the detailed work begins.

---

**Things To Look Out For**

- Most degree courses in Scotland last four years, though many students with good A levels can be exempt from the first year
- Where a university has a split site, check where your course will be based
- Large adverts in the press usually means a university is having difficulty filling its places
- Engineering courses are either MEng or BEng; only the MEng will give maximum credit towards Chartered Engineer status
- Some courses offer the chance of spending a year or part of a year in Europe
- Accommodation might be guaranteed, but check whether it is five miles down the road
- Courses based in two or more departments can feel as if they are based nowhere – check for a 'home' department where you will belong

---

The first source of information will probably be the **undergraduate prospectus**. This is the main recruiting document that universities produce and should include most of what you will need to know, including details of courses, facilities and entry requirements. However, you need to bear in mind that it is not an impartial document, it is a form of advertising designed to make the university seem attractive. Strangely, the sun is always shining in prospectus photographs. They are rarely factually incorrect, but prospectuses can be incomplete or make generalised claims of quality without any supporting evidence (see box, *Tricks of the Prospectus Trade*, p. 35). In addition to the prospectus, many universities will produce a series of **departmental booklets**, which will give more detail about individual subject areas.

One easy way of obtaining a pile of prospectuses and departmental booklets is to visit a **higher education fair** where most universities will have a stand to give out information. You may also get an opportunity to talk to someone from the university if you have particular questions you want to ask.

Alternatively, universities have always been pioneers in using the internet and many have prospectuses available on their **websites**. Departments will usually have their own sites, too, and you can often access student handbooks aimed at current students for all the detail you will ever need about courses, options, teaching methods and assessment.

If you are still unclear about entry requirements, check them out in the *Big Official UCAS Guide*.

Keep firmly in mind that there is no substitute for a personal visit. All universities will offer some kind of **open day** where you can see for yourself what it would be like to go there as a student. If you can't make the date of the open day, many will make arrangements for you to visit more informally during the summer. A few will offer **residential visits**, which allow for a more extended and comprehensive look at the university.

While trawling through all these sources of information, you will no doubt talk to friends, parents, teachers, careers advisers and anyone else who comes within range. While it is good to talk, be critical of what you hear. A parent or teacher may know what they are talking about, but they may be telling you things based on their experiences of 20 or 30 years ago. Universities have changed a lot since then. Alternatively, your next-door neighbour, whom you rarely see, may just happen to work in a university admissions office and be a real source of good advice.

Finally, do a double-check to make sure your chosen university still exists. There are a number of actual and possible mergers around, such as London Guildhall with North London and, possibly, Manchester with UMIST.

In the end only you can decide. It won't be easy, but after all the reading, visiting, surfing and talking, you have got to do it. You have to decide which six will go on your UCAS form. Good luck!

**3**

# Choosing a Course

Choosing a university is a difficult business (see previous chapter) and choosing a course is no easier. Once again the decision is made in the face of enormous diversity, or at least it usually is. For a few the decision is simple: they have always wanted to be a brain surgeon or have always had a passion for Tudor England. For most, however, there is a bewildering variety of courses, many of which are not taught in schools or colleges. Somehow you have to narrow down the thousands of courses to just a few. It will help if the decision is broken down into three main components: the *subject*, what it is you want to study; *the type of course*, precisely how you want to study it; and the *quality* of the course.

## The Subject

When it comes to choosing a subject there are several things you need to take into account. First, you must make sure you understand the nature of the subject you are considering, especially if it is one you have not studied before. A course in ecology, for example, sounds as if it might deal with conservation and 'green' issues. However, many ecology courses are about the scientific study of the interaction between living organisms and may only deal peripherally with conservation

```
Ten Courses You Didn't Know You Could Choose
BA    Adventure Recreation
BA    Animation
BA    Arabic and Amharic
BA    Byzantine Studies
BSc   Equine Science
BA    Packaging Design
BA    Playwork
BSc   Property Valuation
BSc   Science and Football
BA    War Studies

Available for entry in 2002, UCAS website
```

issues. Language courses can vary considerably, from those concerned largely with literature to those which concentrate on translation and contemporary area studies. Psychology is another subject which may not be what is expected. It too can vary depending on whether the course focuses on the social or the neurological end of the subject.

Having made sure you understand the nature of the subject, you must be interested in it. You will spend a large proportion of three or four years immersed in the subject and that will be pretty dull if you find it boring. More important, you will probably perform better if you are excited by what you are studying. You are also likely to perform better if you have an aptitude for the subject. A course may be really interesting and lead to a guaranteed high-flying career, but if you are no good at it, you may end up performing badly or even failing altogether.

| What do Graduates Do? | | | |
|---|---|---|---|
| | Employed (%) | Further Study (%) | Unemployed (%) |
| Civil Engineering | 80.9 | 10.8 | 3.0 |
| Law | 34.0 | 56.2 | 3.7 |
| Building | 75.9 | 15.1 | 3.8 |
| Geography | 59.9 | 26.1 | 4.5 |
| Accountancy | 81.1 | 9.3 | 4.8 |
| Modern Languages | 64.5 | 22.5 | 5.0 |
| Economics | 70.9 | 15.5 | 5.2 |
| Mathematics | 62.0 | 26.1 | 5.3 |
| English | 56.3 | 30.3 | 5.4 |
| Physics | 55.0 | 33.5 | 5.6 |
| History | 56.2 | 30.0 | 5.7 |
| Psychology | 63.3 | 23.1 | 5.7 |
| Biology | 57.3 | 29.2 | 5.8 |
| Sociology | 70.3 | 16.6 | 5.9 |
| Chemistry | 47.8 | 39.3 | 6.0 |
| Business & Management Studies | 77.5 | 8.5 | 6.0 |
| Drama | 71.2 | 14.6 | 6.6 |
| Mechanical Engineering | 71.9 | 13.9 | 6.7 |
| Electrical & Electronic Engineering | 76.3 | 12.2 | 7.5 |
| Information Technology | 79.8 | 7.3 | 7.8 |
| Environmental Science | 63.7 | 19.9 | 8.1 |
| Media Studies | 76.4 | 8.2 | 8.6 |
| Design Studies | 71.5 | 9.6 | 9.0 |
| **All Subjects (2001)** | **69.2** | **19.0** | **5.7** |
| All Subjects (2000) | 67.8 | 19.4 | 6.9 |

*What do Graduates Do?* 2001 AGCAS

Career opportunities are another important factor. If you know what you want to do after university, your subject must provide a suitable basis for that career. The choice may be wider than you think, as just under half of graduate jobs do not specify any particular subject at all. Conversely, a narrowly vocational course could result in your career options being restricted if you subsequently change your mind about the direction you want to go.

Students often refer to employment prospects when they are asked about why they chose their course. However, it is worth looking at the figures. Some courses do, more or less, guarantee a job and the unemployment rates six months after graduation for medicine, veterinary science and education are very low. However,

| Top Ten Most Popular Subjects | |
|---|---|
| 1 Business Management | 28,988 |
| 2 Computer Science | 27,183 |
| 3 Design Studies | 18,098 |
| 4 Law | 16,452 |
| 5 Medicine | 10,231 |
| 6 Psychology | 10,181 |
| 7 Subjects Allied to Medicine | 9,500 |
| 8 Drama | 8,896 |
| 9 English | 8,875 |
| 10 Sports Science | 8,565 |

Applications, entry 2001, UCAS

most subjects fall into a narrow range of about 5–8 per cent still seeking employment after six months. In other words, the employability of most subjects is about the same. Interestingly, business studies, a subject that is often considered to be highly employable, comes out below average at 6.0 per cent, and a highly vocational area, design studies, has the highest unemployment rate. Of course there will be some variability within these broad subject groups. Some courses may be tailored towards specific careers and so achieve a very high level of employability, but conversely may be seen as too specialised if you try for an alternative career.

One reason for this similarity in employment prospects is the point mentioned above, that a significant proportion of job vacancies do not specify any subject at all. You can take the most obscure subject in the *UCAS Directory* and still have nearly 50 per cent of jobs open to you. Another reason is that class of degree is important: students with First Class Honours are very rarely unemployed whatever subject they studied.

You also need to consider entry requirements. Some universities have a General Entrance Requirement, a basic minimum set of qualifications that all students have to have. For most students this is not a problem as they will meet the Requirement easily, but it is worth checking to make sure. Most universities will also have various escape clauses to enable them to admit good students with unusual backgrounds even if they don't meet the General Entrance Requirement.

Each course will also have its entry requirements, both in terms of subjects you must already have studied and the examination grades required for entry. Most Mathematics courses, for example, will require previous study of mathematics. The UCAS website or the *Big UCAS Guide* are the easiest ways to check this. If you have the right subjects, the grades required will vary between universities (as discussed in the last chapter) and also between subjects. There is little point in applying for Medicine unless you are confident of getting As and Bs at A level (or their equivalent in other qualifications) while Ds and Es will get you into an engineering course at many less popular universities.

| Top Ten for Average A-Level Score | | Bottom Ten for Average A-Level Score | |
|---|---|---|---|
| 1 Medicine | 28.4 | 1 Social Work | 12.9 |
| 2 Veterinary Science | 28.0 | 2 Education | 13.3 |
| 3 Dentistry | 26.2 | 3 Catering & Institutional Management | 14.1 |
| 4 Ophthalmics | 24.5 | 4 Building | 14.5 |
| 5 Pharmacy | 23.9 | 5 Environmental Technology | 15.0 |
| 6 Mathematics | 23.6 | 6 Teacher Training | 15.4 |
| 7 Physics | 23.5 | 7 Design Studies | 15.5 |
| 8 Classics | 23.4 | 8 Media Studies | 15.5 |
| 9 Philosophy | 23.3 | 9 Industrial Relations | 15.6 |
| 10 Chemical Engineering | 23.0 | 10 Town & Country Planning | 15.6 |

Average Score of new students under the age of 21 (to subjects with at least 100 entrants at universities in *The Times* League Table), HESA 1999–2000

## The Qualifications Jungle

The new post-16 curriculum has made it much more difficult for universities to express their entry requirements. Previously there were A-level grades or Scottish Highers, with a nod in the direction of GNVQ or BTEC qualifications. Now there are choices to be made about the number of units that should be taken, how many A2 or Advanced Highers will be required, whether Key Skills will be compulsory and so on. Inevitably different universities have made different decisions and so you will have to read the websites and prospectuses much more carefully to ensure that you can find your way through the new qualifications jungle.

On some things most universities are in agreement:

- at least two subjects should be taken at A2 (unless a 12-unit vocational A level is taken)
- applicants who do not take AS in Year 12 will not be disadvantaged
- applicants with four or five AS will not be at an advantage
- neither key skills nor the Advanced Extension Tests will be compulsory

On others, however, there are differences:

- some universities will require a total of 21 units, others 18 units
- some will include Key Skills in offers, others will not
- some will use the new UCAS tariff (see *The UCAS Tariff box*, p. 42), others will not

Generally speaking, universities that come higher up *The Times* League Table are more likely to require 21 units rather than 18, not to include Key Skills in offers, and not to use the Tariff. However, there is a lot of variation so it is important to ensure you read small print carefully.

In general, the new universities are more likely to accept vocational A levels for particular courses, and are more likely to use the new UCAS tariff and allow points for key skills. However, in all cases you will need to check the university's prospectus and/or the *Big UCAS Guide* carefully.

Older students, or those with an unorthodox educational background, will generally be treated more flexibly by universities. While you will still be expected

---

### The UCAS Tariff

For many years, A-level grades were often converted to a numerical score with a maximum of 30 (A-level A=10, B=8, ..., E = 2, AS A=5, B=4, ..., E=1). This was sometimes for statistical purposes such as league tables, where an average score could be calculated for a group of students. At other times it was for use in the UCAS offer-making process, where a conditional offer of a place might be expressed as 20 points at A level instead of grades BCC. This scoring system was widely accepted but it had some problems, notably the fact that it only covered A levels/AS and not the increasing diversity of UK qualifications.

As a result, UCAS has developed a new tariff. This allocates a numerical score to a much wider range of qualifications and attainments, establishing an equivalence between them and allowing the aggregation of scores from many different qualifications. The new tariff has also changed the relationship between different levels of achievement from the old A-level points score (for example, on the old points score an E at A-level was worth 20% of an A, while on the new tariff it is worth 33% of an A).

The new tariff is available from 2002 for universities to use in making their offers of places but not all universities are using it. Some do not agree with the equivalences and weights determined by UCAS while others simply prefer to make offers based on specific grades in specific subjects. In general, universities that appear higher up *The Times* League Table are less likely to use the UCAS tariff in making their offers. Even those using it are likely to require specific grades in certain key subjects as well as an overall tariff score.

Full details are on the UCAS web site (www.ucas.ac.uk) but some of the main scores in the new tariff are as follows:

| Score | English Qualifications | | Scottish Qualifications | | Key Skills |
|---|---|---|---|---|---|
| | GCE AS | GCE A Level | Advanced | Higher | |
| | VCE AS | VCE A Level | Higher | | |
| 120 | | A | A | | |
| 100 | | B | B | | |
| 80 | | C | C | | |
| 72 | | | | A | |
| 60 | A | D | | B | |
| 50 | B | | | | |
| 48 | | | | C | |
| 40 | C | E | | | |
| 30 | D | | | | Level 4 |
| 20 | E | | | | Level 3 |

to demonstrate your ability and suitability for the course, you will be able to do this through a wide variety of qualifications or an access course or, in some cases, relevant work experience. The GCSEs you flunked as an unhappy adolescent before diving into the first job that became available will be ignored and the emphasis will be on what you can do now.

Bear in mind that entry standards are essentially market-related. Popular courses at popular universities can afford to be very choosy about who they admit and so have the highest entry standards. That doesn't mean the courses are any tougher at those universities (though they could be for other reasons) but it does mean that most of the students on the courses will be very able.

## Type of Course

Having decided what you want to study, you will be faced with a variety of ways of studying it. The most basic difference is between the levels of the courses. While most higher education courses lead to a degree, some lead to sub-degree qualifications such as a Higher National Diploma (HND) or the new Foundation Degree. In general sub-degree courses will be shorter, more vocationally orientated, and have lower entry requirements. Some will be linked to degree courses, giving you the option of progressing to a degree if you perform well enough on the early parts of the course.

Courses can differ markedly in length, varying from two years for most sub-degree courses to six years for a professional course in architecture, and possibly more for some part-time courses. The majority of full-time courses are three years, but most language courses last four years and there is an increasing number of science and engineering courses which lead to a Master's degree (such as MChem or MEng) after four years. In some cases it is possible to add a foundation year to the beginning of a course, making it a further year in length. These foundation courses vary somewhat in nature and entry requirements. Some are essentially a conversion course for students who have the 'wrong' subjects in their examinations and will expect the same or a similar standard for entry as the courses they lead on to (though key subjects for direct entry will not be required). Others are designed to take students who have performed below the normal entry requirements for a course to bring them up to speed. These courses will often have lower entry requirements.

In some cases the length of a course can be misleading if you intend to go on to a profession in the same subject. Five years of medicine or six of architecture will qualify you to start work as a doctor or an architect (though in both cases there are further hurdles before full qualification). However, three years of law does not qualify you to be a lawyer. You must undertake further training (at your own expense) before you can work as a barrister or a solicitor. In the case of engineering, a four-year MEng course will give you maximum credit towards the status of Chartered Engineer, but if you take a BEng course you will have to undertake further study after you have finished.

Some differences between courses relate to aspects of the subject itself. Only the very largest academic departments have expertise in all aspects of a subject and so, especially in the later years, the course will focus on the particular expertise of the department. You will need to decide whether a particular course offers the areas of the subject you want to study. Of course you may not know, or may change your mind as you go through the course. If you think this is likely, then a course in a large department with a wide range of options might be best.

Even for courses with a similar content, there may nonetheless be significant differences. Some of the opportunities you may want to consider are:

- spending a year or part of a year in Europe under an ERASMUS programme
- taking time out on a work placement
- extending the course to four years to obtain a Masters degree (common for engineering and some science courses)
- being taught part of your course by a media personality or a Nobel prize-winner who is a member of staff in the department

Courses also differ in their structure. Some will concentrate on a single subject, some will allow you to combine two subjects in a single course (often called Dual or Joint Honours courses), and others will involve several subjects. Some will have a large proportion of the course fixed in advance, while others will allow you to choose options to make up a substantial part of the course. There are even 'pick and mix' courses where you can choose from a wide range of very diverse options (though in making choices on such a course it is worth thinking about a choice that will look coherent to an employer).

Some courses are organised on a modular basis, usually with two semesters rather than three terms per year. Each module will require the same amount of study and will usually be assessed separately. This tends to increase the number of examinations and assessments you will have to do. Modular courses are often advertised as being very flexible, allowing you to choose your options from a very wide range of available modules, and indeed they generally are more flexible than traditionally organised courses. However, they may not be as flexible as they appear as timetable clashes will restrict the real choice that is available to you.

There will be differences in teaching methods and assessment. Some courses will make more use than others of particular teaching methods, such as tutorials (though watch out for groups of 15-20 that are still called tutorials), computer-assisted learning or dissertations. If you seize up in formal examinations, you may want a course with a lot of continuous assessment. Alternatively, if you don't like the continuous pressure that this involves, you may prefer one with an emphasis on final examinations.

### Which Subject is Hardest to Get Into?

There is no simple answer to this question. Some courses are very popular – they get a lot of applications – but the standard of those applications may on average be low. For example, primary education makes the top ten most popular subjects but the average A-level score of new entrants is one of the lowest for any subject. Similarly, veterinary science only gets 1,400 applications but has one of the top A-level scores. Generally, the hardest subjects to get into will be those which *both* attract large numbers of applications *and* attract lots of good applicants and so have a high average A-level score. Having said that, an applicant with AAA (or AAAAA in Scotland) in the right subjects will find it easy to get into almost any course he or she wants.

## Quality

Having narrowed down the course options, you can start to check out their quality, and here *The Times* subject tables can be helpful. These rank universities on the basis of their teaching quality, research quality and the entry standards of their new students. The most important aspect of this is the teaching assessment (technically known as a Subject Review) and this is given the highest weight in the subject tables.

The results of each Subject Review are available via the websites of the QAA or the higher education funding councils (HEFCE for England and Northern Ireland, SHEFC for Scotland and HEFCW for Wales). The full reports for England, Northern Ireland and Scotland are also available on the websites, so you can easily find out about the subjects and universities you are interested in (if you haven't got access to the internet you can buy copies). The older reports in England and Wales, which led to an Excellent or Satisfactory rating, were an attempt to judge the absolute level of teaching quality in each university for the subjects covered. The more recent reports, which lead to a score of 1 to 4 on six aspects of teaching (giving a total out of 24), and all reports in Scotland, are an assessment against the universities' own objectives in teaching. This is an important distinction. On the old English system you can be reasonably confident that a department with an Excellent rating was better at teaching than one with a Satisfactory rating (or at least it was back in 1994 or 1995 when the assessment was carried out – a lot could have changed since then). However, on the new English system, all you can say is that a department with a higher score was better at meeting its own objectives than one with a lower score. A department with very high aspirations, trying to offer the best course in the country but not quite succeeding, could end up with a lower score than a much more modest department which aimed to achieve far less but did so completely. So if you read any Subject Reviews, remember to read the section on the department's objectives very carefully.

Every course is different, but every student wants different things, so the chances of finding a perfect match is not that high, despite the huge range of courses. You will almost certainly end up having to decide what is most important to you. Do you want the best course or one which is quite good but offers the options you really want? Do you want the ideal work placement or the course with least continuous assessment? As with choosing a university, the decision will not be easy and only you can make it. More good luck!

# 4

# The Top Universities by Subject

K nowing where a university stands in the pecking order of higher education is a vital piece of information for any prospective student, but the quality of the course is what matters most. The most modest institution may have a centre of specialist excellence and even famous universities have mediocre departments. This section offers some pointers to the leading universities in those subjects assessed by the higher education funding councils. Expert assessors have produced official ratings for research and teaching.

The tables in this chapter cover all the areas in which teaching has been assessed in England. The top 40 universities are given individual scores and full information in the tables. Thereafter, universities are listed in rank order.

The method used to compare universities takes account of three elements: the funding councils' ratings for teaching; the funding councils' ratings for research; and average A-level entry scores. The three indicators are combined using the same methodology and weightings as in the main university League Table: 2.5 for teaching; 1.5 for research; 1 for A levels. To qualify for inclusion in a table, a university had to have data for at least two out of three measures. Where one measure was missing this was taken into account in calculating the overall score. Differences in the gradings used by the Scottish and Welsh funding councils have been accommodated by calculating an equivalent on the English scale.

The tables confirm the dominance of the traditional universities in most areas of higher education. This is to be expected in research, where decades of differential funding have left the former polytechnics struggling to compete. Less predictably, however, the ratings for teaching have usually told the same story. This is partly because the academics who inspect departments take into account facilities such as library stock, while the traditional universities' generally smaller teaching groups also give them an advantage.

There are exceptions, however. In hospitality, for example, Liverpool John Moores collected top ratings for teaching and research and becomes the first new university to take first place in one of *The Times* subject tables. Overall, however, Cambridge is again by far the most successful university, with 16 top placings and a top ten placing in nearly every subject in which it offers undergraduate courses. Oxford has the next highest number of top places with nine.

| | | Appearances in Subject Tables | Top Places | Times in Top Ten | % in Top Ten |
|---|---|---|---|---|---|
| 1 | Cambridge | 42 | 16 | 40 | 95.2 |
| 2 | Oxford | 35 | 9 | 30 | 85.7 |
| 3 | Warwick | 25 | 2 | 18 | 72.0 |
| 4 | York | 25 | 0 | 18 | 72.0 |
| 5 | Wales College of Medicine | 3 | 0 | 2 | 66.7 |
| 6 | Durham | 32 | 1 | 21 | 65.6 |
| 7 | University College London | 38 | 1 | 24 | 63.2 |
| 8 | Imperial College | 18 | 0 | 11 | 61.1 |
| 9 | Nottingham | 47 | 4 | 28 | 59.6 |
| 10 | Sheffield | 45 | 1 | 24 | 53.3 |
| 11 | Edinburgh | 41 | 0 | 21 | 51.2 |
| 12 | London School of Economics | 12 | 3 | 6 | 50.0 |
| 13 | Bristol | 39 | 3 | 19 | 48.7 |
| 14 | Bath | 26 | 3 | 12 | 46.2 |
| 15 | Manchester | 48 | 3 | 21 | 43.8 |
| 16 | SOAS | 12 | 0 | 5 | 41.7 |
| 17 | UMIST | 17 | 0 | 7 | 41.2 |
| 18 | Loughborough | 27 | 2 | 11 | 40.7 |
| 19 | Southampton | 37 | 1 | 14 | 37.8 |
| 20 | St Andrews | 25 | 0 | 9 | 36.0 |

Excludes universities appearing in a single table

The subject rankings demonstrate that there are 'horses for courses' in higher education. Thus the London School of Economics is more than a match for its rivals in social science while Imperial College confirms its reputation in engineering. In their own fields, table-toppers such as East Anglia (environmental science) and Bath (mechanical engineering) are equally well-known.

In all the tables, the following information is provided when it is available:

*TQA (Teaching Quality Assessment).* The assessment is recorded either with a score (with a maximum of 24) or by a letter – E for Excellent, S for Satisfactory and, in Scotland, an additional category, HS for Highly Satisfactory. At the end of each table the dates of the teaching quality assessments in England are given. This tells you how old the English assessments are as some were carried out in the mid-1990s and so are getting quite old. The dates of assessments in Scotland and Wales were usually different but in the majority of subjects took place before those in England. Recently a new cycle of assessments has started in

Scotland but the outcomes are not reported in a way that can easily be translated into a numerical outcome. Instead we have included the results in a footnote to the table.

*RAE (Research Assessment Exercise).* This provides a measure of the average quality of research undertaken in the subject area. The first figure gives a quality rating of 5* (top), 5, 4, 3a, 3b, 2 or 1 (bottom). The letter refers to the proportion of staff included in the numerical assessment, with A including viritually everyone and F hardly anyone. These data are from 2001.

*A Levels.* This is the average A-level score for new students under the age of 21, taken from HESA data for 1999–2000. Each student's best three A level or AS grades are converted to a numerical score (A level A=10, B=8, C=6, D=4, E=2; AS A=5, B=4, C=3, D=2, E=1) and added up to give a score out of 30. HESA then calculates an average score for the university.

The subjects listed below are covered in the tables in this chapter.

Aeronautical and manufacturing engineering
Agriculture and forestry
American studies
Anatomy and physiology
Anthropology
Archaeology
Architecture
Art and design
Building
Business studies
Celtic studies
Chemical engineering
Chemistry
Civil engineering
Classics and ancient history
Communications and media studies
Computer science
Dentistry
Drama, dance and cinematics
East and South Asian studies
Economics
Education
Electrical and electronic engineering
English
Environmental science
Food science
French
General engineering
Geography
Geology
German
History
History of art
Hospitality, leisure, recreation, sport and tourism

Iberian languages
Italian
Land and property management
Law
Librarianship and information management
Linguistics
Materials technology
Mathematics
Mechanical engineering
Medicine
Middle East and African studies
Molecular biosciences
Music
Nursing
Organismal biosciences
Other subjects allied to medicine (see p. 115 for subjects included in this category)
Pharmacology and pharmacy
Philosophy
Physics and astronomy
Politics
Psychology
Russian and East European languages
Social policy
Social work
Sociology
Theology and religious studies
Town and country planning and landscape
Veterinary medicine

## Aeronautical and Manufacturing Engineering

The courses under this heading focus mainly on aeronautical or manufacturing engineering, but includes some with a mechanical title. To add to the confusion, manufacturing degrees often go under the rubric of production engineering. (*See* General Engineering and Mechanical Engineering)

Bath has taken a clear lead at the top of the table, after achieving a 5* rating for research and with entry standards exceeded only by Imperial College. Like a number of universities in the ranking, Bath had its teaching assessed under a different category, so its other scores are averaged to produce an overall result. Imperial, Liverpool, Southampton and Queen's, Belfast, were the other top scorers for research, but none managed more than 22 points out of 24 for teaching.

Only second-placed Nottingham and Kingston, the top-placed new university, were awarded maximum points for teaching. Loughborough was next-best in an assessment that produced an unusually wide spread of points. Glasgow is the top university in Scotland, with Swansea best-placed in Wales.

Failure rates in first-year exams are high – between 32 and 45 per cent in 1998 – but most pass resits. At least two-thirds of graduates go on to further study or training to meet professional requirements and, particularly for the 3,000 aeronautical engineering graduates, employment prospects are bright.

| | | TQA | RAE | | A-Levels | Score |
|---|---|---|---|---|---|---|
| 1 | Bath | | 5* | A | 28.3 | 100.0 |
| 2 | Nottingham | 24 | 5 | B | 19.7 | 87.6 |
| 3 | Imperial College | 22 | 5* | B | 29.1 | 87.1 |
| 4 | Sheffield | | 5 | A | 24.8 | 86.6 |
| 5 | UMIST | | 5 | A | 24.4 | 85.9 |
| 6 | Loughborough | 23 | 5 | B | 22.3 | 83.9 |
| 7 | Southampton | 21 | 5* | A | 27.0 | 82.5 |
| 8 | Bristol | 22 | 4 | B | 27.9 | 79.2 |
| 9 | Queen's, Belfast | 21 | 5* | B | 25.5 | 78.3 |
| 10 | Glasgow | | 4 | A | 21.4 | 73.1 |
| 11 | Kingston | 24 | 3a | C | 12.5 | 72.0 |
| 12 | Liverpool | 20 | 5* | A | 21.2 | 71.8 |
| 13 | Cranfield | 22 | 4 | C | 20.6 | 69.7 |
| 14 | Manchester | 20 | 5 | B | 23.4 | 67.3 |
| 15 | Aston | | 5 | C | 20.6 | 66.2 |
| 16 | Swansea | | 4 | A | 17.0 | 65.9 |
| 17 | Queen Mary | | 5 | B | 15.2 | 65.7 |
| 18 | Brunel | 20 | 5 | C | 19.8 | 60.1 |
| 19 | Hertfordshire | 22 | 3a | D | 15.1 | 59.2 |
| 20 | Birmingham | 20 | 4 | C | 19.2 | 56.9 |
| 21 | Salford | | 3a | A | 13.3 | 51.9 |
| 22 | Sheffield Hallam | 21 | | | 17.3 | 47.7 |
| 23 | UWCN, Newport | S | 3a | D | | 47.2 |
| 24 | City | 19 | 4 | D | 18.0 | 46.0 |
| 25 | Coventry | 18 | 3a | C | 17.0 | 40.6 |
| 26 | UWIC, Cardiff | S | | | 14.1 | 39.2 |
| 27 | Staffordshire | | 3b | A | 9.6 | 38.1 |
| 28 | Anglia | 19 | 2 | C | | 36.9 |
| 29 | Derby | | 3a | D | 12.8 | 35.9 |

## Aeronautical and Manufacturing Engineering (cont.)

|    |                       | TQA | RAE |   | A-Levels | Score |
|----|-----------------------|-----|-----|---|----------|-------|
| 30 | Liverpool John Moores |     | 3a  | E | 15.5     | 34.1  |
| 31 | Plymouth              |     | 4   | E | 14.1     | 34.0  |
| 32 | Bournemouth           | 18  |     |   | 15.9     | 29.0  |
| 33 | South Bank            | 17  | 3a  | D | 11.5     | 27.0  |
| 34 | East London           | 18  |     |   | 10.1     | 24.2  |
| 35 | Leeds Metropolitan    | 17  |     |   | 8.3      | 16.8  |

**TQA (England) 1996–98**

**Firsts and 2:1s:** 53%; 51% (production)

**Employment:** 69.0 %; 76% (production)

**Further study:** 19.0%; 9% (production)

**Unemployment:** 7.0%; 8.0% (production)

New Scottish Academic Review: *Glasgow Caledonian*: confidence in the academic standards; the quality of teaching and learning, student progression and learning resources was commendable.

## Agriculture and Forestry

Nottingham tops the agriculture table with the best teaching score and a research grade matched only by third-placed Reading. Leeds and Bangor also reached grade 5 for research, but entered fewer academics for assessment. Behind Nottingham, there have been several changes since last year, partly because Edinburgh has dropped out, transferring its courses to Aberdeen. Newcastle has taken over second place, despite a disappointing research grade.

Fourth-placed Queen's, Belfast, is the only university where the entrants had an average of a B and two Cs at A level, while at Greenwich, two Ds secured a place. Plymouth is the top-placed new university, thanks to a teaching assessment which was second only to Nottingham's.

This is one of the few subject areas in which no university achieved full marks for teaching or research. Scores in both sets of assessments are tightly bunched, covering only three grades in the case of research.

A quarter of those enrolling for degrees in agriculture and more than a third in forestry do so without A levels, often coming with relevant work experience. As befits a firmly vocational area, employment rates are high.

|    |                  | TQA | RAE |   | A-Levels | Score |
|----|------------------|-----|-----|---|----------|-------|
| 1  | Nottingham       | 23  | 5   | A | 19.3     | 100.0 |
| 2  | Newcastle        | 22  | 4   | B | 18.0     | 89.4  |
| 3  | Reading          | 21  | 5   | A | 18.4     | 88.4  |
| 4  | Queen's, Belfast | 21  | 4   | C | 20.8     | 83.8  |
| 5  | Leeds            | 20  | 5   | B | 19.9     | 82.4  |
| 6  | Imperial College | 22  |     |   | 19.6     | 79.1  |
| 7  | Bangor           | S   | 5   | C | 16.9     | 77.2  |
| 8  | Plymouth         | 22  | 3a  | E | 12.6     | 76.4  |
| 9  | Aberystwyth      |     | 3a  | C | 15.3     | 72.6  |
| 10 | Coventry         | 21  |     |   | 15.2     | 70.1  |
| 11 | Aberdeen         |     | 3a  | C | 13.4     | 69.5  |
| 12 | West of England  | 20  |     |   | 14.3     | 63.9  |
| 13 | Greenwich        | 20  | 3a  | D | 7.6      | 63.6  |
| 14 | Bournemouth      | 20  |     |   | 11.5     | 61.7  |

## Agriculture and Forestry (cont.)

|  | TQA | RAE | A-Levels | Score |
|---|---|---|---|---|
| 15  Lincoln | 19 |  | 15.5 | 59.4 |
| 16  Central Lancashire | 18 |  | 12.6 | 51.6 |

**TQA (England) 1996–98**
**Firsts and 2:1 degrees:** 54% (forestry 57%)
**Employment:** 73% (forestry 75%)
**Further study:** 12% (forestry 15%)
**Unemployment:** 6% (forestry 9%)

## American Studies

Only 18 universities have been assessed for American Studies, although some others offer courses in the subject as part of modular degree schemes. Manchester comes straight in at the top of the ranking, having been assessed for research and issued A-level scores for the first time. Its students' entrance qualifications were easily the highest and only third-placed Nottingham achieved a better research grade.

Although the top six places are filled by traditional universities, Central Lancashire is comfortably in the top ten, sharing with East Anglia and Keele the distinction of a maximum 24 points for teaching. Keele takes second place, despite a much lower A-level score than a number of other universities in the table.

Kent, Ulster and Aberystwyth are new arrivals in the top ten. Birmingham had the best-qualified entrants, averaging more than an A and two Bs at A level. But a C and two Ds would have secured a place at most of the new universities.

Nine out of ten students taking American Studies have A levels or equivalent qualifications and entrance requirements are high. This translates into an impressive level of firsts and 2:1s, although a relatively high proportion remain unemployed six months after graduating.

|  | TQA | RAE | | A-Levels | Score |
|---|---|---|---|---|---|
| 1  Manchester |  | 5 | B | 27.3 | 100.0 |
| 2  Keele | 24 | 5 | B | 18.7 | 97.2 |
| =3  Nottingham | 22 | 5* | B | 25.9 | 94.4 |
| =3  Sussex | 23 | 5 | B | 23.7 | 94.4 |
| 5  East Anglia | 24 | 4 | C | 22.6 | 90.4 |
| 6  Birmingham | 22 | 4 | B | 25.2 | 84.4 |
| 7  Central Lancashire | 24 | 3b | A | 13.1 | 80.9 |
| 8  Kent | 21 | 4 | B | 21.3 | 75.6 |
| 9  Ulster | 22 | 4 | C |  | 74.9 |
| 10  Aberystwyth | S | 4 | B | 18.4 | 67.4 |
| 11  Derby | 21 | 3a | B | 15.3 | 66.8 |
| 12  Hull | 23 |  |  | 23.3 | 66.2 |
| 13  Brunel | 21 | 3a | B | 14.2 | 66.0 |
| 14  Swansea | S | 3a | A | 19.1 | 65.4 |
| 15  Leicester | 23 |  |  | 21.9 | 65.3 |

## American Studies (cont.)

|  | TQA | RAE | | A-Levels | Score |
|---|---|---|---|---|---|
| 16 Wolverhampton | 21 | 4 | C | 10.2 | 63.3 |
| 17 Reading | 21 | | | 20.3 | 51.8 |
| 18 Liverpool John Moores | 21 | | | 14.1 | 47.5 |

**TQA (England) 1996–98**
**Firsts and 2:1s:** 71%
**Employment:** 70%
**Further study:** 15%
**Unemployment:** 7%

## Anatomy and Physiology

Bristol takes over at the top of the ranking, having added a 5* research grade in anatomy to one of the four maximum scores for teaching. King's College London was the other research star in anatomy, while Manchester and Liverpool reached the top grade in physiology.

In a high-scoring teaching quality assessment completed in 2000, Newcastle and Loughborough, in second and third places, joined Bristol on maximum points. Sheffield was the other top-scorer, but the absence of entries in the relevant categories of the Research Assessment Exercise keeps the university out of the top ten. Oxford also misses the top ten, despite having by far the highest entry grades, because it has one of the lowest teaching scores.

Fifth-placed Cardiff and St Andrews, another absentee in the research assessments, also achieved Excellent ratings for teaching in the Welsh and Scottish systems. Only three former polytechnics appear among the 21 universities in the ranking. Sunderland, which achieved a near-perfect teaching score, is the highest-placed, despite having the lowest average entry grades in the table. Elsewhere, only South Bank and Westminster average less than three Cs at A level.

In spite of the generally high marks for teaching, assessors in England found wide variations in some areas. The proportion of students awarded 2:1s, for example, ranged from 30 per cent in one unnamed university to 90 per cent in another. Some equipment was found to be outdated, but students acquired good knowledge of the subjects and skills that are in demand from employers.

|  | TQA | RAE | | | | A-Levels | Score |
|---|---|---|---|---|---|---|---|
|  |  | Anatomy | | Physiology | |  |  |
| 1 Bristol | 24 | 5* | A | 4 | A | 25.9 | 100.0 |
| 2 Newcastle | 24 | | | 5 | A | 20.9 | 99.0 |
| 3 Loughborough | 24 | | | 4 | A | 22.2 | 95.9 |
| 4 Manchester | 23 | | | 5* | B | 22.7 | 94.6 |
| 5 Cardiff | E | 5 | A | | | 20.2 | 92.3 |
| 6 Liverpool | 23 | 4 | A | 5* | A | 18.6 | 91.6 |
| 7 Cambridge | 23 | 5 | A | 4 | B | | 90.2 |
| 8 Nottingham | 22 | | | 5 | A | 25.4 | 89.1 |
| 9 King's College London | 22 | 5* | B | | | 21.2 | 87.5 |

## Anatomy and Physiology (cont.)

| | | TQA | | RAE Anatomy | | Physiology | A-Levels | Score |
|---|---|---|---|---|---|---|---|---|
| 10 | Aberdeen | | | | 5 | B | 19.8 | 87.1 |
| 11 | University College London | 22 | 5 A | | 4 | A | 24.4 | 87.0 |
| 12 | Leeds | 22 | | | 5 | B | 22.4 | 84.9 |
| 13 | Oxford | 21 | 5 B | | 5 | A | 29.3 | 84.4 |
| 14 | Sheffield | 24 | | | | | 25.6 | 79.6 |
| 15 | Sunderland | 23 | | | 3a | B | 10.8 | 77.7 |
| 16 | Salford | 22 | | | 3a | A | | 76.8 |
| 17 | St Andrews | E | | | | | 23.7 | 72.2 |
| 18 | Queen's, Belfast | 22 | | | | | 20.9 | 64.4 |
| 19 | Reading | 21 | | | | | 20.3 | 57.7 |
| 20 | South Bank | 20 | | | 3a | D | 12.5 | 54.2 |
| 21 | Westminster | 21 | | | | | 11.3 | 52.5 |

**TQA (England) 1998–2000**
**Firsts and 2:1s:** 58%
**Employment:** 46%
**Further study:** 41%
**Unemployment:** 7%

## Anthropology

Anthropology offers the best chance of a good degree in the social sciences, but the unemployment rate is also high. Almost one graduate in five goes on to take a higher degree or some form of postgraduate training.

With maximum points for both teaching and research, LSE overtakes Cambridge this year. Fourth-placed University College was the only other institution rated internationally outstanding for research, but it entered fewer academics and had marginally lower entrance qualifications than LSE. Sandwiched between them are Oxford and Cambridge, sharing the highest A-level scores.

Many teaching scores date from the early rounds of assessment, and the subject was not assessed separately for teaching quality in Scotland or Wales. Hull's assessment was carried out under the current English system, giving a maximum of 24 points. Oxford Brookes and East London are the only new universities among the 19 offering the subject.

There is little to choose between Sussex, Manchester, Durham and the SOAS, since all were rated as Excellent for teaching and were graded five for research. Kent has the same assessment grades, but a much lower A-level score. Brunel does not have a single-honours degree in anthropology so its teaching and research scores are averaged to produce a total.

| | | TQA | RAE | | A-Levels | Score |
|---|---|---|---|---|---|---|
| 1 | London School of Economics | E | 5* | A | 26.3 | 100.0 |
| =2 | Cambridge | E | 5 | A | 29.4 | 96.0 |
| =2 | Oxford | E | 5 | A | 29.4 | 96.0 |

## Anthropology (cont.)

| | | TQA | RAE | | A Levels | Score |
|---|---|---|---|---|---|---|
| 4 | University College London | E | 5* | B | 26.2 | 95.4 |
| 5 | Sussex | E | 5 | A | 24.7 | 92.9 |
| 6 | St Andrews | | 5 | A | 23.4 | 92.6 |
| 7 | Edinburgh | | 5 | B | 28.5 | 91.3 |
| 8 | Manchester | E | 5 | B | 26.3 | 90.1 |
| 9 | SOAS | E | 5 | B | 25.3 | 89.4 |
| 10 | Durham | E | 5 | B | 23.8 | 88.5 |
| 11 | Kent | E | 5 | B | 19.5 | 85.7 |
| 12 | Brunel | E | 4 | A | | 85.2 |
| 13 | Oxford Brookes | E | 4 | A | 19.0 | 83.3 |
| 14 | Goldsmiths College | S | 5 | A | 21.4 | 68.4 |
| 15 | Queen's, Belfast | S | 5 | B | 22.5 | 65.3 |
| 16 | Swansea | | 3a | A | 17.7 | 61.1 |
| 17 | East London | | 4 | B | 11.1 | 58.1 |
| 18 | Hull | 20 | 3a | B | | 55.7 |
| 19 | Lampeter | | 3a | A | 12.8 | 54.8 |

**TQA (England) 1994–95**
**Firsts and 2:1 degrees:** 68%
**Employment:** 63%
**Further study:** 19%
**Unemployment:** 9%

## Archaeology

Cambridge tops the first ranking for archaeology, despite not being one of the three English universities with maximum points for teaching. Second-placed Exeter, Leicester and York are the top-rated teaching universities, together with Cardiff and Lampeter in Wales. But the highest entrance qualifications and one of the three 5* research grades carry the day for Cambridge.

Fourth-placed Reading and Oxford were the other top-rated research universities in the 2001 assessments, Oxford also running Cambridge close on A-level scores. Edinburgh is the only Scottish institution in the ranking, while UWCN, Newport and Bournemouth are the only new universities of the 25 offering degrees in the subject.

Outside Oxbridge, where the normal high entry standards apply, only Durham had average entry grades of three Bs at A level in 2000. Two Cs and a D was enough to secure a place even at some traditional universities.

About 1,000 students began courses in archaeology in 2001, more than 150 of them securing their places through clearing. Even in the most lowly rated universities, assessors found high-quality teaching and a broad curriculum.

| | | TQA | RAE | | A-Levels | Score |
|---|---|---|---|---|---|---|
| 1 | Cambridge | 23 | 5* | A | 29.4 | 100.0 |
| 2 | Exeter | 24 | 5 | A | 22.6 | 99.8 |
| 3 | Leicester | 24 | 5 | A | 18.9 | 97.4 |
| 4 | Reading | 23 | 5* | A | 18.9 | 93.0 |

## Archaeology (cont.)

| | | TQA | RAE | | A-Levels | Score |
|---|---|---|---|---|---|---|
| 5 | York | 24 | 3a | A | 24.3 | 92.5 |
| 6 | Durham | 23 | 5 | A | 23.8 | 92.1 |
| 7 | University College London | 23 | 5 | A | 23.3 | 91.7 |
| 8 | Oxford | 22 | 5* | A | 29.0 | 91.1 |
| 9 | Queen's, Belfast | 23 | 5 | A | 21.3 | 90.4 |
| 10 | Cardiff | E | 5 | A | 20.0 | 89.5 |
| 11 | Southampton | | 5 | A | 19.1 | 87.3 |
| 12 | Manchester | 23 | 5 | B | 18.1 | 85.5 |
| 13 | Sheffield | 22 | 5 | A | 21.6 | 82.0 |
| 14 | Lampeter | E | 4 | A | 13.0 | 80.7 |
| 15 | Edinburgh | | 3a | A | 26.8 | 80.6 |
| 16 | Liverpool | 22 | 5 | A | 17.9 | 79.5 |
| 17 | Bristol | 22 | 4 | B | 23.9 | 77.0 |
| 18 | Bradford | 22 | 5 | B | 14.0 | 74.2 |
| 19 | Bangor | | 4 | B | 15.9 | 70.0 |
| 20 | Nottingham | 21 | 4 | A | 21.8 | 69.3 |
| 21 | Birmingham | 21 | 4 | B | 22.3 | 67.4 |
| 22 | UWCN, Newport | | 3a | A | 13.2 | 62.6 |
| 23 | Newcastle | 21 | 3a | B | 19.3 | 61.6 |
| 24 | Bournemouth | 22 | 3a | C | 10.8 | 61.5 |
| 25 | Kent | 22 | | | 15.5 | 53.0 |

**TQA (England) 2000–01**
**Firsts and 2:1 degrees:** 68%
**Employment:** 61%
**Further study:** 23%
**Unemployment:** 9%

New Scottish Academic Review: *Edinburgh*: confidence in the academic standards; the quality of teaching and learning, student progression and learning resources was commendable.

## Architecture

Cambridge holds onto top place for architecture, despite registering a grade 4 for research. The highest entry qualifications, plus one of ten Excellent grades for teaching, just keeps Sheffield in second place. No university was considered internationally outstanding for research, but Sheffield, Bath, Cardiff and Brighton all reached grade 5.

Architecture was among the first subjects to be assessed for teaching quality, and eight universities in England were top-rated. In Scotland, only Strathclyde managed top marks, and in Wales, Cardiff did the same.

East London and Greenwich are the highest-placed of the new universities offering architecture. Both are rated as Excellent for teaching quality. Ulster has been omitted from the table at the request of the university.

A third of all undergraduates enter with qualifications other than A level, Highers or equivalents. There is a wide spread of entrance scores, from an A-level score of almost 30 at Cambridge to fewer than 12 at Huddersfield and Lincoln. Unemployment on graduation is low. Over two-thirds of graduates go on to complete their professional training, either with further study or within a job.

## Architecture (cont.)

| | | TQA | RAE | | A-Levels | Score |
|---|---|---|---|---|---|---|
| 1 | Cambridge | E | 4 | A | 29.4 | 100.0 |
| 2 | Sheffield | E | 5 | B | 27.1 | 99.7 |
| 3 | Bath | E | 5 | B | 26.3 | 99.1 |
| 4 | Cardiff | E | 5 | A | 22.4 | 98.7 |
| 5 | Nottingham | E | 4 | A | 26.6 | 97.9 |
| 6 | University College London | E | 4 | C | 26.2 | 92.1 |
| 7 | Newcastle | E | 4 | C | 24.7 | 90.9 |
| 8 | Strathclyde | E | 4 | C | 22.4 | 89.2 |
| 9 | East London | E | 4 | D | | 85.1 |
| 10 | Edinburgh | HS | 3a | B | 27.3 | 81.7 |
| 11 | Greenwich | E | 3b | E | 13.4 | 72.2 |
| 12 | Liverpool | S | 4 | B | 21.8 | 69.9 |
| 13 | Brighton | S | 5 | B | 13.9 | 67.5 |
| 14 | Nottingham Trent | | 3a | B | 13.5 | 66.6 |
| 15 | Robert Gordon | HS | 3b | D | | 66.2 |
| 16 | De Montfort | S | 4 | A | 13.1 | 65.6 |
| 17 | Queen's, Belfast | S | 2 | B | 23.7 | 60.9 |
| 18 | Oxford Brookes | S | 4 | D | 16.8 | 58.7 |
| 19 | Westminster | S | 4 | D | 15.1 | 57.4 |
| 20 | Portsmouth | S | 3a | D | 16.1 | 56.2 |
| 21 | Liverpool John Moores | S | 3b | C | 15.4 | 56.1 |
| 22 | North London | S | 3a | D | 15.8 | 56.0 |
| 23 | Central England | 20 | 2 | F | 14.4 | 55.3 |
| 24 | Leeds Metropolitan | S | 3b | D | 14.0 | 52.7 |
| 25 | Northumbria | | 3b | D | 14.7 | 52.4 |
| 26 | South Bank | S | 3b | D | | 52.2 |
| 27 | Plymouth | S | | | 20.6 | 52.1 |
| 28 | Glamorgan | | 3b | C | 10.6 | 51.2 |
| 29 | Dundee | S | | | 19.1 | 51.0 |
| 30 | Kingston | S | | | 17.9 | 50.1 |
| 31 | Manchester | S | | | 17.6 | 49.9 |
| 32 | Huddersfield | S | | | 11.6 | 45.4 |
| 33 | Lincoln | S | | | 11.5 | 45.3 |

**TQA (England) 1994**
**Firsts and 2:1s:** 42%
**Employment:** 70%
**Further study:** 22%
**Unemployment:** 4%

New Scottish Academic Review: *Edinburgh, Robert Gordon*: confidence in the academic standards; the quality of teaching and learning, student progression and learning resources was commendable.

## Art and Design

Most courses in art and design are at new universities – often in former art colleges – but it is Oxford and a clutch of old universities that head the ranking. The explanation lies in the high A-level scores, at Oxford averaging almost two As and a B, and also in the recent teaching quality assessments.

Oxford was the only English university to be awarded full marks for teaching, the assessors commenting warmly on the studio-based course. Sixty undergraduates take the Fine Art degree at the Ruskin School of Drawing, almost 90 per

## Art and Design (cont.)

cent of whom generally achieve a first or upper second.

Art and design was one of the few areas to record poorer research grades in 2001 than in previous assessments – no university was rated internationally outstanding. However, as one of six departments awarded grade 5, University College London is clearly second in the ranking. It has a better teaching rating and much higher A-level entry grades than the other research leaders.

Dundee was another top-scorer for teaching quality, rated Excellent under the separate Scottish system and tying with Leeds for third place. UWIC, Cardiff, included in the guide for the first time this year, has the third perfect teaching score, but Aberystwyth's much higher entry standards make it the top university in Wales.

Brighton is the best-placed new university and the only one in the top ten, despite being almost inseparable from Oxford Brookes, which achieved a better rating for teaching quality. London Guildhall is also highly rated for teaching. Although low entry grades and research score cost it a place in the top ten, many artists would argue that these are of less significance than in other subjects.

| | | TQA | RAE | | A-Levels | Score |
|---|---|---|---|---|---|---|
| 1 | Oxford | 24 | 4 | A | 27.6 | 100.0 |
| 2 | University College London | 23 | 5 | B | 22.8 | 92.5 |
| =3 | Dundee | E | 4 | B | | 89.0 |
| =3 | Leeds | 23 | 3a | A | 23.5 | 89.0 |
| 5 | Goldsmiths College | 22 | 5 | B | 21.1 | 86.1 |
| 6 | Aberystwyth | | 3a | A | 20.7 | 85.3 |
| 7 | Lancaster | 23 | 3a | C | 22.4 | 84.9 |
| 8 | City | 23 | 5 | D | | 83.8 |
| 9 | Loughborough | 23 | 4 | C | 15.8 | 82.6 |
| 10 | Brighton | 22 | 5 | B | 14.0 | 81.3 |
| 11 | Oxford Brookes | 23 | 3b | B | 17.3 | 81.0 |
| 12 | Sheffield Hallam | 22 | 5 | C | 17.2 | 80.4 |
| 13 | Southampton | 22 | 4 | C | | 79.2 |
| 14 | UWIC, Cardiff | E | 4 | D | 15.0 | 79.1 |
| 15 | West of England | 22 | 4 | D | 16.7 | 74.9 |
| 16 | Newcastle | 20 | 4 | B | 23.2 | 74.4 |
| 17 | Northumbria | 22 | 4 | D | 15.2 | 73.9 |
| 18 | London Guildhall | 23 | 3b | E | 14.3 | 73.8 |
| 19 | Hertfordshire | 22 | 3a | D | | 73.5 |
| =20 | Reading | 19 | 5 | A | 22.5 | 73.1 |
| =20 | Staffordshire | 22 | 4 | D | 14.0 | 73.1 |
| 22 | Nottingham Trent | 22 | 3a | E | 19.5 | 72.9 |
| 23 | Kingston | 21 | 4 | D | 20.4 | 72.1 |
| =24 | De Montfort | 21 | 4 | C | 14.5 | 71.1 |
| =24 | Central England | 22 | 4 | E | 15.5 | 71.1 |
| =26 | Robert Gordon | HS | 3a | D | | 70.2 |
| =26 | Gloucestershire | 21 | 3a | C | 16.2 | 70.2 |
| =28 | Sunderland | 21 | 4 | C | 12.9 | 70.1 |
| =28 | Coventry | 22 | 3a | D | 11.7 | 70.1 |
| =28 | Plymouth | 21 | 3a | C | 16.0 | 70.1 |

## Art and Design (cont.)

|  | | TQA | RAE | | A-Levels | Score |
|---|---|---|---|---|---|---|
| 31 | Anglia | 21 | 3b | A | 15.2 | 70.0 |
| 32 | Westminster | 21 | 4 | D | 16.6 | 69.5 |
| =33 | Middlesex | 21 | 3a | C | 14.8 | 69.3 |
| =33 | East London | 21 | 4 | D | 16.1 | 69.3 |
| =35 | Manchester Metropolitan | 22 | 4 | E | 12.4 | 69.0 |
| =35 | Bournemouth | 20 | 5 | D | 21.4 | 69.0 |
| 37 | Central Lancashire | 22 | 3b | E | 13.5 | 68.0 |
| 38 | Leeds Metropolitan | 21 | 3a | D | 15.7 | 67.5 |
| 39 | North London | 22 | | | 14.7 | 66.4 |
| 40 | Teesside | 22 | | | 14.1 | 66.0 |

| | | | | | |
|---|---|---|---|---|---|
| 41 | Napier | 42 | Luton | 43 | Portsmouth |
| 44 | Ulster | 45 | South Bank | 46 | Huddersfield |
| 47 | Wolverhampton | 48 | Liverpool John Moores | 49 | Salford |
| 50 | UWCN, Newport | 51 | Derby | 52 | Lincoln |
| 53 | Surrey Roehampton | | | | |

**TQA (England) 1998–2000**
**Firsts and 2:1s:** 56%
**Employment:** 72%
**Further study:** 10%
**Unemployment:** 13%

## Building

Building is one of the most open of the tables because there is less correlation between the top performers in teaching and research. Kingston was the only university to be awarded maximum points for teaching quality, but low entry grades and the absence of a research score in this category restricted it to tenth place. Nottingham, which launched a degree in 1999–2000, takes top place. The teaching quality assessments had already been completed, so the other scores are averaged to produce an overall result.

University College London slips to sixth place after a disappointing research grade, while Loughborough moves to second as one of two universities rated internationally outstanding for research. Salford is the other, but a low teaching score and entry grades restrict the university to 17th place. In Scotland, Heriot-Watt's grade 5 for research helped produce the country's top score.

Universities admit 44 per cent of students with qualifications other than A level. Those who do take the A-level route tend not to require the highest grades – only Loughborough, Nottingham, Reading, UMIST and University College London registered an average of more than three Cs.

Most graduates go straight into jobs, which they combine with further professional training, and unemployment is low. Hertfordshire and Liverpool are omitted at the universities' own request.

## Building (cont.)

| | | TQA | RAE | | A-Levels | Score |
|---|---|---|---|---|---|---|
| 1 | Nottingham | | 4 | A | 22.4 | 100.0 |
| 2 | Loughborough | 22 | 5* | B | 20.4 | 95.7 |
| 3 | Reading | 21 | 5 | B | 20.2 | 88.8 |
| 4 | Ulster | 21 | 5 | A | 17.4 | 88.0 |
| 5 | UMIST | 22 | 4 | C | 18.1 | 87.2 |
| 6 | University College London | | 4 | C | 18.3 | 85.9 |
| 7 | Nottingham Trent | 22 | 3a | B | 14.9 | 84.5 |
| 8 | Oxford Brookes | 23 | 4 | D | 9.7 | 82.2 |
| 9 | Plymouth | 23 | 4 | E | 12.2 | 81.8 |
| 10 | Kingston | 24 | | | 10.7 | 81.6 |
| 11 | Heriot-Watt | S | 5 | B | 15.6 | 80.2 |
| 12 | Coventry | 22 | 3b | C | 13.8 | 80.0 |
| 13 | Liverpool John Moores | 22 | 3b | C | 12.8 | 79.2 |
| =14 | Westminster | 22 | 3a | D | 12.0 | 78.3 |
| =14 | De Montfort | 20 | 4 | A | | 78.3 |
| 16 | Northumbria | 22 | 3b | D | 12.5 | 77.4 |
| =17 | Salford | 18 | 5* | A | 14.7 | 74.3 |
| =17 | Napier | HS | 3b | D | 11.4 | 74.3 |
| 19 | Wolverhampton | 20 | 3a | B | 12.6 | 73.3 |
| 20 | Sheffield Hallam | 21 | 3a | E | 13.4 | 72.8 |
| 21 | Leeds Metropolitan | 21 | 3b | D | 10.8 | 71.4 |
| 22 | Brighton | 20 | 3b | C | 12.9 | 70.1 |
| 23 | Glasgow Caledonian | S | 3a | D | | 69.2 |
| 24 | Anglia | 20 | 2 | B | 12.7 | 69.1 |
| 25 | Greenwich | 21 | 3b | E | 9.4 | 68.7 |
| 26 | West of England | 21 | | | 11.4 | 68.5 |
| 27 | Robert Gordon | S | 3b | D | | 67.6 |
| 28 | Central Lancashire | 20 | 3a | D | 9.0 | 66.5 |
| 29 | Glamorgan | | 3b | C | 10.3 | 65.5 |
| 30 | Portsmouth | 20 | | | 13.1 | 65.3 |
| 31 | Teesside | 19 | 2 | D | | 60.3 |
| 32 | Central England | 18 | 2 | F | 15.1 | 58.0 |
| 33 | South Bank | 18 | 3b | D | | 56.1 |
| 34 | Staffordshire | 17 | | | 11.3 | 49.9 |

**TQA (England) 1996–98**
**Firsts and 2:1s:** 48%
**Employment:** 85%
**Further study:** 5%
**Unemployment:** 5%

## Business Studies

New teaching and research ratings have produced considerable flux in the ranking, but universities could choose whether or not to be reassessed for teaching quality, so there is a mix of new and old-style grades. Third-placed Warwick and Lancaster, in fifth, are the only universities in the table to be rated internationally outstanding for research. But high entry grades and one of seven perfect scores for teaching in the latest round of assessments give the London School of Economics top spot. London and Manchester business schools are

## Business Studies (cont.)

absent because they do not offer first degrees.

Three new universities – Leeds Metropolitan, North London and Oxford Brookes – are among those with top teaching marks, although Hertfordshire is the nearest to the top 20. Strathclyde is the top university in Scotland, the only one to be rated Excellent for teaching. No such distinction was awarded in Wales.

Six universities have average A-level scores of more than an A and two Bs at A level, with others close to that mark. However, three Cs will secure a place at many of the top 50 institutions.

| | | TQA | RAE | | A-Levels | Score |
|---|---|---|---|---|---|---|
| 1 | London School of Economics | 24 | 5 | A | 28.3 | 100.0 |
| 2 | Aston | 24 | 5 | B | 22.7 | 94.0 |
| 3 | Warwick | E | 5* | B | 27.0 | 93.3 |
| 4 | Bath | E | 5 | A | 27.9 | 93.1 |
| 5 | Lancaster | E | 5* | B | 25.8 | 92.4 |
| 6 | UMIST | E | 5 | A | 24.9 | 91.0 |
| =7 | Manchester | 24 | 5 | C | 22.1 | 90.2 |
| =7 | Nottingham | E | 5 | B | 26.6 | 90.2 |
| 9 | Queen's, Belfast | 23 | 4 | B | 26.8 | 87.6 |
| 10 | Imperial College | E | 5 | B | 21.4 | 86.4 |
| 11 | Southampton | 23 | 4 | B | 24.5 | 85.9 |
| 12 | City | 23 | 5 | C | 23.0 | 84.2 |
| 13 | Ulster | 24 | 3a | D | 21.0 | 82.4 |
| 14 | Strathclyde | E | 4 | C | 22.6 | 81.8 |
| 15 | Leeds | 22 | 5 | C | 25.1 | 79.2 |
| 16 | Surrey | E | 4 | C | 17.7 | 78.2 |
| 17 | East Anglia | 23 | 3a | C | 19.8 | 77.5 |
| 18 | Edinburgh | HS | 4 | B | 25.6 | 76.8 |
| 19 | Exeter | 22 | 4 | C | 24.4 | 76.4 |
| 20 | St Andrews | HS | 4 | A | 22.6 | 76.3 |
| 21 | Bangor | | 5 | B | 13.7 | 75.7 |
| =22 | Loughborough | 22 | 4 | C | 22.6 | 75.2 |
| =22 | Cranfield | E | 4 | D | 17.9 | 75.2 |
| 24 | Hertfordshire | 23 | 3a | C | 16.2 | 74.9 |
| 25 | Oxford | S | 5 | A | 29.8 | 74.7 |
| 26 | Oxford Brookes | 24 | 2 | F | 17.4 | 74.1 |
| 27 | West of England | 23 | 3a | D | 17.8 | 73.5 |
| 28 | De Montfort | E | 3a | C | 13.9 | 73.3 |
| 29 | Leeds Metropolitan | 24 | 2 | F | 14.9 | 72.3 |
| 30 | Stirling | HS | 4 | B | 19.2 | 72.2 |
| 31 | Nottingham Trent | E | 3b | D | 18.0 | 72.1 |
| =32 | North London | 24 | 3b | E | 10.3 | 71.2 |
| =32 | Manchester Metropolitan | 23 | 3a | E | 18.1 | 71.2 |
| =32 | Royal Holloway | 21 | 4 | B | 22.4 | 71.2 |
| 35 | Reading | 21 | 5 | C | 22.6 | 70.7 |
| 36 | Kingston | E | 3a | E | 16.5 | 70.0 |
| 37 | Liverpool | 23 | | | 20.4 | 69.4 |
| 38 | Keele | 21 | 4 | B | 18.5 | 68.3 |
| 39 | Glamorgan | E | 3b | D | 12.4 | 68.1 |

## Business Studies (cont.)

| | | TQA | | RAE | A-Levels | Score |
|---|---|---|---|---|---|---|
| 40 | Cardiff | S | 5 | B | 23.0 | 67.8 |

| | | | | | | |
|---|---|---|---|---|---|---|
| 41 Birmingham | 42 Cambridge | 43 Sheffield |
| 44 Wolverhampton | =45 King's College London | =45 Bournemouth |
| 47 Kent | 48 Glasgow | 49 Liverpool John Moores |
| 50 Northumbria | 51 Central Lancashire | 52 Hull |
| 53 Newcastle | 54 Middlesex | 55 Brunel |
| 56 Derby | 57 Coventry | 58 Bradford |
| 59 Portsmouth | 60 Heriot-Watt | =61 London Guildhall |
| =61 Aberdeen | =61 Leicester | 64 Salford |
| =65 Swansea | =65 Durham | 67 Robert Gordon |
| =68 Gloucestershire | =68 Aberystwyth | 70 Central England |
| 71 Glasgow Caledonian | =72 Brighton | =72 Plymouth |
| 74 Westminster | 75 Lincoln | 76 Sheffield Hallam |
| 77 Anglia | =78 South Bank | =78 Huddersfield |
| 80 Staffordshire | 81 Queen Mary | 82 Luton |
| 83 Napier | 84 UWIC, Cardiff | 85 East London |
| 86 Paisley | 87 Sunderland | 88 Greenwich |
| 89 Abertay Dundee | 90 UWCN, Newport | 91 Teesside |
| 92 Thames Valley | | |

**TQA (England) 1994**
**Firsts and 2:1s:** 47%
**Employment:** 79%
**Further study:** 8%
**Unemployment:** 7%

New Scottish Academic Review: *Abertay Dundee*: confidence in the academic standards.
*Edinburgh*: confidence in the academic standards; the quality of teaching and learning, student progression and learning resources was commendable.

## Celtic Studies

Only a whisker separates Cambridge and Aberystwyth in Celtic studies, a group of subjects fully assessed for teaching quality only in the past year. Under the scoring system, Cambridge benefits from not having a separate A-level score to register – Celtic studies was assessed for teaching and research as part of a larger group of subjects. However, the entrance qualifications of all Cambridge students would have been more than enough to secure top spot.

Aberystwyth could have done no more in its assessments for Welsh – like Bangor, it has maximum points for both teaching and research. Bangor loses out to Queen's University, Belfast, which has higher entry scores, as well as a near-perfect score for teaching quality.

Not surprisingly, universities in Wales and Northern Ireland dominate the table. There was no category of Celtic studies in the Scottish assessments of teaching quality. The subjects have relatively small enrolments, but both Welsh and Irish studies have been attracting more applicants recently.

| | | TQA | RAE | | A-Levels | Score |
|---|---|---|---|---|---|---|
| 1 | Cambridge | 23 | 5* | A | | 100.0 |
| 2 | Aberystwyth | E | 5* | A | 21.3 | 99.6 |
| 3 | Queen's, Belfast | 23 | 5 | A | 22.4 | 98.6 |

## Celtic Studies (cont.)

|  | TQA | RAE | | A-Levels | Score |
|---|---|---|---|---|---|
| 4 Bangor | E | 5* | A | 19.1 | 96.5 |
| 5 Ulster |  | 5* | B | 18.3 | 88.2 |
| 6 Swansea |  | 5 | A | 18.5 | 87.7 |
| 7 Cardiff | S | 5 | A | 22.0 | 85.8 |
| 8 Lampeter | S | 3b | C |  | 69.9 |

**TQA (England) 2000-01**
**Firsts and 2:1s:** 66%
**Employment:** 41%
**Further study:** 52%
**Unemployment:** 2%

## Chemical Engineering

There is little to separate Imperial College, London and Cambridge at the top of the chemical engineering table. Cambridge is fractionally ahead as the university with the best teaching score, although Imperial has a 5* rating for research. Birmingham and University College London are also considered internationally outstanding for research, but their teaching scores keep them out of the top five.

No university in England was awarded top marks for teaching, but Swansea was rated Excellent under the Welsh system. Only two new universities offer this subject, both of them at the bottom of the ranking.

Chemical engineering is one of the smaller branches of engineering. Four out of five students have A levels or equivalent qualifications, and average entry grades are the highest for any engineering subject. This helps produce engineering's largest proportion of firsts and 2:1s but, while two-thirds of the students go straight into jobs, the unemployment rate could be lower.

Assessors said the overall standard in English universities was high in relation to international competition, with most courses offering industrial placements in the final year and leading to Chartered Engineer status. The size of departments varied widely, but nowhere was the student/staff ratio more than 16:1.

|  | TQA | RAE | | A-Levels | Score |
|---|---|---|---|---|---|
| 1 Cambridge | 23 | 5 | A |  | 100.0 |
| 2 Imperial College | 22 | 5* | A | 28.5 | 99.6 |
| 3 UMIST | 22 | 5 | A | 25.7 | 94.4 |
| 4 Swansea | E | 4 | A | 18.5 | 90.3 |
| 5 Loughborough | 22 | 4 | A | 23.4 | 89.5 |
| 6 Birmingham | 21 | 5* | A | 22.1 | 89.4 |
| 7 University College London | 20 | 5* | A | 24.9 | 86.9 |
| 8 Sheffield | 21 | 4 | B | 26.0 | 85.3 |
| 9 Newcastle | 21 | 5 | B | 22.7 | 85.2 |
| 10 Queen's, Belfast | 21 | 4 | A | 23.5 | 84.8 |
| 11 Nottingham | 21 | 4 | B | 23.4 | 83.2 |
| 12 Bath | 20 | 4 | A | 24.6 | 80.9 |

## Chemical Engineering (cont.)

|    |             | TQA | RAE |   | A-Levels | Score |
|----|-------------|-----|-----|---|----------|-------|
| 13 | Heriot-Watt | 19  | 4   | A |          | 72.3  |
| 14 | Edinburgh   | 19  | 4   | C | 24.1     | 71.5  |
| 15 | Aston       | 19  | 5   | C | 16.9     | 67.5  |
| 16 | Leeds       | 19  | 5   | C | 16.4     | 67.1  |
| 17 | Bradford    | 20  | 3a  | D | 15.7     | 64.8  |
| 18 | Surrey      | 18  | 4   | B | 17.8     | 63.9  |
| 19 | South Bank  | 18  | 3a  | E |          | 52.6  |
| 20 | Teesside    | 17  | 2   | D |          | 45.8  |

**TQA (England) 1995-96**
**Firsts and 2:1s:** 56%
**Employment:** 67%
**Further study:** 21%
**Unemployment:** 7%

New Scottish Academic Review: *Paisley*: confidence in the academic standards; the quality of teaching and learning, and learning resources was commendable.

## Chemistry

A much-improved set of research assessments produced challengers for Oxford and Cambridge for the first time, but the pair lead the ranking again. Both were among the 19 institutions rated as Excellent for teaching quality and they were two of the six universities rated internationally outstanding for research.

Durham is now the nearest challenger, as the only other 5* research university entering the maximum number of academics for assessment. Imperial College, London, Bristol and University College London were the other top scorers for research. Edinburgh is the top university in Scotland, Cardiff the leader in Wales.

Chemistry, the biggest of the physical sciences, is old university territory, with only Nottingham Trent representing the former polytechnics in the first 30 places. With Robert Gordon, it was the only new university considered Excellent for teaching quality. The teaching assessments are dated, but are generally consistent with the other two measures in the table.

Chemistry has more than 12,000 full-time degree students. Almost nine out of ten undergraduates have A levels or their equivalent, but entry requirements are not far above the average for all subjects. About half of the graduates go straight into jobs and the unemployment rate is low.

|     |                  | TQA | RAE |    | A-Levels | Score |
|-----|------------------|-----|-----|----|----------|-------|
| 1   | Oxford           | E   | 5*  | A  | 29.7     | 100.0 |
| 2   | Cambridge        | E   | 5*  | A  |          | 98.1  |
| 3   | Durham           | E   | 5*  | A  | 25.9     | 97.6  |
| 4   | Imperial College | E   | 5*  | B  | 27.6     | 95.6  |
| 5   | Bristol          | E   | 5*  | B  | 25.6     | 94.2  |
| 6   | Nottingham       | E   | 5   | A  | 24.8     | 92.7  |
| =7  | Southampton      | E   | 5   | A  | 22.4     | 91.2  |
| =7  | Edinburgh        | E   | 5   | A  | 22.4     | 91.2  |
| 9   | Strathclyde      | E   | 4   | A  | 24.8     | 88.6  |
| 10  | Leeds            | E   | 5   | B  | 20.9     | 87.5  |
| 11  | Manchester       | E   | 5   | B  | 18.6     | 86.1  |

## Chemistry (cont.)

| | | TQA | RAE | | A-Levels | Score |
|---|---|---|---|---|---|---|
| 12 | St Andrews | E | 5 | C | 24.7 | 85.6 |
| 13 | Leicester | E | 4 | A | 19.0 | 84.9 |
| 14 | Cardiff | E | 4 | A | 18.5 | 84.6 |
| 15 | Glasgow | E | 4 | C | 22.1 | 81.0 |
| 16 | Hull | E | 4 | C | 15.3 | 76.5 |
| 17 | Bangor | E | 3a | A | 12.2 | 76.3 |
| 18 | Warwick | S | 5 | A | 24.5 | 72.8 |
| 19 | York | S | 5 | A | 23.9 | 72.4 |
| 20 | University College London | S | 5* | B | 22.1 | 72.3 |
| 21 | Heriot-Watt | HS | 4 | A | 14.5 | 72.1 |
| 22 | Sheffield | S | 5 | B | 23.5 | 69.5 |
| 23 | Liverpool | S | 5 | A | 18.2 | 68.7 |
| 24 | Birmingham | S | 5 | B | 20.8 | 67.8 |
| 25 | Sussex | S | 5 | A | 15.9 | 67.2 |
| 26 | Nottingham Trent | E | 3a | D | 10.5 | 67.1 |
| 27 | Bath | S | 4 | A | 21.8 | 67.0 |
| 28 | East Anglia | S | 5 | B | 18.9 | 66.5 |
| 29 | Queen's, Belfast | S | 4 | A | 19.9 | 65.7 |
| 30 | Aberdeen | HS | 3a | C | | 64.4 |
| =31 | Swansea | S | 4 | A | 17.5 | 64.2 |
| =31 | UMIST | S | 4 | B | 20.9 | 64.2 |
| 33 | King's College London | S | 4 | B | 20.1 | 63.6 |
| 34 | Loughborough | S | 4 | B | 19.4 | 63.2 |
| =35 | Greenwich | S | 4 | A | | 63.1 |
| =35 | Reading | S | 4 | A | 15.9 | 63.1 |
| 37 | Bradford | S | 4 | B | 18.8 | 62.8 |
| 38 | Exeter | S | 4 | B | 18.1 | 62.4 |
| 39 | Salford | S | 4 | A | 12.4 | 60.9 |
| 40 | Surrey | S | 3a | A | 18.4 | 60.7 |

| | | | | | |
|---|---|---|---|---|---|
| 41 Keele | 42 Aston | 43 Brighton |
| 44 Newcastle | 45 Plymouth | 46 Paisley |
| 47 Queen Mary | 48 Sunderland | 49 Huddersfield |
| 50 North London | 51 Kent | 52 Kingston |
| 53 De Montfort | 54 Northumbria | 55 Dundee |
| 56 Lancaster | 57 Manchester Metropolitan | 58 Coventry |
| 59 Liverpool John Moores | 60 Glamorgan | 61 Sheffield Hallam |
| 62 Anglia | | |

**TQA (England) 1993-94**
**Firsts and 2:1s:** 49%
**Employment:** 49%
**Further study:** 40%
**Unemployment:** 6%

## Civil Engineering

An all-Welsh confrontation takes place at the top of the civil engineering ranking, with Cardiff coming out ahead of Swansea because of higher entry standards and a larger proportion of academics entered for the 2001 Research

## Civil Engineering (cont.)

Assessment Exercise. Both were rated Excellent at teaching and were among five universities considered internationally outstanding for research. The others were Bristol, Imperial College and Southampton.

Unusually, no university in England, Scotland or Northern Ireland gained full marks for teaching quality. Plymouth, the top-placed new university, boasts the best score, with 23 points. Eight universities managed 22 points for teaching, but none of the Scottish universities was rated better than Highly Satisfactory.

Imperial has the highest entry standards, but Nottingham's strength across the board leaves it in third place. A-level scores vary more than in most subjects, from more than two As and a B at Imperial to barely more than a D and two Es at East London.

More than 40 universities have civil engineering degrees, about a third of them former polytechnics. Nearly four out of ten undergraduates are admitted with A levels or the equivalent, their grades close to the average for all subjects. More than 11,000 students take full-time degree courses and the unemployment rate is one of the lowest.

| | | TQA | RAE | | A-Levels | Score |
|---|---|---|---|---|---|---|
| 1 | Cardiff | E | 5* | A | 21.7 | 100.0 |
| 2 | Swansea | E | 5* | B | 20.2 | 96.5 |
| 3 | Nottingham | 22 | 5 | A | 23.1 | 90.8 |
| 4 | Bristol | 22 | 5* | C | 25.4 | 89.1 |
| 5 | Bath | 22 | 5 | B | 23.3 | 88.8 |
| 6 | Queen's, Belfast | 22 | 5 | B | 23.1 | 88.7 |
| 7 | Imperial College | 21 | 5* | B | 28.4 | 88.3 |
| 8 | UMIST | 22 | 5 | C | 25.0 | 86.5 |
| 9 | Dundee | HS | 5 | A | | 86.3 |
| 10 | Edinburgh | HS | 5 | B | 24.2 | 86.0 |
| 11 | Liverpool | 22 | 4 | A | 19.3 | 84.9 |
| =12 | Loughborough | 22 | 4 | B | 19.5 | 83.3 |
| =12 | Southampton | 21 | 5* | B | 21.2 | 83.3 |
| 14 | Heriot-Watt | HS | 4 | A | | 82.2 |
| 15 | Sheffield | 21 | 5 | B | 23.4 | 81.9 |
| 16 | Surrey | 22 | 4 | C | 20.5 | 81.0 |
| 17 | Plymouth | 23 | 4 | E | 14.2 | 77.0 |
| =18 | Aberdeen | HS | 4 | C | | 76.4 |
| =18 | Glasgow | HS | 4 | C | | 76.4 |
| =18 | Napier | HS | 4 | C | | 76.4 |
| =18 | Strathclyde | HS | 4 | C | | 76.4 |
| 22 | Birmingham | 21 | 5 | C | 19.4 | 75.6 |
| =23 | Paisley | HS | 3a | C | | 73.5 |
| =23 | Kingston | 22 | 3a | C | 13.0 | 73.5 |
| 25 | Newcastle | 20 | 5 | B | 20.2 | 72.7 |
| 26 | University College London | 19 | 5 | A | 21.1 | 68.5 |
| 27 | Leeds Metropolitan | 21 | 3a | B | 11.0 | 67.5 |
| 28 | Bradford | 20 | 4 | B | 16.5 | 67.2 |
| 29 | Ulster | 19 | 5 | A | 18.4 | 66.6 |
| 30 | Salford | 19 | 5* | A | 12.4 | 65.7 |
| =31 | Aston | 20 | 5 | C | 14.4 | 65.2 |

## Civil Engineering (cont.)

|  |  | TQA | RAE |  | A-Levels | Score |
|---|---|---|---|---|---|---|
| =31 | Brighton | 21 | 3b | C | 14.3 | 65.2 |
| 33 | Nottingham Trent | 20 | 3a | B | 14.6 | 63.0 |
| 34 | Greenwich | 21 | 3b | E |  | 61.3 |
| 35 | Portsmouth | 20 | 3a | C | 15.3 | 61.2 |
| 36 | City | 19 | 4 | B | 17.2 | 60.8 |
| =37 | Oxford Brookes | 21 |  |  | 12.6 | 57.4 |
| =37 | East London | 21 | 2 | D | 8.4 | 57.4 |
| 39 | Leeds | 19 | 5 | D | 18.7 | 57.3 |
| 40 | Coventry | 19 | 3b | C | 13.8 | 50.9 |
| 41 | Glamorgan |  |  | 42 | Sheffield Hallam | |

**TQA (England) 1996–98**
**Firsts and 2:1s:** 45%
**Employment:** 78%
**Further study:** 11%
**Unemployment:** 6%

New Scottish Academic Review: *Glasgow Caledonian, Paisley*: confidence in the academic standards; the quality of teaching and learning, and learning resources was commendable.

## Classics and Ancient History

The table sees Oxford pip Cambridge to top place by virtue of a slightly higher A-level score. Like third-placed King's College London, both universities have maximum points for teaching and research. UCL matched the top three with a 5* rating and ten of the remaining 18 universities reached grade 5.

Six of the 18 universities in the teaching quality assessment for England achieved perfect scores – Birmingham, Manchester and Nottingham being the others – and only Leeds was awarded less than 21 points out of 24. Lampeter and Swansea were both considered Excellent in the older Welsh assessment. There was no separate category in Scotland, although Edinburgh and St Andrews have among the highest entry scores in Britain.

No new universities appear in the table, although some offer the subjects as part of a modular degree scheme. A-level grades in classics are among the highest for any group of subjects, but most universities teach the subject from scratch, as well as to more practised students. As a result, entrants to five of the universities in the table averaged three Cs or less at A level.

|  |  | TQA | RAE |  | A-Levels | Score |
|---|---|---|---|---|---|---|
| 1 | Oxford | 24 | 5* | A | 29.5 | 100.0 |
| 2 | Cambridge | 24 | 5* | A | 29.1 | 99.8 |
| 3 | King's College London | 24 | 5* | A | 21.9 | 94.7 |
| 4 | Birmingham | 24 | 5 | A | 22.8 | 91.0 |
| 5 | University College London | 23 | 5* | B | 25.2 | 88.2 |
| 6 | Nottingham | 24 | 4 | A | 24.8 | 88.0 |
| 7 | Manchester | 24 | 5 | B | 19.8 | 86.1 |
| 8 | Warwick | 23 | 5 | A | 23.5 | 85.9 |
| 9 | Royal Holloway | 23 | 5 | A | 21.1 | 84.2 |
| 10 | St Andrews | | 5 | B | 24.2 | 83.3 |

## Classics and Ancient History (cont.)

| | | TQA | RAE | | A-Levels | Score |
|---|---|---|---|---|---|---|
| =11 | Queen's, Belfast | 23 | 4 | A | | 80.7 |
| =11 | Swansea | E | 4 | A | | 80.7 |
| 13 | Keele | | 5 | A | 18.0 | 80.2 |
| 14 | Exeter | 22 | 5 | A | 21.9 | 79.2 |
| 15 | Edinburgh | | 4 | B | 26.0 | 78.1 |
| 16 | Reading | 22 | 5 | A | 16.9 | 75.8 |
| 17 | Bristol | 21 | 5 | B | 26.0 | 73.8 |
| 18 | Durham | 21 | 5 | B | 25.5 | 73.4 |
| 19 | Newcastle | 22 | 3a | A | 21.3 | 70.2 |
| 20 | Liverpool | 22 | 4 | A | 14.3 | 69.6 |
| 21 | Lampeter | E | 3a | C | 16.5 | 67.4 |
| 22 | Leeds | 19 | 4 | B | 21.1 | 55.4 |
| 23 | Kent | 22 | | | 16.5 | 49.9 |

**TQA (England) 2000–01**
**Firsts and 2:1s:** 66%
**Employment:** 54%
**Further study:** 30%
**Unemployment:** 7%

New Scottish Academic Review: *Edinburgh*: confidence in the academic standards; the quality of teaching and learning, and student progression and learning resources was commendable.

## Communication and Media Studies

The two subjects are mainly the preserve of the new universities, although nine of the top ten places are filled by older institutions. Loughborough, which did not have a teaching assessment but was one of three universities rated internationally outstanding for research, tops the table. No university achieved maximum points for teaching quality, but Warwick, East Anglia and Westminster were only a point away.

East Anglia and Goldsmiths College took the other research stars. Westminster, the only former polytechnic in the top ten, was one of six universities on grade 5. Stirling is the top institution in Scotland; Cardiff the leader in Wales.

Warwick has the highest entry standards of almost two As and a B. Of the rest, only Leeds, Sussex, Sheffield and Birmingham average more than three Bs. Nearly three-quarters of the students enter with A levels, but requirements are generally modest, some courses averaging less than three Ds.

Media studies has been growing in popularity as opportunities have expanded. Assessors found that courses varied from conventional academic degrees to advanced vocational training. Their main concern was a shortage of resources in a fast-changing area of study. Three-quarters of the graduates find jobs within six months of graduation.

| | | TQA | RAE | | A-Levels | Score |
|---|---|---|---|---|---|---|
| 1 | Loughborough | | 5* | A | 23.2 | 100.0 |
| 2 | Warwick | 23 | 5 | B | 27.3 | 93.1 |
| 3 | East Anglia | 23 | 5* | A | 19.8 | 92.8 |
| 4 | Royal Holloway | | 5 | B | 23.8 | 90.4 |

## Communication and Media Studies (cont.)

| | | TQA | RAE | | A-Levels | Score |
|---|---|---|---|---|---|---|
| 5 | Goldsmiths College | 22 | 5* | C | | 83.5 |
| 6 | Leeds | 22 | 4 | C | 26.2 | 81.7 |
| 7 | Sussex | 21 | 4 | A | 25.0 | 80.8 |
| =8 | Sheffield | | 4 | C | 24.6 | 80.0 |
| =8 | Westminster | 23 | 5 | D | 19.7 | 80.0 |
| 10 | Stirling | HS | 5 | C | 21.5 | 78.2 |
| =11 | Ulster | 21 | 4 | B | 22.0 | 76.8 |
| =11 | Birmingham | | 3a | C | 25.5 | 76.8 |
| 13 | Cardiff | S | 5 | B | 23.7 | 76.2 |
| 14 | West of England | 22 | 4 | C | 18.1 | 75.8 |
| 15 | Glasgow Caledonian | HS | 3a | B | | 74.9 |
| 16 | Leicester | 21 | 3a | B | 20.8 | 73.0 |
| 17 | Central Lancashire | 22 | 3b | C | 18.1 | 71.2 |
| 18 | Nottingham Trent | 21 | 5 | D | 19.5 | 70.4 |
| 19 | Plymouth | 21 | 3a | C | | 69.0 |
| 20 | Liverpool John Moores | 22 | 3b | E | 19.5 | 68.3 |
| 21 | Bournemouth | 22 | | | 22.3 | 67.8 |
| 22 | Napier | HS | 3a | D | 16.3 | 67.2 |
| 23 | Sunderland | 22 | 3a | D | 12.8 | 67.0 |
| 24 | South Bank | 20 | 4 | B | 13.9 | 66.1 |
| 25 | De Montfort | 20 | 3a | B | 16.3 | 65.0 |
| 26 | Luton | 22 | 3a | E | 11.7 | 63.5 |
| 27 | Oxford Brookes | 21 | | | 20.0 | 61.3 |
| 28 | Northumbria | | 4 | D | 14.9 | 59.2 |
| 29 | Middlesex | | 3a | D | 16.7 | 58.5 |
| 30 | Staffordshire | 20 | 4 | D | 11.9 | 58.4 |
| 31 | Leeds Metropolitan | 19 | 3a | D | 19.7 | 57.8 |
| 32 | City | 19 | 3b | D | 21.6 | 57.6 |
| 33 | Brunel | 20 | | | 20.1 | 56.7 |
| 34 | Sheffield Hallam | 19 | 3a | E | 19.1 | 54.7 |
| 35 | Greenwich | 19 | 3b | C | 12.1 | 52.6 |
| 36 | Gloucestershire | 20 | | | 14.0 | 52.2 |
| 37 | Wolverhampton | 19 | 2 | E | 13.1 | 48.4 |
| 38 | Teesside | | 2 | A | 9.4 | 47.6 |
| 39 | Coventry | 18 | 3b | E | 13.8 | 45.1 |
| 40 | Anglia | 18 | | | 15.9 | 44.1 |
| | | | | | | |
| 41 | Thames Valley | 42 | North London | | 43 East London | |
| 44 | London Guildhall | 45 | Lincoln | | | |

**TQA (England) 1996–98**
**Firsts and 2:1s:** 56%
**Employed:** 73%
**Further study:** 10%
**Unemployment:** 9%

## Computer Science

Computing is now the most popular subject in terms of size, with 99 universities in the table. The fact that more than four out of five graduates are in work within six months of leaving university helps to explain this.

## Computer Science (cont.)

Cambridge tops the table with a perfect score: maximum points in both teaching and research assessments and an average of practically three As at A level at entry. Imperial College, York, Edinburgh, Southampton and Manchester also record top marks for both teaching and research, although only Edinburgh entered a full complement of academics for the latest Research Assessment Exercise.

Edinburgh is the top Scottish university, with Swansea the leader in Wales. Only Surrey, in 18th place, and Salford, in 26th, achieved 5* research grades without securing an Excellent teaching rating. Teesside is the only new university in the top 20, despite recording the lowest research grade. There is a wide spread of entry standards, but several of those at the top of the table average two As and a B at A level.

| | | TQA | RAE | | A-Levels | Score |
|---|---|---|---|---|---|---|
| 1 | Cambridge | E | 5* | B | 29.9 | 100.0 |
| =2 | Imperial College | E | 5* | B | 28.9 | 99.3 |
| =2 | York | E | 5* | B | 28.8 | 99.3 |
| 4 | Oxford | E | 5 | A | 29.9 | 99.3 |
| 5 | Edinburgh | E | 5* | A | 23.4 | 97.9 |
| 6 | Southampton | E | 5* | B | 25.3 | 97.0 |
| =7 | Manchester | E | 5* | B | 24.4 | 96.4 |
| =7 | Warwick | E | 5 | B | 28.1 | 96.4 |
| 9 | Glasgow | E | 5 | B | 21.0 | 91.8 |
| 10 | Swansea | E | 5 | B | 20.8 | 91.6 |
| 11 | Exeter | E | 4 | B | 22.3 | 90.1 |
| 12 | Kent | E | 4 | B | 21.4 | 89.5 |
| 13 | St Andrews | HS | 5 | A | 20.7 | 80.3 |
| 14 | Heriot-Watt | HS | 4 | A | 16.4 | 74.8 |
| 15 | Teesside | E | 2 | F | 12.8 | 72.1 |
| 16 | University College London | S | 5 | A | 26.2 | 70.8 |
| 17 | Bristol | S | 5 | A | 25.6 | 70.4 |
| 18 | Surrey | S | 5* | A | 18.9 | 68.9 |
| 19 | Cardiff | S | 5 | A | 22.4 | 68.4 |
| 20 | Strathclyde | HS | 3a | D | | 68.0 |
| =21 | Nottingham | S | 5 | B | 24.5 | 67.9 |
| =21 | Bath | S | 4 | A | 26.0 | 67.9 |
| 23 | Sussex | S | 5 | A | 21.4 | 67.8 |
| 24 | Sheffield | S | 5 | B | 24.2 | 67.7 |
| 25 | Lancaster | S | 5 | A | 20.8 | 67.3 |
| 26 | Salford | S | 5* | A | 15.0 | 66.4 |
| 27 | Birmingham | S | 5 | B | 22.0 | 66.3 |
| 28 | Durham | S | 4 | B | 25.4 | 66.0 |
| 29 | Queen's, Belfast | S | 4 | A | 22.8 | 65.8 |
| 30 | Newcastle | S | 5 | B | 20.7 | 65.4 |
| 31 | Royal Holloway | S | 5 | B | 19.8 | 64.9 |
| 32 | King's College London | S | 4 | B | 23.6 | 64.8 |
| 33 | Liverpool | S | 5 | B | 17.4 | 63.4 |
| 34 | Reading | S | 4 | B | 20.7 | 63.0 |
| 35 | Queen Mary | S | 4 | B | 19.6 | 62.3 |
| 36 | Dundee | S | 4 | A | | 62.1 |

## Computer Science (cont.)

| | TQA | | RAE | A-Levels | Score |
|---|---|---|---|---|---|
| =37 Leicester | S | 4 | B | 19.2 | 62.0 |
| =37 Aberystwyth | S | 4 | A | 16.9 | 62.0 |
| =37 East Anglia | S | 4 | B | 19.1 | 62.0 |
| 40 City | S | 4 | B | 18.3 | 61.4 |

| | | |
|---|---|---|
| =41 Aston | =41 Loughborough | 43 UMIST |
| 44 Leeds | 45 Essex | 46 Bangor |
| 47 Hertfordshire | 48 Aberdeen | 49 Liverpool John Moores |
| 50 Hull | 51 Paisley | 52 De Montfort |
| 53 Keele | 54 Stirling | 55 Ulster |
| 56 Sunderland | 57 West of England | 58 Manchester Metropolitan |
| 59 Glamorgan | 60 Goldsmiths College | =61 Northumbria |
| =61 Oxford Brookes | =61 Plymouth | =64 Nottingham Trent |
| =64 Robert Gordon | 66 Bradford | 67 Napier |
| 68 Greenwich | 69 Leeds Metropolitan | 70 Brighton |
| 71 Brunel | 72 Kingston | 73 Huddersfield |
| 74 Sheffield Hallam | 75 Portsmouth | 76 Bournemouth |
| 77 Cranfield | 78 Glasgow Caledonian | 79 Abertay Dundee |
| 80 South Bank | 81 Middlesex | 82 Wolverhampton |
| 83 Coventry | 84 Gloucestershire | 85 Staffordshire |
| 86 North London | =87 Westminster | =87 Central Lancashire |
| =87 Anglia | 90 Central England | 91 UWCN, Newport |
| 92 Lincoln | 93 Derby | 94 UWIC, Cardiff |
| 95 East London | 96 Luton | 97 London Guildhall |
| 98 Surrey Roehampton | 99 Thames Valley | |

**TQA (England) 1994**
**Firsts and 2:1s:** 47%
**Employment:** 81%
**Further study:** 7%
**Unemployment:** 9%

New Scottish Academic Review: *Dundee*: confidence in the academic standards; the quality of teaching and learning, student progression and learning resources was commendable.

## Dentistry

One of the first two 5* research ratings in dentistry allows King's College London to leap to the top of the ranking. It was already one of four universities with full marks for teaching, and only Queen's, Belfast and Leeds have higher entry standards. Manchester, Queen Mary and Queen's, Belfast, are the other top-scorers for teaching, but University College London's consistency carries it to second place.

There are surprising variations among the 14 universities offering dentistry, judging by the three indicators in our table. Although it entered a low proportion of academics for assessment, bottom-placed Bristol achieved the other top rating for research. By contrast, Queen's, Belfast, which had the best A-level and teaching scores, has one of the two lowest grades for research.

No top grades were awarded in Scotland, although both Dundee and Glasgow were rated Highly Satisfactory for teaching. The University of Wales College of

## Dentistry (cont.)

Medicine, which was awarded an Excellent teaching grade, offers the only dentistry degree in Wales.

Dentistry has predictably high entry standards, averaging more than three Bs at A level, and excellent employment prospects. Most degrees last five years, although several universities offer a six-year option for those without the necessary scientific qualifications.

| | | TQA | RAE | | A-Levels | Score |
|---|---|---|---|---|---|---|
| 1 | King's College London | 24 | 5* | C | 27.2 | 100.0 |
| 2 | University College London | 23 | 5 | B | | 97.8 |
| 3 | Manchester | 24 | 4 | B | 26.2 | 96.6 |
| 4 | Queen Mary | 24 | 5 | B | 23.7 | 95.6 |
| 5 | Queen's, Belfast | 24 | 3a | C | 28.7 | 95.5 |
| =6 | Sheffield | 23 | 5 | C | 26.2 | 92.3 |
| =6 | Leeds | 23 | 4 | C | 27.6 | 92.3 |
| 8 | Wales College of Medicine | E | 4 | C | | 90.8 |
| 9 | Newcastle | 23 | 5 | D | 27.2 | 90.1 |
| 10 | Liverpool | 21 | 4 | C | 25.8 | 82.0 |
| 11 | Dundee | HS | 5 | D | 25.4 | 81.5 |
| 12 | Glasgow | HS | 3a | D | 27.0 | 80.9 |
| 13 | Birmingham | 22 | 4 | D | 24.7 | 80.6 |
| 14 | Bristol | 19 | 5* | D | 27.1 | 76.5 |

**TQA (England) 1998-2000**
**Firsts and 2:1s:** 58%
**Employment:** 99%
**Further study:** 1%
**Unemployment:** 0%

## Drama, Dance and Cinematics

Two universities – Warwick and Bristol – are rated internationally outstanding for research in this collection of performing arts, but Warwick takes top place with the better teaching grade. It is one of five institutions on maximum points for teaching quality, the others being Kent, Lancaster, Reading and Hull. Bristol takes second place by virtue of its research grade and high entry standards.

There were no Excellent ratings in Scotland, but Glamorgan reached the standard in Wales. However, one of the four lowest research grades and modest entry standards keep Glamorgan out of the top 20. Brighton is the highest-placed new university, with Manchester Metropolitan also making the top 20.

The gulf in entry standards between new and old universities is particularly noticeable in this table: entrants to several of the older foundations averaged three Bs at A level, while only Bournemouth, Liverpool John Moores and Sheffield Hallam, of the former polytechnics, averaged three Cs. Manchester had the highest entry standards.

## Drama, Dance and Cinematics (cont.)

Freelancing and periods of temporary employment are common throughout the performing arts, but the 3,000 students taking cinematics seem to have more trouble finding work than the 9,000 studying drama. The 16 per cent unemployment rate for cinematics is high.

| | | TQA | RAE | | A-Levels | Score |
|---|---|---|---|---|---|---|
| 1 | Warwick | 24 | 5* | B | 26.5 | 100.0 |
| 2 | Bristol | 23 | 5* | A | 26.2 | 97.0 |
| 3 | Kent | 24 | 5 | B | 22.5 | 93.9 |
| 4 | Lancaster | 24 | 4 | A | 23.0 | 93.1 |
| 5 | Reading | 24 | 5 | B | 21.4 | 93.0 |
| 6 | Royal Holloway | 23 | 5 | B | 24.5 | 90.2 |
| 7 | Hull | 24 | 4 | C | 23.4 | 88.6 |
| 8 | Loughborough | 23 | 5 | C | 22.9 | 85.3 |
| 9 | Goldsmiths College | 22 | 4 | A | 24.6 | 83.8 |
| 10 | Exeter | 22 | 4 | B | 26.3 | 83.4 |
| 11 | Brunel | 23 | 3a | B | 19.7 | 80.5 |
| 12 | Glasgow | HS | 4 | B | 25.2 | 79.9 |
| 13 | East Anglia | 21 | 4 | A | 23.5 | 77.7 |
| 14 | Manchester | 21 | 5 | C | 24.3 | 75.9 |
| 15 | Brighton | | 5 | B | 14.0 | 75.3 |
| 16 | Birmingham | 21 | 4 | C | 25.8 | 74.7 |
| =17 | Queen's, Belfast | | 3b | A | 22.3 | 72.6 |
| =17 | Manchester Metropolitan | 23 | 3a | D | 16.2 | 72.6 |
| 19 | Ulster | 22 | 3a | B | 15.7 | 72.1 |
| 20 | Aberystwyth | S | 5 | B | 20.6 | 71.4 |
| =21 | Bournemouth | 22 | 3b | D | 22.8 | 70.9 |
| =21 | Surrey | 20 | 4 | A | 21.5 | 70.9 |
| 23 | Nottingham Trent | | 5 | C | 15.7 | 70.7 |
| 24 | Surrey Roehampton | 21 | 4 | B | 15.7 | 69.8 |
| 25 | Glamorgan | E | 2 | C | 14.5 | 69.3 |
| 26 | De Montfort | 22 | 3a | C | 14.4 | 68.7 |
| 27 | Middlesex | 22 | 3a | D | 16.1 | 67.3 |
| 28 | Northumbria | 22 | 2 | C | 17.6 | 66.4 |
| 29 | Liverpool John Moores | 21 | 2 | E | 19.1 | 59.7 |
| 30 | North London | 22 | | | 13.8 | 59.1 |
| 31 | Sunderland | 21 | 2 | D | 12.6 | 55.9 |
| 32 | Salford | 21 | | | 15.9 | 55.5 |
| 33 | Plymouth | 21 | | | 15.1 | 54.9 |
| 34 | Staffordshire | 20 | | | 13.8 | 48.5 |
| 35 | Central Lancashire | 20 | | | 13.4 | 48.2 |
| 36 | Sheffield Hallam | 19 | | | 18.3 | 46.8 |
| 37 | East London | 19 | | | 13.1 | 42.8 |
| 38 | Wolverhampton | 19 | | | 12.0 | 41.9 |
| 39 | Huddersfield | 17 | 3a | D | 16.0 | 40.9 |
| 40 | Derby | 18 | | | 13.7 | 37.9 |

**TQA (England) 1996–98**

**Firsts and 2:1s:** 67% (drama), 66% (cinematics)

**Employment:** 73% (drama), 72% (cinematics)

**Further study:** 15% (drama), 9% (cinematics)

**Unemployment:** 7% (drama), 16% (cinematics)

## East and South Asian Studies

The group of languages which make up South and East Asian Studies produced a high-scoring teaching quality assessment, although none was awarded maximum points. The latest research grades were even higher, with both Oxford and Cambridge rated internationally outstanding. Cambridge takes the top spot by virtue of a higher teaching score.

The subjects have not been assessed separately in Scotland, but Edinburgh takes third place, behind the School of Oriental and African Studies, on the strength of its other results. Westminster – the only new university in the ranking – did well to join Cambridge, Leeds and SOAS as top-rated for teaching, as well as reaching grade 5 for research.

Fewer than 1,000 students take the languages as their main subject, with Chinese and Japanese vying to be the largest recruiter. Four out of five undergraduates enter with above-average A-level scores, so degree classifications are also high. There is strong demand for graduates, and unemployment consistently low.

| | | TQA | RAE | | A-Levels | Score |
|---|---|---|---|---|---|---|
| 1 | Cambridge | 23 | 5* | B | | 100.0 |
| 2 | SOAS | 23 | 5 | B | 24.8 | 97.1 |
| 3 | Edinburgh | | 5 | B | 25.5 | 96.2 |
| 4 | Oxford | 22 | 5* | B | 29.8 | 94.3 |
| 5 | Leeds | 23 | 5 | C | 20.3 | 90.7 |
| 6 | Hull | 22 | 5 | A | | 87.6 |
| 7 | Westminster | 23 | 5 | E | | 86.0 |
| 8 | Sheffield | 22 | 4 | D | 22.1 | 78.5 |
| 9 | Durham | 21 | 4 | C | 26.4 | 75.4 |

**TQA (England) 1996–98**
**Firsts and 2:1s:** 63% (Chinese); 69% (Japanese)
**Employment:** 56% (Chinese);75% (Japanese)
**Further study:** 28% (Chinese); 13% (Japanese)
**Unemployment:** 11% (Chinese); 8% (Japanese)

## Economics

Essex, University College London and Warwick all have perfect scores for teaching and research, but only UCL entered the maximum proportion of its academics for the latest Research Assessment Exercise. Essex suffers in our table for the relatively low A levels achieved by entrants – barely more than three Cs on average. Oxford and Cambridge students averaged almost three As.

A total of 15 universities offering economics achieved maximum points for teaching quality. Among them were the new universities of Leeds Metropolitan, Oxford Brookes and Staffordshire, although low A-level scores prevented any of them breaking into the top 30 places. Controversially, LSE was not among them, dropping a point, despite being one of the four universities rated internationally outstanding for research and having the highest A-level score after Oxbridge.

## Economics (cont.)

Nottingham takes third place, ahead of Cambridge, with top marks for teaching and consistently high scores in the other two categories. St Andrews is the leading university in Scotland and Aberystwyth is top-placed in Wales. Hertfordshire is the top new university. Napier was omitted at the university's own request. Economics remains a popular option for undergraduates, and employers favour the subject because they see it as combining the skills of the sciences and the arts.

| | | TQA | RAE | | A-Levels | Score |
|---|---|---|---|---|---|---|
| 1 | University College London | 24 | 5* | A | 26.8 | 100.0 |
| 2 | Warwick | 24 | 5* | B | 27.8 | 98.0 |
| 3 | Nottingham | 24 | 5 | A | 28.5 | 97.6 |
| 4 | Cambridge | 24 | 5 | B | 29.6 | 96.1 |
| 5 | York | 24 | 5 | A | 25.2 | 95.2 |
| =6 | Southampton | 24 | 5 | A | 24.6 | 94.8 |
| =6 | London School of Economics | 23 | 5* | A | 28.9 | 94.8 |
| 8 | Bath | 24 | 5 | B | 25.4 | 93.0 |
| 9 | Essex | 24 | 5* | B | 18.8 | 91.5 |
| 10 | Durham | 24 | 4 | B | 27.0 | 91.0 |
| 11 | Manchester | 24 | 4 | B | 26.4 | 90.5 |
| 12 | Leicester | 24 | 5 | B | 20.9 | 89.8 |
| 13 | Oxford | 23 | 5 | B | 29.6 | 89.3 |
| 14 | Queen's, Belfast | 24 | 4 | B | 23.3 | 88.3 |
| 15 | Bristol | 23 | 4 | A | 26.4 | 85.7 |
| 16 | Birmingham | 23 | 4 | B | 25.4 | 83.1 |
| 17 | St Andrews | E | 4 | B | 23.9 | 82.0 |
| 18 | Kent | 23 | 4 | A | 19.1 | 80.4 |
| 19 | Stirling | E | 4 | A | 18.5 | 80.0 |
| 20 | East Anglia | 23 | 4 | B | 19.2 | 78.6 |
| 21 | Aberdeen | E | 3a | A | | 78.5 |
| =22 | Exeter | 22 | 5 | B | 23.6 | 78.2 |
| =22 | Newcastle | 23 | 4 | C | 23.1 | 78.2 |
| 24 | Loughborough | 23 | 3a | B | 22.1 | 77.5 |
| 25 | Surrey | 23 | 3a | A | 19.4 | 77.0 |
| 26 | Keele | 23 | 3a | A | 16.9 | 75.3 |
| 27 | Brunel | 22 | 4 | A | 20.3 | 74.6 |
| 28 | Royal Holloway | 22 | 4 | B | 22.8 | 74.4 |
| 29 | Liverpool | 22 | 4 | B | 20.3 | 72.6 |
| 30 | Queen Mary | 21 | 5 | B | 20.7 | 69.4 |
| 31 | City | 22 | 3a | B | 19.9 | 69.1 |
| 32 | Ulster | 22 | 4 | C | 19.7 | 68.9 |
| 33 | Aberystwyth | E | 3b | C | 16.7 | 68.3 |
| 34 | Hull | 22 | 4 | C | 18.5 | 68.1 |
| 35 | Hertfordshire | 23 | 3a | C | 12.3 | 67.8 |
| 36 | Oxford Brookes | 24 | | | 16.3 | 67.4 |
| 37 | Sussex | 21 | 4 | B | 22.1 | 67.1 |
| 38 | SOAS | 21 | 4 | B | 21.0 | 66.4 |
| 39 | Leeds Metropolitan | 24 | | | 14.5 | 66.1 |
| 40 | Sheffield | 21 | 3a | B | 24.9 | 65.9 |

41 Staffordshire    42 Reading    43 Cardiff

## Economics (cont.)

| | | | | | |
|---|---|---|---|---|---|
| 44 | Edinburgh | 45 | London Guildhall | 46 | Glasgow |
| 47 | Leeds | 48 | Nottingham Trent | 49 | Swansea |
| 50 | West of England | 51 | Coventry | 52 | Portsmouth |
| 53 | Bangor | 54 | Northumbria | 55 | Dundee |
| 56 | Wolverhampton | 57 | Goldsmiths College | 58 | Liverpool John Moores |
| 59 | Bradford | 60 | Salford | =61 | Paisley |
| =61 | Strathclyde | 63 | Heriot-Watt | 64 | East London |
| 65 | Middlesex | 66 | Kingston | 67 | Central England |
| 68 | Plymouth | 69 | Anglia | =70 | Greenwich |
| =70 | South Bank | | | | |

**TQA (England) 2000–01**
**Firsts and 2:1s:** 54%
**Employment:** 71%
**Further study:** 16%
**Unemployment:** 6%

New Scottish Academic Review: *Abertay Dundee, Dundee, Edinburgh*: confidence in the academic standards; the quality of teaching and learning, student progression and learning resources was commendable.

## Education

The education table sees more change than almost any other because it includes both new research grades and new teaching quality assessments. The most spectacular difference is a 16–place leap by Bristol, which now tops the ranking with full marks for both teaching and research. Like a number of universities in the table, Bristol does not have an A-level score because it does not offer undergraduate courses. Such institutions qualify for inclusion because they have two of the three scores used to compile the ranking, and their position is a guide to the quality of PGCE courses. Oxford, last year's table topper, did not have a teaching score when the guide went to press and could not be placed.

More than a dozen of the universities offering education as a separate subject have full marks for teaching quality and Cardiff was rated Excellent under the Welsh system. Surprisingly, none of the new universities – many of which contain former teacher training colleges – were among the top scorers, although South Bank and Central Lancashire made it into the top 20.

The latest research grades saw Cardiff, as well as Bristol judged internationally outstanding, while another nine universities reached grade 5. Of those universities running BEd degrees, Northumbria had the highest entry standards, its students averaging more than three Bs at A level. But three Ds was more than enough to secure a place on some of the courses in the table.

Education is the third-biggest subject at degree level with more than 100,000 applications for courses beginning in 2002. Employment levels are high.

| | | TQA | RAE | | A-Levels | Score |
|---|---|---|---|---|---|---|
| 1 | Bristol | 24 | 5* | A | | 100.0 |
| 2 | Sheffield | 24 | 5 | A | | 97.0 |
| 3 | Warwick | 24 | 4 | B | 23.0 | 95.0 |

## Education (cont.)

| | | TQA | RAE | | A-Levels | Score |
|---|---|---|---|---|---|---|
| 4 | Lancaster | 24 | 5 | B | 19.8 | 94.5 |
| 5 | Leeds | 24 | 4 | B | 20.8 | 93.2 |
| 6 | Leicester | 24 | 4 | B | | 92.5 |
| =7 | Cardiff | E | 5* | A | 18.2 | 91.9 |
| =7 | York | 24 | 4 | B | 19.2 | 91.9 |
| 9 | Exeter | 24 | 5 | C | 17.7 | 90.2 |
| 10 | Keele | 24 | 3a | B | 19.6 | 90.1 |
| 11 | Southampton | 24 | 4 | C | | 89.8 |
| =12 | Bath | 23 | 5 | B | | 88.6 |
| =12 | Cambridge | 23 | 5 | B | | 88.6 |
| =12 | King's College London | 23 | 5 | B | | 88.6 |
| 15 | Durham | 23 | 5 | C | 19.8 | 86.8 |
| =16 | Queens, Belfast | 23 | 4 | B | | 86.0 |
| =16 | South Bank | 23 | 4 | B | | 86.0 |
| =16 | Surrey | 23 | 4 | B | | 86.0 |
| 19 | Central Lancashire | 24 | 3b | C | | 85.6 |
| 20 | Manchester | 23 | 4 | C | 19.5 | 84.8 |
| =21 | Ulster | | 3a | D | 22.3 | 83.3 |
| =21 | Birmingham | 21 | 5 | B | 24.9 | 83.3 |
| 23 | Northumbria | 24 | 3b | E | 18.5 | 82.9 |
| =24 | Goldsmiths College | | 4 | C | 17.6 | 82.6 |
| =24 | Aberystwyth | | 3a | B | 17.5 | 82.6 |
| 26 | Sussex | 22 | 5 | B | | 82.2 |
| 27 | West of England | 24 | 3a | E | 15.1 | 80.8 |
| 28 | Reading | | 3a | C | 18.4 | 80.7 |
| 29 | Brunel | 23 | 3a | C | 16.5 | 80.6 |
| 30 | Newcastle | 22 | 4 | B | | 79.5 |
| 31 | Stirling | HS | 4 | C | 21.4 | 78.7 |
| 32 | Edinburgh | | 4 | D | 17.8 | 78.1 |
| =33 | Nottingham | 22 | 4 | C | | 76.8 |
| =33 | Leeds Metropolitan | 23 | 3a | E | 16.6 | 76.8 |
| =33 | Sheffield Hallam | 23 | 3a | E | 16.6 | 76.8 |
| =36 | Strathclyde | HS | 4 | E | 19.8 | 72.4 |
| =36 | Nottingham Trent | 22 | 3b | D | 16.6 | 72.4 |
| 38 | Wolverhampton | 23 | 2 | F | 12.7 | 71.2 |
| 39 | Middlesex | 22 | 2 | D | 15.1 | 69.9 |
| 40 | Hertfordshire | 22 | 3b | E | 14.8 | 69.4 |

| | | | | | |
|---|---|---|---|---|---|
| 41 | Plymouth | 42 | Derby | 43 | Gloucestershire |
| =44 | Paisley | =44 | Surrey Roehampton | 46 | Central England |
| 47 | Huddersfield | 48 | Brighton | 49 | Hull |
| 50 | Oxford Brookes | 51 | Sunderland | 52 | Liverpool John Moores |
| 53 | Manchester Metropolitan | 54 | Bangor | 55 | Greenwich |
| 56 | De Montfort | 57 | North London | 58 | Anglia |
| 59 | East London | | | | |

**TQA (England) 2001**
**Firsts and 2:1s:** 53%
**Employment:** 93%
**Further study:** 1%
**Unemployment:** 3%

## Electrical and Electronic Engineering

Southampton tops the table for electrical and electronic engineering with a perfect record in the teaching and research assessments. Sheffield, last year's leader, matched this feat, but entered a lower proportion of academics for the Research Assessment Exercise, slipping to third behind consistent Bristol. Imperial College, London, is tied for third by virtue of its high entry standards.

Six universities rated internationally outstanding for research in the new assessments, while ten English universities achieved maximum points for teaching quality. Three Scottish universities and three in Wales were rated Excellent for teaching in their separate systems, although only Edinburgh was considered internationally outstanding for research. Huddersfield was only new university among those with 24 points for teaching quality, while Glamorgan was rated Excellent in Wales.

Entry standards vary enormously among the 70 universities in the table, from close to three As at Imperial to less than two Ds and an E at a number of former polytechnics. About half of the students – more in electrical engineering – come with qualifications other than A level. Yet it is electrical engineering which has the higher proportion of firsts and 2:1s, as well as a marginally better employment rate. About three-quarters of both sets of graduates go straight into jobs.

|    |                          | TQA | RAE |   | A-Levels | Score |
|----|--------------------------|-----|-----|---|----------|-------|
| 1  | Southampton              | 24  | 5*  | A | 25.9     | 100.0 |
| 2  | Bristol                  | 24  | 5   | A | 26.6     | 96.6  |
| =3 | Sheffield                | 24  | 5*  | B | 24.9     | 96.1  |
| =3 | Imperial College         | 24  | 5   | B | 29.0     | 96.1  |
| 5  | Queen's, Belfast         | 24  | 5   | A | 25.3     | 95.5  |
| 6  | Edinburgh                | E   | 5*  | B | 24.7     | 90.5  |
| 7  | Surrey                   | 23  | 5*  | A | 19.6     | 89.1  |
| 8  | York                     | 24  | 3a  | A | 24.6     | 86.7  |
| =9 | Essex                    | 24  | 5   | B | 16.5     | 85.1  |
| =9 | Cardiff                  | E   | 5   | A | 19.7     | 85.1  |
| =9 | University College London| 22  | 5   | A | 25.8     | 85.1  |
| 12 | Birmingham               | 24  | 5   | C | 21.3     | 85.0  |
| 13 | Strathclyde              | E   | 5   | B |          | 84.6  |
| 14 | Loughborough             | 22  | 5   | B | 23.2     | 80.1  |
| 15 | UMIST                    | 22  | 5   | B | 22.3     | 79.4  |
| 16 | Nottingham               | 22  | 4   | A | 23.2     | 78.7  |
| 17 | Swansea                  | E   | 4   | C | 21.5     | 76.9  |
| 18 | Hull                     | 24  | 4   | C | 15.2     | 76.8  |
| 19 | Leeds                    | 23  | 5*  | D | 21.1     | 76.5  |
| =20| Liverpool                | 21  | 5   | A | 20.7     | 75.1  |
| =20| Newcastle                | 21  | 5   | A | 20.7     | 75.1  |
| 22 | Heriot-Watt              | E   | 4   | B | 14.2     | 74.0  |
| 23 | Reading                  | 21  | 5   | B | 21.7     | 73.4  |
| 24 | Lancaster                |     | 4   | B | 19.5     | 71.2  |
| 25 | Manchester               | 20  | 5*  | B | 19.2     | 69.4  |
| 26 | Brunel                   | 21  | 5   | B | 14.7     | 67.2  |
| 27 | Aston                    | 21  | 5   | C | 18.9     | 66.6  |
| 28 | Glasgow                  | S   | 5   | B |          | 64.3  |

## Electrical and Electronic Engineering (cont.)

| | | TQA | RAE | | A-Levels | Score |
|---|---|---|---|---|---|---|
| 29 | Bath | 20 | 4 | C | 23.8 | 62.6 |
| 30 | Huddersfield | 24 | 3b | F | 13.6 | 62.2 |
| 31 | Kent | 21 | 4 | C | 16.0 | 61.2 |
| 32 | Queen Mary | 21 | 3a | B | 14.3 | 59.7 |
| 33 | Bangor | S | 4 | B | 14.4 | 58.0 |
| 34 | King's College London | 20 | 5 | D | 20.1 | 57.2 |
| =35 | Aberdeen | S | 4 | C | | 55.2 |
| =35 | Bradford | 21 | 4 | E | 18.6 | 55.2 |
| 37 | Ulster | 20 | 3b | A | 17.6 | 54.8 |
| =38 | Northumbria | 22 | 3b | C | 8.6 | 54.4 |
| =38 | Westminster | 21 | 4 | D | 12.9 | 54.4 |
| 40 | City | 21 | 3a | C | 10.2 | 53.2 |

| | | | | | |
|---|---|---|---|---|---|
| 41 | Glamorgan | 42 | Paisley | 43 | West of England |
| 44 | Sussex | 45 | Brighton | 46 | Staffordshire |
| =47 | Hertfordshire | =47 | De Montfort | 49 | Nottingham Trent |
| 50 | Robert Gordon | 51 | Glasgow Caledonian | 52 | Teesside |
| 53 | Manchester Metropolitan | 54 | South Bank | 55 | Portsmouth |
| 56 | Anglia | 57 | Coventry | 58 | Bournemouth |
| 59 | Liverpool John Moores | =60 | Salford | =60 | Oxford Brookes |
| 62 | Derby | 63 | Greenwich | 64 | Plymouth |
| 65 | Luton | 66 | Leeds Metropolitan | 67 | Central England |
| 68 | Sheffield Hallam | 69 | Central Lancashire | 70 | East London |

**TQA (England) 1996–98**

**Firsts and 2:1s:** 51%, 45% (electronic)

**Employment:** 75%, 74% (electronic)

**Further study:** 13%, 13% (electronic)

**Unemployment:** 9%, 10% (electronic)

New Scottish Academic Review: *Glasgow Caledonian, Paisley*: confidence in the academic standards; the quality of teaching and learning, and learning resources was commendable.

## English

Oxford retains the leadership of the table as one of nine universities with maximum points for both teaching and research. Differences at the top are slight. Cambridge, for example, is one of the nine and has the highest entry standards, but misses the top five on its decision not to enter a full complement of staff in the Research Assessment Exercise.

The teaching assessments are dated, but students looking for an excellent undergraduate programme have a wide choice, with all but one of the top 20 receiving that rating. A further 11 universities, including the former polytechnics of Sheffield Hallam, Anglia, West of England, Kingston, Northumbria, Oxford Brookes and North London, fall into the same category. Glasgow is the top-placed Scottish university; Aberystwyth the leader in Wales.

Entry standards remain high: the average A-level score is 25 or above for all but five of the top 20: Glasgow, Queen Mary, Liverpool, Lancaster and Queen's, Belfast. Only six of the top 40 universities have average entry grades of less than three Cs at A level.

## English (cont.)

Competition is certain to remain intense. The 47,000 applicants for places on courses beginning in 2002 represented a 12 per cent increase on 2001. The proportion of English students gaining a first or upper second, at seven out of ten, was among the highest in any subject. Almost a third of all graduates go on to further study.

| | | TQA | RAE | | A-Levels | Score |
|---|---|---|---|---|---|---|
| 1 | Oxford | E | 5* | A | 29.5 | 100.0 |
| 2 | University College London | E | 5* | A | 29.2 | 99.8 |
| 3 | York | E | 5* | A | 28.3 | 99.1 |
| 4 | Durham | E | 5* | A | 28.2 | 99.0 |
| 5 | Leeds | E | 5* | A | 27.1 | 98.3 |
| 6 | Cambridge | E | 5* | B | 29.6 | 96.9 |
| 7 | Warwick | E | 5* | B | 26.9 | 95.0 |
| 8 | Nottingham | E | 5 | A | 27.9 | 94.7 |
| 9 | Southampton | E | 5 | A | 25.8 | 93.1 |
| =10 | Liverpool | E | 5* | B | 24.0 | 92.8 |
| =10 | Leicester | E | 5 | A | 25.4 | 92.8 |
| =10 | Newcastle | E | 5 | A | 25.3 | 92.8 |
| 13 | Glasgow | E | 5* | B | 23.9 | 92.7 |
| =14 | Lancaster | E | 5 | A | 23.7 | 91.6 |
| =14 | Sheffield | E | 5 | B | 27.4 | 91.6 |
| 16 | Queen's, Belfast | E | 5 | A | 23.4 | 91.3 |
| 17 | Queen Mary | E | 5 | A | 23.0 | 91.1 |
| 18 | Sussex | E | 5 | B | 26.7 | 91.0 |
| 19 | Exeter | E | 5 | B | 25.7 | 90.3 |
| 20 | Edinburgh | HS | 5* | A | 29.2 | 89.5 |
| 21 | Bristol | E | 5 | C | 28.5 | 87.8 |
| 22 | Birmingham | E | 5 | C | 27.6 | 87.1 |
| 23 | Stirling | E | 5 | B | 20.6 | 86.6 |
| 24 | St Andrews | HS | 5* | B | 26.6 | 84.4 |
| 25 | West of England | E | 4 | B | 20.9 | 83.0 |
| 26 | Dundee | E | 4 | A | 17.4 | 82.7 |
| 27 | Sheffield Hallam | E | 4 | B | 20.3 | 82.6 |
| 28 | Aberystwyth | E | 4 | B | 20.2 | 82.5 |
| 29 | Oxford Brookes | E | 5 | C | 19.8 | 81.4 |
| 30 | Anglia | E | 5 | C | 14.6 | 77.7 |
| 31 | Kingston | E | 3a | B | 15.3 | 75.2 |
| 32 | Northumbria | E | 3a | C | 19.2 | 75.0 |
| 33 | Cardiff | S | 5* | B | 26.4 | 74.0 |
| 34 | Strathclyde | HS | 5 | B | 17.1 | 73.8 |
| 35 | Royal Holloway | S | 5 | A | 25.4 | 72.2 |
| 36 | Reading | S | 5* | B | 23.6 | 72.0 |
| 37 | North London | E | 3a | C | 14.1 | 71.3 |
| 38 | Manchester | S | 5 | B | 26.2 | 70.1 |
| =39 | Goldsmiths College | S | 5 | A | 22.1 | 69.8 |
| =39 | Aberdeen | HS | 4 | B | 16.8 | 69.8 |

| | | | |
|---|---|---|---|
| 41 East Anglia | 42 Hull | 43 Kent | |
| 44 Salford | 45 King's College London | 46 Keele | |
| 47 De Montfort | 48 Swansea | 49 Loughborough | |

## English (cont.)

| | | |
|---|---|---|
| 50 Glamorgan | =51 Nottingham Trent | =51 Lampeter |
| 53 Essex | 54 Bangor | 55 Gloucestershire |
| 56 Ulster | 57 South Bank | =58 Surrey Roehampton |
| =58 Brunel | 60 Liverpool John Moores | 61 Plymouth |
| 62 Hertfordshire | =63 Portsmouth | =63 Manchester Metropolitan |
| 65 Central Lancashire | 66 Sunderland | 67 Middlesex |
| 68 Central England | 69 Thames Valley | 70 Staffordshire |
| 71 Westminster | 72 Derby | =73 Wolverhampton |
| =73 Luton | 75 Greenwich | 76 Teesside |
| 77 London Guildhall | | |

**TQA (England) 1994–95**

**Firsts and 2:1s:** 70%

**Employment:** 56%

**Further study:** 31%

**Unemployment:** 6%

New Scottish Academic Review: *Strathclyde*: confidence in the academic standards; the quality of teaching and learning, student progression and learning resources was commendable.

## Environmental Science

Comparisons in environmental science are complicated by the fact that the teaching ratings were not all compiled in the same round of assessment. Third-placed Nottingham's 23 points out of 24 are worth more, under the new scoring system for the tables, than the old Excellent grades achieved by 11 other universities. East Anglia and Reading, in first and second place, are the only universities with maximum points for both teaching and research. UEA nudges ahead on the higher average A-level points of its students.

Plymouth is the highest-placed new university, although it has slipped out of the top ten after the latest research assessments. Although it improved its performance, it could not match the grades of Manchester and Keele, both new entrants to the ranking. Oxford Brookes, Hertfordshire and Greenwich also make the top 20.

Seventh-placed Aberystwyth is the top university in Wales, while Stirling, one place lower, is the leader in Scotland. Salford is the third university rated internationally outstanding for research, but a Satisfactory teaching grade and low entry standards keep it out of the top 20. A-level grades are generally modest, none of the 49 universities in the table averaging three Bs.

Nearly half of all environmental science graduates achieve a first or upper second class degree. Two-thirds go straight into employment, while one in five signs up for further study after graduating.

| | | TQA | RAE | | A-Levels | Score |
|---|---|---|---|---|---|---|
| 1 | East Anglia | E | 5* | A | 23.6 | 100.0 |
| 2 | Reading | E | 5* | A | 22.8 | 99.4 |
| 3 | Nottingham | 23 | 5 | A | 17.9 | 97.8 |
| 4 | Southampton | E | 5 | A | 22.3 | 96.4 |

## Environmental Science (cont.)

| | | TQA | RAE | | A-Levels | Score |
|---|---|---|---|---|---|---|
| 5 | Keele | | 5 | A | 18.9 | 93.0 |
| 6 | Imperial College | | 4 | A | 21.7 | 92.3 |
| 7 | Aberystwyth | E | 4 | A | 17.6 | 90.1 |
| 8 | Stirling | E | 3a | B | 18.3 | 87.0 |
| 9 | Birmingham | | 4 | B | 19.7 | 86.4 |
| 10 | Manchester | | 5 | B | 16.7 | 86.3 |
| 11 | Plymouth | E | 4 | C | 14.7 | 84.2 |
| 12 | Oxford Brookes | 23 | 2 | C | 15.0 | 83.9 |
| 13 | Leeds | | 5 | C | 18.7 | 83.8 |
| 14 | Ulster | E | 3b | A | 15.5 | 83.4 |
| 15 | Newcastle | | 4 | B | 17.1 | 82.3 |
| 16 | Aston | | 5 | C | 17.5 | 82.0 |
| 17 | Hertfordshire | E | 2 | B | 14.3 | 79.4 |
| =18 | Lancaster | E | | | 18.5 | 78.3 |
| =18 | Greenwich | E | 3b | C | 11.8 | 78.3 |
| 20 | Sheffield | S | 4 | B | 21.5 | 77.1 |
| 21 | Salford | S | 5* | A | 12.9 | 76.9 |
| 22 | Liverpool | E | | | 15.2 | 75.7 |
| 23 | Bangor | S | 4 | A | 16.6 | 74.7 |
| 24 | Kent | S | 5 | B | | 74.5 |
| 25 | Nottingham Trent | | 3a | B | 14.6 | 73.8 |
| 26 | Exeter | | 4 | A | 9.6 | 73.2 |
| 27 | Manchester Metropolitan | S | 4 | C | 13.4 | 68.5 |
| 28 | Portsmouth | | 3b | A | 12.5 | 67.5 |
| 29 | Anglia | S | 3b | A | | 67.0 |
| 30 | Central Lancashire | S | 3b | B | 12.9 | 65.8 |
| 31 | Wolverhampton | S | 3b | A | 10.8 | 65.0 |
| 32 | Liverpool John Moores | S | 3b | B | 11.7 | 64.8 |
| 33 | Kingston | S | 3b | B | 11.5 | 64.7 |
| 34 | Westminster | S | 3b | C | | 64.3 |
| 35 | Northumbria | S | 3b | C | 12.5 | 64.1 |
| 36 | Bradford | S | 3b | D | 13.4 | 63.3 |
| 37 | Staffordshire | S | 2 | A | 10.4 | 62.1 |
| 38 | Surrey Roehampton | S | 2 | C | | 62.0 |
| 39 | West of England | S | 2 | C | 12.0 | 61.9 |
| =40 | Sussex | S | | | 16.1 | 61.8 |
| =40 | Sunderland | S | 3b | C | 9.6 | 61.8 |
| 42 | Derby | | 43 Bournemouth | | | 44 Middlesex | |
| 45 | Coventry | | 46 Gloucestershire | | | =47 Huddersfield | |
| =47 | Teesside | | 49 De Montfort | | | | |

**TQA (England) 1994–97**
**Firsts and 2:1s:** 48%
**Employment:** 62%
**Further study:** 20%
**Unemployment:** 10%

New Scottish Academic Review: *Abertay Dundee*: confidence in the academic standards; the quality of student progression was commendable.

*Edinburgh, Stirling*: confidence in the academic standards; the quality of student progression and learning resources was commendable.

## Food Science

Nottingham's lead at the top of the Food Science table is cut, after the university slipped a grade in the latest research assessments. However, it still has the best teaching score and the highest entry standards. Sixth-placed Leeds retained its 5* research rating, but entered a relatively low proportion of its academics for assessment. Surrey was the real research star, moving up to third place behind Reading.

UWIC, Cardiff, new to the guide this year as a full member of the University of Wales and Universities UK, takes fourth place and is the top new university. Like Robert Gordon, in fifth, it is rated Excellent for teaching, but has a relatively low research grade.

Most of the 18 universities in the ranking are former polytechnics, with Greenwich, Leeds Metropolitan and Lincoln all making the top ten. Only Nottingham has average entry standards of a B and two Cs at A level, while a C and two Ds would have secured a place on several other food science courses.

Nearly four out of five graduates in food science find employment directly after leaving university. Almost a third of entrants to the course arrive with alternative qualifications to A levels. Assessors in England were concerned at the high drop-out rate on more than half of the courses: more than 20 per cent of students failed to progress to the next stage of their degree.

|  | | TQA | RAE | | A-Levels | Score |
|---|---|---|---|---|---|---|
| 1 | Nottingham | 23 | 5 | A | 20.6 | 100.0 |
| 2 | Reading | 22 | 5 | A | 17.8 | 92.8 |
| 3 | Surrey | 21 | 5* | A | 19.5 | 92.6 |
| 4 | UWIC, Cardiff | E | 3b | C | 15.7 | 86.3 |
| 5 | Robert Gordon | E | 3b | E | | 85.6 |
| 6 | Queen's, Belfast | 21 | 4 | C | | 82.3 |
| 7 | Leeds | 20 | 5* | C | 18.0 | 82.1 |
| 8 | Greenwich | | 3a | A | 14.1 | 76.6 |
| 9 | Leeds Metropolitan | | 3b | C | 16.8 | 73.6 |
| 10 | Lincoln | 20 | 3b | C | | 72.8 |
| 11 | Oxford Brookes | 20 | | | 13.5 | 66.5 |
| 12 | Manchester Metropolitan | 19 | | | 17.5 | 66.1 |
| 13 | North London | 19 | | | 16.1 | 64.7 |
| 14 | Huddersfield | 20 | | | 11.5 | 64.4 |
| 15 | Bournemouth | 19 | | | 14.3 | 62.9 |
| 16 | South Bank | 18 | 3a | E | 13.3 | 60.1 |
| 17 | Teesside | 17 | 2 | B | | 55.6 |
| 18 | Plymouth | | 3a | E | 9.0 | 53.6 |

**TQA (England) 1996–98**
**Firsts and 2:1s:** 58%
**Employment:** 78%
**Further study:** 9%
**Unemployment:** 5%

## French

A 5* rating in the latest Research Assessment Exercise takes Aberdeen to the top of the ranking for French. The university benefits from not having a separate score for entry standards, but with one of two Excellent scores under the Scottish system, it boasts the only perfect record for both teaching and research. Cambridge slips to second, despite retaining its 5* research grade and recording the highest entry standards.

No English university was awarded maximum points for teaching quality, but two new universities – Westminster and Portsmouth – share the best teaching record in England with fifth-placed Queen Mary. In Wales, none of the teaching grades was better than Satisfactory.

Oxford, Royal Holloway, Southampton and Manchester are the other institutions rated internationally outstanding for research. The subject still commands high entry grades, with most of the traditional universities averaging at least 22 points at A level.

French remains the most popular language for a first degree, with more than 4,000 full-time undergraduates, nine out of ten of whom enter with A levels or equivalents. It also has one of the lowest unemployment rates of modern language subjects. The teaching assessments were carried out at least five years ago and, at the time, assessors said that some universities had failed to think through the new teaching approaches that they were applying. However, some departments have changed radically in the intervening period.

|  |  | TQA | RAE | | A-Levels | Score |
|---|---|---|---|---|---|---|
| 1 | Aberdeen | E | 5* | A | | 100.0 |
| 2 | Cambridge | 22 | 5* | A | 29.7 | 94.9 |
| 3 | Glasgow | E | 5 | B | 23.6 | 89.9 |
| 4 | Oxford | 21 | 5* | A | 29.5 | 89.1 |
| 5 | Queen Mary | 23 | 5 | A | 18.6 | 88.7 |
| 6 | Durham | 22 | 5 | B | 27.1 | 86.8 |
| 7 | Liverpool | 22 | 5 | A | 23.5 | 86.7 |
| =8 | Royal Holloway | 21 | 5* | A | 22.9 | 84.3 |
| =8 | Newcastle | 22 | 4 | A | 25.4 | 84.3 |
| 10 | Warwick | 21 | 5 | A | 26.2 | 83.0 |
| 11 | Sussex | 22 | 4 | A | 23.5 | 82.9 |
| 12 | St Andrews | 22 | 4 | B | 26.0 | 82.7 |
| 13 | University College London | 21 | 5 | A | 25.6 | 82.6 |
| 14 | Leeds | 22 | 4 | B | 25.1 | 82.1 |
| 15 | Exeter | 22 | 4 | B | 23.6 | 81.0 |
| 16 | Sheffield | 21 | 5 | B | 26.7 | 80.9 |
| 17 | Edinburgh | HS | 5 | C | 28.0 | 80.7 |
| 18 | King's College London | 21 | 5 | A | 22.7 | 80.5 |
| 19 | Aston | 22 | 5 | C | 23.4 | 80.1 |
| 20 | Oxford Brookes | 22 | 5 | B | 15.9 | 78.7 |
| 21 | Bristol | 20 | 5 | A | 27.8 | 78.6 |
| 22 | Portsmouth | 23 | 5 | C | 13.2 | 78.3 |
| 23 | Stirling | HS | 5 | B | 18.5 | 77.8 |
| 24 | Strathclyde | 22 | 4 | C | | 76.9 |

## French (cont.)

|  |  | TQA | RAE |  | A-Levels | Score |
|---|---|---|---|---|---|---|
| 25 | Reading | 21 | 5 | B | 21.0 | 76.8 |
| 26 | Heriot-Watt | 21 | 4 | B | 24.7 | 76.1 |
| 27 | Cardiff | S | 5 | A | 24.0 | 75.7 |
| 28 | Salford | 20 | 5 | A | 21.8 | 74.2 |
| 29 | Loughborough |  | 5 | B | 18.6 | 72.7 |
| 30 | Queen's, Belfast | 20 | 4 | A | 24.4 | 72.3 |
| 31 | Hull | 21 | 4 | B | 19.0 | 72.0 |
| 32 | Kingston | 21 | 4 | A | 14.9 | 71.0 |
| 33 | Swansea | S | 4 | A | 20.7 | 69.6 |
| 34 | Westminster | 23 | 3a | D | 12.0 | 69.0 |
| 35 | Southampton | 18 | 5* | A | 23.5 | 67.9 |
| 36 | York | 22 |  |  | 27.6 | 67.6 |
| 37 | Northumbria | 23 | 3b | E | 14.9 | 67.0 |
| 38 | Aberystwyth | S | 3a | A | 20.4 | 65.7 |
| 39 | Manchester | 19 | 5* | C | 22.6 | 65.4 |
| 40 | Ulster | 20 | 4 | C | 19.8 | 63.6 |

| | | |
|---|---|---|
| 41 Kent | 42 North London | 43 Central Lancashire |
| 44 Birmingham | 45 Leicester | 46 Bangor |
| 47 Keele | 48 Wolverhampton | 49 Nottingham |
| 50 Surrey | =51 Anglia | =51 Brighton |
| 53 Plymouth | 54 West of England | 55 Surrey Roehampton |
| 56 Coventry | 57 East Anglia | 58 Lancaster |
| 59 Staffordshire | 60 Bath | =61 London Guildhall |
| =61 Middlesex | 63 Bradford | 64 Nottingham Trent |
| 65 UMIST | 66 Liverpool John Moores | 67 Goldsmiths College |
| 68 De Montfort | | |

**TQA (England) 1995–96**
**Firsts and 2:1s:** 64%
**Employment:** 64%
**Further study:** 24%
**Unemployment:** 5%

## General Engineering

Cambridge shades ahead of Oxford at the top of the general engineering table with marginally higher entry standards. Indeed, they could hardly be any higher, at a fraction of a point off three As at A level. Like Southampton and Imperial College, in third and fourth places, both universities have near-perfect teaching scores and are rated internationally outstanding for research.

No university was awarded maximum points for teaching quality in a subject that was not assessed separately in Scotland. Sheffield Hallam achieved the best score in the new universities, with 21 points out of 24, giving it a place in the top 20, just above Hertfordshire. Liverpool John Moores held onto an exceptional grade 5 for research, but had among the lowest entry grades and teaching score.

As in the specialist branches of engineering, entry grades vary considerably, from almost the maximum three As at Oxbridge to little more than three Es at

## General Engineering (cont.)

Coventry. Only nine of the 23 universities reporting separate A-level scores for general engineering averaged more than three Cs.

More than 10,000 undergraduates take general engineering courses, rather than specialising. Employment prospects are close to the norm for all engineering courses, with nearly three-quarters going straight into jobs. The assessors found that the courses nurtured the transferable skills required for later specialisation, but they worried about first-year drop-out rates.

| | | TQA | RAE | | A-Levels | Score |
|---|---|---|---|---|---|---|
| 1 | Cambridge | 23 | 5* | A | 29.9 | 100.0 |
| 2 | Oxford | 23 | 5* | A | 29.7 | 99.9 |
| 3 | Southampton | 23 | 5* | A | | 97.2 |
| 4 | Imperial College | 23 | 5* | B | | 92.6 |
| 5 | Durham | 22 | 5 | B | 25.6 | 78.9 |
| 6 | Brunel | 22 | 5 | B | | 76.1 |
| 7 | Nottingham | | 4 | B | 27.1 | 74.9 |
| 8 | Lancaster | 22 | 4 | B | 19.6 | 68.5 |
| 9 | Warwick | 21 | 5 | B | 22.6 | 66.9 |
| 10 | Leicester | 20 | 5 | A | 20.7 | 59.2 |
| 11 | Sussex | | 5 | B | 13.4 | 56.0 |
| 12 | Surrey | | 4 | B | 16.7 | 53.9 |
| 13 | Aberdeen | | 4 | C | 16.7 | 45.2 |
| 14 | Leeds | | 5 | C | 12.8 | 44.2 |
| 15 | Wolverhampton | 20 | 3a | B | | 43.1 |
| 16 | Exeter | 20 | 4 | C | 14.1 | 40.8 |
| 17 | Bradford | 20 | 3b | C | 20.0 | 39.8 |
| 18 | Cranfield | 20 | 4 | D | | 36.8 |
| 19 | Sheffield Hallam | 21 | 3a | F | | 35.0 |
| 20 | Hertfordshire | 20 | 3a | D | 13.4 | 32.6 |
| 21 | Liverpool John Moores | 18 | 5 | A | 9.0 | 29.7 |
| 22 | Central Lancashire | 20 | 3a | E | | 28.8 |
| 23 | Queen Mary | 19 | | | 19.5 | 20.5 |
| 24 | Oxford Brookes | | 3b | D | 12.3 | 16.6 |
| 25 | Northumbria | | 3b | C | 8.7 | 15.2 |
| 26 | West of England | | 3b | D | 11.5 | 15.0 |
| 27 | Central England | 19 | 3b | F | 9.5 | 11.5 |
| 28 | Greenwich | 17 | 3a | B | | 9.7 |
| 29 | Bournemouth | 18 | 3b | F | 12.3 | 5.4 |
| 30 | Leeds Metropolitan | 17 | 3b | C | 12.3 | 5.4 |
| 31 | Coventry | 18 | | | 7.1 | 1.0 |

**TQA (England) 1996–98**
**Firsts and 2:1s:** 46%
**Employment:** 73%
**Further study:** 13%
**Unemployment:** 9%

## Geography

There is little to choose between the top three geography departments: each has teaching graded Excellent and the highest rating for research. Their positions reflect differences in the average A-level points of their undergraduates, ranging from almost two As and a B at Bristol to nearly an A and two Bs at University College London. Cambridge still has the highest entry standards but slips to fourth after losing its 5* research grade.

Two other universities are rated internationally outstanding for research, and both miss the top ten. Edinburgh is 11th after a Highly Satisfactory grade for teaching, under the Scottish system, while Royal Holloway was restricted to Satisfactory in England. Almost half of the 64 universities in the ranking were rated Excellent in teaching assessments that were among the first to be completed and are now dated.

Edinburgh is the top university in Scotland, Swansea just leads Aberystwyth in Wales. Plymouth is the highest-placed new university. Like Portsmouth, Coventry, Gloucestershire and Oxford Brookes, it is rated Excellent for teaching.

Geography has benefited from rising interest in 'green' issues among the young: there was an increased demand for places on courses starting in 2002 in both human and physical geography. Just 5 per cent of recent geography graduates were unemployed in 2000, although the proportion was slightly higher where the subject was studied purely as a physical science.

|  |  | TQA | RAE | | A-Levels | Score |
|---|---|---|---|---|---|---|
| 1 | Bristol | E | 5* | A | 27.7 | 100.0 |
| 2 | Durham | E | 5* | A | 27.2 | 99.6 |
| 3 | University College London | E | 5* | A | 25.8 | 98.6 |
| 4 | Cambridge | E | 5 | A | 29.7 | 97.7 |
| 5 | Sheffield | E | 5 | A | 26.9 | 95.6 |
| 6 | Southampton | E | 5 | A | 25.1 | 94.2 |
| =7 | Nottingham | E | 5 | B | 27.9 | 93.8 |
| =7 | Oxford | E | 4 | A | 29.6 | 93.8 |
| 9 | Leeds | E | 5 | B | 24.8 | 91.5 |
| 10 | East Anglia | E | 4 | A |  | 89.1 |
| 11 | Edinburgh | HS | 5* | A | 26.6 | 88.7 |
| 12 | Reading | E | 4 | A | 22.7 | 88.6 |
| 13 | Exeter | E | 4 | B | 24.6 | 88.0 |
| =14 | Birmingham | E | 4 | B | 24.3 | 87.7 |
| =14 | Lancaster | E | 4 | A | 21.5 | 87.7 |
| 16 | Queen Mary | E | 5 | A | 16.1 | 87.5 |
| 17 | King's College London | E | 4 | A | 21.1 | 87.4 |
| 18 | Manchester | E | 4 | B | 23.5 | 87.2 |
| 19 | St Andrews | E | 4 | B | 23.3 | 87.0 |
| 20 | Swansea | E | 4 | A | 20.4 | 86.9 |
| 21 | Aberystwyth | E | 4 | A | 19.1 | 85.9 |
| 22 | Glasgow | E | 4 | C | 23.0 | 83.4 |
| 23 | Plymouth | E | 4 | B | 16.5 | 81.9 |
| 24 | Aberdeen | E | 4 | B | 16.4 | 81.8 |
| 25 | Portsmouth | E | 3a | B | 17.7 | 79.4 |
| 26 | Strathclyde | E | 3a | C |  | 78.9 |

## Geography (cont.)

| | | TQA | RAE | | A-Levels | Score |
|---|---|---|---|---|---|---|
| 27 | Coventry | E | 3a | B | 14.1 | 76.7 |
| 28 | Royal Holloway | S | 5* | A | 20.8 | 73.9 |
| 29 | London School of Economics | S | 5 | A | 25.6 | 73.7 |
| 30 | Gloucestershire | E | 3a | C | 12.4 | 72.6 |
| 31 | Newcastle | S | 5 | A | 23.8 | 72.4 |
| =32 | Loughborough | S | 5 | B | 21.2 | 68.0 |
| =32 | Hull | S | 5 | B | 21.2 | 68.0 |
| 34 | Queen's, Belfast | S | 4 | A | 20.6 | 66.1 |
| 35 | Liverpool | S | 4 | A | 20.0 | 65.7 |
| 36 | Oxford Brookes | E | | | 16.4 | 65.2 |
| 37 | Dundee | S | 4 | A | 19.2 | 65.1 |
| 38 | Sussex | S | 4 | B | 21.0 | 64.4 |
| 39 | Leicester | S | 4 | B | 20.7 | 64.2 |
| 40 | SOAS | S | 4 | B | 20.0 | 63.7 |

| | | | | | |
|---|---|---|---|---|---|
| 41 | Keele | 42 | Salford | 43 | Nottingham Trent |
| 44 | Brunel | 45 | Anglia | 46 | Kingston |
| 47 | Brighton | 48 | Middlesex | 49 | Ulster |
| 50 | Staffordshire | 51 | Northumbria | 52 | Sunderland |
| 53 | Westminster | 54 | Huddersfield | 55 | West of England |
| 56 | South Bank | 57 | Manchester Metropolitan | 58 | Bradford |
| 59 | Greenwich | 60 | Hertfordshire | 61 | Central Lancashire |
| 62 | Liverpool John Moores | 63 | Wolverhampton | 64 | Surrey Roehampton |

**TQA (England) 1994–95**

**Firsts and 2:1s:** 61%

**Employment:** 62%

**Further study:** 23%

**Unemployment:** 5%

New Scottish Academic Review: *Dundee*: confidence in the academic standards; the quality of teaching and learning, student progression and learning resources was commendable.

## Geology

Oxford and Cambridge remain the only universities with maximum scores for both teaching and research in geology, but the scoring system for the table rewards Oxford for its high entry qualifications. Cambridge does not list geology separately. Excellent teaching was recorded at all the top 20 departments except Bristol and Cardiff, where it was Satisfactory, and Lancaster, which was not assessed. The top scorers for teaching included three new universities: Derby, Kingston and Plymouth. Edinburgh is the top university in Scotland, where Glasgow was also rated Excellent at teaching. Cardiff, which reached grade 5 for research, is the only entrant from Wales.

Bristol was the only university, apart from Oxford and Cambridge, to be considered internationally outstanding in the latest Research Assessment Exercise, but ten others reached grade 5. Entry standards range from close to three As at Oxford to less than two Ds and an E at Greenwich.

Geology was among the first subjects to be assessed for teaching quality, so the ratings are dated. Only 21 of the 36 English universities covered by the

## Geology (cont.)

assessment were visited because departments could opt for self-assessment if they were prepared to be rated as merely Satisfactory and 17 of them were given top scores. The assessors found wide variations in the proportion of undergraduates awarded firsts or upper seconds, and expressed concern about a number of universities where drop-out rates exceeded 20 per cent.

| | | TQA | RAE | | A-Levels | Score |
|---|---|---|---|---|---|---|
| 1 | Oxford | E | 5* | A | 29.6 | 100.0 |
| 2 | Cambridge | E | 5* | A | | 96.2 |
| =3 | Edinburgh | E | 5 | A | 23.5 | 91.6 |
| =3 | Leeds | E | 5 | A | 23.5 | 91.6 |
| 5 | Newcastle | E | 5 | A | | 91.3 |
| 6 | Southampton | E | 5 | A | 20.9 | 89.7 |
| 7 | University College London | E | 5 | B | 22.9 | 88.6 |
| 8 | Liverpool | E | 5 | A | 18.3 | 87.8 |
| 9 | Durham | E | 4 | B | 25.8 | 87.2 |
| 10 | Royal Holloway | E | 5 | B | 20.2 | 86.6 |
| 11 | Manchester | E | 5 | B | 20.0 | 86.5 |
| 12 | Glasgow | E | 4 | B | | 83.7 |
| =13 | Reading | E | 3a | B | 17.3 | 77.4 |
| =13 | Birmingham | E | 3a | C | 21.1 | 77.4 |
| 15 | Bristol | S | 5* | A | 23.8 | 75.4 |
| 16 | Plymouth | E | 4 | C | 12.9 | 74.2 |
| 17 | Kingston | E | 3b | B | 14.4 | 71.8 |
| 18 | Lancaster | | 5 | B | 11.0 | 69.9 |
| 19 | Cardiff | S | 5 | A | 18.8 | 67.8 |
| 20 | Imperial College | E | | | 21.8 | 67.0 |
| 21 | Aberdeen | HS | 4 | C | | 66.5 |
| 22 | Leicester | S | 4 | A | 16.0 | 61.8 |
| 23 | Keele | S | 3a | B | 15.8 | 56.0 |
| 24 | Portsmouth | S | 3b | A | 12.6 | 51.4 |
| 25 | Gloucestershire | S | 3a | C | | 50.3 |
| 26 | Greenwich | S | 3b | C | 9.4 | 45.7 |
| 27 | Exeter | S | | | 13.6 | 40.6 |
| 28 | Oxford Brookes | S | | | 11.3 | 39.0 |
| 29 | Staffordshire | S | | | 11.1 | 38.9 |

**TQA (England) 1994–95**
**Firsts and 2:1s:** 53%
**Employment:** 54%
**Further study:** 30%
**Unemployment:** 7%

New Scottish Academic Review: *Aberdeen*: confidence in the academic standards; the quality of teaching and learning, student progression and learning resources was commendable.
*Edinburgh*: confidence in the academic standards; the quality of student progression and learning resources was commendable.

## German

Exeter takes over top place for German after a spectacular improvement in its research grade. It is now the only university with top marks for both teaching and research. Swansea was rated as Excellent for teaching under the Welsh

## German (cont.)

system, but was not among the ten universities rated internationally outstanding for research. Second-placed UCL (one of the research stars), Warwick, Queen Mary and Northumbria all came close to maximum points for teaching quality. Kingston is the highest-placed new university and the only one in the top 20.

Sixty universities offer German, but the total number of students is now below 2,000, including certificate and diploma courses. Nine out of ten enter with A levels or equivalent qualifications, and entry standards are relatively high, especially at the leading universities. Only nine of the top 50 averaged less than three Cs in 2000.

Those who opt for German enjoy enviable employment prospects, only 6 per cent taking longer than six months to find a job. The teaching assessment extended to Dutch and Scandinavian languages, as related languages, and the assessors were impressed with the general standard of provision. The main difficulty facing the subject is a shortage of A-level candidates, but some universities teach it *ab initio* as part of a languages package.

| | | TQA | RAE | | A-Levels | Score |
|---|---|---|---|---|---|---|
| 1 | Exeter | 24 | 5* | A | 23.4 | 100.0 |
| 2 | University College London | 23 | 5* | A | 25.0 | 96.2 |
| 3 | Cambridge | 22 | 5* | A | 29.7 | 94.8 |
| 4 | Nottingham | 22 | 5* | A | 27.9 | 93.5 |
| 5 | Warwick | 23 | 5 | A | 25.6 | 93.4 |
| 6 | Swansea | E | 5 | A | 20.8 | 89.9 |
| 7 | Queen Mary | 23 | 5 | A | 17.7 | 87.6 |
| 8 | Durham | 22 | 4 | A | 27.4 | 86.5 |
| 9 | Oxford | 21 | 5 | A | 29.3 | 86.3 |
| 10 | Edinburgh | 21 | 5* | B | 27.6 | 85.8 |
| 11 | Aberdeen | 22 | 4 | A | | 84.3 |
| 12 | Newcastle | 22 | 4 | A | 22.1 | 82.6 |
| 13 | Manchester | 21 | 5* | B | 22.7 | 82.2 |
| 14 | Bristol | 21 | 5 | B | 25.5 | 81.4 |
| 15 | King's College London | 20 | 5* | A | 24.4 | 81.0 |
| 16 | Aston | 22 | 5 | C | 22.8 | 80.8 |
| 17 | St Andrews | 22 | 4 | C | 25.2 | 80.2 |
| 18 | Leeds | 22 | 4 | C | 24.2 | 79.5 |
| 19 | Glasgow | 22 | 4 | C | | 78.5 |
| 20 | Kingston | 21 | 4 | A | | 78.1 |
| 21 | Heriot-Watt | 21 | 4 | B | 24.7 | 77.8 |
| 22 | Cardiff | S | 5 | A | 22.5 | 76.3 |
| 23 | Sheffield | 20 | 4 | A | 26.7 | 76.1 |
| 24 | Salford | 20 | 5 | A | 21.2 | 75.3 |
| 25 | Strathclyde | 22 | 3b | B | | 74.8 |
| 26 | Birmingham | 19 | 5* | B | 23.8 | 73.1 |
| 27 | Liverpool | 19 | 5 | A | 23.8 | 72.3 |
| 28 | Aberystwyth | S | 4 | A | 20.0 | 71.1 |
| 29 | Southampton | 18 | 5* | A | 23.7 | 70.5 |
| 30 | Northumbria | 23 | 3b | E | 16.5 | 70.0 |
| =31 | York | 22 | | | 26.4 | 69.8 |
| =31 | Reading | 20 | 4 | B | 20.5 | 69.8 |

## German (cont.)

| | | TQA | RAE | | A-Levels | Score |
|---|---|---|---|---|---|---|
| 33 | Portsmouth | 21 | 5 | C | 13.5 | 68.9 |
| 34 | Leicester | 21 | 3b | A | 19.0 | 68.8 |
| 35 | Royal Holloway | 19 | 5* | C | 23.5 | 68.7 |
| 36 | Hull | 21 | 3a | C | 18.9 | 68.2 |
| 37 | Stirling | 20 | 4 | C | 20.5 | 66.8 |
| 38 | North London | 20 | 3a | B | | 66.1 |
| 39 | Queen's, Belfast | 19 | 4 | A | | 65.8 |
| 40 | Kent | 19 | 4 | B | 20.2 | 64.5 |

| | | | | | |
|---|---|---|---|---|---|
| =41 Central Lancashire | =41 Bangor | | 43 Oxford Brookes | | |
| 44 Keele | 45 Surrey | | 46 Ulster | | |
| 47 Brighton | 48 Anglia | | 49 West of England | | |
| 50 Plymouth | 51 East Anglia | | 52 Coventry | | |
| 53 London Guildhall | 54 Bath | | 55 Sussex | | |
| 56 Robert Gordon | 57 Lancaster | | 58 Bradford | | |
| 59 Wolverhampton | 60 Goldsmiths College | | 61 Liverpool John Moores | | |
| 62 Nottingham Trent | 63 UMIST | | 64 De Montfort | | |

**TQA (England) 1995–96**
**Firsts and 2:1s:** 62%
**Employment:** 69%
**Further study:** 22%
**Unemployment:** 6%

## History

History was one of the first subjects to be assessed for teaching quality, and there have been big changes in some departments. Almost 20 universities were rated as Excellent, but some of the most popular, such as Bristol and Nottingham, were considered only Satisfactory. Some were not even visited, since the system allowed for self-assessment if a department did not claim to be excellent.

Four institutions scored maximum points for teaching and research: Cambridge, Durham, King's College London and the LSE. Cambridge holds onto top place by virtue of average entry qualifications of almost three As at A level, but Durham is not far behind. Eight universities were rated internationally outstanding in the 2001 Research Assessment Exercise, including Oxford Brookes, making it the only new university in the top 30.

Ninth-placed Edinburgh is the top university in Scotland, finishing ahead of St Andrews because of its high entry standards. Swansea triumphs in Wales, as the only institution rated Excellent for teaching quality.

History remains one of the most popular subjects. Of the top 40, only Dundee, Oxford Brookes and Salford had average entry grades of less than three Cs in 2000. Almost a third of all graduates go on to higher degrees or professional courses.

## History (cont.)

| | | TQA | RAE | | A-Levels | Score |
|---|---|---|---|---|---|---|
| 1 | Cambridge | E | 5* | A | 29.7 | 100.0 |
| 2 | Durham | E | 5* | A | 28.4 | 99.2 |
| 3 | King's College London | E | 5* | A | 25.1 | 97.1 |
| 4 | London School of Economics | E | 5* | B | 28.5 | 96.0 |
| 5 | Oxford | E | 5 | A | 29.4 | 95.5 |
| 6 | Warwick | E | 5 | A | 27.0 | 94.0 |
| 7 | York | E | 5 | A | 26.9 | 93.9 |
| 8 | University College London | E | 5 | A | 25.9 | 93.3 |
| 9 | Edinburgh | E | 5 | B | 27.5 | 91.5 |
| 10 | Royal Holloway | E | 5 | A | 22.5 | 91.1 |
| 11 | Sheffield | E | 5 | B | 26.6 | 91.0 |
| 12 | Birmingham | E | 5 | B | 25.4 | 90.2 |
| 13 | Leicester | E | 5 | A | 21.0 | 90.2 |
| 14 | St Andrews | E | 5 | B | 24.2 | 89.5 |
| 15 | Hull | E | 5 | A | 19.5 | 89.2 |
| 16 | Queen's, Belfast | E | 5 | B | 21.9 | 88.0 |
| =17 | Liverpool | E | 5 | B | 20.8 | 87.2 |
| =17 | Lancaster | E | 4 | A | 23.1 | 87.2 |
| 19 | Swansea | E | 4 | A | 19.8 | 85.1 |
| 20 | Stirling | HS | 5 | A | 20.1 | 80.0 |
| 21 | Glasgow | HS | 5 | B | 23.9 | 79.6 |
| 22 | Dundee | HS | 5 | B | 17.5 | 75.6 |
| 23 | Bradford | S | 5* | A | | 74.9 |
| =24 | Aberdeen | HS | 4 | B | | 73.3 |
| =24 | Strathclyde | HS | 4 | B | | 73.3 |
| =24 | East Anglia | S | 5* | B | 22.9 | 73.3 |
| 27 | Exeter | S | 5 | A | 24.1 | 72.9 |
| 28 | Oxford Brookes | S | 5* | A | 16.9 | 72.7 |
| 29 | Southampton | S | 5 | A | 23.2 | 72.4 |
| 30 | SOAS | S | 5* | B | 20.7 | 71.8 |
| 31 | Cardiff | S | 5 | A | 22.1 | 71.7 |
| 32 | Leeds | S | 5 | B | 25.8 | 71.3 |
| 33 | Nottingham | S | 4 | A | 27.1 | 70.6 |
| 34 | Bristol | S | 4 | A | 26.1 | 70.0 |
| 35 | Manchester | S | 5 | B | 23.5 | 69.8 |
| 36 | Keele | S | 5 | A | 18.3 | 69.2 |
| =37 | Newcastle | S | 4 | A | 24.8 | 69.1 |
| =37 | Essex | S | 5 | A | 18.0 | 69.1 |
| 39 | Sussex | S | 4 | A | 24.4 | 68.9 |
| 40 | Salford | S | 5 | A | 15.8 | 67.7 |

| | | | | | |
|---|---|---|---|---|---|
| 41 | Queen Mary | 42 | Coventry | 43 | Huddersfield |
| 44 | Hertfordshire | 45 | Aberystwyth | 46 | Reading |
| =47 | Sheffield Hallam | =47 | Kent | 49 | West of England |
| 50 | Central Lancashire | 51 | Goldsmiths College | 52 | Lampeter |
| 53 | Surrey Roehampton | 54 | Ulster | 55 | Bangor |
| 56 | Wolverhampton | 57 | De Montfort | 58 | Kingston |
| 59 | Liverpool John Moores | 60 | Teesside | 61 | Nottingham Trent |
| 62 | Portsmouth | 63 | Westminster | 64 | Greenwich |
| 65 | Sunderland | 66 | Northumbria | 67 | North London |
| 68 | Thames Valley | 69 | Plymouth | 70 | Gloucestershire |
| 71 | Manchester Metropolitan | =72 | Glamorgan | =72 | London Guildhall |

## History (cont.)

| | | |
|---|---|---|
| 74 Anglia | 75 Middlesex | 76 Staffordshire |
| 77 Derby | 78 Leeds Metropolitan | 79 Brunel |

**TQA (England) 1993–94**
**Firsts and 2:1s:** 68%
**Employment:** 54%
**Further study:** 32%
**Unemployment:** 7.0%

## History of Art

London University's Courtauld Institute takes over at the top of the table in Art History, after achieving the only 5* rating in the latest Research Assessment Exercise. Only second-placed UCL and the SOAS have better teaching scores, and only Cambridge, in third, has higher entry standards.

St Andrews is the top university in Scotland, overtaking Edinburgh, its average entry score rising by the equivalent of more than a full A-level grade between 1999 and 2000. Oxford Brookes, which was only one point off a perfect teaching score, is the top new university, matching St Andrews for a place in the top ten. Middlesex also makes the top 20, squeezing out older rivals such as Bristol, where entry standards are among the highest.

Fewer than 4,000 undergraduates have been taking degrees in the history of art up to now, although another 1,000 are registered in part-time courses. The majority of students are female. Outside Cambridge, entry standards range from the equivalent of almost two As and a B at Edinburgh to three Ds at some new universities. Assessors in England found that most students were well supported, although about a third of libraries were under pressure.

| | | TQA | RAE | | A-Levels | Score |
|---|---|---|---|---|---|---|
| 1 | Courtauld Institute | 23 | 5* | A | 27.0 | 100.0 |
| 2 | University College London | 24 | 5 | B | 24.8 | 98.6 |
| 3 | Cambridge | 22 | 5 | A | 29.5 | 92.0 |
| 4 | SOAS | 24 | 3a | A | 22.0 | 91.8 |
| 5 | Reading | 23 | 4 | A | 21.6 | 89.0 |
| 6 | Birmingham | 22 | 5 | A | 24.7 | 88.7 |
| 7 | Leeds | 23 | 3a | A | 24.2 | 87.2 |
| =8 | St Andrews | HS | 5 | A | 22.2 | 83.9 |
| =8 | Oxford Brookes | 23 | 3a | A | 19.4 | 83.9 |
| =10 | Warwick | 21 | 5 | A | 25.2 | 82.9 |
| =10 | Essex | 22 | 5 | B | 19.8 | 82.9 |
| =10 | Glasgow | HS | 5 | B | 24.1 | 82.9 |
| 13 | Leicester | 22 | 4 | A | 21.4 | 82.7 |
| 14 | East Anglia | 22 | 5 | B | 18.2 | 81.8 |
| 15 | Edinburgh | HS | 4 | B | 27.1 | 81.7 |
| 16 | York | 21 | 5 | A | 23.2 | 81.5 |
| 17 | Nottingham | 23 | 3b | C | 25.5 | 81.4 |
| 18 | Kent | 22 | 3a | B | 22.2 | 78.1 |

## History of Art (cont.)

|  |  | TQA | RAE |  | A-Levels | Score |
|---|---|---|---|---|---|---|
| 19 | Manchester | 21 | 5 | B | 20.4 | 77.3 |
| 20 | Middlesex | 22 | 5 | D |  | 75.6 |
| 21 | Sussex | 20 | 5 | A | 23.2 | 75.4 |
| 22 | Aberdeen | HS | 4 | C |  | 74.1 |
| =23 | Plymouth | 21 | 5 | A | 11.2 | 73.2 |
| =23 | Brighton | 21 | 5 | B | 14.5 | 73.2 |
| 25 | Manchester Metropolitan | 22 | 4 | C | 12.3 | 71.3 |
| 26 | Bristol | 20 | 3a | B | 26.7 | 69.1 |
| 27 | Southampton | 20 | 4 | B | 16.9 | 65.5 |
| 28 | De Montfort | 21 | 3b | C |  | 63.8 |
| 29 | Northumbria | 21 | 3a | D |  | 63.3 |
| 30 | Aberystwyth | S | 3a | A | 14.8 | 62.3 |
| 31 | Kingston | 20 | 4 | D | 16.3 | 58.1 |
| 32 | Goldsmiths College | 19 | 3b | A | 21.6 | 57.3 |
| 33 | Sheffield Hallam | 20 |  |  | 14.2 | 47.8 |
| 34 | Anglia | 18 | 3b | A |  | 44.8 |

**TQA (England) 1996–98**
**Firsts and 2:1s:** 70%
**Employment:** 60%
**Further study:** 22%
**Unemployment:** 9%

## Hospitality, Leisure, Recreation, Sport and Tourism

Liverpool John Moores tops the table in this portmanteau category, with perfect scores for both teaching and research. Loughborough and Birmingham matched JMU for research (as did eighth-placed Manchester Metropolitan) but they dropped one and two points respectively for teaching quality.

Strathclyde, the top-placed university in Scotland, had by far the highest entrance qualifications, averaging the equivalent of almost three Bs at A level. At JMU, by contrast, a C and two Ds were enough to secure a place. The subjects are mainly offered by new universities and, apart from Strathclyde, only Ulster and Manchester Metropolitan averaged more than three Cs. Several universities, including Birmingham, Brunel and Loughborough did not declare separate A-level scores for these subjects.

The category covers a variety of courses, most directed towards management in the leisure and tourism industries. Employment rates are generally healthy, although starting salaries for graduates are often low. Sports science, in particular, has been growing in popularity. Demand for places in 2002, with 31,000 applications, was very healthy.

|  |  | TQA | RAE |  | A-Levels | Score |
|---|---|---|---|---|---|---|
| 1 | Liverpool John Moores | 24 | 5* | B | 13.4 | 100.0 |
| 2 | Loughborough | 23 | 5* | C |  | 94.1 |
| 3 | Birmingham | 22 | 5* | A |  | 92.9 |
| 4 | Brunel | 23 | 4 | B |  | 92.5 |

## Hospitality, Leisure, Recreation, Sport and Tourism (cont.)

|    |                         | TQA | RAE |   | A-Levels | Score |
|----|-------------------------|-----|-----|---|----------|-------|
| 5  | De Montfort             | 23  | 4   | B |          | 92.5  |
| 6  | Sheffield Hallam        | 24  | 4   | E | 16.7     | 91.3  |
| 7  | Ulster                  | 23  | 4   | D | 19.6     | 90.3  |
| 8  | Manchester Metropolitan | 22  | 5*  | C | 18.6     | 89.5  |
| 9  | Hertfordshire           | 23  | 3a  | C | 17.2     | 89.0  |
| 10 | Westminster             | 24  | 3a  | D | 11.4     | 88.1  |
| 11 | Surrey                  |     | 4   | C | 17.5     | 88.0  |
| 12 | Bath                    | 23  | 3a  | C |          | 87.6  |
| 13 | Strathclyde             | HS  | 4   | C | 23.2     | 86.9  |
| 14 | Manchester              | 22  | 4   | C | 18.2     | 85.7  |
| 15 | Brighton                | 22  | 4   | A | 13.8     | 85.5  |
| 16 | Bangor                  |     | 5   | A | 8.7      | 85.2  |
| 17 | Plymouth                | 23  | 3a  | E | 12.5     | 81.2  |
| 18 | Nottingham Trent        | 22  | 3a  | C |          | 80.3  |
| 19 | Leeds Metropolitan      | 22  | 3a  | D | 14.4     | 78.9  |
| 20 | South Bank              | 22  | 3a  | D |          | 77.8  |
| 21 | Bournemouth             | 22  |     |   | 16.3     | 75.7  |
| 22 | Staffordshire           | 22  | 3a  | E |          | 75.3  |
| 23 | Oxford Brookes          | 22  |     |   | 15.2     | 74.8  |
| 24 | Central Lancashire      | 22  |     |   | 13.7     | 73.6  |
| 25 | Huddersfield            | 22  |     |   | 11.7     | 72.0  |
| 26 | Northumbria             | 21  |     |   | 17.3     | 70.7  |
| 27 | Dundee                  | HS  |     |   | 13.3     | 70.4  |
| 28 | Surrey Roehampton       | 21  | 3b  | D |          | 68.9  |
| 29 | Thames Valley           | 22  |     |   | 7.4      | 68.5  |
| 30 | Gloucestershire         | 21  | 3b  | E | 11.2     | 67.7  |
| 31 | Portsmouth              | 21  |     |   | 13.4     | 67.5  |
| 32 | Coventry                | 21  |     |   | 13.3     | 67.4  |
| 33 | Napier                  | HS  |     |   | 9.5      | 67.3  |
| 34 | UWIC, Cardiff           |     | 3a  | F | 13.9     | 66.7  |
| 35 | Derby                   | 21  |     |   | 12.1     | 66.5  |
| 36 | Lincoln                 | 21  |     |   | 11.9     | 66.3  |
| 37 | North London            | 21  |     |   | 10.0     | 64.7  |
| 38 | Teesside                | 21  |     |   | 9.4      | 64.2  |
| 39 | Glasgow Caledonian      | S   |     |   | 12.0     | 60.5  |
| 40 | Sunderland              | 20  | 3b  | E |          | 59.7  |
| =41 | Anglia                 |     | =41 | Salford | | |

**TQA (England) 2000–01**
**Firsts and 2:1s:** 46%
**Employment:** 81%
**Further study:** 7%
**Unemployment:** 6%

## Iberian Languages

There is no change at the head of the table for Iberian languages, with Cambridge well ahead of the field, but there is plenty of flux in other positions. Swansea, for example, drops from second to seventh, despite improving its research grade, while Newcastle jumps from 15th to sixth.

## Iberian Languages (cont.)

As well as recording the highest entry standards, Cambridge was one of six universities to be rated 5* for research. The others were Queen Mary, King's College London, Manchester, Southampton and Nottingham, the final two missing the top 20 because of low teaching grades.

A tough teaching assessment in England saw second-place Hull awarded the only maximum score. Queen Mary and Northumbria were the only institutions to come close to this mark, although Swansea was rated Excellent under the Welsh system. Oxford Brookes was the highest new university and Edinburgh the top university in Scotland.

Spanish is growing in popularity as an alternative to French in schools, and is a common choice as an element of a broader modern languages degree. Although six out of ten graduates take jobs within six months of leaving university and many others go on to postgraduate courses, employment prospects have not been as good as in French or German.

| | | TQA | RAE | | A-Levels | Score |
|---|---|---|---|---|---|---|
| 1 | Cambridge | 22 | 5* | A | 29.7 | 100.0 |
| 2 | Hull | 24 | 4 | A | 20.8 | 97.2 |
| 3 | Queen Mary | 23 | 5* | A | 16.8 | 95.5 |
| 4 | King's College London | 22 | 5* | A | 22.4 | 94.1 |
| 5 | St Andrews | 22 | 5 | A | 25.8 | 93.1 |
| 6 | Newcastle | 22 | 5 | A | 24.7 | 92.1 |
| 7 | Swansea | E | 5 | B | 19.5 | 91.5 |
| 8 | Birmingham | 22 | 5 | A | 23.6 | 91.3 |
| 9 | Edinburgh | 21 | 5 | A | 28.1 | 88.9 |
| 10 | Sheffield | 21 | 5 | A | 27.1 | 88.1 |
| 11 | Oxford | 21 | 5 | B | 29.5 | 87.6 |
| 12 | Bristol | 22 | 4 | B | 24.9 | 86.4 |
| 13 | Leeds | 22 | 4 | B | 24.4 | 86.1 |
| 14 | Manchester | 20 | 5* | A | 21.9 | 81.6 |
| 15 | Queen's, Belfast | 21 | 4 | A | 23.6 | 81.4 |
| =16 | Glasgow | 22 | 3a | B | | 80.9 |
| =16 | Strathclyde | 22 | 4 | C | | 80.9 |
| =18 | Heriot-Watt | 21 | 4 | B | 24.7 | 80.2 |
| =18 | Liverpool | 21 | 4 | A | 22.1 | 80.2 |
| 20 | Cardiff | S | 5 | A | 22.8 | 78.6 |
| 21 | Royal Holloway | | 4 | A | 21.7 | 77.8 |
| 22 | Oxford Brookes | 22 | 3a | C | | 77.5 |
| 23 | Salford | 20 | 5 | A | 21.3 | 77.3 |
| 24 | Aberdeen | 22 | 4 | D | | 76.0 |
| 25 | Exeter | 20 | 4 | B | 23.7 | 73.5 |
| 26 | Northumbria | 23 | 3b | E | 16.1 | 71.8 |
| 27 | University College London | 19 | 4 | A | 25.6 | 71.0 |
| 28 | Southampton | 18 | 5* | A | 22.5 | 70.1 |
| 29 | Kent | | 4 | B | 19.2 | 69.7 |
| 30 | Nottingham | 17 | 5* | A | 27.5 | 68.1 |
| 31 | Aberystwyth | S | 3a | A | 18.1 | 67.1 |
| 32 | North London | 20 | 3a | B | | 65.8 |
| 33 | Central Lancashire | 21 | 3b | A | 13.0 | 65.2 |
| 34 | Wolverhampton | 20 | 4 | C | 13.5 | 61.7 |

## Iberian Languages (cont.)

|    |                 | TQA | RAE |   | A-Levels | Score |
|----|-----------------|-----|-----|---|----------|-------|
| 35 | Paisley         | 19  | 4   | C |          | 58.3  |
| 36 | Surrey          | 18  | 5   | C | 20.3     | 57.9  |
| 37 | Anglia          | 21  | 2   | C | 10.9     | 57.4  |
| 38 | Surrey Roehampton | 19 | 3a | A | 12.7     | 56.7  |
| 39 | West of England | 21  |     |   | 16.0     | 56.6  |
| 40 | Plymouth        |     | 3b  | A | 17.7     | 56.2  |

| 41 Lancaster | 42 Coventry | 43 Kingston |
|---|---|---|
| 44 Stirling | 45 Durham | 46 Portsmouth |
| 47 Bradford | 48 Liverpool John Moores | 49 London Guildhall |
| 50 Westminster | 51 Nottingham Trent | |

**TQA (England) 1995–96**
**Firsts and 2:1s:** 70% (Spanish)
**Employment:** 60% (Spanish)
**Further study:** 26% (Spanish)
**Unemployment:** 6% (Spanish)

## Italian

Italian is offered in 28 universities, with Cambridge leading the field. Competition is fiercer since the latest Research Assessment Exercise, when the top three all achieved 5* grades. Second-placed Oxford was a point behind its two chief rivals in the teaching assessment, while Birmingham's average A-level score was three grades lower than the ancient universities'.

Unusually, no institution was awarded more than 22 points out of 24 for teaching quality in England or Scotland, although fourth-placed Swansea was rated as Excellent under the Welsh system. Cambridge was one of the eight top scorers for teaching, a group that includes fifth-placed St Andrews, the top university in Scotland. Portsmouth is the only new university in the top 20, although Central Lancashire has a better teaching score.

The top research grades were widely spread in 2001, after a sharp improvement on the previous assessments. As well as the top three, UCL, Reading and Leeds were all rated internationally outstanding, although Leeds entered a relatively low proportion of its academic staff .

Fewer than 500 students take the language at degree level, although others include Italian in combined degree programmes. Assessors found some cases of overcrowding, but were satisfied with learning resources, which generally included satellite television. Most students have no previous knowledge of the language, but there is a high completion rate.

|   |            | TQA | RAE |   | A-Levels | Score |
|---|------------|-----|-----|---|----------|-------|
| 1 | Cambridge  | 22  | 5*  | A | 29.7     | 100.0 |
| 2 | Oxford     | 21  | 5*  | A | 28.7     | 93.1  |
| 3 | Birmingham | 22  | 5*  | B | 22.6     | 92.4  |
| 4 | Swansea    | E   | 4   | A | 17.2     | 90.6  |

## Italian (cont.)

| | TQA | RAE | | A-Levels | Score |
|---|---|---|---|---|---|
| 5 St Andrews | 22 | 4 | B | 25.1 | 88.2 |
| 6 Bristol | 21 | 5 | A | 25.1 | 87.1 |
| 7 Warwick | 21 | 5 | A | 24.1 | 86.3 |
| 8 Exeter | 22 | 4 | B | 22.3 | 86.1 |
| 9 Edinburgh | 21 | 4 | A | 27.9 | 85.6 |
| 10 University College London | 20 | 5* | A | 24.4 | 83.7 |
| 11 Strathclyde | 22 | 4 | C | | 83.6 |
| 12 Royal Holloway | 21 | 4 | A | 22.0 | 81.4 |
| 13 Glasgow | 22 | 3b | A | | 81.2 |
| 14 Cardiff | S | 5 | A | 23.4 | 79.6 |
| 15 Reading | 20 | 5* | A | 17.4 | 78.7 |
| 16 Salford | 20 | 5 | A | 21.7 | 78.4 |
| 17 Hull | 22 | 3a | C | 17.2 | 77.0 |
| 18 Leicester | 20 | 4 | A | 18.6 | 72.8 |
| 19 Portsmouth | 20 | 5 | C | | 71.0 |
| 20 Manchester | 19 | 5 | B | 21.9 | 70.1 |
| 21 Kent | 19 | 4 | B | 24.4 | 68.8 |
| 22 Central Lancashire | 21 | 3b | A | 13.0 | 68.3 |
| 23 Leeds | 19 | 5* | D | 24.3 | 65.7 |
| 24 Anglia | 21 | 2 | C | 10.9 | 61.4 |
| 25 Westminster | 19 | 4 | C | | 60.1 |
| 26 Coventry | 21 | | | 14.3 | 59.4 |
| 27 Lancaster | 20 | | | 20.8 | 57.8 |
| 28 Sussex | 17 | 4 | A | 22.2 | 56.6 |
| 29 Bath | 19 | | | 23.2 | 53.2 |
| 30 Liverpool John Moores | 19 | | | 16.2 | 48.2 |

**TQA (England) 1995–96**
**Firsts and 2:1s:** 71%
**Employment:** 77%
**Further study:** 11%
**Unemployment:** 6%

## Land and Property Management

Cambridge's usual high entry standards have kept the university ahead of Reading at the top of the land and property management table. Both have the same research and teaching grades. Only Kingston achieved maximum points for teaching quality. However, it did not enter academics in the relevant research category and, with low entry grades, cannot reach the top five.

Research ratings improved significantly in 2001. Salford, which was assessed under this category for the first time, was rated internationally outstanding, while Cambridge and Reading both reached grade 5. However, Salford has the lowest teaching rating (with South Bank and Central England) so is only half way up the table.

All but three universities in the ranking are former polytechnics. Oxford Brookes is the top-placed of them, just beating Liverpool John Moores on teaching and research. De Montfort joined Oxford Brookes on 23 points for teaching, eclipsing both Cambridge and Reading on this indicator. Entry standards are

## Land and Property Management (cont.)

generally modest and completion rates tend to be higher at the universities with more demanding entrance requirements.

Only about 2,000 students are taking land and property at degree or diploma level, although the subjects are often included in wider environmental programmes. Over three-quarters of graduates go straight into jobs, but the proportion still out of work six months after leaving university is the highest of the business subjects.

|    |                        | TQA | RAE |   | A-Levels | Score |
|----|------------------------|-----|-----|---|----------|-------|
| 1  | Cambridge              | 22  | 5   | B | 28.5     | 100.0 |
| 2  | Reading                | 22  | 5   | B | 22.9     | 94.8  |
| 3  | Oxford Brookes         | 23  | 4   | C |          | 90.0  |
| 4  | Liverpool John Moores  | 22  | 3a  | A |          | 83.0  |
| 5  | West of England        | 22  | 3a  | B |          | 80.2  |
| 6  | Kingston               | 24  |     |   | 12.3     | 73.3  |
| 7  | Leeds Metropolitan     | 21  | 3a  | B |          | 70.4  |
| 8  | Plymouth               | 22  | 3a  | E |          | 64.9  |
| 9  | Sheffield Hallam       | 21  | 4   | D | 14.2     | 64.2  |
| 10 | Salford                | 18  | 5*  | A |          | 63.1  |
| 11 | De Montfort            | 23  |     |   | 8.5      | 61.9  |
| 12 | Nottingham Trent       | 20  | 3a  | B |          | 60.5  |
| 13 | Northumbria            | 22  |     |   | 13.7     | 58.9  |
| 14 | Portsmouth             | 20  | 3a  | B | 10.8     | 58.5  |
| 15 | Greenwich              | 21  | 3b  | E | 11.4     | 53.0  |
| 16 | City                   | 19  | 3a  | C |          | 46.0  |
| 17 | Westminster            | 19  | 3a  | D | 11.9     | 43.6  |
| 18 | Anglia                 | 19  | 2   | B |          | 39.0  |
| 19 | South Bank             | 18  | 4   | D |          | 34.1  |
| 20 | Central England        | 18  | 3b  | E | 12.3     | 30.3  |

**TQA (England) 1996–98**
**Firsts and 2:1s:** 53%
**Employment:** 82%
**Further study:** 6%
**Unemployment:** 8%

## Law

Only a fraction of an A-level point separates Cambridge and UCL at the top of the law table. Like the LSE and Durham, they have perfect scores for both teaching and research. Oxford also registered top grades but entered fewer academics than its rivals in the latest Research Assessment Exercise. Southampton, Keele and Queen Mary were also considered internationally outstanding for research, but all three are weighed down by a Satisfactory rating from one of the earliest rounds of teaching assessment which is now dated.

Twenty universities, including three former polytechnics – West of England, Northumbria and Oxford Brookes – were among the Excellent teaching institutions. Five Scottish universities were rated Highly Satisfactory, while in Wales, all four institutions were given Satisfactory grades.

## Law (cont.)

Entry standards in law are notoriously high, with Oxford and Cambridge students averaging close to three As at A level and several other universities close behind. However, entrants at some new universities averaged little more than three Ds, and one in five of the national intake arrives without A levels or their equivalent. With almost 75,000 students seeking places in 2002, law remains one of the most popular subjects.

Because of the requirement for further professional training for solicitors and barristers, less than a third of undergraduates go straight into jobs. But with six out of ten taking additional courses on graduation, the unemployment rate is still among the lowest in higher education.

|  |  | TQA | RAE | | A-Levels | Score |
|---|---|---|---|---|---|---|
| 1 | Cambridge | E | 5* | A | 29.5 | 100.0 |
| 2 | University College London | E | 5* | A | 28.9 | 99.5 |
| 3 | London School of Economics | E | 5* | A | 28.6 | 99.3 |
| =4 | Durham | E | 5* | A | 26.5 | 97.6 |
| =4 | Oxford | E | 5* | B | 29.4 | 97.6 |
| 6 | Nottingham | E | 5 | A | 28.5 | 96.1 |
| 7 | Manchester | E | 5 | A | 27.7 | 95.5 |
| 8 | King's College London | E | 5 | A | 27.5 | 95.3 |
| =9 | Leicester | E | 5 | A | 25.4 | 93.6 |
| =9 | Queen's, Belfast | E | 5 | B | 27.9 | 93.6 |
| 11 | Bristol | E | 5 | B | 26.6 | 92.6 |
| 12 | Warwick | E | 5 | B | 26.0 | 92.1 |
| 13 | SOAS | E | 5 | A | 23.4 | 92.0 |
| 14 | Sheffield | E | 5 | C | 27.9 | 90.3 |
| 15 | East Anglia | E | 5 | B | 22.0 | 88.9 |
| 16 | Liverpool | E | 4 | B | 25.2 | 88.7 |
| 17 | Essex | E | 5 | B | 21.3 | 88.3 |
| 18 | Edinburgh | HS | 5 | B | 28.8 | 81.9 |
| 19 | Glasgow | HS | 5 | B | 27.0 | 80.5 |
| 20 | Strathclyde | HS | 5 | A | | 79.9 |
| =21 | Aberdeen | HS | 5 | B | 24.7 | 78.6 |
| =21 | Oxford Brookes | E | 4 | D | 20.0 | 78.6 |
| 23 | Dundee | HS | 5 | B | 21.7 | 76.2 |
| =24 | West of England | E | 4 | F | 19.4 | 71.9 |
| =24 | Northumbria | E | | | 21.0 | 71.9 |
| 26 | Southampton | S | 5* | B | 26.0 | 70.0 |
| 27 | Leeds | S | 5 | A | 26.8 | 69.9 |
| 28 | Queen Mary | S | 5* | B | 23.3 | 67.9 |
| 29 | Keele | S | 5* | A | 20.3 | 67.8 |
| 30 | Surrey | | 5 | C | 19.7 | 66.9 |
| 31 | Brunel | S | 5 | A | 22.3 | 66.3 |
| 32 | Lancaster | S | 5 | B | 24.5 | 66.0 |
| 33 | City | S | 5 | B | 23.5 | 65.2 |
| 34 | Reading | S | 5 | B | 22.7 | 64.6 |
| =35 | Birmingham | S | 5 | C | 26.5 | 64.3 |
| =35 | Kent | S | 5 | B | 22.3 | 64.3 |
| 37 | Exeter | S | 5 | C | 26.3 | 64.2 |
| 38 | Hull | S | 5 | B | 21.9 | 63.9 |
| 39 | Newcastle | S | 5 | C | 25.6 | 63.6 |

## Law (cont.)

| | TQA | RAE | | A-Levels | Score |
|---|---|---|---|---|---|
| 40 Cardiff | S | 5 | C | 25.0 | 63.1 |

| | | |
|---|---|---|
| 41 Sussex | 42 Aberystwyth | 43 Ulster |
| 44 Swansea | 45 Hertfordshire | 46 North London |
| 47 Leeds Metropolitan | 48 Nottingham Trent | 49 De Montfort |
| 50 Bournemouth | =51 Westminster | =51 Central Lancashire |
| 53 Kingston | 54 Anglia | 55 Plymouth |
| 56 Liverpool John Moores | 57 Sheffield Hallam | 58 East London |
| 59 Wolverhampton | 60 Central England | 61 Greenwich |
| 62 Glamorgan | =63 Middlesex | =63 Staffordshire |
| 65 Coventry | 66 Huddersfield | 67 Lincoln |
| 68 South Bank | =69 Derby | =69 London Guildhall |
| 71 Teesside | 72 Luton | 73 Thames Valley |

**TQA (England) 1993–94**
**Firsts and 2:1s:** 54%
**Employment:** 31%
**Further study:** 60%
**Unemployment:** 4%

New Scottish Academic Review: *Glasgow*: confidence in the academic standards; the quality of teaching and learning, student progression and learning resources was commendable.
*Napier*: confidence in the academic standards; the quality of teaching and learning, and student progression was commendable.

## Librarianship and Information Management

Only ten universities are included in the first table covering librarianship and information management. Loughborough finishes top by virtue of the only maximum score for teaching quality, although second-placed Sheffield is the only university rated internationally outstanding for research.

Fourth-placed University College London has the highest entrance qualifications, ahead of Queen's, Belfast, which is the only other institution where new students averaged more than three Bs at A level. The subjects were not assessed separately for teaching quality in Scotland, and only Aberystwyth registered a score in Wales.

Northumbria is best-placed of the four new universities offering the subjects, although Brighton also scored 22 points out of 24 for teaching quality. As the small size of the tables suggests, librarianship and information management are minority interests at degree level. Many students considering librarianship as a career take postgraduate courses in the subject.

| | TQA | RAE | | A-Levels | Score |
|---|---|---|---|---|---|
| 1 Loughborough | 24 | 5 | B | 20.0 | 100.0 |
| 2 Sheffield | 22 | 5* | A | 23.4 | 92.2 |
| 3 Queen's, Belfast | | 4 | B | 24.1 | 87.5 |
| 4 University College London | 22 | 4 | A | 25.1 | 87.0 |
| 5 Aberystwyth | E | 3a | B | 14.5 | 82.6 |
| 6 City | 21 | 5 | A | | 78.5 |
| 7 Northumbria | 22 | 3b | C | | 72.7 |
| 8 Manchester Metropolitan | 21 | 4 | C | | 68.7 |

## Librarianship and Information Management (cont.)

|   |   | TQA | RAE | | A-Levels | Score |
|---|---|-----|-----|---|----------|-------|
| 9 | Brighton | 22 | 3b | D | 12.2 | 66.6 |
| 10 | Central England | 20 | 3a | B | 16.4 | 60.7 |

**TQA (England) 2000–01**
**Firsts and 2:1s:** 54%
**Employment:** 62%
**Further study:** 8%
**Unemployment:** 15%

## Linguistics

There is little to choose between Queen Mary and Cambridge at the top of the table for linguistics. Cambridge has the better research record, but Queen Mary's superior teaching quality grade makes the difference since neither has separately listed A-level averages. Unusually, no institution achieved the maximum score for teaching, but the latest research assessments saw four rated internationally outstanding. Oxford and University College London joined Cambridge and Queen Mary on the top grade.

All but four of the 24 universities offering linguistics are within three points of each other in the teaching quality assessment, with Bangor rated Satisfactory under the separate Welsh system. The research grades improved dramatically on 1996, with more than half of the universities reaching the top two grades.

Wolverhampton is the best-placed of seven new universities in the table. Hertfordshire, Westminster, Luton and Portsmouth also appear in the top 20.

Fewer than 2,000 students take linguistics either at degree or diploma level, eight out of ten of them arriving with A levels. About a quarter go on to further study, but the unemployment level is relatively high compared with other language graduates.

|   |   | TQA | RAE | | A-Levels | Score |
|---|---|-----|-----|---|----------|-------|
| 1 | Queen Mary | 23 | 5* | A | | 100.0 |
| 2 | Cambridge | 22 | 5* | A | | 93.1 |
| 3 | Lancaster | 23 | 5 | B | 22.3 | 91.3 |
| 4 | Durham | 22 | 5 | B | 27.2 | 89.3 |
| 5 | Newcastle | 22 | 5 | A | 22.9 | 88.1 |
| 6 | York | 22 | 5 | A | 22.8 | 88.0 |
| 7 | Oxford | 21 | 5* | A | | 86.2 |
| 8 | Sussex | 22 | 4 | A | 23.4 | 85.5 |
| 9 | University College London | 22 | 5* | C | 22.6 | 84.8 |
| 10 | Edinburgh | | 5 | C | 28.0 | 84.5 |
| 11 | Manchester | 21 | 5 | B | 21.6 | 79.7 |
| 12 | Essex | 21 | 5 | B | 20.9 | 79.2 |
| 13 | Salford | 20 | 5 | A | | 75.5 |
| 14 | Wolverhampton | 21 | 3a | A | | 75.0 |
| 15 | Sheffield | 22 | | | 26.2 | 73.0 |
| =16 | Hertfordshire | 20 | 3a | A | | 68.1 |

## Linguistics (cont.)

| | TQA | RAE | | A-Levels | Score |
|---|---|---|---|---|---|
| =16  SOAS | 20 | 3a | A | | 68.1 |
| 18  Westminster | 20 | 5 | C | 13.7 | 65.1 |
| 19  Luton | 21 | 3a | E | | 64.6 |
| 20  Portsmouth | | 5 | C | 13.3 | 62.8 |
| =21  Reading | 19 | 3a | B | 20.0 | 62.1 |
| =21  Bangor | S | 3b | B | 16.0 | 62.1 |
| 23  Brighton | 20 | 5 | E | | 60.0 |
| 24  East Anglia | 19 | 3b | B | 19.2 | 58.9 |
| 25  Leeds | 17 | 3a | C | 23.0 | 51.1 |

**TQA (England) 1995–96**
**Firsts and 2:1s:** 61%
**Employment:** 62%
**Further study:** 24%
**Unemployment:** 7%

## Materials Technology

A slight dip in research grades has spread out the scores in the upper reaches of the materials technology ranking, with Oxford taking over at the top. Second-placed Imperial College is the only institution in England with maximum points for teaching, but it could not match Oxford's research grade or entry scores.

Oxford was one of six universities rated internationally outstanding for research, but an average A-level score close to three As left it well ahead of most rivals. Only Cambridge, which matched Oxford's teaching and research grades but did not register separate A-level scores for materials, comes close.

Swansea was rated as Excellent under the different Welsh system, but still finishes out of the top three, after dropping two grades in the latest Research Assessment Exercise. Manchester Metropolitan is the highest-placed new university and the only one in the top ten, although Sheffield Hallam is not far behind. Entry standards vary considerably, with several universities, including De Montfort, averaging a B and two Cs or better, but others requiring only three Ds or their equivalent.

The courses assessed between 1996 and 1998 covered three distinct areas: materials science, mining and engineering; textiles technology and printing; and marine technology. A high proportion of students go on to further study, but fewer than one in 20 is out of work six months after leaving university.

| | TQA | RAE | | A-Levels | Score |
|---|---|---|---|---|---|
| 1  Oxford | 23 | 5* | A | 29.6 | 100.0 |
| 2  Imperial College | 24 | 5 | A | 23.7 | 98.4 |
| 3  Cambridge | 23 | 5* | A | | 95.5 |
| 4  Swansea | E | 4 | A | 21.5 | 89.0 |
| 5  Sheffield | 22 | 5* | A | 20.1 | 87.2 |

## Materials Technology (cont.)

| | TQA | RAE | | A-Levels | Score |
|---|---|---|---|---|---|
| 6 Manchester Metropolitan | 22 | 4 | A | | 82.9 |
| 7 Surrey | 22 | 4 | B | | 81.4 |
| 8 Southampton | 23 | | | 24.8 | 80.0 |
| 9 Manchester | 21 | 5* | B | 19.5 | 79.5 |
| =10 Liverpool | 21 | 5 | A | 18.3 | 78.0 |
| =10 Nottingham | 21 | 5 | B | 20.2 | 78.0 |
| 12 Sheffield Hallam | 22 | 5 | D | | 77.2 |
| 13 Birmingham | 20 | 5* | A | 19.4 | 75.8 |
| 14 Loughborough | 21 | 4 | B | | 74.6 |
| 15 UMIST | 20 | 5* | B | 19.5 | 74.1 |
| 16 Queen Mary | 20 | 5 | B | 20.7 | 73.0 |
| 17 Newcastle | 20 | 4 | B | 18.1 | 68.8 |
| 18 Heriot-Watt | | 3b | B | 19.1 | 67.6 |
| 19 Leeds | 20 | 5 | C | 15.5 | 66.3 |
| 20 De Montfort | 19 | 4 | A | 20.0 | 66.2 |
| 21 Exeter | 21 | | | 16.0 | 62.3 |
| 22 Nottingham Trent | 20 | 3b | D | 17.2 | 61.2 |
| 23 East London | | 2 | D | 15.9 | 54.7 |
| 24 Plymouth | 19 | 4 | E | 15.5 | 54.4 |
| 25 London Guildhall | 20 | | | 11.8 | 53.7 |
| 26 Liverpool John Moores | | 3b | D | 13.6 | 53.4 |
| 27 North London | 19 | 3b | D | | 52.5 |

**TQA (England) 1996–98**
**Firsts and 2:1s:** 61%
**Employment:** 56%
**Further study:** 33%
**Unemployment:** 5%

## Mathematics

Only two universities in England achieved maximum points for teaching quality in mathematics. Bath continues to top the ranking table, but Birmingham is restricted to fourth by its entry standards and research ratings. Edinburgh and St Andrews were rated Excellent under the Scottish system.

Cambridge would have secured top position if it had not dropped a point in its teaching assessment. It was the only university to be rated internationally outstanding for pure and applied mathematics and statistics, and the students' entry grades were exceeded only by Oxford.

Three different research categories meant that 5* grades were sprinkled liberally among the leading universities. Third-placed Bristol, Oxford, Warwick and Imperial College each achieved two top grades. Even Durham, which misses the top 20 because of three dropped points in the teaching assessment, has one.

Although 79 universities and a number of higher education colleges offer mathematics degrees, all the top 30 places are filled by traditional universities. Coventry and Portsmouth are the only former polytechnics in the top 40. Only Cardiff, of the Welsh universities, makes the top 50.

## Mathematics (cont.)

Although identified as a subject most likely to lead to a high salary, graduate employment rates are not as high as for some vocational areas. Maths is still one of the top 20 subjects in terms of student numbers, but applications for places in 2002 were down by 12 per cent, perhaps a result of unexpectedly poor AS-level grades in the first year of the remodelled examination.

| | | TQA | Pure | | Applied | | Statistics | | A-Levels | Score |
|---|---|---|---|---|---|---|---|---|---|---|
| 1 | Bath | 24 | 5 | A | 5* | B | 5 | B | 26.4 | 100.0 |
| 2 | Cambridge | 23 | 5* | A | 5* | A | 5* | B | 29.7 | 98.3 |
| 3 | Bristol | 23 | 5 | B | 5* | A | 5* | A | 27.4 | 96.1 |
| 4 | Birmingham | 24 | 5 | C | 5 | B | 4 | B | 24.0 | 94.6 |
| 5 | Nottingham | 23 | 5 | B | 5 | B | 5 | A | 29.3 | 93.2 |
| 6 | Edinburgh | E | 5* | A | 5 | B | 4 | C | 26.7 | 92.8 |
| 7 | UCL | 23 | 5 | B | 5 | B | 5 | B | 27.2 | 91.8 |
| 8 | St Andrews | E | 5 | B | 5 | B | 5 | A | 25.5 | 91.4 |
| 9 | East Anglia | 23 | 5 | A | 4 | B | | | 22.1 | 89.0 |
| 10 | Oxford | 22 | 5* | B | 5 | A | 5* | C | 29.8 | 88.6 |
| 11 | Warwick | 22 | 5 | B | 5* | A | 5* | B | 29.0 | 88.4 |
| 12 | Imperial College | 22 | 5* | B | 5* | B | 5 | B | 27.9 | 88.1 |
| 13 | Newcastle | 23 | 5 | C | 4 | B | 5 | A | 22.1 | 87.9 |
| 14 | Liverpool | 23 | 5 | B | 5 | B | 4 | A | 19.1 | 87.4 |
| 15 | Sussex | 23 | 4 | A | 5 | B | 4 | A | 19.6 | 87.0 |
| 16 | York | 22 | 5 | B | 5 | A | | | 26.5 | 86.3 |
| =17 | Lancaster | 22 | 4 | A | | | 5* | B | 22.9 | 84.7 |
| =17 | City | 23 | | | 4 | A | 3a | C | 24.5 | 84.7 |
| 19 | Leeds | 22 | 5 | B | 5 | B | 5 | B | 25.3 | 84.2 |
| 20 | Manchester | 22 | 5 | B | 5 | A | 4 | B | 23.2 | 83.9 |
| 21 | Exeter | 22 | 4 | A | 5 | A | 4 | A | 23.1 | 83.3 |
| 22 | LSE | 22 | | | | | 4 | B | 28.8 | 83.0 |
| 23 | UMIST | 22 | 5 | A | 4 | A | 4 | C | 23.0 | 82.2 |
| 24 | Leicester | 22 | 5 | B | 5 | B | | | 17.8 | 80.3 |
| 25 | Brunel | 22 | | | 5 | A | 4 | B | 19.0 | 80.1 |
| 26 | Durham | 21 | 5 | B | 5* | B | 4 | B | 28.7 | 80.0 |
| 27 | Reading | 22 | 3a | A | 5 | A | 4 | B | 20.4 | 79.7 |
| 28 | Loughborough | 22 | | | 4 | B | | | 22.2 | 79.6 |
| =29 | Royal Holloway | 22 | 5 | C | | | | | 22.3 | 79.0 |
| =29 | Dundee | HS | | | 5 | B | | | | 79.0 |
| =31 | Glasgow | HS | 5 | D | 5 | A | 5 | A | 24.4 | 78.7 |
| =31 | Heriot-Watt | HS | | | 5 | B | 5 | C | 23.1 | 78.7 |
| 33 | Hull | 22 | 4 | B | 4 | A | | | 18.3 | 78.5 |
| 34 | Keele | 22 | 2 | C | 5 | A | 3a | A | 18.5 | 77.9 |
| 35 | Strathclyde | HS | | | 5 | B | 4 | C | 22.4 | 77.7 |
| 36 | Surrey | 21 | | | 5 | A | 5 | A | 19.1 | 76.5 |
| 37 | Coventry | 23 | | | 3a | C | 3a | E | 15.2 | 75.8 |
| 38 | Portsmouth | 22 | | | 5 | C | | | 15.7 | 75.6 |
| 39 | Sheffield | 21 | 5 | B | 4 | B | 5 | C | 25.3 | 75.4 |
| 40 | King's College London | 21 | 5 | C | 5 | B | | | 23.1 | 75.1 |

| | | | | | |
|---|---|---|---|---|---|
| 41 | Queen's, Belfast | 42 | Aberdeen | 43 | Salford |
| 44 | Abertay Dundee | 45 | Queen Mary | 46 | Oxford Brookes |
| =47 | Stirling | =47 | Kent | 49 | Cardiff |

## Mathematics (cont.)

| | | | | | |
|---|---|---|---|---|---|
| 50 | Southampton | 51 | Brighton | 52 | Sheffield Hallam |
| 53 | Ulster | 54 | Kingston | 55 | Goldsmiths |
| 56 | Swansea | 57 | West of England | 58 | Aberystwyth |
| 59 | Hertfordshire | 60 | Essex | =61 | Glasgow Caledonian |
| =61 | Napier | 63 | Paisley | 64 | Nottingham Trent |
| 65 | North London | 66 | Northumbria | 67 | Aston |
| 68 | Bangor | 69 | Westminster | 70 | Plymouth |
| 71 | De Montfort | =72 | Derby | =72 | Greenwich |
| 74 | Liverpool John Moores | 75 | Wolverhampton | 76 | Glamorgan |
| 77 | Middlesex | 78 | Central Lancashire | 79 | London Guildhall |

**TQA (England) 1998–2000**
**Firsts and 2:1s:** 54%
**Employment:** 63%
**Further study:** 26%
**Unemployment:** 5%

## Mechanical Engineering

Bath's all-round strength leaves the university well clear of the field in mechanical engineering, one of the first subjects in England to be assessed for teaching quality. The only one of the top ten to be rated internationally outstanding for research, Bath boasts one of 11 Excellent teaching quality grades, while its entry standards are exceeded only by Imperial College.

Research ratings improved considerably in 2001, with six universities rated internationally outstanding. However, the grades bear little relation to the increasingly dated teaching scores. Bath was the only top-rated teaching university to reach the 5* grade for research. The other research stars – Imperial College, Southampton, Leeds, Liverpool, University College London and Queen's, Belfast – are all in the lower reaches of the top 20.

Almost half of the universities offering mechanical engineering are former polytechnics, although only Coventry and Hertfordshire, which had a more recent teaching assessment, make the top 20. Manchester Metropolitan was also considered Excellent for teaching. The open access policies pursued by many of the new universities is reflected in the fact that more than a third of the entrants are admitted without A levels or equivalents. Several courses have average entry standards of below three Ds at A level.

Only electronic engineering, within the wider discipline, has more students. The demand for places has been declining, but the subject still offers better employment prospects than most engineering subjects.

| | | TQA | RAE | | A-Levels | Score |
|---|---|---|---|---|---|---|
| 1 | Bath | E | 5* | A | 28.5 | 100.0 |
| =2 | Bristol | E | 5 | A | 26.6 | 95.5 |
| =2 | Sheffield | E | 5 | A | 26.5 | 95.5 |
| 4 | Strathclyde | E | 5 | B | | 93.1 |

## Mechanical Engineering (cont.)

| | TQA | RAE | | A-Levels | Score |
|---|---|---|---|---|---|
| 5 Nottingham | E | 5 | B | 25.8 | 92.9 |
| 6 Cardiff | E | 4 | A | 23.8 | 90.4 |
| 7 Manchester | E | 5 | B | 20.2 | 89.2 |
| 8 Reading | E | 5 | B | 18.2 | 87.9 |
| 9 Cranfield | E | 4 | C | 15.2 | 80.1 |
| 10 Glasgow | HS | 5 | B | | 78.4 |
| 11 Coventry | E | 3a | C | 14.3 | 77.2 |
| 12 Heriot-Watt | HS | 4 | A | | 77.0 |
| 13 Hertfordshire | 22 | 3a | D | 14.8 | 74.9 |
| 14 Imperial College | S | 5* | B | 29.1 | 74.5 |
| 15 Southampton | S | 5* | A | 24.9 | 74.2 |
| 16 Aberdeen | HS | 4 | C | | 71.2 |
| 17 Queen's, Belfast | S | 5* | B | 23.0 | 70.5 |
| 18 Leeds | S | 5* | B | 22.6 | 70.2 |
| 19 Liverpool | S | 5* | A | 18.6 | 70.0 |
| =20 University College London | S | 5 | B | 25.0 | 68.9 |
| =20 UMIST | S | 5 | A | 21.8 | 68.9 |
| 22 Manchester Metropolitan | E | | | 14.1 | 68.2 |
| 23 Loughborough | S | 5 | B | 21.3 | 66.5 |
| 24 Bradford | S | 5 | B | 17.4 | 63.9 |
| 25 Newcastle | S | 4 | B | 21.1 | 63.5 |
| 26 Robert Gordon | HS | 3b | D | | 63.0 |
| 27 Paisley | HS | 2 | C | | 62.6 |
| =28 Edinburgh | S | 4 | C | 23.7 | 62.3 |
| =28 Swansea | S | 4 | A | 16.7 | 62.3 |
| =28 Surrey | S | 4 | B | 19.3 | 62.3 |
| 31 Queen Mary | S | 5 | B | 14.4 | 61.9 |
| =32 King's College London | S | 5 | C | 18.8 | 61.4 |
| =32 Aston | S | 5 | C | 18.8 | 61.4 |
| 34 Birmingham | S | 4 | C | 21.3 | 60.7 |
| 35 Ulster | S | 4 | A | 12.8 | 59.7 |
| 36 Brunel | S | 5 | C | 15.4 | 59.1 |
| 37 Salford | S | 3a | A | 11.0 | 55.3 |
| 38 City | S | 4 | D | 14.7 | 53.0 |
| 39 De Montfort | S | 4 | C | 9.0 | 52.5 |
| 40 Kingston | S | 3a | C | 11.8 | 52.1 |

| | | |
|---|---|---|
| 41 Portsmouth | =42 Leeds Metropolitan | =42 Brighton |
| =44 Staffordshire | =44 Greenwich | =46 Derby |
| =46 Glasgow Caledonian | =46 South Bank | =46 UWCN, Newport |
| 50 Nottingham Trent | 51 Huddersfield | 52 Plymouth |
| =53 Lancaster | =53 Anglia | 55 Sussex |
| 56 Northumbria | 57 Oxford Brookes | 58 Liverpool John Moores |
| 59 West of England | 60 Sheffield Hallam | 61 Hull |
| 62 Central England | | |

**TQA (England) 1993–94**
**Firsts and 2:1s:** 47%
**Employment:** 72%
**Further study:** 14%
**Unemployment:** 8%

New Scottish Academic Review: *Paisley*: confidence in the academic standards; the quality of teaching and learning, and learning resources was commendable.

# Medicine

There is a tendency to assume that there is little to choose between Britain's medical schools, but both teaching and research assessments suggest otherwise. At a time when most teaching reviews saw traditional universities dropping only one or two points out of 24, medicine produced real variation.

Three English universities achieved maximum points, although top-placed Oxford was not among them. Its rise from last year's third place stems from the fact that it was the only medical school to achieve 5* grades with a full complement of academics in all three areas it entered. Third-placed Cambridge matched the grades, but with a lower proportion of staff.

Second-placed Newcastle and Manchester, which ties with Cambridge for third, boast maximum scores for teaching. So do Southampton and Liverpool, which are held back by their research grades. Aberdeen, Dundee, Glasgow, Cardiff and the University of Wales College of Medicine were all rated Excellent under the Scottish and Welsh systems.

The subject is a notoriously difficult one in which to win a place: Government quotas mean that candidates with three or four As at A level are frequently turned away. This pressure should be eased to some extent by an expansion in places, which has resulted in a series of unconventional courses and the first new medical schools for more than 20 years. Undergraduates have to be prepared to work long hours, particularly towards the end of the course, but the employment prospects are among the best in the higher education system.

| | | TQA | Clin Lab | | Community | | Hospital | | Pre-Clin | | A-Levels | Score |
|---|---|---|---|---|---|---|---|---|---|---|---|---|
| 1 | Oxford | 21 | 5* | A | 5* | A | 5* | A | | | 29.8 | 100.0 |
| 2 | Newcastle | 24 | 5* | D | 5 | C | 5 | C | | | 29.5 | 99.2 |
| =3 | Manchester | 24 | 4 | B | 5 | C | 5 | C | 5* B | | 28.8 | 98.7 |
| =3 | Cambridge | 21 | 5* | A | 5* | B | 5* | B | | | 29.9 | 98.7 |
| 5 | Southampton | 24 | 5 | A | 3a | B | 5 | B | | | 27.8 | 98.5 |
| 6 | Glasgow | E | 5 | B | 4 | C | 5 | C | | | 28.5 | 95.5 |
| 7 | Liverpool | 24 | 5 | B | 4 | B | 4 | B | | | 26.4 | 94.5 |
| 8 | Edinburgh | HS | | | 4 | B | 5* | C | | | 29.7 | 94.3 |
| 9 | Leicester | 23 | 4 | B | 3a | B | 4 | B | | | 28.5 | 94.1 |
| =10 | Wales College of Med | E | 5 | C | 4 | B | 4 | B | | | 28.0 | 93.8 |
| =10 | St George's Hospital | 23 | 4 | A | 4 | B | 4 | A | 5 A | | 27.2 | 93.8 |
| 12 | Aberdeen | E | 4 | B | 5 | C | 4 | B | | | 27.6 | 93.0 |
| 13 | Imperial College | 21 | 5* | B | 5 | B | 5* | B | 5 B | | 27.8 | 92.9 |
| 14 | King's College London | 22 | 5 | C | 4 | C | 4 | B | 5 C | | 28.2 | 90.6 |
| 15 | UCL | 21 | | | 4 | B | 5 | B | | | 28.1 | 90.4 |
| 16 | Dundee | E | 5* | B | 4 | D | 5 | E | | | 26.8 | 90.3 |
| 17 | Queen's, Belfast | 22 | 4 | C | 5 | E | 3a | C | | | 29.4 | 89.2 |
| 18 | Nottingham | 21 | 3a | B | 3a | C | 4 | B | 5 A | | 29.0 | 87.9 |
| 19 | Birmingham | 20 | 5* | B | 4 | D | 5 | C | 5 C | | 28.6 | 86.4 |
| 20 | Bristol | 20 | 5 | A | 5* | C | 3a | B | | | 28.6 | 86.0 |
| 21 | Queen Mary | 21 | 3a | B | 3a | B | 4 | B | | | 27.0 | 84.2 |
| 22 | Sheffield | 19 | | | 4 | B | 5 | C | 5* C | | 28.6 | 83.1 |
| 23 | Leeds | 18 | 5 | C | 4 | C | 4 | C | | | 28.4 | 77.7 |
| 24 | St Andrews | HS | | | | | | | | | 28.5 | 76.3 |

## Medicine (cont.)

**TQA (England) 1998–2000**
**Firsts and 2:1s:** n/a
**Employment:** 99%
**Further study:** 1%
**Unemployment:** 0%

*Note:* A number of new medical schools have been established for which data is not yet available. East Anglia, Peninsula (Plymouth and Exeter) and Warwick medical schools will recruit for entry in 2002, while Brighton and Susssex, Hull and York, and Keele will recruit for entry in 2003. In addition, a number of existing medical schools will introduce or have introduced innovative new courses.

## Middle Eastern and African Studies

Only nine universities offer Middle Eastern or African studies, but there is still a wide range of entry standards. Oxford, which does not have a separate A-level score this year, averages the equivalent of an A and two Bs at A level, whereas three Cs would secure a place at some other universities.

Birmingham takes top place as the only university rated internationally outstanding for research and tying with Cambridge for the best teaching quality grade. Oxford takes over second place, partly because it entered a full complement of academics in the latest Research Assessment Exercise. The School of Oriental and African Studies is third, with a consistent set of scores.

No university was awarded less than 20 points out of 24 for teaching quality, and only Leeds and Durham fell below Grade 5 in the latest Research Assessment Exercise.

Middle Eastern Studies is the larger of two small subjects, in terms of student numbers. Fewer than 100 students were taking African languages, literature or culture at degree level in 1998, compared with just over 500 for Middle Eastern subjects. The vast majority – all, in the case of African studies – come with A levels or their equivalent. Completion rates are good, and a high proportion graduate with first or upper second-class degrees.

|   |            | TQA | RAE |   | A-Levels | Score |
|---|------------|-----|-----|---|----------|-------|
| 1 | Birmingham | 23  | 5*  | A | 20.0     | 100.0 |
| 2 | Oxford     | 22  | 5   | A |          | 95.1  |
| 3 | SOAS       | 22  | 5   | B | 22.3     | 93.9  |
| 4 | Cambridge  | 23  | 5   | C |          | 93.6  |
| 5 | Durham     | 22  | 4   | A | 22.0     | 92.3  |
| 6 | Salford    | 20  | 5   | A |          | 84.4  |
| 7 | Exeter     | 20  | 5   | B |          | 81.8  |
| 8 | Manchester | 20  | 5   | B | 19.4     | 81.0  |
| 9 | Leeds      | 21  | 4   | C |          | 80.0  |

**TQA (England) 1996–98**
**Firsts and 2:1s:** 68% (Mid East), 68% (African)
**Employment:** 48% (Mid East), 55% (African)
**Further study:** 29% (Mid East), 20% (African)
**Unemployment:** 10% (Mid East), 5% (African)

## Molecular Biosciences

Molecular biosciences covers genetics and biochemistry as well as molecular biology. More than half of the undergraduates are awarded firsts or 2:1s and over 40 per cent go on to postgraduate study.

More than a dozen of the 79 universities offering the subjects were awarded full marks for teaching, with another seven in Scotland and Wales also rated as Excellent. Research assessments improved out of all recognition in 2001, with ten universities rated internationally outstanding, compared with only three in the previous exercise.

Cambridge heads a group of four universities with perfect scores for both teaching and research, squeezing ahead of Bristol on higher entry standards. The other two, Sheffield and Newcastle, are relegated to fourth and fifth because they did not enter a full complement of academics in the Research Assessment Exercise. Oxford, with its customary high A-level score, slips past into third place, despite missing the top research grade.

Apart from Kent and Dundee, all the top 20 universities in the ranking have average entry scores of at least two Bs and a C at A level. Nottingham Trent, the best-placed new university, narrowly misses a place in the top 20. Like Kingston, Sunderland and the West of England, it was among the top-scorers for teaching.

More than half of the courses include the option of a year in industry or abroad, and unemployment is low.

| | | TQA | RAE | | A-Levels | Score |
|---|---|---|---|---|---|---|
| 1 | Cambridge | 24 | 5* | A | 29.4 | 100.0 |
| 2 | Bristol | 24 | 5* | A | 27.1 | 98.4 |
| 3 | Oxford | 24 | 5 | A | 29.6 | 96.7 |
| 4 | Sheffield | 24 | 5* | B | 24.7 | 94.1 |
| 5 | Newcastle | 24 | 5* | B | 22.3 | 92.4 |
| 6 | Bath | 24 | 5 | B | 25.7 | 91.7 |
| =7 | York | 24 | 5 | B | 25.4 | 91.5 |
| =7 | Durham | 24 | 5 | B | 25.4 | 91.5 |
| 9 | Nottingham | 23 | 5 | A | 27.6 | 88.1 |
| 10 | Manchester | 23 | 5* | B | 24.4 | 86.7 |
| 11 | Kent | 24 | 4 | A | 17.5 | 84.6 |
| =12 | Warwick | 23 | 5 | B | 25.7 | 84.5 |
| =12 | Edinburgh | E | 5 | A | 22.5 | 84.5 |
| 14 | Cardiff | E | 5 | A | 22.4 | 84.4 |
| 15 | Leeds | 23 | 5 | B | 23.0 | 82.6 |
| 16 | Dundee | E | 5* | B | 18.4 | 82.4 |
| 17 | Birmingham | 23 | 5 | B | 22.1 | 82.0 |
| =18 | Glasgow | E | 5 | B | 21.9 | 81.8 |
| =18 | Imperial College | 22 | 5* | B | 27.5 | 81.8 |
| 20 | St Andrews | E | 5 | B | | 81.1 |
| 21 | Southampton | 23 | 5 | B | 20.7 | 81.0 |
| 22 | Salford | 24 | 3a | A | 14.1 | 78.7 |
| 23 | Nottingham Trent | 24 | 5 | D | 16.6 | 77.2 |
| 24 | University College London | 22 | 5 | B | 25.4 | 77.1 |
| 25 | UMIST | 22 | 5 | A | 21.7 | 76.8 |

## Molecular Biosciences (cont.)

| | | TQA | RAE | | A-Levels | Score |
|---|---|---|---|---|---|---|
| =26 | Leicester | 22 | 5* | B | 20.3 | 76.6 |
| =26 | Bangor | E | 4 | A | 16.3 | 76.6 |
| 28 | Sunderland | 24 | 3a | B | 12.5 | 76.1 |
| 29 | East Anglia | 22 | 5 | B | 22.6 | 75.2 |
| 30 | Ulster | 22 | 5* | A | 14.6 | 75.2 |
| 31 | Swansea | E | 3a | A | 18.2 | 74.5 |
| 32 | Essex | 23 | 4 | B | 15.7 | 74.3 |
| 33 | Sussex | 22 | 5 | B | 20.6 | 73.7 |
| 34 | Aberdeen | E | 5 | C | 15.0 | 73.2 |
| 35 | Kingston | 24 | 3a | C | 11.0 | 72.5 |
| 36 | Portsmouth | 22 | 5 | A | 15.5 | 72.3 |
| =37 | Exeter | 22 | 4 | B | 21.7 | 71.4 |
| =37 | Oxford Brookes | 23 | 3a | A | 13.9 | 71.4 |
| 39 | Aberystwyth | E | 3a | A | 13.5 | 71.2 |
| 40 | Surrey | 21 | 5* | A | 17.9 | 70.4 |

| | | | | | |
|---|---|---|---|---|---|
| 41 | Aston | 42 | Cranfield | 43 | Hull |
| 44 | Queen Mary | 45 | Stirling | 46 | King's College London |
| 47 | Wolverhampton | 48 | Brunel | =49 | Queen's, Belfast |
| =49 | Brighton | 51 | West of England | 52 | Lancaster |
| 53 | Royal Holloway | 54 | Reading | 55 | UWIC, Cardiff |
| 56 | Central Lancashire | 57 | Keele | 58 | Plymouth |
| 59 | Napier | 60 | Manchester Metropolitan | 61 | Paisley |
| 62 | Liverpool John Moores | 63 | Sheffield Hallam | 64 | Liverpool |
| 65 | Hertfordshire | 66 | Staffordshire | 67 | Luton |
| 68 | Northumbria | 69 | Huddersfield | 70 | Westminster |
| 71 | Heriot-Watt | 72 | Greenwich | 73 | Anglia |
| 74 | Bradford | 75 | De Montfort | 76 | South Bank |
| 77 | Coventry | 78 | East London | 79 | North London |

**TQA (England) 1998–2000**
**Firsts and 2:1s:** 58%
**Employment:** 45%
**Further study:** 43%
**Unemployment:** 6%

## Music

The latest research assessments have transformed the music ranking. Nottingham moves to first place after achieving one of nine top scores. King's College London and the School of Oriental and African Studies, slip to fifth and tenth respectively after missing the 5* grade.

Six universities have top ratings for both teaching and research. Cambridge, Birmingham, Southampton, Manchester, City and Nottingham all enjoy this distinction, although not all entered a full complement of academics in the Research Assessment Exercise.

Almost half of the 47 universities offering music were rated Excellent in a dated set of teaching assessments, although the Highly Satisfactory grades at

## Music (cont.)

Edinburgh and Glasgow were the best in Scotland. Missing the top grade almost cost Oxford a place in the leading 20 in the table, although it has now been rated internationally outstanding for research and has entry standards exceeded only by second-placed Cambridge.

Selection is as much a matter of musical ability as academic achievement, but nearly nine out of ten students come with A levels. There can be considerable variation in the character of courses, from the practical and vocational programmes in conservatoires to the more theoretical. Although barely half of the graduates went straight into jobs, the unemployment rate was among the lowest of any subject.

| | | TQA | RAE | | A-Levels | Score |
|---|---|---|---|---|---|---|
| 1 | Nottingham | E | 5* | A | 26.1 | 100.0 |
| 2 | Cambridge | E | 5* | B | 28.9 | 99.5 |
| 3 | Birmingham | E | 5* | B | 26.7 | 97.8 |
| 4 | Southampton | E | 5* | A | 23.2 | 97.7 |
| 5 | King's College London | E | 5 | A | 27.3 | 97.3 |
| 6 | York | E | 5 | A | 25.6 | 96.0 |
| 7 | Manchester | E | 5* | B | 24.1 | 95.8 |
| 8 | Sussex | E | 5 | A | 23.6 | 94.5 |
| 9 | Sheffield | E | 5 | B | 23.5 | 92.1 |
| 10 | SOAS | E | 5 | B | | 91.9 |
| 11 | Goldsmiths College | E | 5 | A | 20.1 | 91.8 |
| 12 | Queen's, Belfast | E | 5 | B | 21.8 | 90.8 |
| 13 | City | E | 5* | C | 21.5 | 89.3 |
| 14 | Lancaster | E | 4 | A | 21.2 | 89.1 |
| 15 | Surrey | E | 3a | A | 22.8 | 86.7 |
| 16 | Leeds | E | 4 | C | 24.6 | 86.6 |
| 17 | Keele | E | 4 | A | 17.6 | 86.3 |
| 18 | Salford | E | 4 | A | 15.6 | 84.8 |
| 19 | Bangor | E | 5 | C | 18.2 | 84.2 |
| 20 | Oxford | S | 5* | A | 28.4 | 83.4 |
| 21 | Huddersfield | E | 5 | C | 16.0 | 82.5 |
| 22 | Westminster | 23 | 4 | D | 13.6 | 80.6 |
| 23 | Edinburgh | HS | 4 | B | 23.9 | 80.1 |
| 24 | Glasgow | HS | 4 | A | | 78.9 |
| 25 | Royal Holloway | S | 5* | B | 23.8 | 77.2 |
| 26 | Bristol | S | 5 | A | 24.1 | 76.6 |
| 27 | De Montfort | | 4 | A | 15.8 | 75.7 |
| 28 | Newcastle | S | 5* | A | 17.9 | 75.3 |
| 29 | Ulster | E | 3a | D | 15.8 | 74.4 |
| 30 | Anglia | E | 3b | B | 12.7 | 74.3 |
| 31 | Central England | E | 3a | E | 18.5 | 73.5 |
| 32 | Durham | S | 4 | A | 24.1 | 73.1 |
| 33 | Hull | S | 5 | B | 17.9 | 69.5 |
| 34 | Exeter | S | 4 | B | 21.3 | 68.9 |
| 35 | Cardiff | S | 5 | C | 21.3 | 68.3 |
| =36 | Liverpool | S | 4 | A | 17.1 | 67.6 |
| =36 | East Anglia | S | 4 | B | 19.6 | 67.6 |
| 38 | Oxford Brookes | S | 3a | A | 17.0 | 64.0 |

## Music (cont.)

| | | TQA | | RAE | A-Levels | Score |
|---|---|---|---|---|---|---|
| 39 | Reading | S | 3a | B | 17.8 | 63.1 |
| 40 | Surrey Roehampton | S | 3a | A | 13.0 | 60.9 |
| | | | | | | |
| 41 | Hertfordshire | 42 Kingston | | | 43 Thames Valley | |
| 44 | Napier | 45 Middlesex | | | 46 Derby | |
| 47 | Wolverhampton | | | | | |

**TQA (England) 1994–95**

**Firsts and 2:1s:** 61%

**Employment:** 54%

**Further study:** 38%

**Unemployment:** 4%

## Nursing

Nursing has been one of the main growth points of higher education since the last Conservative government opted for a graduate profession. A number of universities have taken in nursing and midwifery colleges, sometimes at the expense of their normally high research grades. In the latest assessments, Surrey registered the first 5* nursing grade, although the university still fails to make the top 20 because it has one of the lowest scores for teaching quality.

Manchester retains top place through all-round strength, although other universities had higher scores on all three indicators. Second-placed Northumbria and Central Lancashire, in sixth, were the only universities to be awarded full marks for teaching. New universities account for most of the 46 entries in the table, with Plymouth and Kingston also reaching the top ten.

Glasgow, the highest-ranked Scottish university, had the highest entry standards, the equivalent of more than three Bs at A level. Elsewhere, requirements were much lower, with three Ds securing a place on several courses.

Almost two-thirds of the students arrive without A levels, but there are more than five applicants to every place, nine out of ten of them female. A quarter of those who join pre-registration programmes drop out, but the wastage rate is nearer 10 per cent thereafter. Applications are still growing, with almost 25,000 students seeking places on courses starting in 2002.

| | | TQA | RAE | | A-Levels | Score |
|---|---|---|---|---|---|---|
| 1 | Manchester | 23 | 5 | B | 21.0 | 100.0 |
| 2 | Northumbria | 24 | 3a | C | 18.1 | 96.5 |
| 3 | Portsmouth | 22 | 5 | A | | 95.6 |
| 4 | Sunderland | 23 | 3a | B | | 94.5 |
| 5 | Bradford | 23 | 3b | B | | 91.5 |
| 6 | Central Lancashire | 24 | 3b | E | 16.6 | 90.0 |
| 7 | Nottingham | 22 | 3a | C | 23.7 | 89.8 |
| 8 | Plymouth | 23 | 3b | C | | 89.7 |
| =9 | St George's Hospital | 22 | 3a | A | | 88.9 |

## Nursing (cont.)

| | | TQA | RAE | | A-Levels | Score |
|---|---|---|---|---|---|---|
| =9 | Salford | 22 | 3a | A | | 88.9 |
| =9 | Kingston | 22 | 3a | A | | 88.9 |
| 12 | Liverpool | 22 | 3a | B | 18.2 | 87.2 |
| 13 | Southampton | 22 | 3b | A | 19.8 | 86.9 |
| 14 | York | 21 | 5 | B | | 86.3 |
| 15 | Hertfordshire | 23 | 4 | D | 13.4 | 86.1 |
| 16 | Anglia | 23 | 3a | D | 14.7 | 85.8 |
| 17 | King's College London | 21 | 4 | A | 18.3 | 85.5 |
| 18 | Glasgow | HS | 3a | D | 24.4 | 85.3 |
| 19 | Swansea | | 3b | B | 19.5 | 85.0 |
| 20 | Ulster | 22 | 4 | D | 17.8 | 84.0 |
| =21 | Edinburgh | HS | 3a | B | | 83.9 |
| =21 | West of England | 22 | 3b | C | 18.9 | 83.9 |
| 23 | Surrey | 19 | 5* | A | 20.1 | 81.0 |
| =24 | Leeds | 20 | 4 | A | 19.6 | 80.9 |
| =24 | Birmingham | 22 | 3b | D | 17.3 | 80.9 |
| 26 | Greenwich | 23 | | | 14.7 | 80.6 |
| 27 | De Montfort | 22 | 3a | D | 12.8 | 78.6 |
| 28 | Sheffield | 21 | 5 | D | | 78.5 |
| 29 | Huddersfield | 22 | | | 17.7 | 77.4 |
| 30 | City | 20 | 4 | B | 16.9 | 77.2 |
| 31 | Bournemouth | 22 | 3b | F | 16.4 | 76.9 |
| 32 | Brighton | 22 | 2 | F | | 76.0 |
| =33 | Glasgow Caledonian | HS | 3a | E | | 75.9 |
| =33 | Liverpool John Moores | 21 | 3a | C | 13.7 | 75.9 |
| 35 | Wales College of Medicine | S | 4 | D | 21.3 | 75.6 |
| 36 | Leeds Metropolitan | 21 | 3b | E | 16.4 | 72.8 |
| 37 | Middlesex | 22 | 3a | F | 10.0 | 71.9 |
| 38 | Thames Valley | 20 | 3b | A | | 71.3 |
| 39 | Keele | 21 | 2 | E | | 70.3 |
| 40 | Sheffield Hallam | 21 | | | 15.1 | 69.6 |

| 41 Central England | 42 Oxford Brookes | 43 South Bank |
|---|---|---|
| 44 Wolverhampton | 45 Abertay Dundee | 46 Hull |

**TQA (England) 1999–2000**
**Firsts and 2:1s:** 58%
**Employment:** 95%
**Further study:** 2%
**Unemployment:** 2%

*Note*: Some universities are not in the table largely because they ran only diploma courses in 2000. They include Reading, which was awarded the maximum 24 points for teaching, Luton and Teesside (on 23), Brunel, Coventry, Staffordshire and Queen's, Belfast (22), Manchester Metropolitan and North London (21), Essex (20), Derby (19) and East Anglia (18).

## Organismal Biosciences

Organismal biosciences covers botany, zoology, microbiology and biology. Most courses were assessed for teaching quality with molecular programmes, but some specialist providers kept the subjects apart.

More than a dozen English universities achieved full marks for teaching, including a handful of former polytechnics. Cambridge takes the top spot, as one

## Organismal Biosciences (cont.)

of three universities with perfect teaching and research records. Third-placed Sheffield is the other in England, but entry standards of almost three As at A level help Oxford to the runner-up position. Dundee achieved an Excellent rating for teaching under the Scottish system, but it did not enter a full complement of academics in the Research Assessment Exercise. Five institutions in Wales, led by Cardiff, and five in Scotland, where Edinburgh reached the top ten, were rated Excellent.

There were seven 5* research ratings in 2001, spread through the table as far as Surrey, in 40th place. The disparity between teaching and research scores was such that Liverpool, in 64th place out of 73 universities, reached grade 5 for research. Nottingham Trent is the only new university in the top 30, although Kingston and the West of England also achieved top marks for teaching.

The subjects are popular and two-thirds of all entrants arriving with A levels or their equivalent, but the drop-out rates are high on some courses.

|  |  | TQA | RAE | | A-Levels | Score |
|---|---|---|---|---|---|---|
| 1 | Cambridge | 24 | 5* | A | | 100.0 |
| 2 | Oxford | 24 | 5 | A | 29.7 | 99.5 |
| 3 | Sheffield | 24 | 5* | A | 24.5 | 99.4 |
| 4 | York | 24 | 5 | B | 26.3 | 94.5 |
| 5 | University College London | 24 | 5 | B | 25.8 | 94.1 |
| 6 | Bath | 24 | 5 | B | 24.9 | 93.4 |
| 7 | Durham | 24 | 5 | B | 24.5 | 93.1 |
| 8 | UMIST | | 5 | A | 22.5 | 91.8 |
| 9 | Birmingham | 24 | 5 | B | 21.6 | 91.0 |
| 10 | Edinburgh | E | 5 | A | 25.4 | 88.6 |
| 11 | Manchester | 23 | 5* | B | 22.9 | 87.7 |
| 12 | Dundee | E | 5* | B | | 86.8 |
| 13 | Warwick | 23 | 5 | B | 25.3 | 86.0 |
| 14 | Kent | 24 | 4 | A | 15.7 | 85.3 |
| 15 | Royal Holloway | 24 | 5 | C | 18.8 | 84.8 |
| 16 | St Andrews | E | 5 | B | 23.2 | 84.5 |
| 17 | Southampton | 23 | 5 | B | 22.5 | 84.0 |
| 18 | Imperial College | 22 | 5* | B | 27.0 | 83.0 |
| 19 | Cardiff | E | 4 | A | 22.6 | 82.7 |
| =20 | Bristol | 22 | 5 | A | 26.7 | 81.8 |
| =20 | Salford | 24 | 3a | A | 16.0 | 81.8 |
| 22 | Glasgow | E | 5 | B | 18.8 | 81.3 |
| =23 | Aberdeen | E | 5 | B | 16.9 | 79.8 |
| =23 | Nottingham | 23 | 3a | B | 26.0 | 79.8 |
| 25 | Bangor | E | 4 | A | 17.0 | 78.5 |
| 26 | Newcastle | 22 | 5* | B | 19.4 | 77.4 |
| 27 | Leeds | 22 | 5 | B | 23.0 | 76.6 |
| 28 | Swansea | E | 3a | A | 19.3 | 76.4 |
| 29 | Nottingham Trent | 24 | 5 | D | 13.6 | 76.3 |
| 30 | Sussex | 22 | 5 | B | 21.3 | 75.4 |
| =31 | Sunderland | 24 | 3a | B | 8.9 | 74.9 |
| =31 | Essex | 23 | 4 | B | 14.8 | 74.9 |
| 33 | East Anglia | 22 | 5 | B | 20.4 | 74.7 |
| 34 | Aberystwyth | E | 3a | A | 16.0 | 74.0 |

## Organismal Biosciences (cont.)

| | | TQA | RAE | | A-Levels | Score |
|---|---|---|---|---|---|---|
| 35 | Aston | 23 | 3a | C | 21.0 | 73.3 |
| 36 | Kingston | 24 | 3a | C | 9.8 | 72.8 |
| 37 | Oxford Brookes | 23 | 3a | A | 14.0 | 72.5 |
| 38 | Exeter | 22 | 4 | B | 21.1 | 71.8 |
| 39 | Leicester | 22 | 5 | C | 21.8 | 71.6 |
| 40 | Surrey | 21 | 5* | A | 16.3 | 70.2 |

| 41 Hull | =42 Stirling | =42 Brighton |
|---|---|---|
| 44 Queen Mary | 45 Keele | 46 West of England |
| 47 King's College London | 48 Queen's, Belfast | 49 Reading |
| 50 Brunel | 51 Lancaster | 52 Portsmouth |
| 53 Central Lancashire | 54 Wolverhampton | 55 UWIC, Cardiff |
| 56 Liverpool John Moores | 57 Surrey Roehampton | 58 Plymouth |
| 59 Napier | 60 Ulster | 61 Manchester Metropolitan |
| =62 Luton | =62 Derby | 64 Liverpool |
| 65 Paisley | 66 Staffordshire | 67 Westminster |
| 68 Anglia | 69 Northumbria | 70 Coventry |
| 71 Greenwich | 72 East London | 73 North London |

**TQA (England) 1998–2000**
**Firsts and 2:1s:** 58%
**Employment:** 55%
**Further study:** 30%
**Unemployment:** 8%

## Other Subjects Allied to Medicine

The 'allied to medicine' subject covers audiology, complementary therapies, counselling, health services management, health sciences, nutrition, occupational therapy, optometry, ophthalmology, orthoptics, osteopathy, physiotherapy, podiatry, radiography and speech therapy. Traditional universities dominate the top ten, but big names such as Durham and Nottingham find themselves outside the top 30. Teaching scores were generally high, with all the top 40 scoring at least 21 points out of 24. Glasgow Caledonian, the top-placed Scottish university, was assessed separately for occupational therapy, physiotherapy and radiotherapy, but none of the grades was less than Highly Satisfactory.

Cardiff, rated Excellent at teaching under the Welsh system and internationally outstanding for research, takes top place in the table. Loughborough, last year's leader and one of six English universities with full marks for teaching, slips to second after a disappointing research assessment.

Third-placed UMIST has the highest entry standards, averaging two As and a B at A level. However, some new universities, including Liverpool John Moores (the only former polytechnic in the top ten), average little more than three Ds. Across the whole range of subjects, almost half of the students arrive without A levels.

The demand for places is highest on professional courses such as optometry and physiotherapy, where graduate employment prospects are excellent.

## Other Subjects Allied to Medicine (cont.)

| | | TQA | RAE | | A-Levels | Score |
|---|---|---|---|---|---|---|
| 1 | Cardiff | E | 5* | A | 26.7 | 100.0 |
| 2 | Loughborough | 24 | 4 | A | | 99.2 |
| 3 | UMIST | 23 | 5* | B | 28.0 | 98.6 |
| 4 | Strathclyde | | 5 | A | 21.6 | 95.9 |
| 5 | University College London | 24 | 5 | C | 22.2 | 94.8 |
| 6 | Bradford | 23 | 5 | B | 23.8 | 92.7 |
| 7 | Aston | 23 | 5 | C | 26.7 | 91.5 |
| 8 | King's College London | 23 | 4 | B | 24.2 | 90.2 |
| 9 | York | | 5 | A | 17.7 | 90.0 |
| 10 | Liverpool John Moores | 24 | 4 | A | 12.6 | 89.8 |
| 11 | Portsmouth | 23 | 5 | A | 15.9 | 88.7 |
| 12 | City | 23 | 5 | C | 22.8 | 88.6 |
| 13 | Leeds | 24 | 5 | D | 16.3 | 86.5 |
| 14 | East Anglia | 23 | 3b | A | 25.0 | 86.2 |
| 15 | Manchester | 22 | 5 | B | 23.4 | 85.7 |
| 16 | Newcastle | 24 | | | 25.2 | 83.9 |
| 17 | Birmingham | 24 | | | 24.2 | 83.2 |
| 18 | Surrey | 21 | 5* | A | | 82.2 |
| =19 | Sheffield Hallam | 23 | 4 | D | 17.0 | 78.7 |
| =19 | Glasgow Caledonian | E/HS | 4 | C | 21.4 | 78.7 |
| =21 | Nottingham Trent | 23 | 5 | D | 14.1 | 78.1 |
| =21 | St George's Hospital | 23 | 3a | E | 21.7 | 78.1 |
| 23 | Leeds Metropolitan | 23 | 3a | E | 19.9 | 76.8 |
| 24 | Westminster | 23 | 3a | C | 12.7 | 76.5 |
| 25 | Sheffield | 21 | 4 | B | 23.2 | 76.1 |
| 26 | Kingston | 23 | 3a | C | 12.0 | 76.0 |
| =27 | Salford | 22 | 3a | A | 15.9 | 75.9 |
| =27 | Coventry | 23 | 3a | E | 18.7 | 75.9 |
| 29 | UWIC, Cardiff | E | 3b | D | 16.5 | 75.2 |
| 30 | Brighton | 22 | 5 | C | 12.9 | 74.5 |
| 31 | Teesside | 22 | 3a | C | 18.4 | 74.2 |
| =32 | Nottingham | 21 | 3a | C | 25.8 | 73.0 |
| =32 | Central Lancashire | 22 | 3b | A | 16.2 | 73.0 |
| =34 | West of England | 21 | 3a | B | 22.2 | 72.6 |
| =34 | Brunel | 22 | 3a | E | 23.1 | 72.6 |
| 36 | Durham | 23 | | | 18.3 | 72.2 |
| 37 | Northumbria | 23 | | | 17.5 | 71.5 |
| 38 | Manchester Metropolitan | 22 | 3b | D | 19.4 | 70.7 |
| 39 | Ulster | 22 | 4 | F | 23.1 | 70.4 |
| 40 | Wolverhampton | 22 | 3a | C | 12.5 | 69.7 |

| | | | | | | |
|---|---|---|---|---|---|---|
| 41 | Hertfordshire | 42 | Southampton | 43 | Luton | |
| 44 | Liverpool | 45 | North London | 46 | Central England | |
| 47 | Derby | 48 | Staffordshire | 49 | Robert Gordon | |
| 50 | Queen's, Belfast | 51 | Anglia | 52 | Middlesex | |
| 53 | Lancaster | 54 | De Montfort | 55 | East London | |
| 56 | Keele | 57 | South Bank | =58 | Lincoln | |
| =58 | Cranfield | 60 | Plymouth | 61 | Oxford Brookes | |
| 62 | Bournemouth | 63 | Surrey Roehampton | 64 | Greenwich | |

*Note*: The TQA outcome for Sunderland has not yet been published, and so it does not appear in the table.

## Other Subjects Allied to Medicine (cont.)

**TQA (England) 1998–2000**
**Firsts and 2:1s:** 58%
**Employment:** 84%
**Further study:** 8%
**Unemployment:** 4%

## Pharmacology and Pharmacy

An improved research rating is enough to give Manchester top spot for pharmacy and pharmacology, swapping places with Cambridge. Manchester and third-placed Bath were the only universities rated internationally outstanding for pharmacy in the latest assessments. UCL took the one 5* grade in pharmacology, but only just makes the top 20 because of a low teaching score.

All but four of 23 English universities assessed for teaching quality achieved at least 22 points out of 24. Six were awarded maximum points, but only Manchester has a perfect record for both teaching and research. Cardiff and Strathclyde were both rated Excellent under the separate Welsh and Scottish systems, but neither makes the top five.

Portsmouth is by far the top new university. Full marks for teaching, a grade 5 for research and entry grades averaging a B and two Cs see Portsmouth soar from 15th to fourth place. Greenwich, Brighton and Sunderland are the other former polytechnics in the top 20.

Departments in England are evenly split between those specialising in pharmacy and pharmacology. Only four cover both. Since 1997, pharmacy degrees have been converted to the four-year MPharm, whereas pharmacology is available either as a three-year BSc or as an extended course. Industry, hospitals and other health organisations in both subjects have close links, and employment prospects are good, especially in pharmacy.

| | | TQA | RAE | | A-Levels | Score |
|---|---|---|---|---|---|---|
| | | | Pharmacology | Pharmacy | | |
| 1 | Manchester | 24 | | 5* B | 25.1 | 100.0 |
| 2 | Cambridge | 24 | 5  A | | | 99.5 |
| 3 | Bath | 23 | | 5* A | 25.8 | 97.1 |
| 4 | Portsmouth | 24 | 5  A | | 20.2 | 96.3 |
| 5 | Queen's, Belfast | 24 | | 4  B | 27.9 | 95.6 |
| 6 | Nottingham | 23 | | 5  A | 28.1 | 95.0 |
| 7 | Cardiff | E | | 5  A | 25.7 | 93.6 |
| 8 | School of Pharmacy | 23 | | 5  A | 23.6 | 92.3 |
| 9 | Strathclyde | E | | 5  B | 24.3 | 90.5 |
| 10 | Bristol | 23 | 4  A | | 25.0 | 89.7 |
| 11 | Leeds | 23 | 5  B | | 21.3 | 88.8 |
| 12 | Aston | 24 | | 3a C | 24.6 | 88.1 |
| 13 | Bradford | 23 | | 4  B | 20.4 | 85.2 |
| 14 | King's College London | 22 | | 5  B | 23.2 | 84.0 |
| 15 | Liverpool | 22 | 5  A | | 17.5 | 82.8 |
| 16 | Greenwich | 23 | 4  A | | 9.7 | 80.7 |

## Pharmacology and Pharmacy (cont.)

| | | TQA | RAE | | A-Levels | Score |
|---|---|---|---|---|---|---|
| | | | Pharmacology | Pharmacy | | |
| 17 | Brighton | 23 | 5  C | | 13.5 | 80.5 |
| 18 | University College London | 20 | 5*  A | | 23.1 | 77.6 |
| 19 | Sunderland | 22 | | 3a  B | 22.1 | 77.2 |
| 20 | Newcastle | 24 | | | 21.4 | 76.8 |
| 21 | Liverpool John Moores | 23 | | | 21.6 | 71.0 |
| 22 | Robert Gordon | HS | 3b  C | | 19.6 | 67.8 |
| 23 | Nottingham Trent | | 5  D | | 13.4 | 62.2 |
| 24 | Sheffield | 21 | | | 23.0 | 59.9 |
| 25 | Luton | 22 | | | 10.2 | 58.3 |
| 26 | De Montfort | 21 | | | 19.8 | 58.0 |
| 27 | East London | 19 | | | 13.2 | 42.2 |

**TQA (England) 1998–2000**

**Firsts and 2:1s:** 58% (Pharmacology); 58% (Pharmacy)
**Employment:** 53% (Pharmacology); 98% (Pharmacy)
**Further study:** 34% (Pharmacology); 1% (Pharmacy)
**Unemployment:** 9% (Pharmacology); 0% (Pharmacy)

## Philosophy

Cambridge just beats Oxford to the top of the table for philosophy, although, like third-placed King's College London, both have maximum points for teaching and research. Cambridge has a slightly higher A-level score, its entrants averaging almost three As at A level, and it entered a higher proportion of its academics for the latest Research Assessment Exercise.

The 2001 teaching quality assessment in England was among the most generous for any subject, with 22 out of 33 universities achieving maximum points. It is all the more surprising, therefore, that neither the LSE (which had the highest entry scores outside Oxbridge and a 5* rating for research) nor Bristol (the next most difficult course to get into) appears in the list of perfect scores.

Hertfordshire is the top-placed new university, the only one in the top 20, sharing with Wolverhampton the distinction of maximum points for teaching. Middlesex also did well to reach grade 5 in the Research Assessment Exercise, when only five universities were rated internationally outstanding. Sunderland has been omitted from the table at the university's own request.

Edinburgh was the other 5* university for research, although partly because it entered a relatively low number of academics for assessment, it was beaten to the top place in Scotland by St Andrews. Glasgow recorded the best teaching score north of the border, rated Excellent, like Cardiff, the top-placed institution in Wales.

| | | TQA | RAE | | A-Levels | Score |
|---|---|---|---|---|---|---|
| 1 | Cambridge | 24 | 5* | A | 29.7 | 100.0 |
| 2 | Oxford | 24 | 5* | B | 29.5 | 96.8 |
| 3 | King's College London | 24 | 5* | A | 23.3 | 95.6 |

## Philosophy (cont.)

| | | TQA | RAE | | A-Levels | Score |
|---|---|---|---|---|---|---|
| 4 | Sheffield | 24 | 5 | A | 24.7 | 92.4 |
| 5 | Warwick | 24 | 5 | B | 26.6 | 91.1 |
| 6 | York | 24 | 5 | B | 25.8 | 90.6 |
| =7 | Brighton | 24 | 5 | B | | 90.0 |
| =7 | Durham | 24 | 5 | B | 25.0 | 90.0 |
| 9 | Sussex | 24 | 5 | B | 23.8 | 89.1 |
| 10 | Bristol | 23 | 5 | A | 27.4 | 87.7 |
| 11 | Reading | 24 | 5 | B | 20.6 | 86.9 |
| 12 | Southampton | 24 | 4 | A | 21.9 | 86.3 |
| 13 | East Anglia | 24 | 5 | B | 19.6 | 86.2 |
| 14 | Manchester | 24 | 4 | B | 24.2 | 85.8 |
| 15 | London School of Economics | 22 | 5* | A | 28.0 | 85.6 |
| =16 | Bradford | 24 | 4 | B | | 85.4 |
| =16 | Hertfordshire | 24 | 4 | B | | 85.4 |
| 18 | Liverpool | 24 | 4 | A | 20.4 | 85.3 |
| 19 | Leeds | 24 | 5 | C | 24.5 | 85.2 |
| 20 | Essex | 24 | 5 | B | 17.5 | 84.8 |
| 21 | University College London | 23 | 5 | B | 24.5 | 83.0 |
| 22 | Lancaster | 24 | 3a | B | 21.2 | 80.0 |
| 23 | Keele | 24 | 3a | B | 19.1 | 78.5 |
| 24 | Kent | 24 | 4 | C | 18.6 | 78.2 |
| 25 | Nottingham | 22 | 5 | B | 26.8 | 77.9 |
| =26 | St Andrews | HS | 5 | A | 25.2 | 76.2 |
| =26 | Middlesex | 23 | 5 | C | | 76.2 |
| 28 | Glasgow | E | 4 | C | 23.6 | 75.0 |
| 29 | Edinburgh | HS | 5* | C | 27.5 | 73.6 |
| 30 | Cardiff | E | 3a | C | 22.5 | 71.3 |
| 31 | Stirling | HS | 5 | B | 18.8 | 69.0 |
| 32 | Manchester Metropolitan | 23 | 3a | C | | 68.8 |
| 33 | Hull | 22 | 4 | B | 18.5 | 68.5 |
| 34 | Staffordshire | 23 | 3a | C | 11.5 | 63.6 |
| 35 | Wolverhampton | 24 | | | 15.4 | 61.7 |
| 36 | Birmingham | 21 | 4 | C | 22.3 | 60.8 |
| 37 | Aberdeen | HS | 3a | B | | 60.1 |
| 38 | Queen's, Belfast | | 3a | D | 22.9 | 58.2 |
| 39 | Lampeter | S | 3a | A | 13.4 | 49.7 |
| 40 | Dundee | S | 3a | B | | 47.6 |
| 41 | North London | 42 Greenwich | | | 43 Swansea | |

**TQA (England) 2000–01**
**Firsts and 2:1s:** 68%
**Employment:** 51%
**Further study:** 38%
**Unemployment:** 6%

## Physics and Astronomy

Durham retains top place for physics and astronomy without improving on its grade 5 for research. Unlike the five universities rated internationally outstanding for research, it scored maximum points for teaching quality, as well as

## Physics and Astronomy (cont.)

registering one of the top A-level scores.

Ten of the 39 universities whose teaching was assessed in England scored maximum points, and there were five more Excellent ratings in Scotland and Wales. Edinburgh edges out St Andrews in Scotland, while Swansea is the clear leader in Wales. Although traditional universities monopolise the top 30, Nottingham Trent and Sheffield Hallam both have perfect teaching scores.

In spite of the dearth of physicists going into teaching, the subjects command high entry grades in the traditional universities. Places could be had with little more than three Ds at some new universities, but a dozen of the 48 institutions in the table had average entry grades of three Bs or above.

The profile of undergraduates is among the most traditional: only one in five is female and a similar proportion arrive without A levels or their equivalent. About 5 per cent transfer to other courses or drop out, usually at the end of the first year, but over half of those who remain get firsts or 2:1s.

| | | TQA | RAE | | A-Levels | Score |
|---|---|---|---|---|---|---|
| 1 | Durham | 24 | 5 | A | 27.8 | 100.0 |
| 2 | Warwick | 24 | 5 | A | 27.5 | 99.8 |
| 3 | Oxford | 23 | 5* | A | 29.8 | 98.0 |
| 4 | Manchester | 24 | 5 | A | 23.8 | 97.1 |
| 5 | Cambridge | 23 | 5* | A | | 94.5 |
| 6 | Leeds | 24 | 5 | A | 19.5 | 94.0 |
| 7 | Bath | 24 | 4 | A | 23.0 | 92.4 |
| 8 | Liverpool | 24 | 5 | A | 16.8 | 92.1 |
| 9 | Nottingham | 23 | 5 | A | 26.6 | 91.7 |
| 10 | Bristol | 23 | 5 | A | 25.9 | 91.2 |
| 11 | York | 24 | 4 | B | 24.2 | 91.1 |
| 12 | Queen's, Belfast | 23 | 5 | A | 24.8 | 90.4 |
| 13 | Imperial College | 22 | 5* | A | 28.3 | 89.5 |
| 14 | Edinburgh | E | 5 | B | 26.4 | 88.9 |
| 15 | University College London | 23 | 5 | B | 26.0 | 88.6 |
| 16 | St Andrews | E | 5 | B | 25.6 | 88.3 |
| 17 | Leicester | 23 | 5 | A | 21.6 | 88.1 |
| 18 | Lancaster | 23 | 5* | A | 15.3 | 87.6 |
| 19 | Reading | 24 | 4 | B | 19.0 | 87.3 |
| 20 | Swansea | E | 5 | A | 20.0 | 86.9 |
| 21 | Surrey | 23 | 5 | A | 19.3 | 86.4 |
| 22 | Glasgow | E | 5 | B | | 86.0 |
| 23 | Birmingham | 23 | 5 | B | 22.0 | 85.7 |
| 24 | Royal Holloway | 23 | 5 | B | 21.5 | 85.4 |
| 25 | Strathclyde | E | 4 | A | | 84.2 |
| 26 | Southampton | 22 | 5* | B | 21.6 | 81.6 |
| 27 | Exeter | 22 | 5 | A | 22.4 | 81.2 |
| 28 | Sussex | 22 | 5 | A | 20.9 | 80.1 |
| 29 | Sheffield | 22 | 5 | B | 23.8 | 79.5 |
| 30 | Loughborough | 23 | 4 | C | 21.3 | 77.9 |
| 31 | Salford | 23 | 4 | A | 13.0 | 77.8 |
| 32 | King's College London | 22 | 4 | B | 20.9 | 73.8 |
| 33 | Hull | 23 | 4 | C | 14.9 | 73.3 |
| 34 | Nottingham Trent | 24 | 3a | D | 12.8 | 73.0 |

## Physics and Astronomy (cont.)

| | | TQA | RAE | | A-Levels | Score |
|---|---|---|---|---|---|---|
| 35 | Heriot-Watt | HS | 4 | A | | 70.3 |
| 36 | UMIST | 21 | 4 | A | 22.9 | 70.0 |
| 37 | Northumbria | 23 | 3a | D | | 69.1 |
| 38 | Keele | 22 | 3a | B | 18.1 | 68.2 |
| 39 | Queen Mary | 21 | 5 | B | 17.9 | 67.9 |
| 40 | Sheffield Hallam | 24 | 3a | F | 13.8 | 67.0 |
| | | | | | | |
| 41 | Newcastle | 42 | Cardiff | | 43 | Hertfordshire |
| 44 | Kent | 45 | Aberystwyth | | 46 | Paisley |
| 47 | Staffordshire | 48 | Central Lancashire | | | |

**TQA (England) 1998–2000**

**Firsts and 2:1s:** 52% (Physics); 52% (Astronomy)

**Employment:** 51% (Physics); 41% (Astronomy)

**Further study:** 38% (Physics); 43% (Astronomy)

**Unemployment:** 6% (Physics); 14% (Astronomy)

## Politics

Sheffield heads a group of four English universities with perfect scores for teaching and research in the first politics ranking. It entered a higher proportion of academics than second-placed Oxford in the 2001 Research Assessment Exercise, and has higher entry standards than Essex or King's College London. St Andrews also squeezes ahead of Essex, thanks to some of the highest entry standards in Britain.

Aberystwyth has the other department rated internationally outstanding for research, as well as the only one in Wales to achieve an Excellent rating for teaching. The leading 11 universities in England were all awarded maximum points for teaching, an achievement matched by De Montfort, the highest-placed new university, which narrowly missed a spot in the top 20.

Entry scores vary enormously, with Oxford and Cambridge students averaging almost three As at A level, while three Cs would win a place at Salford or Bradford, both of which have perfect teaching scores. Strathclyde is the only Scottish university to be rated Excellent for teaching. Queen's, Belfast, outperforms Ulster and secures a place in the top 20.

Politics has been enjoying a boom as a degree subject. The applications for courses beginning in 2002 rose by 15 per cent.

| | | TQA | RAE | | A-Levels | Score |
|---|---|---|---|---|---|---|
| 1 | Sheffield | 24 | 5* | A | 26.9 | 100.0 |
| 2 | Oxford | 24 | 5* | B | 29.6 | 98.7 |
| 3 | King's College London | 24 | 5* | A | 23.1 | 97.6 |
| 4 | St Andrews | | 5 | A | 27.4 | 95.7 |
| 5 | Essex | 24 | 5* | A | 18.5 | 94.6 |
| 6 | York | 24 | 5 | A | 24.7 | 94.5 |
| 7 | Warwick | 24 | 5 | B | 26.9 | 93.3 |

## Politics (cont.)

| | TQA | RAE | | A-Levels | Score |
|---|---|---|---|---|---|
| 8 Manchester | 24 | 5 | B | 25.8 | 92.6 |
| =9 Nottingham | 24 | 4 | A | 26.2 | 91.4 |
| =9 Birmingham | 24 | 5 | B | 24.0 | 91.4 |
| 11 Keele | 24 | 5 | A | 18.5 | 90.5 |
| 12 Salford | 24 | 5 | A | 16.6 | 89.3 |
| 13 Aberystwyth | E | 5* | A | 21.2 | 87.8 |
| 14 Bristol | 23 | 5 | A | 27.4 | 87.6 |
| =15 Bradford | 24 | 5 | B | 16.4 | 86.5 |
| =15 Southampton | 24 | 4 | B | 22.0 | 86.5 |
| 17 Cambridge | 23 | 4 | A | 29.6 | 85.0 |
| 18 East Anglia | 24 | 4 | B | 19.4 | 84.9 |
| =19 Queen's, Belfast | 23 | 5 | A | 22.2 | 84.3 |
| =19 Hull | 23 | 5 | A | 22.2 | 84.3 |
| 21 Newcastle | 23 | 5 | B | 24.3 | 83.0 |
| 22 De Montfort | 24 | 5 | B | 10.6 | 82.8 |
| 23 Exeter | 23 | 5 | B | 23.4 | 82.4 |
| 24 Sussex | 23 | 4 | A | 23.5 | 81.1 |
| =25 Loughborough | 23 | 5 | B | 19.7 | 80.0 |
| =25 Leeds | 23 | 4 | B | 25.3 | 80.0 |
| 27 London School of Economics | 22 | 5 | A | 28.7 | 79.9 |
| 28 Liverpool | 23 | 4 | A | 21.6 | 79.8 |
| 29 Strathclyde | E | 5 | B | 17.2 | 78.4 |
| =30 Lancaster | 23 | 4 | B | 22.4 | 78.1 |
| =30 Queen Mary | 23 | 4 | A | 18.9 | 78.1 |
| 32 Brunel | 23 | 4 | B | 17.2 | 74.8 |
| 33 Leicester | 23 | 3a | B | 20.2 | 73.1 |
| 34 Kingston | 23 | 4 | A | 10.6 | 72.7 |
| 35 Reading | 22 | 5 | B | 21.1 | 72.3 |
| 36 Portsmouth | 23 | 5 | C | 13.2 | 71.5 |
| =37 Bath | 24 | | | 24.7 | 70.5 |
| =37 Royal Holloway | | 4 | B | 17.6 | 70.4 |
| 39 Glasgow | HS | 5 | B | 23.9 | 69.8 |
| 40 SOAS | 22 | 4 | B | 22.2 | 69.4 |

| | | |
|---|---|---|
| 41 Durham | 42 Coventry | 43 Nottingham Trent |
| 44 University College London | 45 Edinburgh | =46 Ulster |
| =46 Oxford Brookes | 48 Huddersfield | 49 Aberdeen |
| 50 Westminster | 51 Dundee | 52 Wolverhampton |
| 53 Stirling | 54 Cardiff | 55 Manchester Metropolitan |
| 56 Plymouth | 57 London Guildhall | 58 South Bank |
| =59 Middlesex | =59 Northumbria | 61 Kent |
| 62 Liverpool John Moores | 63 Central England | 64 West of England |
| 65 Goldsmiths College | =66 Staffordshire | =66 Swansea |
| 68 Lincoln | 69 Central Lancashire | 70 North London |
| 71 Greenwich | | |

**TQA (England) 2000–01**
**Firsts and 2:1s:** 54%
**Employment:** 64%
**Further study:** 22%
**Unemployment:** 7%

New Scottish Academic Review: *Stirling*: confidence in the academic standards; the quality of teaching and learning, student progression and learning resources was commendable.

# Psychology

The psychology table shows less change than any of the mainstream subjects. The top six positions remain unchanged, and Newcastle is the only new entrant to the top ten, swapping places with Leicester.

The top three all have maximum scores for both teaching and research, as do Reading and Newcastle, which both entered a lower proportion of academics for the Research Assessment Exercise. Cardiff, Bangor and Glasgow have done the same in the separate Welsh and Scottish systems. Oxford's average entry grades of almost three As at A level carry the day. Entry qualifications for psychology are mixed in with other subjects at Cambridge, while York's average is a full grade behind Oxford.

Another eleven English universities were awarded full marks for teaching in an unusually high-scoring assessment. None of the top 40 achieved less than 22 points out of 24. Of the new universities, only Sheffield Hallam and Hertfordshire feature in the top 30 of 78 places in the table. Sheffield Hallam, Westminster and Central Lancashire all received full marks for teaching quality. The Scottish and Welsh assessments were equally generous, with seven universities rated as Excellent. The latest research grades showed considerable improvement on 1996, with a dozen universities rated internationally outstanding.

Psychology has been among the fastest-growing subjects of the past decade. Most undergraduate programmes are accredited by the British Psychological Society, which ensures that key topics are covered, but the clinical and biological content of courses still varies.

|    |                          | TQA | RAE |   | A-Levels | Score |
|----|--------------------------|-----|-----|---|----------|-------|
| 1  | Oxford                   | 24  | 5*  | A | 29.2     | 100.0 |
| 2  | Cambridge                | 24  | 5*  | A |          | 98.4  |
| 3  | York                     | 24  | 5*  | A | 27.0     | 98.3  |
| 4  | Nottingham               | 24  | 5   | A | 28.0     | 96.1  |
| 5  | Royal Holloway           | 24  | 5   | A | 24.1     | 93.1  |
| 6  | Reading                  | 24  | 5*  | B | 22.9     | 93.0  |
| 7  | Lancaster                | 24  | 5   | A | 22.5     | 92.0  |
| 8  | Newcastle                | 24  | 5*  | C | 25.5     | 91.2  |
| 9  | Bristol                  | 23  | 5*  | A | 27.1     | 90.9  |
| 10 | St Andrews               | E   | 5*  | A | 26.5     | 90.5  |
| 11 | Queen's, Belfast         | 24  | 4   | A | 23.8     | 89.9  |
| 12 | Cardiff                  | E   | 5*  | A | 25.5     | 89.7  |
| 13 | Leicester                | 24  | 4   | B | 24.3     | 88.6  |
| 14 | Loughborough             | 24  | 4   | B | 24.0     | 88.4  |
| 15 | Bath                     |     | 5   | B | 26.1     | 88.0  |
| 16 | Bangor                   | E   | 5*  | A | 20.7     | 86.2  |
| 17 | Durham                   | 23  | 5   | A | 23.4     | 85.1  |
| 18 | Exeter                   | 23  | 5   | B | 25.4     | 84.6  |
| 19 | Birmingham               | 23  | 5*  | C | 23.6     | 82.2  |
| 20 | Leeds                    | 23  | 5   | C | 26.4     | 82.1  |
| 21 | Glasgow                  | E   | 5*  | C | 23.1     | 81.8  |
| 22 | Stirling                 | E   | 5   | A | 18.7     | 81.6  |
| 23 | University College London | 22 | 5*  | B | 27.7     | 81.5  |

## Psychology (cont.)

| | | TQA | RAE | | A-Levels | Score |
|---|---|---|---|---|---|---|
| 24 | Sheffield | 22 | 5 | A | 27.6 | 80.8 |
| 25 | Swansea | E | 4 | A | 21.0 | 80.3 |
| 26 | Sheffield Hallam | 24 | 3b | C | 22.0 | 79.8 |
| 27 | Keele | 23 | 4 | B | 20.9 | 78.6 |
| 28 | Surrey | 22 | 5 | A | 23.7 | 77.9 |
| 29 | Manchester | 22 | 5 | B | 25.8 | 77.5 |
| 30 | Hertfordshire | 23 | 4 | B | 18.1 | 76.5 |
| 31 | Dundee | E | 4 | B | 17.6 | 76.1 |
| 32 | Plymouth | 23 | 5 | C | 17.1 | 75.2 |
| 33 | Hull | 23 | 3a | C | 22.6 | 75.0 |
| 34 | Essex | 22 | 5 | A | 19.6 | 74.8 |
| 35 | Westminster | 24 | 3a | D | 15.4 | 74.6 |
| 36 | Central Lancashire | 24 | 3a | E | 17.7 | 73.9 |
| 37 | Edinburgh | HS | 5 | C | 28.9 | 72.7 |
| 38 | Goldsmiths College | 22 | 4 | A | 20.7 | 72.6 |
| 39 | Oxford Brookes | 23 | 3a | C | 19.3 | 72.5 |
| 40 | Aston | 22 | 5 | C | 23.3 | 72.3 |

| | | | | | | |
|---|---|---|---|---|---|---|
| 41 | Kent | 42 | Brunel | 43 | Sussex | |
| 44 | Southampton | 45 | Warwick | 46 | Portsmouth | |
| 47 | Ulster | 48 | London School of Economics | 49 | Liverpool | |
| 50 | Nottingham Trent | 51 | Staffordshire | 52 | East London | |
| 53 | Strathclyde | 54 | City | 55 | Aberdeen | |
| 56 | Northumbria | 57 | Manchester Metropolitan | 58 | UWIC, Cardiff | |
| 59 | Paisley | 60 | Greenwich | 61 | De Montfort | |
| 62 | Surrey Roehampton | 63 | Abertay Dundee | 64 | London Guildhall | |
| =65 | Glasgow Caledonian | =65 | West of England | 67 | Anglia | |
| 68 | Luton | 69 | Wolverhampton | 70 | Lincoln | |
| 71 | South Bank | 72 | Middlesex | 73 | Coventry | |
| 74 | Derby | 75 | Gloucestershire | 76 | Sunderland | |
| 77 | Leeds Metropolitan | 78 | Huddersfield | 79 | Thames Valley | |
| 80 | Teesside | 81 | Liverpool John Moores | 82 | North London | |

**TQA (England) 1998–2000**

**Firsts and 2:1s:** 58%

**Employment:** 64%

**Further study:** 22%

**Unemployment:** 7%

## Russian and East European Languages

Sheffield extends its lead at the top of the ranking for Russian and East European languages, as the only university in Britain with maximum points for teaching quality and one of three with 5* research grades. Cambridge and UCL have neither, but consistent scoring keeps them in a tie for second place.

Oxford and Bristol are the other universities rated internationally outstanding for research, but neither has sufficiently high teaching scores to challenge the top three. The number of universities in the ranking has dropped since last year, several having given up degrees recently. Most of the remaining institutions in

## Russian and East European Languages (cont.)

the ranking are old universities, but Wolverhampton is 13th with a teaching quality grade bettered by only four universities in England.

Entry grades are surprisingly variable: more than half of the universities declaring separate A-level scores averaged more than three Bs, but others require little more than a C and two Ds.

Only 700 students take Russian at degree level, but fewer than half of the universities assessed in England offered Russian as a single-honours degree. Most of the students were learning the language *ab initio*, and there was a high drop-out rate from some universities, despite an 'excellent rapport' between staff and students. Employment prospects are relatively good, with more than six out of ten graduates in work six months after graduation.

|    |                          | TQA | RAE |   | A-Levels | Score |
|----|--------------------------|-----|-----|---|----------|-------|
| 1  | Sheffield                | 24  | 5*  | A | 26.5     | 100.0 |
| =2 | Cambridge                | 22  | 5   | A | 29.7     | 86.9  |
| =2 | University College London| 23  | 5   | A | 22.7     | 86.9  |
| 4  | Oxford                   | 21  | 5*  | B | 29.3     | 81.9  |
| 5  | Queen Mary               | 23  | 5   | C |          | 80.5  |
| 6  | St Andrews               | 22  | 4   | A | 26.8     | 80.2  |
| 7  | Edinburgh                | 21  | 4   | A | 28.2     | 75.6  |
| 8  | Glasgow                  | 22  | 4   | B |          | 74.3  |
| 9  | Bristol                  | 20  | 5*  | A |          | 73.9  |
| 10 | Strathclyde              | 22  | 3a  | A |          | 71.8  |
| 11 | Heriot-Watt              | 21  | 4   | B | 24.7     | 70.3  |
| 12 | Nottingham               | 19  | 5   | A | 25.1     | 66.0  |
| 13 | Wolverhampton            | 22  | 3a  | A | 14.3     | 65.6  |
| 14 | Exeter                   | 20  | 5   | B |          | 64.9  |
| 15 | Leeds                    | 20  | 4   | B | 24.8     | 64.7  |
| 16 | Northumbria              | 23  | 3b  | E |          | 62.1  |
| 17 | Surrey                   | 18  | 5   | A | 19.9     | 56.0  |
| 18 | Coventry                 | 21  |     |   | 14.3     | 42.8  |
| 19 | Portsmouth               | 18  | 5   | D |          | 38.1  |
| 20 | Bath                     | 19  |     |   | 20.9     | 36.8  |
| 21 | Bradford                 | 18  | 4   | D |          | 35.3  |
| 22 | Liverpool John Moores    | 19  |     |   | 16.2     | 33.0  |
| 23 | Sussex                   | 17  | 4   | D |          | 28.2  |
| 24 | Nottingham Trent         | 17  |     |   | 13.6     | 19.4  |

**TQA (England) 1995–96**
**Firsts and 2:1s:** 64%
**Employment:** 62%
**Further study:** 24%
**Unemployment:** 9%

## Social Policy

The social policy ranking is complicated by the fact that, even in England, universities were assessed for teaching quality under two different systems. But, with an Excellent grade for teaching and one of only two 5* ratings for

## Social Policy (cont.)

research, the LSE remains the leader. Second-placed Kent has equally good teaching and research ratings, but much lower entry standards.

Thirteen universities were considered Excellent at teaching, while Warwick scored the maximum 24 points under the assessment system which was introduced in England in 1995. Sheffield Hallam, which, like London Guildhall, has an Excellent teaching grade, is the only new university in the top 20.

Five more universities are included in the ranking this year, although some of those offering the subject are still missing because they chose to be assessed under sociology. Average entry standards are comparatively low. Although two-thirds of entrants come with A levels or their equivalent, some courses cater very largely for mature students: at the extreme, De Montfort is listed with average grades of less than two E grades.

The proportion of students getting firsts or 2:1s is also low, but still seven out of ten graduates go straight into employment.

|    |                          | TQA | RAE |   | A-Levels | Score |
|----|--------------------------|-----|-----|---|----------|-------|
| 1  | London School of Economics | E | 5* | A | 25.2 | 100.0 |
| 2  | Kent                     | E   | 5*  | A | 16.5 | 93.4 |
| 3  | York                     | E   | 5   | A | 20.5 | 92.4 |
| 4  | Bath                     | E   | 5   | B | 23.7 | 92.3 |
| 5  | Sheffield                | E   | 5   | B |      | 90.9 |
| 6  | Manchester               | E   | 5   | B | 19.3 | 88.9 |
| 7  | Newcastle                | E   | 4   | B | 21.3 | 86.9 |
| =8 | Edinburgh                | E   | 4   | B |      | 86.5 |
| =8 | Glasgow                  | E   | 4   | B |      | 86.5 |
| 10 | Southampton              | 21  | 5   | A | 20.1 | 85.7 |
| 11 | Nottingham               | 21  | 4   | A | 23.5 | 84.3 |
| =12 | Warwick                 | 24  |     |   | 23.6 | 84.1 |
| =12 | Hull                    | E   | 4   | B | 17.5 | 84.1 |
| 14 | Leeds                    | 20  | 5   | A | 23.6 | 81.9 |
| 15 | Royal Holloway           | 21  | 4   | B | 18.4 | 78.3 |
| 16 | Ulster                   | E   | 4   | C | 13.9 | 77.8 |
| 17 | Salford                  | 22  | 3a  | A | 11.2 | 77.4 |
| 18 | Sheffield Hallam         | 22  | 3a  | C | 16.7 | 77.0 |
| 19 | Bristol                  | S   | 5   | A | 22.8 | 74.9 |
| 20 | Loughborough             | 23  |     |   | 19.3 | 74.5 |
| 21 | Queen's, Belfast         | 19  | 5   | A | 21.1 | 73.7 |
| 22 | Cardiff                  | S   | 5   | A | 19.1 | 72.1 |
| 23 | London Guildhall         | E   | 3a  | E |      | 70.3 |
| 24 | Goldsmiths College       | S   | 4   | A | 18.2 | 67.5 |
| 25 | Birmingham               | S   | 4   | C | 20.1 | 63.2 |
| 26 | Bangor                   | S   | 3a  | A | 15.7 | 61.6 |
| 27 | Swansea                  | S   | 3a  | B | 17.7 | 61.4 |
| =28 | Nottingham Trent        | S   | 3a  | B |      | 58.0 |
| =28 | Middlesex               | 19  | 4   | C |      | 58.0 |
| 30 | Portsmouth               | S   | 3a  | B | 11.6 | 56.7 |
| 31 | Bradford                 |     | 4   | D | 14.0 | 55.5 |
| 32 | Coventry                 | 21  |     |   | 9.8  | 54.5 |
| =33 | Luton                   | S   | 3a  | C |      | 54.4 |
| =33 | North London            | S   | 3a  | C |      | 54.4 |

## Social Policy (cont.)

|   | | TQA | RAE | | A-Levels | Score |
|---|---|-----|-----|---|----------|-------|
| 35 | Plymouth | S | 4 | D | | 52.9 |
| 36 | Brighton | S | 3b | C | 13.3 | 52.4 |
| 37 | Westminster | 18 | 3a | B | | 50.0 |
| 38 | Lincoln | S | 3a | D | 10.6 | 49.9 |
| 39 | Central Lancashire | S | 3a | D | 8.8 | 48.5 |
| 40 | East London | S | 3b | D | | 47.8 |
| 41 | Wolverhampton | | 42  De Montfort | | | |

**TQA (England) 1994–95**

**Firsts and 2:1s:** 49%

**Employment:** 69%

**Further study:** 16%

**Unemployment:** 9%

New Scottish Academic Review: *Stirling*: confidence in the academic standards; the quality of teaching and learning, student progression and learning resources was commendable.

## Social Work

Lancaster and York remain tied for first place in applied social work, but East Anglia slips to third after entering fewer academics in the latest Research Assessment Exercise. Bristol was the only university rated internationally outstanding for research, but it entered fewer still. Like many of the universities in the table, neither of the leaders has separately listed A-level grades. Both were among the 14 universities rated Excellent at teaching.

Almost half of the 52 universities offering social work are former polytechnics. Only Anglia, Huddersfield and Robert Gordon make it to the top 20. Anglia and Huddersfield are the sole members of the group with Excellent teaching grades.

Entry standards are low in most of the universities registering separate grades for the subject, although some offer only postgraduate courses. Bath had the highest average in 2000, with almost two Bs and a C at A level, but only 14 per cent of entrants in the UK had grades better than the average for all subjects.

Social work is unusual for having more students taking certificate or diploma courses than degrees. Almost two-thirds of all students were selected on qualities or qualifications other than A level. The vocational nature of the subject helps produce the highest proportion in all the social sciences of graduates going straight into employment.

|   | | TQA | RAE | | A-Levels | Score |
|---|---|-----|-----|---|----------|-------|
| =1 | Lancaster | E | 5 | A | | 100.0 |
| =1 | York | E | 5 | A | | 100.0 |
| =3 | East Anglia | E | 5 | B | | 97.1 |
| =3 | Keele | E | 5 | B | | 97.1 |
| =3 | Sheffield | E | 5 | B | | 97.1 |
| 6 | Bristol | E | 5* | C | 21.2 | 96.1 |
| 7 | Durham | E | 4 | A | | 95.5 |
| =8 | Edinburgh | E | 4 | B | | 93.1 |
| =8 | Oxford | E | 4 | B | | 93.1 |

## Social Work (cont.)

| | | TQA | RAE | | A Levels | Score |
|---|---|---|---|---|---|---|
| =8 | Queen's, Belfast | E | 4 | B | | 93.1 |
| 11 | Salford | 22 | 3a | A | | 91.1 |
| =12 | Hull | E | 3a | B | | 89.2 |
| =12 | Southampton | E | 3a | B | | 89.2 |
| 14 | Huddersfield | E | 5 | C | 9.1 | 85.2 |
| 15 | Stirling | HS | 5 | B | | 85.0 |
| 16 | Anglia | E | 3a | D | | 82.3 |
| 17 | Dundee | HS | 4 | B | | 81.0 |
| 18 | Robert Gordon | HS | 3a | A | | 79.0 |
| 19 | Bath | S | 5 | B | 21.7 | 78.4 |
| =20 | Cardiff | S | 5 | A | | 75.8 |
| =20 | Swansea | S | 5 | A | | 75.8 |
| 22 | Manchester | S | 5 | B | | 72.9 |
| 23 | Sussex | S | 4 | A | | 71.4 |
| =24 | Liverpool | S | 4 | B | | 69.0 |
| =24 | Royal Holloway | S | 4 | B | | 69.0 |
| =24 | South Bank | S | 4 | B | | 69.0 |
| 27 | Bangor | S | 3a | A | | 66.9 |
| 28 | Northumbria | S | 3a | B | 13.0 | 66.0 |
| 29 | Bradford | S | 4 | D | 17.9 | 65.7 |
| 30 | Nottingham Trent | S | 3a | B | | 65.0 |
| =31 | Birmingham | S | 4 | C | | 64.9 |
| =31 | Kent | S | 4 | C | | 64.9 |
| =31 | Middlesex | S | 4 | C | | 64.9 |
| 34 | Ulster | S | 3b | D | 20.9 | 64.1 |
| 35 | Plymouth | S | 4 | D | 13.8 | 62.9 |
| 36 | Sunderland | S | 3a | B | 8.1 | 62.6 |
| 37 | Nottingham | S | 3b | A | | 62.4 |
| 38 | Luton | S | 3a | C | | 61.8 |
| 39 | Exeter | S | 4 | D | | 60.4 |
| 40 | Liverpool John Moores | S | 3b | C | 12.0 | 60.2 |

| | | | |
|---|---|---|---|
| 41 Staffordshire | 42 Brunel | 43 De Montfort | |
| 44 Coventry | =45 East London | =45 Reading | |
| 47 Central Lancashire | 48 Oxford Brookes | 49 Manchester Metropolitan | |
| 50 Leeds Metropolitan | 51 Hertfordshire | 52 UWCN, Newport | |

**TQA (England) 1995**
**Firsts and 2:1s:** 49%
**Employment:** 83%
**Further study:** 7%
**Unemployment:** 7%

New Scottish Academic Review: *Stirling*: confidence in the academic standards; the quality of teaching and learning, student progression and learning resources was commendable.

## Sociology

Warwick tops the sociology table as one of the three universities scoring a maximum 24 points for teaching quality, although four others have higher entry standards and seven are rated more highly for research. The university's all-round quality edges out Cambridge, which had the best-qualified entrants, and Sussex, one of the other top-scorers for teaching quality.

## Sociology (cont.)

Edinburgh – like Aberdeen, Glasgow and Stirling, rated Excellent for teaching in Scotland – takes fourth place. Birmingham was the other English university to be awarded maximum points for teaching, but a low research grade keeps it out of the top ten. The West of England is the top-rated new university, with one of the best teaching quality assessments.

Still the biggest of the social sciences, despite a popular image stuck in the 1960s and a high rate of unemployment among graduates, sociology has more than 17,000 undergraduates. There was a slight decline in demand for courses beginning in 2002, but still more than 20,000 applications came in.

Other subjects such as criminology, urban studies, women's studies and some communication studies were also covered in the teaching assessment, which included a large number of institutions where sociology is taught as part of a combined studies or modular programme.

| | | TQA | RAE | | A-Levels | Score |
|---|---|---|---|---|---|---|
| 1 | Warwick | 24 | 5 | A | 25.4 | 100.0 |
| 2 | Cambridge | 23 | 5 | A | 29.6 | 98.2 |
| 3 | Sussex | 24 | 4 | A | 25.7 | 96.5 |
| 4 | Edinburgh | E | 5 | A | 26.6 | 95.8 |
| 5 | Loughborough | 23 | 5* | A | 21.7 | 95.7 |
| 6 | Aberdeen | E | 5 | A | | 93.2 |
| 7 | York | 23 | 5 | A | 22.4 | 92.5 |
| 8 | Sheffield | E | 5 | B | 22.8 | 90.4 |
| 9 | Glasgow | E | 4 | A | 23.7 | 89.7 |
| 10 | Stirling | E | 5 | B | 20.7 | 88.7 |
| 11 | Essex | 22 | 5* | A | 18.7 | 88.2 |
| 12 | Brunel | 22 | 5 | A | 22.3 | 87.3 |
| 13 | Manchester | 21 | 5* | A | 21.7 | 85.4 |
| 14 | Birmingham | 24 | 3a | C | 21.5 | 85.1 |
| 15 | Surrey | 21 | 5* | A | 18.6 | 83.0 |
| =16 | Keele | 22 | 5 | B | 19.9 | 82.9 |
| =16 | Kent | 21 | 5* | A | 18.5 | 82.9 |
| 18 | Lancaster | 21 | 5* | B | 21.5 | 82.4 |
| 19 | West of England | 23 | 3a | B | | 81.7 |
| =20 | Bristol | 21 | 5 | B | 24.5 | 81.4 |
| =20 | Aston | | 5 | B | 20.6 | 81.4 |
| 22 | Goldsmiths College | 21 | 5* | A | 16.0 | 80.9 |
| 23 | London School of Economics | 20 | 5 | A | 27.0 | 80.7 |
| 24 | Nottingham | 21 | 4 | A | 24.8 | 80.3 |
| 25 | Leeds | 20 | 5 | A | 25.2 | 79.3 |
| 26 | Southampton | 21 | 5 | A | 18.5 | 79.1 |
| 27 | Durham | 21 | 4 | A | 22.0 | 78.1 |
| 28 | Exeter | 21 | 5 | B | 20.2 | 78.0 |
| 29 | Reading | 22 | 3a | B | 21.5 | 77.5 |
| 30 | Oxford Brookes | 21 | 4 | A | 19.5 | 76.2 |
| 31 | Cardiff | S | 5 | A | 20.5 | 75.5 |
| 32 | Newcastle | | 4 | B | 20.7 | 74.8 |
| 33 | Greenwich | 23 | 3a | B | 10.9 | 74.3 |
| 34 | Royal Holloway | 21 | 4 | B | 18.9 | 73.6 |
| 35 | Liverpool | 21 | 4 | B | 18.7 | 73.5 |

## Sociology (cont.)

| | | TQA | | RAE | A-Levels | Score |
|---|---|---|---|---|---|---|
| 36 | Strathclyde | HS | 3a | B | | 72.1 |
| 37 | Queen's, Belfast | 19 | 5 | A | 21.1 | 70.9 |
| 38 | Kingston | 21 | 4 | A | 12.5 | 70.5 |
| 39 | Bath | 19 | 5 | B | 22.6 | 69.7 |
| =40 | Glasgow Caledonian | HS | 3a | C | | 68.7 |
| =40 | Paisley | HS | 3a | C | | 68.7 |

| | | | | | |
|---|---|---|---|---|---|
| 42 Salford | 43 Hull | 44 City |
| 45 Leicester | 46 Sunderland | 47 Northumbria |
| 48 Bangor | 49 Manchester Metropolitan | 50 Portsmouth |
| 51 Plymouth | 52 Sheffield Hallam | 53 Nottingham Trent |
| 54 East London | 55 South Bank | 56 Surrey Roehampton |
| 57 Middlesex | 58 Anglia | 59 Coventry |
| 60 Teesside | 61 Swansea | 62 Huddersfield |
| 63 Westminster | 64 Gloucestershire | 65 Wolverhampton |
| 66 Brighton | 67 Central Lancashire | 68 North London |
| 69 Bradford | 70 Derby | 71 Ulster |
| 72 Liverpool John Moores | 73 Staffordshire | 74 Central England |
| 75 Luton | 76 London Guildhall | 77 De Montfort |
| 78 East Anglia | 79 Lincoln | |

**TQA (England) 1995–96**
**Firsts and 2:1s:** 52%
**Employment:** 69%
**Further study:** 18%
**Unemployment:** 8%

## Theology and Religious Studies

Oxford tops the first ranking of theology and religious studies, largely because of the scoring system. It is the only university among the 30 in the table not to have a final score from the teaching assessments recently completed in England. Oxford's 5* research rating and entry grades, bettered only by Cambridge, produce an overall result that condemns Manchester to second place, despite it being the only university with perfect scores for both teaching and research.

Lancaster and Sheffield are the only other English universities to record maximum points for teaching quality, although Stirling and Bangor have top ratings in the Scottish and Welsh systems. Nottingham and Cardiff are the other universities considered internationally outstanding for research. Gloucestershire, which was awarded university status only in 2001, is the best-placed new university, with Derby also reaching the top 20. Both originated from church colleges.

Entry qualifications vary considerably, with students at sixth-placed Sheffield averaging only three Cs at A level, compared with almost three As at Cambridge, two places higher up the table. Three Ds would secure a place studying theology at some of the other universities.

## Theology and Religious Studies (cont.)

| | | TQA | RAE | | A-Levels | Score |
|---|---|---|---|---|---|---|
| 1 | Oxford | | 5* | B | 28.8 | 100.0 |
| 2 | Manchester | 24 | 5* | B | 20.1 | 96.7 |
| 3 | Lancaster | 24 | 5 | A | 20.3 | 96.0 |
| 4 | Cambridge | 23 | 5 | A | 29.3 | 95.2 |
| 5 | Nottingham | 23 | 5* | A | 24.0 | 95.0 |
| 6 | Sheffield | 24 | 5 | A | 17.9 | 94.3 |
| 7 | Exeter | 23 | 5 | A | 22.4 | 90.3 |
| 8 | Durham | 23 | 5 | B | 23.8 | 89.0 |
| 9 | Birmingham | 23 | 5 | B | 22.7 | 88.2 |
| 10 | Leeds | 23 | 4 | A | 21.2 | 85.9 |
| 11 | SOAS | 22 | 5 | B | 25.1 | 82.8 |
| 12 | Newcastle | 22 | 5 | A | 20.3 | 81.5 |
| 13 | Edinburgh | HS | 5 | A | 24.6 | 81.1 |
| =14 | Stirling | E | 5 | C | 17.0 | 80.3 |
| =14 | Bangor | E | 4 | B | 16.1 | 80.3 |
| 16 | St Andrews | HS | 5 | A | 21.6 | 78.9 |
| 17 | Gloucestershire | 23 | 4 | B | 12.2 | 77.4 |
| 18 | Glasgow | HS | 5 | B | | 74.8 |
| 19 | King's College London | 21 | 5 | A | 20.2 | 74.3 |
| 20 | Derby | 22 | 3a | B | | 71.4 |
| 21 | Hull | 23 | 3a | D | 14.7 | 70.7 |
| 22 | Cardiff | S | 5* | A | 19.7 | 70.3 |
| 23 | Aberdeen | HS | 5 | B | 12.0 | 69.7 |
| 24 | Bristol | 20 | 5 | B | 24.1 | 67.6 |
| 25 | Oxford Brookes | 23 | 1 | D | | 66.8 |
| 26 | Surrey Roehampton | 21 | 4 | A | 12.2 | 64.9 |
| 27 | Queen's, Belfast | 22 | | | 22.5 | 62.3 |
| 28 | Lampeter | S | 5 | C | 14.6 | 57.0 |
| 29 | Kent | 20 | 3a | D | 19.9 | 52.8 |
| 30 | Wolverhampton | 21 | | | 11.4 | 47.0 |

**TQA (England) 2000–01**
**Firsts and 2:1s:** 68%
**Employment:** 45%
**Further study:** 43%
**Unemployment:** 7%

New Scottish Academic Review: *Aberdeen, Glasgow*: confidence in the academic standards; the quality of teaching and learning, student progression and learning resources was commendable.

## Town and Country Planning and Landscape

Cambridge takes over from Cardiff at the head of the ranking, largely thanks to the university's normal high entry standards. Cambridge is making its first appearance in the table, having registered an A-level score for the first time in 2000, although it does not have a score for teaching quality.

Second-placed Cardiff is one of two universities rated internationally outstanding for research, the other being Leeds, which misses the top ten because of a low teaching score. Three new universities turned the tables on their older-established peers in the English assessments of teaching quality, with Oxford Brookes,

## Town and Country Planning and Landscape (cont.)

Greenwich and Kingston recording the only perfect scores. Oxford Brookes and the West of England both feature in the top ten.

Little more than a dozen old universities offer degrees in a subject which was once available only at postgraduate level in most institutions. More than 5,000 students now take first degree courses, with almost another 1,000 taking certificate or diploma programmes. The size of departments varies from more than 500 students to less than 150, with about a third of the total postgraduates.

Fewer than half of the students are awarded firsts or 2:1s, but employment prospects are good, with three-quarters of graduates going straight into jobs.

|    |                        | TQA | RAE |   | A-Levels | Score |
|----|------------------------|-----|-----|---|----------|-------|
| 1  | Cambridge              |     | 5   | B | 28.5     | 100.0 |
| 2  | Cardiff                | E   | 5*  | A | 20.4     | 93.1  |
| 3  | Sheffield              | 23  | 5   | A | 21.8     | 90.7  |
| 4  | Nottingham             | 23  | 4   | A |          | 86.0  |
| 5  | Reading                | 22  | 5   | B | 23.1     | 84.5  |
| 6  | Liverpool              | 23  | 4   | A | 16.2     | 82.9  |
| 7  | Oxford Brookes         | 24  | 4   | C | 14.9     | 81.8  |
| 8  | Newcastle              | 21  | 5   | B | 18.5     | 75.9  |
| 9  | Queen's, Belfast       | 22  | 3b  | A | 22.1     | 75.4  |
| 10 | West of England        | 23  | 3a  | B | 11.0     | 73.7  |
| 11 | Kingston               | 24  |     |   | 17.8     | 72.0  |
| 12 | Gloucestershire        | 21  | 4   | A | 12.5     | 69.9  |
| 13 | Leeds                  | 19  | 5*  | A |          | 69.7  |
| 14 | South Bank             | 22  | 4   | D |          | 69.0  |
| 15 | Greenwich              | 24  |     |   | 12.5     | 67.8  |
| 16 | Manchester             | 20  | 4   | B | 18.4     | 67.7  |
| 17 | Nottingham Trent       |     | 3a  | B | 15.7     | 67.3  |
| 18 | Sheffield Hallam       | 22  | 4   | D | 13.4     | 67.0  |
| 19 | Leeds Metropolitan     | 21  | 3a  | B | 14.0     | 66.1  |
| 20 | Aberdeen               | 19  | 5   | B | 16.3     | 64.1  |
| 21 | Dundee                 | 21  | 3b  | D | 14.2     | 59.1  |
| 22 | Salford                | 22  |     |   | 9.3      | 55.3  |
| 23 | Northumbria            | 21  |     |   | 13.7     | 53.7  |
| 24 | Westminster            | 20  | 3a  | D | 9.5      | 52.1  |
| 25 | Strathclyde            | 19  | 3a  | C |          | 51.5  |
| 26 | Liverpool John Moores  | 18  | 3a  | A | 10.6     | 49.9  |
| 27 | Central England        | 20  | 3b  | E | 10.9     | 49.3  |
| 28 | Anglia                 | 19  | 2   | B |          | 46.9  |
| 29 | Heriot-Watt            | 17  | 3a  | B |          | 42.1  |

**TQA (England) 1996–98**
**Firsts and 2:1s:** 49%
**Employment:** 74%
**Further study:** 11%
**Unemployment:** 9%

## Veterinary Medicine

No subject has such high entry standards as veterinary medicine: there are more than 20 candidates for each place. Ironically, the only university with average entry grades of less than two As and a B at A level in 2000 was top-placed Liverpool. An improved research grade secured the leadership for Liverpool, which was also one of three English veterinary schools awarded 24 points for teaching quality.

The ranking is perhaps the closest of any subject. In the 1996 Research Assessment Exercise, for example, all six schools were awarded grade 4; in 2001 they had all moved up to grade 5, having entered similar numbers of academics. Liverpool owes its top place to a slightly larger entry than the Royal Veterinary College and Bristol.

The two Scottish veterinary schools – Glasgow and Edinburgh – were both rated Excellent under the separate Scottish system. Only Cambridge scored less than maximum points for teaching quality, and it had the highest entry standards, with every entrant achieving three As at A level or the equivalent.

Vets' final qualifications are not classified, but between 5 and 15 per cent are awarded a commendation. The five-year courses have to meet the requirements of the Royal College of Veterinary Studies, but they vary in size from 65 to 155 students. Up to 10 per cent drop out, but those who complete the course are in high demand for general practice.

|   |                          | TQA | RAE |   | A-Levels | Score |
|---|--------------------------|-----|-----|---|----------|-------|
| 1 | Liverpool                | 24  | 5   | B | 26.7     | 100.0 |
| 2 | Royal Veterinary College | 24  | 5   | C | 29.2     | 98.7  |
| 3 | Bristol                  | 24  | 5   | C | 28.7     | 97.8  |
| 4 | Cambridge                | 23  | 5   | B | 30.0     | 96.8  |
| 5 | Edinburgh                | E   | 5   | B | 29.3     | 95.7  |
| 6 | Glasgow                  | E   | 5   | B | 29.1     | 95.3  |

**TQA (England) 1999–2000**
**Firsts and 2:1s:** n/a
**Employment:** 77%
**Further study:** 13%
**Unemployment:** 5%

# Applying to University

Once you have made your decisions about what you want to study and where, you can heave a huge sigh of relief because the really hard part is over. The next stage, making an application, is much easier. However, there are still enough issues and decisions to warrant a closer look at the process and how to go about it.

All applications to UK universities for full-time courses are made through UCAS, the Universities and Colleges Admissions Service. While the *Good University Guide* is only concerned with universities, many colleges of one sort or another also recruit through UCAS and so you will find over 300 institutions listed in the *UCAS Directory*. If you are interested in a part-time course you will need to contact universities individually to find out how to apply.

The Application Form, the accompanying guidance *How to Apply*, the *UCAS Directory* (which lists the 50,000 or so courses available) and numerous booklets and leaflets are available from your school, college, local careers service, nearest British Council Office, or direct from UCAS. (The UCAS address is: UCAS, PO Box 130, Cheltenham, GL52 3ZF. This includes a CD-ROM of the *UCAS Directory* but a charge of £6 is made if you want a paper copy of the *Directory*.)

At the time of writing, the detailed procedures for 2003 entry had not been finalised, so do check for any changes from what is given here.

## Filling in the UCAS Form

The UCAS Application Form may only be four pages of A4 paper, or a few screens in the case of the Electronic Application System, but it still looks rather daunting. There is no substitute for reading *How to Apply* and then going slowly and carefully through the form, checking back against *How to Apply* as you go. For most applicants, what you (and your referee) put on the form will be all the university uses to make a decision, so it is important to get it right. A good idea is to take a photocopy of the form and fill that in first as a trial run. Don't forget that the form is scanned at UCAS and reproduced half size for universities, and some of it is read by computer, so write clearly and neatly.

Provided that you follow *How to Apply* carefully, most of the form is straightforward, but on the following pages are a few points about some of the more significant sections.

## Address

This looks simple, and it is, but don't just fill in your current address and then forget about it. If your address changes, make sure you tell UCAS immediately. UCAS will automatically notify your university choices of the change but there is no harm in contacting them directly as well just to make sure. If you don't keep UCAS informed of your change of address you will find letters (which might be offers or a confirmation of a place) go to the wrong place. It is surprisingly common for applicants at a boarding school to put down their school address on the form but then forget to tell UCAS when they go home for the summer. They then find that the letter confirming a place at university goes to the school instead of to them at home.

## Examination Results

Make sure you get the details of your examinations to be taken exactly right. If you are taking English Language and Literature, put the full title and not just English, even if everyone in your school or college calls it English. This is important because any mistakes could mean that UCAS cannot match your application with your examination results straightaway in the summer, resulting in a delay in universities making their decisions. Listing the full module details of a BTEC award or Vocational A level is also important to avoid confusion over precisely what you are studying.

If you are taking the examinations of another country do not try to give a UK equivalent. Always state exactly what you are doing and let the university decide the equivalence so as to avoid any confusion. If the column headings on the form are inappropriate, then ignore them.

And be honest! Never be tempted to massage your results to make them look a little better. UCAS has some sophisticated fraud-busting techniques and admissions tutors are remarkably good at spotting dodgy applications. If you are found to be giving false or incomplete information, you will be promptly ejected from UCAS and lose any chance of a place at university that year. Even if you manage to slip through all the detection devices, you will probably be asked by the university to present your certificates. Any sign of tampering, or lame excuses about them having been eaten by the dog, will result in a check with the records of the examining board. When the board points out that the ABB on your form was really DDD, you will politely be shown the door.

## Personal Statement

This is your chance to say anything you like, in your own words, to persuade admissions tutors that yours is the brightest and best application ever to have crossed their desk. You can write what you like, but the key things probably include:

• why you want to study your chosen subject
• what particular qualities and experience you can bring to it

- details of any work experience or voluntary activity, especially if it is relevant to your course
- any other evidence of achievement, such as the Duke of Edinburgh award
- details of any sponsorship or placements you have secured or applied for
- your career aspirations
- any wider aspects of life that make you an interesting and well-rounded student
- if your first language is not English, describe any opportunities you have had to use English (such as an English-speaking school or work with a company that uses English)

If there is anything about your application that is even slightly unusual, then explain why. If you want to defer your entry to the following year, say why and what you intend to do with your year out. If you have listed more than one subject among your choices this can suggest a lack of commitment, so explain why. If you are a mature student, explain why you want to enter higher education.

As with examinations, be honest. If you say you are interested in philosophy and then get called for interview, you can almost guarantee that some learned professor will ask you about Plato's Theory of Forms or Spinoza's ethics. If you can't talk sensibly about philosophy, you will look rather silly and will be unlikely to get an offer.

There is no ideal way to structure your statement, but it is a good idea to use paragraphs or sub-headings to make the presentation clear and easy for an admissions tutor to read. If you want to say more than there is space available, do not write outside the box or send additional papers to UCAS; they will not automatically be passed on to your chosen universities. If you really can't make it fit, then send any additional material directly to the universities to which you have applied but wait until you have received your application number from UCAS, so that you can include this with your papers and make sure they are matched with the correct application form. And, once again, remember that the form will be reduced at UCAS, so write clearly.

| Timetable | |
|---|---|
| May – Sept | Research and make choices about universities and courses |
| 1 Sept – 15 Oct | Apply for Cambridge or Oxford or Medicine, Dentistry or Veterinary Science/Medicine in any university |
| 1 Sept – 15 Jan | All other applications from the UK (except Art and Design Route B) |
| 1 Sept – 30 June | All other applications from outside the UK (except Art and Design Route B) |
| 1 Jan – 24 March | Art and Design Route B |
| 16 Dec – 30 June | Late applications from the UK considered at universities' discretion |
| 17 Mar – 30 June | UCAS Extra |
| 1 July onwards | Applications go straight into the Clearing procedure |

## Choice of Courses

By the time you fill in your form, you should have your choice of courses ready. You are allowed six, but you don't have to use them all. (Indeed if you only use one choice there is a lower application fee.) If you want to apply for Medicine, Dentistry or Veterinary Science/Medicine, you are only allowed to use four choices for these courses, though you can use the other two for different subjects if you wish. Make sure you get the university and course codes exactly right. If they don't match up, your application will be delayed while UCAS sorts out what you ought to have put down.

From 2003 each university will only see details of its own application and so they will not know where else you have applied or whether all the courses on the form are the same.

---

**Should I Apply Early?**

Universities are required by UCAS rules to treat all applications received by the appropriate deadline on an equal basis. This means that applying early or late should make no difference, as long as the deadline is met, and in practice this is the case for virtually all applicants. Indeed if you are applying for a low-demand subject you will probably get equal treatment even if your application arrives well after the deadline.

It can be a good idea to avoid submitting an application close to the main deadline as there is a peak in the number of application forms arriving at UCAS then. This will not affect your chances of an offer, but it does create something of a backlog at UCAS and so you may have to wait rather longer before you receive any decisions.

Occasionally, in very high-demand subjects such as Medicine, English or Law, a very popular university may experience a sudden increase in applications which only becomes apparent after it has started making decisions. It will then be faced with a choice of either carrying on making offers in the same way and ending up with an intake way above target, or tightening up its criteria and admitting the right number. Neither of these outcomes is desirable: too many students means large classes and over-worked staff; tightening the criteria means being slightly tougher with some applicants. The university may choose the latter course, in which case a few of the later applicants might be rejected whereas, if they had applied earlier, before the increased number of applications was apparent, they might have received an offer. This situation is very rare, but the conclusion is that applying early never does any harm while applying later to high-demand subjects very occasionally might.

---

In all sections of the form, make sure the grammar and punctuation are correct. It is a good idea to show the form to someone else as a final check. When you have finally finished, take a copy and pass the form on to your referee (usually someone from your school or college) with the appropriate fee (£15 for entry in 2003, or £5 if you are only applying for one). Don't forget to sign the form as UCAS will not process it until they have a signature.

All being well, your referee will fill in the section for the reference and send the form off to UCAS at the appropriate time.

The form can arrive at UCAS any time between 1 September and 15 January (or 15 October if Oxford or Cambridge or any medical, dental or veterinary course is among your choices – see the *Timetable* box for this and other exceptions). In some circumstances there can be a small advantage in applying early (see box, *Should I Apply Early?*) but generally it will not make any difference. If you apply after the appropriate deadline your form will still be processed by UCAS but universities do not have to consider it. They can, if they wish, reject you on the grounds that they have received enough applications already. However, if you are applying for one of the less competitive courses or are applying from overseas you will probably find your application is treated just like those that arrived on time.

## What Happens Next?

The first thing to happen after you have submitted your application to UCAS is the arrival of a confirmation of the courses and universities you have chosen and your application number. It is important to check this carefully to make sure there is no mistake and keep your application number safe as you will probably need it later. Then there is nothing to do but wait. Universities are increasingly aware that applicants don't like to be kept hanging around so you may find some decisions arriving fairly soon. However, if your form arrived at UCAS close to the main deadline it can take several weeks to make its way through UCAS processing and on to your universities. When any decisions do arrive, they will be one of the following:

| | |
|---|---|
| Unconditional Offer (U) | This means you have already met all the entry requirements for the course |
| Conditional Offer (C) | This means the University will accept you if you meet certain additional requirements, usually specified grades in the examinations you will be taking |
| Rejection (R) | This means that either you have not got, and are unlikely to get, some key requirement for the course, or that you have lost out in competition with other, better applicants |

If you receive an offer, you will almost certainly be invited to visit the university concerned. This is a good chance to find out much more about the course and university than you can through reading prospectuses and looking at websites. However, bear in mind that the occasion is designed to encourage you to accept the offer as well as to give you the opportunity to find out more. So, just like reading prospectuses, you have to be critical of what you are told and look for evidence for any claims.

Sometimes you may be invited for an interview before a decision is made. This could be the normal practice for that particular course, or it could be because your application is unusual in some way and the university wants to check that you are really suitable (perhaps you are a mature student without the usual formal qualifications). In some cases interviews are not quite what they seem (see box, *When is an Interview not an Interview?*), but you can never be sure, so it is best to treat any interview as a real interview.

If you do get called for interview, then go – you are unlikely to be made an offer if you don't turn up – and be sure that you arrive on time. Prepare yourself in advance, particularly for the obvious questions such as why you want to study the subject and why you want to go to that university. Re-read the copy of your application form to remind yourself what is in your personal statement. And dress smartly. While it is not necessary to look as if you are going to a wedding, an interview is not the time to make a fashion statement.

All being well, particularly if you have chosen your universities carefully, you will get several offers. You can hold on to any offer you receive until all your chosen universities have made their decisions, but then you have to choose which ones you want to accept.

---

#### When is an Interview not an Interview?

Interviews come in two forms. Outwardly both look the same, but in fact they have very different purposes. The first type of interview is the 'real' interview, where a genuine attempt is being made to assess your suitability for the course and your performance in the interview will make a difference to your chances of being made an offer. The second type of interview is the 'psychological' interview. It looks like an interview, feels like an interview, but actually doesn't make any difference. The university has already decided to make you an offer and the interview is merely a psychologically clever way of encouraging you to accept the offer. If you travel half way across the country, answer some tough questions and then get made an offer of a place, it makes you feel good, both about yourself and about the university. Hence you are more likely to accept that offer in favour of one which just arrived in the post. At least that is the idea behind the psychological interview.

The problem for you is that it is hard to tell which type of interview you are facing. Generally speaking, interviews for medical and medically related professions and for education are real (though it is still common for 80 per cent or more of interviewees to be made an offer). Interviews at very competitive universities such as Oxford and Cambridge are also usually real, and interviews for applicants who have an unusual background or lack the usual qualifications are generally genuine attempts to assess suitability. However, interviews for less popular courses, such as chemistry or engineering, at anywhere other than the most competitive universities for these subjects are often the psychological type of interview.

---

### Replies to Offers

You can accept one offer as your firm acceptance (often called your UF choice if the offer was unconditional or your CF choice if it was conditional). If your firm acceptance is CF, then you can accept a second offer as your insurance acceptance (often called your CI choice), but you must decline any others. Most applicants who have more than one conditional offer will accept as CF their first choice university and then a university which has made a lower offer as their CI choice.

You can, in fact, decline all your offers if you wish. Perhaps you have realised that you have made a dreadful mistake in your choice of subject and now wish to look for another subject in UCAS Extra or the Clearing procedure (see below). However, normally you will want to accept one offer as your firm acceptance.

Once you have done that, you and the university are bound together by the rules of UCAS. If you firmly accept an unconditional offer then you have a definite place at that university. If you firmly accept a conditional offer and then meet all the conditions, the university is obliged to accept you and you are obliged to go there. In making your firm acceptance, assuming you have conditional offers, you will have to balance your desire to attend a particular university against your estimate of whether you can meet the conditions. If you expect to get ABB at A level and the offers are all BCC or below, then it is easy: choose the place you want to go. If, however, you think you will get BCC and your offers are ABB, BBB, BCC and CDD, the decision is more difficult, especially if you really want to go to the university that offered ABB.

This is where the insurance acceptance comes in. If you want to, you can just have a firm acceptance and decline the rest. However, most applicants with more than one offer choose an insurance acceptance as well. If you are accepted by your firm choice then that is it, and the insurance choice becomes irrelevant. However, if your firm choice turns you down because you don't meet their conditions, you might still be accepted by your insurance choice, so you get a second chance before heading for Clearing. Obviously, it makes sense to choose a lower offer for your insurance choice so as to maximise your chances of getting at least one of your two choices. However, make sure it is somewhere you would still like to go because if that is where you are placed, the UCAS rules require you to go there. Remember that in some subjects such as chemistry or electronic engineering, places in Clearing, even at prestigious universities, are easy to obtain, so you could be better off choosing just a firm choice rather than two choices, one of which you don't really want. In fact, holding an insurance offer just for the sake of it would delay your entry into Clearing. If all this sounds rather complicated, the flowchart *Firm and Insurance Offers on Results Day* may help.

Finally, make sure you do reply to your offers. If you don't, and ignore the reminders UCAS will send you, you will be 'declined by default' and lose your offers.

## UCAS Extra

If you are unlucky enough not to receive any offers from any of your six choices, or you have a change of heart and decide to decline any offers you do have, a new feature of the UCAS scheme for 2003 comes into play. This is UCAS Extra and, in effect, it allows you to make a seventh choice of university. If you become eligible for UCAS Extra, UCAS will send you all the details you need and courses at universities willing to consider UCAS Extra applications will be available on the UCAS website. You can then either use the UCAS website to make an application or contact a university directly. If you are made an offer, either unconditional or conditional, you can firmly accept or decline it just like any offer in the main UCAS scheme. If you don't get an offer (or decide to decline your offer), you can opt to make another UCAS Extra choice and so on, until either you get an offer or you run out of time (the scheme ends in July).

Once you have an offer and accept it, you become unconditional firm (UF) or conditional firm (CF) for that university (there is only one choice at any time in

UCAS Extra so there is no question of an insurance choice). You are committed to it in exactly the same way as the main UCAS scheme.

### Results Day

If you accepted an unconditional offer, all you have to do is wait for the start of your course and roll up to register. However, most of you will be anxiously waiting for examination results before you find out whether you have been accepted. If you are taking Scottish Highers, an access course or a BTEC qualification, then your results will usually come out before A levels in England. This can be helpful if you don't get accepted as you will then have a chance to find a place somewhere else before the scramble for places after A-level results are published.

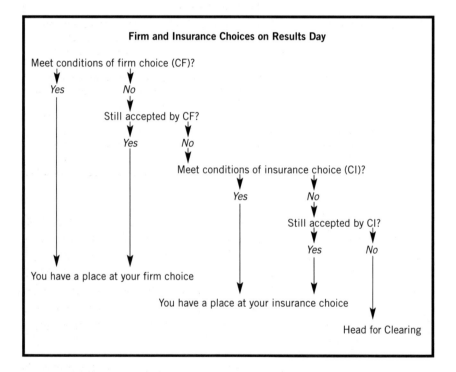

**Firm and Insurance Choices on Results Day**

If you find that your results mean you have met all the conditions of your firm choice, congratulations! You have a place at your chosen university and you can relax, at least for now. Do check carefully though, especially if you have an offer expressed in terms of points rather than grades. UCAS has introduced a new points system, the UCAS tariff, covering Vocational A levels and Scottish qualifications as well as A levels, for entry in 2002 (see page 42). It is not yet clear how many universities will use the new tariff for making offers, but the details of any offer will be clearly explained in your UCAS offer letter.

If you are sure you have met all the conditions, you don't have to do anything. In a day or two you will receive confirmation of your place from UCAS, with a form to sign to confirm that you still want it, and details of when and where to register from your chosen university will follow a little while later. If you are not sure, or just need reassurance, you can ring the university to check, though bear in mind that several thousand others will be doing the same thing, so it may take a little while to get through. If you do ring, make sure you have your UCAS number handy.

Even if you have not met all the conditions, you may still find your place is confirmed. The university may be short of applicants that year or the other offer-holders had worse results than you (see box, *What if I Just Miss my Grades?*). If you are just one grade down, your chances will often be quite good; more than that and your chances will be much less.

---

**What if I Just Miss My Grades?**

Suppose you are offered BBC at A level and get BCC: will you still be accepted? This will depend on two main factors. First, did you drop a grade in a critical subject? If you were asked for a B in, say, chemistry and that was the subject where you got a C, that will reduce the chances of your being accepted. Second, what did everyone else with an offer for the course get? If the university has 50 places and 40 get the grades, they will look first for the extra 10 among those who just missed the offer and you will probably be accepted. However, if 60 get the grades, they will probably reject anyone who didn't meet the offer precisely, and you may well not be accepted. There is nothing you can do about this. Universities are financially penalised for admitting the wrong number of students, so they will always want to admit as near as possible to their target number.

---

## Clearing

If you find that you don't have a place then you will be eligible for the UCAS Clearing scheme, a way of matching universities without students to students without universities. Essentially, it is up to you to find a university that is prepared to accept you. The best way to do this is to ring a university and tell them what you want to do. Usually, if they have vacancies, they will take your details and either give you a decision straightaway or very soon afterwards. Just keep going until somewhere offers you a place. Here are some points to remember if you end up in this position:

- prepare in advance – unless you are very confident you will get the grades, do some contingency planning before results day. Make a list of possible courses and universities where you might be prepared to go in priority order. This will be easy to check against the Clearing vacancy lists when they are published
- be there – don't go on holiday at the critical time
- if you think you may not have a place, check with your firm and insurance choices as soon as possible
- check the Clearing vacancy lists in newspapers, the UCAS website, or the websites of individual universities to find where there are vacancies in your subject
- think about alternative courses (perhaps a joint course with another subject instead of a single subject course) to maximise the choice available

- start ringing possible universities straight away (places at good universities can be filled very quickly)
- always ring yourself – universities are less impressed by people ringing on your behalf
- if you can't get through, keep trying, but also send an e-mail or fax

There will be a few vacancies not listed in the official vacancy lists because the universities know they can fill them with speculative callers and do not need the extra calls generated by the vacancy lists. If there is somewhere you really want to go, it might just be worth ringing even if they are not in the lists. However, such vacancies will be taken within hours, at most within a day of A-level results being published.

Some applicants find that their results are much better than they expected and they are qualified for a much better university than the one where they accepted an offer, or for a high-demand course such as medicine for which they never thought they would be accepted. If you find yourself in this position, you can do one of three things:

1 Carry on with your existing choice, as long as you are sure that is what you want to do now.
2 Find an alternative university which is prepared to accept you and then negotiate with the university where you have been placed to be released into the Clearing scheme. The university is not obliged to do this, and will probably try to persuade you not to, but most will eventually give way if it is clear that you have genuinely thought through what you are doing. Once in the Clearing scheme your alternative university can accept you.
3 Withdraw completely from UCAS and apply again the following year.

If your results are much worse than you expected, the situation can be more difficult. If there were genuine extenuating circumstances (perhaps you were taken ill during your examinations or there was a bereavement in your family) your school should have told the examining board and university about this already. Neither will be impressed by being told about it after your low grades have been published. If the results are just plain surprising, you may wish to seek a re-mark by the examining board. If this brings to light an error, and your grades go up, the university will review its decision, though if you miss the deadline the university may say it can only accept you for the following year.

Trying to get a place in Clearing is not as difficult as it sounds. There is always a lot of talk about 'chaos' and 'scrambling', but in fact universities are getting much better at dealing with large numbers of enquiries very quickly. After all, they have a strong interest in signing up good students as they suffer severe financial penalties if they under-recruit by a large margin. And the range of courses available in Clearing is huge. In 2001, for example, there were a number of vacancies on courses in law and English, two very high-demand subjects. They may not have been precisely the right course or in an ideal part of the country, but they were there and anyone with the right grades who acted quickly could have obtained a place. If you wanted chemistry or engineering you could have had a choice of a number of prestigious universities, even with quite low grades in some cases.

Having said that, trying to find a place in Clearing is not much fun for anyone. The best way to avoid it is to be sensible and realistic early on in the application process. If you apply for courses and universities where you have a good chance of being made an offer and accept offers you have a good chance of achieving, then you will probably be able to avoid Clearing altogether. That is much better for both you and the universities.

## Do I Apply This Year?

Some students take a year out between finishing at school or college and starting university, often known as a gap year. About 8 per cent of the applicants are accepted for deferred entry to the following year. If you are thinking about doing this it is still best to apply during your final year at school or college as a 'deferred applicant'. When you fill in your UCAS form, you should put a D in the 'defer entry' column in section 3 of the UCAS form. This should mean that you get your university place sorted out before starting your job or travels and so don't have to worry about it during your gap year. Indeed, for the more adventurous travellers, trying to fill in a UCAS form on the back of a Mongolian yak or half way across the Australian desert is not recommended. Also, if things go badly wrong in your examinations and you don't get a place, you do get an opportunity to rethink your career options or resit your exams and still start at university when you planned to.

In general, gap years are a good thing. You get a chance to do something useful or interesting, such as work or travel, and maybe save up some money to finance your course. And you will arrive at university a little bit older and wiser. In a few subjects, it may take you a little while to get back into serious study – mathematics is notorious for being a bit harder to take up again after a year away from study – but most students soon catch up again.

In general, universities are happy to consider deferred applicants but, if the prospectus does not make a clear statement about the university's policy, it would be sensible to check.

# Paying Your Way

The head of one university tells the story of a photographer at Graduation asking the student to place a hand on her parent's shoulder, only to hear the riposte from the parent, "Wouldn't it be more appropriate to have a hand in my pocket!" It is an apocryphal tale but one which will ring true for many parents, given the financial support required of them. Going to university these days can be an expensive family business and student debt, a bit like a house mortgage, has become an accepted fact of life. Indeed, it is not uncommon for students to graduate with a debt of £2,500 or more, over and above their maximum student loan. You will need to muster all the resources you can lay your hands on unless you are one of that small band who has a regular private income. The vast majority of students have to rely on loans, savings, earnings, overdrafts and the generosity of family and friends. But all of that is in the distant future.

## Parental Contributions

Parental contribution towards university tuition fees and a student's living cost is means-tested and is based on their so-called Residual Income. This is their gross income from all sources less certain defined allowances. Currently, below a Residual Income of £20,480 no parental contribution is expected. Above this figure, there is a sliding scale of contribution until at £30,502 your parents would be expected to pay the full tuition fee of £1,100. At higher income levels, your parents would also be expected to contribute towards part of your day-to-day living costs. If your parents no longer live together, then only the income of the one with whom you live will normally be assessed. On any remarriage without adoption, the income of a step-parent is not considered when working out your financial support.

## Mature Students

If, however, you have supported yourself for at least three years prior to becoming a student, your parents will not be expected to contribute to either tuition fees or living costs. In addition, bursaries may be available to students with adult dependants, for student parents for childcare, and for students who are single parents. Such mature students will be used to managing their finances, but for others reading this we begin with a breakdown of expected expenditure and income.

## Expenditure

*Tuition fees*

Since 1998, full-time undergraduates whose homes are in the UK or in other EU and EEA countries have been liable to pay means-tested fees direct to the university (frequently by instalment), subject to the maximum shown in the table:

| Year | £ Sterling | |
|------|-----------|------|
| 1999–2000 | £1,025 | (£510)* |
| 2000–2001 | £1,050 | (£520) |
| 2001–2002 | £1,075 | (£530) |
| 2002–2003 | £1,100 | (£540) |

*Figures in brackets are fees for students on full year sandwich/industry placements or studying abroad (except for EU exchange programmes such as SOCRATES and ERASMUS students).

However, most students can get a contribution towards these fees, the level of which is dependent on their – and their family's – income. In fact, it is estimated that almost half of all students are fully exempt from paying anything and only about a third pay the full fee. Any such state contribution towards tuition fees is not a loan and does not have to be repaid. English and Welsh students must apply through the Local Education Authority (LEA) where they normally live for assessment of any contribution. Scottish students must apply through the Student Awards Agency for Scotland (SAAS) and those in Northern Ireland to their local Education and Library Board. You should do so as soon as you have received an offer – even a conditional offer – of a university place. Other EU students are sent an application form by the university offering a place.

In a dramatic move (January 2000), the Scottish Parliament agreed to abolish fees with effect from autumn 2000 for students resident in Scotland who stay there to study and for mainland EU full-time students studying in Scotland (but not for other UK students studying in Scotland). However, those students not paying fees will be expected after graduation to pay £2,000 into a Graduate Endowment Fund for less well-off students on essentially the same basis as repayment of a student loan (see later). Students resident in Scotland but studying elsewhere in the UK will continue to pay income-assessed tuition fees to their universities.

*Tuition fees for overseas students*

Overseas students normally resident in countries outside the EU and EEA pay full-cost tuition fees in all of the UK and these are likely to be in the range:

| Subject | £ Sterling | $US |
|---------|-----------|-----|
| Humanities and Social Sciences | £6,500–£7,300 | $9,100–$10,220 |
| Sciences and Engineering | £7,000–£9,500 | $9,800–$13,300 |
| Clinical Subjects | £17,500–£18,200 | $24,500–$25,480 |

Conversion rate £1.00:$1.40

Whilst many overseas students coming to Britain receive financial support from their home countries, it must be emphasised that UK scholarships and bursaries, whether from the UK government, sponsors or the individual universities themselves are limited. Students from overseas are strongly advised, therefore, to make sure they have sufficient funds for the above full tuition fees and all necessary living costs before leaving home. Indeed, you will almost certainly be asked to guarantee in writing that you have sufficient funds for the complete duration of your course. You should also make sure that you have some ready money or travellers' cheques with you for immediate use on arrival to cover food, travel and other essentials. In that context, a cash card with the Cirrus or Maestro signs allows you to draw money at a UK bank.

*Living costs*
For all students the biggest expenditure items will be regular living costs: accommodation, food and even, perhaps, some clothes! There is evidence to suggest that most university entrants don't know what it costs to be a student and can seriously underestimate these items by as much as 50 per cent. An increasing number, particularly in London, are staying at home and travel daily to their nearest university and that is probably the cheapest option. Home comforts might also feature in this decision, given that a recent UNITE survey indicated that more than 20 per cent of first-year male students and half as many female students couldn't cook or use a washing machine – it's never too late to start learning! However, most first-year students take up a guaranteed place in a university residence. Whilst this is by far the most sensible decision from a social perspective, it can be a relatively expensive and inflexible one. You may perhaps be expected to pay for full-board with all meals even if you choose not to eat in all the time. Of growing interest to many is the possible half-way house of self-catering university accommodation where heating and lighting – no small matters of cost – may still be included but where you can at least control the food bills. You might even be able to engage in a spot of discounted bulk food buying with fellow residents and hence stretch the money further. Ironically, with so much written about student debt, the more expensive university accommodation – often en-suite and with internet access – is oversubscribed whilst some basic facilities are hard to fill.

If you find yourself heading for private-sector accommodation, make sure it is approved by the university and carefully check the terms of any lease you are asked to sign. This is a binding legal document so read and understand the small print. Think, too, about those with whom you plan to share. You never really know someone until you've actually lived with them, and many students before you have fallen out over the state of the kitchen and bathroom, the shared telephone bill, or for using the last drop of milk! With mortgage interests at an historic low, property prices and rents soaring, and the stock market in the doldrums, some parents are opting to buy accommodation for their offspring, perhaps defraying the expense by charging rent to fellow students.

Given that these are the biggest items of expenditure – rent alone could account for 70 per cent of weekly income – it is well worth giving the various accommodation options serious thought, making sure that you maintain maximum flexibility within any arrangements. Check what rent you may have to pay in advance and whether or not you have to pay a retainer in the vacations. As a general rule, accommodation and travel costs are highest in London, southeast England and East Anglia and least expensive in Wales, Scotland and northeast England.

*Studying costs*

Next come costs associated with course work and the essentials: books, stationery, equipment and perhaps fieldwork or electives, here and overseas. After all, you are at university to get a degree! Such additional course work is often compulsory and, whilst you might get some financial support for this, it is unlikely to meet the full costs of a language year, medical elective, or archaeological dig overseas or a residential geography field trip away from the university. The recommended reading list might be long and expensive. You would be well advised not to rush out and buy the lot but rather get to know how to use the library at the earliest opportunity. Students' unions often organise second-hand book sales and access to the internet is easy and free via the university network. Are some textbooks you want available through these sources, at the very least to buy at discount prices? Or is it feasible to share books with a fellow student?

*Other costs*

But university most definitely shouldn't be all work. Again, the students' union will cater for play in all its guises at a fraction of the cost demanded by commercial providers. In fact, university is a great time – perhaps the only time – to pursue the most common or esoteric of interests at a price you can easily afford. However, expenditure on the social scene, whether it be launderette (that washing machine again!), cinema or nightclub, drinking or occasional eating out, is still likely to be a significant cost for most students.

Phone bills can be another sizeable item, especially if you ring the old folks at home or that distant loved one for an hour or so every day and they happen to be in Tokyo or San Francisco! Competition for your custom is fierce and the students' union may well be able to advise on the best deals amongst a growing army of call providers. Selecting an appropriate package for your mobile from the many options will also be important.

*Insurance*

Most students own desirable items like TVs, CD and DVD players, laptops, mobile phones and bikes, and a quarter of them fall victims of crime. Insurance cover is essential but might be possible under existing parental policies at home. If not, there are a number of insurance companies which tailor policies to student belongings and lifestyle. Premiums are usually linked to postal codes, and halls of residence often provide cheaper cover than student houses. It is worth the precaution of photographing expensive items and keeping serial numbers in a safe place.

*Travel costs*

Finally, there are travel costs, where most students rely on public transport; and this is not just between home and university, perhaps two or three times a year, but also from your accommodation to the university every day. This could be a key factor when choosing where to live, both in terms of time and money. It may well pay you to purchase a Student Card on local or national transport, or better still to opt to live a stone's throw from the university or on frequent bus, train or tram routes to it. Whilst most students manage to live less than three miles from the campus, a recent NUS survey showed that the average distance in East Anglia and Scotland is over four and five miles respectively, and in London about half an hour away.

As a general rule, the cost of living is lower the further north and west you choose to study in the UK. That, then, is a brief look at what you will need money for. Try looking at your own personal situation to draw up an annual expenditure list and return to it on a regular basis throughout the year to see how you're doing. In other words, begin to estimate an annual budget. This is shown in the chart of income and expenditure at the end of the chapter.

## Income

*Earning before university*

One possible source of earnings to consider prior to coming to university is a gap year – another is sponsorship. Taking a year out is attractive to a growing number of students, whether to gain experience, to earn money or both. There are essentially four main possibilities: cultural exchanges and courses, expeditions, volunteering, and structured work placements. These can be here in the UK or overseas and some could require considerable funding by you whilst others would pay a wage. You need to question, therefore, your own motivation and means before embarking on a year out. The reasons for taking a gap year seem to be shifting from solely an opportunity for personal development to more one to boost the bank balance ahead of becoming a student. In other words, a shift away from altruism and towards utilitarianism. This understandable short-term expediency needs to be carefully measured against the somewhat longer-term but less tangible benefits of a placement, here or overseas, of real service to the community, but perhaps with less monetary reward. These days, universities take careful note of extracurricular experience and interests alongside good exam grades and generally support a gap year but utter occasional reservations for those planning to study the mathematical sciences. Employers, too, operating increasingly in a global economy, look more and more to the development of self-reliance and teamwork skills and expertise beyond academic performance and class of degree.

Work placements might be structured as, for example, with the 'Year in

Industry Scheme' or 'GAP Activity Projects', or casual. Both provide invaluable experience to put on your CV. Sponsorship is available mostly to those wishing to study engineering or business; a good source of information is the *Student Support Sponsorship Funding Directory* published by CRAC/Hobsons.

*Student loans*

The government used to operate a system of student grants, but these were finally abolished altogether for the 1999–2000 academic year. However, grants in the form of NHS Bursaries do still exist for students on most health-related degree courses. Since October 1999, government support for other university students is wholly through a loan. For most UK students going to university now, therefore, a significant source of income will be this student loan from the Student Loan Company. As with an application for contributions towards tuition fees, so with a student loan you must apply without delay in the first instance to your LEA or funding agency, and you should do this even if you feel you do not qualify

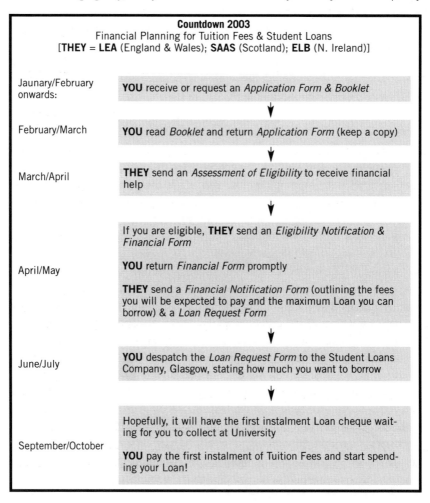

**Countdown 2003**
Financial Planning for Tuition Fees & Student Loans
[**THEY** = **LEA** (England & Wales); **SAAS** (Scotland); **ELB** (N. Ireland)]

Jaunary/February onwards:
**YOU** receive or request an *Application Form & Booklet*

February/March
**YOU** read *Booklet* and return *Application Form* (keep a copy)

March/April
**THEY** send an *Assessment of Eligibility* to receive financial help

April/May
If you are eligible, **THEY** send an *Eligibility Notification & Financial Form*

**YOU** return *Financial Form* promptly

**THEY** send a *Financial Notification Form* (outlining the fees you will be expected to pay and the maximum Loan you can borrow) & a *Loan Request Form*

June/July
**YOU** despatch the *Loan Request Form* to the Student Loans Company, Glasgow, stating how much you want to borrow

September/October
Hopefully, it will have the first instalment Loan cheque waiting for you to collect at University

**YOU** pay the first instalment of Tuition Fees and start spending your Loan!

for a government contribution towards your tuition fees. A timetable for Tuition Fee and Student Loan application is summarised in *Countdown 2003* opposite, and you can also apply for support online at the DfES website.

You don't have to take out this loan – although about 80 per cent of students do – but if and when you do, you will be entering into a legal contract to repay the loan in full **after** leaving university. When and what you repay will depend on your total income and will normally be deducted from your pay. You will repay nothing until your income exceeds £10,000 a year and some graduates might be exempt repayment if, for example, they take up and remain teaching certain key shortage subjects in schools. The interest rate on the loan is linked to the rate of inflation so you will be asked to repay no more, in real terms, than you actually borrowed. Middle-class students are more likely to view debt (from what is essentially an interest-free Student Loan) as an investment whereas many working-class students see it as a burden. It has been argued, therefore, that the current system encourages the development of a debt culture in some but dissuades others from coming to university.

Since the loans-only system was introduced, the **maximum** annual loan rates, apart from the last year at university, have been as shown in the table:

|  | **1999–2000** | **2000–2001** | **2001–2002** | **2002–2003** |
|---|---|---|---|---|
| Living at home: | £2,875 | £2,950 | £3,020 | £3,090 |
| Living away from home: |  |  |  |  |
|     London | £4,480 | £4,590 | £4,700 | £4,815 |
|     Elsewhere | £3,635 | £3,725 | £3,815 | £3,905 |

The amount of loan you can obtain depends, amongst other things, on how much you and your family will be expected to contribute to your living costs. However, 75 per cent of the maximum loan is available regardless of family income.

Only UK students can be considered for a student loan or the other support systems outlined below.

*Student loans for Scottish students*

For students starting courses in Scotland from autumn 2002, a proportion of the student loan may be replaced by the Young Students' Bursary (which is not repaid). The maximum bursary is £2,050 for those whose family income is less than £10,240, declining to zero when family income exceeds £26,400. Depending on family income, some of the total loan will be replaced by a bursary. This is partly because Scottish students studying in Scotland receive free tuition. For Scottish students studying elsewhere in the UK, the maximum bursary is £510 when the family income is less than £15,360 declining to zero when family income exceeds £18,400. Whilst the loan totals given above are the same, a greater proportion is assessed on the basis of family income compared with students from the rest of the UK. Full details are given on the SAAS website (www. saas.gov.uk). An Additional Loan of up to £510 is also available to some students studying in Scotland who are receiving a bursary.

*Further financial support*

Whilst we said earlier that the government has, since 1998, gradually replaced non-repayable maintenance grants by repayable loans, there has been a partial reversal of that policy this past year as part of the drive to encourage young students from less affluent homes to come to university. This has lead to the introduction of **Opportunity Bursaries** for school and college pupils from disadvantaged neighbourhoods within 'Excellence in Cities' areas or Education Action Zones. These Bursaries are worth £2,000 and are for able students from low-income families with little or no experience of university education. They are advertised and administered by the individual universities, some of which, themselves, provide similar scholarships for local applicants.

There are two further sources of modest government help to students on university courses, namely Hardship Loans and Hardship Funds, both of which are allocated by the universities themselves to undergraduates in financial difficulties. They decide which students need support and what the level of that support will be. **Hardship Loans** are, as the name implies, another loan, usually in amounts from £100 up to £500, and are added to any existing student loan. **Hardship Funds** are a back-stop and are normally given as a non-repayable grant according to need. They may be available as a one-off sum or in the form of a bursary payable every year.

The information in this chapter was correct at the time of writing (April 2002) but the rules and regulations for all of these contributions towards tuition fees, student loans or funds and other **Supplementary Grants** (for disabled students, students with dependants, single parent students, care leavers, and for some essential travel costs) are somewhat complicated and you had best consult your own copy of the Department for Education and Skills (DfES) booklet *Financial Support for Higher Education Students, Student Support in Scotland* (SAAS) or *Financial Support for Students in Higher Education* (DHFETE).

In fact, the Prime Minister has admitted that there was widespread criticism of the student support system during the 2001 General Election campaign, and this has now prompted a Government review. That review is expected to report late in 2002 with any recommendations likely to be implemented for the academic year 2003–4 at the earliest. Press reports suggest that the proposed changes could be quite radical and will, no doubt, home in on the balance between state and family contributions to student support. Mention has been made of a return to a system of grants or bursaries targeted at all – or probably at the less well-off – to cover both tuition fees and maintenance costs. But it is still likely that students and their families will be asked to contribute, perhaps through a graduate tax or levy. This might be a flat-rate contribution not tied to the amount of any Government suppport received, or perhaps the replacement of the current inflation-only interest rate on the student loan by the going rate in the market. Some of the universities have also argued for the intoduction of differential tuition fees – so-called top-up fees – but, to date, this has been resisted by Whitehall. However, all agree that the student support system needs to be simplified so changes will be made. *We can't emphasise too strongly that all the above is informed speculation and it is most important that you check the regulations at the time you come to make your application to university.*

If you are ineligible for any of the above financial support, you may still be able to apply for a **Career Development Loan**, available through some major high street banks in partnership with the DfES. Students on a wide range of vocational courses can borrow from £300 to £8,000 to help you fund up to two years of training and not pay anything back until you finish your studies.

### Part-time work

Some firms, particularly the big supermarket chains, offer continuing part-time employment to their school employees when they go away to university. The last few years have also seen a significant growth in student employment offices on university campuses, no doubt a response, in part, to the introduction of fees and loans. About half of all undergraduates now have a part-time job. These offices act as agencies introducing employers with work to students seeking work, perhaps even in the university itself, throughout the academic year. They are also guardians of the student interest, abiding by Codes of Practice which regulate such things as minimum wages, maximum hours worked in term (typically 15 hours a week – so as to avoid adverse effect on studies), non-discrimination, etc. Most universities now have a student employment office run by their careers service or the students' union and they make a welcome contribution to the local economy. This is hardly surprising given the enormous range of skills and knowledge residing in any student community.

### Vacation work

Vacations, too, offer an opportunity to earn cash whilst developing skills for that CV. As with the gap year, such work experience can be casual, formalised in a scheme like the 'Shell Technology Enterprise Programme', or even as part of a sponsorship programme.

### Banks

Finally, banks are well disposed to today's university students in the certain knowledge that many will be tomorrow's high-earning professionals. They are sympathetic to the student cause and will generally permit modest overdrafts on your account to ease cash flow problems without pain. It pays – literally – to shop around for the best offers when transferring or opening your account. Check to see if the bank offers a 24-hour service via the internet or telephone and make sure that its cash machines are accessible around the clock. Branches near universities often have dedicated student advisers to tell you about interest-free overdrafts, mobile phones, discount PCs, insurance or travel, CD vouchers and other offers to lure you inside.

## Your Annual Budget

You can now complete your estimated annual budget by listing all expected income, including any savings you will bring with you to university. See how this compares with expenditure in the hope that the balance sheet almost balances or, better still, that you are left with spare cash in the bank for doing what you've always wanted to do. However, budgeting accurately is never an easy process, and PricewaterhouseCoopers have constructed this simple annual income and expenditure summary to make monitoring and controlling your finances easier:

| Income | £ | Expenses | £ |
|---|---|---|---|
| Student loan | 3,432 | Tuition fees | 1,100 |
| Parental contribution | | Rent | 2,000 |
| to loan | 473 | Electricity, gas, water | 200 |
| to fees | 1,100 | Telephone | 200 |
| Term time/vacation work | 1,500 | Insurance | 60 |
| | | Food, drink | 1,500 |
| *Total Income* | 6,505 | Toiletries | 200 |
| | | Laundry | 100 |
| | | Books, stationery | 170 |
| | | Clothes, shoes | 300 |
| | | Travel | 270 |
| | | Going out | 900 |
| | | Home entertainment | 200 |
| | | Sports, leisure | 150 |
| | | Holidays, presents | 400 |
| | | Emergencies | 200 |
| | | | |
| | | *Total Expenses* | 7,950 |
| | | | |
| | | **(Deficit)** | (1,445) |

It can be difficult to predict accurately some variable expenses such as entertainment. Start by identifying bills which *must* be paid and include in this a small contingency fund. This will leave you with the 'flexible' part of your income to take weekly from the bank. Don't be too optimistic in your first budget, and do be aware of how much you actually spend. Also, do budget for balls at the end of terms, birthdays and parties, or you may find yourself missing out on the best social events of the year. If there is a big gap between budget and actual, perhaps your spending habits need attention rather than your budgeting. Above all, remember to keep a check on your finances so that money worries do not detract from your studying and from enjoying university life. Apparently, women undergraduates are more likely to budget and, as a result, incur lower debt but, even so, tend to worry more about that debt! Clearly, your patterns of expenditure will differ significantly between term-time and vacations and you will need to allow for this. In this example, we have assumed that you are not required to pay full tuition fees of £1,100.

# 7

# Coming from Overseas

It is difficult enough for individuals living in the UK when faced with the bewildering choice amongst the 100 or so universities. How much more so if you live on the other side of the world where, in addition, you will want to consider the significant costs of living and studying in another country. You will need a great deal of information – considerably more than is available within this chapter – but this, and the previous chapter on funding, will give you a good start and point you in the right direction.

## The Country
The British Isles comprise two sovereign and independent states of the European Union, the UK and the Republic of Ireland. Within the UK there are three further countries: England, Scotland and Wales – sometimes collectively called Great Britain – and the province of Northern Ireland. Of the 101 universities covered in *The Times Good University Guide*:
- 78 are in England
- 13 are in Scotland
- 8 are in Wales
- 2 are in Northern Ireland.

In 1999, a Parliament in Scotland and an Assembly in Wales were established, each with devolved powers. These bodies are already having a positive impact on university education in these countries. For example, EU students at Scottish universities do not pay up-front tuition fees, but do contribute after graduation to an endowment for future generations of disadvantaged students. In fact, Scottish universities have seen a surge in numbers of overseas applicants, no doubt as a result of such policy change. Some may also have benefited from Prince William's decision to study at St Andrews!

## The Weather
Most students coming to the UK will find the climate different! Given its position west of the European mainland, Britain tends to have low humidity, warm sum-

mers and mild winters. Although there are four distinct climatic seasons, spring, summer, autumn and winter, the weather is unpredictable and liable to change and change again in the course of a day. Rainfall is highest in and close to the hilly regions in the north and west – typically over 1,000 mm a year – whilst average daily temperatures range from 5 °C in January to 20 °C in July. Snow falls for a short time most winters and there is even a short ski season in the Scottish highlands. As a general rule, southeast England is relatively dry and sunny and northwest Scotland wet and cloudy.

### Entry and Employment Regulations

There are four main receiving countries for university students in the English-speaking world – the USA, the UK, Australia and Canada – and all four have their distinctive characteristics. All four have restrictions on entry and employment for foreign nationals, and since the September 11 attacks on the World Trade Centers, reports from the US and elsewhere suggest that visas for students from some countries might be harder to come by or, at very least, are subject to greater scrutiny, so early application is essential. However, in June 1999 the Prime Minister, Tony Blair, launched a worldwide campaign to encourage overseas students to come to the UK's universities. As part of this initiative, the government is making the passage much easier by streamlining visa and entry procedures. In addition, overseas students can now work for up to 20 hours a week during the academic year and full-time in the vacations without the need for a work permit. Similarly, if you are staying in the UK for a year or more, then your spouse and children will be able to take paid employment even if they are here for a shorter period. You can also now apply to remain in the UK after graduation, perhaps for professional training, work experience or a graduate induction programme. This is the latest package of new measures on immigration and work experience designed to make the UK a more attractive place to study. The government has promised more.

In addition to a valid passport, some students – called 'visa nationals' – coming to university in Britain will need to obtain a visa from the British Embassy or High Commission before arrival and this could take weeks to arrange. Non-visa nationals do not, as the name implies, require a visa for entry but it might be wise for you to submit your study documents to the British Consulate in your own country just to be on the safe side. In doing so, you can obtain an official entry certificate. Nationals of an EU country, Liechtenstein, Norway and Iceland are free to travel to the UK without a visa to study or work.

### How and When to Apply

Chapter 5 deals with this matter and you should read the information there in conjunction with what follows. If you are applying for a full-time first degree course you will need to fill in a UCAS application form and you can send for one through the UCAS website. You can even complete the form electronically and send it via the internet at some schools and British Council offices.

If you are applying from within an EU country, your application form must be received at UCAS by 15 January otherwise you will be treated as a late applicant. Different, usually earlier, dates apply for Oxford and Cambridge, and medical and art and design courses (see page 137).

If you are applying from a non-EU country, you can send your form to UCAS at any time between 1 September and 30 June preceding the academic year in which you plan to commence your studies. However, most students apply well before 30 June to make sure that places are still available and to allow plenty of time to make immigration, travel and accommodation arrangements.

## British Universities
The UK universities have their origins in the ancient seats of learning at Oxford (1096), Cambridge (1209) and St Andrews (1411). They enjoy a worldwide reputation for the quality of their courses, teaching and research which are rigorously assessed by these independent bodies:

- Higher Education Funding Councils
- Quality Assurance Agency for Higher Education
- Office for Standards in Education

The appointment of external examiners at each university also guarantees good standards. These, in turn, are reflected in high entry requirements, short and intensive courses of study, and high completion rates, the latter resulting from an infrastructure which offers strong student support.

This support for overseas students is more comprehensive than in most countries and begins long before students arrive in the UK. Most universities have advisers, even offices, in other countries and they are likely to put students in touch with current students or graduates and answer any queries. Then there may well be pre-departure receptions for students and their families and certainly full written pre-arrival information on all aspects of living and studying in Britain. Arriving in the UK, there are often arrangements made to meet and greet students at the nearest coach or rail station or airport, a guarantee of warm and comfortable university accommodation, an orientation programme – often lasting several days – to meet friends and to help students adjust to their new surroundings, and courses in the English language for those who need them. But it's not all work. Each university has a students' union which organises social, cultural, religious and sporting clubs and events, including many specifically for overseas students, such as short visits to other European countries. Both the university and its students' union are most likely to have full-time staff whose sole purpose is to look after the welfare of overseas students.

And that's not all! Students receive free medical and subsidised dental and optical treatment under the National Health Service, full access to a professional counselling service and a university careers service network – with an enviable reputation throughout the world – to help you decide what to do on completion of your studies. The fact that degree courses here are more intensive, and thus shorter, than those in many other countries has an obvious financial advantage, not only in study and living costs, but also in the opportunity to enter, or re-enter, the employment market sooner.

### Where Overseas Students Study

Most of what follows in this chapter refers to the tables within it. It must be emphasised that these are based solely on the numbers of overseas students attending and say nothing about the quality of the university. It is very important, therefore, that you cross refer to the League Table on pages 23–29 and the individual subject tables (pages 49–133) which are concerned with quality

The data are based on overseas students enrolling in all years of first degree courses at UK universities in 1999–2000 and are the latest figures available. They exclude those students whose complete study programmes were outside the UK but include the majority of students taking part in European Union exchange programmes such as ERASMUS, TEMPUS and LINGUA at UK universities. First degrees are mostly awarded at Bachelor level (BA, BEng, BSc, etc.) and last for three or four years. There are also some so-called 'enhanced' first degrees (MEng, MChem) which take four years to complete. Vocational courses like architecture, dentistry and medicine are one or two years longer. Some universities offer one-year foundation courses, including English language tuition, to act as a bridge for overseas students whose qualifications are insufficient for direct entry to a degree course.

Recent shifts in countries of origin are noteworthy. Whilst Asia remains hugely important as a source of international students (Malaysia, Hong Kong, Singapore, Japan, Taiwan and Brunei), some countries there, like Malaysia, have been beset with economic problems and this, in turn, has affected demand for study overseas. At the same time, there has been a huge growth in student numbers from China and, to a lesser extent, from the Indian subcontinent and the Americas, particularly Latin America. In many UK universities you could expect to have fellow students from over 100 countries across the world. The British university system is truly a global one and increasingly so with more than one in ten of its student population – a much higher figure than the USA – coming from countries overseas.

Tables 1 and 2 give a broad overview of overseas students in Britain. You can see where students come from and what they study here. Greece and Malaysia are prominent as major sending countries, and most students, regardless of where they come from, pursue courses of study which are strongly vocational in that they lead to careers in business, industry and the professions.

**Table 1** *Which countries do overseas students come from?*

| EU countries | | % | Non-EU countries (Top 20) | | % |
|---|---|---|---|---|---|
| Greece | 17,178 | 36.1 | Malaysia | 6,396 | 15.1 |
| Irish Republic | 6,538 | 13.7 | Hong Kong | 4,120 | 9.7 |
| Germany | 5,191 | 10.9 | Singapore | 3,389 | 8.0 |
| France | 4,951 | 10.4 | Norway | 2,451 | 5.8 |
| Spain | 2,994 | 6.3 | Cyprus | 2,221 | 5.3 |
| Sweden | 2,001 | 4.2 | Japan | 1,604 | 3.8 |
| Italy | 1,889 | 4.0 | Kenya* | 1,479 | 3.5 |
| Finland | 1,647 | 3.5 | China* | 1,339 | 3.2 |
| Belgium | 1,191 | 2.5 | United States | 1,226 | 2.9 |
| Netherlands | 970 | 2.0 | Nigeria* | 1,082 | 2.6 |
| Portugal | 938 | 2.0 | India* | 899 | 2.1 |
| Denmark | 752 | 1.6 | Taiwan* | 810 | 1.9 |
| Austria | 521 | 1.1 | Brunei | 781 | 1.8 |
| Luxembourg | 440 | 0.9 | Mauritius* | 677 | 1.6 |
| Gibraltar | 412 | 0.9 | Oman* | 627 | 1.5 |
| | | | Israel | 607 | 1.4 |
| *All EU students* | 47,613 | | Sri Lanka* | 573 | 1.4 |
| | | | Pakistan* | 543 | 1.3 |
| | | | Switzerland | 522 | 1.2 |
| | | | Turkey* | 509 | 1.2 |

*All non-EU students*    42,276

\* Students from these non-EU countries and the Turkish Republic of North Cyprus require a visa to study in the UK.

**Table 2** *What do overseas students study?*

| Subject group | EU students | Non-EU students | Total |
|---|---|---|---|
| Engineering and technology | 8,293 | 8,715 | 17,008 |
| Business and administrative studies | 8,209 | 8,277 | 16,486 |
| Social, economic and political studies | 4,449 | 2,945 | 7,394 |
| Computer studies | 2,183 | 2,579 | 4,762 |
| Legal studies | 1,580 | 2,995 | 4,575 |
| Biological sciences | 3,278 | 1,275 | 4,553 |
| Languages | 3,435 | 1,259 | 4,694 |
| Creative arts and design | 2,297 | 1,875 | 4,172 |
| Subjects allied to medicine* | 2,165 | 1,818 | 3,983 |
| Architectural studies | 1,699 | 1,546 | 3,245 |
| Physical sciences | 1,766 | 782 | 2,548 |
| Medicine and dentistry | 430 | 1,956 | 2,386 |
| Librarianship and information science | 881 | 556 | 1,437 |
| Humanities | 791 | 412 | 1,203 |
| Mathematical sciences | 460 | 593 | 1,053 |
| Education | 373 | 615 | 988 |
| Agriculture | 419 | 160 | 579 |
| Veterinary science | 40 | 181 | 221 |
| Combined studies | 4,865 | 3,737 | 8,602 |

*Subjects allied to medicine include Pharmacy and Nursing.

Table 3 lists those universities with large numbers of overseas students. Ulster owes much of its popularity to its close proximity to the Republic of Ireland whilst big numbers at Middlesex, particularly in business and administrative studies, include students on large exchange programmes. EU students are well represented in the new universities whereas students from other countries gravitate to all parts of the sector. This pattern of distribution largely reflects chosen fields of study and the universities where these subjects are available. As emphasised earlier, you must satisfy yourself about quality by going back to Chapters 1 and 4.

**Table 3** *Where do overseas students study?*

| Institution | EU students | Institution | Non-EU students |
|---|---|---|---|
| Ulster | 1,419 | Nottingham | 1,142 |
| Coventry | 1,193 | London School of Economics | 1,127 |
| Portsmouth | 1,169 | Middlesex | 1,097 |
| Middlesex | 1,143 | Imperial College | 988 |
| Brighton | 1,069 | Manchester | 936 |
| North London | 1,018 | University College London | 885 |
| Kingston | 911 | Sheffield | 844 |
| Greenwich | 884 | King's College London | 796 |
| Luton | 864 | Westminster | 764 |
| Glamorgan | 841 | Leeds | 750 |
| Lincoln | 831 | Warwick | 750 |
| Anglia | 829 | Cambridge | 745 |
| Essex | 818 | Oxford Brookes | 729 |
| Westminster | 803 | Birmingham | 715 |
| Kent | 786 | Northumbria | 714 |
| Sussex | 752 | Portsmouth | 707 |
| Wolverhampton | 730 | Hertfordshire | 697 |
| Manchester Metropolitan | 713 | UMIST | 696 |
| Hertfordshire | 706 | Cardiff | 678 |
| Salford | 688 | Oxford | 651 |
| London Guildhall | 677 | Central England | 627 |
| East London | 667 | East London | 624 |
| Sunderland | 659 | Wolverhampton | 611 |
| Plymouth | 658 | Edinburgh | 601 |
| Liverpool John Moores | 608 | Bristol | 584 |
| | | | |
| *All EU students* | 47,613 | *All Non-EU students* | 42,276 |

Probably the most useful information is to be found in Table 4 which lists the universities by numbers of overseas students in the 22 most popular subjects, each of which has at least a thousand overseas students. Again, use this information in conjunction with the tables that measure quality in the earlier chapters. The subjects are listed in order of popularity.

**Table 4** *The most popular subjects and universities for overseas students*

| Business Studies | EU students | Non-EU students |
|---|---|---|
| Lincoln | 444 | 216 |
| Westminster | 308 | 245 |
| Brighton | 329 | 184 |
| Oxford Brookes | 213 | 244 |
| Northumbria | 165 | 256 |
| Wolverhampton | 271 | 91 |
| Luton | 184 | 150 |
| Greenwich | 235 | 92 |
| Middlesex | 177 | 132 |
| Plymouth | 213 | 93 |
| *All overseas students* | 7,351 | 5,287 |

| Computer Science | EU students | Non-EU Students |
|---|---|---|
| Central England | 21 | 238 |
| Coventry | 61 | 87 |
| Westminster | 48 | 95 |
| Hertfordshire | 44 | 88 |
| Oxford Brookes | 19 | 105 |
| Portsmouth | 68 | 56 |
| UMIST | 49 | 75 |
| Staffordshire | 73 | 45 |
| Teesside | 87 | 28 |
| Ulster | 114 | 1 |
| *All overseas students* | 2,183 | 2,579 |

| Electrical and Electronic Engineering | EU students | Non-EU Students |
|---|---|---|
| UMIST | 45 | 163 |
| Hertfordshire | 7.7 | 103 |
| Sussex | 102 | 66 |
| Sheffield | 21 | 146 |
| Portsmouth | 109 | 53 |
| Essex | 100 | 59 |
| Kent | 105 | 46 |
| Brighton | 104 | 30 |
| Central Lancashire | 15 | 112 |
| Leeds | 41 | 81 |
| *All overseas students* | 2,282 | 2,337 |

| Law | EU students | Non-EU Students |
|---|---|---|
| Wolverhampton | 20 | 240 |
| King's College London | 94 | 142 |
| Kent | 94 | 99 |
| Coventry | 141 | 45 |
| Cardiff | 7 | 165 |
| London School of Economics | 23 | 139 |
| Nottingham | 6 | 148 |
| Bristol | 6 | 132 |
| Essex | 74 | 61 |
| Sheffield | 4 | 128 |
| *All overseas students* | 1,580 | 2,995 |

| Economics | EU students | Non-EU Students |
|---|---|---|
| London School of Economics | 83 | 342 |
| Anglia | 214 | 15 |
| Essex | 168 | 61 |
| Greenwich | 136 | 12 |
| Portsmouth | 121 | 13 |
| Cambridge | 32 | 89 |
| Warwick | 38 | 80 |
| University College London | 33 | 76 |
| Leicester | 5 | 99 |
| Manchester Metropolitan | 88 | 11 |
| *All overseas students* | 2,270 | 1,644 |

| Mechanical Engineering | EU students | Non-EU Students |
|---|---|---|
| Portsmouth | 112 | 60 |
| Imperial College | 22 | 96 |
| Brighton | 80 | 18 |
| Coventry | 59 | 37 |
| UMIST | 21 | 75 |
| Leeds | 39 | 54 |
| Nottingham | 2 | 89 |
| Birmingham | 12 | 77 |
| Hertfordshire | 34 | 52 |
| Sheffield | 4 | 77 |
| *All overseas students* | 1,501 | 1,637 |

| Civil Engineering | EU students | Non-EU Students |
|---|---|---|
| Portsmouth | 141 | 80 |
| East London | 118 | 80 |
| Hertfordshire | 78 | 78 |
| Brighton | 134 | 13 |
| Leeds | 62 | 52 |
| Imperial College | 32 | 82 |
| University College London | 31 | 75 |
| Coventry | 68 | 35 |
| Salford | 72 | 29 |
| Nottingham | 8 | 88 |
| *All overseas students* | 1,860 | 1,274 |

| Accountancy and Financial Management | EU students | Non-EU Students |
|---|---|---|
| London School of Economics | 17 | 254 |
| Lincoln | 3 | 244 |
| Middlesex | 40 | 122 |
| Lancaster | 8 | 118 |
| Portsmouth | 40 | 64 |
| Essex | 39 | 65 |
| Cardiff | 11 | 84 |
| City | 40 | 52 |
| Kent | 9 | 71 |
| Sheffield | 0 | 68 |
| *All overseas students* | 561 | 2,380 |

| Art and Design Studies | EU students | Non-EU Students |
|---|---|---|
| Surrey Institute | 143 | 131 |
| Middlesex | 83 | 115 |
| Central England | 48 | 113 |
| Wolverhampton | 62 | 56 |
| Ulster | 114 | 3 |
| Westminster | 63 | 53 |
| De Montfort | 75 | 33 |
| Goldsmiths College | 36 | 58 |
| West of England | 35 | 58 |
| Nottingham Trent | 19 | 67 |
| *All overseas students* | 1,462 | 1,297 |

| Psychology | EU students | Non-EU Students |
|---|---|---|
| Middlesex | 116 | 18 |
| Luton | 98 | 14 |
| Ulster | 95 | 0 |
| Sussex | 53 | 18 |
| University College London | 22 | 47 |
| Queen's, Belfast | 66 | 1 |
| East London | 39 | 25 |
| Essex | 53 | 7 |
| Aberdeen | 49 | 9 |
| Royal Holloway | 43 | 14 |
| *All overseas students* | 1,465 | 558 |

| Architecture | EU students | Non-EU Students |
|---|---|---|
| Greenwich | 89 | 40 |
| North London | 68 | 32 |
| Oxford Brookes | 64 | 35 |
| Westminster | 58 | 34 |
| East London | 53 | 38 |
| Huddersfield | 77 | 14 |
| Portsmouth | 61 | 30 |
| Manchester Metropolitan | 29 | 54 |
| Robert Gordon | 36 | 47 |
| De Montfort | 63 | 12 |
| *All overseas students* | 1,172 | 708 |

| Other Subjects Allied to Medicine | EU students | Non-EU Students |
|---|---|---|
| Ulster | 155 | 24 |
| Queen Margaret | 32 | 89 |
| Anglia | 23 | 73 |
| King's College London | 31 | 55 |
| Salford | 50 | 33 |
| Bangor | 59 | 4 |
| Northumbria | 10 | 42 |
| Glasgow Caledonian | 34 | 15 |
| Bradford | 23 | 24 |
| City | 22 | 24 |
| *All overseas students* | 974 | 825 |

| Catering and Institutional Management | EU Students | Non-EU Students |
|---|---|---|
| Surrey | 114 | 96 |
| Oxford Brookes | 69 | 65 |
| Brighton | 66 | 41 |
| North London | 79 | 20 |
| Bournemouth | 48 | 48 |
| Glasgow Caledonian | 6 | 88 |
| Luton | 46 | 33 |
| Queen Margaret | 19 | 58 |
| Leeds Metropolitan | 27 | 24 |
| Manchester Metropolitan | 28 | 20 |
| *All overseas students* | 961 | 807 |

| General Engineering | EU students | Non-EU Students |
|---|---|---|
| Coventry | 276 | 27 |
| Central Lancashire | 11 | 178 |
| Cambridge | 32 | 133 |
| Warwick | 16 | 81 |
| Oxford | 21 | 70 |
| De Montfort | 61 | 19 |
| Portsmouth | 43 | 27 |
| Lincoln | 29 | 31 |
| Glasgow Caledonian | 15 | 16 |
| Durham | 11 | 16 |
| *All overseas students* | 725 | 750 |

| Molecular Biosciences | EU Students | Non-EU Students |
|---|---|---|
| Imperial College | 32 | 40 |
| King's College London | 45 | 24 |
| University College London | 30 | 33 |
| Sussex | 45 | 6 |
| Leeds | 34 | 16 |
| Portsmouth | 28 | 20 |
| Aberdeen | 29 | 18 |
| Loughborough | 8 | 35 |
| Greenwich | 28 | 14 |
| Brighton | 28 | 10 |
| *All overseas students* | 956 | 518 |

| Organismal Biosciences | EU Students | Non-EU Students |
|---|---|---|
| Edinburgh | 90 | 32 |
| Essex | 56 | 3 |
| Aberdeen | 53 | 2 |
| Imperial College | 32 | 20 |
| Kingston | 44 | 1 |
| Ulster | 38 | 1 |
| Bangor | 25 | 13 |
| Leeds | 22 | 15 |
| Sussex | 36 | 1 |
| Hertfordshire | 26 | 6 |
| *All overseas students* | 1080 | 300 |

| Aeronautical and Manufacturing Engineering | EU Students | Non-EU Students |
|---|---|---|
| Coventry | 56 | 52 |
| Kingston | 50 | 41 |
| Hertfordshire | 33 | 46 |
| Imperial College | 31 | 48 |
| Brunel | 47 | 31 |
| Salford | 36 | 35 |
| Nottingham | 8 | 44 |
| UMIST | 15 | 31 |
| Central Lancashire | 8 | 37 |
| East London | 35 | 8 |
| *All overseas students* | 661 | 678 |

| Politics | EU Students | Non-EU Students |
|---|---|---|
| London School of Economics | 88 | 125 |
| Sussex | 114 | 36 |
| Kent | 65 | 31 |
| Aberystwyth | 40 | 17 |
| Warwick | 19 | 22 |
| Brunel | 8 | 31 |
| Plymouth | 30 | 7 |
| St Andrews | 11 | 24 |
| Birmingham | 27 | 7 |
| Reading | 20 | 13 |
| *All overseas students* | 760 | 501 |

| English | EU Students | Non-EU Students |
|---|---|---|
| Luton | 123 | 13 |
| Salford | 36 | 51 |
| Wolverhampton | 56 | 15 |
| Kent | 53 | 11 |
| Anglia | 45 | 6 |
| North London | 40 | 4 |
| Portsmouth | 23 | 18 |
| Chichester | 0 | 41 |
| Central England | 31 | 9 |
| York | 14 | 24 |
| *All overseas students* | 816 | 442 |

| Pharmacology and Pharmacy | EU Students | Non-EU Students |
|---|---|---|
| Strathclyde | 16 | 112 |
| Brighton | 92 | 34 |
| Liverpool John Moores | 34 | 89 |
| Robert Gordon | 87 | 30 |
| Sunderland | 95 | 15 |
| Portsmouth | 45 | 29 |
| Nottingham | 0 | 62 |
| King's College London | 23 | 34 |
| Bradford | 30 | 22 |
| Bath | 6 | 26 |
| *All overseas students* | 500 | 585 |

| Building | EU Students | Non-EU Students |
|---|---|---|
| Northumbria | 17 | 106 |
| Wolverhampton | 9 | 87 |
| Glamorgan | 68 | 13 |
| Nottingham Trent | 10 | 70 |
| Ulster | 68 | 3 |
| Greenwich | 3 | 58 |
| UMIST | 5 | 38 |
| Portsmouth | 3 | 33 |
| Napier | 30 | 6 |
| South Bank | 13 | 18 |
| Salford | 5 | 26 |
| *All overseas students* | 359 | 709 |

| Mathematics | EU Students | Non-EU Students |
|---|---|---|
| Imperial College | 35 | 48 |
| Cambridge | 37 | 36 |
| Heriot-Watt | 21 | 32 |
| City | 8 | 41 |
| University College London | 12 | 32 |
| Oxford | 12 | 27 |
| London School of Economics | 5 | 33 |
| North London | 17 | 15 |
| Queen Mary | 7 | 25 |
| Lancaster | 25 | 6 |
| *All overseas students* | 449 | 567 |

**Further information**

Advice and information on the UK universities are available through the British Council and its Educational Counselling Service. The Council maintains a comprehensive network of information centres in cities throughout the world and organises more than 50 university exhibitions in some 25 key countries every year. Its 'Virtual Campus' is a good guide to studying and living in Britain. It is worth visiting at: www.britishcouncil.org/eis/campus/htm

The individual universities have their own profiles in the 'Virtual Campus' where you can find further details of their support services for overseas students. There is also information on course fees, living costs and English language requirements. Website addresses are also given in each of the university profiles in chapter 9 of this book. UKCOSA, the Council for International Education, is another useful source of advice and information to overseas students. Its web site can be viewed at: www.ukcosa.org.uk

# 8

# Oxbridge

Oxbridge (as Oxford and Cambridge are called collectively) is another world when it comes to university admissions. Although part of the UCAS network, the two universities have different deadlines from the rest of the system, and applications are made through UCAS direct to colleges. There is little to choose between them in terms of entrance requirements, but a formidable number of successful applicants have the maximum possible A-level score.

However, that does not mean the talented student should be shy about applying: both Oxford and Cambridge have fewer applicants per place than many less prestigious universities, and admission tutors are always looking to extend the range of schools and colleges from which they can recruit. For those with a realistic chance of success, there is little to lose except the possibility of a wasted space on the UCAS form. While a few universities are said to have looked askance at candidates who consider them second best to any other institution, from 2003 UCAS will no longer show a chosen university the applicant's other choices.

Overall, there are about three applicants to every place at Oxford and Cambridge, but there are big differences between subjects and colleges. As the tables in this chapter show, competition is particularly fierce in subjects such as medicine and English, but those qualified to read metallurgy or classics have a high chance of success. The pattern is similar to that in other universities, although the high degree of selection (and self-selection) that precedes an Oxbridge application means that even in the less popular subjects the field of candidates is likely to be strong.

These two universities' power to intimidate prospective applicants is based partly on myth. Both have done their best to live down the *Brideshead Revisited* image, but many sixth-formers still fear that they would be out of their depth there, academically and socially. In fact, the state sector produces about half the entrants to Oxford and Cambridge, and the drop-out rate is lower than at many other universities. The 'champagne set' is still present and its activities are well publicised, but most students are hard-working high achievers with the same concerns as their counterparts on other campuses. A joint poll by the two universities' student newspapers showed that undergraduates were spending much of their time in the library or worrying about their employment prospects, and relatively little time on the river or in the college bar.

## State School Applicants

Student organisations at both universities have put in a great deal of effort trying to encourage applications from state schools, and some colleges have launched their own campaigns. Such has been the determination to convince state school pupils that they will get a fair crack of the whip that a new concern has grown up of possible bias against independent school pupils. In reality, however, the dispersed nature of Oxbridge admissions discounts any conspiracy. Some colleges set relatively low-standard offers to encourage applicants from the state sector, who may reveal their potential at interview. Some admissions tutors may give the edge to candidates from comprehensive schools over those from highly academic independent schools because they consider theirs the greater achievement in the circumstances. Others stick with tried and trusted sources of good students. The independent sector still enjoys a degree of success out of proportion to its share of the school population.

## Choosing the Right College

Thorough research to find the right college is therefore very important. Even within colleges, different admissions tutors may have different approaches, so personal contact is essential. The college is likely to be the centre of your social life, as well as your home and study centre for at least a year, so you need to be sure not only that you have a chance of a place, but that you want one at that college. Famously sporty colleges, for example, can be trying for those in search of peace and quiet.

The tables in this chapter give an idea of the relative academic strengths of the colleges, as well as the varying levels of competition for a place in different subjects. But only individual research will suggest which is the right place for you. For example, women may favour one of the few remaining single-sex colleges (St Hilda's at Oxford; New Hall, Newnham and Lucy Cavendish at Cambridge). Men have no such option.

Neither the Norrington Table, for Oxford, nor the Tompkins Table, for Cambridge, is published by the university concerned. Indeed, Oxford tried without success to make compilation impossible. However, both tables give an indication of where the academic power-houses lie – information which can be as useful to those trying to avoid them as those seeking the ultimate challenge. Although there can be a great deal of movement year by year, both tables tend to be dominated by the rich, old foundations.

In both universities, teaching for most students is based in the colleges. In practice, however, this arrangement holds good in the sciences only for the first year. One-to-one tutorials, which are Oxbridge's traditional strength for undergraduates, are by no means universal. However, teaching groups remain much smaller than in most universities, and the tutor remains an inspiration for many students.

Both Oxford and Cambridge give applicants the option of leaving the choice of college to the university. For those with no ready source of advice on the colleges, this would seem an attractive solution to an intractable problem, but it is also a risky one: a lower proportion succeeds in this way than by applying to a particular college and, inevitably, you may end up somewhere that you hate.

## The Applications Procedure

Both universities have set a deadline of 15 October 2002 for entry in 2003. At the same time as your UCAS form is submitted, an Oxford Application Form or Cambridge Preliminary Application Form (PAF), which your school can obtain direct from the relevant university, must be sent direct to Oxford or Cambridge. You may apply to only one of Oxford or Cambridge in the same admissions year, unless you are seeking an Organ award at both universities. Interviews take place in September for those who have left school or applied early, but in December for the majority. By the end of October, the first group can expect an offer, a rejection or deferral of a decision until January. The main group of applicants to Oxford will receive either a conditional offer or a rejection by Christmas, while in Cambridge the news arrives early in the new year. There are other differences between the two universities, however. Some Cambridge colleges ask candidates to sit the university's Sixth Term Examination Papers. Oxford abolished its entrance examination because of claims that it favoured candidates from independent schools. Applicants are now given conditional offers in the normal way, although they may be asked to sit tests when they are called for interview. Oxford is more likely than Cambridge to make an offer as low as two E grades if it is sure that it wants the applicant, but the practice is no longer common.

For general information about Oxford and Cambridge universities, see pages 344 and 234 respectively.

## The College League Tables

Both tables are compiled from the degree results of final-year undergraduates. A first is worth five points, a 2:1 four, a 2:2 three, a third one point. The total is divided by the number of candidates to produce each college's average.

### CAMBRIDGE  The TompkinsTable 2001

| 2001 | 2000 | | 2001 | 2000 | |
|---|---|---|---|---|---|
| 1 | 1 | Christ's | 13 | 21 | Fitzwilliam |
| 2 | 3 | Emmanuel | 14 | 19 | Robinson |
| 3 | 2 | Trinity | 15 | 17 | Trinity Hall |
| 4 | 4 | St John's | 16 | 23 | Sidney Sussex |
| 5 | 5 | Queens' | 17 | 18 | Girton |
| 6 | 9 | Clare | 18 | 11 | St Catharine's |
| 7 | 6 | Pembroke | 19 | 14 | Peterhouse |
| 8 | 12 | Gonville and Caius | 20 | 10 | Corpus Christi |
| 9 | 15 | Churchill | 21 | 20 | King's |
| 10 | 8 | Downing | 22 | 22 | Magdalene |
| 11 | 13 | Jesus | 23 | 16 | New Hall |
| 12 | 7 | Selwyn | 24 | 24 | Newnham |

## OXFORD  The Norrington Table 2001

| 2001 | 2000 |  | 2001 | 2000 |  |
|------|------|--|------|------|--|
| 1 | 9 | Balliol | 16 | 24 | St Anne's |
| 2 | 2 | St John's | 17 | 14 | Keble |
| 3 | 18 | Brasenose | 18 | 13 | Trinity |
| 4 | 6 | New College | 19 | 23 | St Hugh's |
| 5 | 4 | Christ Church | 20 | 22 | St Catherine's |
| 6 | 3 | Magdalen | 21 | 25 | Queen's |
| 6 | 1 | Merton | 21 | 7 | Wadham |
| 8 | 21 | Lincoln | 23 | 27 | Pembroke |
| 9 | 19 | Corpus Christi | 24 | 16 | Lady Margaret Hall |
| 10 | 5 | Exeter | 25 | 28 | St Hilda's |
| 11 | 15 | Oriel | 26 | 20 | St Edmund Hall |
| 12 | 10 | Hertford | 27 | 29 | Mansfield |
| 13 | 11 | University | 28 | 8 | Somerville |
| 14 | 17 | Worcester | 29 | 26 | St Peter's |
| 15 | 12 | Jesus | 30 | 30 | Harris Manchester |

## Oxford Applications and Acceptances by Course

| | Applications | | Acceptances | | %places to applications | |
|---|---|---|---|---|---|---|
| **ARTS** | 2001 | 2000 | 2001 | 2000 | 2001 | 2000 |
| Ancient and Modern History | 54 | 53 | 17 | 15 | 31.5 | 28.3 |
| Archaeology and Anthropology | 52 | 69 | 21 | 30 | 40.4 | 43.5 |
| Classical Archaeology and Ancient History | 60 | | 14 | | 23.3 | |
| Classics | 175 | 196 | 118 | 127 | 67.4 | 64.8 |
| Classics and English | 31 | 36 | 11 | 11 | 35.5 | 30.6 |
| Classics and Modern Languages | 37 | 17 | 13 | 9 | 35.1 | 52.9 |
| Economics and Management | 495 | 502 | 88 | 80 | 17.8 | 15.9 |
| English | 854 | 928 | 249 | 254 | 29.2 | 27.4 |
| English and Modern Languages | 102 | 111 | 28 | 29 | 27.5 | 26.1 |
| European and Middle Eastern Languages | 13 | 12 | 6 | 5 | 46.2 | 41.7 |
| Fine Art | 104 | 103 | 17 | 19 | 16.3 | 18.4 |
| Geography | 246 | 239 | 97 | 93 | 39.4 | 38.9 |
| Law | 805 | 839 | 241 | 229 | 29.9 | 27.3 |
| Law with Law Studies in Europe | 214 | 246 | 26 | 27 | 12.1 | 11.0 |
| Mathematics and Philosophy | 71 | 70 | 31 | 25 | 43.7 | 35.7 |
| Modern History | 735 | 690 | 253 | 287 | 34.4 | 41.6 |
| Modern History and Economics | 57 | 58 | 8 | 12 | 14.0 | 20.7 |
| Modern History and English | 66 | 64 | 12 | 15 | 18.2 | 23.4 |
| Modern History and Modern Languages | 87 | 77 | 25 | 24 | 28.7 | 31.2 |
| Modern History and Politics | 189 | 198 | 37 | 45 | 19.6 | 22.7 |
| Modern Languages | 432 | 397 | 203 | 206 | 47.0 | 51.9 |
| Modern Languages & Linguistics | 11 | | 3 | | 27.3 | |
| Music | 114 | 89 | 60 | 49 | 52.6 | 55.1 |
| Oriental Studies | 60 | 69 | 35 | 28 | 58.3 | 40.6 |
| Philosophy and Modern Languages | 48 | 53 | 21 | 23 | 43.8 | 43.4 |
| Philosophy and Theology | 65 | 50 | 19 | 24 | 29.2 | 48.0 |
| Physics and Philosophy | 48 | 46 | 10 | 16 | 20.8 | 34.8 |
| PPE | 880 | 878 | 264 | 252 | 30.0 | 28.7 |
| Theology | 92 | 66 | 47 | 42 | 51.1 | 63.6 |
| **Total Arts** | 6,197 | 6,156 | 1,974 | 1,976 | 31.9 | 32.1 |

| SCIENCE | 2001 | 2000 | 2001 | 2000 | 2001 | 2000 |
|---|---|---|---|---|---|---|
| Biochemistry | 202 | 157 | 93 | 91 | 46.0 | 58.0 |
| Biological Sciences | 229 | 203 | 108 | 93 | 47.2 | 45.8 |
| Chemistry | 261 | 254 | 174 | 183 | 66.7 | 72.0 |
| Computer Science | 131 | 105 | 27 | 22 | 20.0 | 21.0 |
| Earth Sciences (Geology) | 51 | 74 | 26 | 30 | 51.0 | 40.5 |
| Engineering Science | 315 | 263 | 135 | 134 | 42.9 | 51.0 |
| Engineering and Computer Science | 60 | 55 | 14 | 13 | 23.3 | 23.6 |
| Engineering, Economics and Management | 60 | 82 | 18 | 25 | 30.0 | 30.5 |
| Engineering and Materials | 13 | 6 | 4 | 0 | 30.8 | 0.0 |
| Experimental Psychology | 172 | 172 | 43 | 37 | 25.0 | 21.5 |
| Human Sciences | 121 | 132 | 40 | 39 | 33.1 | 29.5 |
| Mathematics | 36 | 479 | 24 | 193 | 66.7 | 40.3 |
| Mathematics and Computer Science | 447 | 74 | 185 | 28 | 41.4 | 37.8 |
| Medicine | 87 | 532 | 28 | 117 | 32.2 | 22.0 |
| Metallurgy and MEM | 563 | 32 | 148 | 19 | 26.3 | 59.4 |
| Physics | 371 | 362 | 166 | 168 | 44.7 | 46.4 |
| Physiological Sciences | 33 | 32 | 16 | 13 | 48.5 | 40.6 |
| PPP | 199 | 170 | 42 | 40 | 21.1 | 23.5 |
| **Total Sciences** | **3,351** | **3,184** | **1,291** | **1,245** | **38.5** | **39.1** |
| **Total** | **9,548** | **9,340** | **3,265** | **3,221** | **34.2** | **34.5** |

NB: The dates refer to the year in which the acceptances were made.

## Cambridge Applications and Acceptances by Course

| | Applications | | Acceptances | | %places to applications | |
|---|---|---|---|---|---|---|
| **ARTS** | 2001 | 2000 | 2001 | 2000 | 2001 | 2000 |
| Anglo-Saxon | 23 | 34 | 13 | 18 | 56.5 | 52.9 |
| Archaeology and Anthropology | 128 | 145 | 55 | 60 | 43.0 | 41.4 |
| Architecture | 199 | 214 | 42 | 39 | 21.1 | 18.2 |
| Classics | 118 | 105 | 75 | 74 | 63.6 | 70.5 |
| English | 669 | 834 | 192 | 201 | 28.7 | 24.1 |
| Geography | 233 | 247 | 90 | 94 | 38.6 | 38.1 |
| History | 543 | 575 | 210 | 195 | 38.7 | 33.9 |
| History of Art | 85 | 95 | 22 | 20 | 25.9 | 21.1 |
| Modern and Medieval Languages | 445 | 509 | 201 | 177 | 45.2 | 34.8 |
| Music | 158 | 144 | 64 | 61 | 40.5 | 42.4 |
| Oriental Studies | 70 | 62 | 29 | 24 | 41.4 | 38.7 |
| Philosophy | 192 | 181 | 58 | 53 | 30.2 | 29.3 |
| Theology and Religious Studies | 80 | 79 | 38 | 43 | 47.5 | 54.4 |
| **Total Arts** | **2,943** | **3,224** | **1,089** | **1,059** | **37.0** | **32.8** |
| **SOCIAL SCIENCES** | 2001 | 2000 | 2001 | 2000 | 2001 | 2000 |
| Economics | 714 | 722 | 169 | 157 | 23.7 | 21.7 |
| Land Economy | 96 | 116 | 33 | 39 | 34.4 | 33.6 |
| Law | 992 | 921 | 222 | 231 | 22.4 | 25.1 |
| Social and Political Sciences | 357 | 362 | 100 | 93 | 28.0 | 25.7 |
| Total Social Sciences | 2,159 | 2,121 | 524 | 520 | 24.3 | 24.5 |
| **SCIENCE AND TECHNOLOGY** | 2001 | 2000 | 2001 | 2000 | 2001 | 2000 |
| Computer Science | 527 | 499 | 111 | 88 | 21.0 | 17.6 |
| Mathematics | 784 | 861 | 251 | 252 | 32.0 | 29.3 |
| Natural Sciences | 1723 | 1,816 | 610 | 617 | 35.4 | 34.0 |
| Engineering | 870 | 1,016 | 295 | 253 | 33.9 | 24.9 |

| | Applications | | Acceptances | | %places to applications | |
|---|---|---|---|---|---|---|
| | 2001 | 2000 | 2001 | 2000 | 2001 | 2000 |
| Medical Sciences | 1141 | 1,130 | 292 | 281 | 25.6 | 24.9 |
| Veterinary Medicine | 494 | 716 | 76 | 65 | 15.4 | 9.1 |
| **Total Science and Technology** | 5,539 | 6,038 | 1,635 | 1,556 | 29.5 | 25.8 |
| **Total** | 10,641 | 11,383 | 3,248 | 3,135 | 30.5 | 27.5 |

NB: The dates refer to the year in which the accpeances were made.
Mathematics includes those applying for Mathematics, Mathematics with Computer Science, and Mathematics with Physics.
The tripos courses at Cambridge in Chemical Engineering and Information Sciences, History of Art, Management Studies, and Manufacturing Engineering can only be taken after a part of another tripos. The entries for these courses are recorded under the first-year subjects taken by the students involved.

# OXFORD COLLEGE PROFILES

## BALLIOL
Balliol College, Oxford OX1 3BJ (tel. 01865-277748)
Undergraduates: 404 Male/female ratio: 60/40
www.balliol.ox.ac.uk admissions@balliol.ox.ac.uk

Famous as the alma mater of many prominent post-war politicians, including Harold Macmillan, Denis Healey and Roy Jenkins, the university's current Chancellor, Balliol has maintained a strong presence in university life and is usually well represented in the Union. Academic standards are formidably high, as might be expected in the college of Wycliffe and Adam Smith, notably in the classics and social sciences. PPE in particular is notoriously oversubscribed. Library facilities are good and include a 24-hour law library. Balliol began admitting overseas students in the 19th century and has cultivated an attractively cosmopolitan atmosphere, of which the lively JCR (Junior Common Room) is a natural focus. Most undergraduates are offered accommodation in college for three years, while the 147 graduate students are usually lodged in the Graduate Centre at Holywell Manor. Centrally located with a JCR pantry that is open all day, Balliol is convenient as well as prestigious.

## BRASENOSE
Brasenose College, Oxford OX1 4AJ (tel. 01865-277510)
Undergraduates: 371 Male/female ratio: 67/33
www.bnc.ox.ac.uk brasinfo@bnc.ox.ac.uk

Brasenose may not be the most famous Oxford college but it makes up for its discreet image with a consistently healthy academic performance, an advantageous position in the centre of town, and lesser known attractions such as

Gertie's Tea Bar. Brasenose was one of the first colleges to become co-educational in the 1970s, although men still take two-thirds of the places. In its defence, the college prospectus points out that the major undergraduate office, President of the JCR, has been filled as often by a woman as a man. But BNC, as the college is often known, still has the image of a rugby haven. Named after the door knocker on the 13th-century Brasenose Hall, the college has a pleasant, intimate ambience which most find conductive to study. Law, PPE and modern history are traditional strengths and competition for places in these subjects is intense. Sporting standards are as high as at many much larger colleges and the college's rowing club is one of the oldest in the university. The college has restructured accommodation charges for its students. An annex, the St Cross Building, means all undergraduates can live in. Most third years live in the Brasenose annex at Frewin Court, just a few minutes' walk away.

## CHRIST CHURCH
**Christ Church College, Oxford OX1 1DP (tel. 01865-276181)**
**Undergraduates:** 417 **Male/female ratio:** 56/44
**www.chch.ox.ac.uk   tutor.admissions@chch.ox.ac.uk**

The college founded by Cardinal Wolsey in 1525 and affectionately known as The House has come a long way since Evelyn Waugh mythologised its aristocratic excesses in *Brideshead Revisited*. The social mix at Christ Church is much more varied than most applicants suspect and the college has gone out of its way recently to become something of a champion of political correctness. The male/female ratio has been improving steadily and a code of practice on sexual harassment has been implemented. Academic pressure at Christ Church is reasonably relaxed, although natural high-achievers prosper and the college's history and law teaching is highly regarded. The magnificent 18th-century library, housing 100,000 books, is one of the best in Oxford. It is supplemented by a separate law library. Christ Church has its own art gallery, which holds over 2,000 works of mainly Italian Renaissance art. Sport, especially rugby, is an important part of college life. The playing fields are a few minutes' walk away through the Meadows. The river is also close at hand for the aspiring oarsman, and the college has good squash courts. Accommodation is rated by Christ Church students as excellent and includes flats off Iffley Road as well as a number of beautifully panelled shared sets (double rooms) in college. The modern bar adds to the lustre of a college justly famous for its imposing architecture and cathedral, the smallest in England.

## CORPUS CHRISTI
**Corpus Christi College, Oxford OX1 4JF (tel. 01865-276693)**
**Undergraduates:** 214 **Male/female ratio:** 67/33
**www.ccc.ox.ac.uk   admissions.office@ccc.ox.ac.uk**

Corpus, until recently Oxford's smallest college, is naturally overshadowed by its Goliath-like neighbour, Christ Church, but makes the most of its intimacy, friendly atmosphere and exquisite beauty. Like The House it has an exceptional view across the Meadows. Although the college has only 307 students including postgraduates, it has an admirable library open 24 hours a day. Academic expectations are high and English, PPE and medicine are especially well established. The college is beginning to make the most of ties with its namesake at Cambridge, establishing a joint lectureship in history in 1999. Corpus is able to offer accommodation to all its undergraduates, one of its many attractions to those seeking a smaller community in Oxford.

## EXETER
**Exeter College, Oxford OX1 3DP (tel. 01865-279648)**
**Undergraduates:** 314 **Male/female ratio:** 60/40
**www.exeter.ox.ac.uk admissions@exeter.ox.ac.uk**

Exeter is the fourth oldest college in the university and was founded in 1314 by Walter de Stapeldon, Bishop of Exeter. Nestling halfway between the High Street and Broad Street, site of most of the city's bookshops, it could hardly be more central. The college boasts handsome buildings, the exceptional Fellows' garden and attractive accommodation for most undergraduates for all three years of their university careers. Exeter's academic record is strong and the college is a consistent high performer in the Norrington Table. It is, however, often accused of being rather dull. Given its glittering roll-call of alumni, which includes Martin Amis, J.R.R. Tolkien, Alan Bennett, Richard Burton, Imogen Stubbs and Tariq Ali, this seems an accusation that on the face of it at least is hard to sustain. College food is not rated highly by students although the bar is popular with students from other colleges. The social scene is livelier than the male/female ratio might suggest.

## HARRIS MANCHESTER
**Harris Manchester College, Oxford OX1 3TF (tel. 01865-271009)**
**Undergraduates:** 75 **Male/female ratio:** 44/56
**www.hmc.ox.ac.uk college.office@hmc.ox.ac.uk**

Founded in Manchester in 1786 to provide education for non-Anglican students, Harris Manchester finally settled in Oxford in 1889 after spells in both York and London. A full university college since 1996, its central location with fine buildings and grounds in Holywell Street is very convenient for the Bodleian, although the college itself does have an excellent library. Harris Manchester admits only mature students of mostly 25 years and above to read for both undergraduate and graduate degrees, predominantly in the arts. There are also groups of visiting students from American universities and some men and women training for the ministry. Most of its members live in and all meals are provided, indeed the college encourages its members to dine regularly in hall. The college has few sporting facilities but its students do still manage to represent Harris

Manchester in football, cricket, swimming and chess as well as playing on other college or university teams. Other outlets include the college Drama Society and also the chapel, a focal point to many there.

## HERTFORD
**Hertford College, Oxford  OX1 3BW (tel. 01865-279404)**
**Undergraduates:** 367  **Male/female ratio:** 52/48
**www.hertford.ox.ac.uk  admissions@hertford.ox.ac.uk**

Though tracing its roots to the 12th century, Hertford is determinedly modern. It was one of the first colleges to admit women (in 1976). Hertford also helped set the trend towards offers of places conditional on A levels, which paved the way for the abolition of the entrance examination. It is still popular with state school applicants. The college lacks the grandeur of Magdalen, of which it was once an annex, but has its own architectural trademark in the Bridge of Sighs. It is also close to the History Faculty library (Hertford's neighbour), the Bodleian and the King's Arms, perhaps Oxford's most popular pub. Academic pressure at Hertford is not high but the quality of teaching, especially in English, is generally thought admirable. Accommodation is improving, thanks in part to the Abingdon House complex, and the college can now lodge almost all its undergraduates at any one time. Like most congenial colleges, Hertford is often accused of being claustrophobic and inward-looking – a charge most Hertfordians would ascribe simply to jealousy.

## JESUS
**Jesus College, Oxford  OX1 3DW (tel. 01865-279720)**
**Undergraduates:** 336  **Male/female ratio:** 60/40
**www.jesus.ox.ac.uk  admissions.tutor@jesus.ox.ac.uk**

Jesus, the only Oxford college to be founded in the reign of Elizabeth I, suffers from something of an unfair reputation for insularity. Its students, whose predecessors include T.E. Lawrence and Harold Wilson, describe it as 'friendly but gossipy' and shrug off the legend that all its undergraduates are Welsh. Close to most of Oxford's main facilities, Jesus has three compact quads, the second of which is especially enticing in the summer. Academic standards are high and most subjects are taught in college. Physics, chemistry and engineering are especially strong. Rugby and rowing also tend to be taken seriously. Accommodation is almost universally regarded as excellent and relatively inexpensive. Self-catering flats in north and east Oxford have enabled every graduate to live in throughout his or her Oxford career. The range of accommodation available to undergraduates is similarly good. The college's Cowley Road development is described by the students' union as 'some of the plushest student housing in Oxford'.

# KEBLE

**Keble College, Oxford OX1 3PG (tel. 01865-272711)**
**Undergraduates:** 444 **Male/female ratio:** 60/40
**www.keble.ox.ac.uk admissions@keb.ox.ac.uk**

Keble, named after John Keble, the leader of the Oxford Movement, was founded in 1870 with the intention of making Oxford education more accessible and the college remains proud of 'the legacy of a social conscience'. With around 450 undergraduates, Keble is one of the biggest colleges in Oxford, while its uncompromising Victorian Gothic architecture also makes it one of the most distinctive. Once famous for the special privileges it extended to rowers, the college is now academically strong, particularly in the sciences where it benefits from easy access to the Science Area, the Radcliffe Science Library and the Mathematical Institute. At the same time, the college's sporting record remains exemplary, providing a large number of rugby Blues in recent years. Undergraduates are guaranteed accommodation in their first two years (or two out of three years), although rent increases have been the cause of some friction between undergraduates and the college authorities. Students who live in must eat in Hall 30 times a year. The Starship Enterprise bar is a particular attraction.

# LADY MARGARET HALL

**Lady Margaret Hall College, Oxford OX2 6QA (tel. 01865-274310/1)**
**Undergraduates:** 391 **Male/female ratio:** 50/50
**www.lmh.ox.ac.uk college.office@lmh.ox.ac.uk**

Lady Margaret Hall, Oxford's first college for women, has been co-educational since 1978 and is now equally balanced. For many students, LMH's comparative isolation – the college is three-quarters of a mile north of the city centre – is a real advantage, ensuring a clear distinction between college life and university activities, and a refuge from tourists. Although the neo-Georgian architecture is not to everyone's taste, the college's beautiful gardens back onto the Cherwell river, which allows LMH to have its own punt house. The students' union describes academic life at the college as 'fairly lax' while commending its record in English, history and law. Accommodation should soon be available to all undergraduates for all years. The college's two recent accommodation buildings have the remarkable attraction of private bathrooms in all their rooms. LMH shares most of its sports facilities with Trinity College though it has squash and tennis courts on site. Recently, it has become one of Oxford's dramatic centres.

# LINCOLN

**Lincoln College, Oxford OX1 3DR (tel. 01865-279836)**
**Undergraduates:** 280 **Male/female ratio:** 60/40
**www.lincoln.ox.ac.uk admissions@lincoln.ox.ac.uk**

Small, central Lincoln cultivates a lower profile than many other colleges with comparable assets. The college's 15th-century buildings and beautiful library – a converted Queen Anne church – combine to produce a delightful environment in which to spend three years. Academic standards are high, particularly in arts subjects, although the college's relaxed atmosphere is justly celebrated. Accommofion, rated 'excellent' by the students' union, is provided by the college for all undergraduates throughout their careers and includes rooms above The Mitre, a medieval inn. Students parade around Oxford in *sub fusc* (formal wear) on Ascension Day while choristers beat the bounds. Graduate students have their own centre a few minutes' walk away in Bear Lane. Lincoln's small size and self-sufficiency have led to the college's being accused of insularity. Lincoln's food is outstanding, among the best in the university. Sporting achievement is impressive for a college of this size, in part a reflection of its good facilities.

## MAGDALEN
**Magdalen College, Oxford  OX1 4AU (tel. 01865-276063)**
**Undergraduates:** 401  **Male/female ratio:** 60/40
**www.magd.ox.ac.uk  admissions@magd.ox.ac.uk**

Perhaps the most beautiful college in Oxford or Cambridge, Magdalen is known around the world for its tower, its deer park and its May morning celebrations when students throw themselves off Magdalen Bridge into the river Cherwell. The college has shaken off its public school image to become a truly cosmopolitan place, with a large intake from overseas and an increasing proportion of state school pupils. Magdalen's record in English, history and law is second to none, while its new science park at Sandford is bound to bolster its reputation in the sciences. Library facilities are excellent, especially in history and law. First-year students are accommodated in the Waynflete Building and allocated rooms in subsequent years by ballot. Undergraduates can be housed in college for all three years. Sets in cloisters and in the palatial New Buildings are particularly sought after. Magdalen is also conveniently placed for the wealth of rented accommodation in east Oxford. The college bar is one of the best in Oxford and the college is a pluralistic place, proud of its drama society and choir. Enthusiasm on the river and sports field makes up for a traditional lack of athletic prowess.

## MANSFIELD
**Mansfield College, Oxford  OX1 3TF (tel. 01865 270982)**
**Undergraduates:** 190  **Male/female ratio:** 55/45
**www.mansfield.ox.ac.uk  info@sea.mansfield.ox.ac.uk**

Mansfield's graduation to full Oxford college status marked the culmination of a long history of development since 1886. Its spacious, attractive site is fairly central, close to the libraries, the shops, the University Parks and the river Cherwell. With only 190 undergraduates, the community is close-knit, although this can verge on the claustrophobic. The male to female ratio is slightly better than for the university as a whole. Women may prefer the less intimidating atmosphere of Mansfield, perhaps helped by its strong representation of state school students. First and third years live in college accommodation. Mansfield students share Merton's excellent sports ground and have numerous college teams although it is in drama that its students truly excel. Despite its former theological background, students are not admitted on the basis of religion and can read a wide variety of subjects. Mansfield is home to the Oxford Centre for the Environment, Ethics and Society (OCEES) and also the American Studies Institute, evidence of the strong links between Mansfield and the United States, which is reflected by some 70 visiting students annually.

## MERTON
**Merton College, Oxford  OX1 4JD (tel. 01865-276329)**
**Undergraduates:** 295  **Male/female ratio:** 60/40
**www.merton.ox.ac.uk   undergraduate-admissions@admin.merton.ox.ac.uk**

Founded in 1264 by Walter de Merton, Bishop of Rochester and Chancellor of England, Merton is one of Oxford's oldest colleges and one of its most prestigious. Quiet and beautiful, with the oldest quad in the university, Merton has high academic expectations of its undergraduates, often reflected in a position at the top of the Norrington Table, as in 2000. History, law, English, physics and chemistry all enjoy a formidable track record. The medieval library is the envy of many other colleges. Accommodation is cheap, of a good standard and offered to students for all three years. Merton's food is among the best in the university; formal Hall is served six times a week. No kitchens are provided for students who live in college, however. Merton's many diversions include the Merton Floats, its dramatic society, an excellent Christmas Ball and the peculiar Time Ceremony, which celebrates the return of GMT. Sports facilities are excellent, although participation tends to be more important than the final score.

## NEW COLLEGE
**New College, Oxford  OX1 3BN (tel. 01865-279551)**
**Undergraduates:** 421  **Male/female ratio:** 55/45
**www.new.ox.ac.uk   admissions@new.ox.ac.uk**

New College is large, old (founded in 1379 by William of Wykeham) and much more relaxed than most expect when first confronting its daunting facade. It is a bustling place, as proud of its excellent music and its bar as of its strength in law, history and PPE. The college has been making particular efforts to increase the proportion of state school students, inviting applications from schools that have never sent candidates to Oxford. The Target Schools Scheme, designed to increase applications from state schools, is well established. From 2001, almost all undergraduates will be able to have college accommodation for three years. The college's library facilities are impressive, especially in law, classics and PPE. The sports ground is nearby and includes good tennis courts.

Women's sport is particularly strong. A new sports complex, named after Brian Johnston, opened in 1997, at St Cross Road. The sheer beauty of New College remains one of its principal assets and the college gardens are a memorable sight in spite of these traditional charms, the college has strong claims to be considered admirably innovative. Music is a feature of college life and the Commemoration Ball, held every three years, is a highlight of Oxford's social calendar.

## ORIEL

**Oriel College, Oxford  OX1 4EW (tel. 01865-276522)**
**Undergraduates:** 292  **Male/female ratio:** 67/33
**www.oriel.ox.ac.uk  admissions@oriel.ox.ac.uk**

In spite of its reputation as a bastion of muscular privilege, Oriel is a friendly college with a strong sense of identity and has adjusted rapidly to co-educational admissions (women were not admitted until 1985). The students' union describes the college as having 'a strong crew spirit' reflecting its traditions on the river. Academic standards are better than legend suggests and the college's well-stocked library is open 24 hours a day. But Oriel's sporting reputation is certainly deserved and its rowing eight is rarely far from the head of the river. Other sports are well catered for, even if their facilities are considerably farther away than the boathouse, which is only a short jog away. Accommodation is of variable quality but Oriel can provide rooms for all three years for those students who require them. Scholars and Exhibitioners chasing firsts in their final year are given priority in the ballot for college rooms. Extensive new accommodation has been completed one mile away off the Cowley Road and at the Island Site on Oriel Street. Oriel also offers a lively drama society, a Shakespearian production taking place each summer in the front quad.

## PEMBROKE

**Pembroke College, Oxford  OX1 1DW (tel. 01865-276412)**
**Undergraduates:** 411  **Male/female ratio:** 55/45
**www.pmb.ox.ac.uk  admissions.secretary@pembroke.ox.ac.uk**

Although its alumni include such extrovert characters as Dr Johnson and Michael Heseltine, Pembroke is one of Oxford's least dynamic colleges. Academic results are solid, and the college has Fellows and lecturers in almost all the major university subjects. Pembroke expects to accommodate all first years and most final-year undergraduates. The Sir Geoffrey Arthur building on the river, ten minutes' walk from the college, offers excellent facilities, in addition to 100 student rooms there is a concert room, computer room and a multi-gym. College food is reasonable, though some find formal Hall every evening rather too rich a diet. Rugby and rowing are strong, with Pembroke second only to Oriel on the river, and squash and tennis courts are available at the nearby sports ground.

# QUEEN'S

Queen's College, Oxford OX1 4AW (tel. 01865-279167)
**Undergraduates:** 318 **Male/female ratio:** 60/40
www.queens.ox.ac.uk admissions@queens.ox.ac.uk

One of the most striking sights of the High Street, Queen's has now shed its exclusive 'northern' image to become one of Oxford's liveliest and most attractive colleges. The college's academic record is good. According to the students' union, 'the general attitude to work is fairly relaxed and seems to bring good results'. Modern languages, chemistry and mathematics are reckoned among the strongest subjects. Queen's does not normally admit undergraduates for the honours school of English language and literature or geography. The library, open till 10 pm, is as beautiful as it is well stocked. All students are offered accommodation, first years being housed in modernist annexes in east Oxford. The college's beer cellar is one of the most popular in the university and the JCR's facilities are also better than average. An annual dinner commemorates a student who is said to have fended off a bear by thrusting a volume of Aristotle into its mouth.

# ST ANNE'S

St Anne's College, Oxford OX2 6HS (tel. 01865-274825)
**Undergraduates:** 459 **Male/female ratio:** 55/45
www.stannes.ox.ac.uk enquiries@st-annes.ox.ac.uk

Architecturally uninspiring (a row of Victorian houses with concrete 'stack-a-studies' dropped into their back gardens), St Anne's makes up in community spirit what it lacks in awesome grandeur. One of the largest colleges, it has a high proportion of state school students. A women's college until 1979, its academic standing is not strong by Oxford's standards, although it has begun to climb the Norrington Table again since slipping to last place in the middle of the last decade. The library is particularly rich in law, Chinese and medieval history texts. Opening hours are long. Accommodation is guaranteed to all undergraduates and the college is just to the north of the city centre. Three new accommodation blocks contain 150 student rooms, including four for disabled students, while the older rooms have been refurbished.

# ST CATHERINE'S

St Catherine's College, Oxford OX13UJ (tel. 01865-271703)
**Undergraduates:** 423 **Male/female ratio:** 62/38
www.stcatz.ox.ac.uk admissions@stcatz.ox.ac.uk

Arne Jacobsen's modernist design for 'Catz', one of Oxford's youngest undergraduate college and fourth largest, has attracted much attention as the most striking contrast in the university to the lofty spires of Magdalen and New College. Close to the university science area and the pleasantly rural Holywell Great Meadow, St Catherine's is nevertheless only a few minutes' walk from the city centre. Academic standards are especially high in mathematics and physics though the college's scholarly ambitions are far from having been exhausted. The undergraduate prospectus used to complain that Fellows were 'increasingly eager to apply more academic pressure in college' The well-liked Wolfson library (famous for its unusual Jacobsen chairs) is open till 1 am on most days. Accommodation is available for first and third years, and plans are underway to extend this to all three years. Rooms are small but tend to be warmer than in other, more venerable colleges. Squash, tennis and netball courts are all on the main college site. There is an excellent theatre, and the college is host to the Cameron Mackintosh Chair of Contemporary Theatre, recent incumbents of which have included Sir Ian McKellen, Alan Ayckbourn and Lord Attenborough. St Catherine's has one of the best JCR facilities in Oxford.

## ST EDMUND HALL

**St Edmund Hall College, Oxford  OX1 4AR (tel. 01865-279008)**
**Undergraduates:** 403  **Male/female ratio:** 67/33
**www.seh.ox.ac.uk   admissions@seh.ox.ac.uk**

St Edmund Hall – 'Teddy Hall' – has one of Oxford's smallest college sites but also one of its most populous with 400 undergraduates swarming through its medieval quads. Some two-thirds of undergraduates are male, but the college is anxious to shed its image as a home for 'hearties', and the authorities have gone out of their way to tone down younger members' rowdier excesses. Nonetheless, the sporting culture at St Edmund Hall is still vigorous and the college usually does well in rugby, football and hockey. Academically, the college has some impressive names among its fellowship as well as a marvellous library, originally a Norman church. The students' union reports that 'a laid-back approach (to work) is the norm'. Accommodation is reasonable and is guaranteed to first and third years, though most second-year students live out. The college has two annexes, one near the University Parks, the other in Iffley Road, where many of the rooms have private bathrooms. Hall food is better than average.

## ST HILDA'S

**St Hilda's College, Oxford  OX4 1DY (tel. 01865-286620)**
**Undergraduates:** 409  **Women only**
**www.sthildas.ox.ac.uk   college.office@st-hildas.ox.ac.uk**

With Somerville co-educational, St Hilda's is now the last bastion of all-women education in Oxford. How long the university will allow it to remain that way is open to question. In spite of its variable academic record, the college is a distinctive part of the Oxford landscape and is usually well represented in university life. The 50,000-volume library is growing fast and plans for its extension are being considered. St Hilda's also boasts one of the largest ratios of state school to independent undergraduates in Oxford. Accommodation is guaranteed to first years and for one of the remaining two years. The college owns its own punts, which are available free for college members and their guests. Many of the rooms offer some of the best river views in Oxford. Social facilities are limited but the standard of food is high.

## ST HUGH'S

**St Hugh's College, Oxford OX2 6LE (tel. 01865-274910)**
**Undergraduates:** 421 **Male/female ratio:** 55/45
**www.st-hughs.ox.ac.uk admissions@st-hughs.ox.ac.uk**

One of Oxford's lesser-known colleges, St Hugh's was criticised by students in 1987 when it began admitting men. There are now fewer women than men at the college, although the male/female ratio is better balanced than at most Oxford colleges. Like Lady Margaret Hall, St Hugh's is a bicycle ride from the city centre and has a picturesque setting. It is an ideal college for those seeking a place to live and study away from the madding crowd, and is well liked for its pleasantly bohemian atmosphere. Academic pressure remains comparatively low, although the students' union says there are signs that this is changing. St Hugh's guarantees accommodation to undergraduates for all three years, although the standard of rooms is variable. Sport, particularly football, is taken quite seriously. The extensive grounds include a croquet lawn and tennis courts

## ST JOHN'S

**St John's College, Oxford OX1 3JP (tel. 01865-277317)**
**Undergraduates:** 371 **Male/female ratio:** 60/40
**www.sjc.ox.ac.uk admissions@sjc.ox.ac.uk**

St John's is one of Oxford's powerhouses, excelling in almost every field and boasting arguably the most beautiful gardens in the university. Founded in 1555 by a London merchant, it is richly endowed and makes the most of its resources to provide undergraduates with an agreeable and challenging three years. The work ethic is very much part of the St John's ethos, and academic standards are high, with English, chemistry and history among the traditional strengths, though all students benefit from the impressive library. There are still fewer undergraduates from state schools than public schools (52/48), but the college compensates to some extent by offering generous hardship funds to those in financial difficulty. As might be expected of a wealthy college, the accommodation is excellent and guaranteed for three or four years. St John's has a strong sporting tradition and offers good facilities, but the social scene is limited.

## ST PETER'S

**St Peter's College, Oxford OX1 2DL (tel. 01865-278863)**
**Undergraduates:** 360 **Male/female ratio:** 60/40
**www.spc.ox.ac.uk admissions@spc.ox.ac.uk**

Opened as St Peter's Hall in 1929, St Peter's has been an Oxford college since 1961. Its medieval, Georgian and 19th-century buildings are in the city centre and close to most of Oxford's main facilities. Though still young, St

Peter's is well represented in university life and has pockets of academic excellence despite finishing near the bottom of the Norrington Table. History tutoring is particularly good. There are no Fellows in classics at the college. Accommodation is offered to students for first and third years and about 60 per cent of second years. Student rooms vary from traditional rooms in college to new purpose-built rooms a few minutes' walk away. The college's facilities are impressive, including one of the university's best JCRs. St Peter's is known as one of Oxford's most vibrant colleges socially. It is strong on acting and journalism and has a recently refurbished bar.

## SOMERVILLE

**Somerville College, Oxford  OX2 6HD (tel. 01865-270629)**
**Undergraduates: 397  Male/female ratio: 50/50**
**www.some.ox.ac.uk  secretariat@somerville.ox.ac.uk**

The announcement, early in 1992, that Somerville was to go co-educational sparked an unusually acrimonious and persistent dispute within this most tranquil of colleges. Protests were doomed to failure, however: the first male undergraduates arrived in 1994 and now account for half the students. Lady Thatcher was one of those who flocked to their old college's defence, illustrating the fierce loyalty Somerville inspires. The college's atmosphere appears to have survived the momentous change, although the culture of protest reappeared when a number of students refused to pay the government's tuition fees in 1998. Accommodation, including 30 small flats for students, is of a reasonable standard, and is guaranteed for first years and students sitting public examinations. Sport is strong at Somerville and the womens' rowing eight usually finishes near the head of the river. The college's hockey pitches and tennis courts are nearby. The 100,000-volume library is open 24 hours a day and is one of the most beautiful in Oxford.

## TRINITY

**Trinity College, Oxford  OX1 3BH (tel. 01865-279910)**
**Undergraduates: 281  Male/female ratio: 56/44**
**www.trinity.ox.ac.uk  admissions@trinity.ox.ac.uk**

Architecturally impressive and boasting beautiful lawns, Trinity is one of Oxford's least populous colleges. It is ideally located, beside the Bodleian, Blackwell's book shop and the White Horse pub. Cardinal Newman, an alumnus of Trinity, is said to have regarded Trinity's motto as 'Drink, drink, drink'. Academic pressure varies, as the college darts up and down the unofficial Norrington Table of academic performance. Nonetheless, the college produces its fair share of firsts, especially in arts subjects. Trinity has shaken off its reputation for apathy, though the early gate closing times can leave the college isolated late at night. Members are active in all walks of university life and the college has its own debating and drama societies. The proportion of state school entrants has been rising. Accommodation is of a reasonable standard and most undergraduates can live in for three years if they wish.

## UNIVERSITY
**University College, Oxford  OX1 4BH (tel. 01865-276601)**
**Undergraduates:** 415  **Male/female ratio:** 67/33
**www.univ.ox.ac.uk  admissions@univ.ox.ac.uk**

University is the first Oxford college to be able to boast a former student in the Oval Office. Indeed, the college seems certain to benefit from its unique links with President Clinton, a Rhodes Scholar at University in the late 1960s. The college is probably Oxford's oldest, though highly unlikely to have been founded by King Alfred, as legend claims. Academic expectations are high and the college prospers in most subjects. Physics, PPE and maths are particularly strong. That said, University has fewer claims to be thought a powerhouse in the manner of St John's, arguably its greatest rival. Accommodation is guaranteed to undergraduates for all three years, with third years lodged in an annexe in north Oxford about a mile and a half from the college site on the High Street. The students' union complains that facilities are poor. Sport is strong and University is usually successful on the river, but the college has a reputation for being quiet socially.

## WADHAM
**Wadham College, Oxford  OX1 3PN (tel. 01865-277947)**
**Undergraduates:** 444  **Male/female ratio:** 48/52
**www.wadham.ox.ac.uk  admissions@wadham.ox.ac.uk**

Founded by Dorothy Wadham in 1609, Wadham is known in about equal measure for its academic track record – the college generally ranks in the top third in examination performance – and its leftist politics. The JCR is famously dynamic and politically active, although the breadth of political opinion is greater than its left-wing stereotype suggests. And for somewhere supposedly unconcerned with such fripperies, its gardens are surprisingly beautiful. The somewhat rough-hewn chapel is similarly memorable. The college has a good 24-hour library. Accommodation is guaranteed for at least two years and there are many large, shared rooms on offer. Journalism and drama play an important part in the life of the college, although sport is there for those who want it. The College also includes the 18th-century Holywell Music Room, a historic concert hall.

## WORCESTER
**Worcester College, Oxford  OX1 2HB (tel. 01865-278391)**
**Undergraduates:** 392  **Male/female ratio:** 60/40
**www.worc.ox.ac.uk  admissions@worc.ox.ac.uk**

Worcester is to the west of Oxford what Magdalen is to the east, an open, rural contrast to the urban rush of the city centre. The college's rather mediocre exterior conceals a delightful environment, including some characteristically muscular Baroque Hawskmoor architecture, a garden and a lake. Though academic pressure has been described as 'tastefully restrained', law, theology and engineering are among the college's strengths. The 24-hour library is strongest in the arts. Accommodation, guaranteed for two years and provided for the majority of third years, varies in quality from ordinary to conference standard in the Linbury Building. The ratio of bathrooms to students (one to four) is better than in many colleges. Sport plays an important part in college life, Worcester having engaged more success recently in rowing and rugby.

# CAMBRIDGE COLLEGE PROFILES

## CHRIST'S

**Christ's College, Cambridge  CB2 3BU (tel. 01223-334953)**
**Undergraduates:** 433  **Male/female ratio:** 65/35
**www.christs.cam.ac.uk  admissions@christs.cam.ac.uk**

Christ's prides itself on its academic strength, topping the Tompkins Table again in 2001. It is also one of the few colleges still to offer places on two E grades at A level, meaning not that entry standards are low but that the college is sufficiently confident of its ability to identify potential high-flyers at interview that it is in effect prepared to circumvent A-levels as the principal criteria for entry. The college has around a 50/50 state-to-independent ratio and women make up almost a third of the students. Though the college has a reputation for being dominated by hard-working natural scientists and mathematicians, it maintains a broad subject range. It has had the best results in the university for history and music over the past five years. The atmosphere is supposedly so cosy that one student described Christ's as 'a cup of Horlicks', but some complain of short bar opening hours and a poor relationship between undergraduates and Fellows. Accommodation in college is guaranteed to all undergraduates, some of whom will be allocated rooms in the infamous New Court 'Typewriter', probably the least attractive building in the city. The Typewriter houses the excellent New Court theatre, home to Christ's Amateur Dramatics Society and Christ's Films, one of the most adventurous student film societies. College sport has flourished in recent years, with teams competing to a good standard. The playing fields (shared with Sidney Sussex) are just over a mile away.

## CHURCHILL

**Churchill College, Cambridge  CB3 ODS (tel. 01223-336202)**
**Undergraduates:** 469  **Male/female ratio:** 70/30
**www.chu.cam.ac.uk  admissions@chu.cam.ac.uk**

Founded in 1960 to help meet 'the national need for scientists and engineers and to forge links with industry', Churchill has been rising again in the Cambridge league table and still has high standards. Maths, natural sciences, engineering and computer science are traditional strengths, but arts results have been disappointing recently. The college has some of the university's best computer facilities. Deferred entry is encouraged in all subjects. Churchill has the joint highest ratio of state to independent pupils (75/25) but one of the lowest proportions of women undergraduates: only one in three. Some are put off by Churchill's unassuming modern architecture and the college's distance from the city centre; others argue that the distance offers much-needed breathing space. One undeniable advantage is Churchill's ability to provide every undergraduate with a room in college for all three years. There are extensive on-site playing fields, and the college does well in rugby, hockey and rowing. The university's only student radio station (broadcasting to Churchill and New Hall) is based here.

## CLARE

Clare College, Cambridge CB2 1TL (tel. 01223-333246)
**Undergraduates:** 473 **Male/female ratio:** 55/45
www.clare.cam.ac.uk admissions@clare.cam.ac.uk

Though for many Clare's outstanding features are its gardens and harmonious buildings, hard-pressed undergraduates are just as likely to praise the rent and food charges, among the lowest in the university. Accommodation is guaranteed for all three years, either in college or nearby hostels. One of the few colleges which openly encourages applications from 'candidates of a good academic standard who have special talents in non-academic fields', Clare tends to feature near the top of the academic tables. Applicants are encouraged to take a gap year. Languages, social and political science and music are especially strong, but science results have been disappointing The ratio of male to female students is better than many colleges, while systematic attempts to raise the proportion of state-educated students has left those from independent schools in a minority. Music thrives. The choir records and tours regularly, and Clare Cellars (comprising the bar and JCR) is rapidly becoming the Cambridge jazz venue as well as providing more contemporary sounds such as drum and bass. Sporting emphasis is as much on enjoyment as competition. The women's teams have had outstanding success in recent years. The playing fields are little more than a mile away.

## CORPUS CHRISTI

Corpus Christi College, Cambridge CB2 1RH (tel. 01223-338056)
**Undergraduates:** 265 **Male/female ratio:** 63/37
www.corpus.cam.ac.uk admissions@corpus.cam.ac.uk

The only college to have been founded by town residents, Corpus's size inevitably makes it one of the more intimate colleges. It prides itself on being a cohesive community, but some find the focus on college rather than university life excessive. Although traditionally broad based academically, it had the best arts results in the university in 1999, but only twelfth for sciences. The kitchen fixed charge is above average but the college is known for a good formal hall.

Almost all undergraduates are allocated a room in college or neighbouring hostels. The library is open 24 hours. There is a fairly even social balance: the independent-to-state ratio is 47/53. The college bar has an enviable atmosphere. The sporting facilities, at Leckhampton (just over a mile away), are among the best in the university and include a swimming pool. The size of the college means that its sporting reputation owes more to enthusiasm than success, however. Drama is also well catered for, and the college owns The Playroom, the university's best small theatre.

## DOWNING

**Downing College, Cambridge CB2 1DQ (tel. 01223-334826)**
**Undergraduates:** 429 **Male/female ratio:** 55/45
**www.dow.cam.ac.uk admissions@dow.cam.ac.uk**

Downing's imposing neo-Classical quadrangle may look more like a military academy than a Cambridge college but the atmosphere here is anything but martial. Founded in 1800 for the study of law, medicine and natural sciences, these are still the college's strong subjects. Indeed Downing is often called 'the law college', although recent results have been better in sciences than arts. A reputation for hard-playing, hard-drinking rugby players and oarsmen is proving hard to shake off. The college claims the best boat club in Cambridge. But while sport undoubtedly enjoys a high profile, pressure to conform to the sporty stereotype is never excessive. Downing currently guarantees a place in college accommodation for two out of three years; the completion of a new accommodation block on 2000 allows students to be housed throughout a first degree. The new library, opened by Prince Charles in 1993, has won an award for its architecture. There is a good balance between students with state and independent school backgrounds. The new student-run bar/party room has improved college social life following three candlelit formal dinners a week.

## EMMANUEL

**Emmanuel College, Cambridge CB2 3AP (tel. 01223-334290)**
**Undergraduates:** 511 **Male/female ratio:** 55/45
**www.emma.cam.ac.uk admissions@emma.cam.ac.uk**

Thanks in no small part to its huge and stylish, strikingly modern bar, Emmanuel has something of an insular reputation; although the students are active in university clubs and societies. Traditionally a mid-table college, with no subject bias, Emmanuel has significantly raised its academic profile recently, gaining strength in medicine and social science, but particularly in English. Deferred entry is greatly encouraged. An almost even state-to-independent ratio contributes to the college's unpretentious atmosphere and nearly half the undergraduates are women. All students are guaranteed accommodation. Second years are housed in college hostels. With self-catering facilities limited, most students eat in Hall. The college offers ten expedition grants to undergraduates every year, and has a large hardship fund. In the summer, the college tennis courts and open-air swimming pool offer a welcome haven from exam pressures. The duck pond is one of the most picturesque spots in Cambridge. The sports grounds are excellent, if some distance away.

## FITZWILLIAM
**Fitzwilliam College, Cambridge CB3 ODG (tel. 01223-332030)**
**Undergraduates:** 490 **Male/female ratio:** 60/40
**www.fitz.cam.ac.uk admissions@fitz.cam.ac.uk**

Based in the city centre until 1963, the college now occupies a large, modern site on the Huntingdon Road. What it may lack in architectural splendour, Fitzwilliam makes up in friendly informality. More than 60 per cent of its undergraduates come from the state sector, and about 40 per cent are women, though the college hopes 'significantly to raise this proportion in the coming years'. College accommodation is now available for all undergraduates with the completion of the Wilson Building. Fitzwilliam's academic record has been improving, with languages and geography the strongest subjects. Arts are generally stronger than sciences. Applications are also encouraged in archaeology and anthropology, classics, social and political sciences and music. As at Christ's, offers of places are sometimes made on the basis of two Es only at A level. On the extracurricular front, the badminton, hockey and football teams are among the best in the university. The playing fields are a few hundred yards away. The twice termly Ents (college entertainments) are exceptionally popular. Music and drama thrive.

## GIRTON
**Girton College, Cambridge CB3 OJG (tel. 01223-338972)**
**Undergraduates:** 532 **Male/female ratio:** 45/55
**www.girton.cam.ac.uk admissions@girton.cam.ac.uk**

The joke about needing a passport to travel to Girton refuses to die. In fact, with the city centre a 15-minute cycle ride away, the college is closer than many hostels at other universities. But if comparative isolation inevitably encourages a strong community spirit, Girtonians still manage to participate in university life at least as much as students at more central colleges and are particularly active in university sports. On the other hand, since Girton stands on a 50-acre site and the majority of second-year students live in Wolfson Court (near the University Library), there is no question of over-crowding: rooms are available for the entire course. Some find that the long corridors remind them of boarding school. Since becoming co-educational in 1979, the college has maintained a balanced admissions policy. Almost 60 per cent of undergraduates are from state schools. Girton also has the highest proportion of women Fellows in any mixed college (50 per cent). The on-site sporting facilities, which include a swimming pool, are excellent. The college is active in most sports and particularly strong in football. The formal hall is excellent and popular, but held only once a week.

# GONVILLE AND CAIUS

**Gonville and Caius College, Cambridge  CB2 1TA (tel. 01223-332447)**
**Undergraduates:** 525  **Male/female ratio:** 65/35
**www.cai.cam.ac.uk   admissions@cai.cam.ac.uk**

Gonville and Caius College – to confuse the outsider, the college is usually known as Caius (pronounced 'keys') – is among the most beautiful of Cambridge's colleges, as well as one of the most central. It has an excellent academic reputation, especially in medicine and history, though maths and law are also highly rated. Recent results have been better in sciences than arts. Book grants are available to all undergraduates. The library has been refurbished and computer facilities improved. Accommodation is split between the central site on Trinity Street and Harvey Court, a five-minute walk away across the river. Rooms are guaranteed for all first and third years. The majority of second years live in college hostels, none of which is more than a mile away. Undergraduates are obliged to eat in Hall at least 45 times a term, a ruling some find restrictive but which at least ensures that students meet regularly. The college has something of a Home Counties or public school reputation especially for its 'It' girls, society high-fliers. In 2001 acceptances for state school pupils fell to under 40 per cent. However, Caius is 'eager to extend the range of its intake'. Caius tends to do well in rowing and hockey, but most sports are fairly relaxed. A lively social scene is helped by the student-run Late Night Bar.

# HOMERTON

**Homerton College, Cambridge  CB2 2PH  (tel. 01223-507114)**
**Undergraduates:** 535  **Male/female ratio:** 13/87
**www.homerton.cam.ac.uk   admissions@homerton.cam.ac.uk**

In August 2001 Homerton became the newest college of the university (formerly an 'Approved Society'), though its students had been university members for a quarter of a century. The college will continue to specialise in education, including teacher training – through the BA degree and the postgraduate certificate in education (PGCE) courses offered by the Faculty of Education – but has started to offer places for many of the other courses offered by the university at both undergraduate and postgraduate level. All first years have rooms in college in new accommodation blocks. In the second year accommodation may be in college or in private rented houses, but final-year students can live in if they wish. There is a 77/23 state-independent split, with men, at the moment, making up no more than 13 per cent of undergraduates. The college's position, a mile from the city centre in its own large grounds, means that the onus is on Homerton students to take the initiative and get involved in university activities. Many do. Homerton is like the other undergraduate colleges in what it offers, and students can take advantage of Formal Hall, sport (there are on-site playing fields), music and drama.

# JESUS

**Jesus College, Cambridge CB5 8BL (tel. 01223-339495)**
**Undergraduates:** 505 **Male/female ratio:** 60/40
**www.jesus.cam.ac.uk admissions@jesus.cam.ac.uk**

For those of a sporting inclination Jesus is perhaps the ideal college. Within its spacious grounds there are football, rugby and cricket pitches as well as three squash courts and no less than ten tennis courts, while the Cam is just a few hundred yards away. With these facilities, it is hardly surprising that sports, in particular rowing, rugby and hockey, rate high on many students' agendas. That said, sporting prowess is far from the whole story. The music society thrives, and has extensive practice facilities. Although Jesus lacks a theatre of its own, the college is active in university drama. On the academic front, the Fellows-to-undergraduates ratio is generous and, while philosophy and politics are among the college's strong suits, the balance between arts and sciences is fairly even. There is an excellent and stylish new library. Rooms in college are guaranteed for all first and third-year students. The majority of second years live in college houses directly opposite the college. Over half the undergraduates are state educated and the college is keen to encourage more applications from the state sector. The college grounds – particularly The Chimney walkway to the porter's lodge – are attractive.

# KING'S

**King's College, Cambridge CB2 1ST (tel. 01223-331417)**
**Undergraduates:** 406 **Male/female ratio:** 55/45
**www.kings.cam.ac.uk undergraduate.admissions@kings.cam.ac.uk**

The reputation of King's as the most right-on place in the university has become something of an in-joke. It is true that the college has a 4:1 state-to-independent ratio and that it has banned Formal Hall and abandoned May Balls in favour of politically correct June Events. The college is involved in an initiative to increase the number of candidates from socially and educationally disadvantaged backgrounds, and is also keen to encourage applications from ethnic minorities and from women. The students' union is active politically. The college has fewer undergraduates than the grandeur of its buildings might suggest, one result being that accommodation is guaranteed, either in college or in hostels a few hundred yards away. With the highest ratio of Fellows to undergraduates in Cambridge, it is not surprising that King's has been one of the most academically successful colleges. No subjects are especially favoured, but recent results have been better in arts than sciences. Applications are not accepted in veterinary medicine and there are few law students. Sport at King's is anything but competitive. An extremely large bar/JCR is the social focal point, while the world-famous chapel and choir form the heart of an outstanding music scene.

## LUCY CAVENDISH

Lucy Cavendish College, Cambridge  CB3 OBU  (tel. 01223-330280)

Undergraduates: 96  **Women only**

www.lucy-cav.cam.ac.uk  lcc-admissions@lists.cam.ac.uk

Since its creation in 1965, Lucy Cavendish has given hundreds of women over the age of 21 the opportunity to read for Tripos subjects. A number of its students had already started careers and/or families when they decided to enter higher education. The college seeks to offer financial support to those with family responsibilities, though as yet it has no child care facilities. Accommodation is provided for all who request it, either in the college's three Victorian houses or in its three modern residential blocks. The college's small size enables all students to get to know one another. Plans to increase the intake are unlikely to alter the intimate and informal atmosphere. Law is still the dominant subject in terms of numbers of students, but veterinary science is also strong and the college welcomes applications in the sciences and other disciplines. All the Fellows are women. For subjects not covered by the Fellowship, there is a well-established network of university teachers.

## MAGDALENE

Magdalene College, Cambridge  CB3 OAG  (tel. 01223-332135)

Undergraduates: 356  **Male/female ratio:** 60/40

www.magd.cam.ac.uk  magd-admissions@lists.cam.ac.uk

As the last college to admit women (1988), Magdalene has still to throw off a lingering image as home to hordes of public school hearties. In fact, around 45 per cent of its undergraduates are from the state sector while over a third are women. That said, the sporty emphasis, on rugby and rowing in particular, is undeniable. The nearby playing fields are shared with St John's and the college has its own Eton fives court. Despite finishing closer to the foot of the academic league tables than its Fellows would wish, Magdalene is strong in architecture, law and social and political science. Students are heavily involved in university-wide activities from drama to journalism as well as sport. Accommodation is provided for all undergraduates, either in college or in one of 21 houses and hostels, 'mostly on our doorstep'. Living in is more expensive than in most colleges. Magdalene is proud of its river frontage, the longest in the university, which is especially memorable in the summer.

## NEW HALL

New Hall College, Huntingdon Road, Cambridge  CB3 ODF (tel. 01223-762229)

Undergraduates: 374  **Women only**

www.newhall.cam.ac.uk  admissions@newhall.cam.ac.uk

One of three remaining all-women colleges, New Hall enjoys a largely erroneous reputation for feminism and academic underachievement not helped by a much-publicised whitewash on *University Challenge*. Founded in 1954 to increase the number of women in the university, it occupies a modern grey-brick site next door to Fitzwilliam. Students are split 55/45 between state and independent schools. The college lays claim to certain paradoxes. While a rent strike early in the 1990s attested to a degree of political activism, tradition is far from rejected. The following year saw New Hall's first-ever May Ball, an event hosted jointly with Sidney Sussex. Its results regularly place the college near the bottom of the academic league, but it must be remembered that women's results lag behind men's throughout the university. Natural sciences, medicine, economics, and English are New Hall's strongest areas. The college is known for its unusual split-level bar, but many students choose to socialise elsewhere. Sport is a good mixture of high-fliers and enthusiasts, with grounds, shared with Fitzwilliam, half a mile away. The college is particularly proud of its collection of contemporary women's art.

## NEWNHAM

**Newnham College, Cambridge CB3 9DF (tel. 01223-335783)**
**Undergraduates:** 438 **Women only**
**www.newn.cam.ac.uk admissions@newn.cam.ac.uk**

Newnham has long had to battle with a blue-stocking image. Its entry in the university prospectus used to insist that it 'is not a nunnery' and that the atmosphere in this all-women college is no stricter than elsewhere. It even has a 'Newnham Nuns' drinking club to make the point. With an even state–independent ratio, the college has also successfully cast off a reputation for public school dominance. Newnham is in the perfect location for humanities students, with the lecture halls and libraries of the Sidgwick Site just across the road. The college is, however, keen to encourage applications in engineering, maths and the sciences, and recent results in these subjects have been better than in the arts. All of the Fellows are women. Around 95 per cent of students live in for all three years. This is not to say that ventures into the social, sporting and artistic life of the university are the exception rather than the rule. Newnham students are anything but insular. As well as being blessed with the largest and most beautiful lawns in Cambridge, Newnham has its playing fields on site. The boat club has been notably successful, while college teams compete to a high standard in tennis, cricket and a number of minority sports.

## PEMBROKE

**Pembroke College, Cambridge CB2 1RF (tel. 01223-338154)**
**Undergraduates:** 443 **Male/female ratio:** 58/42
**www.pem.cam.ac.uk admissions@pem.cam.ac.uk**

Another college with a reputation for public school dominance (but actually with a current state-to-independent ratio of around 50/50), Pembroke's image is changing. Rowing and rugby still feature prominently, but with a female population of about 42 per cent the heartiness is giving way to a more relaxed if still somewhat insular atmosphere. Around two-thirds of all undergraduates live in college, including all first years. The rest are housed in fairly central college hostels, though the standards of these are variable. Academically, Pembroke is considered solid rather than spectacular. Engineering and natural sciences have the largest number of undergraduates, but the subject range is wide with history, classics and English recent strengths. The bar is inevitably the social focal point, but a restriction on advertising means that Pembroke bops attract few students from other colleges. The Pembroke Players generally stage one play a term in the Old Reader, which also doubles as the college cinema, and many Pembroke students are involved in university dramatics. The Old Library is a popular venue for classical concerts. Indeed music is a Pembroke strength. In a city of memorable college gardens, Pembroke's are among the best.

## PETERHOUSE
**Peterhouse College, Cambridge  CB2 1RD  (tel. 01223-338223)**
**Undergraduates:** 251  **Male/female ratio:** 70/30
**www.pet.cam.ac.uk  admissions@pet.cam.ac.uk**

The oldest and among the smallest of the colleges, Peterhouse is another that has had to contend with an image problem. But while by no means as reactionary as its critics would have it, Peterhouse is certainly not overly progressive. There is a 2/1 male-to-female split, while the state-to-independent ratio is around 45/55, having seen a decline in state school applicants. The college's diminutive size – its entire student population is the same as one year's intake at Trinity – inevitably makes for an intimate atmosphere. But this does not mean that its undergraduates never venture beyond the college bar. Peterhouse is known above all as 'the history college'. But while history is indeed a traditional strength and results are excellent, there are in fact no more history students than there are taking natural science or engineering. Academically, the college is generally a mid-table performer, with a better record in arts than sciences. The 13th-century candle-lit dining hall provides a fitting setting for what by common consent is the best food in the university. Rents are below average, and undergraduates live in for at least two years, the remainder choosing rooms in college hostels, most within one or two minutes' walk. The sports grounds are shared with Clare and are about a mile away. The college teams have a less than glittering reputation, not surprisingly, given its size.

## QUEENS'
**Queens' College, Cambridge  CB3 9ET  (tel. 01223-335540)**
**Undergraduates:** 538  **Male/female ratio:** 59/41
**www.quns.cam.ac.uk  admissions@quns.cam.ac.uk**

There is a strong case for claiming that Queens' is the most tightly knit college in the university. With all undergraduates housed in college for the full three years, a large and popular bar (open all day) and outstanding facilities, including Cambridge's first college nursery, it is easy to see why. Queens' also has the distinction of attracting an above-average number of applicants. The state-to-independent ratio is around 55/45, and more than a third of students are female.

Though not to all tastes, the mix of architectural styles, ranging from the medieval Old Court to the 1980s Cripps Complex, is as great as any in the university. In addition to three excellent squash courts, the Cripps Complex is also home to Fitzpatrick Hall, a multipurpose venue containing Cambridge's best-equipped college theatre and the hub of Queens' renowned social scene. Friday and Saturday night bops are extremely popular. Queens' has perhaps the foremost college drama society and a thriving cinema. Law, maths, engineering and natural sciences are the leading subjects in a college with an enviable academic record across the board. Apart from squash, Queens' is not especially sporty. The playing fields (one mile away) are shared with Robinson.

## ROBINSON
**Robinson College, Cambridge CB3 9AN (tel. 01223-339143)**
**Undergraduates:** 419 **Male/female ratio:** 58/42
**www.robinson.cam.ac.uk undergraduate-admissions@robinson.cam.ac.uk**

Robinson is the youngest college in Cambridge and admitted its first students in 1979. Its unspectacular architecture has earned it the nickname 'the car park'. On the other hand, having been built with one eye on the conference trade, rooms are more comfortable than most and the majority have their own bathrooms and online links to the university computer network. Almost all students live in college or in houses in the attractive gardens. The college is one of the few with rooms adapted for disabled students. Robinson has sometimes been close to the bottom of the academic tables, but it improved its position in 2001. There is no particular subject bias, but recent results have been better in sciences than arts. One in four Fellows are women, the second highest proportion in any mixed college. Its youth and balanced admissions policy (36 per cent are from independent schools, and there is a 44 per cent female intake) ensure that Robinson has one of the more unpretentious atmospheres. The auditorium is the largest of any college and is a popular venue for films, plays and concerts. The college fields (shared with Queens') are home to excellent rugby and hockey sides, and the boat club is also successful.

## ST CATHARINE'S
**St Catharine's College, Cambridge CB2 1RL (tel. 01223-338319)**
**Undergraduates:** 467 **Male/female ratio:** 51/49
**www.caths.cam.ac.uk undergraduate.admissions@caths.cam.ac.uk**

Known to everyone as 'Catz', this is a medium-sized, 17th-century college standing opposite Corpus Christi on King's Parade. The principal college site, with its distinctive three-sided main court, though small, provides accommodation for all its first-year students. The majority of second years live in flats at St Chad's Court, a ten-minute walk away. Catz is not considered one of the leading colleges academically, but it has a reputation as a friendly place. Geography and law are usually the strongest subjects. More than a third of the students are women, and the split between independent and state school pupils is about even. A new library and JCR have improved the facilities considerably, and there is a strong musical tradition. College social life centres on the large bar, which has been likened, among other things, to a ski chalet or sauna. With a reputation for being sporting rather than sporty, Catz is one of the few colleges that regularly puts out three rugby XVs, and also has a good record in football and hockey. The playing fields are about a ten-minute walk away.

## ST JOHN'S
St John's College, Cambridge CB2 1TP  (tel. 01223-338685)
Undergraduates: 588  Male/female ratio: 61/39
www.joh.cam.ac.uk  admissions@joh.cam.ac.uk

Second only to Trinity in size and wealth, St John's has an enviable reputation in most fields and is sometimes resented for it. The wealth translates into excellent accommodation in college for almost all undergraduates throughout their three years, as well as book grants and a new 24-hour library. First years are housed together, which can hinder integration. There is no particular subject bias and St John's has a formidable academic record. English and natural sciences have been recent strengths. A reputation for heartiness persists and the female intake is 39 per cent, slightly below average. The state-to-independent split is about 50/50. The boat club has a powerful reputation, but rugby, hockey and cricket are all traditionally strong. In such a large community, however, all should be able to find their own level. Extensive playing fields shared with Magdalene are a few hundred yards away and the boathouse is extremely good. The college film society organises popular screenings in the Fisher Building, which also con-tains an art studio and drawing office for architecture and engineering students. Music is dominated by the world-famous choir. Excellent as the facilities are, some students find that the sheer size of St John's can be daunting and this makes it hard to settle into.

## SELWYN
Selwyn College, Cambridge  CB3 9DQ  (tel. 01223-335896)
Undergraduates: 376  Male/female ratio: 54/46
www.sel.cam.ac.uk  admissions@sel.cam.ac.uk

Described by one undergraduate as 'the least overtly intellectual college', Selwyn has a down-to-earth and relatively unpressured atmosphere. Located behind the Sidgwick Site, it is in an ideal position for humanities students, and its academic prowess has traditionally been on the arts side although engineering is an emerging strength. One of the first colleges to go mixed (1976) now approaching half of Selwyn's undergraduates are female. Its state-to-independent ratio stands at about 50/50. Accommodation is provided for all students, either in the college itself or in hostels, all of which are close by. The college has been a leader in IT provision: all college rooms have online connections to the university computer network and there are two well-strocked computer rooms. As well as the usual college groups, the Music Society is especially well-supported. The bar is popular if a little 'hotel-like'. In sport, the novice boat crews have done well in recent years, as have the hockey and badminton sides, but the emphasis is as much on enjoyment as achievement. The grounds are shared with King's and are three-quarters of a mile away.

## SIDNEY SUSSEX

Sidney Sussex College, Cambridge  CB2 3HU  (tel. 01223-338872)
Undergraduates: 343  Male/female ratio: 58/42
www.sid.cam.ac.uk  admissions@sid.cam.ac.uk

Students at this small, central college are forever the butt of jokes about Sidney being mistaken for the branch of Sainsbury's over the road. Two other, more serious, aspects of life at Sidney stand out: almost every year its undergraduates raise more for the Rag Appeal than any others; while rents are comfortably the lowest in the university (all students are housed either in college or one of 11 nearby hostels). Exam results generally place the college in the middle of the academic leagues; 2001 saw the college return to this level after a disasterous performance in 2000. Engineering, geography and law are generally the strongest subjects. Sidney has a good social balance, with a nearly even state-to-independent ratio, while more than 40 per cent of the undergraduates are women. There is a large student-run bar which is the venue for fortnightly bops, an active drama society (SADCO) and plenty of involvement in university activities. The sports grounds are shared with Christ's and are a 10-minute cycle ride away. Sidneyites are enthusiastic competitors, but the college does not have a reputation for excellence in any individual sports. Sidney's size means that the college is a tight-knit community. Some students find such insularity suffocating rather than supportive.

## TRINITY

Trinity College, Cambridge  CB2 1TQ  (tel. 01223-338422)
Undergraduates: 716 Male/female ratio: 67/33
www.trin.cam.ac.uk  admissions@trin.cam.ac.uk

The legend that you can walk from Oxford to Cambridge without ever leaving Trinity land typifies Cambridge undergraduates' views about the college, even if it is not true. Indeed, the college is almost synonymous with size and wealth. Founded by Henry VIII, its endowment is almost as big as the other colleges' put together. However, the view that every Trinity student is an arrogant public schoolboy is less easily sustained. That said, it is true that only about a third of Trinity undergraduates are women, the lowest proportion in any of the mixed colleges. On the other hand, there is little obvious bias in the admissions policy. Being rich, Trinity offers book grants to every student as well as generous travel grants and spacious, reasonably priced rooms in college for all first and third-year students as well as many second years. The college generally features in the top ten academically and was third in the Tompkins Table in 2001. Generally better for sciences than arts, the strongest subjects are engineering, maths and natural sciences. Trinity rarely fails to do well in most sports, with cricket in the fore-front. The playing fields are half a mile away. A new and larger bar should improve the social scene. The Trinity Sweatys attract students from all over the university.

## TRINITY HALL

**Trinity Hall, Cambridge  CB2 1TJ  (tel. 01223-332535)**
**Undergraduates:** 362  **Male/female ratio:** 55/45
**www.trinhall.cam.ac.uk   admissions@trinhall.cam.ac.uk**

The outstanding performance of its oarsmen has ensured the prevailing view of Trinity Hall as a 'boaty' college, but it is also known for its drama, music and bar. The Preston Society is one of the better college drama groups and stages regular productions both in the college theatre and at other venues. Weekly recitals keep the Music Society busy. The small bar is invariably packed. Not sur-prisingly, many undergraduates rarely feel the need to go elsewhere for their entertainment, although there has been considerable involvement in the stu-dents' union recently. Notwithstanding an unusually low position in the last two years' tables, the college is strong academically. Law is a traditional speciality and results have been excellent in modern languages recently. Though the nat-ural sciences are well represented, the college is much stronger in the arts. Approaching half of the undergraduates are women and around half are from state schools. All first years and approximately half the third years live in the col-lege, which is situated on the Backs behind Caius. The remainder take rooms either in two large hostels close to the sports ground (a mile from college), or in college accommodation about five minutes' walk away.

# University Profiles

Some famous names are missing from our university listings: the Open University, the separate business and medical schools, Birkbeck College and Cranfield University among them. Their omission is no reflection on their quality, simply a function of their particular roles. The guide is based on provision for full-time undergraduates and the factors judged to influence this. The Open University (www.open.ac.uk), though Britain's biggest university, with 75,000 students, could not be included because most of the measures used in our listing do not apply to it. As a non-residential, largely part-time institution, Birkbeck College, London (www.bbk.ac.uk), could also not be compared in many key areas. Although Cranfield (www.cranfield.acuk), for example, offers undergraduate degrees in two of its campuses, the Institute is primarily for graduate students. Manchester Business School (www.mbs.ac.uk) and London Business School (www.lbs.ac.uk) were excluded for the same reason. Similarly, specialist institutions such as the Royal College of Art (www.rca.ac.uk) and the medical schools could not fairly be compared with generalist universities. A number of colleges with degree-awarding powers also do not appear because they have yet to be granted university status. However, at the end of the book, we list higher education colleges with their addresses and websites.

Each university profile includes some standard information, which is described below:

*Telephone* This is the telephone number for admission enquiries.

*Website* This is the address of the main university website.

*e-mail* This is the e-mail address for admissions and prospectus enquiries.

*The Times rankings* These figures are taken from the main League Table. See pages 15–29 for this table and the sources of the data. The headings used match those in the main League Table apart from '*Work and further study*' which is entitled '*Graduate destinations*' in the main table and '*Expected completion rate*' which is entitled '*Efficiency*' in the main table. Please refer to p. 21 for a full explanation of these measures.

*Undergraduates* The first figure is for full-time undergraduates. The second figure (in brackets) gives the number of part-time undergraduates. The figures are for 1999–2000, and are the most recent provided by HESA.

*Postgraduates* The first figure is for full-time postgraduates. The second figure (in

202 Good University Guide 2003

brackets) gives the number of part-time postgraduates. The figures are for 1999–2000, and are the most recent provided by HESA.

*Mature students* This figure is the percentage of First degree acceptances in 2001 who were over 21. The figures were compiled by UCAS.

*Overseas students* This figure is the number of undergraduate overseas students (both EU and non–EU) as a percentage of full-time undergraduates. All figures relate to 1999–2000 and are based on HESA data.

*Applications/place*. This figure is the number of applicants per place for 2001 as calculated by UCAS.

*From State sector* This figure gives the number of young full-time undergraduate entrants from state schools or colleges in 1999–2000 as a percentage of total young entrants. The figures were compiled by the Higher Education Funding Councils.

*From working-class homes* The number of young full-time undergraduate entrants in 1999–2000 whose parental occupation is skilled, manual, semi-skilled or unskilled (Social Classes IIIM–V) as a percentage of total young entrants. The figures were compiled by the Higher Education Funding Councils.

*Teaching quality assessments* Quality Assurance Agency for Higher Education assessments published up to March 2002. See pages 19–20 for an explanation of the teaching assessment ratings.

*Accommodation* The information was obtained through a survey made of all university accommodation services, and their help in compiling this information is gratefully acknowledged.

Comments on campus facilities apply to the universities' own sites only. New universities, in particular, operate 'franchised' courses at further education colleges, which are likely to have lower levels of provision. Prospective applicants should check out the library and social facilities before accepting a place away from the parent institution.

## The University of London

The University of London is a federal university composed of a number of institutions. In this profile section, the pages on the University of London (pages 312–3) outline the colleges of the university that are not listed separately in this guide. There are separate entries on the leading undergraduate colleges.

## University of Wales

The University of Wales is also a federal university. General details are given below. Separate profiles can be found for the following institutions: Aberystwyth, Bangor, Cardiff, Cardiff, University of Wales Institute (UWIC), Lampeter, Newport, University of Wales College (UWCN) and Swansea.

Founded in 1893, it celebrated its centenary in 1993 and is second only to London, its federal counterpart in terms of full-time student numbers, with more than 42,000 full-time undergraduates. Like London, it is surrendering more power to its colleges. At the same time, however, intercollegiate links have been increasing, especially in research. A new structure was introduced in 1996, bringing the university colleges in Cardiff and Newport into the fold. See www.wales.ac.uk.

*Not listed separately:*

**University of Wales College of Medicine**, Heath Park, Cardiff CF4 4XN (*tel:* 029-2074-7747; *e-mail:* uwcmadmissions@cf.ac.uk; *website:* www.uwcm.ac.uk). Founded 1931. Full-time students: 2,030. Based at the University Hospital of Wales, two miles from the centre of Cardiff.

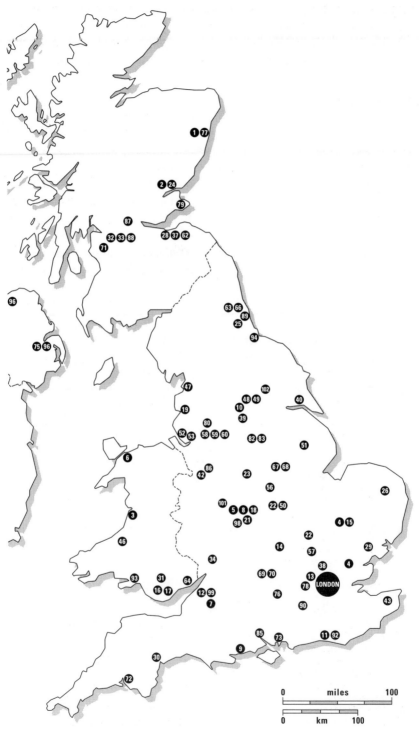

## Location of Universities

The map opposite shows the locations of the universities covered in this book. The following universities in London are not shown separately: 20, 27, 35, 36, 41, 44, 45, 54, 55, 65, 74, 81, 84, 91, 95, 97, and 100. In the key, the name of the university is given first and the town where it is located second.

1 Aberdeen *Aberdeen*
2 Abertay *Dundee*
3 Aberystwyth *Aberystwyth*
4 Anglia Polytechnic *Chelmsford, Cambridge*
5 Aston *Birmingham*
6 Bangor *Bangor*
7 Bath *Bath*
8 Birmingham *Birmingham*
9 Bournemouth *Bournemouth*
10 Bradford *Bradford*
11 Brighton *Brighton*
12 Bristol *Bristol*
13 Brunel *Uxbridge*
14 Buckingham *Buckingham*
15 Cambridge *Cambridge*
16 Cardiff *Cardiff*
17 Cardiff, UWIC *Cardiff*
18 Central England *Birmingham*
19 Central Lancashire *Preston*
20 City *London EC1*
21 Coventry *Coventry*
22 De Montfort *Leicester, Bedford*
23 Derby *Derby*
24 Dundee *Dundee*
25 Durham *Durham*
26 East Anglia *Norwich*
27 East London *London E15*
28 Edinburgh *Edinburgh*
29 Essex *Colchester*
30 Exeter *Exeter*
31 Glamorgan *Pontypridd*
32 Glasgow *Glasgow*
33 Glasgow Caledonian *Glasgow*
34 Gloucestershire *Gloucester, Cheltenham*
35 Goldsmiths College *London SE14*
36 Greenwich *Greenwich, London SE10*
37 Heriot-Watt *Edinburgh*
38 Hertfordshire *Hatfield*
39 Huddersfield *Huddersfield*
40 Hull *Hull*
41 Imperial College *London SW7*
42 Keele *Keele*
43 Kent at Canterbury *Canterbury*
44 King's College London *London WC2*
45 Kingston *Kingston, Surrey*
46 Lampeter *Lampeter*
47 Lancaster *Lancaster*
48 Leeds *Leeds*
49 Leeds Metropolitan *Leeds*
50 Leicester *Leicester*
51 Lincoln *Lincoln*

52 Liverpool *Liverpool*
53 Liverpool John Moores *Liverpool*
54 London Guildhall *London EC3*
55 London School of Economics *London WC2*
56 Loughborough *Loughborough*
57 Luton *Luton*
58 Manchester *Manchester*
59 UMIST *Manchester*
60 Manchester Metropolitan *Manchester*
61 Middlesex *London N17*
62 Napier *Edinburgh*
63 Newcastle *Newcastle*
64 Newport, UWCN *Newport*
65 North London *London N7*
66 Northumbria *Newcastle*
67 Nottingham *Nottingham*
68 Nottingham Trent *Nottingham*
69 Oxford *Oxford*
70 Oxford Brookes *Oxford*
71 Paisley *Paisley*
72 Plymouth *Plymouth*
73 Portsmouth *Portsmouth*
74 Queen Mary *London E1*
75 Queen's University, Belfast *Belfast*
76 Reading *Reading*
77 Robert Gordon *Aberdeen*
78 Royal Holloway *Egham, Surrey*
79 St Andrews *St Andrews*
80 Salford *Salford*
81 SOAS *London WC1*
82 Sheffield *Sheffield*
83 Sheffield Hallam *Sheffield*
84 South Bank *London SE1*
85 Southampton *Southampton*
86 Staffordshire *Stoke on Trent*
87 Stirling *Stirling*
88 Strathclyde *Glasgow*
89 Sunderland *Sunderland*
90 Surrey *Guildford*
91 Surrey Roehampton *London SW15*
92 Sussex *Brighton*
93 Swansea *Swansea*
94 Teeside Middlesborough
95 Thames Valley *Ealing, London W5*
96 Ulster *Coleraine, Belfast*
97 University College London *London WC1*
98 Warwick *Coventry*
99 West of England *Bristol*
100 Westminster *London W1*
101 Wolverhampton *Wolverhampton*
102 York *York*

# University of Aberdeen

Times ranking: 19 (2002 ranking:19)

Founded: 1495

**Contact details**
*Address:* King's College,
Aberdeen AB24 3FX
*Tel:* 01224 272090/91
*Website:* www.abdn.ac.uk
*e-mail:* sras@abdn.ac.uk

**The Times rankings**
*Teaching assessment:* =34 (21.3)
*Research assessment:* =43 (4.7)
*Entry standards:* =40 (19.7)
*Student–staff ratio:* =7 (11.0)
*Library/IT spend/student:* 12 (£712)
*Facilities spend/student:* 5 (£290)
*Firsts and 2:1s:* 15 (72.4%)
*Work and further study:* =10 (97%)
*Expected completion rate:* =62 (84.0%)

**Students**
*Undergraduates:* 7,460 (1,590)
*Postgraduates:* 1,140 (1,060)
*Mature students:* 20.6%
*Overseas students:* 10.2%
*Applications per place:* 4.9
*From state sector schools:* 81%
*From working class homes:* 20%

**Teaching quality assessments**
*1993–98 Rated Excellent:* cellular
biology; economics; French; geography;
medicine; organismal biology; sociology
*1993–98 Rated Highly Satisfactory:*
accounting; chemistry; civil engineering;
English; geology; history of art; law;
mathematics; mechanical engineering;
philosophy; politics; psychology; theology.
*2001 Rated Commendable:* earth and
environmental sciences; geology; theology.

## Overview

Aberdeen registered one of the biggest rises in last year's league table, and has since celebrated a sharply improved performance in the latest Research Assessment Exercise. The university described the results as a 'triumph', as the number of internationally rated departments shot up from two to ten. The relatively small French department achieved the only 5* rating, but other top grades were divided among four faculties.

The previous research grades had been disappointing, but the university succeeded in boosting its external research funds from £14 million to £35 million over five years. It already enjoyed consistently good teaching scores, with only three subjects rated less than Highly Satisfactory. French, biology, sociology and community-based medicine now have top ratings for both teaching and research.

Aberdeen considers itself a 'balanced' university because roughly half of its students are men and half women, half study medicine, science or engineering, half the arts or social sciences. Most students are not even admitted to a particular department, allowing them to try out three or four subjects before committing themselves at the end of their first or even second year. The modular system is so flexible that the majority of students change their intended degree before graduation.

Medicine, law and divinity head Aberdeen's traditional strengths – the university established the English-speaking world's first chair in law and has seen its share of medical advances. The new

Institute of Medical Sciences brought together all Aberdeen's work in this area with a dozen new professorships. It will be extended in 2002, when an initial fundraising target of £40 million is expected to be reached.

Biological sciences have developed considerably in recent years, becoming second only to the social sciences in terms of size. Biomedicine is particularly strong and the university's links with the oil industry show in geology's high reputation. Agriculture, which is part of a new European university network, will benefit from an agreement to take over Edinburgh University's stake in the subject. Senior academic posts have been strengthened in a variety of areas, from Celtic and Spanish to international relations since the university recovered from financial problems in the 1980s.

Today's university is a fusion of two ancient institutions which came together in 1860. With King's College dating back to 1495 and Marischal College following almost a century later, Aberdeen likes to boast that for 250 years it had as many universities as the whole of England. The original King's College buildings are the focal point of an appealing and quiet campus, complete with cobbled main street and some sturdily handsome Georgian buildings, about a mile from the city centre. Medicine is at Foresterhill, a 20–minute walk away, adjoining the Aberdeen Royal Infirmary. Buses link the two sites with the Hillhead residential complex, and the students' union runs a free late-night service. The Aberdeen arm of Northern College has now joined the fold, restoring the university's original involvement in teacher training, as well as swelling the ranks of the social sciences. The college will move to Old Aberdeen within the next four years.

Almost half of the students come from the north of Scotland, but taking one in ten from outside Britain ensures a cosmopolitan atmosphere. Bursaries of £1,000 are available to mature students in the region who join degree courses from the university's ten-week access summer school. Students from England and further afield are generally prepared for Aberdeen's remote location and long and often bitter winters. They find the city lively and welcoming but expensive, although its prosperity does provide a good selection of part-time jobs from the JobLink service.

Student facilities are generally good. There is an impressive ICT network and recreational facilities include a mountain hut in the Cairngorms. The university has been increasing its residential stock in recognition of the limited private market and now houses almost half of all undergraduates.

## Accommodation

Number of places and costs refer to 2002–03

*University-provided places:* about 3,200

*Percentage catered*: 28%

*Costs for catered accommodation:* £77.50–£91.75 a week.

*Costs for self-catered accommodation:* £44.25–£94.00 a week including fuel.

*Policy for first-year students:* accommodation is guaranteed. There are no restrictions for students whose homes are close to the university.

*Policy for international students:* accommodation is guaranteed.

*Contact for further information:* m.d.irvine@abdn.ac.uk

# University of Abertay Dundee

**Times ranking:** 64 (2002 ranking: 68)

Founded: Royal charter 1994, formerly
Dundee Institute of Technology

**Contact details**
*Address:* Bell Street, Dundee DD1 1HG
*Tel:* 01382 308080
*Website:* www.abertay.ac.uk
*e-mail:* ro@abertay.ac.uk

**The Times rankings**
*Teaching assessment:* =79 (20.2)
*Research assessment:* =90 (2.0)
*Entry standards:* =95 (11.8)
*Student–staff ratio:* 56 (17.1)
*Library/IT spend/student:* 4 (£1,016)
*Facilities spend/student:* =56 (£152)
*Firsts and 2:1s:* =64 (50.2%)
*Work and further study:* 74 (92.6%)
*Expected completion rate:* =37 (88.0%)

**Students**
*Undergraduates:* 3,320 (250)
*Postgraduates:* 300 (180)
*Mature students:* 25.1%
*Overseas students:* 8.9%
*Applications per place:* 4.7
*From state sector schools:* 98%
*From working class homes:* 40%

**Teaching quality assessments**
*1993–95 Rated Highly Satisfactory:* cellular and molecular biology; chemistry; civil engineering; mechanical engineering; mathematics and statistics; psychology.
*2001 Rated Commendable:* economics; engineering.
*2001 Rated Approved:* business.

## Overview

Scotland's newest university has been proving highly popular with applicants, bucking the downward trend north of the border in 1999 and sharing in the boom since up-front tuition fees were abolished for Scottish students. Still less than 5,000 strong, the former central institution has enjoyed a series of good teaching scores, although drop-out rates have increased. Almost a quarter of 1998 entrants were expected to transfer to other courses or leave without a qualification.

However, more than a third of the undergraduates come from socially deprived areas, almost twice the average for the subjects offered. Almost all the students attended state schools and four out of ten come from working-class homes.

The former Dundee Institute of Technology was made to wait for university status, which only came two years after the polytechnics were promoted. But the institute had already established its academic credentials, with teaching in economics rated more highly than in some of Scotland's elite universities. Subsequent assessments have been solid, without living up to that early promise. More than half of the subjects have been rated better than Satisfactory.

Research is not being ignored; Abertay is proud of its record in establishing a series of specialist centres, in areas as diverse as wood technology, waste water and Chinese business, during its first five years as a university. The latest research assessments showed a big improvement on 1996, although the university's claim of a 'stunning rise to prominence' might be stretching a point when only environmental science reached any of the top three grades.

Abertay plays to its strengths with a limited range of courses, and is not shy about its achievements. Among them is a high-tech approach that permeates all four of the university's schools. Its website offers prospective students 'better networking than Oxford', claiming to spend twice as much as the ancient university on computers.

Based mainly in the centre of Dundee, all the university's buildings are within 15 minutes' walk of each other. The imposing Dudhope Castle dominates recruitment literature, although it is an exclusively postgraduate management centre. Other buildings are more modern and functional. New facilities are gradually being added, notably the £8 million learning resources centre opened by the Queen. A £6 million student centre is next on the list, with construction scheduled to start at the end of 2002.

Entrance requirements for most courses are modest, but the boom in applications has cut the number of places filled through clearing. Degrees are predominantly vocational, with more subjects being added every year. The world's first degree in computer games technology was a recent high-profile example, with visiting professors from the games industry adding their expertise. Forest products technology was another tailored precisely to job opportunities in the region, as was the new degree in golf tourism. All courses can be taken on a part-time basis, and the aim is for new courses to offer students the chance to spend at least 30 per cent of their time in industry.

The modular scheme means that undergraduates normally take five subjects per 15–week semester. Each module consists of an introduction and further study, with assessment by examination, coursework or project. Students can complete a Certificate of Higher Education after one year, a diploma after two, an ordinary degree after three, or honours in four years.

With the student population still relatively small, that translates into a moderate social scene, particularly at weekends. However, Dundee has a large student population and is improving as a youth centre, and the cost of living is low. Over 25 per cent of the undergraduates are over 21 on entry, many living locally. This lifts the pressure on university-owned beds sufficiently to allow all first-years from outside the area to be guaranteed accommodation.

## Accommodation

Number of places and costs refer to 2002–03

*University-provided places:* 720

*Percentage catered:* 0%

*Costs for catered accommodation:* n/a

*Costs for self-catered accommodation:* £36.70–£55.60 a week inclusive of heat and light.

*Policy for first-year students:* places guaranteed for all first-year entrants who apply before 1 September in their year of study. No restriction on local students.

*Policy for international students:* first entrants guaranteed. Senior students allocated 25% of all accommodation on a first-come basis.

*Contact for further information:* accommo@abertay.ac.uk

# Aberystwyth, University of Wales

**Times ranking:** 49 (2002 ranking: 34)

---

**Founded:** 1872

**Contact details**
*Address:* Old College, King Street,
Aberystwyth, Ceredigion SY23 2AX
*Tel:* 01970 622021
*Website:* www.aber.ac.uk
*e-mail:* ug-admissions@aber.ac.uk

**The Times rankings**
*Teaching assessment:* =52 (20.9)
*Research assessment:* 50 (4.5)
*Entry standards:* 50 (18.7)
*Student–staff ratio:* =76 (19.0)
*Library/IT spend/student:* 38 (£507)
*Facilities spend/student:* 14 (£246)
*Firsts and 2:1s:* 45( 57.9%)
*Work and further study:* 88 (91.3%)
*Expected completion rate:* =22 (90%)

**Students**
*Undergraduates:* 6,020 (2,000)
*Postgraduates:* 800 (1,390)
*Mature students:* 14%
*Overseas students:* 7.9%
*Applications per place:* 4.2
*From state sector schools:* 93%
*From working class homes:* 22%

**Teaching quality assessments**
*1993–95 Rated Excellent:* accounting and
finance; biological sciences; Celtic
studies; earth studies; economics; English;
environmental science; geography;
information and library studies; politics;
Welsh.

---

## Overview

Although the oldest of the Welsh university colleges, Aberystwyth has long prided itself on a modern outlook. The modular degree system has been running since 1993, covering academic and vocational courses, and the principle of flexibility was established long before that. Uniquely in the UK, every student is offered the opportunity of a year's work experience in commerce, industry or the public sector, either at home or abroad. Students who have taken advantage of the scheme have achieved better than average degrees and enhanced their employment prospects. The college was forced to make cuts in the 1990s, but has since expanded significantly. A new School of Management and Business as well as a department of Sports and Exercise Science has opened recently.

An attractive seaside location does the university no harm when the applications season comes around. A new £3.6 million centre for theatre, film and television studies is the latest addition to the Penglais campus, which overlooks the town. Aber is always heavily oversubscribed even though the number of places has increased substantially in recent years. Almost a third of the students are Welsh.

More than 90 per cent of the undergraduates come from state schools or colleges – a far higher proportion than the mix of subjects would imply – but only 22 per cent come from working-class homes and half that number from areas that send few students to higher education. The drop-out rate of 8 per cent is among the lowest in Wales and also lower than the funding council's 'benchmark' figure for the institution.

Merger with the Welsh Agricultural College produced a new Institute of Rural Studies in 1997, allowing Aber to claim the widest range of land-related courses in the UK. The institute shares the Llanbadarn campus with information and library studies and a further education college. Teaching ratings have been impressive, especially in the arts and social sciences. Mathematics and science courses accept general studies as full A or AS levels as long as applicants have passed two other subjects. Celtic studies and politics were rated internationally outstanding in the latest research assessments, while theatre, film and television studies reached the next rung of the ladder.

More than 40 entrance scholarships are available, worth up to £1,150 a year with a guarantee of university accommodation for three years. There are also £400 music awards and 50 merit awards of £400 are on offer to those who are not awarded scholarships. Candidates sit two papers in their schools or colleges, or on campus, in February. Poor performances are not held against those who pursue their applications. Aber boasts one of higher education's most informative websites and also publishes a 12-page guide for parents. There is 24-hour access to the computer network, and the four university libraries are complemented by the National Library of Wales.

The town of Aberystwyth is compact and travel to other parts of the UK slow, so applicants should be sure that they will be happy to spend three years or more in a tight-knit community. Most

are: 94 per cent of first-year students responding to the annual satisfaction survey said they would make the same choice again. Although applications for courses beginning in 2002 dropped slightly, a 13 per cent increase in student numbers the previous year left Aber well in credit. The students' guild is the largest entertainments venue in the region and the arts centre has been extended at a cost of £3.5 million.

The student-produced Alternative Prospectus describes the traditional seaside town of 25,000 people as the 'Welsh California'. They say it has 'plenty of life and vitality, and a certain *je ne sais quoi*'. It also offers plenty of out-of-season accommodation to supplement the university's 3,600 places, all of which will be online by 2004. Sports facilities are good for the size of institution, with 50 acres of pitches, a swimming pool and specialist outdoor facilities for water sports.

**Accommodation**
Number of places and costs refer to 2001–02
*University-provided places:* 3,605
*Percentage catered:* 28%
*Costs for catered accommodation:* £47.29–£69.19 a week.
*Costs for self-catered accommodation:* £33.43–£61.29 a week.
*Policy for first-year students:* all first years guaranteed accommodation in halls, including local residents and those coming through clearing.
*Policy for international students:* all international students are guaranteed accommodation in hall for the duration of their courses.
*Contact for further information:* mew@aber.ac.uk
website: www.aber.ac.uk/residential

# Anglia Polytechnic University

**Times ranking:** =92 (2002 ranking: 78)

**Founded:** University status 1992, formerly Anglia Polytechnic

**Contact details**
*Address:* Rivermead Campus: Chelmsford, Essex CM1 1SQ
Cambridge Campus: East Road, Cambridge CB1 1PT
*Tel:* 0845 271 3333 (enquiries)
*Website:* www.apu.ac.uk
*e-mail:* answers@apu.ac.uk

**The Times rankings**
*Teaching assessment:* =79 (20.2)
*Research assessment:* =99 (1.5)
*Entry standards:* =76 (13.6)
*Student–staff ratio:* 88 (20.3)
*Library/IT spend/student:* =98 (£295)
*Facilities spend/student:* =88 (£100)
*Firsts and 2:1s:* 80 (47.7%)
*Work and further study:* =57 (93.6%)
*Expected completion rate:* =93 (76%)

**Students**
*Undergraduates:* 9,680 (6,450)
*Postgraduates:* 460 (2,650)
*Mature students:* 32.9%
*Overseas students:* 18.1%
*Applications per place:* 5.1
*From state sector schools:* 94%
*From working class homes:* 32%

**Teaching quality assessments**
*1993–95 Rated Excellent:* English; music; social work.
*From 1995 (top score 24):* **24** philosophy. **23** health subjects; nursing; theology. **22** psychology. **21** art and design; modern languages; molecular biosciences; organismal biosciences. **20** building and civil engineering; politics; sociology; electrical and electronic engineering; land management; politics; town planning. **19** education. **18** history of art; hospitality; media studies.

## Overview

The last university to retain the polytechnic title tried unsuccessfully to drop it, in order to avoid confusion among employers and overseas applicants. After rejecting a series of alternative names, it appears that APU is here to stay. The university has not been standing still, however: teacher training courses have been relocated to the new Rivermead campus in Chelmsford and further developments are in the pipeline.

An amalgamation of two well-established higher education colleges made Anglia the first regional polytechnic, but the twin bases in Chelmsford and Cambridge remain distinct. The two very different locations are far enough apart to ensure that there is little contact, although electronic networking and a central administration mean that key academic facilities are available throughout the university. The university claims to have Europe's biggest learning technology research centre, in Ultralab, a source of ideas for the Government as well as local academics and students.

The regional ideal extends to a network of more than 20 partner colleges in Cambridgeshire, Essex, Norfolk and Suffolk. One, at Benfleet, in Essex, has become a 'local campus' of the university. East Anglia has always lagged behind other parts of England for participation in higher education and, although numbers have risen since 1999, the university has sometimes struggled to fill its places.

Most teaching ratings have been solid, rather than spectacular, although there has been an improvement recently. Nursing and theology (a postgraduate subject only) have produced the best scores, but the hospitality, sport, leisure and tourism course added to the low scores in 2001. The latest research grades also showed improvement, but only one university submitted a lower proportion of academics for assessment, and only English made the top three categories. The guide's new 'benchmarking' system, which takes account of the mix of subjects, is only partly responsible for a big drop in this year's *Times* League Table.

The university has a strongly European outlook, encouraging students to take a language option and providing an unusually large number of exchange opportunities in Malaysia and China, as well as Europe and the United States. Each undergraduate has an adviser to help compile a degree package which looks at the chosen subject from different points of view to maximise future job prospects.

Employers play a part in planning courses which are integrated into a modular system extending from degree level to professional programmes. Anglia is taking a leading role in the development of the Government's two-year foundation degrees, which are designed as partnerships between the academic and business worlds. Three courses began in 2001: in e-commerce, land-based industries and transport.

The university's cramped town centre site in Chelmsford is due to close in 2005, moving progressively to the more spacious and attractive Rivermead campus on the edge of town. The next big development will be the £8 million Ashcroft International Business School, named after the former Conservative Party Treasurer and alumnus, Lord Ashcroft, who is meeting most of the cost. Due to open in 2002, the pavilion-style building will contain personal study and teaching facilities, including a 250-seat auditorium.

Anglia's Cambridge site is small, but well-provided with academic and recreational facilities for a relatively small student population. There is limited collaboration with Cambridge University, for example on a new cricket academy and a base for Anglia's rowing club.

The social scene inevitably varies between the two campuses. Cambridge students enjoy the advantages of a great university city, but have to shrug off the tag of attending the lesser institution, while at the Essex end of the university, students can find Chelmsford dull. Neither is far from London by train.

## Accommodation

Number of places and costs refer to 2001–02

*University-provided places:* Cambridge, about 850; Chelmsford, 685

*Percentage catered:* 0%

Costs for catered accommodation: n/a

*Costs for self-catered accommodation:* Cambridge: £51–£63 (shared houses); £63–£67 (shared communal facilities); £69.50 (en-suite) a week. Chelmsford: £48–£62 a week.

*Policy for first-year students:* approximately 80% of first years accommodated; restriction within 30–mile radius of Cambridge campus and 20–mile radius of Chelmsford campus.

*Policy for international students:* bed-spaces are equally divided between home and international students.

*Contact for further information:* Cambaccom@anglia.ac.uk

# Aston University

**Times ranking:** 36 (2002 ranking: 41)

**Founded:** 1895, Royal charter 1966

**Contact details**
*Address:* Aston Triangle,
Birmingham B4 7ET
*Tel:* 0121 359 6313 (admissions
enquiries only)
*Website:* www.aston.ac.uk
*e-mail:* prospectus@aston.ac.uk

**The Times rankings**
*Teaching assessment:* =43 (21.1)
*Research assessment:* =37 (5.0)
*Entry standards:* =30 (22.0)
*Student–staff ratio:* 82 (19.4)
*Library/IT spend/student:* 60 (£433)
*Facilities spend/student:* 16 (£236)
*Firsts and 2:1s:* 35 (61.3%)
*Work and further study:* =14 (96.3%)
*Expected completion rate:* =53 (85%)

**Students**
*Undergraduates:* 4,780 (10)
*Postgraduates:* 490 (1,300)
*Mature students:* 11.3%
*Overseas students:* 6.2%
*Applications per place:* 6.7
*From state sector schools:* 84%
*From working class homes:* 33%

**Teaching quality assessments**
*1993–95 Rated Excellent:* none.
*From 1995 (top score 24):* **24** business
and management; pharmacy. **23** health
subjects; molecular biosciences; organismal biosciences. **22** French; German;
psychology. **21** electrical and electronic
engineering. **20** civil engineering.
**19** chemical engineering; mathematics.

## Overview

Aston has always gloried in its role as a tight-knit, vocational, urban university, which has swum against the tide of British higher education over the past decade. Small and lively, set in the heart of Birmingham, it has remained resolutely specialist in science and technology, business and languages, concentrating on the sandwich degrees which have served its graduates so well in the employment market. Having rejected the option of merger with its much larger neighbour, Birmingham University, it is now having to chart a new course.

The university's refusal to take more than the current 5,000 students has made for a bumpy ride financially – the funding council has had to provide special help several times to avoid damaging budget cuts. At one stage, it was relying on the Government allowing higher tuition fees to make the books balance in the long term. But the strategy has paid off to some extent with encouraging rises in applications and big grants from industry, which have allowed the university to boost staffing in business, engineering and languages.

The changes produced much-improved research grades at the end of 2001, with four of the five subject areas judged to be producing work of international quality. Business and management, European studies, general engineering and neurosciences all achieved top scores, although the proportion of academics entered for assessment was low for a traditional university. Academic restructuring, designed mainly to break down barriers between departments, has reduced the number of schools to four.

As befits a one-time college of advanced technology, Aston's strengths are on the science side, although the business school is highly rated and accounts for almost half the students. After a bruising introduction to the teaching quality assessments, in which none of the first six departments was considered excellent, ratings have improved considerably. Aston achieved the first maximum score for pharmacy in 1999, building on high grades for optometry and biological sciences. Recent assessments have veered from a disappointing 19 points in maths and statistics to another maximum for business and management. There is a wide range of combined honours programmes for those who prefer not to specialise.

Four out of five Aston graduates go straight into jobs, spurning the postgraduate courses and training programmes which have become the first port of call for many of their counterparts in the old universities. Often they are returning to the scene of work placements, which have become the norm for 70 per cent of Aston's undergraduates.

The university is flexible about entry requirements for mature students, but school-leavers are generally asked for at least the equivalent of a B and two Cs at A level. The actual entry grades are often even higher, and the rising demand for places is likely to prolong the trend. The drop-out rate has been rising, reaching 13 per cent in the most recent projections. Socially, the intake is diverse, with three out of ten undergraduates coming from working-class homes.

The 40-acre campus, a ten-minute walk from the centre of Birmingham, is barely recognisable from the university's early days. Carefully landscaped, it is nearing the end of a £16 million building plan, which will see Aston's residential and academic accommodation concentrated on the same site. The first 650 students moved into the Lakeside halls in autumn 1999. New developments in residential and sporting facilities are being considered, but will take time to complete.

Aston was among the pioneers of 'smart cards', giving students access to university facilities and enabling them to make purchases on campus, once they have money in their accounts. There is plenty of opportunity to use them in a buzzing social scene, which most students find to their taste. The guild of students, which has an informative website (to be found at www.astonguild.org.uk) has always been among the most active both socially and politically.

## Accommodation

Number of places and costs refer to 2002–03

*University-provided places:* 1,950

*Percentage catered:* 0%

*Costs for catered accommodation:* n/a

*Costs for self-catered accommodation:* £43.20 (standard); £63.00 (en-suite) a week.

*Policy for first-year students:* all first years are guaranteed a place provided Aston is their first-choice university.

*Policy for international students:* international fee-paying students are guaranteed places for duration of course, but must apply each year.

# Bangor, University of Wales

**Times ranking:** =56 (2002 ranking: 47)

**Founded:** 1884

**Contact details**
*Address:* Bangor, Gwynedd LL57 2DG
*Tel:* 01248 382016
*Website:* www.bangor.ac.uk
*e-mail:* admissions@bangor.ac.uk

**The Times rankings**
*Teaching assessment:* =52 (20.9)
*Research assessment:* =43 (4.7)
*Entry standards:* 60 (16.3)
*Student–staff ratio:* =69 (18.4)
*Library/IT spend/student:* =33 (£530)
*Facilities spend/student:* 61 (£147)
*Firsts and 2:1s:* =64 (50.2%)
*Work and further study:* =85 (91.5%)
*Expected completion rate:* =37 (88%)

**Students**
*Undergraduates:* 5,500 (1,350)
*Postgraduates:* 860 (1,140)
*Mature students:* 19.8%
*Overseas students:* 7.5%
*Applications per place:* 4.5
*From state sector schools:* 93%
*From working class homes:* 27%

**Teaching quality assessments**
*1993–98 Rated Excellent:* biology;
chemistry; forestry; music; ocean sciences;
psychology; Russian; theology; Welsh.

## Overview

Bangor's community focus dates back to a 19th-century campaign which saw local quarrymen putting part of their weekly wages towards the establishment of a college. The Community University of North Wales, which provides modular courses throughout the area, continues that tradition, but the college has also built a worldwide reputation in areas such as ocean sciences and environmental studies.

The latest research assessments were an improvement on 1996, although only psychology and Welsh were rated internationally outstanding. Three-quarters of the researchers were placed in the top three categories of seven. Teaching assessments have been more impressive, with half of the subjects rated as excellent. As well as traditional strengths such as biology and forestry, the list includes music, placing Bangor in *The Times* top twenty for the subject. There is a high proportion of small-group teaching and tutorials. A range of £1,000 scholarships, including new awards for sport, is available to offset the cost of tuition fees.

Bangor merged with a nearby teacher training college, Coleg Normal, in 1996. All other departments are within walking distance of each other, apart from ocean sciences, which is two miles away near the Menai Bridge. Departments such as philosophy and physics closed in a major restructuring designed to enable the college to concentrate on its strengths. Recent changes have seen departments coming together, for example with a School of Informatics encompassing electronic engineering, computer systems and mathematics.

A new School for Business and Regional Development has been created by bringing together banking, accounting, economics, business and marketing as well as community development, tourism, leisure and heritage management. Bangor has an international reputation in banking and finance, but the new school is being shaped to serve the needs of the Welsh economy. Another significant reorganisation has established the School of Arts and Humanities, bringing together languages (including Welsh and English), history, religious studies and communications. Like the other clusters, the new school is intended to encourage inter-disciplinary research and more flexible degrees.

Based a little more than a stone's throw from Snowdonia, Bangor is an expanding centre for Welsh-medium teaching. As well as a single honours degree in Welsh, some media courses are only available in Welsh while others are offered in either English or Welsh. More than 10 per cent of the students speak the language and one of the seven halls of residence is Welsh-speaking. The college also has a flourishing international exchange programme, with some unusual partner institutions: Poland and Italy are favourite destinations for linguistics students, while biologists tend to head for Sweden or Norway. All biology, chemistry or engineering degrees carry the option of a year abroad. The university has also cut its fees by £1,000 for students from the world's poorest countries.

Bangor does better than most traditional universities when judged against access benchmarks. More than nine out of ten students come from state schools or colleges, and over quarter come from working-class homes. Even the 13 per cent of students from areas without a tradition of higher education matches the national average for the subjects offered, while the 12 per cent drop-out rate is lower than at most universities with similarly diverse intakes.

Bangor is not the remote location that English students may imagine: Liverpool is less than an hour away and even Ireland is easily accessible by ferry. The university is the focus of social and cultural life in the small town (officially a city) where the 7,000 students account for a third of the population during term-time. Nightlife is inevitably limited, although the students' union has opened its own £1 million club with a capacity of 800. Sports facilities are good enough to host a National Coaching Foundation centre. A £1.7 million sports hall has improved them yet further.

## Accommodation

Number of places and costs refer to 2002–03

*University-provided places:* about 2,300 rox.*Percentage catered:* 34.2%

*Costs for catered accommodation:* £72.10 (standard); £80.99 (en-suite); £84.21 (en-suite plus datapoint) a week.

*Costs for self-catered accommodation:* £44.52 – £47.46 (standard); £61.11 (en-suite) £64.40 (en-suite plus datapoint) a week.

*Policy for first-year students:* accommodation is guaranteed to all first years.

*Policy for international students:* international postgraduate students have priority.

*Contact for further information:* ao5017@bangor.ac.uk

# University of Bath

Times ranking: 4 (2002 ranking: 9)

**Founded:** 1894 (in Bristol), Royal charter 1966

**Contact details**
*Address:* Claverton Down, Bath BA2 7AY
*Tel:* 01225 323019
*Website:* www.bath.ac.uk
*e-mail:* admissions@bath.ac.uk

**The Times rankings**
*Teaching assessment:* =27 (21.4)
*Research assessment:* =10 (5.7)
*Entry standards:* =11 (25.4)
*Student–staff ratio:* 23 (14.0)
*Library/IT spend/student:* 9 (£789)
*Facilities spend/student:* 1 (£403)
*Firsts and 2:1s:* 21 (70.1%)
*Work and further study:* =18 (96.2%)
*Expected completion rate:* =4 (95%)

**Students**
*Undergraduates:* 5,800 (10)
*Postgraduates:* 1,130 (2,830)
*Mature students:* 5.1%
*Overseas students:* 10.3%
*Applications per place:* 7.9
*From state sector schools:* 79%
*From working class homes:* 17%

**Teaching quality assessments**
*1993–95 Rated Excellent:* architecture; business and management; mechanical engineering; social policy.
*From 1995 (top score 24):* **24** economics; mathematics; molecular biosciences; organismal biosciences; physics; politics. **23** education; leisure management; pharmacy; sports science. **22** civil engineering. **21** materials technology. **20** chemical engineering; electrical and electronic engineering. **19** modern languages; sociology.

## Overview

Bath is in the middle of a £70 million expansion plan but, for the moment, it remains a relatively small technological university of 8,000 students. The extra places will cater to some degree for the burgeoning demand for places at an institution which enjoys both an attractive location and a high academic reputation. At one time, applications increased by 22 per cent in a single year and entrance requirements rose by the equivalent of a full grade at A level. Bath's healthy showing in league tables may be one reason for the surge – it has never been out of the top 20 in *The Times* table and is now well-established in the top ten.

Students like the 'small and friendly' image the university projects, and one of the lowest drop-out rates in Britain suggests that they are well supported. Few can fail to be impressed by the magnificence of the city's architecture. The modern campus, with some undistinguished buildings dating from the 1960s, offers an unfortunate contrast. But the 200-acre site is functional, and major developments will see enhanced academic, recreational and residential facilities in close proximity. A new building for chemistry opened in 2000 and for chemical engineering in 2002, whilst 450 study bedrooms, new lecture theatres and computer laboratories will follow.

The allocation of an extra 900 places for British students allowed the university to begin the current phase of growth. The establishment of a campus in nearby Swindon will help, although it will take five years to reach its full complement of

1,000 students. The development, based initially in school premises and featuring community courses, will bring higher education to one of the few remaining counties without a university. Strong collaborative links exist between Bath and Bath Spa University College, and include a joint bid for a New Technology Institute for the area.

Research is Bath's greatest strength, with applied mathematics, mechanical engineering and pharmacy all rated internationally outstanding in the latest assessments. Teaching assessments have confirmed the university's excellence in science and technology, with molecular and organismal biosciences achieving maximum points for teaching quality in 1999 and maths and statistics following in 2000. Arts and social science ratings have been mixed, with recent successes in economics and politics, but some other subjects have been less impressive. More than 20 new professorships were added in the 1990s, as Bath undertook limited academic reorganisation. Most courses have a practical element, and assessors have praised the university for the work placements it offers. The majority of students take sandwich courses, which help to produce consistently outstanding graduate employment figures.

The university's other great claim to fame lies in its sports facilities, which are already among the best in Britain and are set to improve further with the aid of £20 million of Lottery money. The campus has already acquired an international-standard swimming pool by this route, to which it has added an indoor running track, new sports hall and even a simulated bobsleigh start area. There is a strong tradition in competitive sports, encouraged by sports scholarships worth up to £12,000 a year for performers of international calibre, which Bath introduced to Britain more than 20 years ago. There are now courses to do the facilities justice, as recognised in a near-perfect score for teaching quality in sport and leisure in 2001.

Students find the campus quiet at weekends and struggle to afford some of Bath's attractions, but value its location. When they tire of the beauty of Bath, the nightlife of Bristol is only a few minutes away. The two cities have a combined student population of more than 30,000.

## Accommodation

Number of places and costs refer to 2001–02

*University-provided places:* 4,645

*Percentage catered:* 4%

*Costs for catered accommodation:* £70.09 a week for bed, breakfast and evening meal Monday–Friday for standard room with washbasin.

*Costs for self-catered accommodation:* Undergraduate – £46.28 (standard); £56.00 (en-suite) a week.

*Policy for first-year students:* all first-year full-time full-degree undergraduates and new overseas fee-paying postgraduates are guaranteed university residence. No restrictions on local students.

*Policy for international students:* as above plus international exchange students are housed on a reciprocal pro-rata basis. EU postgraduates are not guaranteed places, but priority is given to international postgraduates who apply by 1 July.

*Contact for further information:* accommodation@bath.ac.uk

# University of Birmingham

**Times ranking:** 17 (2002 ranking: 14)

**Founded:** 1828, Royal charter 1900

**Contact details**
*Address:* Edgbaston, Birmingham B15 2TT
*Tel:* 0121 414 3374 (general admission enquiries)
*Website:* www.bham.ac.uk
*e-mail:* prospectus@bham.ac.uk

**The Times rankings**
*Teaching assessment:* =13 (21.7)
*Research assessment:* =26 (5.3)
*Entry standards:* 19 (23.7)
*Student–staff ratio:* =18 (13.5)
*Library/IT spend/student:* 28 (£560)
*Facilities spend/student:* 18 (£223)
*Firsts and 2:1s:* 14 (72.9%)
*Work and further study:* =28 (95.6%)
*Expected completion rate:* =22 (90%)

**Students**
*Undergraduates:* 13,960 (2,860)
*Postgraduates:* 2,950 (5,780)
*Mature students:* 8.8%
*Overseas students:* 7.4%
*Applications per place:* 6.8
*From state sector schools:* 74%
*From working class homes:* 19%

**Teaching quality assessments**
*1993–95 Rated Excellent:* English; geography; geology; history; music.
*From 1995 (top score 24):* **24** electrical and electronic engineering; health subjects; mathematics; organismal biosciences; politics; sociology. **23** economics; Middle Eastern and African studies; molecular biosciences; physics; psychology; theology. **22** American studies; dentistry; history of art; hospitality; Iberian languages; Italian; nursing; sport. **21** archaeology; business and management; chemical engineering; civil engineering; drama, dance and cinematics; education; philosophy. **20** mechanical engineering; materials science; medicine. **19** German. **18** French.

## Overview

Strength across the board is Birmingham's aim, and its secure position among the top 20 universities in *The Times* ranking suggests that it is hitting its target. Despite offering an unusually wide range of subjects, its teaching and research ratings seldom slip. The university had been intending to become even larger by merging with neighbouring Aston, but is having to revise its long-term plans and shed staff following Aston's withdrawal.

Students come to Birmingham from more than 100 countries, but the university enjoys particularly high prestige in its own region, where it is widely regarded as the next best thing to Oxbridge. Entry standards are high, averaging the equivalent of more than three Bs at A level. With nearly seven applicants for each place, they are likely to remain so, but aspiring students still flock to the largest open days in Britain each spring. There is also an admissions forum in September.

The university's enduring reputation is based on its research, with two-thirds of its departments considered nationally or internationally outstanding in the new assessments. A dozen 5* ratings tripled the number awarded in 1996, with language departments doing particularly well: French, German, Italian and Russian all reached the top level.

Many of the teaching scores have also been impressive, with maths, organismal biosciences and physiotherapy following sociology and electrical and electronic engineering in recording maximum points. Economics only just missed out in 2001 and there was a string of 'excellent' verdicts in the early rounds of assessments.

Birmingham's highly regarded medical school was granted the biggest expansion in Britain when quotas for the subject were reviewed in 1999. Engineering has been reorganised, following a year-long review, to promote an interdisciplinary approach, responding to employers' wish for more flexibility. Students can enter either a BA or BSc degree programme, combining Technology with subjects ranging from Latin or modern Greek to the management of floods and other natural disasters.

The 230-acre campus in leafy Edgbaston is dominated by a 300-foot clocktower, which is one of the city's best-known landmarks, and boasts its own station. Only dentistry is located elsewhere. Most of the halls and university flats are conveniently located in an attractive parkland setting nearby. There are more than 5,000 university-owned beds and private sector accommodation is also plentiful.

The campus is less than three miles from the centre of Birmingham, but Edgbaston has plenty of shops, pubs and restaurants of its own. With five nightclubs among the facilities on campus, some students do not even stray that far, but the city is acquiring a growing reputation among the young, which is helping to make the university even more popular.

Pressure on teaching space was eased to some extent in 1999 with the creation of the University of Birmingham, Westhill, a joint venture with a Free Church college whose education and theology degrees the university had validated for many years. The site will be used for part-time degrees and continuing educa-tion, as well as the existing courses, under an agreement which saw the university take over the management of nine partner colleges in all.

Student facilities are on a par with the best in the country, with four restaurants and two bars on campus, and an outdoor pursuits centre on Coniston Water. Birmingham has always been concerned with the body as well as the mind; compulsory exercise was only abandoned in 1968. The Active Lifestyles Programme, the voluntary modern-day equivalent, attracts 4,000 students to 150 different courses. Tutors with national qualifications run classes from beginner to advanced level.

## Accommodation

Number of places and costs refer to 2002–03

*University-provided places:* 5,100
*Percentage catered:* 32%
*Costs for catered accommodation:* £85.70–£129.70 a week depending upon room size, provision of en-suite facilities and location.
*Costs for self-catered accommodation:* £51.30–£77.70 a week depending upon location and room size.
*Policy for first-year students:* a 'Freshers Guarantee Scheme' guarantees accommodation to all first years, subject to the terms of the guarantee. No restrictions for local students.
*Policy for international students:* First-year undergraduate and postgraduate international students are guaranteed university accommodation, subject to the terms of the guarantee.
*Contact for further information:* ugradaccom@bham.ac.uk (undergraduate enquiries)
J.Dhanda@bham.ac.uk (private sector housing enquiries)

# University of Bournemouth

Times ranking: 80 (2002 ranking: 83)

**Founded:** University status 1992, formerly Bournemouth Polytechnic, originally Dorset Institute of Higher Education

**Contact details**
*Address:* Talbot Campus, Fern Barrow, Poole, Dorset BH12 5BB
*Tel:* 01202 524111
*Website:* www.bournemouth.ac.uk
*e-mail:* prospectus@bournemouth.ac.uk

**The Times rankings**
*Teaching assessment:* 97 (19.6)
*Research assessment:* =92 (1.9)
*Entry standards:* =54 (17.6)
*Student–staff ratio:* 45 (16.2)
*Library/IT spend/student:* =75 (£393)
*Facilities spend/student:* 100 (£45)
*Firsts and 2:1s:* 60 (51.5%)
*Work and further study:* =67 (93.0%)
*Expected completion rate:* =31 (89%)

**Students**
*Undergraduates:* 7,930 (1,970)
*Postgraduates:* 810 (740)
*Mature students:* 19.2%
*Overseas students:* 5.8%
*Applications per place:* 5.4
*From state sector schools:* 91%
*From working class homes:* 21%

**Teaching quality assessments**
*1993–95 Rated Excellent:* none.
*From 1995 (top score 24):*
**22** archaeology; business; communication and media studies; nursing; television and video production. **20** agriculture; art and design; health subjects. **19** electrical engineering; food science. **18** mechanical engineering; modern languages.

## Overview

Always an institution with an eye for the distinctive, Bournemouth's strategic plan declares that it will 'dare to be different and stand out from the crowd'. Study boundaries are set by areas of social or economic activity, rather than traditional academic disciplines, because the aim is to be a 'pre-eminent vocational university'. Thus, there is no Faculty of Arts but there is a School of Service Industries.

Bournemouth's forte is in identifying gaps in the higher education market and then filling them with innovative programmes. Degrees in public relations, licensed retail management, scriptwriting and tax and revenue law are among the examples. The university also boasts a National Centre of Computer Animation. The mix has been popular with students – Bournemouth was one of the few new universities to see applications rise in 2002 and the drop-out rate is among the lowest.

The university claims a number of firsts in its growing portfolio of courses, notably in the area of tourism, media studies and conservation, which won a Queen's Anniversary Prize in 1994. It was no surprise to find the university among the successful bidders for the first Foundation Degrees – two-year highly vocational courses, which are at the heart of the Government's expansion plans for higher education. The new degrees are being delivered in further education colleges from Cornwall to Salisbury, supporting the needs of business in the creative arts, media and tourism.

Many of the existing courses contain a language element and all students are encouraged to improve their linguistic ability. A majority of undergraduates take sandwich courses, and 70 per cent do work placements. The result is an employment rate which is the university's proudest achievement: four out of five graduates went straight into jobs in 2000. The Retail Management degree has notched up eight successive years of full employment. The university has put its graduates' success down to the in-depth knowledge of the business world which they acquire.

Teaching ratings have improved after a poor start – none of the subjects assessed in the early rounds of assessments was considered excellent and modern languages only passed at the second attempt, after an unusually low score. Those initial failings partly account for Bournemouth's low position in *The Times* ranking.

More recently, however, archaeology, television and video production, media studies and nursing have all passed with flying colours. Media courses are a particular strength, with entry requirements well above the university's modest average. A joint venture with Microsoft saw the launch of a pioneering and award-winning internet radio station, which will be used by aspiring broadcaster and web designers. Computer animation was the star performer in the 2001 research assessments, which saw much-needed improvement on 1996.

Bournemouth has come a long way since its days as a struggling college of education. University status arrived only two years after the success of a protracted battle to become a polytechnic. Student numbers doubled in four years and, inevitably, resources were stretched.

New teaching and residential accommodation has been added in recent years. There are now two campuses – the original Talbot site on the way to Poole and a collection of buildings in the town centre – as well as associate colleges in Yeovil, Poole and the Isle of Wight.

The southern seaside location and the subject mix attract more middle-class students than most new universities. Students are discouraged from bringing cars (which are banned within a mile of the town centre campus) but many still do. The area has plenty to offer students during the summer season. Although it naturally becomes less lively in the winter months – party conferences apart – cheap and plentiful accommodation then is a compensation.

**Accommodation**
Number of places and costs refer to 2001–02
*University-provided places:* about 2,200
*Percentage catered:* about 25% in privately-owned hotels and guest houses.
*Costs for catered accommodation:* £66.50–£84.50 a week (private hotels).
*Costs for self-catered accommodation:* £53–£64 a week for university-rented shared houses and halls of residence (includes utilities).
*Policy for first-year students:* the university expects to offer all first years a place to live. Halls places are not offered to students living within 15 miles, but university-shared houses are available.
*Policy for international students:* the university expects to offer all international students who request accommodation a place to live, mainly in halls of residence.
*Contact for further information:* accommodation@bournemouth.ac.uk

# University of Bradford

Times ranking: 54 (2002 ranking: 56)

**Founded:** Royal charter 1966, College of Advanced Technology 1957-66

**Contact details**
*Address:* Richmond Road,
Bradford BD7 1DP
*Tel:* 01274 233081
*Fax:* 01274 236260
*Website:* www.bradford.ac.uk
*e-mail:* enquiries@bradford.ac.uk

**The Times rankings**
*Teaching assessment:* =79 (20.2)
*Research assessment:* =51 (4.4)
*Entry standards:* 53 (17.8)
*Student–staff ratio:* =41 (15.8)
*Library/IT spend/student:* 53 (£461)
*Facilities spend/student:* 15 (£243)
*Firsts and 2:1s:* 73 (48.7%)
*Work and further study:* =24 (95.8%)
*Expected completion rate:* =53 (85%)

**Students**
*Undergraduates:* 6,380 (2,000)
*Postgraduates:* 710 (2,300)
*Mature students:* 29%
*Overseas students:* 10.0%
*Applications per place:* 6.3
*From state sector schools:* 91%
*From working class homes:* 33%

**Teaching quality assessments**
*1993–95 Rated Excellent:* none.
*From 1995 (top score 24):* **24** philosophy; politics. **23** health subjects; nursing; pharmacy. **22** archaeology. **21** economics; electrical and electronic engineering. **20** chemical engineering; civil engineering; general engineering; molecular biosciences. **18** modern languages. **17** sociology.

## Overview

Having experienced an involuntary transformation in the 1980s as the result of Government spending cuts, Bradford is volunteering for even more radical change in the new century. The university is considering a merger with the city's main further education college to create an institution that it sees as a model for an expanding sector. Students would be able to join a course after GCSE and stay on to postgraduate level, if they wished.

Bradford already has an alliance with Leeds Metropolitan University, which will see collaboration in a number of subjects and help boost participation in a region where it is among the lowest in Europe. Bradford students will be able to use their partner institution's services, including its job shops and placement schemes.

Huddersfield University will make it a three-way arrangement for the delivery of new two-year Foundation Degrees, which are intended to fill 1,500 places by 2004. Bradford will concentrate on health and social care. The university has already expanded local opportunities in this field, bringing about a fourfold increase in nursing enrolments by young women from South Asian families.

The university has also carved out a niche for itself with mature students, who relish its vocational slant and the accent on sandwich courses, which regularly place Bradford near the top of the graduate employment tables. Admissions tutors let it be known that they are less obsessed by high A-level grades than most of their counterparts in the old universities. To some extent, they are making a virtue of necessity because a substantial slice of Bradford's intake is in engineering and languages – two notoriously difficult recruitment fields. Only one university experienced a bigger fall in applications for places in 2002.

The relatively small, lively campus is close to the city centre. Apart from Bradford and Airedale College of Health, incorporated in 1996, only business and management students are taught elsewhere. The highly rated management centre is three miles away in a period building surrounded by parkland.

Teaching assessments have seen sudden and dramatic improvement since 1999, when no subject had been rated as excellent or amassed the 22 points regarded as its equivalent. Since then, nursing, pharmacy and other health studies have all managed 23 points out of 24, while politics and the interdisciplinary human studies programme, which combines philosophy with the study of psychology, literature and sociology, have been awarded full marks.

Research grades improved again in the latest assessment exercise, with European studies achieving the coveted 5* and archaeology, biomedical sciences and politics on the next rung of the ladder. Politics includes the university's best-known offering of peace studies, which has acquired an international reputation.

Around one-third of undergraduates take sandwich courses, which are a legacy of Bradford's previous existence as a college of advanced technology. Engineers and scientists take a majority of the places, but many take management or a language as part of their degree. The university has launched the world's first Internet law degree, marrying the expertise of the law school and social scientists with the Department of Cybernetics, Internet and Virtual Systems. Bradford was already offering courses in e-commerce and internet computing, alongside BScs in computer animation and special effects, and interactive systems and video games design. Computer-assisted learning is increasing in many subjects, making use of an unusually extensive network for student use.

More southerners are being attracted to Bradford by the low cost of living, and the 2,000 places in university-owned accommodation are relatively cheap. Some 140 hall rooms were refurbished in 2001, as part of a £7.5m facelift for the university. The senior management group now includes a Dean of Students to ensure that the student voice is heard in future developments. The students' union operates a late-night 'safety bus' for those living within seven miles of the campus.

## Accommodation

Number of places and costs refer to 2001–02

*University-provided places:* 1,955

*Percentage catered:* 0%

*Costs for catered accommodation:* n/a

*Costs for self-catered accommodation:* £43.20–£63.00 a week.

*Policy for first-year students:* all first years placing the university as their first choice are guaranteed accommodation. Students from the Bradford Metropolitan area might not be offered rooms.

*Policy for international students:* all first-year international students are guaranteed accommodation.

# University of Brighton

**Times ranking:** 68 (2002 ranking: 66)

**Founded:** University status 1992, formerly Brighton Polytechnic

**Contact details**
*Address:* Mithras House, Lewes Road, Brighton BN2 4AT
*Tel:* 01273 642828
*Website:* www.brighton.ac.uk
*e-mail:* admissions@brighton.ac.uk

**The Times rankings**
*Teaching assessment:* =57 (20.7)
*Research assessment:* =64 (2.9)
*Entry standards:* =76 (13.6)
*Student–staff ratio:* 92 (21.3)
*Library/IT spend/student:* 63 (£425)
*Facilities spend/student:* 69 (£140)
*Firsts and 2:1s:* 76 (48.5%)
*Work and further study:* =30 (95.5%)
*Expected completion rate:* =66 (83%)

**Students**
*Undergraduates:* 10,470 (3,120)
*Postgraduates:* 670 (1,390)
*Mature students:* 27.9%
*Overseas students:* 17.0%
*Applications per place:* 7.2
*From state sector schools:* 93%
*From working class homes:* 23%

**Teaching quality assessments**
*1993–95 Rated Excellent:* none.
*From 1995 (top score 24):* **24** philosophy. **23** pharmacy. **22** art and design; health subjects; hospitality; librarianship and information management; mathematics and statistics; molecular biosciences; nursing; organismal biosciences. **21** civil engineering; education; history of art and design. **20** building; electrical and electronic engineering; modern languages.

## Overview

The 2003–4 academic year will see Brighton come of age, as one of a select band of new universities to be awarded a medical school. Run jointly with neighbouring Sussex University, the £28.5 million school will train 128 doctors on a curriculum modelled on that at the highly rated counterpart along the coast at Southampton. Brighton was already heavily engaged in other health subjects, recently opening a new building for nursing and midwifery.

The two universities have been collaborating since Brighton was a polytechnic, when a joint degree in engineering was the first between institutions from opposite sides of the binary line. The Sussex Technology Institute has since been established as a partnership for postgraduate courses and there is a joint accord guaranteeing the offer of a place to all suitably qualified applicants from the Channel Island of Jersey.

Only two new universities did as well as Brighton in the latest Research Assessment Exercise, and only one entered such a high a proportion of its academics. Art and design, biomedical sciences and European studies were all rated nationally excellent, with some work of top international quality. Teaching ratings have also been consistently good, with philosophy registering the university's first maximum score in 2001. The plaudits have not gone unnoticed by students, who have been applying in unprecedented numbers.

Brighton's acknowledged strengths in art and design and health subjects were among the areas contributing to the university's rise, but there had been equally good scores in mathematics and pharmacy. The Design Council's national archive is lodged on campus, and the four-year fashion textiles degree has acquired an international reputation, with work placements in the United States, France and Italy, as well as Britain.

The modular course system gives students many options within their own faculty and sometimes across academic fields. Most undergraduates have a personal tutor, who will advise on combinations. One student in five enters through clearing, but this high proportion partly reflects the large numbers who come in their twenties and thirties. Almost a third of the students are over 21, and such students tend to apply later in the year than school-leavers. They are attracted by strongly vocational courses and the prospect of three years in 'London by the sea'.

Three sites in and around Brighton, plus one in Eastbourne, house the five faculties. Art and design has the prime location opposite the Royal Pavilion, with sports science at Eastbourne and the other subjects on the outskirts of Brighton, at Falmer and Moulsecoomb, the university's headquarters. Each site has distinctive characteristics, although all are linked by shuttle bus.

Numerous European links give most courses an international flavour, often involving a period of study on the Continent. The university has a cosmopolitan air, with more overseas students than most of the former polytechnics.

The 1990s saw £45 million spent on new facilities, particularly in Eastbourne, where there is a new library and exten-sive sports and leisure facilities. A new sports centre with three gymnasia and dance studio, a refurbished swimming pool and new fitness facilities, opened in 2000. New sport science laboratories followed and further grants will see improvements to the learning resources centre, lecture theatres and refectory. The extensive modernisation of the Falmer campus continues, with a library, nursing and midwifery centre, accommodation and the new medical school.

Students like Brighton, although the cost of living is high, and the acquisition of a nightclub in the town has added to the attractions. Eastbourne is also suprisingly popular, despite its retirement home image. Both towns offer plentiful accommodation to supplement the university's stock.

**Accommodation**

Number of places and costs refer to 2002–03

*University-provided places:* 1,780

*Percentage catered:* 0%

*Costs for catered n/a*

*Costs for self-catered accommodation:* £49–£68 a week.

*Policy for first-year students:* only students holding unconditional offers are guaranteed accommodation. Students living in East or West Sussex are not offered halls accommodation.

*Policy for international students:* accommodation guaranteed.

*Contact for further information:* accommodation@brighton.ac.uk

# University of Bristol

**Times ranking:** 7 (2002 ranking: 4)

**Founded:** 1876, Royal charter 1909

**Contact details**
*Address:* Senate House, Tyndall Avenue,
Bristol BS8 1TH
*Tel:* 0117 928 9000
*Website:* www.bris.ac.uk
*e-mail:* admissions@bris.ac.uk

**The Times rankings**
*Teaching assessment:* =19 (21.6)
*Research assessment:* =10 (5.7)
*Entry standards:* =5 (26.5)
*Student–staff ratio:* =12 (12.8)
*Library/IT spend/student:* 29 (£559)
*Facilities spend/student:* 3 (£352)
*Firsts and 2:1s:* 3 (88.1%)
*Work and further study:* =20 (95.9%)
*Expected completion rate:* =6 (94%)

**Students**
*Undergraduates:* 9,360 (3,190)
*Postgraduates:* 1,820 (3,540)
*Mature students:* 6.5%
*Overseas students:* 8.5%
*Applications per place:* 11
*From state sector schools:* 57%
*From working class homes:* 11%

**Teaching quality assessments**
*1993–95 Rated Excellent:* chemistry; English; geography; law; mechanical engineering; social work.
*From 1995 (top score 24):* **24** anatomy and physiology; education; electrical and electronic engineering; molecular biosciences; veterinary medicine.
**23** drama, dance and cinematics; economics; mathematics and statistics; pharmacology; philosophy; physics; politics; psychology. **22** aeronautical engineering; archaeology; civil engineering; Iberian languages; organismal biosciences. **21** classics and ancient history; German; Italian; sociology. **20** French; history of art; medicine; Russian; theology. **19** dentistry.

## Overview

Bristol is a traditional alternative to Oxbridge, favoured particularly by independent schools, whose pupils account for more than a third of the intake. But the university has instituted radical plans to widen its appeal, encouraging departments to make lower offers to promising applicants from schools with poor records at A level. It has also set about doubling the number of students recruited from local schools.

Like Oxford and Cambridge, the university has found it difficult to attract working-class teenagers, who fear that they would be out of place socially, if not academically. Tiny numbers are recruited from the thousands of schools in the bottom half of the A-level league tables. Trying to reverse the trend may spread alarm in the traditional recruiting grounds, but Bristol believes the prize is worth the risk if previously untapped sources of bright students can be brought to the surface.

The city is one of the most attractive in Britain, as well as possessing a vibrant youth culture. It is also prosperous, offering job opportunities to students and graduates alike. The university merges into the centre, its famous Gothic tower dominating the skyline from the junction of two of the main shopping streets. Departments dot the hillside close to the picturesque harbour area.

Having recovered from financial difficulties at the start of the 1990s, the university has embarked upon modest expansion and is living up to expectations in assessments of teaching and research.

A third of the staff assessed for research are in departments considered internationally excellent and three-quarters saw their departments reach one of the top two grades.

Research is Bristol's traditional strength. The 2001 assessments saw the university's tally of 5* subjects shoot up from one to 15, with another 21 subjects on the next of the seven grades. Only Cambridge, Oxford and University College London had more maximum scores. The 33 Excellent teaching ratings also represent one of the largest totals in the university system, with veterinary medicine, molecular biosciences, anatomy, electronic engineering and, most recently, education all achieving perfect scores.

A funding appeal which has raised more than £86 million has enabled Bristol to create new chairs and embark on a number of building projects. The highly rated chemistry department, for example, moved into a well-appointed new centre in 2000, allowing new medical science laboratories to be constructed in the department's former premises. Equine studies, archaeology and policy studies are among the other departments to benefit, and a new sports centre was started in 2001. The developments are much needed after 11 per cent growth in full-time undergraduate numbers over a five-year period when funding levels were reduced consistently, and projects costing another £140 million are in the pipeline.

Entry standards have remained among the highest in Britain, however, ranging from almost three As at A level, or their equivalent, for medicine to more than an A and two Bs for social sciences. A mod-ular course system is now well established, although the majority of students still take single or dual honours degrees.

Most students enjoy life in Bristol, although some do find the high cost of living the main drawback, together with security concerns in some parts of the city. The students' union is less of a social centre than in some universities, but it runs an evening bus service to the halls of residence, and there is a free late-night service for women from the library and the union to their homes.

## Accommodation

Number of places and costs refer to 2001–02

*University-provided places:* about 4,000

*Percentage catered:* 52%

*Costs for catered accommodation:*
£84–£96 (single); £68–£77 (shared) a week.

*Costs for self-catered accommodation:*
£44–£74 (single); £33–£48 (shared) a week.

*Policy for first-year students:* accommodation is guaranteed for new full-time undergraduate students during their first year of study provided they apply by the deadline (12 July), are unaccompanied and live outside the Bristol area.

*Policy for international students:* accommodation is guaranteed for unaccompanied postgraduates paying overseas fees during their first year of study, who have accepted a place for a full academic year in Bristol, and who apply by the deadline (12 August).

*Contact for further information:*
Accom-office@bris.ac.uk

# Brunel University

**Times ranking:** 50 (2002 ranking: 52)

**Founded:** Royal charter 1966

**Contact details**
*Address:* Uxbridge, Middlesex UB8 3PH
*Tel:* 01895 203214 (admissions office)
*Website:* www.brunel.ac.uk
*e-mail:* admissions@brunel.ac.uk

**The Times rankings**
*Teaching assessment:* =39 (21.2)
*Research assessment:* =53 (4.3)
*Entry standards:* =51 (18.3)
*Student–staff ratio:* 87 (20.2)
*Library/IT spend/student:* =58 (£440)
*Facilities spend/student:* 51 (£161)
*Firsts and 2:1s:* =56 (52.4%)
*Work and further study:* =8 (97.2%)
*Expected completion rate:* =62 (84%)

**Students**
*Undergraduates:* 8,570 (1,250)
*Postgraduates:* 1,210 (2,740)
*Mature students:* 23%
*Overseas students:* 7.0%
*Applications per place:* 6.8
*From state sector schools:* 85%
*From working class homes:* 30%

**Teaching quality assessments**
*1993–95 Rated Excellent:* anthropology; social policy
*From 1995 (top score 24):* **23** drama and dance; education; politics; sports science. **22** economics; general engineering; health subjects; mathematics; molecular biosciences; nursing; psychology; sociology. **21** American studies; electrical and electronic engineering. **20** materials science; mechanical engineering; media studies.

## Overview

Brunel has changed in size and character in recent years. The west London university has taken in the former West London Institute of Higher Education, a teacher training centre with an illustrious record in sport, set up its own business school after years of collaboration with Henley Management College and started to move away from the sandwich courses which were once the norm.

About half of all undergraduates still take four-year degrees with six-month placements in each of the first three years, but new developments have tended to be conventional three-year arts and social science programmes. New courses include multimedia design, e-commerce, and internet engineering while other options are creative music technology and ballet and contemporary dance.

The sandwich system and technological emphasis in Brunel's original portfolio have served graduates well in the employment market, as well as providing them with an income from work placements. Almost a third of the students are taking more than one subject, and all have the option of including language or business elements in their degrees.

Although the university has quadrupled in size, only 5,500 students share Brunel's spacious, if uninspiring, main campus at Uxbridge, on the end of the Metropolitan Line. Another former higher education college provides a more picturesque site on the Thames, at Runnymede, for industrial design, while sport, health, social work and education are south of the river at Osterley and Twickenham. The latter also houses the Rambert School of Ballet and Contemporary Dance. Courses generally do not require students to travel between campuses, but a university bus service links the four campuses.

The sporting traditions of the former Borough Road College are being maintained, with gold medal-winning boxer and alumnus Audley Harrison providing the latest reminder at the Sydney Olympics. Close relationships remain with Henley and Buckinghamshire Chilterns University College, where Brunel still validates research degrees. The London Bible College is an associae institute.

Teaching assessments have been consistently good in recent years, with education, sport science and government matching drama and dance in 2001 for the best scores. All the assessments since the millennium have produced scores of at least 22 points out of 24. The latest research assessments also showed further improvement, although only 61 per cent of the academics were entered and design lost its 5* rating. General and mechanical engineering, library and information studies, law and sociology all reached grade 5, and a £14 million investment in 60 more research posts should produce further progress.

Unusually, most applicants are interviewed. Brunel was also among the first of the traditional universities to introduce access courses, run in further education colleges, to bring underqualified applicants up to the necessary standard for entry. With information systems and electronic and computer engineering among the biggest departments, the impact on completion rates could have been considerable – the subjects have the highest drop-out rate nationally – but the projected total of 16 per cent leaving without a qualification is lower than the funding council expected. However, the strain shows in a greater reliance on clearing than most traditional universities would expect: 17.5 per cent of undergraduates arrive via that route.

Student union facilities are good, especially at Uxbridge, and students like Brunel's intimacy. Some feel cut off at Runnymede, but the recent expansion has made for a livelier social scene overall.

Accommodation prospects, like the recreational facilities, vary between sites. The 2,800 university beds at Uxbridge and Runnymede are enough to guarantee first years a place, but some at Twickenham and Osterley still miss out.

## Accommodation

Number of places and costs refer to 2001-02

*University-provided places:* 3,180

*Percentage catered:* 10%

*Costs for catered accommodation:* £65–£69 a week.

*Costs for self-catered accommodation:* £48.50–£62.50 a week.

*Policy for first-year students:* all first-year students are eligible for on-campus accommodation irrespective of home address.

*Policy for international students:* all new international students are given on-campus accommodation.

*Contact for further information:* accom-uxb@brunel.ac.uk

# University of Buckingham

**Founded:** 1974, Royal charter 1983

**Contact details**
*Address:* Hunter Street,
Buckingham MK18 1EG
*Tel:* 01280 824081 (admissions)
*Website:* www.buckingham.ac.uk
*e-mail:* admissions@buckingham.ac.uk

**Students**
*Undergraduates:* 403 (56)
*Postgraduates:* 90 (40)
*Mature students:* 45.5%
*Overseas students:* 60%
*Applications per place:* 19.2
*From state sector schools:* n/a
*From working class homes:* n/a

**Teaching quality assessments:** not carried out because the Higher Education Funding Council has no jurisdiction.

**Main subject areas:** accounting; business studies; computer science; English; history; history of art and heritage management; hotel management and economics; law; politics; psychology.

## Overview

Britain's only private university is its smallest by far, but no longer the youngest. Nor, it claims since the introduction of tuition fees elsewhere, should it be considered any more expensive than other universities, especially if you are well qualified. Its intensive two-year degrees cut maintenance costs, and a scholarship scheme reduces the £10,000-a-year fees by more than a third for applicants with three Bs at A level. The threshold is reduced to three Cs for those who go to school or live in Buckinghamshire and the surrounding counties of Bedfordshire, Berkshire, Hertfordshire, Northamptonshire and Oxfordshire who achieve three Cs at A level or the equivalent in the International Baccalaureate or other elements of the Curriculum 2000 programme. The same fee reductions are also available for any other students who achieved 3 Bs at A level or its equivalent.

The university, which celebrated its 25th anniversary in 2001, has no ambitions to follow its peers into the mass higher education market: it values the personal approach that comes with having only ten students to each member of staff. One-to-one tutorials, which have all but disappeared outside Oxbridge and are by no means universal there, are common at Buckingham. The average teaching group contains about six students.

However, the scholarship initiative, which is open to British and foreign students, could bring modest growth and breathe new life into the university. A Conservative-backed experiment of the 1970s, Buckingham had to wait almost ten years for its royal charter, but is now an accepted part of the university system. Although in 1992 it installed Lady Thatcher as chancellor and recently honoured her husband Sir Denis with an honorary degree, the university has no party political ties. Dr Terence Kealey, a biochemist from Cambridge University, became the latest vice-chancellor in April 2001, declaring an ambition for Buckingham to 'one day' challenge the cream of American higher education.

Buckingham's private status excludes it from the funding councils' assessment of teaching and research, making it impossible to place in our league table. However, the university's degrees carry full currency in the academic world and teaching standards are high. Law and business are particularly popular.

The university runs on calendar years, rather than the traditional academic variety, although law students have the option of entering in July. Between October and December, students taking degrees including French are offered a ten-week course in Lille. Degree courses run for two 40–week years, minimising disruptive career breaks for the many mature students. More than half of the students are from overseas, but the proportion from Britain has been growing.

The two-year degree has been fully assessed by Professor John Clarke, a founder member of the university staff. Although hardly neutral, he concluded that the individual tuition given to Buckingham students, made possible by unusually generous staffing levels, allowed the system to succeed. However, he acknowledges that 'undercapitalisation' has prevented the university achieving as much as it hoped.

New courses in 2001 included degrees in multimedia journalism and media communications, both paired with English. The university is also focusing on e-commerce, with a Certificate in Internet Technologies and an MSc in e-business.

Campus facilities have improved considerably in recent years, although they cannot compare with those available at traditional universities. Buckingham operates on three sites, all within easy walking distance of each other, including a business school which opened in 1996. An academic centre containing computer suites, lecture theatres and student facilities provides a focal point that was missing previously.

The social scene is predictably quiet, given the size of the university and the workload, especially at weekends. The town is pretty and has its share of pubs and restaurants. Milton Keynes or Oxford are near, except that Buckingham has no station.

## Accommodation
Number of places and costs refer to 2001–02

*University-provided places:* 450

*Percentage catered:* 0%

*Costs for catered accommodation:* n/a

*Costs for self-catered accommodation:* £59–£105 a week; £35–£40 a week during vacation (students may stay in their allocated room during vacation).

*Policy for first-year students:* all students are guaranteed accommodation for a minimum period of six months.

*Policy for international students:* all students are guaranteed accommodation for their first year.

*Contact for further information:* admissions@buckingham.ac.uk

# University of Cambridge

**Times ranking:** 2 (2002 ranking: 1)

**Founded:** 1209

**Contact details**
*Address:* Kellet Lodge, Tennis Court Road,
Cambridge CB2 1QJ
*Tel:* 01223 333308
*Website:* www.cam.ac.uk
*e-mail:* ucam-undergraduate-
admissions@lists.cam.ac.uk

**The Times rankings**
*Teaching assessment:* 1 (22.7)
*Research assessment:* 1 (6.6)
*Entry standards:* 1 (29.7)
*Student–staff ratio:* 10 (11.9)
*Library/IT spend/student:* 5 (£959)
*Facilities spend/student:* 60 (£150)
*Firsts and 2:1s:* 1 (93.4%)
*Work and further study:* 3 (98.5%)
*Expected completion rate:* 1 (98%)

**Students**
*Undergraduates:* 11,000 (2,730)
*Postgraduates:* 4,220 (2,350)
*Mature students:* 4.3%
*Overseas students:* 10.5%
*Applications per place:* 3.3
*From state sector schools:* 52%
*From working class homes:* 9%

**Teaching quality assessments**
*1993–95 Rated Excellent:* anthropology;
architecture; chemistry; computer science;
English; geography; geology; history; law
music.
*From 1995 (top score 24):* **24** classics and
ancient history; economics; molecular
biosciences; organismal biosciences;
pharmacy; philosophy; psychology.
**23** anatomy and physiology;archaeology;
Celtic studies; chemical engineering;
education; general engineering; materials
science; mathematics; Middle Eastern and
African studies; physics; politics;
sociology; theology; veterinary medicine.
**22** history of art; land management;
linguistics; modern languages.
**21** medicine.

## Overview

Until this year, Cambridge had enjoyed an unbroken run at the top of *The Times* League Table, and even now it is practically inseparable from first-placed Oxford. The university has the best record in the teaching and research assessments, and loses out by a statistically insignificant three points out of 1,000 Traditionally supreme in the sciences, where an array of subjects boast top ratings for teaching and research, the university has added strength in the arts and social sciences. A new Centre for Research in the Arts, Social Sciences and Humanities, designed to compete with similar institutes in Australia, Germany and the United States, should accelerate this trend. The Judge Management School is also well established now.

All but one of the subjects assessed in the first rounds of teaching quality assessment were considered excellent and none has dropped more than two points out of 24 under the current system. Classics and economics were added to the subjects on full marks in 2001. Almost three-quarters of the academics entered for research assessment were in subjects rated internationally outstanding, and only three subjects failed to reach the next-highest grade. The tripos system was a forerunner of the currently fashionable modular degree, allowing students to change subjects (within limits) mid-way through their courses, as well as providing two degree classifications.

More students now come from state schools than the independent sector – a trend the university is keen to continue –

but the proportion of working-class undergraduates remains low. Summer schools, student visits and, in some colleges, sympathetic selection procedures, are helping to attract more applications from comprehensive schools. Cambridge escaped largely unscathed from the controversy over Laura Spence's rejection at Oxford, although the university acknowledged that it could just as easily have been the centre of attention.

A lively alternative prospectus, available from the students' union, says there is no such thing as Cambridge University, just a collection of colleges. Where applications are concerned, this is true, as it is to some extent socially. Making the right choice of college is crucial, both to maximise the chances of winning a place and to ensure an enjoyable three years if you are successful. However, teaching is university-based, especially in the sciences, and a shift of emphasis towards the centre has been taking place with the aid of a £250 million funding appeal. Applicants can take pot luck by opting to go straight into the pool of colleges, but this route is not as successful on average.

The university's leading place in British higher education was underlined by its success in attracting Microsoft's first research base outside the United States. This was one of a series of recent technological partnerships with the private sector, several of which benefit undergraduates as well as researchers. Cambridge was also chosen for a Government-sponsored partnership with the Massachusetts Institute of Technology to promote entrepreneurship.

Such is the scale of development that almost £500 million worth of building is either planned or under construction. The medical school's facilities are being upgraded at Addenbrookes Hospital but, with the city choking with traffic and short of sites for development, the university is looking to the outskirts to expand. The West Cambridge site will take a mixture of teaching and research buildings, and there are plans for more on green-belt land further north. In the long term, up to three new colleges could be built as the university adds 5,000 extra places.

For the moment, however, entrance requirements will remain the toughest in Britain. With fewer than four applicants for each place – fewer still if you choose your subject carefully – the competition for places appears less intense than at the popular civic universities. The difference is that almost nine out of ten entrants have at least three A-grade A levels. The pressure does not end there: the amount of high-quality work to be crammed into eight-week terms can prove too much for some students, although the 1 per cent drop-out rate is the lowest in Britain.

The college system ensures that student facilities are among the best, especially for sport. Students do not pick Cambridge for the clubbing, which is just as well. With two universities within its boundaries, the city caters well for students in many respects, but it is never going to be among the leading lights for its youth scene.

*See Chapter 8 for information about individual colleges.*

# Cardiff University ....

**Times ranking:** 34 (2002 ranking: 29)

**Founded:** Royal charter 1988, formerly University College (founded 1883) and University of Wales Institute of Science and Technology (founded 1866), merged 1988

**Contact details**
*Address:* PO Box 921, Cardiff CF10 3XQ
*Tel:* 029 2087 4839
*Website:* www.cardiff.ac.uk
*e-mail:* admissions@cardiff.ac.uk

**The Times rankings**
*Teaching assessment:* =43 (21.1)
*Research assessment:* =10 (5.7)
*Entry standards:* 24 (22.8)
*Student–staff ratio:* =57 (17.2)
*Library/IT spend/student:* 45 (£487)
*Facilities spend/student:* 22 (£216)
*Firsts and 2:1s:* 31 (62.7%)
*Work and further study:* =49 (94.4%)
*Expected completion rate:* =31 (89%)

**Students**
*Undergraduates:* 12,140 (2,890)
*Postgraduates:* 2,610 (1,510)
*Mature students:* 9.4%
*Overseas students:* 9.0%
*Applications per place:* 5.2
*From state sector schools:* 84%
*From working class homes:* 19%

**Teaching quality assessments**
*1993–95 Rated Excellent:* accounting and finance; anatomy and physiology; archaeology; architecture; biochemistry; biology; chemistry; civil engineering; dentistry; education; environmental engineering; English language; electrical and electronic engineering; maritime studies; mechanical engineering; medicine; optometry; pharmacy; philosophy; psychology; town planning.

## Overview

Cardiff has established itself as the front-runner in Welsh higher education after a period of financial instability. Although still part of the University of Wales, there is little sign of the federal university in Cardiff's promotional material. With more than 16,000 students, including over 3,000 postgraduates, it is a match for most rivals in teaching and research. A third of the students come from Wales, but the 1,400 from overseas testify to Cardiff's international reputation. Seven subjects – city and regional planning, civil engineering, English, education, optometry, psychology and theology – were rated internationally outstanding in the latest research assessments, compared with only one in 1996. Almost nine out of ten researchers were placed in the top two of the seven categories, one of the highest proportions in Britain.

Research income is healthy, too, with industrial collaboration by the Manufacturing Engineering Centre winning a Queen's Anniversary Prize in 2001. Teaching quality is also highly rated. The 21 subjects graded as excellent represent more than half of the university. An overall audit by the Quality Assurance Agency complimented the university on its 'powerful academic vision and well-developed and effectively articulated mission to achieve excellence in teaching and research'. Student support services, including counselling facilities and the help offered to dyslexics, were among the features singled out for praise.

Humanities and social sciences take the largest share of places. A partial reorganisation has created two 'super schools' of biosciences and social sciences, while a new Centre for Lifelong Learning co-ordinates 700 courses, which are offered at 100 regional centres. Many full-time degrees share a common first year, and the introduction of a modular system has made undergraduate study more flexible.

The university enjoys a central location in the Welsh capital, occupying a significant part of the civic complex around Cathays Park. In recent years, £160 million has been invested in new buildings and equipment, and extensive refurbishment. The flagship projects involved a £30 million centre for engineering, physics and computer science, with facilities comparable with the best in Britain, and a £3.5 million refurbishment of the chemistry department. The latest phase of the programme involves a new building for the school of biosciences and upgraded halls of residence.

Entry requirements have been rising, despite recent expansion, and the graduate employment record is good. There was a 13 per cent rise in applications for courses beginning in 2002, when the average entrance requirement was expected to be three Bs at A level. One undergraduate in six comes from an independent school – less than the funding council anticipated – but still almost 20 per cent have a working-class background. The 6 per cent drop-out rate is the lowest in Wales and among the lowest in Britain.

Merger talks were under way with the University of Wales College of Medicine as this guide went to press. The Cardiff-based college was already a partner institution, with the university teaching pre-clinical courses and collaborating in spin-off research. The city of Cardiff is popular with students, offering all the attractions of a large conurbation without such high prices as students experience elsewhere.

The university's own facilities are good. In recent years £40 million has been invested in student accommodation, almost half of the money going into a single residential development which has provided more than 1,000 extra places. Two-thirds of the study bedrooms are en-suite, and most are within walking distance of lectures.

The main residential site at Talybont boasts a 'sports village', with three multi-purpose sports halls, a fitness suite and outdoor pitches. There is also a city centre fitness suite and a sports ground that was used as a training facility for the rugby union World Cup.

## Accommodation

Number of places and costs refer to 2001–02

*University-provided places:* about 4,700

*Percentage catered:* 13%

*Costs for catered accommodation:* £56–£68 a week.

*Costs for self-catered accommodation:* £43–£51 a week.

*Policy for first-year students:* a guarantee of accommodation is given to all first years entering through the normal admissions cycle. No restrictions are placed on those who live locally.

*Policy for international students:* as above for first-year students. They are also guaranteed accommodation for the duration of their course.

*Contact for further information:* residences @cardiff.ac.uk

# Cardiff, University of Wales Institute (UWIC)

Times ranking: 65

**Founded:** University status as a constituent member of the University of Wales, 1996

**Contact details**
*Address:* Western Avenue,
Cardiff CF5 2YB
*Tel:* 029 2041 6070
*Website:* www.uwic.ac.uk
*e-mail:* uwicinfo@uwic.ac.uk

**The Times rankings**
*Teaching assessment:* =43 (21.1)
*Research assessment:* =72 (2.7)
*Entry standards:* =63 (15.8)
*Student–staff ratio:* =31 (15.2)
*Library/IT spend/student:* =92 (£333)
*Facilities spend/student:* 93 (£91)
*Firsts and 2:1s:* 67 (49.8%)
*Work and further study:* =85 (91.5%)
*Expected completion rate:* =37 (88%)

**Students**
*Undergraduates:* 5,230 (1,140)
*Postgraduates:* 520 (680)
*Mature students:* 20.7%
*Overseas students:* 6.9%
*Applications per place:* 5.3
*From state sector schools:* 94%
*From working class homes:* 28%

**Teaching quality assessments**
*1993–95 Rated Excellent:* art and design; biomedical sciences; environmental health; nutrition; podiatry; psychology; speech therapy.

## Overview

The Institute, which is usually known as UWIC, is included in the guide for the first time this year, as a full member of the University of Wales and Universities UK. It has a national reputation for sport, but is no slouch in some academic fields either. The combination has been attracting record numbers of applicants, with 17 per cent more seeking places in 2002 despite a reduction in advertising. Almost 9,000 had applied when the official deadline passed, a total which placed UWIC among the most popular new universities.

The 8,000 enrolments in 2001 were more than ever before. Two-thirds of the students are Welsh, half of them from Cardiff or the Vale of Glamorgan. Over 90 per cent attended state schools and 28 per cent come from working-class homes. The 17 per cent who come from areas sending few students to higher education is significantly ahead of the 'benchmark' set according to the mix of courses. The drop-out rate is lower than the average for new universities.

UWIC is one of Britain's leading centres for university sport, with team performances to match some excellent facilities. The Institute has had British university champions in acrobatics, trampolining, athletics, rugby union, rugby league, boxing, squash, archery, weightlifting and judo. More than 240 past or present students are internationals in 28 sports, world and Olympic champions among them. The £7 million national indoor athletics centre is the Institute's pride and joy, but other facilities are also of high quality.

Academically, art and design is the star performer, with teaching in ceramics, fine art and internal architecture rated excellent, and the whole area considered nationally excellent for research. The four faculties were reorganised into nine schools in 1999-2000 for maximum flexibility. All six teacher training courses are rated excellent for teaching and there have been top scores in several sciences, but fewer than one academic in five was entered for the latest Research Assessment Exercise, leaving UWIC near the bottom of the research table in terms of average grades per member of staff.

Entrance requirements are generally low, but the menu of largely vocational courses means that many students come with qualifications other than A levels. About a third are mature students and there is a relatively high proportion from overseas.

UWIC has six sites, all within four miles of the centre of Cardiff. The Cyncoed campus, which houses education and sport, is the centre of activity, particularly for first-year students. The athletics centre is there, together with a multitude of outdoor facilities and also the Welsh Sports Centre for the Disabled. Student facilities, including the Institute's largest bar, have been upgraded recently.

Howard Gardens, by contrast, is the home of fine art, while the Llandaff campus hosts design, engineering and the health courses, which now account for the largest number of students. Llandaff has a new £3 million student centre, which includes a dyslexia support unit among a number of advice and representation services. Business, leisure and food are taught at the Colchester Avenue campus, and there are two other sites containing student accommodation.

Students tend to like Cardiff as a city, and UWIC's enterprising union does its best to make their time at the union as lively as possible. It bought Reds nightclub and Stamps Bar in the city centre to add to the campus choices. Before the recent expansion, all first years were guaranteed accommodation, and 90 per cent still live in halls.

## Accommodation

Number of places and costs refer to 2002–03

*University-provided places:* 1,062

*Percentage catered:* 42%

*Costs for catered accommodation:* £72 a week.

*Costs for self-catered accommodation:* £51–£57 a week.

*Policy for first-year students:* accommodation is guaranteed if applications made before the end of May.

*Policy for international students:* acccommodation is guaranteed if applications are made through the International Office.

*Contact for further information:* accomm@uwic.ac.uk
www.uwic.ac.uk

# University of Central England in Birmingham

**Times ranking:** 87 (2002 ranking: 92)

**Founded:** University status 1992, formerly Birmingham Polytechnic

**Contact details**
*Address:* Perry Barr, Birmingham B42 2SU
*Tel:* 0121 331 5595
*Website:* www.uce.ac.uk
*e-mail:* recruitment@uce.ac.uk

**The Times rankings**
*Teaching assessment:* =93 (19.9)
*Research assessment:* =85 (2.2)
*Entry standards:* 74 (14.1)
*Student–staff ratio:* 95 (22.5)
*Library/IT spend/student:* 89 (£354)
*Facilities spend/student:* =64 (£145)
*Firsts and 2:1s:* =56 (52.4%)
*Work and further study:* 56 (93.9%)
*Expected completion rate:* =80 (81%)

**Students**
*Undergraduates:* 10.540 (5,540)
*Postgraduates:* 1,170 (2,110)
*Mature students:* 29.5%
*Overseas students:* 12.0%
*Applications per place:* 5.6
*From state sector schools:* 95%
*From working class homes:* 37%

**Teaching quality assessments**
*1993–95 Rated Excellent:* music.
*From 1995 (top score 24):* **22** art and design; education; health subjects.
**21** business; economics. **20** architecture; librarianship and information management; nursing; town planning.
**19** agriculture; electrical and electronic engineering; mechanical engineering.
**18** building; land and property management; sociology.

## Overview

UCE describes itself as 'the responsive university', emphasising its willingness to act on students' wishes as well as serving the needs of the Second City. The annual satisfaction survey goes to half of the student body, in a model that may soon be part of a national system of quality assurance and has already been adopted by other universities in Britain and abroad. The results are taken seriously: more than £1 million was spent on library stock after one survey, and a more recent exercise has led to the introduction of internet tutorials in engineering and new help with research for undergraduates in law and social science. The longstanding initiative is just one of the activities of the influential Centre for Research into Quality, which is headed by one of the university's most senior academics.

The university has a proud record of extending access to higher education: almost 40 per cent of its students come from working class homes and 95 per cent attended state schools. But one in five drop out – a slightly higher rate than expected, even given the social and subject mix. About half of the full-time students come from the West Midlands, many from ethnic minorities. UCE also has one of the largest programmes of part-time courses in Britain, making it the biggest provider of higher education in the region. Students also enter through the network of 15 associated further education colleges, which run foundation and access programmes.

One of the university's best-known features is its Conservatoire, housed in part of Birmingham's smart convention centre. Courses from opera to world music have given it a reputation for innovation, which was recognised in an 'excellent' rating for teaching. Most other teaching ratings have been mediocre, however, although the teacher education courses produced the best scores among the former polytechnics in the Teacher Training Agency's performance indicators. Those for secondary teachers were bettered only by Oxford and Cambridge.

Education, health subjects and art and design have registered the best scores among the recent assessments. The university has been building up its portfolio of high-tech courses with new degrees in electronic commerce, electronic systems, communications and network engineering and mechanical engineering systems.

UCE opted out of the first research assessment exercise – the only university to do so – as a statement of its priority for teaching. The latest assessments showed improvement on 1996, but only art and design reached any of the top three grades. However, income from research contracts has been healthy throughout.

Seven campuses straggle across Birmingham, but the majority of students are concentrated on the modern Perry Barr site three miles north of the city centre. The large teacher training centre moved there from the southern suburb of Edgbaston in 2001, and the university has bought an adjacent 43-acre site to improve sporting provision, which was poorly positioned and inadequate for 25,000 students. The indoor facilities, clubhouse and pitches are to be upgraded and extended.

The Institute of Art and Design, refurbished at a cost of £20 million, spreads further south to Bourneville, where it occupies part of the Cadbury 'village'. It is the largest in Britain, and includes a school of jewellery in the city centre. The recent relocation of engineering and computing to the city's Millennium Point high-tech development provided a new focus for the university. Facilities in the £114 million Lottery-funded centre are open to the public.

University-owned accommodation is only guaranteed for some first years. But the high proportion of locally-based mature students and the relatively cheap and plentiful private sector housing make this less of a problem. Students have been critical of the union facilities, but the city's youth scene is highly rated.

## Accommodation

Number of places and costs refer to 2001–02

*University-provided places:* 2,289

*Percentage catered:* 6.3%

*Costs for catered accommodation:* £60–£71 a week.

*Costs for self-catered accommodation:* £44.50–£69.50 a week.

*Policy for first-year students:* all first-years who have firmly accepted an offer by 31 May will be allocated a room in halls. Students living in the Greater Birmingham area are excluded from this guarantee, but if sufficient places remain they will normally be allocated a room.

*Policy for international students:* guaranteed a room in the halls of residence for the duration of their course.

*Contact for further information:* Accommodation@uce.ac.uk

# University of Central Lancashire

Times ranking: =78 (2002 ranking: 74)

**Founded:** University status 1992, formerly Lancashire (originally Preston) Polytechnic

**Contact details**
*Address:* Preston PR1 2HE
*Tel:* 01772 201201
*Website:* www.uclan.ac.uk
*e-mail:* cenquiries@uclan.ac.uk

**The Times rankings**
*Teaching assessment:* =70 (20.5)
*Research assessment:* =85 (2.2)
*Entry standards:* 71 (14.5)
*Student–staff ratio:* 86 (20.1)
*Library/IT spend/student:* 90 (£346)
*Facilities spend/student:* =62 (£146)
*Firsts and 2:1s:* 85 (45.9%)
*Work and further study:* =80 (92.0%)
*Expected completion rate:* 88 (77.4%)

**Students**
*Undergraduates:* 13,300 (7,880)
*Postgraduates:* 430 (1,830)
*Mature students:* 22.5%
*Overseas students:* 9.3%
*Applications per place:* 4.9
*From state sector schools:* 97%
*From working class homes:* 33%

**Teaching quality assessments**
*1993–95 Rated Excellent:* none.
*From 1995 (top score 24):* **24** American studies; education; nursing; psychology. **22** art and design; business; health subjects; linguistics; media studies; molecular biosciences; organismal biosciences; politics; tourism and leisure. **21** modern languages. **20** building; drama, dance and cinematics; general engineering. **19** history of art; mathematics; physics and astronomy. **18** agriculture; sociology. **15** electrical and electronic engineering.

## Overview

A big university at the heart of England's newest city, Central Lancashire does not dominate Preston to the extent that Cambridge or Durham do, but students account for a sixth of the population during termtime. The balance will shift much further in their favour if the university succeeds in its aim of expanding to 50,000 students by the end of the decade. The modern, town centre campus has seen considerable development, as the university has doubled in size, and still the building continues. A £12 million Lottery-funded sports centre opened in 1999 followed by a 'knowledge park' for technology transfer in 2000.

Amid the expansion, the university has revamped its pioneering credit accumulation and transfer system, allowing undergraduates to mix and match from a menu of more than 3,000 courses. Electives are used to broaden the curriculum, so that up to 11 per cent of students' time is spent on subjects outside their normal range. There is particular encouragement to include a language as part of the package, and more than 2,000 students do so. A growing proportion also take advantage of the numerous international exchange programmes, which are available in all subject areas. The university's website is even available in Chinese.

The former polytechnic has acquired a high reputation in some apparently unlikely fields. American studies and psychology both achieved perfect scores for teaching quality, followed more recently by nursing and education. Journalism, which also scored well, is sufficiently popular to be able to demand the equivalent of three Bs at A level. Astrophysics benefits from two observatories, including Britain's most powerful optical telescope. Although its teaching quality score was disappointing, it was one of the successes of the latest research assessments. These were a definite improvement on 1996 but, apart from physics and astronomy, only history and law rated in the top three categories. New courses include a degree in policing and investigation, and a new range of joint honours was launched in 2000.

The university took in an agricultural college at Newton Rigg, in Cumbria, in 1998 – its first excursion beyond Preston. Further education in land-based subjects are continuing there and new programmes across a broader curriculum are being developed at degree and postgraduate level for a county with little higher education provision. A £3.5 million learning resources centre has been added.

A high proportion of Central Lancashire's students are local people in their twenties or thirties, many of whom come through the well-established lifelong learning networks run in colleges throughout the North West. No fewer than 14 per cent of the university's students are taught in colleges but, unlike some institutions involved in 'franchising', Central Lancashire has carried out a thorough review of the quality of its external programmes. Applications have been low for the number of places on offer, but there was a big improvement in 2001. Even so, more than 30 per cent of undergraduates enter through clearing.

The social scene in Preston may not compare with Manchester or Liverpool, but neither do the security risks and the cost of living is low. Both cities are within easy reach, and the student union's 'Feel' club nights have won national recognition. Although still not the most fashionable university, Central Lancashire commands great loyalty among its students.

Rents for the 1,700 places in university accommodation are among the lowest in Britain and the new 60–acre Preston Sports Arena, built in partnership with the local authority, is among the best in any higher education institution. Three miles from the main campus, the centre is staffed, managed and maintained by the university, but available to clubs throughout the region.

## Accommodation

Number of places and costs refer to 2001–02

*University-provided places:* 1,700

*Percentage catered:* 0%

*Costs for catered accommodation:* n/a

*Costs for self-catered accommodation:* £30–£64 a week.

*Policy for first-year students:* the Student Accommodation Service guarantees to help all first years find suitable accommodation either in university-managed housing or in the private sector. No restrictions for local students.

*Policy for international students:* as above, with priority given to first years.

*Contact for further information:* saccommodation@uclan.ac.uk

# City University

**Times ranking:** 47 (2002 ranking: 49)

**Founded:** 1894, Royal charter 1966

**Contact details**
*Address:* Northampton Square,
London EC1V 0HB
*Tel:* 020 7040 5060
*Website:* www.city.ac.uk
*e-mail:* ugadmissions@city.ac.uk

**The Times rankings**
*Teaching assessment:* =57 (20.7)
*Research assessment:* =51 (4.4)
*Entry standards:* 36 (20.5)
*Student–staff ratio:* 20 (13.6)
*Library/IT spend/student:* 49 (£481)
*Facilities spend/student:* 42 (£178)
*Firsts and 2:1s:* =49 (55.8%)
*Work and further study:* =20 (95.9%)
*Expected completion rate:* =66 (83%)

**Students**
*Undergraduates:* 4,950 (4,640)
*Postgraduates:* 1,700 (3,680)
*Mature students:* 24%
*Overseas students:* 18.7%
*Applications per place:* 7.6
*From state sector schools:* 78%
*From working class homes:* 28%

**Teaching quality assessments**
*1993–95 Rated Excellent:* music.
*From 1995 (top score 24):* **23** art and
design; business and management; health
subjects; mathematics. **22** economics.
**21** electrical and electronic engineering;
librarianship and information
management; psychology. **20** nursing.
**19** civil engineering; land management;
mechanical engineering; media studies;
sociology.

## Overview

Originally a college of advanced technology, a third of City students now study business, a third health subjects and a third study law, computing, engineering, journalism, and the arts. But the university has maintained its links with business, industry and the professions, reaping the benefits with consistently good graduate employment figures. Courses have a practical edge, and many of the staff hold professional, as well as academic, qualifications. The university has been reviewing its mission since the arrival of Professor David Rhind as vice-chancellor, but that is one characteristic which will not alter.

The new strategy has more to do with increasing the size of the university, which is comparatively small, especially for an institution where more than a third of the students are postgraduates. Numbers doubled during the 1990s, partly due to the incorporation of a nursing and midwifery college at nearby St Bartholomew's Hospital. But growth came to a halt at the end of the decade, despite one of the highest ratios of applicants to places in the university system.

Limited development has already taken place at the university's headquarters, on the borders of the City of London, but the most ambitious plan is the new £42 million home for the business school, in the financial district of the City of London. Opening in summer 2002, the new building, spread over eight floors, doubles the school's usable space, enabling it to expand its academic activity and executive programmes. The business school is, not surprisingly, one of City's great strengths. It recently became the first Western university to forge links with the Bank of China, planning an Executive MBA programme in Shanghai as the first step to a wider role in business education throughout South East Asia.

The university had already boosted its legal provision by incorporating the Inns of Court School of Law. The new Institute of Law, which includes the university's original department, offers London's only 'one-stop shop' for legal training, from undergraduate to professional courses. City has also agreed to work with Queen Mary, University of London, in a range of subjects, starting with medicine.

City has a particularly high reputation in music, where it is associated with the Guildhall School of Music and Drama, with its teaching rated as excellent and research internationally outstanding. The subject achieved the university's only 5* rating in the 2001 Research Assessment Exercise, but business, law, information science, arts policy and optometry all reached the next grade.

Until recently, however, most teaching assessments had been disappointing. The university's response was to establish an educational development unit to enhance the quality of teaching and launch a review of the effectiveness of personal tutoring. It set a target of 22 points out of 24 for each teaching assessment, a mark that has since been met by all but two subjects, which only narrowly missed out. There have been near-perfect scores in maths and statistics, arts management and health subjects (language and communication science, optometry and radiography).

New degrees include environmental engineering and Anglo-American law whilst the journalism department is well regarded. There is also a flourishing sub-degree programme for adults, which ranges from sitcom writing to e-business.

Official performance indicators for higher education have brought mixed news: although the 18 per cent drop-out rate is among the highest in the traditional universities, this is less than the funding council expects, given City's subject mix. Students tend to be more concerned by their inability to afford the attractions of a trendy part of London. Most fall back on the extended students' union, but this is usually shut at weekends.

## Accommodation

Number of places and costs refer to 2001–02

*University-provided places:* 982

*Percentage catered:* 33%

*Costs for catered accommodation:* £93 a week.

*Costs for self-catered accommodation:* £77.50–£79.50 a week.

*Policy for first-year students:* guaranteed if an offer has been firmly accepted, accommodation has been applied for by 15 May, and the student is normally resident outside the Greater London area.

*Policy for international students:* preference is given to overseas students , but halls will have a mix of UK and international students.

*Contact for further information:* accomm@city.ac.uk www.city.ac.uk/accommodation

# Coventry University

Times ranking: 67 (2002 ranking: 75)

**Founded:** University status 1992, formerly Coventry (originally Lanchester) Polytechnic

**Contact details**
Address: Priory Street, Coventry CV1 5FB
Tel: 024 7688 7688
Website: www.coventry.ac.uk
e-mail: info.reg@coventry.ac.uk

**The Times rankings**
Teaching assessment: =57 (20.7)
Research assessment: 89 (2.1)
Entry standards: =80 (13.5)
Student–staff ratio: =50 (16.7)
Library/IT spend/student: 57 (£441)
Facilities spend/student: 28 (£194)
Firsts and 2:1s: 91 (44.4%)
Work and further study: =39 (95.1%)
Expected completion rate: =74 (82%)

**Students**
Undergraduates: 10,850 (2,660)
Postgraduates: 670 (1,140)
Mature students: 23.3%
Overseas students: 16.7%
Applications per place: 6
From state sector schools: 94%
From working class homes: 36%

**Teaching quality assessments**
1993–95 Rated Excellent: geography; mechanical engineering.
From 1995 (top score 24): **23** economics; health subjects; history; mathematics; politics. **22** art and design; building; business and management; nursing. **21** agriculture; hospitality; modern languages; psychology; sociology. **19** civil engineering; town planning; molecular biosciences; organismal biosciences. **18** electrical and electronic engineering; media studies; aeronautical and manufacturing engineering.

## Overview

Coventry's origins go back to the foundation of the Coventry College of Design in 1843 and its links with the motor industry of the Midlands was reflected in its earlier title of Lanchester Polytechnic, named after a leading figure in that industry. The campus of the university is confined to an area close to the city centre, with all its departments within walking distance of each other. There has been an ambitious building plan after a decade in which student numbers have doubled. A £20 million library, a media and arts centre, a technology park and enhanced student facilities, including new student accommodation and a second students' union building, are transforming the university.

The university's financial base is sound, its income more than doubling in the 1990s, but not all its recruitment targets were met. After recording its first deficit in 2000, the position was turned around the following year. Although some class sizes increased, students have been benefiting from an innovative approach to computer-assisted learning, supported by an expanded computer network and a showpiece library, almost entirely naturally ventilated and lit. A former cinema is the site of a £7 million arts centre and the conversion of a former working men's club provides much needed space for the students' union with dedicated facilities for mature and international students.

Its predominantly vocational curriculum has a strong sense of direction, and its computing and engineering courses have proved particularly popular with overseas students. A rough balance is maintained between arts, technology, business and health studies in order to preserve an all-round educational environment. Most full-time and sandwich students take advantage of the university's modular system to ensure that their degree programme meets their needs, within faculty limits. The majority of students exercise their right to take 'free choice modules' that cover the full range of university provision, with IT skills and languages particularly popular. Coventry has been building up its portfolio of courses, having introduced eye-catching degrees in subjects such as disaster management, forensic chemistry, criminology and boat design. Degrees in automotive engineering and design courses are developed in collaboration with the city's motor industry. The vocational slant of its courses ensures that the university always enjoys a healthy graduate employment rate. A selection of franchised courses are run at local colleges of further education.

Teaching ratings have been good recently, with history and politics, economics, health subjects and maths achieving near-perfect scores. Business and art and design, two of the biggest areas of the university, were close behind, as was the growing field of nursing. Research grades improved considerably in the 2001 assessment exercise, but only design, materials and politics reached any of the top three categories. Design should benefit further from a revolutionary digital modelling workshop, due to open in December 2002, which will provide full-scale vehicle modelling facilities for undergraduates as well as researchers.

Dr Mike Goldstein, the vice-chancellor,

claims that a 'quiet revolution' has taken place in recent years, and the university has acquired the confidence to take new initiatives. As well as the bricks and mortar, this has meant measures such as the introduction of tangible rewards for excellent teaching and further development of electronic learning.

More than most universities, Coventry is a creature of its city, and the civic-minded approach of the university has created many links between town and gown. The main buildings open out from the ruins of the bombed cathedral, as university and public facilities mingle in the city centre. Students welcome the relatively low cost of living in Coventry, and, as at most new universities, the student body encompasses a wide range of ages.

**Accommodation**
Number of places and costs refer to 2002–03

*University-provided places:* 2,700

*Percentage catered:* 24%

*Costs for catered accommodation:* £76 a week (10 meals).

*Costs for self-catered accommodation:* £45–£64 a week.

*Policy for first-year students:* guaranteed offer of accommodation to all first years, in university-owned or managed accommodation if application made before 6 September. No restriction on students who live close to campus.

*Policy for international students:* international students are given priority for university-owned accommodation.

*Contact for further information:* accomm.ss@coventry.ac.uk

# De Montfort University

**Times ranking:** 86 (2002 ranking: 85)

**Founded:** University status 1992, formerly Leicester Polytechnic

**Contact details**
*Address:* The Gateway, Leicester LE1 9BH
*Tel:* 0645 454647 (Enquiry Centre)
*Website:* www.dmu.ac.uk
*e-mail:* enquiry@dmu.ac.uk

**The Times rankings**
*Teaching assessment:* =90 (20.0)
*Research assessment:* 60 (3.1)
*Entry standards:* =80 (13.5)
*Student–staff ratio:* 79 (19.1)
*Library/IT spend/student:* 73 (£399)
*Facilities spend/student:* 98 (£52)
*Firsts and 2:1s:* 47 (56.4%)
*Work and further study:* =57 (93.6%)
*Expected completion rate:* 87 (78%)

**Students**
*Undergraduates:* 15,540 (2,860)
*Postgraduates:* 1,400 (2,460)
*Mature students:* 22.6%
*Overseas students:* 6.4%
*Applications per place:* 6.3
*From state sector schools:* 94%
*From working class homes:* 34%

**Teaching quality assessments**
*1993–95 Rated Excellent:* business and management.
*From 1995 (top score 24):* **24** politics. **23** hospitality, leisure and tourism; land management; sports science. **22** drama, dance and cinematics; nursing; psychology. **21** art and design; history of art; molecular biosciences; pharmacy; town planning. **20** building; education; health subjects; mathematics and statistics; media studies. **19** electrical and electronic engineering; general engineering; materials technology; modern languages (Bedford). **17** modern languages; sociology.

## Overview

Like the 13th-century earl of Leicester, after whom the university is named, De Montfort has a fiefdom of sorts: in this case a network of campuses in a 50–mile radius. Based on what was Leicester Polytechnic, the new university spread ever outwards, making it the biggest in the region. The addition of a nursing and midwifery college provided a third campus in and around Leicester, but the announcement that the Milton Keynes outpost will close in 2003 and the transfer of campuses in Lincolnshire to Lincoln University have brought a sudden and unexpected end to the process.

From 2003, there will be five campuses in Bedford and Leicester. In Bedford, besides the traditional teacher training, physical education and humanities, sports science, management, performing arts and contemporary studies will also be on offer. Agriculture and horticulture have transferred to Lincoln University, with conservation and craft courses. DMU is putting £50 million into consolidating more manageable estate, catering for more than 30,000 students, when part-timers are included. Another ten colleges are associates, linked in to the university's network and offering its courses. A formal agreement commits the colleges, which stretch from North Oxfordshire to Grantham, to work with each other as well as with De Montfort.

Professor Kenneth Barker, who retired as vice-chancellor in 1999, set out the university's uncompromising philosophy: 'Higher education has been too busy chasing Nobel prizes, instead of giving industry and the community the service they really need.' His successor, Professor Philip Tasker, is not changing the vocational emphasis, but he is giving a new emphasis to research. The approach paid off in the 2001 Research Assessment Exercise, when DMU registered the highest proportion of subjects of any new university in the top three categories. Politics and English were only one grade off the top of the seven-point scale, while the 11 subjects on the next grade was easily the highest total among the former polytechnics.

Teaching ratings were patchy until recently, with only one excellent rating in the first 11 attempts. There has been a marked improvement, however, since land management's near-perfect score. Politics was given full marks in 2001, while the hospitality, leisure and tourism courses were only one mark short of the maximum.

However, recruitment stalled in 2000, causing the financial problems which have led to the withdrawal from Milton Keynes campus. Degrees in business, computing, engineering and social sciences will transfer to other centres. The range of programmes has been expanding, but the drop-out rate remains worryingly high. More than a quarter of students who began degrees in 1998 are projected to transfer to other courses or leave without a qualification. However, the university was one of the first to set up an employment agency to help students find part-time work during their course of study, as well as find careers upon graduation.

Inevitably, the quality of student life varies widely among the different campuses, but technology ensures that everyone has access to the same academic support and resources. Not surprisingly, Leicester, which has by far the largest concentration of students, also has the best facilities. The energy-efficient School of Engineering and Manufacture, for example, has won architectural prizes. A new £6 million library opened in Bedford in 2001, however, and with a former physical education college on one of its two sites, students there are already well-served for sport. Students should find it easier to relate to the reduced scale of De Montfort. Accommodation difficulties will be eased when a further 1,400 rooms become available in 2003. Given the logistical difficulties it faces, the university is still remarkably successful at providing good-quality higher education.

## Accommodation

Number of places and costs refer to 2001–02

*University-provided places:* 1,692

*Percentage catered:* 28%

*Costs for catered accommodation:* £64.00 including breakfast and evening meal Monday to Friday.

*Costs for self-catered accommodation:* £48.45–£61.00 a week.

*Policy for first-year students:* not all first years are guaranteed accommodation. First years over 23 are not allocated accommodation. First years having a home address with 'LE' postcodes are also not allocated housing, but can apply if there are exceptional circumstances.

*Policy for international students:* guaranteed accommodation.

# University of Derby

**Times ranking:** 98 (2002 ranking: 91)

**Founded:** University status 1992, formerly Derbyshire College of Higher Education

**Contact details**
*Address:* Kedleston Road,
Derby DE22 1GB
*Tel:* 01332 622289
*Website:* www.derby.ac.uk
*e-mail:* Admissions@derby.ac.uk

**The Times rankings**
*Teaching assessment:* 96 (19.7)
*Research assessment:* =99 (1.5)
*Entry standards:* 91 (12.4)
*Student–staff ratio:* 100 (30.8)
*Library/IT spend/student:* =92 (£333)
*Facilities spend/student:* =84 (£111)
*Firsts and 2:1s:* 86 (45.6%)
*Work and further study:* =77 (92.2%)
*Expected completion rate:* =53 (85%)

**Students**
*Undergraduates:* 8,400 (1,840)
*Postgraduates:* 220 (970)
*Mature students:* 28.8%
*Overseas students:* 2.8%
*Applications per place:* 5.4
*From state sector schools:* 97%
*From working class homes:* 33%

**Teaching quality assessments**
*1993–95 Rated Excellent:* geology
*From 1995 (top score 24):* **24** pharmacy.
**22** business; education; health subjects; organismal biosciences; theology and religious studies. **21** American studies; hospitality; mathematics; psychology. **20** art and design. **19** civil engineering; electrical and electronic engineering; history of art; nursing. **18** drama, dance and cinematics; modern languages; sociology. **17** media studies.

## Overview

Derby sees itself as a prototype for the modern university, providing courses at all levels from the age of 16 into retirement. Although not as extensive as the original plans for spanning further and higher education in the same institution, a merger with High Peak College and the creation of a county-wide education network have created a university of 30,000 students, around 7,000 of whom study overseas on franchised courses. While accepting that Derby will never scale the heights in league tables such as ours, Sir Christopher Ball, the chancellor, has set Derby the target of becoming the pre-eminent university of its type by 2020. His yardsticks are student satisfaction, employability and cost-effectiveness.

As the only higher education college promoted to university status with the polytechnics, Derby had to run to keep up with its peers in its early days. Student numbers doubled in four years, the residential stock increased fivefold and extra teaching space was built.

The pace of expansion inevitably imposed strains, and at one time Derby was the only university with two 'unsatisfactory' verdicts in the teaching assessments. Although still not spectacular, scores have improved recently. Indeed, a failure in pharmacy turned into maximum points on reinspection after provision was rationalised. Business and theology have also scored well recently, as did biosciences and other health subjects before them.

Funding council statistics send conflicting messages on the drop-out rate.

The first projection, in 1999, put Derby in a better position than many new universities, with 19 percent expected to miss out on a degree – less than the 'benchmark' figure, which takes account of the social and subject mix. However, a more pessimistic picture emerged in later reports, with 27 per cent expected to drop out in the most recent projections.

Development is still continuing, with an £8 million art and design centre on the horizon and ambitious plans to bring higher education to the Peak District through the High Peak campus, near Buxton. There were six sites already – the legacy of a series of mergers in the 1970s and 1980s. The Kedleston Road site, two miles north of the city centre, is the largest, catering for most of the main subjects as well as the students' union headquarters. The Mickleover campus, which specialises in education and health, is also in a suburban location, while art and design have smaller, more central sites.

The Further Education School, in the old High Peak campus, is the only element outside the Derby area. But the purchase of the Devonshire Royal Hospital, in Buxton, for a nominal fee will provide a home for a new school of tourism and hospitality management. The landmark building, which has a dome bigger than St Paul's Cathedral's, will house a 4* training hotel and health spa, in addition to academic facilities. There are also plans for a multifaith centre on the Kedleston Road campus, which has attracted the support of the Prince of Wales.

Courses are modular and a foundation programme allows students to begin work at a partner college before transferring to the university. Distance learning is a growth area either online or through Derby's nine regional centres. Business and management is by far the biggest academic area, but work placements are encouraged in all subjects. The accent on employability continued with an eight-week course on key skills such as CV preparation and interview technique. Derby has also been in the forefront of the adoption of new teaching methods, pioneering the use of interactive video for a national scheme.

The university has spent £30 million in five years to maintain its guarantee of accommodation for all first years. Students seem to appreciate the university's efforts because it comes out well in satisfaction surveys.

## Accommodation

Number of places and costs refer to 2001–02

*University-provided places:* 2,350

*Percentage catered:* 0%

*Costs for catered accommodation:* n/a

*Costs for self-catered accommodation:* £34.62 (twin room ); £48.38–£57.49 (standard single room); £68 (en-suite single room) a week; all costs inclusive of utilities and energy costs based on 39-week agreements.

*Policy for first-year students:* all new students who wish to live in halls will be accepted; priority is given to international students or those with special needs.

*Policy for international students:* policy as above; priority given to new students.

*Contact for further information:* Accommodation@derby.ac.uk

# University of Dundee

Times ranking: 37 (2002 ranking: 35)

**Founded:** 1881, part of St Andrews University until 1967

**Contact details**
*Address:* Nethergate, Dundee DD1 4HN
*Tel:* 01382 344160
*Website:* www.dundee.ac.uk
*e-mail:* srs@dundee.ac.uk

**The Times rankings**
*Teaching assessment:* =48 (21.0)
*Research assessment:* =35 (5.1)
*Entry standards:* 39 (19.8)
*Student–staff ratio:* 6 (10.9)
*Library/IT spend/student:* 35 (£528)
*Facilities spend/student:* 41 (£181)
*Firsts and 2:1s:* 11 (79.1%)
*Work and further study:* =20 (95.9%)
*Expected completion rate:* =62 (84%)

**Students**
*Undergraduates:* 7,300 (1,580)
*Postgraduates:* 590 (1,980)
*Mature students:* 18.1%
*Overseas students:* 9.0%
*Applications per place:* 5.7
*From state sector schools:* 90%
*From working class homes:* 23%

**Teaching quality assessments**
*1994–97 Rated Excellent:* cellular biology; English; finance and accounting; graphic and textile design; medicine; organismal biology; psychology.
*1994–97 Rated Highly Satisfactory:* civil engineering; dentistry; environmental science; fine art; history; hospitality studies; law; mathematics; physics; politics; social work; statistics.
*From 1998:* **21** planning and landscape.
*2001 Rated Commendable:* computing; economics; geography.

**Overview**

Dundee describes itself as 'Scotland's most enterprising university' and, while there would be other claimants to that title, it has certainly been among the liveliest in recent years. Already on a roll after a series of good quality ratings and the acquisition of education, nursing and art colleges, which increased its scope and size, the university has also extended its horizons by going into partnership with St Andrews. Merger is not on the agenda, but the programme will see the pooling of areas of excellence, beginning with a joint degree in electronics and optoelectronics. Working groups are examining the potential for collaboration in five areas, from engineering to art history, with the intention of developing more teaching and research links over the next two years.

The initiative predated the arrival of a new Principal, Sir Alan Langlands, who is equally determined to build up Dundee's industrial links. Dundee has doubled its student population in recent years and is challenging Scotland's elite universities in a growing number of areas. But it is still relatively small, and is looking outwards to achieve the 'critical mass' which experts regard as essential to break into the higher education elite.

Dundee is best known for the life sciences, where research into cancer and diabetes is recognised as worldclass. The University is currently involved in an initiatives with the other Scottish medical schools aiming to take advantage of new technology and e-learning in the training of future doctors. The medical school won a Queen's Anniversary Prize in 1998, as well as an excellent rating for teaching and a 5* research grade for clinical laboratory sciences in the latest research assessments. Set in 20 acres of parkland, it is the one of several components of the university outside the compact city-centre campus – nursing and midwifery students are 30 miles away in Kirkcaldy, and education and social work are located at the Northern College campus, 2 miles outside the centre.

Biochemistry is the flagship department, moving into the £13 million Wellcome Trust Building in 1997. Its academics were the first in Britain to be invited to take part in Japan's Human Frontier science programme and are now the most-quoted researchers in their field. The biological sciences won Dundee's other 5* research rating, while six more subjects were on the next rung of the research assessment ladder, leaving half of the university's researchers in departments rated in the top two categories.

Teaching ratings have been almost uniformly impressive, with only philosophy judged less than highly satisfactory. Vocational degrees predominate, helping to produce the university's consistently good graduate employment record. The law department is the only one on either side of the border to offer both Scots and English law. The highly rated design courses are taught at the former Duncan of Jordanstone College of Art, which overlooks the River Tay.

There has been an emphasis on opportunities for women ever since Dundee's separation from St Andrews University in 1967. The incorporation of Northern College's local arm will increase the female majority in the university, adding teacher education to the portfolio of courses. The Bank of Scotland is funding a more general access initiative, which will help 100 students from poor backgrounds attend a university summer school and provide 25 of them with £1,000-a-year bursaries.

Two-thirds of Dundee's students are from Scotland and nearly one in ten from Northern Ireland. They enjoy a welcoming atmosphere and a cost of living which is lower than in most university cities. Private accommodation is plentiful for those who are not housed by the university. New students even have their own website. The city is profiting from recent regeneration programmes and becoming more fashionable. The university has been trading on this reputation with a recruitment campaign which some saw as risqué. Spectacular mountain and coastal scenery are close at hand, but social life tends to be concentrated on the students' union, which is one of the largest in Scotland.

## Accommodation

Number of places and costs refer to 2002–03

*University-provided places:* 1,700

*Percentage catered:* 22%

*Costs for catered accommodation:* £77.70 a week (16 meals).

*Costs for self-catered accommodation:* £39.27–£68.95 a week.

*Policy for first-year students:* entrant students guaranteed accommodation if they apply by 15 September for October entry. No restrictions for local students.

*Policy for international students:* entrant students guaranteed accommodation if they apply by 15 September for October entry.

# University of Durham

Times ranking: 13 (2002 ranking: 15)

Founded: 1832

Contact details
*Address:* University Office, Old Elvet,
Durham DH1 3HP
*Tel:* 0191 374 2000
*Website:* www.dur.ac.uk
*e-mail:* admissions.office@dur.ac.uk

The Times rankings
*Teaching assessment:* =9 (21.9)
*Research assessment:* =10 (5.7)
*Entry standards:* =11 (25.4)
*Student–staff ratio:* =27 (14.4)
*Library/IT spend/student:* 24 (£575)
*Facilities spend/student:* 9 (£269)
*Firsts and 2:1s:* =28 (63.4%)
*Work and further study:* =53 (94%)
*Expected completion rate:* =6 (94%)

Students
*Undergraduates:* 9.010 (630)
*Postgraduates:* 1,430 (1,930)
*Mature students:* 8.7%
*Overseas students:* 5.4%
*Applications per place:* 6.3
*From state sector schools:* 62%
*From working class homes:* 13%

Teaching quality assessments
*1993–95 Rated Excellent:* anthropology;
chemistry; English; geography; geology;
history; law; social work
*From 1995 (top score 24):* **24** economics;
molecular biosciences; organismal
biosciences; philosophy; physics.
**23** archaeology; education; health
subjects; psychology; theology.
**22** engineering; French; German;
linguistics; Middle Eastern and African
studies; politics. **21** classics and ancient
history; East and South Asian studies;
mathematics and statistics; sociology.
**20** Italian; Russian. **16** Iberian languages.

## Overview

Long established as a leading alternative
to Oxford and Cambridge, Durham even
delays selection to accommodate those
applying to the ancient universities. A collegiate structure and picturesque setting
add to the Oxbridge feel, attracting a
largely middle-class student body and,
although more than a third come from
independent schools, the university is
attracting more applicants from non-traditional backgrounds. Those who receive
offers without interview are invited to a
special open day to see if Durham is the
university for them. Since more than 80
per cent of undergraduates come from
outside the north-east of England, most
are seeing the small cathedral city for the
first time. The proportion of regional students is much higher at the Stockton
campus.

Applications have to be made to one of
the 14 colleges, all but one of which is
mixed. They range in size from 300 to
900 students and are the focal point of
social life, although all teaching is done in
central departments. There are significant
differences in atmosphere and student
profile, ranging from the historic University College, in Durham Castle, to modern
buildings overlooking the river on the outskirts of the city.

Winning a place is far from easy –
entrance requirements are among the
highest in Britain – but the drop-out rate
of 5 per cent is also among the lowest in
the higher education system. Six subjects
(chemistry, applied maths, geography, law,
English and history) reached the pinnacle
of the last research assessment exercise,

and 14 others were considered nationally outstanding. Most of the teaching ratings have also produced high scores. Biological sciences, physics and chemistry are particularly strong on the science side; history, philosophy, econ-omics and theology among the stars of the arts. A £3 million grant to establish a centre for fundamental physics is intended to place Durham at the forefront of world research on the structure of the universe.

Durham is on the whole quite traditional. Wherever possible, teaching takes place in small groups and most assessment is by written examination. Resits are permitted only in the first year, although the dropout rate compares favourably with other universities. Two partnerships have broken the mould of tradition, however. The first saw the establishment in the city of the Teikyo University of Japan, while the second produced the Stockton Campus. Initially a joint venture with Teesside University, Stockton is now Durham's own venture into community education. Entry standards are 18.3 points at A level, compared with an average of 26 for the main university, and subjects such as sport, health and exercise, human sciences and geography and cities help broaden the university's intake.

The Stockton campus has also seen the fulfilment of Durham's long-held ambition to restore the medical education it lost when Newcastle University went its own way more than 35 years ago. In another joint project, this time with Newcastle, 95 students will do the first two years of their training on Teesside, concentrating on community medicine.

Medicine has added to the 80 subjects available at degree level. Undergraduates are also offered a variety of generalist 'free elective' modules, such as environmental economics and personal language learning. The aim is to make Durham graduates even more employable.

The university dominates the city of Durham to an extent to which sometimes causes resentment. For those looking for nightlife, or just a change of scene, Newcastle is a short train journey away. Sports facilities are excellent, and Durham is among the premier universities in national competitions. Among the alumni are the England cricket captain, Nasser Hussain, and former England rugby captain Will Carling. The university is hosting one of the England's new centres for cricketing excellence

## Accommodation

Number of places and costs refer to 2001–02

*University-provided places:* 5,094

*Percentage catered:* 88%

*Costs for catered accommodation:* £93 a week.

*Costs for self-catered accommodation:* £45–£55 (Durham); £35 (Stockton) a week.

*Policy for first-year students:* almost all first years are offered accommodation. Only one of the collegiate bodies (St Cuthbert's Society) offers some non-residential places, usually for mature students living locally. No restrictions based on home address.

*Policy for international students:* normally all first-year and final-year international students are offered a place in college-owned accommodation.

*Contact for further information:* admissions@durham.ac.uk

# University of East Anglia

**Times ranking:** 40 (2002 ranking: =39)

**Founded:** Royal charter 1964

**Contact details**
*Address:* University Plain,
Norwich NR4 7TJ
*Tel:* 01603 592216
*Website:* www.uea.ac.uk
*e-mail:* admissions@uea.ac.uk

**The Times rankings**
*Teaching assessment:* =48 (21.0)
*Research assessment:* =24 (5.4)
*Entry standards:* 33 (21.1)
*Student–staff ratio:* =76 (19.0)
*Library/IT spend/student:* =47 (£482)
*Facilities spend/student:* 34 (£187)
*Firsts and 2:1s:* 26 (64.4%)
*Work and further study:* =64 (93.3%)
*Expected completion rate:* =18 (91%)

**Students**
*Undergraduates:* 6,500 (2,880)
*Postgraduates:* 1,520 (1,460)
*Mature students:* 16.9%
*Overseas students:* 10.1%
*Applications per place:* 4.7
*From state sector schools:* 88%
*From working class homes:* 20%

**Teaching quality assessments**
*1993–95 Rated Excellent:* development studies; environmental studies; law; social work.
*From 1995 (top score 24):* **24** American studies; philosophy; politics. **23** business and management; economics; mathematics and statistics; communication and media studies; health subjects. **22** history of art; molecular biosciences; organismal biosciences. **21** drama, dance and cinematics. **19** education; electrical and electronic engineering; modern languages. **18** nursing. **16** sociology.

## Overview

UEA is best-known for its star-studded creative writing course and extensive art collections, but some of the broad subject combinations which the university pioneered from its origins in the 1960s are equally highly regarded in the academic world. Development studies and environmental sciences are two such areas, which have attracted top ratings for teaching and research.

The university has almost completed an ambitious building programme, which has allowed its residential stock to keep pace with the expansion in student numbers and is adding extensive new sports facilities. Other recent developments on the 320-acre campus just outside Norwich have included academic buildings for the highly rated School of Social Work and the School of Occupational Therapy and Physiotherapy. Health studies have been among UEA's fastest-developing areas, and now the university has achieved its ultimate ambition with the establishment of the School of Medicine, Health Policy and Practice – one of the first new medical schools for 20 years. More than 110 students will be in the first intake in September 2002. A new £6 million school of nursing and midwifery, opening in 2002 and catering for 2,500 students, is next on the health blueprint.

With successive 5* ratings for research and an excellent teaching grade, environmental sciences is the flagship school. The Climatic Research Unit is among the leaders in the investigation of global warming and the prestigious Jackson Environment Unit's move to UEA in 1999 has strengthened it further. The university is the base for a Government-funded unit bringing together scientists, economists, social scientists and engineers in nine institutions. History and film studies added to the 5* research grades in 2001.

Philosophy and politics have joined American studies as the top performers in the teaching assessments. Like the English degrees, one of which includes creative writing, American studies is heavily oversubscribed. With Andrew Motion, the Poet Laureate, taking up where the late Malcolm Bradbury left off, the attraction of creative writing for both undergraduates and postgraduates remains undimmed. Art history is another strong subject, aided by the presence of the Sainsbury Centre for the Visual Arts, perhaps the greatest resource of its type on any British campus. The centre houses a priceless collection of modern and tribal art, in a building designed by Sir Norman Foster.

Since 1999, most students have had the opportunity of work experience as part of their course. The modular course system allows undergraduates to construct their own degrees, with the help of an academic adviser, who monitors progress right through to graduation.

Most UEA students come from outside the region, despite the presence of unusually large numbers of mature students for a traditional university. However, the university reaches some 3,500 local people with its programme of evening and day courses at 50 locations in Norfolk and Suffolk. The drop-out rate is low, at 9 per cent.

The number of university-owned beds has increased considerably in recent years, ensuring that first years can still be guaranteed accommodation. Sporting facilities are excellent: a £17.5 million sports park, with an Olympic-size swimming pool and climbing wall, opened in 2000, and the university was chosen as the base for the English Institute of Sport in the East, developing a sports science network for the region.

The university is situated in parkland, formerly a golf course, on the outskirts of the medieval city of Norwich, which can boast a pub for every day of the year. Rail links to London can be slow, but Norwich airport links to Amsterdam and world-wide connections in little more than an hour.

**Accommodation**

Number of places and costs refer to 2001–02

*University-provided places:* 3,000+

*Percentage catered:* 0%

*Costs for catered accommodation:* n/a

*Costs for self-catered accommodation:* £34.09–£69.86 a week.

*Policy for first-year students:* all first years are guaranteed accommodation if they have been offered and accepted a place by the deadline date. Those living within a 12-mile radius are not offered a place until all the guaranteed students accepting accommodation have been housed.

*Policy for international students:* international undergraduates are guaranteed accommodation for the whole of their course provided they apply each year when requested to do so. Postgraduates are guaranteed housing for the first year providing they have not studied at the university previously.

*Contact for further information:* accom@uea.ac.uk; www.uea.ac.uk/menu/admin/rsd/accom

# University of East London

Times ranking: 99 (2002 ranking: 96)

**Founded:** University status 1992, formerly Polytechnic of East London, originally North East London Polytechnic

**Contact details**
*Address:* Romford Road, London E15 4LZ
*Tel:* 020 8223 2835
*Website:* www.uel.ac.uk
*e-mail:* admiss@uel.ac.uk

**The Times rankings**
*Teaching assessment:* 100 (19.2)
*Research assessment:* =76 (2.5)
*Entry standards:* 90 (12.5)
*Student–staff ratio:* 75 (18.7)
*Library/IT spend/student:* 79 (£385)
*Facilities spend/student:* 78 (£131)
*Firsts and 2:1s:* =83 (47.0%)
*Work and further study:* 101 (86.4%)
*Expected completion rate:* =95 (75%)

**Students**
*Undergraduates:* 7.880 (1,550)
*Postgraduates:* 880 (2.070)
*Mature students:* 54%
*Overseas students:* 16.7%
*Applications per place:* 4.3
*From state sector schools:* 96%
*From working class homes:* 38%

**Teaching quality assessments**
*1993–95 Rated Excellent:* architecture; English.
*From 1995 (top score 24):* **23** psychology. **21** art and design; civil engineering. **20** economics; health subjects. **19** drama, dance and cinematics; education; molecular biosciences; organismal biosciences; pharmacy; sociology. **18** mechanical engineering; modern languages. **16** media studies. **15** electrical and electronic engineering.

## Overview

East London's £40 million Docklands campus, which opened in 1999, offers a new lease of life to a university which had struggled to recapture the sparkle it had as a pioneering polytechnic. Student residences and recreational facilities stand side by side with academic buildings in a prize-winning development which will eventually cater for 7,000 students.

The capital's first new campus for 50 years, which borders on London City Airport, has given the university a new focal point, with its modern version of traditional university features like cloisters and squares. Students of fashion, fine art, graphic design, media and cultural studies, electrical and manufacturing engineering have moved into the futuristic premises near the Thames, which also house a technology centre promoting links with local business and industry. More courses, including the School of Architecture, will move to the site as expansion takes place over the next five years.

UEL's two original campuses are in Barking and Stratford, where the university caters particularly for the large ethnic minority population. A successful mentoring scheme for black and Asian students has become a model for other institutions, while classes in English as a second language, designed mainly for overseas students, are available free of charge. Stratford is to be redeveloped to concentrate on part-time and day release students, while the present Barking campus will close in 2005 to be replaced by a life-long learning centre run in partnership with the neighbouring further education college.

With research in media studies judged to be nationally outstanding and sociology and art and design on the next grade, UEL was among the top ten new universities in the latest research assessments. However, teaching assessments have also been patchy, largely accounting for the university's low position in our rankings, despite a requirement for all new lecturers to take a teaching qualification if they do not already have one. Psychology did well, and both English and architecture have excellent ratings, but communication and media studies and electrical and electronic engineering both registered unusually low scores. Recent assessments, in health subjects and art and design, both produced solid ratings.

UEL's mission is more concerned with extending access to higher education than competing with the elite universities. Over half of the new first year intake now arrive with A levels and more than half are over 21 on entry. Most degrees are vocational and employers, notably Ford, with whom there is a longstanding relationship, are closely involved in course planning. About one student in seven takes a sandwich course.

Almost four out of ten UEL students come from working-class homes and there has been some success in attracting candidates from areas without a tradition of higher education. A Widening Participation Unit provides advice and guidance sessions for people considering returning to education. The downside is that only one university had a worse projected drop-out rate in the funding councils most recent survey, with almost a third not expected to finish their degree, and graduate unemployment is high.

University-owned accommodation is relatively sparse for the number of students, although many choose to live at home, so that all first years who request accommodation are housed. Students in private accommodation complain of racism in some areas, but there is a community feel within the university. The social mix also means that UEL is not the place to look for the archetypal partying student lifestyle, although the new campus is beginning to change this. Sports facilities, including a 30-metre swimming pool, are some miles away in Dagenham, where full membership of the centre costs students £108 a year.

**Accommodation**

Number of places and costs refer to 2001–02

*University-provided places:* 1,433

*Percentage catered:* 0%

*Costs for catered accommodation:* n/a

*Costs for self-catered accommodation:* £41–£68 a week.

*Policy for first-year students:* first years given priority. No distance restrictions.

*Policy for international students:* rooms reserved in numbers to meet anticipated demand, and guaranteed to this number only.

*Contact for further information:* telephone 020 8223 2835.

# University of Edinburgh

**Times ranking:** 15 (2002 ranking: 8)

**Founded:** 1583

**Contact details**
*Address:* Old College, South Bridge,
Edinburgh EH8 9YL
*Tel:* 0131 650 4360
*Website:* www.ed.ac.uk
*e-mail:* slo@ed.ac.uk

**The Times rankings**
*Teaching assessment:* =23 (21.5)
*Research assessment:* =17 (5.6)
*Entry standards:* =5 (26.5)
*Student–staff ratio:* 21 (13.8)
*Library/IT spend/student:* 10 (£742)
*Facilities spend/student:* 17 (£234)
*Firsts and 2:1s:* 4 (86.6%)
*Work and further study:* =20 (95.9%)
*Expected completion rate:* =49 (86 %)

**Students**
*Undergraduates:* 15,200 (2,350)
*Postgraduates:* 2,550 (2,070)
*Mature students:* 10.4%
*Overseas students:* 8.1%
*Applications per place:* 7.9
*From state sector schools:* 63%
*From working class homes:* 14%

**Teaching quality assessments**
*1993–98 Rated Excellent:* biology;
cellular biology; chemistry; computing;
electrical and electronic engineering;
finance and accounting; geology; history;
mathematics and statistics; physics;
organismal biology; social policy; social
work; sociology; veterinary medicine.
*1993–98 Rated Highly Satisfactory:* architecture; civil engineering; English, French;
geography; history of art; law; medicine;
music; nursing; philosophy, politics,
psychology, theology.
*From 1998 (top score 24):* **21** European
languages. **19** chemical engineering.
*2001 Rated Commendable:* archaeology,
architecture; business and management;
classics and ancient history; economics.
*2001 Rated Approved:* earth and environmental sciences

## Overview

Although overtaken by St Andrews in this
year's League Table, Edinburgh retains a
special status in Scotland, where the
university is regarded as the nearest thing
to Oxbridge north of the border. The university has dropped out of the top ten for
the first time, partly due to the new
scoring system, which takes account of
the mix of subjects.

Edinburgh has raised a £40 million
investment bond to ensure long-term
financial stability, and has embarked on a
five-year restructuring plan. The process
will involve abandoning some subjects
and cutting staff, but there will also be
investment in new buildings and extra
posts in selected areas. First to go will be
degree courses in agriculture, which are
transferring to Aberdeen. Then comes a
fundraising campaign and consultation
over how to save or raise £3 million a year.

Early plans include a 40 per cent
increase in overseas students, who already
number more than 2,000, testifying to
Edinburgh's worldwide reputation.
Demand from England has also held up,
despite the expense of a four-year degree.

The addition of Moray House as a new
faculty of education has made Edinburgh
the largest university in Scotland, with
more than 18,000 students. Yet entry
standards are among the highest in
Britain, whether in A levels or Highers.
The university's buildings are scattered
around the city, but most border the historic Old Town. The science and engineering campus is two miles to the south. The
Cramond education campus, six miles
west of the city, is to close, concentrating

its activities on the former college's Holyrood site.

The latest research assessments showed a big improvement on a disappointing outcome in 1996, when only electrical and electronic engineering reached the top grade. This time, nine subjects were awarded the coveted 5* and another 19 achieved grade 5, accounting for three-quarters of those entered for the exercise. The 15 subjects rated as Excellent for teaching already amounted to the biggest haul in Scotland. Despite having to settle for Highly Satisfactory in its teaching assessment, medicine is a traditional strength and the law faculty is the largest north of the border. The university enjoys a reputation for high quality across the board.

Departments organise visiting days in October for those thinking of applying and in the spring for those holding offers. There is also an annual open day in June. New students join one of the nine faculties and generally take three subjects in their first year and two in their second. Every student has a Director of Studies to help them narrow down the selection of a final degree and give personal advice when necessary.

Some £850,000 has been spent making the university more accessible to disabled students, who can also call on the services of a disability office. All students are issued with a smart card for access to university facilities, which can be loaded with money to pay for a variety of goods and services. A new student venue has added to the already impressive facilities.

The city is a treasure-trove of cultural and recreational opportunities, even away from the Festival period. Most students thrive on Edinburgh life, even though the cost of living can make it difficult to do it justice. Some scientists complain of isolation, although there is a regular bus link with George Square. The university has always attracted a high proportion of middle-class candidates and is a favourite in independent schools. It has been trying to redress the balance with an eight-week summer school for teenagers from Lothian schools. This has been supplemented since 2001 with 50 bursaries funded by the Royal Bank of Scotland, providing £1,000 a year for Scottish students who otherwise could not have afforded to go to university.

## Accommodation
Number of places and costs refer to 2001–02

*University-provided places:* about 5,400

*Percentage catered:* about 32%

*Costs for catered accommodation:* £95–£101 a week.

*Costs for self-catered accommodation:* £56–£69 a week.

*Policy for first-year students:* first years are guaranteed an offer of accommodation providing they are confirmed by UCAS by 1 September, have submitted an accommodation form by that date, and do not reside within the City of Edinburgh.

*Policy for international students:* visiting undergraduates on formal exchanges are guaranteed if they have applied by 1 September. Visiting non-EU undergraduates are also guaranteed if they apply by that date. Non-EU international postgraduates are guaranteed accommodation if they are confirmed and have applied by 16 September.

*Contact for further information:* accommodation@ed.ac.uk

# University of Essex

**Times ranking:** 25 (2002 ranking: 31)

**Founded:** Royal charter 1965

**Contact details**
*Address:* Wivenhoe Park, Colchester,
Essex CO4 3SQ
*Tel:* 01206 873666
*Website:* www.essex.ac.uk
*e-mail:* admit@essex.ac.uk

**The Times rankings**
*Teaching assessment:* =13 (21.7)
*Research assessment:* =17 (5.6)
*Entry standards:* =51 (18.3)
*Student–staff ratio:* 37 (15.5)
*Library/IT spend/student:* 18 (£618)
*Facilities spend/student:* 8 (£270)
*Firsts and 2:1s:* 55 (53.1%)
*Work and further study:* =43 (95.0%)
*Expected completion rate:* =66 (83%)

**Students**
*Undergraduates:* 4,380 (990)
*Postgraduates:* 1,260 (800)
*Mature students:* 18.4%
*Overseas students:* 31.3%
*Applications per place:* 5.7
*From state sector schools:* 91%
*From working class homes:* 24%

**Teaching quality assessments**
*1993–95 Rated Excellent:* law.
*From 1995 (top score 24):* **24** economics;
electrical and electronic engineering;
hospitality, sport, leisure and tourism;
philosophy; politics. **23** molecular
biosciences; organismal biosciences.
**22** history of art; psychology; sociology.
**21** linguistics. **20** mathematics and
statistics; nursing.

## Overview

Essex has long since moved out of the shadow of its radical past when the university was a hotbed of student unrest, acquiring a reputation for high-quality research, especially in the social sciences. Its small size and arts bias has held it back in previous university rankings, although there are plans for a 20 per cent increase in student numbers by 2005.

Law was top-rated in the early teaching quality assessments and sociology is among the leading departments in Britain, attracting a series of prestigious research projects as well as a high score for teaching. Both sociology and government achieved their second successive 5* grades in the latest research assessments, with economics joining them on the top grade. With eight subjects on grade 5, three-quarters of the researchers are in departments doing work of international quality.

Although still the junior partners, the sciences have been growing in strength and the recently merged biological and chemical sciences department is the largest in the university. Electronic engineering recorded a perfect score for teaching quality to add to an improved research rating, and biosciences almost repeated the feat. Computer science is also strong and a new BSc in computer games and internet technology shows Essex keeping pace with changing demands in graduate employment. The last three teaching assessments – for hospitality, philosophy and politics – have all seen full marks.

But improvements in the university's academic performance could not disguise the fact that the glass and concrete campus on the outskirts of Colchester was showing distinct signs of a quarter of a century's wear and tear. The university has embarked on a programme of refurbishment at the same time as expanding student facilities. Teaching and administration blocks, which cluster around a network of squares, are gradually being transformed and extra catering and residential facilities added.

A £9.5 million development, the university's largest ever, provided another 500 study bedrooms in 2000, enabling Essex to accommodate half its students on campus. There are plans to build a further 750 en-suite rooms for 2004. More office and teaching accommodation for history, accounting and management became available in 2002. The library had already been extended to provide 950 reader spaces and almost 80 hours access a week.

Essex was originally expected to grow rapidly to become a medium to large university, but Government cuts intervened and it has remained among the smallest, despite recent growth. There are still just over 6,000 students and the incorporation of the East 15 acting school, in Loughton, has added only 130 places. The arrangement had more to do with enhancing the university's provision in theatre studies, but it is the university's first venture beyond Colchester.

Like the other universities established in the 1960s, Essex champions academic breadth. In each of the four schools of study, undergraduates follow a common first year before specialising. They may take four or five different subjects before committing themselves to a particular degree. Essex's student population is also unusually diverse for a traditional university, with high proportions of mature and overseas students. Almost a quarter of the undergraduates are from working-class homes and the same goes for state school entrants, who make up 91 per cent of the intake – a higher proportion than the subject mix would suggest.

Social and sporting facilities are good, due in part to an extension of the Sports Centre, but town–gown relations in the garrison base of Colchester have not always been smooth. The 200-acre parkland campus can be bleak in winter and tends to empty at weekends, but there is a strong community atmosphere and students do not doubt the university's academic quality.

## Accommodation

Number of places and costs refer to 2001–02

*University-provided places:* 2,973

*Percentage catered:* 0%

*Costs for catered accommodation:* n/a

*Costs for self-catered accommodation:* £39.41 (off campus); £43.12 (on campus shared facilities); £62.16 (on campus en-suite) a week.

*Policy for first-year students:* new undergraduates are guaranteed accommodation provided that forms are submitted before the closing date in September.

*Policy for international students:* new students are guaranteed accommodation; priority given to students in 2nd and 3rd year.

*Contact for further information:* newug@essex.ac.uk (undergraduates) newpg@essex.ac.uk (postgraduates)

# University of Exeter

Times ranking: 35 (2002 ranking: 36)

Founded: Royal charter 1955

**Contact details**
Address: Northcote House, The Queen's Drive, Exeter EX4 4QJ
Tel: 01392 263035
Fax: 01392 263857
Website: www.exeter.ac.uk
e-mail: admissions@exeter.ac.uk

**The Times rankings**
Teaching assessment: =27 (21.4)
Research assessment: =31 (5.2)
Entry standards: =21 (23.0)
Student–staff ratio: 67 (18.2)
Library/IT spend/student: =58 (£440)
Facilities spend/student: 73 (£133)
Firsts and 2:1s: 24 (66.2%)
Work and further study: =53 (94.0%)
Expected completion rate: =6 (94%)

**Students**
Undergraduates: 7,270 (970)
Postgraduates: 1,490 (2,040)
Mature students: 8.1%
Overseas students: 5.7%
Applications per place: 7.3
From state sector schools: 69%
From working class homes: 14%

**Teaching quality assessments**
1993–95 Rated Excellent: computer science; English; geography.
From 1995 (top score 24):
24 archaeology; education; German.
23 politics; psychology; theology.
22 business and management; classics and ancient history; drama, dance and cinematics; economics; French; Italian; mathematics and statistics; molecular biosciences; organismal biosciences; physics.
21 materials technology; Middle Eastern and African studies; sociology; education.
20 general engineering; Iberian languages; Russian. 16 linguistics.

## Overview

Exeter is one of Britain's most popular universities, in terms of first-choice applications, not only in its traditional strong suit, the arts, but increasingly in the sciences and social sciences. Three out of ten undergraduates came from independent schools in 1999–2000, the most recent year for which figures have been published. This was a much higher proportion than the national average for the subjects Exeter offers, and placed the university among the dozen with the lowest state school intake. The share of places going to working-class students and those from areas without a tradition of higher education were among the lowest in the country. In response, the university has appointed its own Widening Participation Officer to help ensure wider recruitment and is specifically targeting schools and colleges in the rural South West.

Location is partly responsible for the relatively rarified social mix. There is no large industrialised centre of population to draw on, and seemingly sleepy cathedral cities in the southwest are not what every teenager is looking for. However, the academic reputation is strong and there have been exciting developments recently.

Chief among them is the establishment of the Peninsula Medical School, in association with Plymouth University. Opening in October 2002 with 127 students, the school will be the first in the region, with outposts in Torbay, Truro and Barnstaple. Among the entrants will be graduates from other health-related disciplines.

The university has undergone a complete academic and administrative reorganisation, introducing semesters and replacing faculties with 18 schools. The modular system allows students to build a degree from a wide range of courses at the end of their first year, and a single model of assessment is being developed, balancing coursework and examination.

Gradual expansion has produced a medium-sized university, and having entered the franchising business, any significant growth is likely to be outside Devon. Some £30 million has been invested in residential accommodation over the past 15 years so that there are more than 4,000 beds. Another £32 million will go on the replacement of sub-standard stock by 2005.

The main Streatham Campus, close to the centre of Exeter is one of the most attractive in the country. The highly rated schools of education and health studies are a mile away in the former St Luke's College. The university is also part of the Combined Universities in Cornwall (a partnership with Falmouth College of Arts, Plymouth University and FE colleges in Cornwall). A new £50 million campus is being built outside Falmouth, and the Cambourne School of Mines (with whom Exeter is developing new degree programmes) will move there in 2004.

There is a long tradition of European integration, exemplified by the popular European Law degree. All students are offered tuition in European languages and a number of degrees include the option of a year abroad. Language degrees have scored well in the teaching assessments, with German achieving a perfect score matched recently by education and archaeology. Arabic and Islamic studies have benefited from investment from the Middle East. The latest research assessments were an improvement on 1996: although only German was considered internationally outstanding, another 18 reached the next-highest grade. Computer science was one of the top-rated courses for teaching, and politics, psychology and theology did well more recently. English literature, drama and history are among the most heavily subscribed courses in their fields.

Exeter has an increasing number of pubs and clubs catering for students in the city. There is also a lively social scene on campus, the students being kept informed by a thriving print and broadcast media. The Northcott Theatre, on campus, is one of the cultural centres of the region, and the area's beautiful countryside and enticing beaches are within easy reach.

## Accommodation

Number of places and costs refer to 2001–02

*University-provided places:* 4,023

*Percentage catered:* 44.4%

*Costs for catered accommodation:* £94.57–£102.97 a week (21 meals).

*Costs for self-catered accommodation:* £44.31–£80.08 a week (options for 34, 39 or 50-week lets).

*Policy for first-year students:* all first years are guaranteed accommodation. There are no restrictions for local students.

*Policy for international students:* all first years and postgraduates are provided with accommodation.

*Contact for further information:* Hallaccommodation@exeter.ac.uk Selfcateringaccommodation@exeter.ac.uk

# University of Glamorgan

Times ranking: =81 (2002 ranking: 79)

**Founded:** University status 1992, formerly Polytechnic of Wales

**Contact details**
*Address:* Llantwit Road, Treforest, Pontypridd, Mid Glamorgan CF37 1D
*Tel:* 01443 480480
*Website:* www.glam.ac.uk

**The Times rankings**
*Teaching assessment:* =74 (20.4)
*Research assessment:* =80 (2.4)
*Entry standards:* 84 (13.1)
*Student–staff ratio:* =48 (16.6)
*Library/IT spend/student:* 77 (£389)
*Facilities spend/student:* =48 (£165)
*Firsts and 2:1s:* =81 (47.6%)
*Work and further study:* 93 (90.3%)
*Expected completion rate:* =89 (77%)

**Students**
*Undergraduates:* 9,490 (5,100)
*Postgraduates:* 650 (1,850)
*Mature students:* 26.2%
*Overseas students:* 13.9%
*Applications per place:* 4.4
*From state sector schools:* 97%
*From working class homes:* 35%

**Teaching quality assessments**
*1993–98 Rated Excellent:* accounting and finance; biology; business studies; creative writing; drama; earth studies; electrical and electronic engineering; English; information and library studies; media; mining surveying; public sector schemes; Welsh.

## Overview

Wales's second university was the smallest of the polytechnics. Although still not large by modern university standards, Glamorgan has been making up for lost time, largely by franchising courses to colleges at home and abroad. Twinning programmes operate in five overseas centres, while in Wales a growing number of further education colleges offer the university's courses. Pembrokeshire College has become an associate college, providing an outpost in west Wales, which guarantees places on degree courses if students fulfil set conditions.

The university's own campus is 20 minutes by train from Cardiff in Treforest, overlooking the market town of Pontypridd. Originally based in a large country house, Glamorgan now has purpose-built premises for the science and technology departments. There has also been a £5 million refurbishment of teaching accommodation for maths and computing. The law, nursing and midwifery schools are housed in Glyntaff in corporate-style buildings a short walk from the campus.

Glamorgan is committed to retaining its vocational slant, tailoring a diploma in management to the needs of the Driver and Vehicle Licensing Agency, for example. It has a large business school, and there is also an Institute of Chiropractic, housing the UK's only undergraduate course in the subject. The university is among the first providers of the two-year foundation degree, based on a combination of academic and work-based learning. Glamorgan's courses will focus on human resources management and marketing, business and accounting.

The vocational approach pays dividends for graduate employment, which is consistently good, although the drop-out rate is also the highest among the university institutions in Wales. With 12 per cent of students either transferring to other universities or dropping down to a different level, the funding council expected only six out of ten of those starting degree courses in 1998 to complete their course at Glamorgan. The drop-out rate reflects an intake which is more socially diverse than elsewhere in Wales. More than a third of the undergraduates come from working-class homes and almost a quarter are from areas with no tradition of higher education – one of the highest figures at any UK university.

The university is one of the top scorers among the former polytechnics in teaching quality assessments, which have now been completed in Wales. Eight subjects have been rated as Excellent at degree level, and there have also been awards for the remaining further education course provision. The best-known courses are in engineering and professional studies, although the university has caused a stir with a degree in science fiction and modules on aliens and UFOs. The success of the English and creative writing programmes is reflected in the establishment at the university of the National Centre for Writing, opening in 2002. The School of Technology has been designated a centre of excellence for Wales, while three National Partnership awards testify to high standards in course design and delivery.

Many of the 12,000 full-time undergraduates live around Pontypridd, while others choose Cardiff, which is both livelier than Pontypridd and a better source of accommodation. However, the campus has been developing, with the addition of a recreation centre and an extension to the students' union, which is the focus of social life. Its bars are the only part of the university where smoking is allowed.

The sports facilities are good enough for Glamorgan to have been awarded the 2001 British University Games and to become one of six centres of excellence in cricket. The university is successful in student competitions, especially in rugby, and offers a number of sports bursaries for students with international potential. But there is also a wide range of health and fitness classes for those with lower aspirations.

## Accommodation

Number of places and costs refer to 2001–02

*University-provided places:* 1,200

*Percentage catered:* 8%

*Costs for catered accommodation:* £80 a week.

*Costs for self-catered accommodation:* £47–£56 a week.

*Policy for first-year students:* no restrictions except for those living in the immediate locality.

*Policy for international students:* all international students are allocated a place in hall if they require one.

*Contact for further information:* accom@glam.ac.uk

# University of Glasgow

Times ranking: 28 (2002 ranking: 20)

**Founded:** 1451

**Contact details**
*Address:* University Avenue,
Glasgow G12 8QQ
*Tel:* 0141 339 8855 (main switchboard,
university admits by faculty)
*Website:* www.gla.ac.uk
*e-mail:* sras@gla.ac.uk

**The Times rankings**
*Teaching assessment:* =13 (21.7)
*Research assessment:* =31 (5.2)
*Entry standards:* =15 (24.2)
*Student–staff ratio:* 22 (13.9)
*Library/IT spend/student:* 25 (£573)
*Facilities spend/student:* 47 (£166)
*Firsts and 2:1s:* 9 (80.5%)
*Work and further study:* =61 (93.5%)
*Expected completion rate:* =53 (85%)

**Students**
*Undergraduates:* 14,870 (3,830)
*Postgraduates:* 1,930 (2,070)
*Mature students:* 13.3%
*Overseas students:* 5.7%
*Applications per place:* 5.5
*From state sector schools:* 85%
*From working class homes:* 21%

**Teaching quality assessments**
*1993–98 Rated Excellent:* cellular
biology; chemistry; computing science;
English; French; geography; geology;
medicine; physics; philosophy; psychology,
organismal biology; social policy;
sociology; veterinary medicine.
*1993–98 Rated Highly Satisfactory:* civil
engineering; dentistry; drama; finance and
accounting; history; history of art; mathematics and statistics; mechanical
engineering; music; nursing; politics;
social work.
*From 1998 (top score 24):* **22** European
languages.
*2001 Rated Commendable:* law; theology.

## Overview

Glasgow enjoys the rare distinction of having been established by Papal Bull, and begun its existence in the Chapter House of Glasgow Cathedral in 1451. Since 1871 it has been based next to Kelvingrove Park in the city's fashionable west end on the Gilmorehill campus, with its many listed buildings. The latest addition, to house the prestigious medical school, will open in 2002.

The university has taken in St Andrew's College to form a new faculty of education, which will be based from summer 2002 on the Park campus, between Gilmorehill and the city centre. The campus, formerly the Queen's College, has been acquired from Glasgow Caledonian University, and will provide the extra teaching accommodation needed to locate the education faculty close to the main campus. The Vet school and outdoor sports facilities are located at Garscube, a few miles away, while the first students will shortly graduate from the new Crichton campus in Dumfries.

More distinctively Scottish than its rivals in Edinburgh or St Andrews, almost half of the students come from within 30 miles of Glasgow and three-quarters are from north of the border. There was a high proportion of home-based students long before the city became fashionable, but it also attracts students from some 80 countries.

The university has adopted a increasingly outward-looking style under the leadership of Sir Graeme Davies, marked by two Queen's Anniversary prizes, for opening up artistic, scientific and cultural resources and taking computing to local communities. A 'synergy' agreement with neighbouring Strathclyde University has led to the development of teaching and research partnerships, the latest establishing a single department of naval architecture and marine engineering. Meanwhile, the innovative Crichton College campus in Dumfries is taking higher education to southwest Scotland with unusual three-year degrees.

Not that Glasgow is a stranger to innovation: it was the first university to have a school of engineering, for example. The huge science faculty – the biggest outside London – is strong, having received top ratings for teaching in six subjects. Applications for science degrees reflect this quality, having risen by 25 per cent since the mid-1990s. Overall, applications for courses starting in 2002 rose by more than 10 per cent on the previous year, 224 coming from schools taking part in the university's access scheme.

The latest research assessments were an improvement on a disappointing set of results in 1996, with arts and social sciences leading the way. Four subjects were rated internationally outstanding – English, European studies, psychology and sports science – a further 19 achieving grade 5 and 95 per cent of researchers were in the top three categories. The university has opened an office in California's Silicon Valley in order to make the most of its research successes.

Overseas recruitment has remained strong, especially in engineering. Glasgow is also taking an active role in the Universitas 21 worldwide group of universities, involving partnerships on five continents and eventual shared teaching arrangements. But the home market has not been overlooked: the Century 21 Club has enrolled 20 firms to sponsor undergraduates at £1,000 a year, as part of an arrangement to forge closer links with local business. Another ten scholarships for students from poor backgrounds will commemorate the life of Donald Dewar, Scotland's late First Minister. The scheme is the first of a number of memorials planned for one of the university's best-known graduates.

More than a fifth of the students are from working-class homes, one in six from an area without a tradition of higher education. Most like the combination of campus and city life, with the relatively low cost of living an added attraction. They have the choice of two student unions, plus a sports union supporting 50 different clubs and activities.

## Accommodation

Number of places and costs refer to 2001–02

*University-provided places:* 3,800

*Percentage catered:* 15%

*Costs for catered accommodation:* £66–76 (standard room); £88 (en-suite).

*Costs for self-catered accommodation:* £45–51 (standard); £65 (en-suite).

*Policy for first-year students:* first years living beyond commuting distance are guaranteed accommodation if they apply by 1 September in their year of entry. Those living in and around Glasgow have to commute in the first instance until places become available.

*Policy for international students:* first years are guaranteed accommodation if they apply by 1 September.

*Contact for further information:* accom@gla.ac.uk

# Glasgow Caledonian University

**Times ranking:** 72 (2000 ranking 72)

**Founded:** University status 1992, formerly Queen's College (founded 1875) and Glasgow Polytechnic (founded 1972)

**Contact details**
*Address:* City Campus, 70 Cowcaddens Road, Glasgow G4 0BA
*Tel:* 0141 331 3000
*Website:* www.caledonian.ac.uk
*e-mail:* admissions@gcal.ac.uk

**The Times rankings**
*Teaching assessment:* =57 (20.7)
*Research assessment:* =76 (2.5)
*Entry standards:* 57 (17.1)
*Student–staff ratio:* =48 (16.6)
*Library/IT spend/student:* 101 (£220)
*Facilities spend/student:* 97 (£63)
*Firsts and 2:1s:* 59 (51.7%)
*Work and further study:* =67 (93.0%)
*Expected completion rate:* =93 (76%)

**Students**
*Undergraduates:* 10,050 (2,560)
*Postgraduates:* 860 (1,250)
*Mature students:* 29.9%
*Overseas students:* 5.7%
*Applications per place:* 5.3
*From state sector schools:* 96%
*From working class homes:* 36%

**Teaching quality assessments**
*1993–98 Rated Excellent:* chemistry; physiotherapy.
*1993–98 Rated Highly Satisfactory:* biology; cellular biology; consumer studies; finance and accounting; mathematics and statistics; mass communications; nursing; nutrition and dietetics; occupational therapy; physics; psychology; social work; sociology.
*2001 Rated Commendable:* engineering.

## Overview

Glasgow Caledonian, or 'The Cally' as it is known locally, is in the process of putting the difficulties of the last decade firmly behind it, when even naming the new institution was unexpectedly fraught. The original choice of The Queen's University, Glasgow, was considered too like its namesake in Belfast. Glasgow Caledonian eventually emerged from a ballot of students and staff. Dramatic expansion has put facilities under strain, but the estate is improving, along with the teaching ratings.

Caledonian is in the top four UK universities for attracting students from areas without a tradition of higher education, with 36 per cent of its undergraduates coming from working-class homes. The university has argued forcefully that extending access should be rewarded more generously if such students are to receive the support they need to make a success of higher education.

However, the latest performance indicators suggested that more than a third of Caledonian's undergraduates would fail to complete the degree they embarked upon, 27 per cent dropping out and a further 7 per cent transferring to other institutions or lesser courses. Even this was better than the estimates made 12 months earlier, but the university has since introduced a series of measures which should improve matters. Telltale signs are being monitored, such as non-attendance at lecures, and better academic, social and financial support offered to those at risk of dropping out.

Consolidated on its city-centre campus,

Caledonian's original five sites have now been reduced to one with the sale of the Park Campus, in the west end of the city, to Glasgow University. It has taken a £350 million building programme to get this far, and more will have to be spent to meet the university's desire for a single, high-quality campus in the city centre. Proposed additions include a state-of-the-art Learning Centre. A start was made in 2001, when a new health building was opened by Thabo Mbeki who named it in honour of his father. Physiotherapy is the only subject since chemistry's success in 1993 to be rated excellent for teaching, and Caledonian now boasts among the most extensive health programmes in Britain.

A string of other subjects (mainly on the science side) are considered Highly Satisfactory. Business is the other big area, the Caledonian Business School boasting more undergraduates than any other institution in Scotland, with over 1,000 in each year group. The university pioneered subjects such as entrepreneurial studies and risk management – the only university in the country to do so – and offers highly specialist degrees, such as tourism management, fashion and marketing, leisure management and consumer protection.

Degrees in all areas are strongly vocational, and are complemented by a wide portfolio of professional courses. A high proportion of students choose sandwich courses, and the university operates on a modular system. REAL@Caledonian is a new student facility combining enhanced learning technology with a informal cyber-café atmosphere. With more than 14,000 students, only Edinburgh and Glasgow universities are bigger north of the border.

The legacy of Queen's College, which catered mainly for women, has ensured that the proportion of female students is the highest of any university in Britain. Sports and social facilities have been among the priorities in the building programme, and the library has been extended and upgraded recently. Some students find that the high proportion of their peers living at home detracts from the social scene, but Glasgow is a very lively city with a large student population.

## Accommodation

Number of places and costs refer to 2001–02

*University-provided places:* 847

*Percentage catered:* 0%

*Costs for self-catered accommodation:* £55–£60; £68 en-suite a week.

*Policy for first-year students:* priority for students under 19 living outside the Glasgow area.

*Policy for international students:* priority for non-EU international students applying before August.

*Contact for further information:* accommodation@gcal.ac.uk

# University of Gloucestershire

Times ranking: =81

**Founded:** University status 2001, formerly Cheltenham and Gloucester College of Higher Education

**Contact details**
*Address:* The Park Campus, PO Box 220, The Park, Cheltenham GL50 2QF
*Tel:* 01242 543477 (prospectus)
*Website:* www.glos.ac.uk
*e-mail:* admissions@glos.ac.uk

**The Times rankings**
*Teaching assessment:* =86 (20.1)
*Research assessment:* =61 (3.0)
*Entry standards:* =82 (13.4)
*Student–staff ratio:* 98 (22.9)
*Library/IT spend/student:* 86 (£371)
*Facilities spend/student:* 87 (£101)
*Firsts and 2:1s:* 89 (44.9%)
*Work and further study:* =30 (95.5%)
*Expected completion rate:* =62 (84%)

**Students**
*Undergraduates:* 5,570 (1,540)
*Postgraduates:* 430 (1,830)
*Mature students:* 22%
*Overseas students:* 2.5%
*Applications per place:* 5
*From state sector schools:* 95%:
*From working class homes:* 28%

**Teaching quality assessments**
*1993–95 Rated Excellent:* geography
*From 1995 (top score 24):* **23** theology. **21** art and design; hospitality and leisure; psychology; town and country planning. **20** media studies; sociology.

## Overview

The latest university to be established in England is also the first for more than a century to have formal links with the Church of England. Although its religious origins have been played down in recent years, Gloucestershire University will maintain an association that includes church appointees on its governing body. Not surprising, then, that theology is the top-rated subject, with good scores for both teaching and research, but the rechristened institution has much wider interests.

Cheltenham and Gloucester College of Higher Education had been pressing for university status almost since it came into existence in 1990. The product of a merger between a church college and the higher education wing of a college of arts and technology, it had the breadth of study necessary to meet the Government's exacting criteria for promotion, including the power to award doctorates as well as first degrees.

Teaching ratings were good enough to satisfy the assessors, without being spectacular, and the latest research grades suggested that Gloucestershire would not be out of place in the university system. More than 40 per cent of academics were entered for the Research Assessment Exercise – a figure exceeded by only four former polytechnics – and the average score per member of staff placed the new university fifth among that group. English matched theology's grade 4, denoting national excellence in virtually all of the work submitted.

After considerable expansion during the

1990s, there are now almost 10,000 students, including 3,300 part-timers, and 1,000 academic and support staff. The main subject areas are management and IT, the arts, media and design, humanities, the environment, teacher education, leisure and tourism, social sciences and sport. The university prides itself on a good range of work placements, which range from British Aerospace to Disneyworld.

The main campus is on the attractive site of the former College of St Paul and St Mary, a one-time botanical garden two miles outside Cheltenham, but a new base is being developed in Gloucester on the site of a closed comprehensive school. The contrast mirrors differences between middle-class Cheltenham and more working-class Gloucester, but the two campuses are only seven miles apart and students will not be as isolated as they are in some split-site institutions. There are also two smaller sites in Cheltenham: Pittville for art and design, and Francis Close Hall for a range of subjects, including environment, sport and social sciences.

Gloucestershire's intake is as diverse as its locations, with 95 per cent of undergraduates from state schools, but only 28 per cent from working-class homes. As with the 12 per cent from areas without a tradition of higher education, the funding council expected more, given the mix of subjects. The drop-out rate, at 19 per cent, was also slightly above the benchmark set for the university. The new Oxstalls campus, in Gloucester, where participation in higher education has always been low, will focus particularly on access initiatives.

Sports facilities include a swimming pool, sports hall and tennis courts, but are not extensive for a university of 10,000 students. Likewise accommodation: with fewer than 1,000 beds, students need to be quick off the mark at the start of the academic year, although first years are given priority in the allocation of places. However, 'enhancement of the student experience' is one of the priorities in the university's strategic plan. Although Cheltenham and Gloucester are not clubbers' paradises, neither is dull and the college claimed higher education's biggest ball, with 7,000 attending, in 2001.

## Accommodation

Number of places and costs refer to 2001–02

*University-provided places:* 918

*Percentage catered:* 0%

*Costs for catered accommodation:* n/a

*Costs for self-catered accommodation:* £59–£69 a week.

*Policy for first-year students:* all places are reserved for first-year students; 60% of non-local students accommodated.

*Policy for international students:* first year international students are given priority if they request a place in residence.

*Contact for further information:* afolliard@glos.ac.uk

# Goldsmiths College

Times ranking: 63 (2002 ranking: 53)

**Founded:** 1891, Royal charter 1990;
College of the University of London

**Contact details**
*Address:* Lewisham Way, New Cross,
London SE14 6NW
*Tel:* 020 7919 7766
*Website:* www.goldsmiths.ac.uk
*e-mail:* admissions@gold.ac.uk

**The Times rankings**
*Teaching assessment:* =86 (20.1)
*Research assessment:* =26 (5.3)
*Entry standards:* =45 (19.1)
*Student–staff ratio:* 52 (16.8)
*Library/IT spend/student:* 72 (£405)
*Facilities spend/student:* 86 (£109)
*Firsts and 2:1s:* 52 (54.5%)
*Work and further study:* =75 (92.4%)
*Expected completion rate:* =53 (85%)

**Students**
*Undergraduates:* 3,840 (1,180)
*Postgraduates:* 1,100 (900)
*Mature students:* 38.8%
*Overseas students:* 15.5%
*Applications per place:* 6.2
*From state sector schools:* 86%
*From working class homes:* 20%

**Teaching quality assessments**
*1993–95 Rated Excellent:* music.
*From 1995 (top score 24):* **22** art and
design; drama, dance and cinematics;
economics; media studies; politics;
psychology. **21** mathematics; sociology.
**19** history of art. **17** French; German.

**Overview**
Although it has been a London University college for only a decade, Goldsmiths has a long history of community-based courses, mainly in education and the arts. Evening classes are still as popular as conventional degree courses. A tradition of providing educational opportunities for women is reflected in the largest proportion of female students in the British university system – two-thirds at the last count.

Determinedly integrated into its southeast London locality, the college precincts have a cosmopolitan atmosphere. More than half of all students are over 21 on entry, many coming from the area's ethnic minorities, and there is a growing proportion of overseas students. Goldsmiths has also become highly fashionable among the trendier elements of the new left, especially since the arrival of political biographer Ben Pimlott as warden.

The older premises have been likened to a grammar school, with their long corridors of classrooms. But the new Rutherford Information Services Building won an award from the Royal Institute of British Architects, and a former baths building has been converted to provide more space for research and art studios.

Goldsmiths describes itself as specialising in the study of 'creative, cultural and social processes', although there is still room for mathematics in the arts-dominated portfolio of courses. The college has an enduring reputation in the visual arts, with luminaries such as Graham Sutherland, Mary Quant and Damien Hurst among its alumni over the years. Its graduates won the Turner Prize no fewer than five times during the 1990s. The college is hoping to capitalise on such successes with a campaign to raise £12 million for a new arts centre. The controversial architect, Will Alsop, has recently won an international competition to design the centre.

Both media and communications and sociology were rated internationally outstanding in the last research rankings, which were a spectacular success for the college. Anthropology, art and design and music were close behind, leaving more than a third of the academics entered for assessment in the top two of seven categories. The research scores have helped transform Goldsmiths' financial position, allowing more investment in teaching. Art and design, economics, politics and psychology have joined music, media studies and drama, dance and cinematics as the college's best performers for teaching scores so far, but education, which caters mainly for primary teachers, is also well regarded.

Employment prospects are good, especially for a college with such a high proportion of students taking performing arts subjects, where a period of unemployment after graduation is commonplace. Indeed, on postgraduate courses, recent success rates have been among the best in Britain.

Student politics has survived at Goldsmiths to an extent not seen at many universities – even the concert venue was given the name Tiananmen, while a college in which Damon Albarn is only one of a number of successful rock alumni cannot fail to have a thriving music scene.

The surrounding area is enjoying a mini-boom as a prime location for loft apartments, although sky-high prices put them way beyond the reach of the student housing market. However, the college has 1,200 residential places within walking distance of the campus. Sports enthusiasts are less well provided for. Although there is a swimming pool and indoor complex in Deptford, the main pitches are eight miles away.

## Accommodation

Number of places and costs refer to 2002–03

*University-provided places:* 1,039 (college halls); 15 (intercollegiate halls).

*Percentage catered:* 0% (college halls); 100% (intercollegiate halls).

*Costs for catered accommodation:* £65 a week.

*Costs for self-catered accommodation:* £63.00–£83.50 a week.

*Policy for first-year students:* priority is given to new full-time students living outside Travelcard Zone 6 (trains and tubes) if the offer of a place is firmly accepted by mid-August. Students living within Travelcard Zone 6 are placed on a waiting list.

*Policy for international students:* provided the offer of a place is firmly accepted by mid-August, students will normally be accommodated in a college hall. Non -EU students have highest priority.

*Contact for further information:* accommodation@gold.ac.uk

# University of Greenwich

Times ranking: 90 (2002 ranking: =80)

**Founded:** University status 1992, previously Thames Polytechnic

**Contact details**
*Address:* Old Royal Naval College, Park Row, Greenwich, London SE10 9LS
*Tel:* 0800 005006
*Website:* www.gre.ac.uk
*e-mail:* courseinfo@greenwich.ac.uk

**The Times rankings**
*Teaching assessment:* =79 (20.2)
*Research assessment:* =76 (2.5)
*Entry standards:* 98 (11.5)
*Student–staff ratio:* =89 (20.5)
*Library/IT spend/student:* 42 (£495)
*Facilities spend/student:* =52 (£157)
*Firsts and 2:1s:* 97 (40.8%)
*Work and further study:* 66 (93.1%)
*Expected completion rate:* =89 (77%)

**Students**
*Undergraduates:* 9,610 (3,460)
*Postgraduates:* 1,100 (2,700)
*Mature students:* 39.2%
*Overseas students:* 16.4%
*Applications per place:* 6.6
*From state sector schools:* 95%
*From working class homes:* 34%

**Teaching quality assessments**
*1993–95 Rated Excellent:* architecture; environmental studies.
*From 1995 (top score 24):* **24** town and country planning. **23** nursing; pharmacy; sociology. **22** psychology. **21** building; civil engineering; land and property management; philosophy; politics. **20** agriculture; business and management; economics; education; molecular biosciences; organismal biosciences. **19** mathematics and statistics; media studies. **18** health subjects. **17** electrical and electronic engineering; general engineering.

## Overview

Greenwich's move into the former Royal Naval College buildings designed by Sir Christopher Wren at last gives the university a campus worthy of one of the most desirable titles in the higher education world. Its name has always conjured up images of history and science in equal measure. The opening of King William Court, costing £50 million to restore and convert, marks the completion of the new Maritime Campus. The World Heritage site should prove a draw for home and overseas students alike.

Queen Mary Court, at the heart of Wren's baroque masterpiece, opened to the public for the first time in more than two centuries in 2000 and is now being used, with the former Dreadnought Hospital, to teach over half the university's students humanities, business, law, computing and maths. A former nurses' home nearby has been converted into a hall of residence and a conference centre and another development will add a further 230 rooms by autumn 2002.

Greenwich describes itself as a 'regional university' for southeast London and half of Kent, a populous county with only one university of its own, and the real investment is in the Medway campus, at Chatham. Some £20m is going into facilities for the European business school, 'urban renaissance' school and (the university hopes) the first new school of pharmacy for 20 years. The aim is to have 6,000 students at the former HMS Pembroke naval base by 2006.

Other departments are situated in two other sites. As well as a student village,

Avery Hill, a Victorian mansion on the outskirts of southeast London, is home to health and social care, the social sciences, and the large education faculty, one of the few teacher training centres to offer both primary and secondary education courses. Architecture, landscape and construction students remain at Dartford until 2003, while humanities and life sciences have relocated to the Maritime and Medway campuses.

Most teaching assessments have been favourable, with town planning, sociology, nursing and pharmacy the star performers. Where scores have been low, it has generally been the quality assurance procedures that have been found wanting. The university also achieved some respectable results in the latest research assessment exercise, with computing, German and materials leading the way, although less than a third of the academic staff entered. Greenwich does not shy away from assessment, however. It was among the first British universities to be rated by investment analysts, who pored over its academic, administrative and financial standing.

A wide range of degrees is one of the university's strengths, with website architecture and graphic and digital design added in 2001. The School of Engineering, in Chatham continues to buck the national trend in recruitment with a record intake of more than 200 students.

Greenwich has also celebrated a Queen's Anniversary Prize for Higher and Further Education for work on processing, conservation and marketing of food supplies in the developing world. The judges commended the university, saying that its work is of 'international renown'. There are also strong links with European institutions, providing a steady flow of overseas students, as well as exchange opportunities for those at Greenwich. Seven associated colleges in Kent and London teach the university's courses.

A commitment to extending access to higher education has led to low entrance requirements in many subjects and a relatively high proportion of mature students. The downside is a projected drop-out rate of a quarter, with barely more than two-thirds of degree students expected to complete the course they started at Greenwich.

## Accommodation

Number of places and costs refer to 2001–02

*University-provided places:* 2,319

*Percentage catered*: 10.9%

*Costs for catered accommodation:* £77.35 a week.

*Costs for self-catered accommodation:* £47.87–£86.52 a week.

*Policy for first-year students:* first years with home address further than 20 miles away from their campus are guaranteed a place. Priority given to disabled students throughout all years of their study.

*Policy for international students*: as new students they would get priority; in later years they are treated as home students.

*Contact for further information:* accommodation@gre.ac.uk

# Heriot-Watt University

Times ranking: 48 (2002 ranking: 50)

**Founded:** 1821, Royal charter 1966

**Contact details**
*Address:* Riccarton, Edinburgh EH14 4A
*Tel:* 0131 451 3376/77/78
*Website:* www.hw.ac.uk
*e-mail:* admissions@hw.ac.uk

**The Times rankings**
*Teaching assessment:* =64 (20.6)
*Research assessment:* =43 (4.7)
*Entry standards:* 44 (19.3)
*Student–staff ratio:* 26 (14.3)
*Library/IT spend/student:* 16 (£640)
*Facilities spend/student:* 20 (£219)
*Firsts and 2:1s:* 88 (45.2%)
*Work and further study:* 48 (94.5%)
*Expected completion rate:* =49 (86%)

**Students**
*Undergraduates:* 4,650 (130)
*Postgraduates:* 810 (1,340)
*Mature students:* 20.3%
*Overseas students:* 13.5%
*Applications per place:* 4.7
*From state sector schools:* 90%
*From working class homes:* 26%

**Teaching quality assessments**
*1993–95 Rated Excellent:* electrical and electronic engineering.
*1993–98 Rated Highly Satisfactory:* cellular biology; chemistry; civil engineering; computer studies; finance and accounting; mathematics and statistics; mechanical engineering; physics.
*From 1998 (top score 24):* **21** modern languages. **19** chemical engineering.
*2002 Rated Commendable:* computing; engineering.

## Overview

Concentration on technology, languages and business is fitting for a university which commemorates James Watt, the pioneer of steam power, and George Heriot, financier to King James VI. Still evolving more than 30 years after attaining university status, in many ways Heriot-Watt is Scotland's most unconventional university. The main campus, on the outskirts of Edinburgh, was completed only in 1992, and is among the most modern in Britain. Still small in terms of full-time students, the primarily technological university is aiming to double its numbers over 20 years. It already has 10,000 students taking distance learning courses.

For many years, Heriot-Watt's main claim to fame outside the academic community lay in its degree in brewing and distilling. But the university has a wide variety of vocational programmes, as well as more conventional degrees. Research in petroleum engineering is rated internationally outstanding, while modern languages are a more unexpected strength. Electrical and electronic engineering is the only subject area to achieve the maximum score for teaching, but there has been a succession of Highly Satisfactory ratings.

The range of subjects has been extended with the addition of Edinburgh College of Art (planning and housing) and the Galashiels-based Scottish College of Textiles, where the facilities include some of the largest print and weave facilities in the UK. Management and computing have joined textiles on the Borders campus 30 miles from the university headquarters, which has been upgraded since it was taken over by Heriot-Watt.

Science, engineering, management and languages are located on the main campus, a site at Riccarton, which saw £100 million of investment in the last decade. The university has also been investing in people: a five-year programme has seen £3.7 million worth of new appointments. The focus for the new millennium is on the Borders, where higher education provision is still scarce, with a broadband network planned to bring the university together electronically. Heriot-Watt has long been a leader in the use of information technology for teaching, thanks partly to a huge research and development programme.

Heriot-Watt is the most commercially diversified of any British university, with the share of private research funding consistently among the highest in the UK per member of academic staff. About 45 per cent of Heriot-Watt's income, more than £33 million, comes from the research, training and commercial services provided to the commercial sector.

The subject mix also serves graduates well in the jobs market: Heriot-Watt is seldom far from the top of the employment league tables. But the new acquisitions have altered the student profile, with the proportion of women creeping up to 38 per cent. The drop-out rate, at 15 per cent, has also risen but is no higher than the average for other universities offering the same subjects. A bare majority of campus-based students are from Scotland, with 19 per cent from other parts of Britain.

Students at Riccarton complain that the six-mile journey to the city centre leaves them isolated, and the campus is not the liveliest. However, the improved transport links to the city centre, with buses about every ten minutes, should improve the situation. Sports enthusiasts are well provided for, and representative teams do well. Hearts, one of Edinburgh's two premier league clubs, have chosen the campus as the site for its football academy, which will be used by students and local people as well as the young professionals.

**Accommodation**
Number of places and costs refer to 2001–02

*University-provided places:* 1,623

*Percentage catered:* 19%

*Costs for catered accommodation:* £46.55–£64.05 a week (7 meals).

*Costs for self-catered accommodation:* £31.99–£45.99 a week (self-catering flats); £49.98 a week (self-catering halls); £59.99 a week (self-catering halls with en-suite facilities).

*Policy for first-year students:* all new students who apply by 1 September are guaranteed accommodation provided they have firmly accepted an unconditional offer at this stage.

*Policy for international students:* international students are included in the policy for new students as above.

*Contact for further information:* S.W.S@hw.ac.uk

# University of Hertfordshire

Times ranking: =59 (2002 ranking: 63)

**Founded:** University status 1992, formerly Hatfield Polytechnic

**Contact details**
*Address:* College Lane, Hatfield,
Herts AL10 9AB
*Tel:* 01707 284800
*Website:* www.herts.ac.uk
*e-mail:* admissions@herts.ac.uk

**The Times rankings**
*Teaching assessment:* =43 (21.1)
*Research assessment:* =76 (2.5)
*Entry standards:* =68 (15.1)
*Student–staff ratio:* =57 (1.2)
*Library/IT spend/student:* =46 (£483)
*Facilities spend/student:* =80 (£124)
*Firsts and 2:1s:* 63 (50.4%)
*Work and further study:* =64 (93.3%)
*Expected completion rate:* =66 (83%)

**Students**
*Undergraduates:* 12,640 (2,300)
*Postgraduates:* 810 (1,560)
*Mature students:* 23.6%
*Overseas students:* 13.5%
*Applications per place:* 4.6
*From state sector schools:* 95%
*From working class homes:* 35%

**Teaching quality assessments**
*1993–95 Rated excellent:* environmental studies.
*From 1995 (top score 24):* **24** philosophy. **23** business and management; economics; hospitality; nursing; psychology. **22** art and design; education; health subjects; mechanical and aeronautical engineering. **21** mathematics and statistics; molecular biosciences; physics. **20** electrical and electronic engineering; general engineering; linguistics.

## Overview

Hertfordshire has embarked on a new strategy for the third millennium, overtly designed to propel it up the league tables by attracting more highly qualified students. The prime draw will be a new £105 million de Havilland campus, due to open in September 2003, half a mile from the existing headquarters in Hatfield, which will bring the university together for the first time.

Professor Neil Buxton, the vice-chancellor, has told his staff that A-level requirements will rise over the first three years of the new century and the university's academic approach will become 'tougher and more rigorous'. Although Hertfordshire has always been considered among the leading new universities, its average entry scores were lower than rivals such as Manchester Metropolitan, Kingston or Oxford Brookes. After 30 per cent growth in five years, the theory is that the university can afford to be more selective without ignoring the needs of its region.

The strategy had an immediate impact, with the average A-level score of entrants rising by three points in 2000. Art and design will be joined on the new campus, which was once the headquarters of British Aerospace, by business, education and the humanities. The Hertford and Watford campuses will close, but law will remain in its current base in the centre of St Albans.

Under the plans, Hertfordshire will remain one of the few genuinely rural universities. Many students commute from towns and villages in the county, using the most extensive university bus network in

Britain. Academic and social facilities are provided on every site, but the student experience has inevitably suffered from the geographical divisions. For those looking for more sophisticated nightlife, London is only a short train journey away.

Hatfield Polytechnic's reputation was built mainly on engineering, science and computing. However, business studies and healthcare now rival them in terms of size. European links are a speciality, with the range of exchange possibilities growing every year, and half the undergraduates take a language option. For the growing numbers coming in the opposite direction, there is a one-year foundation programme, designed for the natural sciences but also available in other areas.

Half of the students also include work placements in their degrees, the close links with employers sometimes bringing in valuable research and consultancy contracts. All students are encouraged to take 'free choice' courses in subjects outside their degree programmes, which can contribute to their final results. The intake is more diverse than the funding councils expected, given the subject mix: 95 per cent of undergraduates are state-educated and 35 per cent come from working-class homes.

Hertfordshire suffers in *The Times* table for indifferent grades in the early years of teaching assessment, when only environmental studies was rated excellent. More recently, philosophy achieved a perfect score, with business and management, psychology and nursing close behind, while aeronautical and mechanical engineering and art and design have also produced good results. Grades in the latest research assessment exercise showed considerable improvement on 1996, with history rated nationally outstanding and computing, nursing, physics and psychology all in the next category.

Until now, 3,500 university-controlled beds have been a mixture of halls, houses and flats, head leasing properties and lodgings, mostly located on the Hatfield campus. But the new de Havilland campus will include 1,600 residential places, all with en-suite facilities and internet connections in ten new halls. There will also be extensive sports facilities and another learning resources centre to add to the one on the main campus, which is Britain's biggest, with 24–hour access to 1,900 computers.

## Accommodation

Number of places and costs refer to 2002–03

*University-provided places:* 3,000

*Percentage catered:* 0%

*Costs for catered accommodation:* n/a

*Costs for self-catered accommodation:* £49–£67 a week.

*Policy for first-year students:* first years are guaranteed accommodation if they apply before A-level results are published and accept course places by 31 August. No restrictions on geographical location.

*Policy for international students:* overseas students are guaranteed accommodation if they apply before 6 September.

*Contact for further information:* Accommodation@herts.ac.uk

# University of Huddersfield

**Times ranking:** 89 (2002 ranking: 90)

**Founded:** University status 1992, formerly Huddersfield Polytechnic

**Contact details**
*Address:* Queensgate, Huddersfield, West Yorkshire HD1 3DH
*Tel:* 01484 422288
*Website:* www.hud.ac.uk
*e-mail:* admissions@hud.ac.uk

**The Times rankings**
*Teaching assessment:* =70 (20.5)
*Research assessment:* =80 (2.4)
*Entry standards:* =76 (13.6)
*Student–staff ratio:* =84 (19.7)
*Library/IT spend/student:* 97 (£317)
*Facilities spend/student:* 82 (£120)
*Firsts and 2:1s:* =83 (47.0%)
*Work and further study:* 90 (91.1%)
*Expected completion rate:* =89 (77%)

**Students**
*Undergraduates:* 9.570 (3,900)
*Postgraduates:* 860 (1,930)
*Mature students:* 26%
*Overseas students:* 6.7%
*Applications per place:* 5
*From state sector schools:* 97%
*From working class homes:* 36%

**Teaching quality assessments**
*1993–95 Rated Excellent:* music; social work.
*From 1995 (top score 24):* **24** electrical and electronic engineering. **23** politics. **22** education; health subjects; hospitality, leisure and tourism; molecular biosciences; nursing; organismal biosciences. **21** art and design; materials technology; mathematics. **20** food science; psychology; sociology. **18** media studies. **17** drama, dance and cinematics. **15** modern languages.

## Overview

Official performance indicators for higher education have shown Huddersfield living up to its mission to help produce a more diverse student population. More than a third of the full-time students are from working class homes and almost a fifth are from areas without a strong tradition of higher education, one of the highest proportions in Britain. The downside is that a quarter are not expected to complete their degrees, far more than the funding councils' 'benchmark' for the university, which takes account of the courses on offer.

Huddersfield made a fresh start in 1996 under the current vice-chancellor after a difficult period in which the previous management attracted highly public criticism. An immediate aim has been to bring the university together on one campus, selling the Holly Bank site, where the School of Education and Professional Development was based, and extending the Queensgate campus in the town centre. This has been completed recently.

The university is capitalising on Huddersfield's industrial past to ease the strain on facilities struggling to cope with expansion which reached 13 per cent a year at its peak. Canalside, a refurbished mill complex, has provided new space for mathematics and computing, and education will occupy another mill site – this time a £4 million recreation of the original. The university is even creating 'pocket parks' and a landscaped area along the reopened Narrow Canal to provide additional green space. Human and health sciences have already acquired new premises and precision engineering is next on the list.

A tradition of vocational education dates back to 1841, and the university has a long-established reputation in areas such as textile design and engineering. But there are less obvious gems such as music and social work, both of which were rated excellent for teaching and nationally outstanding for research. Teaching assessments have ranged from the sublime (maximum points for electrical and electronic engineering) to the ridiculous (only 15 out of 24 for modern languages). Recent results have shown more consistency, the last seven assessments all producing either 21 or 22 points, with politics, education and hospitality, leisure and tourism doing well in 2001.

The university adopted a much more selective approach to the latest research assessments, entering half the number of academics it did in 1996. History matched social work and music's grade 5, with mechanical engineering in the next category. A flourishing relationship with industry produces more private income than is achieved in many larger institutions, as well as influencing courses.

Many arts courses, which now attract the majority of students, have a vocational slant. Politics, for example, includes a six-week work placement, which often takes students to the House of Commons. A third of the students in all subjects take sandwich courses, one of the highest proportions in Britain, and more than 4,000 have some element of work experience. The approach pays off with consistently good graduate employment figures.

Additional accommodation is available at Ashenhurst, just over a mile from the campus, but most residential accommodation is now concentrated in the Storthes Hall Park student village. Despite recent developments, the 1,713 residential places are not enough to guarantee accommodation to first years. Private housing is cheap, if not always plentiful. Students are also encouraged to follow a structured fitness programme at the upgraded campus sports centre. Town–gown relations are good and the cost of living low. Most students like the town's friendly atmosphere, although they tend to base their social life on the students' union. The description of Huddersfield in the prospectus as a 'happening town' may be stretching things, but it is not far to Leeds for those in search of serious clubbing.

## Accommodation
Number of places and costs refer to 2000–01

*University-provided places:* 1,713

*Percentage catered:* 0%

*Costs for catered accommodation:* n/a

*Costs for self-catered accommodation:* £38.50–£59.50 a week.

*Policy for first-year students:* a 'Reservation of Halls' scheme operates which guarantees a place in halls for any first year who has made Huddersfield first choice, no matter where they live.

*Policy for international students:* all international students who choose to go into university halls accommodation are allocated places, provided the application form arrives in time.

*Contact for further information:* m.salter@hud.ac.uk

# University of Hull

Times ranking: 43 (2002 ranking: 42)

**Founded:** 1928, Royal charter 1954

**Contact details**
Address: Cottingham Road, Hull HU6 7RX
Tel: 0870 126 2000
Website: www.hull.ac.uk
e-mail: admissions@admin.hull.ac.uk

**The Times rankings**
Teaching assessment: =34 (21.3)
Research assessment: =53 (4.3)
Entry standards: 43 (19.5)
Student–staff ratio: 55 (17.0)
Library/IT spend/student: =47 (£482)
Facilities spend/student: 92 (£93)
Firsts and 2:1s: 43 (58.5%)
Work and further study: =10 (97%)
Expected completion rate: =10 (93%)

**Students**
Undergraduates: 7,480 (3,640)
Postgraduates: 1.150 (1,780)
Mature students: 24.1%
Overseas students: 8.0%
Applications per place: 5.1
From state sector schools: 89%
From working class homes: 24%

**Teaching quality assessments**
1993–95 Rated Excellent: chemistry; history; social policy; social work.
From 1995 (top score 24): **24** drama; electrical and electronic engineering; Iberian languages. **23** American studies; molecular biosciences; organismal biosciences; physics; politics; psychology; theology. **22** East and South Asian studies; economics; Italian; mathematics and statistics; philosophy. **21** French; German. **20** anthropology; Dutch; education; sociology. **19** Scandinavian. **17** nursing.

## Overview

After years of relative stability, Hull has been expanding rapidly, both on its spacious home campus and through mergers. It has already added nursing to its portfolio of courses with the acquisition of the former Humberside College of Health, but the more substantial change was the merger with University College Scarborough in August 2000, which will bring the university's full-time student population close to 10,000, with many more taking part-time and distance learning courses.

The 94-acre main campus has seen considerable development recently, with new buildings for languages and chemistry, a Graduate Research Institute and the acquisition of the Cottingham campus from the University of Lincoln. The campus, with its art gallery and highly automated library, is less than three miles from the centre of Hull. Although neither would be considered fashionable, both the city and the university inspire strong loyalty among students. Philip Larkin, once the university librarian, described the city as 'in the world, yet sufficiently on the edge of it to have a different resonance.'

The modest cost of living and ready availability of accommodation have much to do with Hull's popularity with students, but the quality of courses is also high. Teaching has been rated excellent in most subjects, with drama, electronic engineering and Iberian languages all achieving perfect scores. Politics and theology almost repeated the feat in 2001, but nursing recorded an unusually low score the previous year, with criticism of student support and quality management on the course. These issues have been addressed, and a new nursing facility has since opened at Willerby.

Strength in politics – confirmed by one of three grade 5 assessments for research, as well as the teaching quality success – is reflected in a steady flow of graduates into the House of Commons. A longstanding focus on Europe shows in the wide range of languages available at degree level, with the purpose-built Language Institute heavily used by students of all subjects.

No subject was rated internationally outstanding in the latest research assessments, but law and geography joined politics in the next category. Social work collected a Queen's Anniversary Prize and was also rated excellent for teaching. An Institute for Learning was established in 1997 to try to put research findings into practice, developing training courses for lecturers and encouraging the university's interest in lifelong learning.

Hull has always maintained a roughly equal balance between science and technology and the arts and social sciences, believing that this promotes a harmonious atmosphere, although the new Scarborough campus will tip the scales firmly towards the arts. However, the university's patient development, in collaboration with the local health authority, of a postgraduate medical school has now been rewarded with approval for a traditional medical school to be run jointly with York University from 2003.

Only one traditional university has a higher proportion of state-educated students than Hull's 89 per cent. Almost a quarter are from working-class homes and the drop-out rate, at 5 per cent, is among the lowest in Britain, far below

the funding council's 'benchmark' for the subjects offered. In an effort to broaden its intake further, the university is offering conditional places to local 16-year-olds if they take part in a Science Experience Programme. Many of the youngsters have been attending a university science club once a month since the age of 11 or 12, and have access to the library and computer facilities. The initiative, which has drawn praise from Tony Blair, should help to raise participation in higher education in an area where it has traditionally been low.

Student leisure facilities, which were always good but becoming crowded, have been upgraded as part of the campus building programme. Further development of the students' union, which was rated the best in Britain in one survey, is underway.

## Accommodation
Number of places and costs refer to 2002–03
*University-provided places:* 2,825 (owned stock); 310 (leased/associated stock)
*Percentage catered:* 50%
*Costs for catered accommodation:* £89.11 a week (catered; 31 weeks); £65.80 a week (semi-catered; 33 weeks).
*Costs for self-catered accommodation:* £51.17 a week (student houses; 42 weeks); £49.56 a week (self-catered halls; 33 weeks); £64.16 a week (on-campus en-suite flats; 50 weeks).
*Policy for first-year students:* accommodation for unaccompanied first years is guaranteed, excepting late applicants.
*Policy for international students:* accommodation for new unaccompanied undergraduate and postgraduate international students is guaranteed, excepting late applicants.
*Contact for further information:* rooms@hull.ac.uk

# Imperial College of Science, Technology and Medicine

**Times ranking:** 3 (2002 ranking: 3)

**Founded:** 1907
College of the University of London

**Contact details**
*Address:* Exhibition Road,
South Kensington, London SW7 2AZ
*Tel:* 020 7594 8014
*Website:* www.ic.ac.uk
*e-mail:* admissions@ic.ac.uk

**The Times rankings**
*Teaching assessment:* =5 (22.0)
*Research assessment:* =3 (6.4)
*Entry standards:* 4 (27.9)
*Student–staff ratio:* 2 (8.1)
*Library/IT spend/student:* 6 (£933)
*Facilities spend/student:* 2 (£369)
*Firsts and 2:1s:* 2 (93.1%)
*Work and further study:* 7 (97.7%)
*Expected completion rate:* =31 (89%)

**Students**
*Undergraduates:* 6,780 (0)
*Postgraduates:* 2,850 (910)
*Mature students:* 3.2%
*Overseas students:* 21.8%
*Applications per place:* 6.1
*From state sector schools:* 60%
*From working class homes:* 17%

**Teaching quality assessments**
*1993–95 Rated Excellent:* business and management; chemistry; computer science; geology.
*From 1995 (top score 24):* **24** electrical and electronic engineering; materials science. **23** general engineering. **22** aeronautical engineering; agriculture; chemical engineering; mathematics; molecular biosciences; organismal biosciences; physics. **21** civil engineering; medicine.

## Overview

After years of running Oxford close in *The Times* rankings, London's specialist science and engineering college briefly moved ahead but is now back in third place. Over 800 academic staff include Nobel prize-winners and 44 Fellows of the Royal Society. Three-quarters of the academics entered for assessment in the latest research assessment exercise were in departments considered internationally outstanding – the highest proportion in any university – and almost all were in one of the top two categories.

Teaching scores have been up to the same high standard, with electrical and electronic engineering and materials science achieving maximum points. Recent grades have not quite reached that level, but physics and maths both scored 22 points out of 24, and medicine also did well. Imperial is not recommended for academic slouches, but tough entrance requirements ensure that they are a rare breed in any case. Such is the level of competition that applications have dropped in the last two years, but even though many of the subjects struggle for candidates elsewhere, and entrants average better than an A and two Bs at A level. Four out of ten undergraduates are from independent schools – one of the highest proportions at any university.

Engineering courses last four years and lead to a Masters qualification. Almost all branches of engineering achieved the coveted 5* rating for research. The college has been expanding its range of European exchanges, with a variety of prestigious technological institutions available for courses such as the MSc in physics.

Medicine was the main area of development in the 1990s: mergers with the St Mary's, Charing Cross and Westminster teaching hospitals producing one of the biggest medical schools in the country. Top ratings for research in clinical medicine were a source of pride, given its size. With 200 undergraduate places a year, the school has the status of a constituent college, and handles its own admissions. Further mergers in 2000 brought in the Kennedy Institute of Rheumatology and Wye College, the university's agricultural and environmental centre in Ashford, Kent, which added 2,000 students and extended Imperial's range of subjects.

Facilities on the main campus, in the heart of South Kensington's museum district, have been expanded with the construction of a new biosciences building and extra space for earth studies, engineering and environmental science. There are also fieldwork facilities and more laboratories at Sillwood Park, near Ascot.

A growing management school, rated excellent for teaching, is the main concession to the academic world beyond science and technology. Dr Gary Tanaka, an Imperial graduate and successful technology investment manager, has donated £25 million to provide a new home for the school (in the former Royal School of Mines building) by 2004. The gift is the largest personal donation in the history of the college.

The Undergraduate Research Opportunities Programme provides opportunities for 'hands-on' experience of the research activities of college staff and postgradu-ates. A voluntary scheme open to all undergraduates, it is especially popular in the summer vacation, when students can be paid bursaries and international undergraduates can participate without needing a work permit. There is also a Vacation Training Scheme during the summer for undergraduates to acquire work experience.

Imperial's specialisms have the effect of making it the most male-dominated university institution in Britain. This shows in a social scene which many students find limited, despite the impressive selection of clubs and societies on offer. Outdoor sports facilities are remote, but Wednesday afternoons are left free to encourage students to make the effort to exercise.

## Accommodation

Number of places and costs refer to 2002–03

*University-provided places:* 3,059

*Percentage catered:* 6%

*Costs for catered accommodation:* £69.04 (double); £90.74 (single) a week.

*Costs for self-catered accommodation:* £40 (triple); £80.92 (single); £105 (single studio flat) a week.

*Policy for first-year students:* first years are guaranteed accommodation provided that they will be studying for the full academic year and have not stayed in college accommodation while studying full-time at a UK university.

*Policy for international students:* for undergraduates, as above; although not guaranteed accommodation, overseas postgraduate students are given first consideration (with the same provisos as above).

*Contact for further information:* student.accom@ic.ac.uk

# Keele University

Times ranking: 46 (2002 ranking: 51)

**Founded:** 1949, formerly University College of North Staffordshire

**Contact details**
*Address:* Keele, Staffordshire ST5 5BG
*Tel:* 01782 584005
*Website:* www.keele.ac.uk
*e-mail:* aaa30@keele.ac.uk

**The Times rankings**
*Teaching assessment:* =39 (21.2)
*Research assessment:* =48 (4.6)
*Entry standards:* =47 (18.9)
*Student–staff ratio:* 61 (17.6)
*Library/IT spend/student:* 100 (£272)
*Facilities spend/student:* =70 (£139)
*Firsts and 2:1s:* 27 (64.1%)
*Work and further study:* =36 (95.2%)
*Expected completion rate:* =13 (92%)

**Students**
*Undergraduates:* 4,740 (2,310)
*Postgraduates:* 880 (1,850)
*Mature students:* 11.6%
*Overseas students:* 7.1%
*Applications per place:* 5.8
*From state sector schools:* 89%
*From working class homes:* 22%

**Teaching quality assessments**
*1993–95 Rated Excellent:* music; social work.
*From 1995 (top score 24):* **24** American studies; education; philosophy. politics. **23** economics; psychology. **22** mathematics and statistics; organismal biosciences; physics; sociology. **21** business; molecular biosciences; nursing;. **20** French; health subjects; Russian. **19** German.

## Overview

The general foundation course, which used to give a quarter of Keele's undergraduates a four-year degree programme, has been a victim of the rising cost of studying: there has to be a good reason to take extra time nowadays. But the university remains committed to breadth of study and has set itself the target of being the leading interdisciplinary institution in Britain. Nine out of ten students take more than one subject for their degree, with a subsidiary from the other side of the arts/science divide in the first year. Among the more outlandish combinations are Latin and astrophysics, or biochemistry and electronic music. Most programmes provide the opportunity of a semester abroad, which the university would like a quarter of all undergraduates to take.

American studies, education, philosophy and politics have all produced perfect scores in recent teaching assessments, but international relations and the many dual honours programmes – especially those featuring politics or music – are the university's traditional strengths. Law was the only subject to be rated internationally outstanding for research, but seven more reached grade 5. The improvement on the previous assessments, in 1996, was enough to win the university a modest budget increase for 2002-3.

Science subjects have been improving, as was demonstrated by the recruitment of two top scientists from ICI to run the inorganic chemistry and materials science group. Biosciences and physics both

scored well in recent teaching assessments. However, it is in health subjects
that the main development has been
focused. Physiotherapy, nursing and midwifery have been added in recent years,
but the big news was the success of a
joint bid with Manchester University to
introduce clinical medicine in 2002.
Students will spend their first two years
in Manchester, with the choice of completing their training there or moving to
Keele and North Staffordshire hospital.

All the existing courses are modular,
and the traditional academic year has
been replaced by two 15–week semesters, with breaks at Christmas and
Easter. The university has committed
itself to maintaining a generous staffing
ratio of one academic to every 15 students throughout its extended period of
growth. Keele remains relatively small by
modern university standards, but student
numbers rose by 75 per cent in five years
during the 1990s. The proportion of
postgraduates has also been growing,
with a third of the students now taking
higher degrees.

Nearly nine out of ten undergraduates
are state-educated, a figure exceeded by
only one traditional university in England. But the proportion of working-class
students, at 22 per cent, is less than the
national average for the subjects on offer.
The 12 per cent drop-out rate is relatively low, and better than the funding
council expected. Keele has been pro-
active in trying to broaden its intake, targeting 12 and 13-year-olds with a
special website, as well as running mas-
terclasses in local schools and hosting a
summer school at the university.

The attractive 617-acre campus near
the M6 outside Stoke-on-Trent could
take many more students. A development
plan is underway, beginning with a new
arts complex. Seven out of ten students
and some staff live on campus, which
inevitably dominates the social scene as
well as providing part-time employment
for hundreds of students. The students'
union has six bars, and sports facilities
are good for those seeking a more active
lifestyle. Although the cost of living is relatively low in the Potteries, it is not an
area famous for youth culture. The normal
overstated section on the attractions of
the locality is noticeably absent from the
prospectus.

**Accommodation**
Number of places and costs refer to
2002–03

*University-provided places:* 3,200

*Percentage catered:* 0%

*Costs for catered accommodation:* n/a

*Costs for self-catered accommodation:*
£46, £52.50, £76 a week.

*Policy for first-year students:* first years
holding Keele as first choice or insurance
place are guaranteed accommodation on
campus. Every effort is made to
accommodate students through clearing
and usually all are housed. No restrictions
on those living locally.

*Policy for international students:* guaranteed accommodation for the duration of
the course.

*Contact for further information:*
hpa03@kfm.keele.ac.uk

# University of Kent at Canterbury

Times ranking: 42 (2002 ranking: 46)

**Founded:** Royal charter 1965

**Contact details**
*Address:* Canterbury, Kent CT2 7NZ
*Tel:* 01227 827272
*Fax:* 01227 827077
*Website:* www.ukc.ac.uk
*e-mail:* recruitment@ukc.ac.uk

**The Times rankings**
*Teaching assessment:* =48 (21.0)
*Research assessment:* =41 (4.8)
*Entry standards:* 38 (20.2)
*Student–staff ratio:* =63 (17.9)
*Library/IT spend/student:* 31 (£534)
*Facilities spend/student:* 59 (£151)
*Firsts and 2:1s:* =49 (55.8%)
*Work and further study:* 5 (97.9%)
*Expected completion rate:* =37 (88%)

**Students**
*Undergraduates:* 6,310 (2,670)
*Postgraduates:* 950 (790)
*Mature students:* 17.9%
*Overseas students:* 23.1
*Applications per place:* 5
*From state sector schools:* 85%
*From working class homes:* 22%

**Teaching quality assessments**
*1993–95 Rated Excellent:* anthropology; computer science; social policy.
*From 1995 (top score 24):* **24** drama and theatre studies; molecular biosciences; organismal biosciences; philosophy. **23** economics. **22** archaeology; classics and ancient history; history of art; psychology. **21** American studies; business and management; electrical and electronic engineering; health subjects; mathematics; physics; sociology. **20** media studies; theology. **19** modern languages.

## Overview

Kent has capitalised sensibly on its position near the Channel ports, specialising in international programmes, as well as the flexible degree structures that are the hallmark of most 1960s universities. Interdisciplinary study is encouraged, and many courses include the option of a year spent elsewhere in Europe or in the United States. Almost a quarter of the undergraduates take a language for at least part of their degree, and European studies are among the most popular subject combinations. Changes of specialism are allowed up to the end of the first year.

The low-rise campus, set in 300 acres of parkland overlooking Canterbury, is tidy rather than architecturally distinguished. A new psychology building opened in 2000 and the Jean Monnet Centre will coordinate European research in Kent and beyond. Among other recent developments is a long-desired student centre with a nightclub big enough to attract big-name bands. The university also assumes a regional role, with a joint stake in 26 access courses throughout the county, which allow students to upgrade their qualifications to degree entry standard. The main focus is on the Medway towns, with a base in the old Chatham dockyard and now a campus near Rochester Airport shared with Mid-Kent College. Bridge Warden's College, in the dockyard's 18th-century Clocktower Building, provides short courses and Masters degrees, while the new Medway Higher Education Campus will pass control of Mid-Kent's degree courses to the university. Further education programmes will continue under the aegis of the college. Kent has been awarded more than £3 million of additional funding in order to provide another 1,000 places in subjects including business studies, the performing arts, information technology, travel and tourism, and law. The majority will be concentrated in the Medway area. The new places may help to reverse a decline in applications, which took place at the end of the 1990s, and reduce average entry grades which reach an A and two Bs at A level in some subjects.

The university is strongest in the social sciences, although biosciences, philosophy and drama, dance and theatre studies have taken pride of place in the teaching assessments, each registering a maximum score. The university takes teaching standards seriously, encouraging all academics to take a Postgraduate Certificate in Higher Education. Social policy and statistics were rated internationally outstanding in the latest research assessments, which showed marked improvement on the disappointing grades in 1996.

Kent, which has taken to using the acronym UKC, has been trying to build up its science departments, among which computing is particularly well regarded. Six new chemistry degrees – three of them with a year's placement in industry – and a joint honours programme in physics and computer science were added in 2001. But still two-thirds of the students take arts or social sciences. Graduates of all disciplines fare well in the employment market – a jobless rate below 4 per cent is impressive for an arts-dominated institution.

The university has a more mixed intake than many in the south of England: 85 per cent are from state schools and 22 per cent come from working-class homes, although its location does not lend itself to strong recruitment from areas without a tradition of higher education. Significant numbers of American and European students give the university a cosmopolitan feel, but some complain that the campus is empty at weekends, while Canterbury itself is expensive and limited socially.

Students are attached to one of four colleges, although they do not select it themselves. The colleges act as the focus of social life, and include academic as well as residential facilities. They provide accommodation for all first years. When it comes to moving out, private housing in Canterbury is limited, but the seaside towns of Whitstable and Herne Bay are fertile ground.

## Accommodation

Number of places and costs refer to 2001–02

*University-provided places:* 3,186

*Percentage catered:* 43%

*Costs for catered accommodation:* £63.07–£70.49 a week for bed and breakfast.

*Costs for self-catered accommodation:* £52.43–£60.06 a week.

*Policy for first-year students:* first years guaranteed accommodation provided they return completed application before 10 September in the year of entry. Those with home addresses in the city of Canterbury are not guaranteed accommodation.

*Policy for international students:* all international fee-paying students are guaranteed accommodation.

*Contact for further information:* accomm@ukc.ac.uk

# King's College London

**Times ranking:** 20 (2002 ranking: 18)

**Founded:** 1829
College of the University of London

**Contact details**
*Address:* Strand, London WC2R 2LS
*Tel:* 020 7848 2929
*Website:* www.kcl.ac.uk
*e-mail:* ceu@kcl.ac.uk

**The Times rankings**
*Teaching assessment:* =13 (21.7)
*Research assessment:* =19 (5.5)
*Entry standards:* 17 (24.1)
*Student–staff ratio:* =7 (11.0)
*Library/IT spend/student:* 19 (£609)
*Facilities spend/student:* 43 (£174)
*Firsts and 2:1s:* 6 (84.5%)
*Work and further study:* =57 (93.6%)
*Expected completion rate:* =18 (91%)

**Students**
*Undergraduates:* 10,910 (1,820)
*Postgraduates:* 2,330 (3,040)
*Mature students:* 16.2%
*Overseas students:* 13.7%
*Applications per place:* 7.1
*From state sector schools:* 66%
*From working class homes:* 19%

**Teaching quality assessments**
*1993–95 Rated excellent:* geography;
history; law; music.
*From 1995 (top score 24):* **24** classics and
ancient history; dentistry; philosophy; war
studies. **23** education; health subjects;
Portuguese. **22** anatomy and physiology;
medicine; molecular biosciences;
organismal biosciences; pharmacy; physics
and astronomy; Spanish. **21** French;
Institute of Psychiatry; mathematics and
statistics; nursing; theology. **20** electrical
and electronic engineering; German.

## Overview

The second largest of London University's colleges, King's has completed an extended period of redevelopment, leading to concentration on three campuses close to the Thames. Most departments are now within walking distance of each other, on the original Strand site or the new Waterloo campus, with medicine and dentistry based not far away at London Bridge.

Medical subjects are the main growth point. Two nursing schools have been amalgamated, building on the college's longstanding BSc in nursing studies, while the merger in 1998 with the United Medical Schools of Guy's and St Thomas's Hospitals has made King's a major centre for medical education. Among more than 2,500 students training to become doctors or dentists will be mature students on a new course designed to provide more variety in the medical profession. The university is in the final stages of the £350 million merger relocation project, with biomedical sciences, medicine, and the Dental Institute acquiring purpose-built facilities on the Guy's Campus, and 2,000 students in health and life sciences moving from Kensington and Chelsea to the largest university building in London, near Waterloo Station.

Another property deal has brought together the college's libraries at the former Public Record Office on the other side of the river, in Chancery Lane. A £4 million donation by a graduate has underwritten the spectacular new Maughan Library with 1,250 networked reader places.

Although best known for science, King's offers a wide range of subjects in ten schools of study, including such unusual features as Britain's only department devoted entirely to Portuguese – one of four language departments rated internationally outstanding in the latest research assessments. War studies, developmental biology, dentistry, history, philosophy and psychiatry completed the college's impressive haul of 5* grades. Almost one in three of those entered for the exercise were in such departments. A further 14 departments achieved a 5 grade.

Classics, dentistry, war studies and philosophy are all top-rated for teaching. Other recent teaching assessments included medicine, where 22 points out of 24 was more of an achievement than in areas where grading has been more lenient. Throughout the college, scientists remain in a majority, and are now offered a wide range of interdisciplinary combinations, such as chemistry and philosophy, or French and mathematics.

King's was one of the two founding colleges of London University, but has tended to be the forgotten member of the capital's academic elite. The full extent of the college's ambitions is clear from its mission statement, which includes having all its departments rated excellent for both teaching and research. The college was among the first to follow the example of American universities by submitting to a credit rating, which took account of its academic and financial standing. The 'AA minus' result was better than many big cities have achieved.

King's is also a solid bet for a good degree for those who satisfy its demanding entry requirements. Every student is allocated a personal tutor, and much of the teaching is in small groups. Over 60 per cent of undergraduates can expect a first or upper-second class degree. There are more than 2,700 residential places, the new halls at the Waterloo and Guy's campus providing 1,300, all en-suite. Some of the outdoor sports facilities are rather dispersed.

## Accommodation

Number of places and costs refer to 2001–02

*University-provided places:* 2,734 (college places); 450 (intercollegiate places)

*Percentage catered:* 17.3% (college); 100% (intercollegiate places)

*Costs for catered accommodation:* £92.68 a week.

*Costs for self-catered accommodation:* £50.33– £82.95 a week.

*Policy for first-year students:* all full-time students, entering the college for the tirst time on a programme lasting 2 or more years, are guaraneed one year (not always the first) in College or Intercollegiate residence. Students who have firmly accepted a conditional or unconditional offer, and submit their completed accommodation application by 30 June, will receive an offer of a place in residence for their first year.

*Policy for international students:* within the undergraduate and postgraduate quotas, priority for vacancies is given to intending overseas applicants who have not previously lived or studied in the UK.

*Contact for further information:* 020 7848 2759

# Kingston University

Times ranking: =72 (2002 ranking: 58)

**Founded:** University status 1992, formerly Kingston Polytechnic

**Contact details**
*Address:* Kingston upon Thames, Surrey KT1 1LQ
*Tel:* 020 8547 2000
*Website:* www.kingston.ac.uk
*e-mail:* admissions-info@kingston.ac.uk

**The Times rankings**
*Teaching assessment:* =39 (21.2)
*Research assessment:* =72 (2.7)
*Entry standards:* =72 (14.2)
*Student–staff ratio:* 96 (22.7)
*Library/IT spend/student:* =75 (£393)
*Facilities spend/student:* =74 (£132)
*Firsts and 2:1s:* 70 (49.2%)
*Work and further study:* =53 (94%)
*Expected completion rate:* =95 (75%)

**Students**
*Undergraduates:* 10,640 (1,160)
*Postgraduates:* 660 (2,040)
*Mature students:* 25.1%
*Overseas students:* 12%
*Applications per place:* 5
*From state sector schools:* 90%
*From working class homes:* 31%

**Teaching quality assessments**
*1993–95 Rated Excellent:* business and management; English; geology.
*From 1995 (top score 24):* **24** building and land management; mechanical and aeronautical engineering; molecular biosciences; organismal biosciences; town and country planning. **23** health subjects; mathematics; politics. **22** civil engineering; nursing; sports science. **21** art and design; economics; electrical and electronic engineering; modern languages; sociology. **20** history of art.

## Overview

Kingston has established itself as one of the leading new universities, despite slipping in this year's League Table. It has scored impressively in a number of subject rankings, while investing heavily in a new building programme. No department has scored less than 20 points out of 24 in the current teaching assessments. The vice-chancellor, Professor Peter Scott, is now trying to spread the message more widely to reduce the surprisingly large numbers recruited through clearing. He seems to be succeeding: a 16 per cent rise in applications in 2000 was the largest at any English university, and in 2001 Kingston was one of the few former polytechnics to register an increase.

The university has four campuses in southwest London: two close to Kingston town centre, another two miles away at Kingston Hill and the fourth in Roehampton Vale, where a new technology block occupies a site once used as an aerospace factory. A new flight simulator continues the tradition. An unusually extensive, 1,400-terminal computer network links them all.

Over the last decade Kingston has invested more than £65 million in new buildings, which include facilities such as a 300-seat lecture theatre, additional teaching space and a high-tech learning resources centre. At the main Penrhyn Road campus, recent development has provided a new four-storey science building which has provided additional space for an extended learning resources centre with state-of-the-art computing facilities and increased library space. New laboratories and extra teaching and office space will be created by demolishing the oldest remaining part of the campus in the next phase of the redevelopment.

Research grades in the latest assessment exercise showed improvement, with European studies, history and history of art scoring well, but teaching scores have shown Kingston's real strength. The School of Life Sciences joined building and mechanical, aeronautical and manufacturing engineering in recording perfect scores, following on from some good performances under the original quality system. Politics almost joined the club in 2001, when nursing also produced a good result. Nursing is part of the Faculty of Health and Social Care Sciences, a successful collaboration with St George's Hospital Medical School.

Private research income is healthy, with all academics encouraged to extend their interests beyond teaching. The business school has been especially successful with its services for small firms, and the university has also become a world leader in GIS – geographical information systems. The successful work-based MSc has allowed, for example, employees from the satellite company Astrium, to embark on a series of projects, in this case to reduce production lead-times, and earn postgraduate degrees.

Kingston has one of the lower drop-out rates among the new universities, at 18 per cent, despite filling a third of its places with mature students and a similar proportion from working-class families – both groups with low completion rates nationally. That only 10 per cent come from areas sending few students to higher education is mainly a matter of the university's location on the borders of prosperous Surrey.

To make the university more responsive to its students, it provides a 'one-stop shop', which deals with student issues ranging from careers and accommodation to complaints and internal discipline, while the Dean of Students has become a member of the university executive. Over £20 million has been spent on halls of residence in recent years, and further refurbishment is planned to begin in 2002. Kingston claims to be a particularly safe university, following the introduction of extra security measures. Students like the location, on the fringe of London, although complaints about the high cost of living are common.

## Accommodation

Number of places and costs refer to 2002–03

*University-provided places:* 2,300

*Percentage catered:* 0%

*Costs for catered accommodation:* n/a

*Costs for self-catered accommodation:* £53.25–£75.50 a week.

*Policy for first-year students:* places are guaranteed provided an application is received by 30 August. UCAS applicants must have an unconditional firm offer and Kingston must have received a returned UCAS AS12 acceptance slip or Clearing Entry Form and the applicant's home must be more than 10 miles from Kingston town centre.

*Policy for international students:* the same policy applies for international students studying for at least one academic year.

*Contact for further information:* Accommodation@kingston.ac.uk

# Lampeter, University of Wales

**Times ranking:** 70 (2002 ranking: 65)

**Founded:** Founded 1822, part of University of Wales since 1971

**Contact details**
*Address:* College Street, Lampeter, Ceredigion SA48 7ED
*Tel:* 01570 422351
*Website:* www.lamp.ac.uk
*e-mail:* admissions@lampeter.ac.uk

**The Times rankings**
*Teaching assessment:* =64 (20.6)
*Research assessment:* =43 (4.7)
*Entry standards:* =82 (13.4)
*Student–staff ratio:* =72 (18.5)
*Library/IT spend/student:* =39 (£502)
*Facilities spend/student:* 50 (£162)
*Firsts and 2:1s:* 68 (49.6%)
*Work and further study:* 98 (87.3%)
*Expected completion rate:* =31 (89%)

**Students**
*Undergraduates:* 1,160 (1,180)
*Postgraduates:* 90 (370)
*Mature students:* 34.4%
*Overseas students:* 9.9%
*Applications per place:* 3.4
*From state sector schools:* 88%
*From working class homes:* 31%

**Teaching quality assessments**
*1993–95 Rated Excellent:* archaeology; classics and ancient history.

## Overview

In the whole of England and Wales, only Oxford and Cambridge were awarding degrees before Lampeter. Yet only Buckingham University is smaller today. In fact, Lampeter claims to be the smallest publicly funded university in Europe, making a virtue of its size by stressing its friendly atmosphere and intimate teaching style. It remains to be seen whether small remains beautiful when the recommendations of the Welsh Assembly review of higher education are implemented, however. The politicians favour collaboration between the Principality's small higher education institutions

Based on an ancient castle and modelled on an Oxbridge college, St David's College (as it was originally known) was established to train young men for the Anglican ministry. That title receded into the small print, as the University of Wales allowed its member institutions to drop their college titles. But the original quadrangle remains and the chapel is in daily use.

There have been significant changes in the last few years – notably a big expansion in distance learning and the introduction of such subjects as anthropology, IT, management, and film and media studies. There are now 300 course combinations available in the joint honours programme. Australian studies is unique to Lampeter, while Victorian studies and medieval studies are other unusual constructs. However, there is no immediate aim to go beyond 1,700 full-time students, itself almost double the numbers taken a decade ago.

Lampeter remains an arts-dominated

haven in rural Wales. Even IT leads to a BA, and the Bachelor of Divinity is the only other undergraduate degree. Lampeter is best known for languages and theology, one of the two top-rated research departments, the other being English. The small campus includes a mosque for the growing number of Muslim students attracted by a well-endowed programme of Islamic studies. But students are opting increasingly for broad courses such as medieval studies, which includes archaeology, classics and theology, as well as history, English and Welsh. The university won a Queen's Anniversary Award for a degree in voluntary sector studies, developed from a series of sub-degree courses.

Modular degrees have been introduced, but degrees are still divided into two parts, with the first year designed to ensure breadth of study. Undergraduates are encouraged to try a new language, such as Arabic, Greek or Welsh. Part two normally takes a further two years, although languages and philosophy take three. Lampeter is deep in Welsh-speaking West Wales, and both the university and the students' union have strong bilingual policies. The university is also taking Welsh to a wider audience, with the only university course teaching the language over the Internet.

Although only four hours from London and two from Cardiff, Lampeter's geographical position could be a problem for the unprepared. The town has only 4,000 inhabitants, with among the lowest crime rates in Britain, and the nearest station is more than 20 miles away at Carmarthen. A high proportion of the students run cars. The students' union is the centre of social life – not

surprising when the university's guide to the town lists its attractions as 'cafés, pubs, a curry house and a French patisserie'. Most students have made a deliberate choice to avoid the bright lights, and many would like to remain in the area after graduation, although jobs are scarce. The location helps to produce a relatively high proportion of students from areas with little tradition of higher education and, more surprisingly, almost a third come from working-class homes. The 13 per cent drop-out rate, although higher than at many traditional universities, is well below the funding council's 'benchmark', taking account of the subject mix.

## Accommodation

Number of places and costs refer to 2002–03

*University-provided places:* 600

*Percentage catered:* 10%

*Costs for catered accommodation:* £70.00 a week (18 meals).

*Costs for self-catered accommodation:* £39.00 (standard); £47.00 (en-suite) a week.

*Policy for first-year students:* all first years who wish to live in can be accommodated. No restriction on those living close to the university.

*Policy for international students:* all international students who apply can be accommodated in the university.

*Contact for further information:* p.thomas@lampeter.ac.uk

# Lancaster University

Times ranking: 21 (2002 ranking: =23)

**Founded:** Royal charter 1964

**Contact details**
*Address:* Bailrigg, Lancaster LA1 4YW
*Tel:* 01524 65201
*Website:* www.lancs.ac.uk
*e-mail:* ugadmissions@lancaster.ac.uk

**The Times rankings**
*Teaching assessment:* =19 (21.6)
*Research assessment:* =7 (5.8)
*Entry standards:* =28 (22.1)
*Student–staff ratio:* 68 (18.3)
*Library/IT spend/student:* 30 (£544)
*Facilities spend/student:* 11 (£258)
*Firsts and 2:1s:* 33 (61.7%)
*Work and further study:* =67 (93.0%)
*Expected completion rate:* =13 (92%)

**Students**
*Undergraduates:* 7,050 (1,140)
*Postgraduates:* 1,230 (1,770)
*Mature students:* 8.4%
*Overseas students:* 9.7%
*Applications per place:* 5.9
*From state sector schools:* 89%
*From working class homes:* 22%

**Teaching quality assessments**
*1993–95 Rated Excellent:* business and management; English; environmental studies; geography; history; music; social policy; social work.
*From 1995 (top score 24):* **24** drama, dance and cinematics; education; philosophy; psychology; theology. **23** art and design; linguistics; physics; politics. **22** general engineering; mathematics. **21** health subjects; molecular biosciences; organismal biosciences; sociology. **20** French; Italian; Spanish. **19** German.

## Overview

Lancaster has recovered from its financial difficulties of the mid-1990s and recently an investment analysts' rating, which examines academic and financial issues, has given the university a clean bill of health. The student experience seems not to have suffered. Indeed, a new vice-chancellor returning to the town from Australia is taking over an institution that is thriving academically.

The rating placed Lancaster among the top dozen universities for research and in the top 20 for teaching. Despite continuing high debt charges, the university was deemed financially sound and capable of competing for students and research funds on a national and international level. Official assessments place Lancaster higher still: its latest research grades were in the top ten and teaching ratings have continued to be consistently excellent. An audit by the Quality Assurance Agency in 2000 gave top marks to all teaching areas.

Results from the 2001 Research Assessment Exercise were an improvement on an already strong performance five years earlier. Business and management, physics, sociology and statistics were all rated internationally outstanding and, with another ten subjects achieving grade 5, more than 70 per cent of the academics were in departments placed in the top two categories.

Social work, which has a dozen applications for every place, attracted one of a number of glowing reports for teaching. Education, philosophy and theology joined psychology and drama, dance and cinematics on maximum scores in 2001. With politics also recording a near-perfect score, Lancaster departments had gone more than two years without dropping one point out of 24 in teaching assessments. A £10 million environment centre to be shared with the Natural Environment Research Council opens in 2003 and will reinforce the university's strength in environmental science.

Nevertheless, Lancaster is not just a ratings factory. The university has always had a high proportion of mature students for a traditional university, aided by an innovative scheme, subsequently adopted by the polytechnics, which allows adults to join courses through their local further education colleges. Provision for students with special needs has been rewarded with a Queen's Anniversary Prize.

Lancaster is another of the campus universities of the 1960s which has always traded on its flexible degree structure. Undergraduates take three subjects in their first year, and only select the one in which they intend to specialise at the end of it. Combined degree programmes, with 200 courses to choose from, are especially popular. Some offer 'active learning courses', in which outside projects count towards final results.

The drop-out rate has fluctuated but, at 8 per cent, the latest figure is much lower than the average for the subjects on offer. Lancaster has matched the funding council's expectations for the recruitment of working-class pupils in disadvantaged areas and exceeded them by taking almost nine out of ten undergraduates from state schools.

The largely uninspiring campus overlooking Morecombe Bay has benefited from refurbished lecture theatres, sports facilities and residences, and is a ten-minute bus ride from Lancaster, three miles away. Students join one of nine residential colleges, which run their own 'freshers' weeks' and become the centre of most students' social life. Most house between 400 and 800 students in self-catering accommodation, giving Lancaster 4,600 residential places in all. The campus has a reputation for being one of the safest in the UK. The university has forged links with the local community, including many business-based initiatives.

Sports facilities are good and conveniently-placed. For those who want the outdoor life, the Lake District is within easy reach. Road and rail communications are good, but some students still find the location more isolated than they expected.

## Accommodation

Number of places and costs refer to 2002–03

*University-provided places:* 4,600

*Percentage catered:* 0%

*Costs for catered accommodation:* £18–£30 a week for dining club arrangement depending on number of meals.

*Costs for self-catered accommodation:* £40.60–£49.00 (single study) a week; £62.30–£63.70 (single en-suite) a week.

*Policy for first-year students:* it is normally possible to accommodate all first years, but insurance, clearing and very late applicants are not guaranteed places.

*Policy for international students:* international students are guaranteed accommodation throughout their studies.

*Contact for further information:* CRO@lancaster.ac.uk

# University of Leeds

**Times ranking:** 29 (2002 ranking: 28)

**Founded:** 1874, Royal charter 1904

**Contact details**
*Address:* Leeds, West Yorkshire LS2 9JT
*Tel:* 0113 233 2332
*Website:* www.leeds.ac.uk
*e-mail:* admissions@leeds.ac.uk

**The Times rankings**
*Teaching assessment:* =34 (21.3)
*Research assessment:* =26 (5.3)
*Entry standards:* 18 (23.8)
*Student–staff ratio:* =31 (15.2)
*Library/IT spend/student:* 23 (£578)
*Facilities spend/student:* 72 (£137)
*Firsts and 2:1s:* 25 (65.9%)
*Work and further study:* =18 (96.2%)
*Expected completion rate:* =18 (91%)

**Students**
*Undergraduates:* 17,110 (3,200)
*Postgraduates:* 3,120 (2,960)
*Mature students:* 9.5%
*Overseas students:* 7.8%
*Applications/place:* 7.3
*From State sector schools:* 71%
*From working class homes:* 16%

**Teaching quality assesments**
*1993–95 Rated Excellent:* chemistry;
English; geography; geology; music.
*From 1995 (top score 24):* **24** education;
health subjects; philosophy; physics.
**23** art and design; dentistry; East and
South Asian studies; electrical and
electronic engineering; history of art;
molecular biosciences; pharmacy; politics;
psychology; theology. **22** anatomy and
physiology; business; drama, dance and
cinematics; economics; French; German;
media studies; Iberian languages;
mathematics and statistics; organismal
biosciences. **21** art and design; Middle
Eastern and African studies.
**20** agriculture; food science; materials
technology; nursing; Russian; sociology.
**19** chemical engineering; civil engineering;
classics and ancient history; Italian.
**18** medicine. **17** linguistics.

## Overview

The rise of Leeds as a clubbing mecca to
rival Manchester has added to the attractions of a university which has long been
one of the giants of the higher education
system. It has more full-time students
than any institution outside London and is
always among the most popular in Britain.
An unusually wide range of degrees gives
applicants more than 500 undergraduate
programmes to choose from, with over
1,000 academic staff teaching more than
20,000 students.

The university occupies a 140-acre site,
two-thirds of which is designated a conservation area, close to Leeds Metropolitan University and within walking distance
of the city centre. The buildings are a mixture of Victorian and modern, the latest of
which have extended the library, provided
more space for biology and moved the
business school into new £10 million
premises.

After 30 months of negotiation, a
merger has gone ahead with Bretton Hall
College, near Wakefield, with its sculpture
park and established reputation in the
performing and visual arts. Investment
totalling £9 million has gone into the
main college campus, and the university
has based a new Academy of Performing
Arts and Cultural Industries there. The
agreement boosts the university's local
links since half of Bretton Hall's 2,000
students came from Yorkshire. Nine other
colleges in various parts of the county
offer Leeds courses, but handle their own
admissions.

Further afield, Leeds is now part of a
'worldwide network' which brings together

four American and four British universities to collaborate initially on research, postgraduate degree programmes, and continuing professional development. There was already a thriving European programme involving more than 100 Continental partners and a flow of students in both directions. More students take languages than any other subject, and the free-standing language unit also caters for casual learners.

Leeds has followed the fashion for modular courses, enabling its students to take full advantage of a growing range of interdisciplinary degrees. Almost a quarter now take dual honours or combinations such as communications, women's studies or international studies. Business and management is increasingly popular, the business school having moved into the former Leeds Grammar School site.

Electrical and mechanical engineering, English, food science, Italian and town planning were all rated internationally outstanding for research in 2001, when Leeds had among the largest number of academics in the national assessment exercise. Teaching ratings have generally been good, if sometimes less than outstanding. Education and philosophy have joined physics and healthcare studies on maximum points for teaching, but 18 points out of 24 was disappointing for medicine and the assessment of classics highlighted student dissatisfaction with some aspects of the courses.

Student facilities are generally first-rate. Leeds teams regularly excel in competition and the university has been awarded one of five centres of cricketing excellence. The 8,000 computer workstations are among the most at any university and the library one of the biggest.

It all contributes towards a low drop-out rate of 7 per cent.

The already large students' union, famous for its long bar and big-name rock concerts, has been extended to cope with the latest phase in the university's expansion. The £4 million upgrade has provided a new venue, more shops and catering facilities. Most students like the broad mix of backgrounds within the university, although official performance tables have shown a surprisingly low proportion of working-class students and even fewer from areas without a tradition of higher education. Town–gown relations are traditionally good.

**Accommodation**
Number of places and costs refer to 2001–02
*University-provided places:* 6,620
*Percentage catered:* 28%
*Costs for catered accommodation:* £64.16–£98.71 a week (single room) for a 31-week contract.
*Costs for self-catered accommodation:* £27.63–£62.65 a week (single room) for 40-week contract.
*Policy for first-year students:* single first years submitting an application by 1 June and not coming through clearing are guaranteed a place. There are no restrictions for students who live locally.
*Policy for international students:* full fee-paying undergraduates are guaranteed accommodation provided they submit applications by the required deadlines. New postgraduates are guaranteed accommodation until the end of the academic session in which they arrive.
Contact for further information: accom@adm.leeds.ac.uk

# Leeds Metropolitan University

Times ranking: =78 (2002 ranking: 86)

**Founded:** University status 1992, formerly Leeds Polytechnic

**Contact details**
*Address:* City Campus, Leeds,
West Yorkshire LS1 3HE
*Tel:* 0113 283 3113
*Website:* www.lmu.ac.uk
*e-mail:* course-enquiries@lmu.ac.uk

**The Times rankings**
*Teaching assessment:* =86 (20.1)
*Research assessment:* =85 (2.2)
*Entry standards:* =65 (15.4)
*Student–staff ratio:* =76 (19.0)
*Library/IT spend/student:* =39 (£502)
*Facilities spend/student:* =80 (£124)
*Firsts and 2:1s:* 66 (50.0%)
*Work and further study:* 87 (91.4%)
*Expected completion rate:* =66 (83%)

**Students**
*Undergraduates:* 11,780 (6,900)
*Postgraduates:* 710 (2,570)
*Mature students:* 20.2%
*Overseas students:* 7.7%
*Applications per place:* 6.6
*From state sector schools:* 93%
*From working class homes:* 29%

**Teaching quality assessments**
*1993–95 Rated Excellent:* none.
*From 1995 (top score 24):* **24** business and management; economics.
**23** education; health subjects. **22** cinematics; hospitality. **21** art and design; building; civil engineering; land and property management; nursing; town planning. **20** psychology. **19** media studies; modern languages. **17** electrical and electronic engineering; mechanical engineering.

## Overview

The incorporation of a large further education college in Harrogate is bringing Leeds Metropolitan closer to its goal of creating a 'comprehensive' post-school institution, in which students can take courses at all levels and progress through a network of qualifications. The university was already moving in this direction following a review of its activities to prepare for the new century.

The former polytechnic's commitment to open access and concentration on teaching, rather than research, have done it no favours in the league tables, but it remains a popular choice for students. Four out of ten come from Yorkshire and Humberside region, and over half are over 21 on entry. Fewer than half of the students are taking conventional full-time degrees, such is the popularity of sandwich and part-time courses. The drop-out rate has been improving and the latest figure of 18 per cent was well below the benchmark, which takes account of the subject mix. As part of its efforts to widen access, LMU runs the Government-funded ENABLE scheme, which teaches business studies to unemployed young people in depressed parts of the city. A summer school for Asian women was another innovation.

Leeds Metropolitan was also among the first universities offering two-year foundation degrees, working with a dozen further education colleges and Bradford University, with which LMU has a formal partnership arrangement. Information technology has been particularly popular, as has the programme in exercise science and sports leadership, which was LMU's main contribution to the initial menu of courses.

There are two campuses in Leeds: the main site close to the city centre and Leeds University, and Beckett Park, a former teacher training college three miles away in 100 acres of park and woodlands. The latter boasts outstanding sports facilities, as well as teaching accommodation for education, informatics, law and business. Over 7,000 students take part in some form of sporting activity, despite higher charges than in many other universities.

Teaching scores have improved after a poor start: no subjects were rated excellent under the original assessment system and it took until 2001 for business, management and economics to record the first perfect scores. Education and the large Science for Health programme, which caters for more than 900 students, were close behind. Only 12 subjects were entered for the latest research assessment exercise, with librarianship and information management the only one to reach the top three categories of seven.

Students are included on the committees that design and manage courses. There is a growing emphasis on educational technology, which has been enhanced by a new £20 million learning resources centre. More than 400 computers, audio-visual presentation studios and study areas are available all hours. It follows a £4.5 million project on the Beckett Park campus, completing a total upgrade in the space of two years.

Contacts with small and medium-sized businesses have been carefully fostered as part of the university's successful attempts to maintain a good record in graduate employment. The links even attracted a Queen's Anniversary Prize in the last set of awards. Most undergraduate courses are determinedly vocational, although the modular system gives students considerable control over their what makes up their degree.

Sports facilities are excellent on the Beckett Park campus, a former physical education college, and include the £2 million Carnegie Regional Tennis Centre, which opened in November 2000. Like its older neighbour, Leeds Metropolitan is benefiting from the city's growing reputation for nightlife. But it is making its own contribution with a famously lively entertainments scene. Young and mature students seem to mix well socially.

## Accommodation

Number of places and costs refer to 2001–02

*University-provided places:* 2,361

*Percentage catered:* 0%

*Costs for catered accommodation:* n/a

*Costs for self-catered accommodation:* £43.10–£64.40 a week.

*Policy for first-year students:* allocations are mainly for first years or for students new to Leeds. Criteria are based on age and the distance a student lives from Leeds. Students living in Leeds or nearby would not be allocated university accommodation.

*Policy for international students:* international students are guaranteed accommodation if they apply by 31 July.

*Contact for further information:* accommodation@lmu.ac.uk

# University of Leicester

**Times ranking:** 26 (2002 ranking: 33)

**Founded:** 1921, Royal charter 1957

**Contact details**
*Address:* University Road,
Leicester LE1 7RH
*Tel:* 0116 252 5281
*Website:* www.le.ac.uk
*e-mail:* admissions@le.ac.uk

**The Times rankings**
*Teaching assessment:* =13 (21.7)
*Research assessment:* =37 (5.0)
*Entry standards:* 32 (21.9)
*Student–staff ratio:* 34 (15.3)
*Library/IT spend/student:* =43 (£491)
*Facilities spend/student:* 33 (£188)
*Firsts and 2:1s:* 37 (60.4%)
*Work and further study:* =39 (95.1%)
*Expected completion rate:* =13 (92%)

**Students**
*Undergraduates:* 7,300 (610)
*Postgraduates:* 1,880 (7,370)
*Mature students:* 11.4%
*Overseas students:* 7.9%
*Applications per place:* 5.5
*From state sector schools:* 85%
*From working class homes:* 21%

**Teaching quality assessments**
*1993–95 Rated Excellent:* chemistry;
English; history; law.
*From 1995 (top score 24):*
**24** archaeology; ancient history;
economics; education; museum studies;
psychology. **23** American studies;
medicine; physics and astronomy; politics.
**22** history of art; mathematics; molecular
biosciences; organismal biosciences.
**21** media studies; German. **20** general
engineering; Italian. **19** French; sociology.

## Overview

Leicester is beginning to take off, after many years living in the shadow of the big city universities. A string of excellent assessments for teaching and research have coincided with rising student enrolments and a campus development programme that has produced a buzz around the university.

Though the university celebrated its 80th anniversary in 2001, it is only now approaching the size of most of its traditional counterparts after growing by more than 60 per cent in recent years. The accent has been on achieving a viable size for a leading institution by expanding both full-time and the now substantial distance learning numbers. Less than half of the 18,500 registered students are full-time campus-based undergraduates.

Professor Robert Burgess, the vice-chancellor, has declared his intention to focus on the university's provision for lifelong learning, as well as strengthening its research. In addition to opening in 2002 the Institute of Lifelong Learning, Leicester was one of the few traditional universities to offer the new, two-year foundation degrees. It is collaborating with the Security Industry Training Organisation on a course in security and risk management, which was launched in 2001 on the back of a new Honours degree in Criminology. Efforts to broaden the university's intake have included the introduction of a summer school for 11-year-olds from local schools. Almost nine out of ten undergraduates come from state schools, but the drop-out rate, at 6 per cent, is among the lowest in Britain.

Teaching ratings have improved considerably after a sound, rather than spectacular, start. The last dozen assessments have all produced at least 22 points out of 24, with archaeology, ancient history, economics, education, museum studies and psychology making six in a row on full marks. Close behind are American studies, politics, medicine and physics and astronomy – a predictable success for a leader in space science and the recipient of a Queen's Anniversary Award in 1994. The university hosts the National Science Centre, thanks to a £52 million grant from the Millennium Commission, and a Challenger learning centre opened in 1999 to bring science to life for schoolchildren. By contrast, Leicester has also been chosen to promote good teaching practice in archaeology.

The medical school, which was the youngest in Britain until the latest allocation of places, registered one of the best teaching quality scores for the subject. It has developed a new style of medical degree with Warwick University, allowing graduates in the life sciences to qualify in four years. The school has among the most modern facilities in Britain, and the siting of a medically based interdisciplinary research centre at the university was another indication of growing strength. Genetics achieved the only 5* ratings in the latest research assessments, but a dozen subjects in the next category enabled Leicester to outperform a clutch of civic universities in terms of average grades per member of staff.

Other than clinical medicine at Leicester's General Hospital, all teaching and most residential accommodation is concentrated in a leafy suburb a mile from the city centre. Recent campus developments have included a new arts and social science centre and upgrades of engineering, chemistry and archaeology facilities. An audio-visual centre is heavily used for teaching in a wide range of subjects.

An equal opportunities code for admissions has helped raise the proportion of mature students and the Richard Attenborough Centre has given the university a particular reputation for catering for disabled students. Extensive residential accommodation includes a £2.6 million refurbishment of ageing halls of residence, which are within easy reach of the teaching areas. The £16 million maintenance programme has also included a new sports ground and pavilion.

## Accommodation
Number of places and costs refer to 2001–02

*University-provided places:* 3,804

*Percentage catered:* 49%

*Costs for catered accommodation:* £77.70 a week (14 meals a week) for a 30-week contract; includes telephone rental.

*Costs for self-catered accommodation:* £44.80 a week for a 39-week contract; includes telephone rental.

*Policy for first-year students:* a guarantee is offered to all first-year students.

*Policy for international students:* a guarantee of university accommodation is offered to all new international students with priority to return in subsequent years.

*Contact for further information:* accommodation@le.ac.uk

# University of Lincoln

Times ranking: 91 (2002 ranking: 88)

**Founded:** University status 1992. Humberside University until 1996; Lincolnshire and Humberside until 2001

**Contact details**
*Address:* Brayford Pool, Lincoln LN6 7TS
*Tel:* 01522 882000
*Website:* www.lincoln.ac.uk
*e-mail:* marketing@lincoln.ac.uk

**The Times rankings**
*Teaching assessment:* =98 (19.5)
*Research assessment:* 97 (1.7)
*Entry standards:* 75 (13.7)
*Student–staff ratio:* =84 (19.7)
*Library/IT spend/student:* 52 (£464)
*Facilities spend/student:* 96 (£80)
*Firsts and 2:1s:* 90 (44.8%)
*Work and further study:* =77 (92.2%)
*Expected completion rate:* =53 (85%)

**Students**
*Undergraduates:* 7,960 (2,390)
*Postgraduates:* 930 (1,170)
*Mature students:* 26.1%
*Overseas students:* 20.4%
*Applications per place:* 4.8
*From state sector schools:* 97%
*From working class homes:* 34%

**Teaching quality assessments**
*1993–95 Rated Excellent:* none.
*From 1995 (top score 24):* **24** education management. **22** politics and international relations. **21** health subjects; tourism; psychology. **20** art and design; food science. **19** agriculture. **18** mechanical engineering. **17** media studies. **16** sociology.

## Overview

The opening of an impressive purpose-built campus near Lincoln station brought about the most dramatic transformation of any university in recent times. Humberside University, as it then was, even gave its new location pride of place in its title. Now it has gone a step further, selling its original campus and securing the approval of the Privy Council to become plain Lincoln University. While not moving out of Hull entirely, the university is to concentrate its activities on a much smaller city-centre site shared with a further education college.

The decision, which followed a change of vice-chancellor, was all the more unexpected because the university had just won a protracted battle to develop another new campus on a waterfront site in Hull. The £48 million scheme was to have provided academic and recreational facilities for 3,500 students, including 400 residential places. But a continuing decline in enrolments cast doubt on the financial viability of the scheme.

As Lincolnshire and Humberside University, student numbers dropped by 20 per cent over five years, in spite of its geographical expansion. The site in Grimsby was already due to close, but new science laboratories and sports facilities have been completed in Lincoln, bringing the cost of the development to more than £60 million. More student accommodation and a media communications building have been recently started, to be followed by a students' union and event venue. In 2001 there was an increase in admissions.

Despite the change of name, the university remains effectively two institutions 40 miles apart, although a broad-band telecommunications network links the sites – part of the impressive IT provision, which runs to 1,200 computers. A further rationalisation of courses has left Hull with health subjects, art and design, and business and management, with the promise of £4 million of investment over five years so that the site can take 1,500 students.

Lincoln initially concentrated on social sciences, accentuating the university's bias in favour of the arts, but has been building up a wider range of courses. The 40-acre riverside campus attracted architectural as well as educational interest, and represented the end of a saga. The cathedral city had been seeking a university presence for several years, and initially chose Nottingham Trent University to provide it. But the Conservative government's cap on student numbers stopped the deal going ahead and Humberside stepped in. The acquisition of former art and design and agriculture colleges from De Montfort University in 2001 brought the university's student numbers in and around Lincoln to 4,500, with the aim of expanding to 6,000 before long.

Poor performances in both teaching and research assessments account for Lincoln's low position in *The Times* ranking, although results have improved recently. Education achieved the university's first perfect score, while politics and international relations managed 22 points out of 24. Only 21 per cent of the academics were entered for the latest research ratings, but still none reached the top three categories of seven.

All students take the Effective Learning Programme, which uses computer packages backed up by weekly seminars to develop necessary study skills and produce a detailed portfolio of all their work. Research into teaching and learning methods has been aided by a £1 million fund provided by BP. Some degrees can be taken as work-based programmes, with students winning credit for relevant aspects of their employment. The university also has long-established European links, providing a growing number of courses abroad, as well as participating in more than 40 formal partnerships.

The university has a Charter Mark for exceptional service, but the student experience inevitably differs between sites. Overall, one student in three has a working-class background, and the drop-out rate of 18 per cent is now better than the average for the subjects on offer. Lincoln is adapting to its new student population, but will always be quieter than Hull, where a lively waterfront area means that the city is no longer known just for the low cost of living.

## Accommodation

Number of places and costs refer to 2002–03

*University-provided places:* Hull, 200; Lincoln, 1,037

*Percentage catered:* 0%

*Costs for catered accommodation:* n/a

*Costs for self-catered accommodation:* £55–£64 a week.

*Policy for first-year students:* priority given to students living more than 25 miles away.

*Policy for international students:* given detailed information and assistance.

*Contact for further information*: mball@lincoln.ac.uk

# University of Liverpool

**Times ranking:** 38 (2002 ranking: =37)

**Founded:** 1881

**Contact details**
*Address:* Liverpool L69 3BX
*Tel:* 0151 794 5928
*Febsite:* www.liv.ac.uk
*e-mail:* ugrecruitment@liv.ac.uk

**The Times rankings**
*Teaching assessment:* =27 (21.4)
*Research assessment:* =31 (5.2)
*Entry standards:* 35 (20.7)
*Student–staff ratio:* =31 (15.2)
*Library/IT spend/student:* =68 (£412)
*Facilities spend/student:* =70 (£139)
*Firsts and 2:1s:* 23 (67.3%)
*Work and further study:* =30 (95.5%)
*Expected completion rate:* =37 (88%)

**Students**
*Undergraduates:* 10,980 (4,150)
*Postgraduates:* 2,310 (2,570)
*Mature students:* 12.7%
*Overseas students:* 8.2%
*Applications per place:* 6.2
*From state sector schools:* 83%
*From working class homes:* 22%

**Teaching quality assessments**
*1993–95 Rated Excellent:* English; environmental science; geology; history; law. *From 1995 (top score 24):* **24** medicine; philosophy; physics; veterinary medicine. **23** anatomy and physiology; business; mathematics; media studies and politics; town planning. **22** archaeology; civil engineering; classics; economics; French; nursing; pharmacy; psychology. **21** dentistry; electrical and electronic engineering; Iberian languages; materials technology; sociology. **20** health subjects; mechanical engineering. **19** German; molecular biosciences; organismal biosciences. **17** building.

## Overview

Liverpool has been trying to modernise its portfolio of courses while preserving a well-established reputation for research. The introduction of flexible, part-time degrees, with the option of day or evening classes, was the first step in a renewed expansion programme. The top-rated medical school is being extended to cope with a bigger allocation of places and the campus is being upgraded.

Liverpool has been among the top dozen recipients of research council funds for two decades, with outside income increasing dramatically in recent years. Growth of 50 per cent in student numbers over five years also brought more money for teaching, much of which has been invested in new educational technology. The main library has been extended recently and the former Liverpool Royal Infirmary converted into extra teaching accommodation to cope with the influx. Recent expansion has been concentrated on first degrees. Full-time numbers are almost exactly balanced between the sexes.

A series of excellent ratings in the early teaching assessments took time to repeat, but philosophy has now joined veterinary science, medicine and physics on perfect scores, while media studies and politics, maths and town planning have all come close to emulating the feat. Nursing came through a reinspection successfully with a score of 22. Physiology, mechanical engineering and English recorded 5* ratings for research in the latest assessments, when more than half of the academics entered for research assessment were placed in one of the top two categories.

The university prides itself on strength across the board. Interdisciplinary courses have been expanded, introducing engineering with management and European studies, for example. Undergraduate courses are divided into eight units per two-semester year, many with examinations at the end of each semester. The university has withdrawn from teacher training, but it still claims that an unusually high proportion of teaching and research relates to the professions.

Liverpool was among the first traditional universities to run access courses for adults without traditional academic qualifications, but the mix does not show in the drop-out rate of only 10 per cent. The university is awarding record numbers of scholarships and bursaries to widen opportunities further: the 55 in 2001–02 had a total value of more than £100,000. They include five in memory of the Hillsborough disaster victims and 28 in memory of John Lennon, all for Merseyside residents. Other access initiatives include a week-long summer school and the opening of a purpose-built children's centre to help mature students and staff, with 68 subsidised places for children from six weeks to school age.

The university precinct is only half a mile up the hill from the city centre. Recent developments have included an £8 milion management school with courses from undergraduate level to MBA, a £23 million biosciences centre and a new student services centre. The Infirmary development includes new facilities for health care, pharmacy and technology transfer. A former chapel has been converted into a language centre with a television and video conference studio, while a £1.5 million gift from a former student is being used to improve information technology facilities.

Both the university and the city have a loyal following among students, a state of affairs not wasted on recruiters: the Beatles and both Liverpool football teams have featured on the first page of the prospectus. The 3,600 places in halls of residence, self-catering flats and houses are more than enough to guarantee accommodation to all first years. However, the suburban setting of the main halls complex and the focus of social life on the guild of students means that there is less integration than at some other civic universities.

## Accommodation

Number of places and costs refer to 2001–02

*University-provided places:* 3,656

*Percentage catered:* 57%

*Costs for catered accommodation:* £75.74–£82.74 a week.

*Costs for self-catered accommodation:* £52.85–£60.55 a week.

*Policy for first-year students:* students offered and firmly accepting a place who apply by 31 August are guaranteed accommodation. Recently, students who have had the university as insurance choice and some entering through clearing have also been offered housing. The guarantee is not affected by a student's home address.

*Policy for international students:* the accommodation guarantee applies to all categories of international student.

*Contact for further information:* accommodation@liverpool.ac.uk www.liv.ac.uk/accommodation

# Liverpool John Moores University

**Times ranking:** 85 (2002 ranking: 77)

**Founded:** University status 1992, formerly Liverpool Polytechnic

**Contact details**
*Address:* Roscoe Court, 4 Rodney Street, Liverpool L1 2TZ
*Tel:* 0151 231 5090
*Website:* www.livjm.ac.uk
*e-mail:* recruitment@livjm.ac.uk

**The Times rankings**
*Teaching assessment:* =79 (20.2)
*Research assessment:* 75 (2.6)
*Entry standards:* =65 (15.4)
*Student–staff ratio:* =63 (17.9)
*Library/IT spend/student:* 74 (£396)
*Facilities spend/student:* =88 (£100)
*Firsts and 2:1s:* =74 (48.6%)
*Work and further study:* 92 (90.4%)
*Expected completion rate:* =66 (83 %)

**Students**
*Undergraduates:* 13,260 (3,900)
*Postgraduates:* 630 (2,180)
*Mature students:* 21%
*Overseas students:* 9.1 %
*Applications per place:* 5.7
*From state sector schools:* 94%
*From working class homes:* 33%

**Teaching quality assessments**
*1993–95 Rated Excellent:* none.
*From 1995 (top score 24):* **24** health subjects; hospitality; physics.
**23** organismal biosciences; pharmacy.
**22** business and management; economics; land management; media studies; mole-cular biosciences; politics.
**21** American studies; drama, dance and cinematics; education; mathematics and statistics; nursing. **20** civil engineering.
**19** art and design; modern languages; psychology. **18** electrical and electronic engineering; general engineering; sociology; town planning.

## Overview

Naming itself after a football pools millionaire was just the start for one of the most innovative of the new universities. JMU was criticised in 1999 for marketing itself more as a fun factory than a seat of learning, but the former polytechnic prefers to portray itself as 'forward-thinking'. Never afraid to take a direct approach, even the prospectus has the look of an alternative travel guide.

Among the initiatives to its credit was the launching of Britain's first student charter, which became a template for others. Before university status had even been confirmed, it set about transforming itself into a huge, futuristic multimedia institution. The two learning resource centres serving different academic areas and a state-of-the-art media centre, are now open all hours. Computer-based teaching has replaced many lectures, freeing academic staff for face-to-face tutorials, and student numbers have soared.

Mainly concentrated in an area between Liverpool's two cathedrals, the university is now one of Britain's biggest. Arts and science courses occupy separate sites within easy reach of the city centre, with the IM Marsh campus, once a teacher training college, three miles away in the suburbs for education and community studies. JMU has retained a local commitment, with more than 60 per cent of the students drawn from the Merseyside area, some attracted by the range of diploma courses which still supplement the largely vocational degree programme. A 'learning federation' embracing four further education colleges in St Helen's, Southport and

Liverpool itself adds to the regional flavour.

A growing research reputation is a source of particular pride, and is reflected in an unusually large number of postgraduates for a new university. JMU was one of only two new universities to have a subject rated internationally outstanding in the latest research assessment exercise. Sports science made the step up from a grade 5 in 1996, while general engineering succeeded in holding onto that score and four more subjects reached the next category. Astronomy has a growing reputation, with a part share in a telescope in the Canary Islands. An international centre for digital content, a partnership with Mersey Television, is developing a range of new courses, including masters programmes in computer games design and e-commerce. A £1.6 million maritime centre features the UK's most advanced 360–degree shiphandling simulator.

Teaching scores have improved after a poor start, in which none of the subjects assessed under the original quality system was rated as excellent. The impressive range of courses in hospitality, leisure, sport and tourism achieved a perfect score in 2001, as did physics and the healing and human development courses in the School of Health before them, and the last overall audit by the Quality Assurance Agency found that standards had improved since 1993.

JMU is one of the most popular of the new universities, judged in terms of applications per place, although numbers have declined in the last two years. Its efforts to extend access to higher education are successful: there are more state-educated undergraduates and more

from areas of low participation than the funding council expected. The drop-out rate of nearly one in five is high, but still better than in many similar institutions.

Work-based degrees should attract even more 'non-traditional' students. A new programme gives previously unqualified students credit towards their final awards for experience in the workplace and encourages them to build study projects around their job. Degrees can be taken in most subject areas, with at least a fifth of the work taught, usually at JMU.

Facilities for conventional undergraduates have been improving. The conversion of a city-centre hotel was one of a number of residential projects, which have provided enough university-owned beds for most young entrants from outside Merseyside. In addition a number of private halls, with around 3,500 beds, have been developed in collaboration with JMU.

## Accommodation

Number of places and costs refer to 2001–02

*University-provided places:* 880 plus 18,000 bed-spaces on the books of Liverpool Student Homes.

*Percentage catered:* 0%

*Costs for catered accommodation:* n/a

*Costs for self-catered accommodation:* £47.85–£52.43 a week.

*Policy for first-year students:* all first years are guaranteed a place in halls of residence. Students with a Liverpool postcode can apply to the private halls.

*Policy for international students:* international students are guaranteed a place in halls of residence.

*Contact for further information:* Accommodation@livjm.ac.uk

# University of London

**Founded** 1836

**Senate House, Malet Street, London WC1E 7HU (tel. 0171-636 8000)**

**Tel:** 020 7636 8000
**e-mail:** enquiries@eisa.lon.ac.uk
**Website:** www.lon.ac.uk
**Enquiries:** To individual colleges, institutes or schools
**Total students:** 89,500
**Mature students:** 32%
**Overseas students:** 15%

## Overview

The federal university is Britain's biggest by far, even if some of the most prestigious members have considered going their own way. Indeed its colleges and institutes have already seen their autonomy increased considerably. They are bound together by the London degree, which enjoys a high reputation worldwide. The colleges are responsible both for the university's academic strength and its apparently precarious financial position.

London students have access to some joint residential accommodation, sporting facilities and the University of London Union. But most identify with their college, which is their social and academic base.

The following colleges have separate entries, and each also appears within the main university league table. Smaller colleges are listed on the next page.

**Goldsmiths College**
**Imperial College of Science, Technology and Medicine**
**King's College London**
**London School of Economics and Political Science**
**Queen Mary College**
**Royal Holloway College**
**School of Oriental and African Studies**
**University College London**

Many of London's teaching hospitals have now merged with colleges of the university: Imperial College of Science, Technology and Medicine now incorporates St Mary's, Charing Cross and Westminster teaching hospitals.
King's College now incorporates Guys and St Thomas's (the United Medical and Dental Schools of Guys and St Thomas's).
Queen Mary College now incorporates St Bartholomew's and the Royal London School

of Medicine and Dentistry.

University College now incorporates the Royal Free Hospital Medical School and the Eastman Dental Hospital.

In addition the School of Slavonic and Eastern European Studies is now part of University College, and Wye College (in Ashford, Kent, and offering degrees in agriculture, rural affairs and environmental studies) is now part of Imperial College.

*Colleges not listed separately:*

**Birkbeck College**, Malet Street, London WC1E 7HX (*tel.* 020 7631 6000; *e-mail*: admissions@bbk.ac.uk; *website*: www.bbk.ac.uk). 9,780 undergraduates, mainly part-time. Apply direct, not through UCAS.

**Courtauld Institute of Art**, Somerset House, Strand, London WC2R 0RN (*tel.* 020 7848 2645; *e-mail*: ugadmissions@courtauld.ac.uk; *website*: www.courtauld.ac.uk). History of art degree. 115 undergraduates.

**Heythrop College**, Kensington Square, London W8 5HQ (*tel.* 020 7795 6600; *e-mail*: enquiries@heythrop.ac.uk; *website*: www.heythrop.ac.uk). Theological college. 130 undergraduates.

**Institute of Education**, 20 Bedford Way, London WC1H 0AL (*tel.* 020 7612 6000; *e-mail*: info@ioe.ac.uk; *website*: www.ioe.ac.uk). Postgraduate education courses.

**London Business School**, Regent's Park. London NW1 4SA (*tel.* 020 7262 5050; *e-mail*: mbainfo@london.edu; *website*: www.lbs.ac.uk). Postgraduate MBA and other courses.

**London School of Hygiene and Tropical Medicine**, Keppel Street, London WC1E 7HT (*tel.* 020 7636 8636; *e-mail*: registry@lstm.ac.uk; *website*: www.lstm.ac.uk). Postgraduate medical courses.

**Royal Academy of Music**, Marylebone Road, London NW1 5HT (*tel.* 020 7873 7373; *e-mail*: registry@ram.ac.uk; *website*: www.ram.ac.uk). Music degrees. 340 undergraduates.

**Royal Veterinary College**, Royal College Street, London NW1 0TU (*tel.* 020 7468 5148; *e-mail*: registry@rvc.ac.uk; *website*: www.rvc.ac.uk). Degrees in veterinary medicine. 600 undergraduates.

**St George's Hospital Medical School**, Cranmer Terrace, London SW17 0RE (*tel.* 020 8672 9944; *website*: www.sghms.ac.uk). Degrees in medicine. 1,100 undergraduates.

**School of Pharmacy**, 29-39 Brunswick Square, London WC1N 1AX (*tel.* 020 7753 5800; *e-mail*: registry@ulsop.ac.uk; *website*: www.ulsop.ac.uk). Degrees in pharmacy and toxicology. 430 undergraduates.

# London Guildhall University

**Times ranking:** 100 (2002 ranking: 95)

**Founded:** University status 1992, formerly City of London Polytechnic, City of London College founded 1861

**Contact details**
*Address:* 31 Jewry Street,
London EC3N 2EY
*Tel:* 020 7320 1000
*Website:* www.lgu.ac.uk
*e-mail:* enqs@lgu.ac.uk

**The Times rankings**
*Teaching assessment:* =90 (20.0)
*Research assessment:* =92 (1.9)
*Entry standards:* =95 (11.8)
*Student–staff ratio:* =89 (20.5)
*Library/IT spend/student:* =64 (£424)
*Facilities spend/student:* 91 (£99)
*Firsts and 2:1s:* 100 (32.0%)
*Work and further study:* =99 (87.1%)
*Expected completion rate:* 100 (70%)

**Students**
*Undergraduates:* 7,610 (2,760)
*Postgraduates:* 430 (1,340)
*Mature students:* 42.8%
*Overseas students:* 15%
*Applications per place:* 5
*From state sector schools:* 92%
*From working class homes:* 36%

**Teaching quality assessments**
*1993–95 Rated Excellent:* social policy.
*From 1995 (top score 24):* **23** art and design; economics. **22** business and management; politics; psychology. **20** materials technology. **19** modern languages. **18** mathematics. **17** media studies; sociology.

## Overview

In the space of a few dramatic months, London Guildhall provided the first leader of a former polytechnic to head the body representing the university system and then announced plans to amalgamate with North London University. Assuming the merger goes ahead as planned, entrants in 2003 will find themselves at London Metropolitan University, an institution of 25,000 students and an annual budget of £110 million. London Guildhall denies that financial difficulties forced its hand but, like a number of new universities, it has struggled to meet recruitment targets. Applications for courses beginning in 2002 were down by almost 9 per cent.

Spilling over from the Square Mile into the Aldgate area of East London, the university's academic interests reflect the stark contrasts in its location. City traditions are maintained in a wide range of business-related courses, while a variety of craft subjects cater for the neighbouring community. London Guildhall traces its origins back 150 years to the Metropolitan Evening Classes for Young Men, and still boasts the highest proportion students taking further education courses of any university in the country.

More than half of the students are on business courses, many coming from City firms to join part-time degrees or professional courses. The Business School is one of the largest in Britain, taking advantage of its position in the use of guest lecturers from the City to supplement over 300 full and part-time staff. Although not on the same scale, the silversmithing and jewellery courses are the largest in

Britain, while those in furniture restoration and conservation were the first of their kind in Europe. Following the vocational theme that runs through all its courses, the university even offers ground training for civil aviation pilots.

An imaginative twin-track system allows entrants who know what they want to study to enrol on 'early specialist' degrees while others embark on the modular course programme, postponing the choice of single or combined honours until the end of the first year. There is a regular flow of students into the university at this stage, thanks to a well-established credit transfer scheme. Some courses are franchised to colleges in and around London. For those wishing to go further afield, there are 48 partner institutions on the Continent, where students may take one or two semesters of their course.

Quality assessments have been patchy, accounting for London Guildhall's low position in *The Times* table. Economics and business studies did well in recent assessments, but only social policy was rated excellent under the original system and almost half the subjects assessed under the current arrangements have scored less than 20 points out of 24. Fewer than 100 academics were entered for the latest research assessment exercise, and only German reached the top three grades.

The university is finally overcoming teaching accommodation problems that surfaced in its polytechnic days, as leases on key buildings came to an end. Spread over seven main sites, students used to complain that buildings were crowded and in poor condition. But a £3.5 million refurbishment programme has brought improvements, and new purchases are beginning to bring the university together around the Aldgate area. New developments include the Women's Library and the Cass Centre for Silversmithing and Jewellery.

More than one undergraduate in three has a working class background – a bigger share of the intake than the funding council anticipated, given the subject mix. But, perhaps because of the location, the reverse is true of the numbers from areas without a tradition of higher education, which amount to only 12 per cent. Almost a quarter of graduates go into further training or studies, but a third drop out before they reach this point.

London Guildhall's residential accommodation is extremely limited, even given the large number of students who choose to live at home. But the university uses its extensive contacts in the private sector to help place the remainder. The same goes for sports facilities, with arrangements with non-university sports centres topping up London Guildhall's own.

## Accommodation
Number of places and costs refer to 2001–02

*University-provided places:* 492

*Percentage catered:* 0%

*Costs for catered accommodation:* n/a

*Costs for self-catered accommodation:* £70–£80 a week.

*Policy for first-year students:* cannot guarantee; priority given to young and non-local students; students living within Greater London (20–mile radius) not eligible.

*Policy for international students:* non-EU first-years are guaranteed a place if they apply before the third week in August.

*Contact for further information:* accom@lgu.ac.uk

# London School of Economics and Political Science

**Times ranking:** 5 (2002 ranking: 7)

**Founded:** 1895
College of the University of London

**Contact details**
*Address:* Houghton Street,
London WC2A 2AE
*Tel:* 020 7955 7124
*Website:* www.lse.ac.uk
*e-mail:* UG-admissions@lse.ac.uk

**The Times rankings**
*Teaching assessment:* =9 (21.9)
*Research assessment:* =3 (6.4)
*Entry standards:* 3 (28.2)
*Student–staff ratio:* 29 (14.6)
*Library/IT spend/student:* 3 (£1,058)
*Facilities spend/student:* =62 (£146)
*Firsts and 2:1s:* 19 (70.3%)
*Work and further study:* =33 (95.3%)
*Expected completion rate:* =10 (93%)

**Students**
*Undergraduates:* 3,330 (170)
*Postgraduates:* 3,290 (920)
*Mature students:* 5.9%
*Overseas students:* 48%
*Applications per place:* 11.1
*From state sector schools:* 58%
*From working class homes:* 13%

**Teaching quality assessments**
*1993–95 Rated Excellent:* anthropology;
applied social work; management; history;
law; social policy.
*From 1995 (top score 24):* **24** business
and management. **23** economics;
psych-ology. **22** mathematics; media
studies; philosophy; politics. **20** sociology.

## Overview

Always one of the big names of British higher education, the LSE has taken on a new lease of life under its latest director, signing up big names from Oxford, Harvard, Yale and other top universities. Although most are visiting professors or on short-term appointments, the new blood has helped to revitalise an institution which has been back in the limelight since the arrival of Professor Anthony Giddens, the academic face of Tony Blair's 'Third Way'.

Much of the 1990s was taken up with fruitless searches for room to break out from the school's cramped site near London's law courts. The most ambitious – a bid for County Hall – was blocked by the Conservative government, while the possibility of a move to Docklands was rejected by the school itself. Even a contingency plan to levy the first undergraduate fees was overtaken by events, when Labour introduced its national scheme. Proposals to divide the institution into graduate and undergraduate schools were also dropped, but the intention is still to concentrate on masters degrees. One consequence may be to make the LSE even more difficult to get into: only Oxford and Cambridge have higher entry standards. Already half the students are postgraduates, and the accent on research has seen income from this source rise dramatically.

Improvements are being made to the campus. The British Library of Economic and Political Science returned to the Aldwych in the summer of 2001 as part of a

£30 million Norman Foster-designed redevelopment of the Lionel Robbins Building.

More than four out of ten British undergraduates are from independent schools – one of the highest ratios in the country and much higher than the funding councils' 'benchmark' figure. Efforts are being made to attract a broader intake with Saturday classes and a summer school. However, there is a positive side to the current admissions policy in a drop-out rate of only 8 per cent.

The school also has the highest proportion of overseas students at any university, with the nationals of more than 120 countries taking up half the places. Alumni are in influential positions all over the world, not forgetting Britain, where 30 sitting MPs are LSE graduates. The international character not only gives the LSE global prestige, but also an unusual degree of financial independence. Little more than a quarter of its income comes from the Higher Education Funding Council.

Areas of study range more broadly than the name suggests. Law, management and history are among the subjects top-rated for teaching, and there is even a small contingent of scientists. Business, economics, psychology and maths all produced good results recently. Only Cambridge outperformed the LSE in the latest research assessments, which saw half of the school's subjects rated internationally outstanding. The school entered the highest proportion of its academics, at 97 per cent, of any university and just one subject (statistics) slipped below the top two grades.

The LSE does not hide its light under a bushel: it describes itself as 'the world's leading social science institution for teaching and research'. The school's website includes a Director's Home Page, which describes Professor Giddens as the most widely-read and cited social theorist of his generation and includes 'frequently asked questions' such as the meaning of reflexive modernisation and structuration theory.

Partying is not the prime attraction of the LSE for most applicants, who tend to be serious about their subject, but London's top nightspots are on the doorstep for those who can afford them. Despite the high proportion of UK students from independent schools, few can. At least 2,500 residential places for 7,000 full-time students offer a good chance of avoiding central London private sector rents.

## Accommodation

Number of places and costs are approximate and refer to 2003–04

*University-provided places:* 2,525

*Percentage catered:* about 40%

*Costs for catered accommodation:* £53 (shared room) – £110 (single room) a week.

*Costs for self-catered accommodation:* same as above.

*Policy for first-year students:* try to guarantee an offer of a space to every new first year. There are no geographical restrictions placed upon first-year students.

*Policy for international students:* same as domestic students.

*Contact for further information:* accommodation@lse.ac.uk to apply and submit application forms online: www.lse.ac.uk/accommodation

# Loughborough University

Times ranking: 14 (2002 ranking: 21)

**Founded:** 1909, Royal charter 1966

**Contact details**
*Address:* Ashby Road, Loughborough, Leicestershire LE11 3TU
*Tel:* 01509 222498/9
*Website:* www.lboro.ac.uk
*e-mail:* prospectus-enquiries@lboro.ac.uk

**The Times rankings**
*Teaching assessment:* =5 (22.0)
*Research assessment:* =35 (5.1)
*Entry standards:* =30 (22.0)
*Student–staff ratio:* 46 (16.3)
*Library/IT spend/student:* 22 (£583)
*Facilities spend/student:* 7 (£277)
*Firsts and 2:1s:* 41 ( 59.8%)
*Work and further study:* =8 (97.2%)
*Expected completion rate:* =22 (90%)

**Students**
*Undergraduates:* 8,840 (190)
*Postgraduates:* 1,300 (1,940)
*Mature students:* 6.1%
*Overseas students:* 4.7%
*Applications per place:* 5.7
*From state sector schools:* 83%
*From working class homes:* 22%

**Teaching quality assessments**
*1993–95 Rated Excellent:* business and management.
*From 1995 (top score 24):* **24** anatomy and physiology; health subjects; information science; psychology. **23** art and design; drama; economics; hospitality; mechanical engineering; physics; politics; sociology; sport and recreation. **22** business and management; chemical engineering; civil engineering; electrical and electronic engineering; mathematics and statistics. **21** materials science.

## Overview

Best known for its successes on the sports field, Loughborough has enhanced its academic reputation recently, consistently finishing well up *The Times* rankings and rivalling Oxbridge in its teaching ratings, which average no less than 22 points out of 24. Good results are not confined to the technological subjects which used to be the university's raison d'etre: information science achieved a perfect rating for teaching quality, while economics, sociology and drama were only a whisker behind. The news is not lost on schools and colleges: the number of candidates shot up at the end of the 1990s, despite the introduction of tuition fees, and rose by another 9 per cent for courses starting in 2002.

Loughborough has merged with the neighbouring colleges of education and art and design, giving a more balanced mix between art and science, making the university much less male dominated. However, engineering remains by far the biggest subject area, with more than 2,500 students. Aeronautical and automotive engineering are particularly strong, but all branches have fared well in teaching assessments. A £20 million integrated engineering complex opened in 2000, freeing space for a new information and learning resource centre.

The university has been pursuing modest growth recently. The most far-reaching change is the development of a branch campus in Peterborough, a thriving city without a university of its own. A purpose-built academic centre and library offers degrees in business studies, sports science, graphic design, performing arts, theology and information technology.

The original 216-acre campus has recently benefited from a construction programme which included a large student union extension and a new business school, as well as additions to the extensive residential stock. The 5,000 rooms now all have telephone and internet connections. Social activity is concentrated on the union, although Loughborough is only a mile away and both Leicester and Nottingham are within easy reach.

Most subjects are available either as three-year full-time or four-year sandwich courses, which includes a year in industry. This has helped to give graduates an outstanding employment record, as well a drop-out rate of 10 per cent, which is low for the subjects Loughborough offers. The university prides itself on a close relationship with industry, which attracted one of the university's three Queen's Anniversary Prizes.

Only one subject (materials science) has dropped below 22 points since the quality system was changed in 1995, and that by only one point. The built environment, sociology and sports science reached the top rung of the research assessment ladder in 2001, when almost half of the academics entered for assessment were in the top two categories. The university has shown itself prepared to act when subjects are not living up to expectations: primary teacher training and some secondary training specialisms had their last intake in 2000, leaving the university to concentrate on its strengths in physical education, design and science.

For all of its academic progress, sportsmen and women still set the tone of student life. Loughborough remains pre-eminent in British university sport, both in terms of facilities and performance. Representative teams have a record second to none and the programme of sports scholarships is the largest in the university system. Another £21 million is going into one of Sport England's new national network centres, which will be based on the campus. It includes a 50-metre swimming pool, indoor athletics centre, gymnastic, badminton, tennis and hockey facilities, and sports science and medicine centres. In 2001 Loughborough was selected as the permanent site for the England and Wales Cricket Board's national academy.

## Accommodation

Number of places and costs refer to 2001–02

*University-provided places:* 4,732

*Percentage catered:* 65.8%

*Costs for catered accommodation:* £60.43–£95.34 a week.

*Costs for self-catered accommodation:* £41.07–£58.21 a week.

*Policy for first-year students:* guarantee to Loughborough first-choice students, and insurance choice.

*Policy for international students:* guaranteed accommodation for two years of their course.

*Contact for further information:* SAS@lboro.ac.uk

# University of Luton

Times ranking: =72 (2002 ranking: 76)

---

**Founded:** University status 1993, formerly Luton College of Higher Education

**Contact details**
*Address:* Park Square, Luton, Bedfordshire LU1 3JU
*Tel:* 01582 489262
*Website:* www.luton.ac.uk
*e-mail:* admissions@luton.ac.uk

**The Times rankings**
*Teaching assessment:* =52 (20.9)
*Research assessment:* 96 (1.8)
*Entry standards:* 100 (10.6)
*Student–staff ratio:* =35 (15.4)
*Library/IT spend/student:* 71 (£408)
*Facilities spend/student:* =48 (£165)
*Firsts and 2:1s:* =81 (47.6%)
*Work and further study:* 1 (99.4%)
*Expected completion rate:* 97 (74.9%)

**Students**
*Undergraduates:* 7,500 (4,350)
*Postgraduates:* 490 (1,070)
*Mature students:* 33.4%
*Overseas students:* 22.3%
*Applications per place:* 6
*From state sector schools:* 99%
*From working class homes:* 36%

**Teaching quality assessments**
*1993–95 Rated Excellent:* none.
*From 1995 (top score 24):* **23** health subjects; nursing. **22** anatomy and physiology; art and design; building; media studies; molecular biosciences; organismal biosciences; pharmacy; psychology. **21** linguistics. **20** electrical and electronic engineering; modern languages. **18** sociology.

---

## Overview

Luton has been finding its feet as a university, with consistently good teaching ratings, after a shaky start. But under-recruitment in academic subjects, which at one time threatened almost 100 academic posts, showed that it is not yet the finished article. A 27 per cent drop in applications for 2002 was the biggest at any university, although course closures were largely responsible. Never a polytechnic, it had to break all records for expansion to meet the criteria for promotion a year after the other new universities were created. The dash was worth it because tough obstacles have since been placed in the way of other ambitious colleges, but the strains showed in the more exalted company the institution was keeping. None of the first dozen departments to be assessed for teaching quality was considered excellent, and almost all subjects were placed in the bottom two categories in the 1996 research rankings.

Times have changed, however, and Luton is indignant that it is so often the butt of jokes about low standards in higher education. The first official measure of graduate destinations showed the university with the lowest unemployment rate of all. Developments costing some £40 million have transformed the main campus, and in recent teaching assessments the university is averaging 21 points out of 24 – better than many traditional universities. The last six subjects to be assessed for teaching quality all attracted the equivalent of the old 'Excellent' rating, with health subjects and nursing producing the best score.

Research grades improved in the latest assessments, although only history and tourism reached the top three categories.

Although there are outposts in Bedford, Dunstable, Aylesbury and Northampton, most departments are on two sites in Luton town centre. The main Park Square campus, which has seen the addition of an impressive learning resources centre, languages centre and extensive residential accommodation in recent years, is in the midst of the shopping area. The second site, for humanities, is ten minutes' walk away and there is an attractive management centre and conference venue at Putteridge Bury, a neo-Elizabethan mansion three miles outside Luton. The latest addition is a small graduate business school in Aylesbury, which opened in 2000. All are subject to the university's rigid no-smoking rule.

Nursing and midwifery students in the growing Faculty of Healthcare and Social Studies are scattered more widely, with Stoke Mandeville Hospital and Wycombe General Hospital the centres in Buckinghamshire, while Bedford, and Luton and Dunstable Hospitals provide the equivalent for Bedfordshire.

The university's commitment to open access is reflected in a high proportion of mature students, many of whom take access courses to bring them up to degree or diploma standard, while almost half of the school-leavers arrive through the clearing system. Luton claims to have the second most diverse intake in Britain, with almost one student in three coming from an ethnic minority and a similar proportion arriving without traditional academic qualifications. The mix is a classic recipe for a high drop-out rate, but the funding council's estimate of 17 per cent non-completion was well below the expectation for its intake.

Courses are strongly vocational. A new English degree, for example, is entitled Professional Communication, and covers text production, website construction and computer conferencing skills, as well as more traditional English language teaching. The university also makes the most of its high-tech facilities for assessment. More than 10,000 students in disciplines from accountancy to biology are subject to 'computer assisted assessment'.

Luton, although not known for its social scene, has its share of pubs, clubs and restaurants. Students tend to rely on hall or union facilities, and London is only half an hour away by train. Nearly 2,000 residential places have been added since university status arrived – enough to accommodate all first years. Sports facilities are limited, but students make use of the more extensive facilities in town.

## Accommodation

Number of places and costs refer to 2001–02

*University-provided places:* about 1,450

*Percentage catered:* 0%

*Costs for catered accommodation:* n/a

*Costs for self-catered accommodation:* £45.00, £50.00, £57.70, £59.43 and £61.29 a week.

*Policy for first-year students:* those who have accepted places are guaranteed hall places subject to defined cut-off dates, wherever they live.

*Policy for international students:* given priority and allocated to particular halls providing applications made in good time.

# University of Manchester

Times ranking: 12 (2002 ranking: 16

**Founded:** 1851, Royal charter 1903

**Contact details**
*Address:* Oxford Road, Manchester
M13 9PL
*Tel:* 0161 275 2077
*Website:* www.man.ac.uk
*e-mail:* ug.prospectus@man.ac.uk

**The Times rankings**
*Teaching assessment:* =9 (21.9)
*Research assessment:* =10 (5.7)
*Entry standards:* 20 (23.5)
*Student–staff ratio:* =24 (14.1)
*Library/IT spend/student:* 13 (£678)
*Facilities spend/student:* 25 (£205)
*Firsts and 2:1s:* 12 (78%)
*Work and further study:* =14 (96.3%)
*Expected completion rate:* =10 (93%)

**Students**
*Undergraduates:* 16,400 (2,220)
*Postgraduates:* 3,360 (3,610)
*Mature students:* 10.8%
*Overseas students:* 9.0%
*Applications per place:* 6.6
*From state sector schools:* 74%
*From working class homes:* 18%

**Teaching quality assessments**
*1993–95 Rated Excellent:* anthropology; chemistry; computer science; geography; geology; law; mechanical engineering; music; social policy.
*From 1995 (top score 24):* **24** business and management; classics and ancient history; dentistry; economics; medicine; pharmacy; philosophy; physics and astronomy; politics; theology. **23** anatomy and physiology; archaeology; education; molecular biosciences; nursing; organismal biosciences. **22** health subjects; leisure management; mathematics and statistics; psychology. **21** drama, dance and cinematics; German; history of art; linguistics; material science; sociology. **20** aerospace engineering; electrical and electronic engineering; Iberian languages; Middle Eastern and African studies; town planning. **19** French; Italian. **18** civil engineering. **16** Russian.

## Overview

Always among the giants of British higher education, with 22 Nobel prizewinners to its credit, Manchester has emerged from a difficult period in which official assessments suggested that it was underachieving. The university celebrated its 150th anniversary with its best-ever ratings, and has gone on from strength to strength. Another four perfect scores for teaching were followed by much-improved research grades and a 17 per cent leap in applications after two years of decline.

Not surprisingly, Manchester has been climbing *The Times* rankings, as well as reclaiming its place among the three universities with the largest number of applicants. Seven of the last dozen subjects to be assessed have achieved maximum points for teaching quality – a record that none of its rivals can match. Business and management, economics, philosophy and politics are the latest members of this exclusive club.

The rise in research grades in 2001 was also spectacular, with the 12 internationally outstanding subject areas trebling the haul five years earlier. The successful departments were spread equally between the arts and sciences, representing a quarter of the academics entered for assessment. Altogether, three-quarters of the entrants were in subjects placed in the top two categories.

Impressive teaching ratings for the medical school were rewarded with extra places in collaboration with Keele University. A new teaching block will cater for the additional 230 places a year. The university has also upgraded the facilities for chemistry and biosciences, which won a Queen's Anniversary Prize for innovation. More than £40 million is going into a new centre that will establish the university as one of Europe's leading players in biomedical science and biotechnology.

Manchester remains the model of a traditional university, where the computer was invented and Rutherford began the work which led to the splitting of the atom. There is a roughly equal balance between arts and sciences, with school-leavers filling most of the undergraduate places, and more than 5,000 postgraduates underlining the emphasis on research. Graduate schools have been introduced to cater more efficiently for their needs, while a modular system has been introduced for first degrees. Student numbers have been creeping up recently, and might become a quantum leap if proposals for a merger with neighbouring UMIST go ahead. Amalgamation would produce the largest conventional university in Britain, with many world-class departments.

The city's famed youth culture and the university's position at the heart of a huge student precinct shared with two other Manchester universities already help to ensure keen competition for places – and hence high entry standards in most subjects.

A quarter of the undergraduates are from independent schools and fewer than one in five come from working-class homes. Among its efforts to broaden the intake the university has launched a summer school for state-school teenagers and is running a 'bridging course' for those with disappointing A levels. There are about 100 Century Scholarships of £1,500, some reserved for applicants from the Targeted Access Scheme, which guarantees interviews for Manchester teenagers without a family tradition of higher education.

Sports facilities, which are already first-rate, will improve still further with the Commonwealth Games in 2002. An Olympic-sized pool has already opened on campus. The city's reputation for violent crime may be overstated, but the students' union runs late-night minibuses, self-defence classes, and regular safety campaigns. Students tend to be fiercely loyal both to the university and their adopted city.

## Accommodation

Number of places and costs refer to 2002–03. All accommodation is shared with UMIST, and centrally administered.

*University-provided places:* 9,020

*Percentage catered*: 29%

*Costs for catered accommodation:* £73–£97 a week, based on 38-week let.

*Costs for self-catered accommodation:* £42–£71.50 a week, based on 38-week let.

*Policy for first-year students:* all unaccompanied students are guaranteed accommodation provided that they have an unconditional place and have submitted an application for accommodation by 31 August. There are no restrictions on local students.

*Policy for international students:* international students paying the overseas rates of fees are guaranteed two years in university accommodation.

*Contact for further information:* Accommodation@man.ac.uk www.accommodation.man.ac.uk

# UMIST

......................

Times ranking: 31 (2002 ranking: 30)

Founded: Founded 1824, part of
Manchester University 1905-93

Contact details
Address: P O Box 88, Manchester
M60 1QD
Tel: 0161 200 4033/34
Website: www.umist.ac.uk
e-mail: ug.admissions@umist.ac.uk

The Times rankings
Teaching assessment: =64 (20.6)
Research assessment: =19 (5.5)
Entry standards: =25 (22.7)
Student–staff ratio: 3 (9.4)
Library/IT spend/student: 36 (£521)
Facilities spend/student: 24 (£209)
Firsts and 2:1s: 44 (58.2%)
Work and further study: =39 (95.1)
Expected completion rate: =37 (88%)

Students
Undergraduates: 5,000 (0)
Postgraduates: 1,370 (300)
Mature students: 10.6%
Overseas students: 20.3%
Applications per place: 8.3
From state sector schools: 80%
From working class homes: 24%

Teaching quality assessments
1993–95 Rated Excellent: business and
management.
From 1995 (top score 24): 23 health
subjects. 22 building; chemical
engineering; civil engineering; electrical
and electronic engineering; mathematics;
molecular biosciences. 21 physics and
astronomy. 20 building; materials
technology. 18 modern languages.

## Overview

UMIST (University of Manchester Institute of Science and Technology), has been fully independent of Manchester University since 1993, although it still shares services such as student accommodation and careers advice with its parent body. But that may be about to change, with the two institutions considering a full merger as this guide went to press. Specialising in science, engineering, technology and management, it has a high reputation among academics and employers alike. But a merged university would be the biggest in Britain, apart from the federations in London and Wales, bringing obvious advantages in international competition.

UMIST is already involved in a number of joint academic projects and was the first university to win a Queen's Anniversary Prize for innovation three times. It is a full partner in the Manchester Federal School of Business and Management, for example, despite offering its own highly-rated courses in the area. Indeed, UMIST tops The Times undergraduate business ranking with top scores for both teaching and research. A purpose-built management school costing £8 million opened in 1998.

Much of the development planned over the next few years is designed to strengthen an already healthy research base. More than a quarter of the students are postgraduates and two-thirds of the academics in the last research assessment reached one of the top two out of seven categories. Materials technology and health subjects were both 5* rated.

Teaching ratings have also been good, especially in engineering. The latest assessments have seen a near-perfect score for optometry and neuroscience, with maths and statistics not far behind. Undergraduate developments are focusing on combining science or technology with a modern language or environmental study. A new science and enterprise centre will tailor courses even more to the employment market, with modules on business skills. Students already have access to the largest computer centre in Europe and a library that is one of the most high-tech in Britain.

Entry qualifications have remained high throughout UMIST's recent period of expansion: an average close to three Bs at A level is a tall order when many of subjects offered are experiencing a national shortage of well-qualified candidates. UMIST's popularity is due in part to the consistently excellent employment record of its graduates, with several surveys of employers placing it among their favourite recruiting grounds. Students have access to an unrivalled network of industrial sponsorship, while UMIST's graduates were the highest-earning in Britain in a recent survey.

Sited close to the city centre and Manchester's other universities, UMIST's Victorian art nouveau headquarters is now surrounded by modern academic buildings. UMIST's technological bias helps to produce a more socially diverse student population than at most leading universities: one undergraduate in five is from an independent school but almost a quarter are from working-class homes and the share of places going to students from areas without a tradition of higher education is larger than the funding council

anticipated. The drop-out rate, at 12 per cent, is exactly the national average for the subjects on offer.

The social scene is bound up with the other universities and the city's broader youth culture, although UMIST has plenty of facilities of its own. The students' union recently had a £600,000 facelift, and has a popular nightclub as well as bars and restaurants. The sports facilities are benefiting from the city's selection to host the Commonwealth Games. Students get discounted entry to the UMIST-run Manchester Aquatics Centre, with its two 50-metre pools and leisure pool.

## Accommodation

Number of places and costs refer to 2002–03. All accommodation is shared with Manchester University, and centrally administered.

*University-provided places:* 9,020

*Percentage catered:* 29%

*Costs for catered accommodation:* £73–£97 a week, based on 38-week let.

*Costs for self-catered accommodation:* £42–£71.50 a week, based on 38-week let.

*Policy for first-year students:* all unaccompanied students are guaranteed accommodation provided that they have an unconditional place and have submitted an application for accommodation by 31 August. There are no restrictions on local students.

*Policy for international students:* international students paying the overseas rates of fees are guaranteed two years in university accommodation.

*Contact for further information:*
Accommodation@man.ac.uk
www.accommodation.man.ac.uk

# Manchester Metropolitan University...

Times ranking: 75 (2002 ranking:71)

Founded: University status 1992, formerly Manchester Polytechnic

Contact details
Address: All Saints Building, Oxford Road, Manchester M15 6BH
Tel: 0161 247 1035/6/7/8
Website: www.mmu.ac.uk
e-mail: prospectus@mmu.ac.uk

The Times rankings
Teaching assessment: =55 (20.8)
Research assessment: =64 (2.9)
Entry standards: =65 (15.4)
Student–staff ratio: 83 (19.6)
Library/IT spend/student: =80 (£384)
Facilities spend/student: 95 (£81)
Firsts and 2:1s: 92 (44.1%)
Work and further study: =80 (92.0%)
Expected completion rate: =66 (83%)

Students
Undergraduates: 18,620 (5,520)
Postgraduates: 2,060 (3,870)
Mature students: 40%
Overseas students: 5.8%
Applications per place: 6.5
From state sector schools: 93%
From working class homes: 32%

Teaching quality assessments
1993–95 Rated Excellent: mechanical engineering.
From 1995 (top score 24): 23 business and management; drama; philosophy. 22 anatomy and physiology; art and design; health subjects; history of art; hospitality; materials technology; molecular biosciences; organismal biosciences; politics; psychology. 21 dentistry; electrical and electronic engineering; librarianship; modern languages; nursing; sociology. 20 education; mathematics; town planning. 19 food sciences.

## Overview

The largest conventional higher education institution in Britain reached another milestone at the end of 2001 with one of the first 5* ratings for research at a new university. Sports science was the area rated internationally outstanding, while seven other subjects were rated in the top three of seven categories. The assessments confirmed that Manchester Metropolitan has quality as well as quantity: there are more than 30,000 students, including part-timers. Although the former polytechnic could not sustain its lead over Manchester University in applications for 2002, still only a handful of institutions were more popular. Only the Open University and two federations in London and Wales have more students.

Long-standing commitments to extending access are being continued: even among the full-time undergraduates, 40 per cent are over 21 on entry and almost a third are from working-class homes. More than 90 per cent of the undergraduates went to state schools and 17 per cent come from areas without a tradition of higher education. The 400 courses at degree level cover more than 70 subjects, while the seven campuses stretch from the centre of Manchester to Crewe and Alsager, 40 miles to the south.

The university features in The Times top 20 for materials technology, food science and drama, the last of which achieved a near-perfect score in its teaching quality assessment. Only mechanical engineering was rated as excellent in the first rounds of assessment, but recent scores have improved including near-perfect results for business and philosophy and a further four subjects achieving scores of 22 in the last year. The university takes teaching seriously: small groups are used whenever possible and staff are encouraged to take a three-year MA in teaching, which has been running since 1992. Many courses also involve work placements.

Education courses also came out well of the Teacher Training Agency's performance indicators for primary training. Some 800 trainees are at the former Crewe and Alsager College campuses with students taking contemporary arts and sports science, while the remainder are based at Didsbury with those taking community studies, five miles out of Manchester. A new Institute of Education covers both centres.

The Crewe and Alsager campuses are six miles apart, but free transport is provided between the two. Although the rural location inevitably makes for a quieter life than in Manchester, Alsager has an arts centre with two theatres, a dance studio and an art gallery, as well as extensive sports facilities, while the Crewe campus has its own nightclub. Eventually, the university intends to develop Crewe as its Cheshire base, adding sports facilities and residential accommodation, as well as more lecture theatres.

The Didsbury campus will remain, with all other subjects based in Manchester itself, mostly at the extensive All Saints campus, close to the city centre and the other universities. Only the clothing, food and hospitality courses, three miles away on the Hollings campus, are out of walking distance. Overseas links have expanded rapidly in recent years, offering exchange opportunities in Europe and farther afield, as well as establishing teaching bases abroad.

One student in three comes from the Manchester area, easing the pressure on accommodation in a city of 70,000 students. The city's attractions do no harm to recruitment levels, but much depends on where the course is based. Didsbury may offer the best of both worlds, with swift access to the city centre and a peaceful environment, but students at Crewe and Alsager can feel isolated. Some potential applicants are daunted by the sheer size of the university, but individual courses and sites usually provide a social circle.

## Accommodation

Number of places and costs refer to 2002–03

*University-provided places:* 3,600; 5,000 in privately-owned halls.

*Percentage catered:* 30%; 5% in privately-owned halls

*Costs for catered accommodation:* £74.50 a week (16 meals).

*Costs for self-catered accommodation:* £47–£61 (standard); £63.25–£74.00 (en-suite).

*Policy for first-year students:* all new full-time students who apply for accommodation before 31 August will be offered halls somewhere in Manchester (or at Crewe/Alsager if working at a Cheshire campus).

*Policy for international students:* same as above.

*Contact for further information:* accommodation@mmu.ac.uk

# Middlesex University

**Times ranking:** 88 (2002 ranking: =80)

**Founded:** University status 1992, formerly Middlesex Polytechnic

**Contact details**
*Address:* White Hart Lane, Tottenham, London N17 8HR
*Tel:* 020 8362 5898
*Website:* www.mdx.ac.uk
*e-mail:* admissions@mdx.ac.uk

**The Times rankings**
*Teaching assessment:* =74 (20.4)
*Research assessment:* =72 (2.7)
*Entry standards:* 92 (12.3)
*Student–staff ratio:* =80 (19.2)
*Library/IT spend/student:* 41 (£496)
*Facilities spend/student:* 99 (£51)
*Firsts and 2:1s:* 58 (51.9%)
*Work and further study:* 84 (91.6%)
*Expected completion rate:* =89 (77%)

**Students**
*Undergraduates:* 14,510 (2,500)
*Postgraduates:* 1,550 (2,400)
*Mature students:* 36.2%
*Overseas students:* 18.3%
*Applications per place:* 6.1
*From state sector schools:* 96%
*From working class homes:* 36%

**Teaching quality assessments**
*1993–95 Rated excellent:* none.
*From 1995 (top score 24):* **23** philosophy. **22** American studies; business; drama, dance and cinematics; education; health subjects; history of art; nursing; politics. **21** art and design; economics; psychology. **20** mathematics. **19** electrical and electronic engineering; modern languages; sociology.

## Overview

Middlesex has been reassessing its priorities. After two years of serious decline in the number of applications, another drop of almost 4 per cent when the official deadline passed for courses beginning in 2002 represented near-stability. The university has reorganised its schools, largely admitting defeat on engineering (although its product design courses will continue), and focusing instead on its strengths in business, computing and the arts.

Other areas of the university will maintain the successful mixture of community involvement and international operations. There are more than 20,000 students, including part-timers, and a growing network of partner colleges at home and abroad. Half of the full-timers come from London, but one in five is from overseas. The university's long-standing commitment to Europe sees more than 2,000 students coming from the Continent and a healthy flow of British students taking advantage of the exchange programmes. All undergraduates are encouraged to take a language option as part of their modular degrees.

The highly flexible course system allows students to start many courses in February if they prefer not to wait until autumn, and offers the option of an extra five-week session in July and August to try out new subjects or add to their credits. The start of the academic year has been brought forward to early September to squeeze in a full semester before Christmas. Nine out of ten students take vocational courses, many at postgraduate or sub-degree level. Business is the biggest subject area, but almost a quarter of the undergraduates are on multidisciplinary programmes. More than half are over 21 on entry.

Over 95 per cent of the students are from state schools and 36 per cent from working-class homes, but the university is still heavily engaged in access initiatives. About 100 scholarships are available for academic, sporting or community achievement, the fund boosted by £31,000 of sponsorship when the vice-chancellor ran the London Marathon.

The university lists six 'main campuses' dotted around London's North Circular Road, but smaller sites practically double that total. Locations include a picturesque country estate at Trent Park, an innovative warehouse conversion and a house in Hampstead that was once home to the ballerina Anna Pavlova. There is also an outpost in Bedford specialising in dance. Many students have to travel between sites for lectures and seminars.

In the long term, the university plans to concentrate its activities on three sites, with a new main campus for 10,000 students at Tottenham Hale alongside the River Lea. Hendon, Trent Park and the nearby Cat Hill arts site would remain, with only a specialist health campus beyond these confines. Middlesex already has a health partnership with University College London, with a joint campus at the Archway campus, in north London.

Teaching ratings have improved considerably after an unspectacular start, with philosophy recently achieving the university's best score. The subject also registered one of Middlesex's two grade 5 assessments for research, denoting nationally outstanding work and some of international excellence. History of art was the other top scorer. The university has also won three Queen's Anniversary Prizes for innovation – the latest for its flood research.

The number of residential places is planned to double in the next few years from the current 2,400 beds. Sports facilities are also scheduled to improve, with a new speed and conditioning centre planned and the proposed national athletics stadium on the university's doorstep.

## Accommodation

Number of places and costs refer to 2002–03

*University-provided places:* 2,400

*Percentage catered:* 0%

*Costs for catered accommodation:* n/a

*Costs for self-catered accommodation:* £61.60–£73.92 a week.

*Policy for first-year students:* full-year international students have priority, followed by the youngest UK and EU students coming from the furthest distance when Middlesex is their first choice. Students living within a 75-mile radius of their base campus are less likely to be accommodated.

*Policy for international students:* all new full-year international students are guaranteed a room in halls provided the Accommodation Office receives a completed registration form for the start of the academic year and £200 caution deposit by the end of August.

*Contact for further information:* Accomm@mdx.ac.uk

# Napier University

Times ranking: 66 (2002 ranking: =69)

**Founded:** University status 1992, formerly
Napier Polytechnic of Edinburgh

**Contact details**
*Address:* 10 Colinton Road,
Edinburgh EH10 5DT
*Tel:* 0500 35 35 70
*Website:* www.napier.ac.uk
*e-mail:* info@napier.ac.uk

**The Times rankings**
*Teaching assessment:* =79 (20.2)
*Research assessment:* =82 (2.3)
*Entry standards:* =95 (11.8)
*Student–staff ratio:* 62 (17.7)
*Library/IT spend/student:* 62 (£426)
*Facilities spend/student:* 67 (£143)
*Firsts and 2:1s:* 42 (58.6%)
*Work and further study:* =12 (96.9%)
*Expected completion rate:* =46 (87%)

**Students**
*Undergraduates:* 7,360 (1,570)
*Postgraduates:* 820 (820)
*Mature students:* 36.2%
*Overseas students:* 10.4%
*Applications per place:* 3.5
*From state sector schools:* 90%
*From working class homes:* 28%

**Teaching quality assessments**
*1993–95 Rated Excellent:* none.
*1993–97 Rated Highly Satisfactory:*
building; cellular biology; chemistry; civil
engineering; hospitality studies; mass
communications; mathematics; organismal
biology; statistics.
*From 1998 (top score 24):* **19** European
languages.
*2001 Rated Commendable:* accountancy
and economics; law.

## Overview

Napier was Scotland's first and largest polytechnic. Now a university of 13,000 students, 3,000 of whom are part-timers, it has declared an ambition to become a 'world-class modern university'. It has been developing the facilities to make that possible, but has had difficulty convincing potential students. Applications for courses starting in 2002 shot up by more than 20 per cent, in common with other Scottish universities, but they had declined in the previous two years.

A bizarre wrangle over drop-out rates seems to have been partly responsible. The funding council's first performance indicators, published in 1999, showed one in three undergraduates leaving without qualifications – the second worst rate in Britain. The university claimed that the true rate was only half the following year's estimate and the latest projection is for only 9 per cent to drop out – fewer than at neighbouring Edinburgh University and less than half the 'benchmark' figure, which takes account of the subject mix. Instead, 17 per cent are said to be destined for a different qualification to the one they expected, three times as many as at any other university in Scotland.

Ironically, Napier has been held up as a model to other universities trying to reduce wastage rates. It runs 'diagnostic tests' to identify students at risk of dropping out before their second year and follow-up studies have led to changes in the way that courses are run. A scholarship scheme, funded from a credit card for alumni, helps to address financial difficulties.

Two new libraries, a purpose-built music centre and a £2.5 million refurbishment of the science laboratories have underlined Napier's ambitions, and now £43 million is earmarked for a new business school and an arts and social science building, both of which are due to open in 2003. The two new projects follow a 500-seat computer centre on the main campus, completed in 2001.

The university is named after John Napier, the inventor of logarithms. The tower where he was born still sits among the concrete blocks of the Merchiston site, in the student district of Edinburgh. The other main sites are Sighthill, a 1960s development in the west of the city, and nearby Craiglockhart, a one-time military hospital, where the business school is being built. It will feature a glass atrium housing a cyber café and two spherical lecture theatres with a total of 600 seats.

The arts building will be at the newest of Napier's campuses, at Craighouse, in the south of Edinburgh. The futuristic building will feature a combined cinema, concert hall and theatre – dubbed the mediadrome – which will open in the summer onto a terraced roof space covered with artificial turf. A regular university bus service links the main sites, but there are several more teaching outposts where lectures may be scheduled.

Furthest afield is the former Lothian College of Health Studies and the Scottish Borders College of Nursing, whose incorporation gave the university the largest nursing and midwifery facility north of the border. Yet Napier failed to register a single excellent rating before the Scottish system of assessing teaching quality completed its first round of ratings in 1998, despite a string of Highly Satisfactory grades.

The university has its roots as a college of science and technology, which merged with a college of commerce, and these subjects remain the biggest recruiters. The business school is the largest in Scotland. Most of the avowedly vocational courses include a work placement, and the close relationship with industry and commerce helps to produce consistently good graduate employment figures. The modular course system covers independent study and allows movement between courses at all levels. It has also allowed Napier to introduce the option of starting courses in February, rather than September.

The dispersed nature of the university does nothing for the social scene. Despite improvements, some students find life too quiet in the evenings and at weekends.

## Accommodation
Number of places and costs refer to 2001–02

*University-provided places:* 929

*Percentage catered:* 0%

*Costs for catered accommodation:* n/a

*Costs for self-catered accommodation:* £59–£60 a week.

*Policy for first-year students:* a guarantee of a place is given to first years if an application is received before the end of August. They must live 30 miles outside of Edinburgh.

*Policy for international students:* as far as possible, all requests are met if an application is received before the end of August.

*Contact for further information:* accommodation@napier.ac.uk

# University of Newcastle

Times ranking: 16 (2002 ranking: 13)

**Founded:** 1834 (as part of Durham University), Royal charter 1963

**Contact details**
*Address:* Kensington Terrace, Newcastle upon Tyne NE1 7RU
*Tel:* 0191 222 5594
*Website:* www.ncl.ac.uk
*e-mail:* admissions-enquiries@ncl.ac.uk

**The Times rankings**
*Teaching assessment:* =19 (21.6)
*Research assessment:* =31 (5.2)
*Entry standards:* =21 (23.0)
*Student–staff ratio:* =16 (13.3)
*Library/IT spend/student:* 7 (£845)
*Facilities spend/student:* 10 (£263)
*Firsts and 2:1s:* 20 (70.2%)
*Work and further study:* 52 (94.3%)
*Expected completion rate:* =31 (89%)

**Students**
*Undergraduates:* 10.070 (2,780)
*Postgraduates:* 2,020 (2,070)
*Mature students:* 9.6%
*Overseas students:* 7.7%
*Applications per place:* 4.8
*From state sector schools:* 67%
*From working class homes:* 16%

**Teaching quality assessments**
*1993–95 Rated Excellent:* architecture; English; geology; social policy.
*From 1995 (top score 24):* **24** anatomy and physiology; health subjects; medicine; molecular biosciences; pharmacology and pharmacy; psychology. **23** dentistry; economics; mathematics; politics. **22** agriculture; classics and ancient history; education; linguistics; organismal biosciences; modern languages; theology. **21** archaeology; chemical engineering; electrical and electronic engineering; physics; town planning. **20** art and design; civil engineering; marine technology.

## Overview

A string of outstanding teaching assessments ensured that there is little separating Newcastle and its parent university of Durham as the leading university in the North East of England in *The Times* table, although recent results have slipped slightly. Originally a medical school, its excellence in that area was confirmed by maximum points for teaching in medicine, anatomy and physiology, pharmacology and pharmacy, reviewed jointly with molecular biosciences, psychology and its department of speech. Dentistry only just missed out on the same score. The school's reputation has been cemented with its selection as a national centre to disseminate best teaching practice in medicine.

The medical school is growing yet larger in a partnership with Durham, with trainees based at Durham's Stockton campus. Other recent academic developments include Britain's first degree in folk and traditional music, complementing a course in pop and contemporary music, and a four-year business and accounting degree (in conjunction with PricewaterhouseCoopers, which provides a fast-track to professional qualifications.

Buoyed by the popularity of the city among young people, the university grew dramatically in the 1990s, and growth resumed in 2001 after several years of restraint. A 17 per cent increase in applications for courses starting in 2002 will ensure that continues. As well as the normal range of subjects for a traditional university, Newcastle has a number of unusual features, such as a fine art degree which attracts up to 15 applicants per place. It also has a long-standing reputation for agriculture, which recorded good scores for both teaching and research with the benefit of two farms in Northumberland.

Research grades improved in the latest assessments, with biological sciences, clinical laboratory sciences, music and psychology all rated internationally outstanding. Six out of ten academics entered for the exercise were in departments placed in the top two categories.

The campus is spacious and varied, occupying 45 acres close to the main shopping area, civic centre, Northumbria University and Newcastle United's ground, which is overlooked by one of the halls of residence. Half the buildings date from the 1960s onwards. The university also boasts a theatre, an art gallery and three museums.

Although not on the same scale as Durham's intake, Newcastle has become a particular favourite with independent schools, whose applicants now take a third of the places. The university has stepped up its contacts with local state schools in an attempt to broaden its intake. Official performance indicators also reveal a healthy 93 per cent completion rate – better than anticipated, given the subject mix. One student in five is a postgraduate and the same proportion of those taking first degrees take dual or combined honours.

Few students regret choosing Newcastle for a degree, even if the growing number of southerners can find the winter temperatures a shock. The city's nightlife is legendary – eighth best in the world, according to one survey – and the university topped a student poll based on computer facilities and student services, as well as the social scene. The cost of living is reasonable and town–gown relations better than in many cities.

Sport is a particular concern, Newcastle claiming to be one of the top ten universities both in terms of performance and facilities. There are two sports centres on the main university site, with refurbished fitness suites, massage clinics and all the normal indoor services. Some outdoor pitches are conveniently placed, but the main ground is ten miles out of the city, where the university has its own 18–hole golf course. Over £30,000 of sports bursaries are awarded annually to elite athletes.

## Accommodation

Number of places and costs refer to 2002–03

*University-provided places:* 4,140

*Percentage catered:* 37.5%

*Costs for catered accommodation:* £66.36–£90.79 (en-suite) a week.

*Costs for self-catered accommodation:* £41.93–£74.20 (en-suite) a week.

*Policy for first-year students:* a student is guaranteed a room in university-managed accommodation if an offer of a place has been firmly accepted and an application has been returned on time. This guarantee also applies to students who live locally.

*Policy for international students:* the above guarantee applies to international undergraduates.

*Contact for further information:* accommodation-enquiries@ncl.ac.uk

# Newport, University of Wales College (UWCN)

**Times ranking:** 96

**Founded:** 1975 as Gwent College of Higher Education; admitted to the University of Wales 1996

**Contact details**
*Address:* Caerleon Campus, Newport, South Wales NP18 3YG
*Tel:* 01633 432432
*Website:* www.newport.ac.uk
*e-mail:* uic@newport.ac.uk

**The Times rankings**
*Teaching assessment:* =98 (19.5)
*Research assessment:* =61 (3.0)
*Entry standards:* 89 (12.6)
*Student–staff ratio:* 99 (28.5)
*Library/IT spend/student:* =94 (£331)
*Facilities spend/student:* 94 (£84)
*Firsts and 2:1s:* 62 (50.5%)
*Work and further study:* =77 (92.2%)
*Expected completion rate:* =83 (80%)

**Students**
*Undergraduates:* 2,550 (3,720)
*Postgraduates:* 270 (1.070)
*Mature students:* 35.7%
*Overseas students:* 7.9%
*Applications per place:* 3.1
*From state sector schools:* 99%
*From working class homes:* 37%

**Teaching quality assessments**
*1993–95 Rated Excellent:* none.

## Overview

University of Wales College, Newport (UWCN) appears in the guide for the first time this year, as a full member of the University of Wales and Universities UK, at a time when it is enjoying unprecedented popularity. Applications have soared by 23 per cent in two years, and the demand for postgraduate places are up by more than half. Art, media and design, which achieved a grade 5 rating for research in the latest assessments, has been the main attraction, but education, humanities and computing have also recruited well.

Other research and teaching ratings leave much to be desired, but both students and employers appear enthusiastic about UWCN. In the annual student survey, 92 per cent declared themselves very satisfied. An equivalent poll of local employers produced even higher levels of satisfaction.

Just one academic in ten was entered for the latest research assessment exercise, the lowest proportion in the university system. As a result, only one university finished below UWCN for average grades per member of staff. No teaching quality assessments have taken place since 1996, but the eight subjects scrutinised before then were all rated Satisfactory, rather than Excellent. In separate assessments by Estyn, the Welsh schools inspectorate, however, the teacher-training courses were commended for their excellence.

The University College, which was previously Gwent College of Higher Education, now has 9,000 students from 44 different countries. There were merger discussions with Lampeter, University of Wales in 2001, but the two institutions agreed to remain independent. Newport may now join a looser 'cluster' of institutions in South Wales.

Virtually all the full-time undergraduates come from state schools and there is a higher proportion from working-class homes than at any other university institution in Wales. However, the drop-out rate of 25 per cent is higher than the 'benchmark' set according to the subject mix. UWCN operates a number of access schemes, including one offering students at local schools and colleges guaranteed places if they fulfil certain criteria.

The college is actively involved with a range of local businesses. It was rated the number one university in Wales for enterprise education by the Knowledge Exploitation Fund. Among its innovations is the Corus to Campus project for redundant steelworkers (previously employed by Corus), and it is also a leading player in the Community University of the Valleys. The college also hosts the International Film School Wales.

There are two campuses, the smaller of which overlooks Newport, a ten-minute walk away, and focuses on engineering and computing, business and professional studies. The Caerleon campus is further out, with impressive views, and caters for humanities, science, education and art, media and design. It also contains the student village of 660 self-catered study bedrooms. Free buses link the two sites.

A new sports centre at Caerleon has transformed facilities that previously compared unfavourably with those of other universities. The town of Newport has established a reputation for producing successful rock bands, but students in search of serious cultural or clubbing activity gravitate to nearby Cardiff.

## Accommodation

Number of places and costs refer to 2002–03

*University-provided places:* 660

*Percentage catered:* 0%

*Costs for catered accommodation:* n/a

*Costs for self-catered accommodation:* £44.50 (standard), £53 (en-suite) a week.

*Policy for first-year students:* accommoation guaranteed until 6 September.

*Policy for international students:* same as above.

*Contact for further information:* accommodation@newport.ac.uk

# University of North London

**Times ranking:** 97 (2002 ranking: 93)

**Founded:** University status 1992, formerly Polytechnic of North London

**Contact details**
*Address:* 166–220 Holloway Road, London N7 8DB
*Tel:* 020 7753 3355
*Website:* www.unl.ac.uk
*e-mail:* admissions@unl.ac.uk

**The Times rankings**
*Teaching assessment:* =93 (19.9)
*Research assessment:* =82 (2.3)
*Entry standards:* 99 (11.3)
*Student–staff ratio:* 97 (22.8)
*Library/IT spend/student:* =80 (£384)
*Facilities spend/student:* 46 (£167)
*Firsts and 2:1s:* 94 (42.3%)
*Work and further study:* =70 (92.9%)
*Expected completion rate:* 101 (69%)

**Students**
*Undergraduates:* 8,960 (3,300)
*Postgraduates:* 790 (1,530)
*Mature students:* 47.4%
*Overseas students:* 17.4%
*Applications per place:* 7
*From state sector schools:* 96%
*From working class homes:* 41%

**Teaching quality assessments**
*1993–95 Rated Excellent:* English.
*From 1995 (top score 24):* **24** business and management. **22** art and design; drama and cinematics; electrical and electronic engineering; philosophy.
**21** health studies; hospitality; mathematics; nursing; politics.
**20** education; modern languages. **19** food science; materials technology; psychology.
**18** library and information management; molecular biosciences; organismal biosciences. **17** media studies.

## Overview

If merger negotiations with London Guildhall run their course, North London students will find themselves at London Metropolitan University by the time the academic year begins in 2003. Applications for courses beginning in 2002 dropped by 13 per cent and, although the university insists that funding problems have not forced it into the arrangement, the larger institution should be more secure. The new university will have 25,000 students and a budget of £110 million.

In recent years, North London has become known for spreading higher education into ethnic communities otherwise little seen in the university system. More than a third of the students are Afro-Caribbean and the proportion of mature students is the highest in Britain. The university's mission statement commits it to widening opportunities further, as well as expanding international and business links. A high proportion enter through clearing, and barely half are selected on A levels, which average less than three Ds. Almost a quarter of the students are on sub-degree or professional courses.

Quality also features in the mission statement, however, and most of the recent teaching ratings have been encouraging. Business and management, by far the university's biggest subject area, achieved its first perfect score in 2001, but library and information management managed only 18 out of 24. A series of other subjects, including philosophy, art, drama and electronic engineering all scored well. Sandwich and part-time courses in electronic engineering are particularly highly rated, as is the health studies portfolio. American studies was the only subject to make the top three grades in the latest research assessment exercise, although, in contrast to 1996, none of the 17 entries finished in the bottom two categories.

All undergraduates receive information technology training, as part of 'capability curriculum' designed to enhance future employment prospects. Other elements of the curriculum include communication skills and teamworking. Students are also encouraged to take a language option from the menu of modular courses. Many programmes have been designed with the ubiquitous mature student in mind, but they have not prevented the drop-out rate reaching one in three – considerably worse than expected for the intake and among the highest in the country.

Second and third-year students are offered a new assessed and accredited work placement programme as one module of their course. It can be taken during term-time or in a summer vacation. The placement, which may be abroad, has to be relevant to the degree or to the student's career plans. Longer work experience is arranged as sandwich placements, spending a year in industry or commerce between the second and third years of a course. A career planning and personal development module is available in the first year of degree courses.

The university has been improving its facilities, which had become crowded and run-down in parts after continuous expansion. Having added to teaching space and student services, as well as opening a new learning resources centre, North London has built a new tower to transform the computing services and provide a new focal point for the university. The new building, completed in January 2000, has 4,000 square metres of space and 700 open-access computers. A new graduate school, designed by Daniel Libeskind, is planned for 2003.

The five sites are concentrated around the Holloway Road which caters well for students. The mixture of ages and cultures seems to produce a livelier social scene than at most similar universities, but the cost of living is high. There are fewer than 900 residential places but, such is the size of the local intake, first years who accept their offers early are guaranteed accommodation.

## Accommodation
Number of places and costs refer to 2001–02

*University-provided places:* 871

*Percentage catered:* 25%

*Costs for catered accommodation:* £83 a week (5 evening meals).

*Costs for self-catered accommodation:* £71 a week.

*Policy for first-year students:* an offer is guaranteed for first years who live more than 25 miles away, have accepted either a conditional or unconditional offer, and have completed and returned an application by mid August.

*Policy for international students:* the guarantee stated above applies. Once the deadline for the guarantee has passed international students will be considered a priority.

*Contact for further information:* Accommodation@unl.ac.uk

# University of Northumbria at Newcastle

Times ranking: =56 (2002 ranking: 54)

**Founded:** Royal charter 1992, formerly Newcastle Polytechnic

**Contact details**
*Address:* Ellison Terrace,
Newcastle upon Tyne NE1 8ST
*Tel:* 0191 227 4777
*Website:* www.unn.ac.uk
*e-mail:* rg.admissons@unn.ac.uk

**The Times rankings**
*Teaching assessment:* =27 (21.4)
*Research assessment:* =82 (2.3)
*Entry standards:* 59 (16.4)
*Student–staff ratio:* 66 (18.1)
*Library/IT spend/student:* 85 (£380)
*Facilities spend/student:* =56 (£152)
*Firsts and 2:1s:* 69 (49.5%)
*Work and further study:* =70 (92.9%)
*Expected completion rate:* =31 (89%)

**Students**
*Undergraduates:* 13,720 (4,470)
*Postgraduates:* 1,010 (2,360)
*Mature students:* 22.8%
*Overseas students:* 9.8%
*Applications per place:* 4.9
*From state sector schools:* 90%
*From working class homes:* 29%

**Teaching quality assessments**
*1993–95 Rated Excellent:* English; law.
*From 1995 (top score 24):* **24** education; nursing. **23** health subjects; modern languages; physics . **22** art and design; building; business and management; drama, dance and cinematics; economics; electrical and electronic engineering; land and property management; librarianship and information management; physics; politics; psychology. **21** history of art; hospitality; mathematics; molecular biosciences; town planning. **20** sociology.

## Overview

Always among the leading new universities in *The Times* table, Northumbria is also one of the largest, with more than 20,000 students, including the many part-timers. The former polytechnic has benefited from Newcastle's reputation as an exciting student city, but it remains predominantly a local institution. More than half the students are from the north of England, many coming from Tyneside itself and enrolling as mature students.

Entry grades for those with A levels are among the highest in the new universities, but more than half of the students are admitted with other qualifications or on the strength of relevant work experience. Free one-day taster courses run between January and July to give local people an idea of what a university course would be like. The projected drop-out rate of 14 per cent is among the best in the new universities, despite meeting the funding council's benchmarks for widening participation in higher education. University bursaries of £1,000 are available for young students whose parents are on state benefits but who do not qualify for the Government's Opportunity Bursaries.

The last big leap in numbers came with the incorporation of a large college of health studies in 1995. Health subjects are now second only to business studies in terms of student numbers and have been highly successful in teaching assessments: nursing achieved Northumbria's first maximum score and health subjects 23 points out of 24. Education also managed maximum points in 2001, after achieving mixed results in the Teacher Training Agency's performance indicators, its primary school training courses faring much better than those for secondary teachers.

The university has also been expanding geographically, with two campuses for business studies established well away from Newcastle during the 1990s. One in Carlisle has 500 students and may eventually have twice as many; the other, 15 miles north of Newcastle at Longhirst, is for postgraduates and conference delegates. There is also a network of feeder colleges encouraging applications from adults without traditional academic qualifications.

The main campus, with its mainly modern buildings, is just the other side of the civic centre from Newcastle University. The majority of subjects are based there, but health, education and social work are on the Coach Lane campus on the outskirts of the city. An £18 million programme to upgrade its facilities has been completed, including new sports facilities and a learning resource centre.

Northumbria's best-known feature is its fashion school, although modern languages scored well in the teaching quality assessment. Research ratings improved in 2001 but still three subject areas finished in the last category but one. Only psychology and art and design reached the top three grades. Most degrees are available as sandwich courses, with placements of up to a year in business or industry. Law and business studies have the highest entrance requirements.

The university's otherwise smooth progress was interrupted in 2000 first by financial difficulties and then by the resignation of Professor Gilbert Smith, the vice-chancellor, who blamed unspecified differences with the board of governors over their vision for the university. Up to 130 jobs are going in order to save £3.6 million, and stave off deficits which the university said would endanger academic quality.

About 90 per cent of first years from outside the area live in university accommodation. There is a shortfall of about 450 places, but almost 1,000 more beds are on the way in the next stage of the university's building programme.

## Accommodation
Number of places and costs refer to 2002–03

*University-provided places:* 3,100 (includes Carlisle/Longhirst)

*Percentage catered:* 16%

*Costs for catered accommodation:* £57.75 (5 meals, part-board); £74.20 (full board) a week.

*Costs for self-catered accommodation:* £37.00–£56, most commonly £49–£51 a week; £67 a week (en-suite).

*Policy for first-year students:* main Newcastle campus gives priority to non-local first years. Local students (living within 8–10 miles) may take vacant rooms once term has begun. Satellite campuses: no restrictions.

*Policy for international students:* full-year first years can be guaranteed accommodation if application received in good time.

*Contact for further information:* rc.accommodation@unn.ac.uk

# University of Nottingham

Times ranking: 9 (2002 ranking: 11)

**Founded:** 1881, Royal charter 1948

**Contact details**
*Address:* University Park,
Nottingham NG7 2RD
*Tel:* 0115 951 5151
*Website:* www.nottingham.ac.uk
*e-mail:* undergraduate-enquiries@
nottingham.ac.uk

**The Times rankings**
*Teaching assessment:* =13 (21.7)
*Research assessment:* =26 (5.3)
*Entry standards:* 8 (26.2)
*Student–staff ratio:* =24 (14.1)
*Library/IT spend/student:* 11 (£740)
*Facilities spend/student:* 21 (£218)
*Firsts and 2:1s:* 10 (80.1%)
*Work and further study:* =12 (96.6%)
*Expected completion rate:* =4 (95%)

**Students**
*Undergraduates:* 13,440 (4,100)
*Postgraduates:* 2,630 (3,360)
*Mature students:* 6.6%
*Overseas students:* 12%
*Applications per place:* 8.8
*From state sector schools:* 71%
*From working class homes:* 15%

**Teaching quality assessments**
*1993–95 Rated Excellent:* architecture;
business and management; chemistry;
English; geography; law; mechanical
engineering; music.
*From 1995 (top score 24):* **24** classics and
ancient history; economics; manufacturing
engineering; politics; psychology.
**23** agriculture; environmental science,
food science; history of art; mathematics;
molecular biosciences; organismal
biosciences; pharmacy; physics; theology;
town planning. **22** American studies;
anatomy and physiology; civil engineering;
education; electrical and electronic
engineering; German; nursing; philosophy.
**21** archaeology; chemical engineering;
health subjects; materials technology;
medicine; sociology. **19** Russian.
**17** Iberian languages. **16** French.

## Overview

Nottingham became officially the most popular university in Britain in 2002, with 46,000 applicants for 4,500 places. For many years it has been among the institutions with the stiffest competition for each place, but a striking new campus and extra courses have made it even more fashionable. The 17 per cent increase in applications was among the biggest in England.

The university already boasted one of the most attractive campuses in Britain, and has been rising up the pecking order of higher education. In less than 20 years, it has gone from being a solid civic university to a prime alternative to Oxbridge. Constantly among the top dozen universities in *The Times* table, it seldom stands still. A £30 million fundraising target was hit a year ahead of schedule and a series of projects are waiting to eat up the money.

Once in, the highly qualified students tend to stay the course – the drop-out rate is bettered only by Oxford and Cambridge. But the university is trying to broaden an intake which has more independent school students and fewer from working-class homes than the national average for the subjects offered. There is a well-established summer school for state school teenagers and a new bursary scheme for Nottinghamshire students with no history of higher education in their families.

The 30-acre Jubilee campus, which cost £50 million, is barely a mile away from the original parkland site. Futuristic buildings clustered around an artificial lake house the schools of management and finance, computer science and education. The campus also hosts the Government's College of Leadership for school managers, as well as adding 750 residential places. There is space for further development if the university continues to grow, as planned.

Nottingham describes itself as a 'research-led' university. Its £80 million income from research contracts in 2001 placed it among the top four universities and there are 5,000 postgraduates. However, the latest assessments were disappointing by the university's high standards, with only five subjects rated internationally outstanding, none of them from science, engineering or medicine. The top performers were American studies, German, Iberian languages, music and theology, with 26 more subjects on the next assessment grade.

Most teaching assessments have been excellent, with classics, economics and politics joining psychology and manufacturing engineering on perfect scores in 2001. Only one of the last nine assessments produced less than 22 points out of 24, and that by a single point. Nottingham is second only to Cambridge in the number of subjects rated at this level.

Nottingham has long-standing links with the Far East, which provides the majority of its 2,000 overseas students, and has even chosen a Chinese physicist, Professor Fujia Yang, as its chancellor. The university has a campus in Malaysia, the only foreign university to be permitted to establish one, and is an active participant in the Universitas 21 global grouping of universities, which is developing shared teaching and research, as well as offering exchange programmes.

More controversially, the university accepted £3.8 million from British American Tobacco for the study of corporate responsibility, prompting the Cancer Research Campaign to withdraw support for the medical school. As the leading advocate of 'top-up' fees, Sir Colin Campbell, the vice-chancellor, had already shown that he would not shy away from controversy to ensure that Nottingham could compete internationally.

Both main campuses are within three miles of the centre of the city, with a good selection of student-friendly clubs. However, halls of residence and the students' union tend to be the centre of social life for students in both locations. Sports facilities are excellent and residential accommodation plentiful.

### Accommodation

Number of places and costs refer to 2001–02

*University-provided places:* 5,600

*Percentage catered:* 75%

*Costs for catered accommodation:* £20.26 (shared bedroom) to £28.94 (en-suite) for a 31-week contract.

*Costs for self-catered accommodation:* £18.00–£20.86 (plus en-suite supplement where applicable) for a 44-week contract.

*Policy for first-year students:* students who firmly accept a place at Nottingham via UCAS by the correct deadline are guaranteed accommodation if they return their preference form by 1 August.

*Policy for international students:* same guarantee but are given priority of places available after guarantees are sorted.

*Contact for further information:* www.nottingham.ac.uk

# Nottingham Trent University

**Times ranking:** 55 (2002 ranking: 59)

**Founded:** University status 1992, formerly Nottingham (originally Trent) Polytechnic

**Contact details**
*Address:* Burton Street,
Nottingham NG1 4BU
*Tel:* 0115 941 8418
*Website:* www.ntu.ac.uk
*e-mail:* marketing@ntu.ac.uk

**The Times rankings**
*Teaching assessment:* =74 (20.4)
*Research assessment:* =67 (2.8)
*Entry standards:* 56 (17.3)
*Student–staff ratio:* 59 (17.4)
*Library/IT spend/student:* =66 (£419)
*Facilities spend/student:* 23 (£212)
*Firsts and 2:1s:* =74 (48.6%)
*Work and further study:* 6 (97.8%)
*Expected completion rate:* =46 (87%)

**Students**
*Undergraduates:* 14,640 (3,180)
*Postgraduates:* 880 (2,280)
*Mature students:* 12.6%
*Overseas students:* 4.9%
*Applications per place:* 5.3
*From state sector schools:* 91%
*From working class homes:* 26%

**Teaching quality assessments**
*1993–95 Rated Excellent:* business and management; chemistry.
*From 1995 (top score 24):* **24** molecular biosciences; organismal biosciences; physics. **23** health subjects; politics. **22** art and design; building; economics; education; psychology; sports science. **21** mathematics and statistics; media studies. **20** civil engineering; electrical and electronic engineering; land management; materials technology. **19** sociology. **17** modern languages.

## Overview

An ambitious research programme was amply rewarded in the latest assessments, when Nottingham Trent had four subjects judged nationally outstanding, with much of their work considered internationally excellent. The achievements of drama, dance and the performing arts, English, media studies and health subjects was matched by only two other new universities.

Always regarded as one of the leading polytechnics, Nottingham Trent is demonstrating high quality in an unusually wide range of disciplines for a new university. Best known for fashion and other creative arts, which have the largest number of students, it has recorded maximum scores in teaching assessments for physics and biosciences. The law school is one of Britain's largest, offering legal practice courses for both solicitors and barristers, and there is even a prize-winning herd of Jersey cows on a new campus devoted to land-based studies.

The university is particularly proud of the highest entry grades of any new university and a graduate employment record in the first official statistics which saw 98.7 per cent of leavers in work or further study within six months. The drop-out rate, at 16 per cent, is among the better records among the former polytechnics, although the intake is as diverse as most. More than a quarter of the undergraduates come from working class homes and nine out of ten attended state schools or colleges.

An annual opinion survey shows that most of the students are satisfied. These surveys are part of a systematic attempt to involve students in decision-making. Helped by the popularity of Nottingham as a student centre, it grew by a third in five years in the 1990s, and was one of the few new universities to see applications increase for courses beginning in 2002.

Nottingham Trent is among the biggest of the new universities, with more than 23,000 students, including a large contingent of part-timers. The extensive main city site originally housed Nottingham University, but now boasts a mixture of Victorian and modern buildings. Science, mathematics and the humanities are five miles away on the Clifton campus, with teacher education in a new £4 million block. The latest addition to the estate came from a merger with Brackenhurst College, an agricultural college 14 miles from Nottingham. As well as a farm, the new campus has an equestrian centre with a purpose-built indoor riding area.

Improvements to the original campuses have seen a new teacher training block at Clifton and a £2.2 million renovation of the Waveley building, the Victorian headquarters of art and design. The students' union had already had a £3 million upgrade. Health subjects will benefit from BASF's gift of a large research facility, which is said to be the largest corporate donation at any new university.

The largely vocational courses are part of a modular system which gives every student training in information technology, as well as the opportunity to learn a language. A high proportion of students take sandwich degrees, helping Nottingham Trent to a consistently good employment record for both undergraduates and postgraduates.

The university was responsible for the largest programme in the first tranche of two-year foundation degrees, covering 14 subject areas. They ranged from garden design and horse management to more conventional subjects like physics and chemistry. Teaching ratings have been variable, but show recent improvement with politics scoring 23 and education and sports science scoring 22 points out of 24 in 2001.

The student body is diverse, with large numbers of mature and overseas students. The university's residential stock has been increasing, but still is not sufficient to accommodate all first years. Social life varies between campuses, but all have access to the city's lively cultural and clubbing scene. A late-night bus service links the main campuses.

## Accommodation
Number of places and costs refer to 2002–03

*University-provided places:* 3,000

*Percentage catered:* 0%

*Costs for catered accommodation:* n/a

*Costs for self-catered accommodation:* £58.03–£68.77 for a 40 or 48-week contract.

*Policy for first-year students:* students must have unconditional offer before they can apply. Allocation is primarily in date order. Students living within 25-mile radius are not initially offered university accommodation.

*Policy for international students:* international students given as much priority as possible.

*Contact for further information:* www.ntu.ac.uk/sas

# University of Oxford

Times ranking: 1 (2002 ranking: 2)

**Founded:** 1096

**Contact details**
*Address:* University Offices,
Wellington Square, Oxford OX1 2JD
*Tel:* 01865 270207
*Website:* www.ox.ac.uk
*e-mail:* undergraduate.admissions@
admin.ox.ac.uk

**The Times rankings**
*Teaching assessment:* 4 (22.3)
*Research assessment:* 2 (6.5)
*Entry standards:* 2 (29.5)
*Student–staff ratio:* 11 (12.2)
*Library/IT spend/student:* 1 (£1,417)
*Facilities spend/student:* 39 (£184)
*Firsts and 2:1s:* 5 (84.9%)
*Work and further study:* =36 (95.2%)
*Expected completion rate:* =2 (96%)

**Students**
*Undergraduates:* 11,780 (3,820)
*Postgraduates:* 4,480 (1,590)
*Mature students:* 2.4%
*Overseas students:* 9.5%
*Applications per place:* 3.1
*From state sector schools:* 51%
*From working class homes:* 9%

**Teaching quality assessments**
*1993–95 Rated Excellent:* anthropology;
chemistry; computer science; English;
geography; geology; history; law; social
work.
*From 1995 (top score 24):* **24** art and
design; classics and ancient history;
molecular biosciences; organismal
biosciences; philosophy; politics;
psychology. **23** economics; general
engineering; materials technology; physics.
**22** archaeology; East and South Asian
studies; mathematics; Middle
Eastern and African studies. **21** anatomy
and physiology; linguistics; medicine;
modern languages.

## Overview

After eight years of frustration, Oxford has finally toppled Cambridge from top place in *The Times* League Table, albeit by the narrowest of margins. The accolade follows a turnaround in Oxford's fortunes after the debilitating controversy over the rejection of Laura Spence, from a Tyneside comprehensive. Quality assessments have continued to be impressive and the university is celebarating an 18 per cent increase in applications for courses starting in 2002.

The university countered every accusation of elitism, from Gordon Brown's highly-publicised assault onwards, but its critics were not easy to convince. The recovery probably has more to do with the increased efforts to get the message through to teenagers that Oxford is open to all who can meet the exacting entrance requirements. Long-standing student visits to comprehensive schools have been supplemented by summer schools, recruitment fairs and colleges' own initiatives. There are even plans for regional centres, partly funded from £2 million of Government money.

Oxford briefly slipped to third place in our table, partly because of comparatively low central spending on facilities such as careers and sport. The college structure, which produces an enviable student environment, acted as a handicap. However, agreement has now been reached with the Higher Education Statistics Agency on a fairer reflection of spending and this, together with a new scoring system that makes allowance for the mix of subjects in each university, has had a dramatic effect.

Oxford is the oldest and probably the most famous university in the English-speaking world, and it remains almost inseparable from Cambridge in terms of overall quality. Like Cambridge, it attracts world-class academics and takes its share of the brightest students. The pair are head and shoulders above the other non-specialist universities in *The Times* ranking and in the view of most experts.

For all the university's efforts to shed its socially elitist image, funding council figures still show almost half of Oxford's students coming from independent schools – the largest proportion at any university. Only 9 per cent come from working-class homes, but £2,000 bursaries for all undergraduates who are eligible for full fees may help to broaden the mix a little.

Selection is in the hands of the 30 undergraduate colleges, which vary considerably in their approach to this issue and others. Sound advice on academic strengths and social factors is essential for applicants to give themselves the best chance of winning a place and finding a setting in which they can thrive. The choice is particularly important for arts and social science students, whose world-famous individual or small group tuition is based in college. Science and technology, which have benefited from Oxford's phenomenally successful fundraising efforts, are taught mainly in central facilities. Applicants have the option of going straight into the admissions pool without expressing a preference for a particular college, but the success rate is lower than via the conventional route.

Recent developments include the new management school, made possible by a £20 million donation from the controversial Syrian businessman, Wafic Said, which opened in 2001. An even bigger project will see the addition of a £60 million chemistry building to house the western world's largest chemistry department, as well as new premises for economics. A £21 million social sciences library is due to follow in 2004.

There was never much doubt about the strength of Oxford's research but, with 25 out of 46 subject areas rated internationally outstanding and 96 per cent of those entered for assessment placed in the top two categories, the latest grades confirmed the university's high standing. The university had the largest number of top-rated researchers and also attracts the biggest amount of research income, at about £200 million. Most teaching assessments have been similarly impressive, with classics and philosophy recording maximum points in 2001.

A major review of the university's activities resulted in some restructuring in August 2000, with the creation of five academic divisions, each headed by a full-time officer. But there will be no change to the eight-week terms and concentration on final examinations, which some students have found too pressurised. Only two in 100 drop out, however, a proportion bettered only by Cambridge.

*See Chapter 8 for information about individual colleges.*

# Oxford Brookes University...

**Times ranking:** 51 (2002 ranking: 48)

**Founded:** University status 1992, formerly Oxford Polytechnic

**Contact details**
*Address:* Headington Campus, Headington, Oxford OX3 0BP
*Tel:* 01865 484848
*Website:* www.brookes.ac.uk
*e-mail:* query@brookes.ac.uk

**The Times rankings**
*Teaching assessment:* =27 (21.4)
*Research assessment:* =67 (2.8)
*Entry standards:* 61 (16.2)
*Student–staff ratio:* =27 (14.4)
*Library/IT spend/student:* 82 (£383)
*Facilities spend/student:* 13 (£247)
*Firsts and 2:1s:* 54 (53.9%)
*Work and further study:* 46 (94.7%)
*Expected completion rate:* =74 (82%)

**Students**
*Undergraduates:* 8,570 (1,810)
*Postgraduates:* 1,230 (1,780)
*Mature students:* 30%
*Overseas students:* 16.6%
*Applications per place:* 6
*From state sector schools:* 72%
*From working class homes:* 19%

**Teaching quality assessments**
*1993–95 Rated Excellent:* anthropology; English; geography; law.
*From 1995 (top score 24):* **24** business and management; economics; town planning. **23** anatomy and physiology; art and design; biology and environmental science; building; history of art; land management; molecular biosciences; organismal biosciences; psychology; theology. **22** French; hospitality; mathematics; Iberian languages; Italian; politics. **21** civil engineering; education; media studies; sociology. **20** food science; health subjects; nursing. **19** electrical and electronic engineering; German.

## Overview

Now firmly established as the leading new university in *The Times* table, Oxford Brookes was one of a handful of former polytechnics to have a subject rated internationally outstanding in the latest research assessments. That the 5* rating in history placed the department ahead of its world-renowned neighbour can only have added to the sense of achievement. English and French reached the next grade, although the biggest entry in any new university, representing 41 per cent of the academic staff, meant that overall results were unusually variable. Brookes made a leap in size in 2000, taking in Westminster College, a merger which added 2,000 students, mainly in teacher training and the humanities, and forming a £2.5 million Institute of Education. The new arrivals joined an institution that is challenging the traditional universities on their own ground, but retaining a substantial part-time programme and recruiting large numbers of mature students.

As a polytechnic, Oxford pioneered the modular degree system that has swept British higher education. After more than 20 years' experience, the scheme now offers in excess of 2,000 modules in an undergraduate programme which can pair subjects as diverse as history and physical sciences, or catering management and history of art. Each subject has compulsory modules in the first year and a list of others that are acceptable later in the course. Students are encouraged to take some subjects outside their main area of study, and there is a range of possible exit points. They can qualify for a Certificate in Higher Education after a full 24 modules.

The university's location has always been an advantage in student recruitment, but the quality of provision is the real draw. Its departments feature in *The Times* top ten for several subjects, including a fourth place for French. Even the law ranking – normally the preserve of the traditional universities – sees Oxford Brookes in twelfth place. Town planning and economics have achieved perfect scores for teaching, while art and design, and biological and environmental programmes are among a clutch of subjects where only one point has been dropped.

Brookes' strength in hospitality, leisure and tourism has been recognised with the siting of a national centre for teaching and learning there. The university's first two-year foundation degree is in this area and is expected to maintain the consistently excellent record for graduate employment.

The university is to partner Warwick University in hosting the Government's academy for gifted and talented schoolchildren. More than a quarter of the undergraduates come from independent schools – by far the highest proportion among the new universities and twice as many as the 'benchmark' figure calculated from national averages for each subject. The proportion from working-class homes and coming from areas without a tradition of higher education are also well both below funding council expectations.

There are three main sites, two of which are only a mile from the city centre and linked to each other by a footbridge. The original Gipsy Lane site was becoming overcrowded when the chance came to acquire the late Robert Maxwell's 15-acre estate at neighbouring Headington Hill. Computing and business are five miles away at Wheatley. Westminster's campus will offer further scope for expansion. A swimming pool and 18-hole golf course have been added to the already impressive sports facilities. Representative teams have a good record, the cricketers now combining with Oxford University to take on county teams.

The social scene is not the liveliest and Oxford can be expensive, but there is enough going on to satisfy most students. The university has almost 3,000 residential places, but even first years have to live more than 70 miles from Oxford to be sure of securing a place. The accommodation office organises house-hunting weekends in September, with free hall places bookable on 01865 483100.

## Accommodation
Number of places and costs refer to 2001–02

*University-provided places:* 3,500

*Percentage catered*: 30%

*Costs for catered accommodation:* £82–£88 a week.

*Costs for self-catered accommodation:* £52–£75 a week.

*Policy for first-year students:* all accommodation is allocated to first-years by distance from Oxford Brookes. Those students living in Oxfordshire, Berkshire and Buckinghamshire are unlikely to get a place.

*Policy for international students:* the policy is the same for all first years.

*Contact for further information:* accomm@brookes.ac.uk

# University of Paisley

**Times ranking:** =92 (2002 ranking: 89)

**Founded:** University status 1992, formerly Paisley College

**Contact details**
*Address:* Paisley, Renfrewshire PA1 2BE
*Tel:* 0800 027 1000
*Website:* www.paisley.ac.uk
*e-mail:* uni-direct@paisley.ac.uk

**The Times rankings**
*Teaching assessment:* =74 (20.4)
*Research assessment:* 98 (1.6)
*Entry standards:* 94 (12.1)
*Student–staff ratio:* =72 (18.5)
*Library/IT spend/student:* =54 (£450)
*Facilities spend/student:* 83 (£114)
*Firsts and 2:1s:* 96 (41.1%)
*Work and further study:* 97 (87.6%)
*Expected completion rate:* 82 (80.4%)

**Students**
*Undergraduates:* 5,770 (2,490)
*Postgraduates:* 700 (590)
*Mature students:* 46.6%
*Overseas students:* 5.5%
*Applications per place:* 3.2
*From state sector schools:* 97%
*From working class homes:* 42%

**Teaching quality assessments**
*1993–98 Rated Excellent:* none.
*1993–98 Highly Satisfactory:* cellular biology; chemistry; civil engineering; mathematics and statistics; mechanical engineering; organismal biology; psychology; social work; sociology, teacher education.
*From 1998 (top score 24):* **19** European languages.
*2001 Rated Commendable:* engineering.

## Overview

Paisley has enjoyed the biggest surge in popularity of any British university, with a 30 per cent increase in applications for places beginning 2002. Even allowing for the trend among Scottish students to remain north of the border to avoid up-front tuition fees, the rise was remarkable. The university gives the credit to the development of a new range of degrees in subjects such as commercial music, computer games technology and music technology, which saw applications for places on the education and media campus in Ayr grow by 50 per cent in a year.

The university is proud of its record in attracting under-represented groups onto courses. Its proportion of students from areas without a tradition of higher education is by far the highest in Britain, at 35 per cent, and the 42 per cent share of places going to working-class students is exceeded by only three universities. However, the 29 per cent drop-out rate is the highest in Scotland and among the worst in Britain. Access measures are continuing, however, with more than 200 youngsters aged 14 and 15 signing up for the 'University Experience' and sampling a week of student life in Scotland's first scheme targeting this age group.

Only seven miles from Glasgow, Paisley is Scotland's largest town. The university has more than 9,000 students, including the many part-timers, a high proportion coming from the Glasgow area. Student numbers have grown rapidly in recent years, but staffing levels compare favourably with most new universities. Courses are strongly vocational, with business, multimedia and health subjects by far the most popular choices. There are close links with business and industry, notably with the computer giant IBM. All students are offered hands-on computer training, and there is a postgraduate course available in information technology for those who want to move into the industry without a first degree in computing.

No subjects were rated Excellent before the teaching quality system changed in 1998, but a majority were graded Highly Satisfactory. The university pioneered credit transfer in Scotland, giving credit for non-academic achievement, and its modular course system covers day, evening and weekend classes. Most students either take sandwich degrees or have work placements built into their courses, and earn an average of £10,000 in the process, but the impact on graduate employment has not been as great as in some other universities. Research grades improved in the latest assessments, with accountancy achieving the only grade 5 in any new university in Scotland, but still the majority of entrants were placed in the bottom three grades. Applied research and consultancy is concentrated specialist units on subjects such as alcohol and drug abuse and thin film technology.

The main campus, covering 20 acres in the middle of Paisley, has seen substantial development in recent years, including a new library and learning resource centre. The campus in Ayr, acquired through a 1993 merger with a former teacher training college, has seen the establishment of a management centre in an 18th–century mansion. A third campus opened in Dumfries in 1996, in partnership with Glasgow University and a local college. The venture now has over 400 students, and a new teaching centre is increasing the range of courses available for the under-provided southwest of Scotland.

The two main centres could hardly be more different, Paisley industrial and seaside Ayr smaller both as a campus and a town. Social life varies accordingly, although the higher proportion of residential students in Ayr compensates to some extent for the smaller numbers. The university has been investing heavily in improved leisure facilities, with a new students' union already open in Ayr and £5 million town-centre union building now added in Paisley. Sports provision has also been improving: £1.5 million was spent upgrading Paisley's indoor and outdoor facilities.

## Accommodation

Number of places and costs refer to 2001–02

*University-provided places:* 568

*Percentage catered:* 0%

*Costs for catered accommodation:* n/a

*Costs for self-catered accommodation:* £36.79–£43.08 a week.

*Policy for first-year students:* where possible, accommodation is provided for those whose home address lies outside a 25-mile travel zone.

*Policy for international students:* accommodation is provided for those applicants on the waiting list at the time of allocation. Every effort is made to assist late applicants.

*Contact for further information:* accommodation@paisley.ac.uk

# University of Plymouth

Times ranking: 53 (2002 ranking: 57)

Founded: University status 1992, formerly Polytechnic South West, originally Plymouth Polytechnic

**Contact details**
Address: Plymouth, Devon PL4 8AA
Tel: 01752 232232
Website: www.plymouth.ac.uk
e-mail: admissions@plymouth.ac.uk

**The Times rankings**
Teaching assessment: =55 (20.8)
Research assessment: =57 (3.2)
Entry standards: =68 (15.1)
Student–staff ratio: =16 (13.3)
Library/IT spend/student: 21 (£589)
Facilities spend/student: 68 (£142)
Firsts and 2:1s: 71 (49.1%)
Work and further study: =70 (92.9%)
Expected completion rate: =37 (88%)

**Students**
Undergraduates: 14,610 (4,580)
Postgraduates: 580 (2,110)
Mature students: 22%
Overseas students: 8.4%
Applications per place: 5.1
From state sector schools: 91%
From working class homes: 25%

**Teaching quality assessments**
1993–95 Rated Excellent: environmental science; geography; geology; oceanography.
From 1995 (top score 24): **23** building; civil engineering; hospitallity; nursing; psychology. **22** agriculture; education; land management; molecular biosciences; organismal biosciences; politics. **21** art and design; drama, dance and cinematics; history of art; media studies. **20** health subjects; mathematics and statistics; sociology. **19** materials technology. **18** electrical and electronic engineering.

## Overview

Plymouth has been collaborating with Exeter University to establish the Peninsula Medical School, which admits its first students in 2002. The project, which will involve a £23 million building in the city for teaching and laboratory work, made Plymouth the first new university to be awarded a medical school – a genuine accolade and a breakthrough for the sector. As a polytechnic, Plymouth was highly regarded and a persistent advocate of university status; now it is the envy of many older foundations.

The university was already responsible for all nursing and midwifery training in the region, building or adapting premises at Cornwall College in Camborne and at Somerset College of Arts and Technology in Taunton, as well as on its own campuses, in order to fulfil that role. The Institute of Health Studies' close links with the new Medical School will see health professionals training side by side. The medical school will use hospitals in Plymouth, Exeter, Truro, Torbay and Barnstaple.

Naming the university after its Plymouth base conformed to the idea that applicants identify with cities, although attracting students has never been a problem. The university has four main campuses in Devon and is a partner in the Combined Universities in Cornwall (CUC) initiative, which aims to increase the provision of further and higher education in Cornwall.

The other three campuses in Devon have developed out of a school of art and design in Exeter, Seale-Hayne agricultural college near Newton Abbot, and a college of education in Exmouth, each now offering a wider range of courses. The university is widening participation in higher education, franchising courses to the Royal Naval College at Dartmouth and 20 further education colleges in the region – a system that won a Queen's Anniversary Prize in 1994.

Unlike many new universities, Plymouth has 80 per cent of its students on full-time or sandwich courses, most of them degrees. With Staffordshire University, it also has one of the lowest dropout rate of all the former polytechnics. Once best known for marine studies, civil engineering, building, psychology, nursing, and hospitality have produced the best recent teaching scores, each narrowly missing out on full marks.

In both science and technology, foundation courses for those without formal qualifications prepare students for degree courses, and an MEng with an extra year's study is open to high-fliers throughout the faculty of technology. The university hit the headlines for introducing a degree in surfing, but it insists that the oversubscribed course is rigorous as well as vocational, and have followed it with a degree in applied marine sports science, in collaboration with the College of St Mark and St John.

Plymouth has a long-standing commitment to research. More than a third of the academics were entered for the latest research assessment exercise, with computer science, psychology and art history all rated nationally outstanding with significant work of international excellence. For example, the Plymouth Institute of Neuroscience opened this year, drawing upon the expertise in computing and

psychology, while collaborative research work is undertaken with the Eden Project and the National Marine Aquarium.

The standard of facilities and the prospect of securing a place in halls vary between campuses, although all are within easy reach of the sea and the region's areas of natural beauty. Plymouth, which hosts the majority of students, is inevitably the liveliest location, with excellent facilities for water sports. A £15 million scheme has seen the development of a 1,300-bed student village. The remaining sites have an identity and social life of their own. At Seale-Hayne, Exmouth, and Exeter most first years are offered hall accommodation and more rooms are being planned for Plymouth, Exeter and Exmouth.

## Accommodation
Number of places and costs refer to 2001–02

*University-provided places:* 2,393

*Percentage catered:* 0%

*Costs for catered accommodation:* n/a

*Costs for self-catered accommodation:* £42–£95 (95% of rooms less than £71) a week.

*Policy for first-year students:* students are guaranteed an offer if Plymouth is their first choice, the conditions of their original offer are met and they live 25 miles away from the campus where they are studying.

*Policy for international students:* accommodation of their choice is guaranteed providing they are confirmed students and their application is received by the specified date in August.

*Contact for further information:* Plymouth: accommodation@plymouth.ac.uk
Exeter: accomexe@plymouth.ac.uk
Exmouth: accomexm@plymouth.ac.uk
Seale-Hayne: accomsh@plymouth.ac.uk

# University of Portsmouth

**Times ranking:** 62 (2002 ranking: =69)

**Founded:** University status 1992, formerly Portsmouth Polytechnic

**Contact details**
*Address:* Winston Churchill Avenue, Portsmouth PO1 2UP
*Tel:* 023 9284 8484
*Website:* www.port.ac.uk
*e-mail:* admissions@port.ac.uk

**The Times rankings**
*Teaching assessment:* =64 (20.6)
*Research assessment:* =57 (3.2)
*Entry standards:* =63 (15.8)
*Student–staff ratio:* =69 (18.4)
*Library/IT spend/student:* 70 (£409)
*Facilities spend/student:* =84 (£111)
*Firsts and 2:1s:* 78 (48.1%)
*Work and further study:* =14 (96.3%)
*Expected completion rate:* =53 (85 %)

**Students**
*Undergraduates:* 11,320 (2,080)
*Postgraduates:* 770 (2,070)
*Mature students:* 19%
*Overseas students:* 18.2%
*Applications per place:* 4.2
*From state sector schools:* 92%
*From working class homes:* 26%

**Teaching quality assessments**
*1993–95 Rated Excellent:* geography.
*From 1995 (top score 24):* **24** pharmacy.
**23** education; French; health subjects (radiography); politics; psychology.
**22** mathematics; molecular biosciences; nursing; organismal biosciences.
**21** economics; German; hospitality. **20** art and design; building; civil engineering; electrical and electronic engineering; Italian; land management; physics; sociology. **18** Iberian languages; Russian.

## Overview

Portsmouth only narrowly missed university status before the polytechnics were created, and never gave up the chase. Degree work dates from the beginning of the last century and now four out of five students are at this level or above. Postgraduate numbers have been rising steadily and staffing levels are among the most generous in the new universities. Four subjects reached grade 5 of the latest research assessments: biomedical and biomolecular studies, cosmology, European studies and Slavonic studies. No new university managed more, and three grade 4s left 45 per cent of the researchers in the top three of the seven categories. Every faculty was involved in research, and the 38 per cent of academics entered for the assessment was among the most in the former polytechnics.

Completion rates are the best in any former polytechnic and graduate employment is healthy, especially for a university where a high proportion of the students take arts subjects. Languages are Portsmouth's greatest strength, as teaching and research assessments have shown. One student in five takes a language course, and the facilities rival those of many traditional universities. About 1,000 Portsmouth students go abroad for part of their course, and at least as many come from the Continent. French achieved a near perfect teaching score and its research was rated internationally outstanding.

The range of subjects has widened in recent years, with the incorporation of the

Solent School of Nursing and the Portsmouth School of Art, Design and Further Education. Teaching assessments were variable, but there has been a marked improvement recently. Pharmacy recorded a maximum score and education and politics joined radiography and psychology on 23 points out of 24 in 2001.

The main Guildhall campus, dotted around the city centre, is undergoing an £8 million redevelopment, as part of an estates strategy designed to have all the university's buildings in good order by 2004. Developments in the nineties provided some distinctive buildings, including the aluminium-clad St Michael's Centre and the eco-friendly Portland Building, with its solar panels. In 2003 the business school is moving into a new building on main campus from Milton, two miles away. Facilities for design, including workshops for metalworking, woodworking and ceramics, have been upgraded recently. A new student centre opens in 2002, and the modernised sport, exercise and fitness facilities at St Paul's include resistance and cardiovascular training gyms, dance studios and a sports hall. Facilities for media studies and art and design are being refurbished and extended.

Information technology is two miles away at Milton, with education and English a further mile away at the largely residential Langstone campus. Only health studies are off Portsea Island, based at Queen Alexandra Hospital, in Cosham. Almost 30 new degree courses were launched in 2001, in such subjects as internet systems, criminology and e-business.

More than a quarter of the undergraduates come from working-class homes and nine out of ten attended state schools or colleges. Efforts are being made to broaden the intake still further with a website for teenagers, which offers discounts as well as stressing the value of higher education. Portsmouth, which has been described as a Northern industrial city on the south coast, has a larger working-class population and more deprivation than some applicants may realise. But the city also has a vibrant student pub and club scene to supplement a popular students' union. The cost of living is not as high as at many southern universities, and the sea is close at hand. There are not enough hall places to accommodate all first years, but 1,400 places have been added since 2000. The students' union runs 'secure a home' days at the beginning of September to help new arrivals with house-hunting.

## Accommodation

Number of places and costs refer to 2002–03

*University-provided places:* about 2,241

*Percentage catered:* 33.3%

*Costs for catered accommodation:* £78.15–£93.68 a week (36-week let).

*Costs for self-catered accommodation:* £58.26–£78.15 a week (36-week let).

*Policy for first-year students:* those who make Portsmouth their firm choice by 26 April and return an application by the May deadline will be prioritised. A ballot may be necessary if demand exceeds supply. Students whose home addresses are in PO1–17 postcodes are not offered rooms.

*Policy for international students:* new international students are guaranteed a room as long as the application is received by the stated deadline.

*Contact for further information:* Student.housing@port.ac.uk

# Queen Mary, University of London

**Times ranking:** 39 (2002 ranking: =23)

**Founded:** 1882 Westfield College, 1887
Queen Mary College, merged 1989
College of the University of London

**Contact details**
*Address:* Mile End Road, London E1 4NS
*Tel:* 020 7882 5511/5533
*Website:* www.qmw.ac.uk
*e-mail:* admissions@qmw.ac.uk

**The Times rankings**
*Teaching assessment:* =34 (21.3)
*Research assessment:* =37 (5.0)
*Entry standards:* =47 (18.9)
*Student–staff ratio:* 5 (10.8)
*Library/IT spend/student:* 17 (£629)
*Facilities spend/student:* 26 (£200)
*Firsts and 2:1s:* 18 (70.7%)
*Work and further study:* 73 (92.8%)
*Expected completion rate:* =53 (85%)

**Students**
*Undergraduates:* 6.680 (150)
*Postgraduates:* 1,400 (790)
*Mature students:* 16.4%
*Overseas students:* 11.9%
*Applications per place:* 5.8
*From state sector schools:* 79%
*From working class homes:* 28%

**Teaching quality assessments**
*1993–95 Rated Excellent:* English;
geography with environmental studies.
*From 1995 (top score 24):* **24** dentistry.
**23** modern languages; linguistics; politics.
**22** health subjects; molecular biosciences;
organismal biosciences. **21** drama, dance
and cinematics; economics; electrical and
electronic engineering; mathematics and
statistics; medicine; physics and
astronomy. **20** materials technology.
**19** general engineering.

## Overview

More than £100 million is being spent developing London University's East End base into a broadly based institution of 8,000 students. Professor Adrian Smith, Queen Mary's Principal, believes it has been 'punching below its weight' in recent years, and is trying to put that right with a higher profile and impressive new facilities. A £10 million chemistry building is being added to the purpose-built medical school and the student village.

The modern setting is a far cry from the People's Palace, which first used the site to bring education to the Victorian masses, but there is still a community programme as well as conventional teaching and research. In addition to catering for local people, the Open and Distance Learning Unit provides on-line degrees in computer science for adults without scientific qualifications.

The arts-based Westfield College and scientific Queen Mary came together in 1989, but it took time to mould the new institution and overcome financial difficulties. The sale of Westfield's Hampstead base released the necessary capital to modernise the Mile End Road campus with a series of building projects. The new Medical and Dental School, created from mergers with the London and St Bartholomew's teaching hospitals, is not far away, in Whitechapel. The striking new headquarters, complete with a Public Understanding of Science area on the ground floor, will be fully operational by 2004.

Already London University's fourth largest college, Queen Mary is expected to carry on growing. It is one of the federation's designated points of expansion in the sciences, and has been consistently successful in attracting overseas students, who now fill one place in five and make full use of a unit specialising in English as a foreign language. Although by no means a household name, the college title, which led to talk of secession from the university in the mid-1990s, seems not to have held it back. Just to be sure, however, both Westfield and college have disappeared from the nameplate.

Teaching ratings have improved after a patchy start, which saw only two excellent ratings out of the first eight subjects to be assessed. Dentistry has produced the only perfect score, with politics and modern languages close behind. Iberian and Latin American languages, law and linguistics were the only subjects rated internationally outstanding for research in the 2001 assessments, but another 13 reached grade 5, leaving almost half of the researchers in the top two categories of seven. Queen Mary is one of the losers in the switch to a new scoring system in our League Table, making allowance for the mix of subjects in each university. The new method cost it seven places.

The majority of undergraduates take at least one course in departments other than their own, some arts students even migrating to a different campus. Most degree courses are organised in units to allow maximum flexibility. Interdisciplinary study has always been encouraged, recently through the combination of languages, the study of European institutions and a specialism in science or technology. The international theme is reinforced with a flourishing exchange programme, which includes universities in the United States and Japan, as well as Europe. Each student has an adviser to guide them through the possibilities.

Queen Mary attracts a socially diverse intake: almost a quarter of the undergraduates come from independent schools, but a bigger proportion come from the two lowest socio-economic groups. Social life centres on the campus, although the West End is easily accessible by tube. Students welcome the relatively low prices (for the capital) in East London, which is becoming more fashionable and now has more to offer than many expect when they apply.

A 1,000-bed student village close to the campus on the banks of the Regent's Canal will help bring the college together. The existing halls complex, half an hour away by tube on the edge of Epping Forest, will be sold for redevelopment.

## Accommodation
Number of places and costs refer to 2002–03

*University-provided places:* 2,129

*Percentage catered:* 10%; 31% part-catered.

*Costs for catered accommodation:* £73.30 a week (part-catered, single); £105.49–£119.35 a week (fully-catered, single).

*Costs for self-catered accommodation:* £71.07 (single); £90.55 (single en-suite) a week.

*Policy for first-year students:* priority for first years and postgraduates if they apply by 30 June. Offers to those living within a one-hour commute will be deferred until the start of term when final numbers are known (most are housed).

*Policy for international students:* as above, and will treat as highest priority and extend deadline to accommodate late applicants.

*Contact for further information:* residences@qmw.ac.uk

# Queen's University, Belfast

Times ranking: 23 (2002 ranking: 26)

Founded: 1845, Royal charter 1908

Contact details
Address: University Road,
Belfast BT7 1NN
Tel: 028 9024 5133
Website: www.qub.ac.uk
e-mail: admissions@qub.ac.uk

The Times rankings
Teaching assessment: =23 (21.5)
Research assessment: 40 (4.9)
Entry standards: =15 (24.2)
Student–staff ratio: =38 (15.6)
Library/IT spend/student: 50 (£471)
Facilities spend/student: 6 (£287)
Firsts and 2:1s: 30 (62.8%)
Work and further study: =24 (95.8%)
Expected completion rate: =22 (90.1%)

Students
Undergraduates: 11,180 (5,200)
Postgraduates: 1,860 (2,620)
Mature students: 8.9%
Overseas students: 8.0%
Applications per place: 5.5
From state sector schools: 100%
From working class homes: 30%

Teaching quality assessments
1993–95 Rated Excellent: English;
geology; history; law; music; social work.
From 1995 (top score 24): 24 dentistry;
economics; electrical and electronic engineering; pharmacy; psychology.
23 archaeology; business; Celtic studies;
classics and ancient history; education;
physics; politics. 22 anatomy and physiology; civil engineering; mathematics;
medicine; nursing; theology. 21 health
subjects; town planning; agriculture;
chemical engineering; food science;
Iberian languages; mechanical
engineering; molecular biosciences; organismal biosciences. 20 French. 19 German;
sociology.

## Overview

Generally regarded as Northern Ireland's
premier university, Queen's has been
making big changes to improve on a poor
performance in the 1996 research assessments. Four schools have closed, with the
early retirement or redeployment of 80
academics and the recruitment of more
than 100 others as part of a £25 million
investment programme. The strategy
worked to some extent – mechanical engineering was again the only subject rated
internationally outstanding in the latest
assessments, but 15 of the 40 subject
areas reached the next grade.

Queen's enjoyed big increases in applications at the end of the 1990s, as more
of the province's students decided to stay
at home. With 10 per cent more young
people going into higher education in
Northern Ireland than in England, the
result is a university of almost 23,000
students. Queen's was one of three university colleges for the whole of Ireland in
the 19th century, and still draws students
from all over the island. The peace
process even began to revive demand from
mainland Britain.

Teaching assessments have shown the
university's all-round strength. Half of the
subjects assessed under the original quality system were rated excellent, and none
of the 18 areas inspected since 1996–7
have yielded less than 21 points out of
24. The latest of five subjects to achieve
maximum points was economics, but
archaeology, business, Celtic studies, education and politics all came close in
2001. Education at St Mary's and Stranmillis colleges (both associated with

Queen's) also gained maximum scores.

The university district, which is among the most attractive in Belfast, is one of the city's main cultural and recreational areas. Queen's runs a highly successful arts festival each November, opened a new art gallery in 2001 and its cinema is one of the best in the province. Student facilities are being expanded and upgraded to cope with increasing student numbers, with a £50 million student centre to bring services together at the heart of the campus and the building of a student village. A new library has been added recently and more teaching accommodation provided, with better access for the disabled. The university's great hall has had a £2.5 million refurbishment, courtesy of the university's own foundation.

Queen's has been spreading its wings in recent years. It formed a partnership with St Mary's College and Stranmillis College in 1999, with the aim of academic integration, and has established a campus in Armagh City, which now has 400 students. There is a smaller outreach centre in Newcastle, Co. Down. Other teaching and research premises are located at the Royal Victoria Hospital, Belfast City Hospital, a nursing campus at Altnagelvin Hospital and the Marine Biology Station in Portaferry on Strangford Loch.

Courses at Queen's are modular and semesters have been introduced. Students are encouraged to take language programmes from a unique 'virtual' language laboratory, which provides online tuition from any computer in the university. IT facilities are good: Queen's was the first institution to meet the national target of providing at least one computer workstation for every five undergraduate students. An unusually large proportion of graduates go on to further study, which does Queen's no harm in the employment league.

Though the university has been criticised for religious imbalance among its staff, the principle of strictly non-denominational teaching is enshrined in a charter which has guaranteed student representation and equal rights for women since 1908.

Nightlife has returned to the city centre, but the social scene is still concentrated on the students' union and the surrounding area. Sports facilities, which include a university hut in the Mourne mountains, are of a high standard. A rugby academy opened in 2002. Queen's has fewer than 2,000 residential places, but there is plenty of reasonably-priced private housing to rent.

## Accommodation

Number of places and costs refer to 2001–02

*University-provided places:* 1,900

*Percentage catered:* 26%

*Costs for catered accommodation:* £54 (shared room); £62 (single room) a week.

*Costs for self-catered accommodation:* £41–£51; en-suite £61.60 a week.

*Policy for first-year students:* priority given to first-year and final-year students.

*Policy for international students:* international students are given priority.

*Contact for further information:* s.accommodation@qub.ac.uk

# University of Reading

Times ranking: 30 (2002 ranking: 27)

**Founded:** 1892, Royal charter 1926

**Contact details**
*Address:* Whiteknights, PO Box 217,
Reading RG6 6AH
*Tel:* 0118 987 5123
*Website:* www.reading.ac.uk
*e-mail:* information@reading.ac.uk

**The Times rankings**
*Teaching assessment:* =34 (21.3)
*Research assessment:* =26 (5.3)
*Entry standards:* 34 (20.9)
*Student–staff ratio:* =18 (13.5)
*Library/IT spend/student:* =33 (£530)
*Facilities spend/student:* =31 (£189)
*Firsts and 2:1s:* 38 (60.3%)
*Work and further study:* =24 (95.8%)
*Expected completion rate:* =37 (88%)

**Students**
*Undergraduates:* 7,390 (1,010)
*Postgraduates:* 1,990 (3,000)
*Mature students:* 12.4%
*Overseas students:* 9.8%
*Applications per place:* 6.6
*From state sector schools:* 78%
*From working class homes:* 17%

**Teaching quality assessments**
*1993–95 Rated Excellent:* environmental
studies; geography; geology; mechanical
engineering.
*From 1995 (top score 24):* **24** dance,
drama and cinematics; nursing;
philosophy; physics; psychology.
**23** archaeology; history of art; typography.
**22** classics; food science; land
management; mathematics; politics;
sociology; town planning. **21** agriculture;
American studies; anatomy and
physiology; building; business and
management; economics; electrical and
electronic engineering; French; molecular
biosciences; organismal biosciences.
**20** German; Italian. **19** art and design;
education; linguistics.

## Overview

Recent assessments in teaching and research have demonstrated an all-round strength that may have surprised those who knew Reading primarily for its highly regarded agricultural and environmental courses. The university achieved a series of good grades in the arts and social sciences, a perfect score in philosophy following a hat-trick of perfect scores in nursing, physics and psychology around the turn of the millennium. Drama had already achieved this feat.

Several of the successes have come in subjects added when the university took in Bulmershe College a decade ago, although the large education faculty is yet to feature. The college provided a second campus near the original 300-acre parkland site on the outskirts of Reading. The university spent more than £60 million on new buildings in the 1990s, upgrading and extending facilities for meteorology, management and – most recently – for agriculture and archaeology.

Reading was the only university established between the two world wars, having been Oxford's extension college for the first part of the century, but the attractive main campus now has a modern feel. There are also 2,000 acres of university-owned farmland on the Downs, near Reading, for agricultural teaching and research. The university's location, a bus ride away from Heathrow Airport, and an international reputation in agriculture and food sciences ensure that there is a healthy flow of overseas students. More than one in five is from the Continent or further afield.

However, the university was taken to task by the funding council over the social composition of its British intake. Reading was one of six universities criticised for missing all three 'benchmarks' for widening access to higher education and told to investigate the reasons. More than 20 per cent of undergraduates come from independent schools, only 17 per cent have working-class backgrounds and just 8 per cent are from areas without a tradition of higher education. At least the retention rate lived up to expectations, with more than nine out of ten undergraduates who started courses in 1998 expected to graduate at Reading.

Professor Roger Williams, the vice-chancellor, is committed to breaking down the barriers between the arts and sciences. Reading has already taken some steps in this direction, notably in a joint initiative with the Open University to develop standardised course materials to help underqualified students cope with physics degrees. The scheme won an award for innovation, a distinction repeated in 1998 when the university won a Queen's Anniversary Prize. Arts and social science students are encouraged to broaden their horizons by taking three subjects from the modular course scheme in the first year of their degree.

Successes in the latest research assessment exercise were well spread. Archaeology, English, environmental science, Italian and psychology were all rated internationally outstanding, with 58 per cent of the academics entered for assessment placed in the top two categories of seven. Reading is second in *The Times* ranking for environmental science, land management and food science.

The town may not be the most fashionable, but it has plenty of nightlife and London is easily accessible by train, but the cost of living is comparable with the capital without qualifying for the extra financial support available there. More than 4,500 residential places include a landscaped student village, while first-rate sports facilities include accessible rowing and sailing boathouses. Representative teams have a good record in inter-university competitions.

Students praise the social scene, although the high proportion from the South East means that many go home at the weekends. The large students' union had a £500,000 refit to improve and extend its popular main venue, but students who live in town often avoid the trek back out to the campus.

## Accommodation

Number of places and costs refer to 2001–02

*University-provided places:* about 4,500

*Percentage catered:* 55%

*Costs for catered accommodation:* £80–£103 for 30-week year (vacations optional).

*Costs for self-catered accommodation:* £45–£68 for 30-week year (vacations optional).

*Policy for first-year students:* all first-year undergraduates with Reading as first choice are guaranteed a place in halls if they apply by the end of June. Students who apply through Insurance or Clearing after all halls are full are not guaranteed a place.

*Policy for international students:* a proportion of rooms are reserved.

*Contact for further information:* accommodation@reading.ac.uk

# The Robert Gordon University

Times ranking: =59 (2002 ranking: 61)

**Founded:** University status 1992, formerly
The Robert Gordon Institute of Technology

**Contact details**
*Address:* Schoolhill, Aberdeen AB10 1FR
*Tel:* 01224 262105
*Website:* www.rgu.ac.uk
*e-mail:* admissions@rgu.ac.uk

**The Times rankings**
*Teaching assessment:* =64 (20.6)
*Research assessment:* =92 (1.9)
*Entry standards:* =72 (14.2)
*Student–staff ratio:* =53 (16.9)
*Library/IT spend/student:* 56 (£447)
*Facilities spend/student:* =74 (£132)
*Firsts and 2:1s:* 40 (59.9%)
*Work and further study:* 4 (98.1%)
*Expected completion rate:* =74 (82%)

**Students**
*Undergraduates:* 6,630 (1,560)
*Postgraduates:* 680 (1,180)
*Mature students:* 19.7%
*Overseas students:* 12.1%
*Applications per place:* 4.6
*From state sector schools:* 92%
*From working class homes:* 30%

**Teaching quality assessments**
*1994–98 Rated Excellent:* chemistry;
nutrition and dietetics.
*1994–98 Highly Satisfactory:* architecture;
business and management; graphic and
textile design; mathematics and statistics;
mechanical engineering; pharmacy;
physiotherapy; physics; radiography; social
work.
*From 1998 (top score 24):* **19** European
languages.

## Overview

So close are links with the North Sea oil
and gas industries that Robert Gordon has
dubbed itself the Energy University. All
offshore workers must have a certificate
from its Survival Centre, and several
longer courses are tailored to the needs of
an industry which accounts for 40 per
cent of the university's business. The
School of Mechanical and Offshore Engineering is the main link, but other parts of
the university are also involved.

The university's commitment to vocational education is not confined to the
energy industry, however. Courses are flexible, with credit accumulation and transfer making for easy transfer in and out of
the university for an often mobile local
workforce. Many students are accepted
without standard academic qualifications,
often embarking on diploma courses
before transferring to a degree programme. Work placements, which can last
up to a year, are the norm, helping an
employment record that has often been
the best in the new universities.

Efforts to extend access beyond the
normal higher education catchment have
produced a diverse student population,
with almost a third of the undergraduates
coming from working-class homes and 17
per cent from areas sending few students
to higher education. However, the 23 per
cent projected drop-out rate is not as good
as the funding council expected, given the
mix of courses.

Only two of the subjects assessed in the
main rounds of teaching assessment were
rated Excellent, but a majority of the rest
were considered Highly Satisfactory. Only

120 academic staff were entered for the latest research assessment exercise and none of the subjects featured in the top three of the seven categories.

There are now about 140 degrees to choose from. Fleeting talk of a merger with Aberdeen University is long forgotten, but the two institutions have been discussing shared teaching on some courses. Finances are now described as 'sound as a pound', and the most secure of any new university in Scotland. Students from the city's two institutions mix easily, and there is healthy academic rivalry in some areas, despite the obvious differences between the universities. Named after an 18th-century philanthropist, Robert Gordon has two sites around the city and an attractive field study centre at Cromarty, in the Highlands. The main Schoolhill site adjoins Aberdeen art gallery, while Garthdee, based on a Victorian mansion, overlooks the River Dee. Recent developments here have made room for art, architecture and business, and, from autumn 2002, the faculty of health and social care (with 3,000 students).

Like most new universities, especially in Scotland, Robert Gordon recruits most of its students locally. The Scottish Executive has provided £500,000 in European funding to help more people from disadvantaged communities to take courses. The university already offers four-week intensive access programmes in maths, engineering, chemistry and computing during August and September for applicants who narrowly miss the entry requirements to top up their qualifications. If they prefer, prospective students may take access units in these subjects by distance learning, using study packs and with the support of an assigned tutor. The scheme, which runs all year round, is recommended for aspiring students without traditional academic backgrounds.

The university is pinning many of its hopes on new technology. A virtual campus was launched with an online course in e-business for postgraduates, again with European funding, which also enables management undergraduates to receive course materials via an intranet, and other degree and short courses are available.

Aberdeen is a long way to go for English students, but train and air links are excellent, and the city regularly features in the top ten for quality of life. In addition, new sports facilities have been approved for Garthdee. Although private accommodation is notoriously expensive, low prices in the students' union partially compensate, and there are 1,500 residential places for first years from outside the area.

## Accommodation

Number of places and costs refer to 2002–03

*University-provided places:* 1,228

*Percentage catered:* 0%

*Costs for catered accommodation:* n/a

*Costs for self-catered accommodation:* £49–£66 a week.

*Policy for first-year students:* all first-year students who live outside the Aberdeen city area are eligible to apply for student accommodation.

*Policy for international students:* international students are guaranteed accommodation for the duration of their studies.

*Contact for further information:* accommodation@rgu.ac.uk www.rgu.ac.uk/accommmodation

# Royal Holloway, University of London

Times ranking: 22 (2002 ranking: 22)

**Founded:** 1849 Bedford College; 1886 Royal Holloway College; merged 1985 College of the University of London.

**Contact details**
*Address:* Royal Holloway University of London, Egham Hill, Egham, Surrey TW20 0EX
*Tel:* 01784 443883
*Website:* www.rhul.ac.uk
*e-mail:* undergrad-office@rhul.ac.uk

**The Times rankings**
*Teaching assessment:* =39 (21.2)
*Research assessment:* =10 (5.7)
*Entry standards:* =28 (22.1)
*Student–staff ratio:* 30 (15.1)
*Library/IT spend/student:* =43 (£491)
*Facilities spend/student:* 4 (£316)
*Firsts and 2:1s:* 39 (60.2%)
*Work and further study:* =49 (94.4%)
*Expected completion rate:* =18 (91%)

**Students**
*Undergraduates:* 4,610 (40)
*Postgraduates:* 840 (550)
*Mature students:* 18.3%
*Overseas students:* 17.4%
*Applications per place:* 5.5
*From state sector schools:* 75%
*From working class homes:* 18%

**Teaching quality assessments**
*1993–95 Rated Excellent:* geology; history.
*From 1995 (top score 24):* **24** organismal biosciences; psychology. **23** classics and ancient history; drama, dance and cinematics; physics. **22** economics; mathematics. **21** business and management; French; Italian; molecular biosciences; sociology. **19** German.

## Overview

London University's 'campus in the country' occupies 120 acres of woodland between Windsor Castle and Heathrow. The 600-bed Founder's Building, modelled on a French chateau and opened by Queen Victoria, is one of Britain's most remarkable university buildings. The merger with Bedford College, and the sale of Bedford's valuable site in Regent's Park, enabled Royal Holloway to embark on a £24 million building programme, which has since been extended. The earth sciences, life sciences, mathematics and computing, history and social policy have all benefited, and a well-appointed media arts centre and library building have also been added.

The college has now embarked on another ten-year development plan after opening a new sports centre and international building, as well as building up a portfolio of scholarships and bursaries. A new Centre for Victorian Studies, the opening of a Hispanic Studies department and the establishment of a formal link with New York University demonstrate that progress has not just been a matter of bricks and mortar.

Both partners in the merger which formed the college were originally for women only, their legacy now commemorated in the Bedford Centre for the History of Women. There is still an emphasis on the arts and humanities, and a majority of the students are female. French, German, geography and music were considered internationally outstanding in the latest research assessments, when three-quarters of the academics entered for assessment were in departments rated in the top two of seven categories. The successes placed Royal Holloway in the top dozen research institutions.

Drama, dance and theatre studies led the way in teaching assessments, until psychology and biological sciences registered perfect scores in 2000. Physics had almost beaten them to it, and should benefit from the university's decision to develop science subjects at Royal Holloway. The college already offers a science foundation year at further education colleges in the region, and the balance of disciplines is gradually shifting. All the sciences were judged nationally outstanding for research in 2001.

All 20 departments encourage interdisciplinary work, which is facilitated by a modular course structure with examinations at the end of every year. Semesters have been introduced, running from the end of September to April, with a five-week examinations term to follow. An Advanced Skills Programme, covering information technology, communication skills and foreign languages, further encourages breadth of study.

Like other parts of London University, Royal Holloway has experienced financial problems. The £11 million sale of a Turner seascape from Thomas Holloway's valuable art collection helped preserve the Founder's Building, but not without bitter controversy and a court action. Immediate expansion plans centre on distance learning.

The college has an upmarket reputation, with a quarter of its undergraduates recruited from independent schools and fewer than one in five coming from working-class homes. Both proportions are lower than the national average for the subjects offered, and even fewer come from areas without a tradition of higher education. However, the projected dropout rate of only 9 per cent is also better than the funding council's 'benchmark' figure for the college.

New halls of residence have brought the number of college-owned beds to more than 2,000, almost a third of which are in the Founder's Building itself. The rural location at Egham, Surrey, with only slow rail links to the capital, ensures that social life is concentrated on the recently-extended students' union. However, the town is only 20 miles to London for those determined to seek the high life. A high proportion of students come from London and the Home Counties, and the campus can seem empty at weekends.

## Accommodation

Number of places and costs refer to 2001–02

*University-provided places:* 2,470

*Percentage catered:* 67%

*Costs for catered accommodation:* £49–£79 a week (excluding meals). Residents are entitled to a 50% discount on most food from the three dining halls.

*Costs for self-catered accommodation:* £53–£74 a week.

*Policy for first-year students:* all first years applying through UCAS by the deadline are guaranteed accommodation. Distance is not a criterion.

*Policy for international students:* all international undergraduates are guaranteed accommodation.

*Contact for further information:* Accommodation-Office@rhul.ac.uk

# University of St Andrews

Times ranking: 10 (2002 ranking: 10)

**Founded:** 1411

**Contact details**
*Address:* College Gate, North Street,
St Andrews KY16 9AJ
*Tel:* 01334 462150
*Website:* www.st-andrews.ac.uk
*e-mail:* admissions@st-andrews.ac.uk

**The Times rankings**
*Teaching assessment:* =5 (22.0)
*Research assessment:* =10 (5.7)
*Entry standards:* 14 (24.7)
*Student–staff ratio:* 4 (9.8)
*Library/IT spend/student:* 14 (£668)
*Facilities spend/student:* 19 (£221)
*Firsts and 2:1s:* 7 (83.3%)
*Work and further study:* =28 (95.6%)
*Expected completion rate:* =13 (92%)

**Students**
*Undergraduates:* 6,630 (1,560)
*Postgraduates:* 690 (250)
*Mature students:* 4.4%
*Overseas students:*
*Applications per place:* 6.2
*From state sector schools:* 59%
*From working class homes:* 13%

**Teaching quality assessments**
*1994–97 Rated Excellent:* cellular
biology; chemistry; economics; geography;
history; mathematics and statistics;
organismal biology; physics; psychology.
*1994–97 Rated Highly Satisfactory:*
business and management; computer
studies; English; geology; history of art;
medicine; philosophy; theology.
*From 1998 (top score 24):* **22** European
languages.

## Overview

As the oldest Scottish university and the third oldest in Britain, St Andrews has long been both well-known and fashionable among a mainly middle-class clientele. But its fame became truly global since Prince William chose to study there. There was a 44 per cent surge in applications during 2000 – by far the biggest rise at any university. That kind of increase was unsustainable, but even an 8 per cent decline for courses starting in 2002 left St Andrews more popular than at any time in the 20th century. With more than 40 per cent of the students coming from south of the border, St Andrews has earned the nickname of Scotland's English university. But international students from 75 countries give a cosmopolitan feel. Fee concessions for them may encourage further applications.

Whatever the motivation of the newcomers, peer assessments have shown that there is top quality behind the prestige. St Andrews now has the best teaching and research grades in Scotland, and this year for the first time it is the top Scottish university in our League Table. Uniquely, every subject assessed has been rated either Excellent or Highly Satisfactory for teaching, demonstrating quality across the board. Psychology and English were the only starred research departments, but 15 subjects on the next rung of the ladder put the university into the top ten in terms of the average per member of staff.

Unsurprisingly, St Andrews was one of the universities criticised by its funding council in 2000 for the narrowness of its intake. With more than 40 per cent of its undergraduates coming from independent schools, its was further adrift of its 'benchmark' of 77% from the state sector than any university in Britain. Only 13 per cent came from working-class homes and 8 per cent from areas sending few students to higher education. A dedicated Access Centre is trying to broaden the intake.

The town of St Andrews is steeped in history, as well as being the centre of the golfing world. The university at its heart accounts for about a third of the 18,000 inhabitants. There are close relations between town and gown, both cultural and social. Many colourful traditions remain, including a promenade every Sunday in which students process along the pier of St Andrews harbour. New students acquire third and fourth-year 'parents' to ease them into university life, and on Raisin Monday give their academic guardians a bottle of wine in return for a Latin receipt, which can be written on anything. Another unusual feature is that all humanities students are awarded an MA rather than a BA.

Many of the main buildings date from the 15th and 16th centuries, but sciences are taught at the modern North Haugh site a few streets away. Everything is within walking distance, but bicycles are common. Although small, St Andrews offers a wide range of courses. The university's reputation has always rested primarily on the humanities. It has the largest mediaeval history department in Britain, for example. But a full range of physical sciences are offered, with sophisticated lasers and the largest optical telescope in Britain.

An academic partnership with Dundee University is being developed in order to expand teaching and research in areas of common interest. A joint degree in electronics and opto-electronics was the first project, followed by shared teaching in medical education and health sciences, and the launch of a course pooling St Andrews' excellence in art history and Dundee's flair for design.

Students do not come to St Andrews for the nightclubs, but there is no shortage of parties in a tight-knit community. More than 40 per cent of all students live in halls of residence, with another 235 rooms added in 2002, and sports facilities are excellent.

**Accommodation**
Number of places and costs refer to 2002–03

*University-provided places:* 3,125

*Percentage catered:* 65%

*Costs for catered accommodation:* £71.96–£98.70 a week.

*Costs for self-catered accommodation:* £35.91–£61.67 a week.

*Policy for first-year students:* accommodation guaranteed for single entrant undergraduates who apply by 31 May of year of entry. No restrictions on local students.

*Policy for international students:* as above for first-year students.

*Contact for further information:* studacc@st-andrews.ac.uk

# University of Salford

**Times ranking:** 74 (2002 ranking: 67)

**Founded:** 1896, Royal charter 1967

**Contact details**
*Address:* Salford,
Greater Manchester M5 4WT
*Tel:* 0161 295 4545
*Website:* www.salford.ac.uk
*e-mail:* course-enquiries@salford.ac.uk

**The Times rankings**
*Teaching assessment:* =70 (20.5)
*Research assessment:* =53 (4.3)
*Entry standards:* 70 (14.9)
*Student–staff ratio:* =69 (18.4)
*Library/IT spend/student:* 91 (£340)
*Facilities spend/student:* 55 (£154)
*Firsts and 2:1s:* 87 (45.5%)
*Work and further study:* 91 (90.6%)
*Expected completion rate:* =83 (80%)

**Students**
*Undergraduates:* 11,940 (3,990)
*Postgraduates:* 1,060 (2,750)
*Mature students:* 30%
*Overseas students:* 13.9%
*Applications per place:* 5.1
*From state sector schools:* 95%
*From working class homes:* 33%

**Teaching quality assessments**
*1993–95 Rated Excellent:* music.
*From 1995 (top score 24):* **24** molecular
biosciences; organismal biosciences;
politics. **23** physics. **22** anatomy and
physiology; health subjects; nursing; social
policy; social work; town planning. **21** art
and design; drama, dance and cinematics;
mathematics. **20** Arabic; economics;
modern languages; sociology. **19** civil
engineering; hospitality, leisure and
tourism. **18** building; land management.
**16** electrical and electronic engineering.

## Overview

A merger with University College Salford, with which there were already close links, provided a second opportunity to forge a new type of higher education institution. The main victim of higher education budget cuts in the early 1980s, Salford bounced back as the prototype decentralised, customer-oriented university. Now the model, which many commentators expect to set another national trend, is the comprehensive post-school institution. Uniquely among the older universities, almost five per cent of the students are on further education courses.

In the last three years, however, Salford has begun to slip below some of the new universities in *The Times* table. Assessment grades have been variable and the projected drop-out rate of 22 per cent is worse than a number of former polytechnics. Like most of the universities with high drop-out rates, Salford takes large numbers from under-represented groups: more than a third come from working-class homes and almost one in five from areas sending few students to higher education nationally. Many are mature students, who have access to a nursery with 100 places.

The access strategy has been working where applications are concerned: the demand for places has grown in each of the last three years. The other good news has come in improved ratings for teaching quality, which included perfect scores for politics and molecular and organismal biosciences. Of the first 11 subjects assessed, only music was considered excellent, but only leisure and tourism has dipped below that standard in recent years.

Previously a College of Advanced Technology, Salford has retained its technological bias, although business and health subjects are now the biggest recruiters. The university's growing involvement in health has seen the establishment of a national centre for prosthetics and orthotics, and a high reputation for the treatment of sports injuries. Another innovation is the launch of Europe's first nursing course for deaf students, as part of the Government's 'Making a Difference' strategy to attract more nurses.

Engineering is the university's traditional strength, attracting many of the 1,500 overseas students, but teaching grades have been disappointing. Two-thirds of the courses offer work placements, many of them abroad and almost all counting towards degree classifications. The tradition of sandwich courses always serves Salford well in terms of graduate employment. However, the university has made headlines with more unusual areas of teaching and research, such as degrees in surf science and technology and business economics with gambling studies, not to mention the appointment of Britain's first professor of pop music. Among the newer offerings is a two-year foundation degree in 'community governance'.

Salford's extended range of courses meant that fewer than 40 per cent of the academics were entered for the latest research assessment exercise, when the built environment and information management were the only areas considered internationally outstanding. European studies – another long-standing strength – again reached the second rung of the ladder and will benefit from a new £1 million languages centre. The university remains committed to research: it has established six interdisciplinary research centres and a graduate school.

The modern landscaped campus is only two miles from Manchester city-centre and has a mainline railway station. At its heart is a municipal park, a haven of lawns and shrubberies along the River Irwell. Students like the friendly atmosphere and, although Salford may not be terribly fashionable, the legendary Manchester nightlife is on hand. Most of the residential places are either on campus or in a student village 15 minutes' walk away – an important consideration in an area where security is a big issue.

## Accommodation

Number of places and costs refer to 2002–03

*University-provided places:* 4,046

*Percentage catered:* 6%

*Costs for catered accommodation:* £74.62 (standard); £84.42 (en-suite); inclusive of heat, light and power.

*Costs for self-catered accommodation:* £41.09–£53.27; inclusive of heat, light and power.

*Policy for first-year students:* an offer of a place is guaranteed provided the student has an unconditional/firm offer and submitted an application by 1 September. Local students are usually accommodated within the first two weeks of academic year.

*Policy for international students:* the policy outlined above applies.

*Contact for further information:* accommodation@university-management.salford.ac.uk

# School of Oriental and African Studies, London

Times ranking: 27 (2002 ranking: =23)

**Founded:** 1916
College of the University of London

**Contact details**
*Address:* Thornhaugh Street,
Russell Square, London WC1H 0XG
*Tel:* 020 7898 4034
*Website:* www.soas.ac.uk
*e-mail:* study@soas.ac.uk

**The Times rankings**
*Teaching assessment:* =23 (21.5)
*Research assessment:* =19 (5.5)
*Entry standards:* =25 (22.7)
*Student–staff ratio:* =12 (12.8)
*Library/IT spend/student:* 2 (£1,077)
*Facilities spend/student:* =88 (£100)
*Firsts and 2:1s:* 16 (72.2%)
*Work and further study:* 95 (89.1%)
*Expected completion rate:* =66 (83%)

**Students**
*Undergraduates:* 1,840 (40)
*Postgraduates:* 1,120 (730)
*Mature students:* 33%
*Overseas students:* 26.6%
*Applications per place:* 4
*From state sector schools:* 67%
*From working class homes:* 18%

**Teaching quality assessments**
*1993–95 Rated Excellent:* anthropology;
law; music.
*From 1995 (top score 24):* **24** history of
art. **23** East and South Asian Studies.
**22** Middle Eastern and African Studies;
politics; religious studies. **21** economics.
**20** linguistics.

## Overview

As the major national centre for the study of Africa and Asia, SOAS has a global reputation in subjects relating to two-thirds of the world's population. Originally only a specialist Oriental college, the school has always worked closely with the Foreign Office, whose staff attend its extensive range of language courses and briefings. The library, with nearly one million volumes, periodicals and audio-visual materials in 400 languages, attracts scholars from around the world.

Students come from over 100 countries, although more than 80 per cent of undergraduates are British. However, the school has a much wider portfolio of courses than its name would suggest, with 400 degree combinations on offer. Degrees are available in familiar subjects such as law, music, history or the social sciences, but with a different emphasis to other universities.

Student recruitment is on the rise, especially among independent school candidates, who account for a third of the British undergraduates. Applications for places in 2002 were up by almost 15 per cent. The numbers taking first degrees increased significantly in the 1990s, and now the growth area is postgraduate courses, which have helped to tackle a financial deficit. More than 1,000 students (mainly living abroad) are now taking distance learning courses, which won a Queen's Anniversary Prize for innovation in higher education in 1996.

Over 40 per cent of the students are

postgraduates, many attracted by a research record which saw history rated internationally outstanding in the latest assessments. Seven of the 11 subject areas were placed in the top two categories of seven. Teaching assessments have also been good, a maximum score for history of art leading the way, with East and South Asian studies close behind. The latest assessments produced solid results in politics and economics.

Nearly all students take advantage of the unique opportunities for learning one of the wide range of languages on offer: 40 non-European languages are available. There is also an option of spending one, two or three terms of a degree course in one of the school's many partner universities in Africa or Asia. Almost two-thirds of those graduating recently achieved firsts or upper-second class degrees. However, the drop-out rate has fluctuated between an alarming projection of 29 per cent and the most recent figure of 19 percent, which was within the funding council's 'benchmark' for the school. Fewer than one British student in five comes from a working-class home and, perhaps not surprisingly, the proportion from areas without a tradition of higher education is among the lowest at any university.

SOAS is located in Bloomsbury, but in 2001 opened a second campus at Vernon Square, Islington. Less than a mile from the main Russell Square site, and adjacent to the student residences, it provides student-orientated facilities such as an Internet café. The centrepiece is an airy, modern building with gallery space as well as teaching accommodation, a gift from the Sultan of Brunei. There is no separate students'

union building, although the students do have their own bar and catering facilities. The well-equipped and underused University of London Union is close at hand, with swimming pool, gym and bars. The West End is also on the doorstep.

The 500 residential places, which accommodate all first-year students, are within 15 minutes' walk of the school. However, the school has few of its own sports facilities and the outdoor pitches are remote, with no time set aside from lectures. The ethnic and national mix has led to inevitable tensions at times, but SOAS is small enough for most students to know each other, at least by sight, and the normal atmosphere is friendly. Students tend to be highly committed – not surprising since many will return to positions of influence in developing countries.

**Accommodation**
Number of places and costs refer to 2001–02
*University-provided places:* 772 (through Shaftesbury Housing Association); 100 (intercollegiate)
*Percentage catered:* 11.5%
*Costs for catered accommodation:* £91.00–£92.75 a week.
*Costs for self-catered accommodation:* £84.62 a week.
*Policy for first-year students:* every effort is made to provide first years with accommodation although it cannot be guaranteed.
*Policy for international students:* no separate policy for international students, although they are a high housing priority.
*Contact for further information:* student@shaftesburyhousing.org.uk

# University of Sheffield

**Times ranking:** 18 (2002 ranking: 17)

**Founded:** 1828, Royal charter 1905

**Contact details**
*Address:* Western Bank,
Sheffield S10 2TN
*Tel:* 0114 222 8027
*Website:* www.sheffield.ac.uk
*e-mail:* ug.admissions@sheffield.ac.uk

**The Times rankings**
*Teaching assessment:* =5 (22.0)
*Research assessment:* =19 (5.5)
*Entry standards:* =11 (25.4)
*Student–staff ratio:* =41 (15.8)
*Library/IT spend/student:* 51 (£470)
*Facilities spend/student:* =37 (£185)
*Firsts and 2:1s:* 13 (73.8%)
*Work and further study:* =39 (95.1%)
*Expected completion rate:* =22 (90%)

**Students**
*Undergraduates:* 14,320 (2,600)
*Postgraduates:* 3,390 (3230)
*Mature students:* 8.9%
*Overseas students:* 8.3%
*Applications per place:* 7.3
*From state sector schools:* 81%
*From working class homes:* 17%

**Teaching quality assessments**
*1993–95 Rated Excellent:* architecture;
English; geography; history; law;
mechanical engineering; music; social
work; sociology
*From 1995 (top score 24):* **24** anatomy
and physiology; education; electrical and
electronic engineering; molecular
biosciences; organismal biosciences;
philosophy; politics; Russian; theology.
**23** dentistry; town and country planning.
**22** archaeology; East and South Asian
studies; librarianship and information
management; linguistics; materials technology; physics; psychology. **21** chemical
engineering; civil engineering; economics;
French; health subjects; Iberian
languages; mathematics and statistics;
nursing; pharmacy. **20** German.
**19** medicine.

## Overview

Sheffield is enjoying perhaps the most successful period in its history, consistently in or around the top 20 in *The Times* league table thanks to good ratings for both teaching and research. The university's nine excellent ratings in the early rounds of teaching assessment were among the most anywhere, and only one subject (medicine) has scored fewer than 20 points out of 24 under the current system. Three-quarters of the staff assessed for the latest research exercise were placed in the top two categories, with nine starred departments spread around medicine, science, engineering and social science. However, an unusually low number of entries (76 per cent of the academic staff) will limit the financial rewards.

The star performers have been electrical and electronic engineering, the biosciences, politics and Russian, each of which achieved maximum scores for both teaching and research. Education became the latest subject to record a perfect score for teaching during 2001. In the previous year, improvements were acknowledged in medicine on a re-inspection associated with a successful bid for extra places.

Research excellence, which takes pride of place in Sheffield's mission statement, has boosted the university's facilities: £50 million for biological, biomedical and physical sciences, chemistry, physics and social sciences, and a £15 million aerospace manufacturing research centre funded by Boeing, which will form the hub of an advanced manufacturing technology park. The university is the lead institution for systems engineering, smart materials and stem-cell technology in an Anglo–American research network, which also involves Bristol, Leeds, Manchester, Southampton and York universities.

Sheffield has always enjoyed one of the highest ratios of applications to places, despite expanding through much of the 1990s. Only the allocation of more places has brought the university back into clearing recently, and applications for courses starting in 2002 were up by 12 per cent.

Only medicine and dentistry remain outside the modular course system, which operates on semesters. The university has an unusually large number of mature students for a traditional university and also offers courses in a network of further education colleges.

The academic buildings are concentrated in an area about a mile from the city centre on the affluent west side of Sheffield, with most university flats and halls of residence a little further into the suburbs. Most recent investment in bricks and mortar has focused on medicine and health, which now account for about a fifth of the students. Some £14 million went into a new School of Nursing and Midwifery, while a £26 million extension to the medical school will be devoted mainly to obstetrics and gynaecology. Recent developments mean that the main university precinct now stretches into an almost unbroken mile-long 'campus'.

The intake is more diverse than at many leading universities – 81 per cent come from state schools or colleges – and an unexpectedly high drop-out rate in the funding council's first published performance indicators was down to 8 per cent in the latest set of figures. The students' union's long-established student reception service helps new arrivals settle in, visiting those in private accommodation as well as hall-dwellers. Few have much trouble adjusting to the hectic social scene, which is based on the vibrant union's recently extended facilities but also takes full advantage of the city's burgeoning clublife. The union was recently voted 'UK Entertainments Venue of the Year'.

Residential accommodation is plentiful, with most of the 5,200 university-owned places within walking distance of lectures, and private housing reasonably priced. Both the university and the city acquired top-notch sports facilities from the World Student Games in 1991, to which have been added a fitness centre and other facilities.

## Accommodation

Number of places and costs refer to 2001–02

*University-provided places:* 5,198

*Percentage catered:* 56%

*Costs for catered accommodation:* £76.02–£99.26 a week.

*Costs for self-catered accommodation:* £40.32–£66.08 a week.

*Policy for first-year students:* single students accepting by 6 July and confirming a place by 31 August are guaranteed a place (excludes those applying with Sheffield postal codes).

*Policy for international students:* single international undergraduate students are covered by the guarantee above.

*Contact for further information:* housing@sheffield.ac.uk

# Sheffield Hallam University

**Times ranking:** 61 (2002 ranking: 62)

**Founded:** University status 1992, formerly
Sheffield Polytechnic

**Contact details**
*Address:* City Campus, Sheffield S1 1WB
*Tel:* 0114 225 5555
*Website:* www.shu.ac.uk
*e-mail:* undergraduate-admissions@
shu.ac.uk

**The Times rankings**
*Teaching assessment:* =48 (21.0)
*Research assessment:* =61 (3.0)
*Entry standards:* 62 (15.9)
*Student–staff ratio:* 93 (21.4)
*Library/IT spend/student:* =83 (£382)
*Facilities spend/student:* =35 (£186)
*Firsts and 2:1s:* 72 (49.0%)
*Work and further study:* =61 (93.5%)
*Expected completion rate:* =49 (86%)

**Students**
*Undergraduates:* 16,040 (3,190)
*Postgraduates:* 1,280 (3,070)
*Mature students:* 20.2%
*Overseas students:* 4.2%
*Applications per place:* 5.1
*From state sector schools:* 92%
*From working class homes:* 30%

**Teaching quality assessments**
*1993–95 Rated Excellent:* English.
*From 1995 (top score 24):* **24** hospitality,
leisure, sport and tourism; physics;
psychology. **23** education; health subjects;
mathematics and statistics. **22** art and
design; materials technology; molecular
biosciences; sociology; town planning.
**21** building; business; land management;
mechanical engineering; nursing.
**20** history of art. **19** communication
studies; drama, dance and cinematics.
**18** civil engineering; electrical and
electronic engineering.

## Overview

A series of good teaching scores and a good performance in the latest research assessment exercise have cemented Sheffield Hallam's position among the leading new universities in *The Times* table. Teaching grades had been improving steadily after a disappointing start in which only one of the first eight subjects was rated as excellent. But physics and now hospitality, sport, leisure and tourism have followed psychology with perfect scores, with education not far behind in 2001.

The university has been undergoing a £70 million transformation designed to alter its image and cater for an even bigger student population, helping to revitalise the city centre in the process. It considered starting afresh in a less central development area, but will now keep its main site in the heart of Sheffield. Eventually, there are to be only two campuses, but a slump in property prices delayed the final pieces of the reorganisation jigsaw.

Development has been continuing apace, however. New buildings for engineering and information technology have been completed; an atrium provides social space for staff and students; and an innovative library development, the Adsetts Centre, takes pride of place. The Sheffield Business School, which has by far the biggest share of the university's students, has its own city centre headquarters. The Collegiate Crescent campus, a former teacher training college, houses education, health and community studies, while art and design are further away in a former art college. This site will close when the School of Cultural Studies moves to the city centre site.

While most of the money has gone on the main campus, which adjoins the main bus and rail stations, the next stage will see a new School of Health and Social Care on the Collegiate Crescent site. The School of Sport and Exercise Science, which incorporates a new £6 million research centre, won glowing praise from inspectors, and is one of Europe's largest centres of its kind, with more than 2,000 students.

One of the first three polytechnics to be established, Sheffield Hallam traces its origins in art and design back to the 1840s. It is now one of the largest of the new universities, with high proportions of part-time and mature students. More than 1,000 students are taught on franchised courses in further education colleges. Business and industry are closely involved in the development of more than 650 courses, with almost half of the students taking sandwich courses. Research in art and design, history and materials were all rated nationally outstanding with significant work of international standard in the latest research assessments.

The university is creating a 'virtual campus'. All students are being offered e-mail accounts and cheap equipment to give them access to the growing volume of on-line courses, assignments and discussion groups provided by the university, even when they are at home or on work placements, as well as enabling those with laptops to use them on campus. A course in information technology and management was chosen as one of three pilot programmes for the national e-university.

More than 30 per cent of undergraduates come from working-class homes, half of them from areas that send few students to higher education. However, the 15 per cent drop-out rate is lower than at most of the other universities with such a diverse intake and significantly less than the funding council expected, given the entry qualifications and subject mix.

Such is the size of the university that even 2,900 residential places are not enough to guarantee all first years accommodation, although the large local intake means that many live at home. Sports facilities are supplemented by those provided by the city for the World Student Games, including the magnificent Ponds Forge swimming pool on the doorstep of the main campus.

### Accommodation
Number of places and costs refer to 2001–02

*University-provided places:* 2,948

*Percentage catered:* 14%

*Costs for catered accommodation:* £80.00 a week for a 33-week contract

*Costs for self-catered accommodation:* £38–£65 a week; contract lengths vary between 39 and 44 weeks

*Policy for first-year students:* all first years offered accommodation either in University-owned, partnership or private housing.

*Policy for international students:* accommodation is guaranteed but there is a closing date for applications.

*Contact for further information:* accommodation@shu.ac.uk

# South Bank University

Times ranking: 95 (2002 ranking: 94)

Founded: University status 1992, formerly
South Bank Polytechnic

Contact details
Address: 103 Borough Road,
London SE1 0AA
Tel: 020 7815 7815
Website: www.sbu.ac.uk
e-mail: via website

The Times rankings
Teaching assessment: =90 (20.0)
Research assessment: =64 (2.9)
Entry standards: =54 (17.6)
Student–staff ratio: 44 (16.1)
Library/IT spend/student: 96 (£318)
Facilities spend/student: 66 (£144)
Firsts and 2:1s: 99 (37.8%)
Work and further study: =99 (87.1%)
Expected completion rate: 99 (73%)

Students
Undergraduates: 7,460 (4,490)
Postgraduates: 990 (2,090)
Mature students: 56%
Overseas students: 9.5%
Applications per place: 5.8
From state sector schools: 93%
From working class homes: 34%

Teaching quality assessments
1993–95 Rated Excellent: none.
From 1995 (top score 24): 23 education.
22 hospitality; town planning. 21 health
subjects; politics. 20 art and design;
anatomy and physiology; business and
management; civil engineering;
economics; media studies; molecular biosciences; nursing; organismal biosciences;
psychology. 19 electrical and electronic
engineering; sociology. 18 building;
chemical engineering; food science; land
and property management. 17 general
engineering; mechanical engineering.

## Overview

South Bank styled itself 'the university without ivory towers', and its mission statement underlines the point with an emphasis on wealth creation and the labour market. The former polytechnic's links with the local community are such that 70 per cent of students are from the area, many coming from south London's wide range of ethnic minorities. Of more than 17,000 students, a third are part-time and half of the undergraduates are on sandwich courses.

The proportion of mature students is among the highest in Britain, a feat encouraged by initiatives such as the summer school for local people to upgrade their qualifications. The Fast Track to Higher Education programme has been expanded to include numeracy, communication and study skills, as well as the original maths. The courses, some of which are tailored to the needs of mature students and some for younger students, start at the end of June and are limited to 15 hours a week so as not to affect students' benefit entitlement.

South Bank has stayed closer than most of the new universities to the technological and vocational brief given to the original polytechnics. Until the recent explosion in demand for health subjects, engineering was second only to business studies in terms of size. Diploma and degree courses run in parallel so that students can move up or down if they are better suited to another level of study. There have been some good teaching assessments, but the university has not quite matched the general improvement in scores seen elsewhere in recent times. There were better signs in 2001, with education, politics, business and management and economics all reaching at least 20 points out of 24.

No subjects reached the top two categories in the latest research assessments, but more than four out of ten researchers were in departments on the next rung of the ladder. Computer science, electronic engineering, town planning, social policy and English led the way. The results were considerably better than those in 1996, although a higher proportion of academics entered. Specialist facilities such as the Centre for Explosion and Fire Research show that the vocational theme carries through into research.

The main campus is in Southwark, near the Elephant and Castle, and not far from the Riverside Arts Complex. Work is under way on a nine-storey building, due to open in 2003, that will upgrade much of the teaching accommodation and provide a new focal point for the university. A purpose-built site three miles away houses the faculty of the built environment and includes a library with seating for 300 readers and one of largest single collections of its kind in the UK. Some health students are based on the other side of London, in hospitals in Romford and Leytonstone, where there are limited learning resources, supplementing those in Southwark.

The social scene suffers from the fact that the large numbers of mature students are more likely to spend their leisure time with their family or local community than their fellow students. The capital's attractions are on the doorstep but, with a third of the students coming from working-class homes, many cannot afford them. Financial problems are also partly responsible for a drop-out rate of a third, almost the worst in Britain and much higher than the funding councils expected, given the subject mix.

A new hall of residence means that South Bank now has 1,400 residential places within ten minutes' walk of the main campus. It is not enough to guarantee places for first years, but the 2,000 overseas students are all given places if they want them. Sports facilities have improved with the extension of the campus sports centre. Representative teams have been quite successful in recent years and sports bursaries of £500 a year are available for elite performers.

## Accommodation

Number of places and costs refer to 2001–02

*University-provided places:* 1,401

*Percentage catered:* 0%

*Costs for catered accommodation:* n/a

*Costs for self-catered accommodation:* £64–£78 a week.

*Policy for first-year students:* offer of a room not guaranteed; high priority given to first-year UK students who live furthest away.

*Policy for international students:* offer of a room guaranteed to international and EU first-year students. High priority to final years in 150 returner's rooms.

*Contact for further information:* housing@sbu.ac.uk

# University of Southampton

**Times ranking:** 24 (2002 ranking: =37)

**Founded:** 1862, Royal charter 1952

**Contact details**
*Address:* Highfield,
Southampton SO17 1BJ
*Tel:* 023 8059 5000
*Website:* www.soton.ac.uk
*e-mail:* prospenq@soton.ac.uk

**The Times rankings**
*Teaching assessment:* =19 (21.6)
*Research assessment:* =7 (5.8)
*Entry standards:* =21 (23.0)
*Student–staff ratio:* =41 (15.8)
*Library/IT spend/student:* 26 (£567)
*Facilities spend/student:* =31 (£189)
*Firsts and 2:1s:* 46 (57.8%)
*Work and further study:* 45 (94.8%)
*Expected completion rate:* =22 (90%)

**Students**
*Undergraduates:* 13,050 (2,770)
*Postgraduates:* 2,350 (2,610)
*Mature students:* 13.5%
*Overseas students:* 6.0%
*Applications per place:* 7.9
*From state sector schools:* 77%
*From working class homes:* 17%

**Teaching quality assessments**
*1993–95 Rated Excellent:* chemistry;
computer science; English; geography;
geology; music; oceanography; social work.
*From 1995 (top score 24):* **24** economics;
education; electrical and electronic
engineering; medicine; philosophy;
politics. **23** business and management;
general engineering; materials; molecular
biosciences; organismal biosciences.
**22** art and design; nursing; physics.
**21** civil engineering; mechanical
engineering; psychology; sociology.
**20** health subjects; history of art;
mathematics. **18** modern languages.

## Overview

Southampton has been celebrating its 50th anniversary in 2002, but is has been the last decade which has really made its name as an elite university. During that time, student numbers have doubled, and the university has opened two new campuses of its own, as well as acquiring two others in college mergers. At the same time, the university's stock has risen, as both teaching and research assessments have confirmed the high quality of provision. The past year has been no exception, with three perfect scores for teaching quality and a set of research grades that were among the top ten in Britain, resulting in a big rise up our League Table.

The university stresses its research strength: the proportion of income derived from research is among the highest in Britain. The 2001 assessments saw the number of subjects rated internationally outstanding shoot up from two to eight, with three branches of engineering among them. Physics, computer science, European studies, law and music were the other top-scorers. Economics, education and politics are the latest high-fliers for teaching.

The medical school, too, has enhanced its reputation with a maximum score for teaching quality in a set of assessments that has seen more variation than most. It is in the midst of a three-year review with the aim of producing a common core curriculum for the 3,000 medical, nursing and other health students from entry to internship. The New Generation curriculum will be introduced in 2003, giving each professional group transferable skills and a working knowledge of others' roles.

The main Highfield campus, in an attractive location two miles from the city centre, has been the focus of recent development to cater for the expansion in numbers. Nursing, chemistry, electronics and computer science have all benefited, and there is a new commercial services centre as well as a graduate centre for social sciences. A docklands campus opened in 1996 on Southampton's revitalised waterfront. The Oceanography Centre, a £49 million joint project with the Natural Environmental Research Council, is considered Europe's finest. In the same year, the Avenue campus opened near the main site to house the arts departments. Clinical medicine is based at Southampton General Hospital.

A new dimension was added in 1998 when the university took over the former La Sainte Union campus near the city centre to create Southampton New College. Courses are gradually being replaced as part of a £6.8 million plan to increase student numbers from fewer than 2,500 to 13,500, the majority of them part-timers. Among the innovations is a two-year foundation degree in health studies, taught jointly with the School of Nursing and Midwifery and several further education colleges. The new facility has a regional focus, offering opportunities for students from different backgrounds to the norm for a university where entry requirements are high and almost a quarter of the successful candidates come from independent schools. The new Golden Jubilee scholarships in a range of subjects, covering tuition fees, are being introduced as part of the university's attempt to broaden its intake.

Winchester School of Art had already joined the fold, complementing the university's Continental outlook with its own well-established European links, which include an outpost in Barcelona for fashion students. Two new buildings have since doubled the physical size of the school.

The city has plenty to offer culturally and has the attraction of a seaside location, but may prove a disappointment for dedicated nightclubbers. The university's own social facilities have struggled to keep up with the pace of expansion, but the students' union has been refurbished, with the addition of a new nightclub, and a new indoor sports complex and swimming pool are planned.

## Accommodation

Number of places and costs refer to 2001–02

*University-provided places:* 5,000

*Percentage catered:* 25%

*Costs for catered accommodation:* £78–£104 (single room) a week.

*Costs for self-catered accommodation:* £45–£68 (single room) a week.

*Policy for first-year students:* all are guaranteed accommodation for their first year except those living within the Southampton city council area; insurance acceptances initially go into lodgings. Students under 18 years are required to live in hall during their first year.

*Policy for international students:* single overseas fee-paying non-EU students are guaranteed accommodation for the normal duration of their courses.

*Contact for further information:* accommodation@soton.ac.uk website: www.accommodation.soton.ac.uk

# Staffordshire University

Times ranking 81 (2002 ranking: 82)

**Founded:** University status 1992, formerly Staffordshire (originally North Staffs) Polytechnic

**Contact details**
*Address:* College Road,
Stoke-on-Trent ST4 2DE
*Tel:* 01782 294000
*Website:* www.staffs.ac.uk
*e-mail:* admissions@staffs.ac.uk

**The Times rankings**
*Teaching assessment:* =79 (20.2)
*Research assessment:* =85 (2.2)
*Entry standards:* =87 (12.7)
*Student–staff ratio:* 94 (21.6)
*Library/IT spend/student:* =54 (£450)
*Facilities spend/student:* =52 (£157)
*Firsts and 2:1s:* 93 (42.5%)
*Work and further study:* =75 (92.4%)
*Expected completion rate:* 45 (87.2%)

**Students**
*Undergraduates:* 11,120 (3,410)
*Postgraduates:* 620 (1,320)
*Mature students:* 23.5%
*Overseas students:* 7.7%
*Applications per place:* 4.8
*From state sector schools:* 97%
*From working class homes:* 35%

**Teaching quality assessments**
*1993–95 Rated Excellent:* none.
*From 1995 (top score 24):* **24** economics.
**23** philosophy; psychology. **22** art and design; hospitality; health subjects; molecular biosciences; nursing; organismal biosciences; physics and astronomy; sport, health and exercise.
**21** history of art and design; modern languages. **20** drama; electrical and electronic engineering; media studies.
**17** building; materials technology; sociology.

## Overview

The former polytechnic has been expanding on two main sites, the headquarters in Stoke and the other 12 miles away in Stafford. A massive rationalisation plan, designed to cope with rapid and continuing growth, saw two-thirds of the academic staff move offices. The rural Stafford site, inherited from a 1960s teacher training college, features the purpose-built Octagon Centre, in which lecture theatres, offices and walkways surround one the largest university computing facilities in Europe. Health, science and engineering are all based at Stafford, while Stoke specialises in the arts and social sciences. The business school, which acquired a new headquarters in Stoke in 1995, straddles the two campuses in an attempt to foster links with the private sector.

However, a new campus in Lichfield gives a glimpse of the future for Staffordshire and many other new universities. An integrated further and higher education centre, developed in partnership with Tamworth and Lichfield College, is the first purpose-built institution of its kind. The main aim is to act as a resource centre for local businesses. The School of Health has branches in Telford, Shrewsbury and Oswestry, while the business school's Business Development Unit is based in Cannock. Franchised courses spread the university's net much further afield, with 4,500 students around the Pacific Rim, and even an art gallery in New York.

The university also runs courses for more than 1,000 students at further education colleges in its own region, as well as offering incentives for local people to apply. A priority applications scheme guarantees a place to under-21s from Staffordshire, Shropshire or Cheshire as long as they meet the minimum requirements for their chosen course, while mature students are guaranteed at least an interview if they join one of the range of access courses. A growing list of scholarships and bursaries includes £500 awards for up to 30 disadvantaged students from Shropshire, Cheshire and Staffordshire. The policy has been working – more than a third of the students are from the local area.

None of the first 11 subjects to be assessed for teaching quality achieved an excellent rating, but scores have improved recently. Economics registered Staffordshire's first perfect score in 2001, and only one of the last ten assessments has yielded less than 20 points out of 24. The university learnt the lesson of the 1996 research assessments, when almost two-thirds of the academics were entered, but nearly all were placed in the bottom three categories. In the latest exercise, the proportion of entries was halved and, although no subjects reached the top two grades, media studies and art and design were in the next category.

With 97 per cent of its undergraduates state-educated and more than a third coming from working-class homes, Staffordshire comfortably meets all of the 'benchmarks' set by the funding council for widening access to higher education. When it was calculated, the drop-out rate of 15 per cent was not only much better than the funding council expected, but was amongst the best performance of any of the new universities.

Stoke is not the liveliest city of its size, but the campus is close to the railway station, within easy reach of the centre and has a buzzing union. Stafford is much the more attractive setting and offers the best chance of a residential place, but the town is quiet and the campus is a mile and a half outside it. Sports facilities are good, especially in Stafford, where there is a new £1.4 million sports centre and all-weather pitches. Sports scholarships and good coaching have helped attract some outstanding athletes, who have access to a sports performance centre to help with training schedules, psychological support and dietary assessments.

## Accommodation

Number of places and costs refer to 2001–02

*University-provided places:* 1,566 (Stoke campus); 605 (Stafford campus)

*Percentage catered:* n/a

*Costs for catered accommodation:* n/a

*Costs for self-catered accommodation:* £27.00 (twin bedroom) to £54.00 (en-suite bedroom) a week.

*Policy for first-year students:* new first years having Staffordshire as their first choice and living outside a 25–mile radius of the campus, whose applications are received by 31 May have priority. Exceptions to this deadline are made for disabled students and those with a serious medical condition.

*Policy for international students:* first-year students whose applications are received by 1 September have priority.

*Contact for further information:*
Accommodation_stoke@staffs.ac.uk
Accommodation_stafford@staffs.ac.uk

# University of Stirling

Times ranking: =32 (2002 ranking: 32)

**Founded:** Royal charter 1967

**Contact details**
*Address:* Stirling FK9 4LA
*Tel:* 01786 467044
*Website:* www.stir.ac.uk
*e-mail:* admissions@stir.ac.uk

**The Times rankings**
*Teaching assessment:* =27 (21.4)
*Research assessment:* =41 (4.8)
*Entry standards:* =45 (19.1)
*Student–staff ratio:* =50 (16.7)
*Library/IT spend/student:* 27 (£564)
*Facilities spend/student:* =35 (£186)
*Firsts and 2:1s:* 32 (62.2%)
*Work and further study:* 27 (95.7%)
*Expected completion rate:* =22 (90%)

**Students**
*Undergraduates:* 5,720 (840)
*Postgraduates:* 770 (770)
*Mature students:* 12.9%
*Overseas students:* 6.3%
*Applications per place:* 7
*From state sector schools:* 91%
*From working class homes:* 27%

**Teaching quality assessments**
*1993–98 Rated Excellent:* economics;
English; environmental science;
psychology; sociology; theology.
*1993–98 Rated Highly Satisfactory:* business and management; cellular biology;
finance and accounting; French; history;
mass communications; mathematics and
statistics; organismal biology; philosophy;
politics; social work; teacher education.
*From 1998 (top score 24):* **20** European
languages.
*From 2000 Rated Commendable:* conservation science; politics; social policy.
*From 2000 Rated Approved:* environmental sciences.

## Overview

One of the most beautiful campuses in Britain features low-level, modern buildings in a loch-side setting beneath the Ochil Hills on the former Airthrey Estate, close to Bridge of Allan, and two miles from the centre of Stirling. Even after a 20 per cent expansion over four years, the university will still be among the smallest in Britain and is likely to remain so, despite adding 1,300 students with the incorporation of three nursing colleges at Falkirk, Inverness and Stornoway, in the Western Isles. Stirling also has probably the most popular chancellor: spurning the usual dignitaries, the university chose actress Diana Rigg for the post.

Although highly rated in some research fields, the university focuses primarily on teaching. There were no starred departments in the latest research assessments, although ten out of the 22 subject areas reached grade 5, denoting national excellence and significant work of international standard. Excellent teaching ratings for economics, sociology, theology, business studies, psychology and English show Stirling's strength in the arts and social sciences. Only environmental science has redressed the subject balance, although all but one of the subjects assessed have been rated at least Highly Satisfactory. Film and media studies is particularly popular. International exchanges are common, with many students going to American, Asian and European universities each year.

Stirling was the British pioneer of the semester system, which has now become so popular in other universities. The academic year is divided into two 15–week terms, with short mid-semester breaks. Students have the option of starting courses in February, rather than September. Successful completion of six semesters will bring a general degree, eight honours. The emphasis on breadth is such that there are no barriers to movement between faculties. Undergraduates can switch the whole direction of their studies, in consultation with their academic adviser, as their interests develop. The modular scheme allows students to speed up their progress on a Summer Academic Programme, which squeezes a full semester's teaching into July and August. Full-time students are not allowed to use the programme to reduce the length of their course, but part-timers can use it to make more rapid progress.

A 12.5 per cent increase in applications for courses beginning in 2001 was one of the largest anywhere and there was another small rise in 2002. The intake is surprisingly diverse, with 91 per cent of undergraduates state-educated and more than a quarter coming from working-class homes. Almost a quarter come from areas that send few students to higher education, and even before fee differentials encouraged more Scots to stay at home to study, 70 per cent of Stirling's students were from north of the border.

Sports facilities are excellent and still improving. The national tennis and swimming centres are both based on the campus, the latter in a new Olympic-sized pool, and there is even a nine-hole golf course. Sports bursaries worth between £900 and £2,000, according to performance, are open to overseas students, as well as Britons. The campus will house the new Scottish Institute of Sport and the National Swimming Academy.

The almost 3,000 campus residential places are enough to accommodate all the first years and most finalists who want them. Students appreciate the individual attention a small, campus university can offer, although some find the atmosphere claustrophobic. The campus buildings have been beginning to show their age and are being refurbished. Stirling is not the top choice of nightclubbers, but the students' association put on a lively social programme. The surrounding scenery offers its own attractions for walkers.

For nurses and midwives, the Highland campus is based in the grounds of Raigmore Hospital in Inverness, with purpose-built teaching accommodation and student flats. The Western Isles campus is located in Stornoway, where the teaching accommodation is an integral part of the recently built Lewis Hospital.

## Accommodation

Number of places and costs refer to 2001–02

*University-provided places:* 3,000

*Percentage catered:* 0%

*Costs for catered accommodation:* n/a

*Costs for self-catered accommodation:* £45–£68 a week.

*Policy for first-year students:* guaranteed accommodation provided applications received by 1 September.

*Policy for international students:* guaranteed accommodation.

*Contact for further information:* Accommodation@stir.ac.uk

# University of Strathclyde

Times ranking: 41 (2002 ranking: =39)

Founded: 1796 Anderson's Institute. Royal Technical College 1912. Royal charter 1964

Contact details
Address: 16 Richmond Street, Glasgow G1 1XQ
Tel: 0141 548 2813
Website: www.strath.ac.uk
e-mail: j.gibson@mis.strath.ac.uk

The Times rankings
Teaching assessment: =23 (21.5)
Research assessment: =43 (4.7)
Entry standards: 37 (20.4)
Student–staff ratio: 60 (17.5)
Library/IT spend/student: 65 (£421)
Facilities spend/student: 44 (£172)
Firsts and 2:1s: 36 (60.9%)
Work and further study: =33 (95.3%)
Expected completion rate: =74 (82%)

Students
Undergraduates: 11,730 (2,140)
Postgraduates: 2,420 (8,060)
Mature students: 14.7%
Overseas students: 5.6%
Applications per place: 5.4
From state sector schools: 92%
From working class homes: 25%

Teaching quality assessments
1993–98 Rated Excellent: architecture; business and management; chemistry; electrical and electronic engineering; geography; mechanical engineering; pharmacy; physics; politics.
1993–98 Highly Satisfactory: cellular biology; civil engineering; computer studies; English; history; hospitality studies; law; mathematics and statistics; social work; sociology; teacher education.
From 1998 (top score 24): 22 European languages. 20 chemical engineering. 19 planning and landscape.
From 2001 Rated Commendable: English.

## Overview

Even as Anderson's Institution in the 19th century, Strathclyde concentrated on 'useful learning'. Some Glaswegians still refer to it as 'the tech'. But if the nickname does less than justice to the current portfolio of courses, the university has never shrunk from its technological and vocational emphasis. Strathclyde aims to offer courses that are both innovatory and relevant to industry and commerce – hence civil engineering with European studies or mathematics with languages.

Traditional science degrees have continued to prosper, however, with a series of top ratings. All but two of the 26 subjects assessed under Scotland's original system of grading teaching quality were considered Excellent or Highly Satisfactory. The university is in The Times top ten for architecture, chemistry, health subjects, mechanical engineering and pharmacy. Its careers service is also rated among the best. No department was rated internationally outstanding in the latest research assessments, but ten of the 33 subject areas reached the next rung of the ladder.

Strathclyde's main strength, however, is in the top-rated business school, which is one of the largest in Europe. All 340 BA business studies students are provided with laptop computers as an experiment with IBM. The students follow an 'integrative studies' programme, which is designed to place them in a realistic business environment from day one and involves work with a range of major companies.

The engineering faculty is also the largest in Scotland, and has linked with

Glasgow University to provide a joint department of naval architecture and marine engineering.

European focus is evident throughout the university, which has encouraged all departments to adapt their courses to the needs of the single market. Many students combine business or engineering with European studies or languages to give themselves an edge in the job market. The credit-based modular course system has proved particularly attractive to mature students, who now account for a third of the places and have a special organisation to look after their interests. With 20,000 students, including part-timers, Strathclyde is the third-largest university in Scotland, but its numbers are swelled to 56,000 by a growing number of short courses and distance learning programmes.

The main John Anderson campus is in the centre of Glasgow, behind George Square and near Queen Street station. Apart from the Edwardian headquarters, the buildings are mostly modern. A former maternity hospital will provide extra teaching accommodation and a £40 million refurbishment programme is planned, with £10 million to be spent in the current decade. Since 1993, Strathclyde has also had a second campus on the west side of the city, following a merger with Jordanhill College of Education, Scotland's largest teacher training institution. The 67-acre parkland site has views over the Clyde estuary and enabled the university to establish a faculty of education. The campus, which is breaking new ground with Scotland's first part-time teacher training degree, also offers courses in speech and language pathology, community arts, social work,

sport and outdoor education.

The university is losing its image as a 'nine-to-five' institution, thanks to a student village on the main campus, complete with pub, which has brought the number of residential places to more than 2,300. The Millennium Student project has delivered full network access from every study bedroom on campus and it is planned to make extensive high-speed dial-up facilities into the University network available for all students in the Glasgow area. The ten-floor union building attracts students from all over Glasgow with its reputation for hard-drinking revelry. For those with more sophisticated tastes, there are two theatres and the city's own variety of cultural venues.

## Accommodation

Number of places and costs refer to 2001–02

*University-provided places:* 2,275

*Percentage catered:* 22%

*Costs for catered accommodation:* £64.60 (shared room); £70.00 (single room) a week.

*Costs for self-catered accommodation:* £43.60–£68.75 a week.

*Policy for first-year students:* accommodation is offered to those students who live 25 miles from the city centre.

*Policy for international students:* as above.

*Contact for further information:* student.accommodation@mis.strath.ac.uk

# University of Sunderland

Times ranking: 71 (2002 ranking: 73)

**Founded:** University status 1992, formerly Sunderland Polytechnic

**Contact details**
*Address:* Langham Tower, Ryhope Road, Sunderland SR2 7EE
*Tel:* 0191 515 3000
*Website:* www.sunderland.ac.uk
*e-mail:* student-helpline@sunderland.ac.uk

**The Times rankings**
*Teaching assessment:* =57 (20.7)
*Research assessment:* =67 (2.8)
*Entry standards:* =87 (12.7)
*Student–staff ratio:* =72 (18.5)
*Library/IT spend/student:* =94 (£331)
*Facilities spend/student:* =37 (£185)
*Firsts and 2:1s:* 79 (47.9%)
*Work and further study:* =49 (94.4%)
*Expected completion rate:* =85 (79%)

**Students**
*Undergraduates:* 8,500 (2,550)
*Postgraduates:* 640 (820)
*Mature students:* 25%
*Overseas students:* 10.3%
*Applications per place:* 4.6
*From state sector schools:* 97%
*From working class homes:* 35%

**Teaching quality assessments**
*1993–95 Rated Excellent:* none.
*From 1995 (top score 24):* **24** molecular biosciences; organismal biosciences. **23** anatomy and physiology; nursing. **22** media studies; pharmacy. **21** art and design; drama, dance and cinematics; education; history of art; music; sociology. **20** hospitality; politics; psychology; sports science. **19** mechanical engineering. **18** Iberian languages. **17** French; German.

## Overview

One of Britain's newest cities also has among the newest university campuses. Designed for 8,000 students, St Peter's Campus, an award-winning 24-acre site by the banks of the Wear, now houses the business school and the infomatics centre. Next on the list is a £20 million arts, design and media centre, the first phase of which will begin construction soon. The main campus and a third site in one of Sunderland's suburbs are within walking distance. The university doubled in size in four years, and has taken advantage of urban regeneration programmes to expand its facilities to match. A well-appointed science complex opened on the city centre site, language laboratories were upgraded and specialist research centres opened for ecology and Japanese studies.

Developments have been planned with an eye to history, for example incorporating a working heritage centre for the glass industry at the heart of the new campus, which is built around a 7th-century abbey described as one of Britain's first universities. The glass and ceramics design degree carries on a Sunderland tradition – the National Glass Centre is one of the features of the new campus – while the courses in automotive design and manufacture serve the region's new industrial base. The large pharmacy department is another strength and the well-equipped School of Computing, Engineering and Technology is one of the largest in the UK with over 3,000 students.

Teaching assessments have been improving after a poor start. The biosciences recorded the university's only perfect scores, but nursing and anatomy and physiology came close to joining them. The latest research assessments were more impressive, registering a big improvement on 1996 and representing the best performance in any new university in terms of average grades per member of staff. Although no subjects reached the top two grades, the 44 per cent of academics entered for assessment was the most in any former polytechnic, and art and design, English and history all managed grade 4.

Sunderland is making the most of the opportunity to link up with the multinational companies that have arrived on its doorstep. A new institute for automotive and manufacturing advanced practice has a team of 40 researchers and consultants working with local businesses, while nearby Nissan played an important role in designing a course in automotive product development. The Sony media centre is another example, providing students with excellent television and video production facilities.

The university has a determinedly local focus, aiming to double the number of students coming from an area which has little tradition of sending students to higher education. Almost 30 per cent come from 'low participation neighbourhoods', the largest proportion at any English university. A pioneering access scheme offers places to mature students without A levels, as long as they reach the required levels of literacy, numeracy and other basic skills. The Learning North East initiative, based on Sunderland's successful pilot for the University for Industry, even offers free taster courses to take at home.

More than a third of the undergraduates have a working-class background, but the downside of the university's access efforts is a projected drop-out rate of 24 per cent. Particular efforts to cater for the 700 students who are disabled or have other special educational needs, including offering a special course to help dyslexics. There is special provision among the 2,200 residential places. Sunderland itself is fiercely proud of its identity and has the advantage of a coastal location but, despite the city title, with the exception of the impressive new football ground, it has the leisure facilities of a medium-sized town. Those in search of big cultural events or serious nightlife head for the deadly rival, Newcastle, which is less than half an hour away by train or bus.

## Accommodation

Number of places and costs refer to 2002–03

*University-provided places:* 2,100 beds in halls; 450 in head tenancy scheme (private accommodation managed by the university).

*Percentage catered:* 0%

*Costs for catered accommodation:* n/a

*Costs for self-catered accommodation:* £33 for a room in a house; £60 (en-suite) in a hall with free internet access; £80–£100 (family houses and flats) a week.

*Policy for first-year students:* all first years guaranteed a room in hall.

*Policy for international students:* no special arrangements.

*Contact for further information:* accommodation@sunderland.ac.uk

# University of Surrey

Times ranking: =32 (2002 ranking: 44)

**Founded:** 1891, Royal charter 1966

**Contact details**
*Address:* Guildford, Surrey GU2 7XH
*Tel:* 01483 879305
*Website:* www.surrey.ac.uk
*e-mail:* admissions@surrey.ac.uk

**The Times rankings**
*Teaching assessment:* =70 (20.5)
*Research assessment:* =24 (5.4)
*Entry standards:* 42 (19.6)
*Student–staff ratio:* 14 (12.9)
*Library/IT spend/student:* 32 (£531)
*Facilities spend/student:* 12 (£249)
*Firsts and 2:1s:* 51 (55.3%)
*Work and further study:* 2 (99.0%)
*Expected completion rate:* =22 (90%)

**Students**
*Undergraduates:* 5,140 (2,440)
*Postgraduates:* 1,450 (2,420)
*Mature students:* 18.3%
*Overseas students:* 21.5%
*Applications per place:* 4.3
*From state sector schools:* 84%
*From working class homes:* 21%

**Teaching quality assessments**
*1993–95 Rated Excellent:* business and
management; music.
*From 1995 (top score 24):* **23** economics;
education; electrical and electronic
engineering ; physics and astronomy.
**22** civil engineering; materials technology;
psychology. **21** health subjects;
mathematics; molecular biosciences;
organismal biosciences; sociology.
**20** drama, dance and cinematics. **19** art
and design; nursing. **18** chemical
engineering; modern languages.

## Overview

Surrey has remained true to the technological legacy of its predecessor institution, Battersea Polytechnic Institute. Even
some of the arts degrees carry a BSc and
are highly vocational: four out of five
undergraduates in all subjects undertake
work experience. Placements of one (or
two half) years, often taken abroad, mean
that most degrees last four years. The
format and the subject balance combine
to keep UniS, as the institution likes to be
called, at the head of the graduate
employment league, as well as producing
a healthy research income. Expansion in
recent years in healthcare, human sciences and performing arts has seen a
change in emphasis on the traditional
strengths in science and engineering.

Expansion continued in the latter half
of the 1990s, when many universities
were retrenching. Growth has come almost
entirely in full-time courses, and numbers
are rising again as a result of an academic
partnership with the University of Surrey
Roehampton. The two institutions remain
legally separate and employ their own
staff so they are not amalgamated in our
league table, but there are joint mecha-
nisms for the award of degrees and related
academic standards. Surrey has also
announced plans to work closely on a
more informal basis with Kingston University, particularly in health-related subjects.

All students are encouraged to enrol for
a course at the European language centre,
and a growing number of degrees, including a new range in engineering, have a
language component. The cosmopolitan

feel is enhanced by one of the largest proportions of overseas students at any university – a feat which won Surrey a Queen's Anniversary Prize.

Recent teaching assessments have been impressive, with economics and education recording a near-perfect scores to match those for physics and astronomy, and electrical and electronic engineering, one of Surrey's three starred research areas. With health and sociology also top-rated, a third of the researchers were in departments considered internationally outstanding – a proportion bettered by only four universities in Britain. Six out of ten reached one of the top two grades. Another indication of the university's research strength lies in the growing proportion of income derived from sources other than Government grants: up from 10 per cent to about 70 per cent in little over a decade. The Surrey Research Park is one only three science parks still owned, funded and managed by the university that opened it.

Both the proportion of state school pupils (84 per cent) and the 21 per cent share of places going to students from working-class homes were lower than the funding council's 'benchmark' figures, which take account of the subject mix and entry standards. The proportion from areas sending few students to higher education was also low, but still the drop-out rate, at 16 per cent, was still not as good as expected.

The compact campus is a ten-minute walk from the centre of Guildford. Most of the buildings date from the late 1960s, but the gleaming European Institute of Health and Medical Sciences offers a striking contrast. Shaped like a giant ship's prow, the steel and glass building houses the large nursing and midwifery departments. A £12 million management building and an Advanced Technology Institute open in September 2002. The campus includes two lakes, playing fields and enough residential accommodation to enable all first-years and most final-year students to live in.

As a predominantly middle-class town, Guildford has plenty of cultural and recreational facilities, but riotous nightclubs are not encouraged. The campus, inevitably, is the centre of social life, and has seen recent improvements to leisure facilities. The proximity of London – little more than half an hour away by train – is an attraction to many students, but can leave the campus feeling empty at weekends. It also helps account for the high cost of living, which is not mitigated by the allowances available in the capital.

## Accommodation

Number of places and costs refer to 2002–03

*University-provided places:* 3,152

*Percentage catered:* 0%

*Costs for catered accommodation:* n/a

*Costs for self-catered accommodation:* £37.10 (shared room); £72.10 (en-suite) a week.

*Policy for first-year students:* all first years guaranteed a place, with no restrictions regarding home address, date of application, etc.

*Policy for international students:* students designated overseas for fees are guaranteed a place for the duration of their course.

*Contact for further information:* www.surrey.ac.uk/Accommodation/index.html

# University of Surrey Roehampton

**Times ranking:** 76

**Founded:** 1975 Roehampton Institute.
University of Surrey Roehampton, 2000.

**Contact details**
*Address:* Erasmus House, Roehampton
Lane, London SW15 5PU
*Tel:* 020 8392 3232
*Website:* www.roehampton.ac.uk
*e-mail:* enquiries@roehampton.ac.uk

**The Times rankings**
*Teaching assessment:* =86 (20.1)
*Research assessment:* =57 (3.2)
*Entry standards:* =85 (12.8)
*Student–staff ratio:* =89 (20.5)
*Library/IT spend/student:* =98 (£295)
*Facilities spend/student:* =52 (£157)
*Firsts and 2:1s:* 77 (48.4%)
*Work and further study:* =36 (95.2%)
*Expected completion rate:* =53 (85%)

**Students**
*Undergraduates:* 5,260 (800)
*Postgraduates:* 610 (580)
*Mature students:* 28.9%
*Overseas students:* 5%
*Applications per place:* 4.1
*From state sector schools:* 92%
*From working class homes:* 30%

**Teaching quality assessments**
*1993–95 Rated Excellent:*
*From 1995 (top score 24)*: **23** organismal
biosciences. **22** linguistics; psychology.
**21** drama, dance and cinematics;
hospitality. **20** health subjects; sociology.
**19** art and design; modern languages.

## Overview

Students at the former Roehampton Institute, in southwest London, always received their degrees from Surrey University but, since 2000, the two institutions have forged a new relationship, and the institute became the University of Surrey Roehampton. The federal university means separate staffs, courses and admissions systems, but it gives Roehampton a status that other colleges of higher education are denied. Students may find that little has changed for the moment, but there are plans for an extended range of programmes at some point in the future. An explanation of the changes on the Roehampton website talks of 'unique challenges and exciting opportunities' arising out of the federation, but assures students that the ethos, courses and locations will remain as they are for now.

The institute was formed from a merger of four distinctive colleges: the Church of England's Whitelands, in Putney, the Roman Catholic Digby Stuart, the Methodist Southlands, and the Froebel Institute, following the teachings of the humanist Frederick Froebel, all of which are in and around the Roehampton Lane main base. Whitelands is to move in 2004 to the 18th century mansion, Parkstead House, overlooking Richmond Park. The 14-acre site is within walking distance of Roehampton Lane, and will allow some new building as well as refurbishment of the house. The institute had already spent £20 million relocating Southlands, providing a new site for the social sciences.

In order to maintain as much as possible of their original identities, Digby

Stuart continues to concentrate on the arts and humanities, Froebel on education, Southlands on the social sciences and Whitelands on science. The colleges all have their own bars and other leisure facilities, although they are open to all members of the university.

In line with the colleges' teacher training origins, education remains the largest subject area, accounting for more than a quarter of the students, with others taking combined studies programmes.

There are over 400 combinations to choose from, including film studies and biological anthropology, or dance and theology. Dance was rated internationally outstanding in the latest research assessments, with anthropology and history both in the next-highest category. With 45 per cent of the academics entered for assessment – a higher figure than at any of the former polytechnics – Roehampton outperformed all of its new peer group in terms of average grades per member of staff. The institute had already won a Queen's Anniversary Prize for its research into children's literature.

Teaching grades have been less spectacular, but still respectable. Despite the predominance of arts students, biological sciences have produced the best score, with psychology and linguistics close behind. A Work and Study Scheme gives local employees credit towards their degree for relevant tasks performed in the workplace. The programme is designed to help employers recruit and retain key staff, as well as helping those who cannot afford to study full-time.

Nine out of ten undergraduates were educated in state schools and three out of ten come from working-class homes – both figures on or above the national 'benchmark' for the subjects studied. Roehampton's leafy setting is partly responsible for a low proportion of students from areas without a tradition of higher education. Applicants from low-income families now have access to 27 Government-funded Opportunity Bursaries, worth £2,000, to help them with their finances while studying. Although not low, at 19 per cent, the drop-out rate is also better than the funding council expected.

About 60 per cent of first years are offered hall places, with priority going to those who make Roehampton their first preference. Rents are not cheap for those who miss out on a place or prefer the private sector, but students like the proximity of central London and the lively and attractive suburbs around Roehampton.

## Accommodation

Number of places and costs refer to 2001–02

*University-provided places:* 1,555

*Percentage catered:* 26%

*Costs for catered accommodation:* £90 (standard room) a week.

*Costs for self-catered accommodation:* £70 (standard room) a week.

*Policy for first-year students:* students who have nominated Roehampton as their first choice given priority.

*Policy for international students:* many reserved places for new international students who apply early.

*Contact for further information:*
southlands@roehampton.ac.uk
j.marsh@roehampton.ac.uk (Whitelands)
judith.marshall@roehampton.ac.uk (Digby Stuart)
j.rochford@roehampton (Froebel)

# University of Sussex

Times ranking: 44 (2002 ranking: 43)

**Founded:** Royal charter 1961

**Contact details**
*Address:* Falmer, Brighton BN1 9RH
*Tel:* 01273 678416
*Website:* www.sussex.ac.uk
*e-mail:* UG.Admissions@sussex.ac.uk

**The Times rankings**
*Teaching assessment:* =57 (20.7)
*Research assessment:* =19 (5.5)
*Entry standards:* 27 (22.6)
*Student–staff ratio:* =35 (15.4 )
*Library/IT spend/student:* 20 (£593)
*Facilities spend/student:* 30 (£190)
*Firsts and 2:1s:* 34 (61.5%)
*Work and further study:* 82 (91.9%)
*Expected completion rate:* =49 (86%)

**Students**
*Undergraduates:* 6,800 (1,860)
*Postgraduates:* 1,420 (1,280)
*Mature students:* 20.8%
*Overseas students:*17.1%
*Applications per place:* 5.1
*From state sector schools:* 83%
*From working class homes:* 16%

**Teaching quality assessments**
*1993–95 Rated excellent:* anthropology;
English; music.
*From 1995 (top score 24):* **24** philosophy;
sociology. **23** American studies;
mathematics and statistics; politics.
**22** education; French; linguistics;
molecular biosciences; organismal
biosciences; physics. **21** economics;
electrical and electronic engineering;
media studies; psychology. **20** history of
art. **17** modern languages.

## Overview

Its heyday as the most fashionable campus in Britain may have been 30 years ago, but Sussex's all-round academic reputation has seldom been higher. Sir Harry Kroto's 1996 Nobel Prize for Chemistry was the university's third award. Although no subject was considered internationally outstanding in the latest research assessment exercise, more than half were placed in the next category. The university now generates more than a third of its income from private sources, largely in research contracts.

Philosophy has joined sociology on maximum points for teaching quality, with politics also scoring well in 2001. Maths and American studies – a long-established strength – led a series of good scores before that. Applications have been rising steadily, and there are plans for further expansion, particularly in part-time courses and off-campus programmes.

The interdisciplinary approach, which has always been Sussex's trademark, is being re-examined to see whether this 1960s concept needs adaptation for the 21st century. The university hopes to become more creative in the combinations offered to students, although breadth of study is already taken for granted. Social science is by far the biggest area of study, but languages and biological sciences are also substantial.

Sussex is committed to taking candidates with no family tradition of higher education, which partly explains lower average entry scores than in most leading universities. It also has one of the biggest representations of mature students among its peer group of institutions, but the proportion of working-class students and the share of places going to those from areas with little tradition of higher education are both lower than the funding council's 'benchmark' figures. A survey of graduates five years after leaving Sussex showed an enviable employment record, and the drop-out rate, at 14 per cent, is now better than the national average for the subjects on offer.

The university is based in an 18th–century park at Falmer, close to the South Downs and four miles from the centre of Brighton. Sir Basil Spence's original buildings are ageing but have been supplemented by new developments like the Sussex Innovation Centre and the Genome Damage and Stability Centre. The library has been extended and the language centre refurbished.

Relations with neighbouring Brighton University are good. The two institutions succeeded in a joint bid for a medical school, with a syllabus modelled on Southampton University's top-rated medical school, which opens in 2003. The Brighton and Sussex Medical School will be split between the Royal Sussex County Hospital and the Falmer campus.

About a fifth of the full-time students are postgraduates, attracted by the interdisciplinary research units, which include well-known names like the Institute of Development Studies. Undergraduates can take a year abroad in many subjects, and one student in five takes advantage of this facility, either in Europe or North America. Some courses offer joint qualifications with Continental universities, and those returning from a year abroad are given priority, with first years, for the 2,800 residential places on campus.

Sussex has always attracted overseas students in large numbers, but a high proportion of the remainder are from the London area, where many return at weekends. As a result, the well-appointed campus can be quiet, although there is no shortage of social events and Brighton has plenty to offer students. The town centre is 15 minutes away by bus and a has mainline station.

Sports facilities are good, and the university has launched a new initiative to attract top performers. Basketball and hockey are the first sports to be highlighted, bringing in coaches from the Brighton Bears, Sussex Magic and Lewes Hockey Club to make use of the two sports halls and a lottery-funded all-weather playing area.

## Accommodation

Number of places and costs refer to 2001–02

*University-provided places:* 2,850

*Percentage catered:* 0%

*Costs for catered accommodation:* n/a

*Costs for self-catered accommodation:* £51.25–£65.00 (en-suite) a week.

*Policy for first-year students:* undergraduates applying through UCAS who firmly accept the offer of a place for the coming year are given a guarantee of housing. There are no restrictions for students whose homes are close to the university.

*Policy for international students:* certain categories of international students are given priority for housing provided the application is received by 1 August.

*Contact for further information:* housing@sussex.ac.uk

# Swansea, University of Wales

**Times ranking:** 45 (2002 ranking: 45)

**Founded:** Royal charter 1920

**Contact details**

*Address:* Singleton Park,
Swansea SA2 8PP
*Tel:* 01792 295111
*Website:* www.swan.ac.uk
*e-mail:* admissions@swansea.ac.uk

**The Times rankings**

*Teaching assessment:* =43 (21.1)
*Research assessment:* =48 (4.6)
*Entry standards:* =40 (19.7)
*Student–staff ratio:* =38 (15.6)
*Library/IT spend/student:* =66 (£419)
*Facilities spend/student:* 40 (£183)
*Firsts and 2:1s:* 53 (54.2%)
*Work and further study:* 43 (95.0%)
*Expected completion rate:* =46 (87%)

**Students**

*Undergraduates:* 7,460 (1,590)
*Postgraduates:* 1,160 (1,310)
*Mature students:* 15%
*Overseas students:* 7.9%
*Applications per place:* 4.1
*From state sector schools:* 88%
*From working class homes:* 23%

**Teaching quality assessments**

*1993–98 Rated Excellent:* biosciences;
chemical engineering; civil engineering;
classics and ancient history; computer
science; electrical and electronic
engineering; geography; German; history;
Italian; materials engineering; physics;
psychology; Spanish.

## Overview

Although still small enough to feature in merger speculation, Swansea is second only to Cardiff in terms of size within the University of Wales. With an attractive coastal location and accessible to students from outside Wales, it is also a natural alternative to the Welsh capital for thousands of applicants, and numbers have been growing steadily. A wide variety of new courses have been introduced, as part of a development plan stressing language combinations. There are now 450 degree courses in the modular scheme, and undergraduates are encouraged to stray outside their specialist area in their first year. Swansea takes its European interests seriously, with links to more than 90 Continental institutions. The new law school offers options in European and international law, while science students, as well as those on arts courses, can undertake some of their studies abroad.

Swansea has won European funding for some of its recent projects, including Cymru Prosper Wales, which steers students towards small firms through industrial placements and vacation jobs. The most important academic development, however, has come with a successful bid for an undergraduate medical school, 32 years after the first attempt. The university already had a postgraduate school, but collaboration with University of Wales College of Medicine and Swansea NHS Trust saw the Welsh Assembly back plans which led to the first 50 undergraduates entering in September 2001.

About half of the subjects assessed for teaching quality have received excellent ratings. Swansea counts European management science and modern languages among its strengths, and all branches of engineering are highly rated. Civil engineering was the only top-rated subject in the latest research assessments, but a third of the researchers were placed in one of the top two grades.

For all its concentration on international activities, Swansea has not forgotten its local responsibilities. A University of the Valleys offers part-time courses for mature students in an area hard hit by pit closures and the decline of the steel industry. Franchised courses have been introduced in local further education courses and a compact with schools in mid-Glamorgan encourages students in areas of economic disadvantage to aspire to higher education.

The immediate locality is far from depressing, however. The coastal campus two miles from the centre of Swansea offers ready access to the excellent beaches of the Gower Peninsula, and the university occupies an attractive parkland site. Apart from Singleton Abbey, the neo-Gothic mansion which houses the administration, most of the buildings are modern. The city has a reasonable range of leisure facilities, but the campus itself is the focus of social life.

Swansea makes a particular effort to cater for disabled students. There are facilities for the blind, deaf and wheelchair-bound, and graduates are invited to join the Volunteer Student Support Scheme, working with disabled students in exchange for free accommodation and a spending allowance. Other access measures have been reasonably successful: almost a quarter of the undergraduates come from working-class homes and half

that number are from areas sending few students to higher education. The share of places going to applicants from state schools and colleges was higher, at 90 per cent, than the funding council's 'benchmark' for the institution, and the drop-out rate is a respectable 10 per cent.

Sports facilities are good and representative teams (particularly in rugby union) successful. A new Olympic-sized swimming pool will be ready for 2002. The 1,500 computers available for student use represent one of the best ratios at any university. Scholarships worth £700 a year and bursaries worth £350 a year are offered to students who are outstanding in sport or the arts.

## Accommodation

Number of places and costs refer to 2001–02

*University-provided places:* about 2,800

*Percentage catered:* 33% (of which one third is full-catered and two-thirds is part-catered).

*Costs for catered accommodation:* £57.00–£76.60; £60.50 (single in part-catered) for 31-week let.

*Costs for self-catered accommodation:* £34.00–£63.50; £44.20 (standard single) for 40-week let.

*Policy for first-year students:* over 98% housed. Students with firm offers are guaranteed places. No distance restrictions (except for late clearing applicants).

*Policy for international students:* guaranteed for 2 years, but will usually get 3 years if required.

*Contact for further information:* accommodation@swansea.ac.uk

# University of Teesside

Times ranking: =92 (2002 ranking: 84)

**Founded:** University status 1992, formerly Teesside Polytechnic

**Contact details**
*Address:* Borough Road,
Middlesbrough TS1 3BA
*Tel:* 01642 218121
*Website:* www.tees.ac.uk
*e-mail:* reg@tees.ac.uk

**The Times rankings**
*Teaching assessment:* =93 (19.9)
*Research assessment:* =92 (1.9)
*Entry standards:* 93 (12.2)
*Student–staff ratio:* 47 (16.4)
*Library/IT spend/student:* =83 (£382)
*Facilities spend/student:* 79 (£129)
*Firsts and 2:1s:* 98 (39.8%)
*Work and further study:* 89 (91.2%)
*Expected completion rate:* =74 (82%)

**Students**
*Undergraduates:* 7,270 (4.090)
*Postgraduates:* 490 (1,100)
*Mature students:* 31.3%
*Overseas students:* 6.2%
*Applications per place:* 4.5
*From state sector schools:* 98%
*From working class homes:* 45%

**Teaching quality assessments**
*1993–95 Rated Excellent:* computer science.
*From 1995 (top score 24):* **23** nursing.
**22** art and design; health subjects.
**21** electrical and electronic engineering; sport and exercise studies. **20** psychology.
**19** building; sociology. **17** chemical engineering; food science.

## Overview

Teesside dubs itself the Opportunity University, stressing its open access and customer-oriented approach. The past year has shown it making progress on both counts. Teaching ratings have improved sharply and official performance indicators show the former polytechnic well ahead of the access 'benchmarks' set by the funding council. Only one English university draws a larger proportion of undergraduates from state schools or takes more from areas sending few students to higher education. More than four in every ten come from working-class homes, and the drop-out rate, at 21 per cent, is no higher than the average for new universities.

Although it has never been considered a fashionable student destination, applications have been growing at a time when some new universities have been having recruitment problems. There are now nearly 17,000 students, over a third of them on non-degree courses and more than a third part-timers. Enrolments reached an all-time high in 2001, with an increase of 10 per cent on the previous year, largely due to the popularity of computing and health courses. Applications dipped slightly for 2002, but remain comparatively buoyant.

More than 1,000 students are taking Teesside courses at local further education colleges, which will also be involved in two-year foundation degrees in chemical technology, health and public sector management. In the long term, up to a quarter of the university's students are expected to take their courses off campus.

The colleges are also the focus of a 'Passport' scheme which offers help and guidance to students considering going to university. However, the university's best-known access initiative targets a much younger age-group. The prize-winning Meteor scheme gives primary schoolchildren a taste of higher education, even offering them the use of a cyber-café in the centre of Middlesbrough. University students act as mentors and can earn some useful extra cash and gain experience of working in schools.

Only one subject – computer science – was rated excellent in the original teaching assessments. But nursing, design and health subjects have all achieved the equivalent of the old 'excellent' rating. The 4,500 health students are now by far the largest group in the university. The latest research grades were an improvement on 1996, with history rated as outstanding, but the overall results still left Teesside among the bottom ten universities.

The university is based on one town-centre campus in Middlesbrough, where £50 million has been spent in recent years. An £8 million School of Health is the latest addition, while computer science and IT facilities have also been upgraded. Previous improvements in the Campus 2000 scheme have featured a state-of-the-art learning resource centre to replace the main library. The redevelopment programme also included an innovation centre, incorporating virtual reality facilities and an array of other high technology, including a cinema and a 20-seater hemispherium giving a 180-degree field of view. Computer provision is generous, with 1,400 PCs available.

The new facilities are being used to provide degrees in subjects such as computer games design, animation and virtual reality, as well as one in forensic investigation.

Middlesbrough has more nightlife than sceptics might imagine, and the booming student population has attracted new pubs, cafés and student-orientated shops in and around the Southfield Road area. The cost of living is also among the lowest in the country, with the lively students' union claiming to sell some of the cheapest beer and acting as the centre of most undergraduates' social life. Sports facilities are being improved, with a £6 million centre for teaching and recreation, due to open in 2003. A £1.5 million watersports centre is also opening on the River Tees.

## Accommodation

Number of places and costs refer to 2001–02

*University-provided places:* 800 (managed residences); 550 (managed housing)

*Percentage catered:* 0%

*Costs for catered accommodation:* n/a

*Costs for self-catered accommodation:* £30.70–£53.25 (residences), £32.50 (in University-managed housing) a week.

*Policy for first-year students:* all places in university-managed residences are reserved exclusively for first years. Allocations are made on a quota basis: first come, first served.

*Policy for international students:* international and students designated overseas for fees are guaranteed accommodation provided they apply by 1 August.

*Contact for further information:* S.A.Houchen@tees.ac.uk

# Thames Valley University

**Times ranking:** 101 (2002 ranking: 97)

**Founded:** University status 1992, formerly West London Polytechnic

**Contact details**
*Address:* St Mary's Road, Ealing,
London W5 5RF
*Tel:* 020 8579 5000
*Website:* www.tvu.ac.uk
*e-mail:* learning.advice@tvu.ac.uk

**The Times rankings**
*Teaching assessment:* 101 (19.1)
*Research assessment:* 101 (0.5)
*Entry standards:* 101 (10.3)
*Student–staff ratio:* 101 (35.7)
*Library/IT spend/student:* 78 (£387)
*Facilities spend/student:* 101 (£44)
*Firsts and 2:1s:* 101 (30.0%)
*Work and further study:* 96 (88.9%)
*Expected completion rate:* =74 (82%)

**Students**
*Undergraduates:* 6,300 (5,070)
*Postgraduates:* 290 (1,220)
*Mature students:* 48%
*Overseas students:* 8.1%
*Applications per place:* 7.3
*From state sector schools:* 98%
*From working class homes:* 34%

**Teaching quality assessments**
*1993–95 Rated Excellent:* none.
*From 1995 (top score 24):* **22** hospitality, leisure and tourism; linguistics; sociology.
**20** health subjects; nursing; psychology.
**18** media studies; modern languages.
**19** business and management.
**15** American studies.

## Overview

Barely 30 degrees were left after a restructuring in the wake of a disastrous year, which saw official criticism of TVU's academic standards, the resignation of Mike Fitzgerald, the university's high-profile vice-chancellor, and a collapse in the demand for places. The courses are now concentrated in three schools – business, management and law; music and media; and health and human sciences – two of which have recruited heads from other universities. Among the casualties were the two top-rated subjects: sociology and linguistics, which also achieved one of the few grade 5 research assessments in the new universities in 1996.

Amid the reconstruction, new honours degrees have been launched in areas such as e-business, entrepreneurship and web and e-business computing, and the university was among those chosen to trial foundation degrees. TVU is working with Reading and Stratford-upon-Avon colleges and 18 employers, including Compaq, Ealing Studios and the Savoy Hotel Group, to provide courses for 120 students. The two-year courses, in hospitality, music and multimedia technology and internet computing will be delivered partly in the workplace.

An action plan enabled the university to survive, although the pressures showed as TVU plummeted down *The Times* table. Despite some improvement, it still has the worst research record in the university system, entering fewer than one academic in five for the latest assessments. The policy of open access, which ensures that more than a third of the undergraduates come from working-class homes, already put the university at a disadvantage in rankings such as ours. Hospitality, leisure and tourism achieved a good score in the only recent teaching assessment, and the support of students and staff has given the plan a chance of success.

An experienced administrator is at the helm, in Professor Kenneth Barker, the founding vice-chancellor of De Montfort University. Under his leadership, the split-site university is maintaining the unconventional approach which has become its hallmark. However, applications have continued to drop, although the rate of decline had slowed to manageable proportions.

The university describes itself as 'student-driven' and boasts a higher proportion of non-degree students than any of its peers. Some of its vocational courses have a strong reputation: the school of tourism, hospitality and leisure management, for example, is recognised by the Académie Culinaire de France for its culinary arts programmes. Nursing courses, too, are popular and well-regarded.

TVU achieved university status only a year after becoming a polytechnic in a merger between two well-established higher education colleges. The dramatic growth which accompanied the merger may have exacerbated the administrative problems, which caused the Quality Assurance Council to question the university's fitness to award degrees.

The university occupies town-centre sites in Ealing and Slough, which are linked by a free bus service. The business-oriented campus in Slough consists mainly of 1960s buildings, but has been enhanced by an award-winning learning resources centre designed by Sir Richard Rogers. The busier Ealing base was suffering from overcrowding before retrenchment took place. Almost half of the students are from London or Berkshire, despite an unexpectedly large contingent of overseas students.

A large proportion of home-based students makes up to some extent for the absence of residential accommodation, but the remainder find the cost of living high. The mix is not conducive to a socially cohesive and active student body, although the students' union offers a full programme during the week. The Slough campus boasts an impressive gym, but otherwise sports facilities are limited.

## Accommodation

Number of places and costs refer to 2001–02

*University-provided places:* 391

*Percentage catered:* about 40%

Costs for catered accommodation: £58–£117 a week.

*Costs for self-catered accommodation:* £50–£75 a week.

*Policy for first-year students:* at the start of the academic year priority is given to students who live outside the M25.

*Policy for international students:* priority is given to international students.

*Contact for further information:* uas@tvu.ac.uk

# University of Ulster

**Founded:** Royal charter 1984, formerly the New University of Ulster and Ulster Polytechnic (merged 1984)

**Contact details**
*Address:* Cromore Road, Coleraine,
Co. Londonderry BT52 1SA
*Tel:* 08700 400 700
*Website:* www.ulster.ac.uk
*e-mail:* online@ulst.ac.uk

**The Times rankings**
*Teaching assessment:* =57 (20.7)
*Research assessment:* 56 (3.8)
*Entry standards:* =47 (18.9)
*Student–staff ratio:* =53 (16.9)
*Library/IT spend/student:* 87 (£360)
*Facilities spend/student:* =74 (£132)
*Firsts and 2:1s:* =28 (63.4%)
*Work and further study:* =57 (93.6%)
*Expected completion rate:* 30 (89.8%)

**Students**
*Undergraduates:* 12,400 (3,250)
*Postgraduates:* 1,490 (3,190)
*Mature students:* 17%
*Overseas students:* 12.3%
*Applications per place:* 6.6
*From state sector schools:* 100%
*From working class homes:* 38%

**Teaching quality assessments**
*1993–95 Rated Excellnt:* environmental studies; music; social policy.
*From 1995 (top score 24):* **24** business and management. **23** hospitality, tourism and sports management; philosophy; psychology. **22** American studies; drama, dance and cinematics; economics; health subjects; mathematics; molecular biosciences; nursing; politics. **21** building; land management; media studies; organismal biosciences. **20** electrical and electronic engineering; French. **19** art and design; civil engineering; German. **18** Iberian languages. **17** sociology.

## Overview

The establishment of the Northern Ireland Assembly brought with it the culmination of Ulster's campaign for a 'peaceline campus' linking Belfast's two communities. The development of the £370 million Springvale Educational Village is now forging ahead to offer both further and higher education courses, as well as an applied research centre, drawing on UU's work in bioengineering, biomedicine, and multimedia applications. The educational spread is appropriate for the only British university with a charter stipulating that there should be courses below degree level.

The university is hoping to capitalise on the peace process again with the development of a former army base at Fort George, overlooking the River Foyle, in Londonderry. The Millennium Campus would be close to the Magee campus, one of UU's four main sites, focusing on research but also providing leisure facilities, such as a jogging track, cycle paths and landscaped open park areas, for the city.

With more Irish students now choosing to stay in the province to study, there is plenty of scope for expansion, despite the fact that UU already has more than 20,000 students. The main sites in and near Belfast have never been busier, while Magee attracts students from both sides of the border. High technology brings together the university for teaching purposes, but the sites are 80 miles apart at their farthest point and very different in character. Jordanstown, seven miles outside Belfast, has the most students, concentrating on engineering, health and social science. The isolated original university campus, at Coleraine, follows the style of the 1960s, and is the most traditional in outlook, with a focus on science and the humanities. The small Belfast site specialises in art and design, being the former art college. Current development is focusing mainly on Magee, although Jordanstown has acquired improved library and computing facilities. Once the poor relation of the university, confined to adult education, Magee is now a thriving centre. Over the next four years, new programmes are expected to see student numbers grow to about 7,500, including part-timers. There will be new schools of performing arts, computing and electronics, as well as improved provision for education, nursing and Irish studies. The Institute for Legal and Professional Studies will allow graduates to train as barristers and solicitors.

Although often overshadowed by Queen's University, Ulster's community consciousness has made it a popular choice among students in the province. Almost 40 per cent come from blue-collar backgrounds – more than twice the UK average – and the student profile mirrors the religious balance in the wider population. Mature students are well catered for, with a nursery and three playgroups in the university.

Teaching ratings have mainly been sound, rather than spectacular, although business and management registered maximum points in 2001, while drama and American studies have also produced good scores. Research is not Ulster's principal strength, although grades improved in the latest assessments, with Celtic studies and biomedical sciences rated internationally outstanding.

There has never been a big representation from mainland Britain, but 11 per cent of the students come from the Continent or further afield. As with any split-site university, the student experience varies according to the location. Some courses offer lectures on more than one campus, but for the most part students are based on a single site throughout their university life. With more than half of the students living with their parents or at their own home, the university is not always the focus of social life. The exception is Coleraine, a classic campus university, where there are fewer home-based students, although many gravitate towards the nearby seaside towns of Portrush and Portstewart.

## Accommodation
Number of places and costs refer to 2001–02

*University-provided places:* 2,100

*Percentage catered:* 0%

*Costs for catered accommodation:* n/a

*Costs for self-catered accommodation:* £34–£46 a week.

*Policy for first-year students:* 60% of places are allocated to new first years, if applications received before 31 August.

*Policy for international students:* an offer is guaranteed to students paying overseas fees who have firmly accepted a course for at least 1 academic year. A completed accommodation application form must be received by 1 August in the year of entry.

*Contact for further information:* accommodation@ulster.ac.uk

# University College London

Times ranking: 11 (2002 ranking: 5)

Founded: 1826
College of the University of London

Contact details
Address: Gower Street, London WC1E 6BT
Tel: 020 7679 2000
Website: www.ucl.ac.uk
e-mail: via website

The Times rankings
Teaching assessment: =9 (21.9)
Research assessment: =5 (6.0)
Entry standards: 9 (25.8)
Student–staff ratio: 1 (6.7)
Library/IT spend/student: 8 (£837)
Facilities spend/student: 29 (£191)
Firsts and 2:1s: 8 (82.4%)
Work and further study: 63 (93.4%)
Expected completion rate: =13 (92%)

Students
Undergraduates: 10,380 (210)
Postgraduates: 4,080 (3,070)
Mature students: 11.6%
Overseas students: 14.9%
Applications per place: 6.9
From state sector schools: 58%
From working class homes: 14%

Teaching quality assessments
1993–95 Rated Excellent: anthropology;
architecture; English; geography; geology;
history; law.
From 1995 (top score 24): 24 economics;
health subjects; history of art; organismal
biosciences. 23 art and design;
archaeology; classics and ancient history;
dentistry; German; mathematics and
statistics; medicine; physics; philosophy;
politics; Scandinavian. 22 anatomy and
physiology; Dutch; electrical and
electronic engineering; linguistics;
molecular biosciences; psychology.
21 French; medicine. 20 chemical
engineering; Italian. 19 civil engineering;
Iberian languages.

## Overview

Such is the breadth and quality of provision at University College (UCL) that it can fairly describe itself not only as a 'university within a university' but also as one of the top multifaculty institutions in England. Its position in *The Times* rankings has regularly confirmed this, while a recent analysis of research funding, which allowed for subject differences, also showed only Oxford and Cambridge in a better position. The college's excellence is built on a history of pioneering subjects that have become commonplace in higher education: modern languages, geography and fine arts among them.

Already comfortably the largest of London University's colleges, UCL's incorporation of the School of Slavonic and East European Studies has added to the 70 departments. In recent years, the Slade School of Fine Art and the Institutes of Archaeology, Child Health, Neurology and Ophthalmology have all joined the fold. Medicine started the merger trend, with the Middlesex Hospital joining forces with UCL in 1992. The more recent additions of the Royal Free Hospital Medical School and the Eastman Dental Hospital have created a large and formidable unit, although its teaching assessment was a disappointment. A poor rating for learning resources was largely responsible, but new teaching facilities opened in the refurbished Cruciform building during 2000. The acquisitions mean that the college now has outposts in several parts of central and north London, but the main activity remains centred on the original impressive Bloomsbury site.

Anatomy, archaeology, several branches of engineering, modern languages and pharmacology are among the areas rated internationally outstanding for research. One academic in five was in a top-rated department in the last assessments, with two-thirds in the top two categories. History of art and organismal biosciences have recorded maximum points for teaching, but most subjects have scored well. A growing number of degrees take four years, and most are organised on a modular basis.

Almost a quarter of UCL's students are from overseas, including more than 1,000 from other EU countries, reflecting the college's high standing overseas. Suitably-qualified British applicants are interviewed whenever possible before being offered a place and, once accepted, first-year students in many subjects are given peer tutoring by more experienced colleagues to help them adapt to degree study. The college stresses its commitment to teaching in small groups, especially in the second and subsequent years of degree courses. The approach seems to work: almost three-quarters leave with a first or 2:1 and the drop-out rate of 8 per cent is much lower than the funding councils' 'benchmark' figure for the subjects on offer.

UCL is conscious of its traditions as a college founded to expand access to higher education, but the 43 per cent share of places going to independent school students is among the highest in Britain and further behind the council's 'benchmark' than any other institution. Only one undergraduate in seven has a working-class background and a tiny one in 20 comes from an area without a tra-

dition of higher education. The college has established a summer school for state school sixth-formers and increased contact with local schools and further education colleges in an attempt to broaden its intake.

The academic pace can be frantic but, close to the West End and with immediate access to London University's underused central students' union facilities, there is no shortage of leisure options. Residential accommodation is plentiful and mainly of a good standard. Three gyms are close at hand, but the main outdoor sports facilities, though good enough to attract professional football clubs, are a coach ride away in Hertfordshire.

## Accommodation
Number of places and costs refer to 2001–02

*University-provided places:* 4,156 (including 578 intercollegiate places)

*Percentage catered:* 34%

*Costs for catered accommodation:* £73.50–£108.50 a week.

*Costs for self-catered accommodation:* £48.79–£94.01 a week.

*Policy for first-year students:* accommodation guaranteed for all first-year undergraduates who have UCL as their first choice and apply before the end of May prior to intake.

*Policy for international students:* accommodation guaranteed to all undergraduate and postgraduates students who apply by pre-advised deadlines.

*Contact for further information:* Residences@ucl.ac.uk www.ucl.ac.uk/admission/accommodation

# University of Warwick

Times ranking: 6 (2002 ranking: 6)

**Founded:** Royal charter 1964

**Contact details**
*Address:* Coventry CV4 7AL
*Tel:* 02476 523723
*Website:* www.warwick.ac.uk
*e-mail:* ugadmissions@
admin.warwick.ac.uk

**The Times rankings**
*Teaching assessment:* 3 (22.5)
*Research assessment:* =5 (6.0)
*Entry standards:* 7 (26.3)
*Student–staff ratio:* 40 (15.7)
*Library/IT spend/student:* 15 (£657)
*Facilities spend/student:* 45 (£171)
*Firsts and 2:1s:* 17 (72.1%)
*Work and further study:* 47 (94.6%)
*Expected completion rate:* =2 (96%)

**Students**
*Undergraduates:* 8,400 (3,450)
*Postgraduates:* 2,480 (4,210)
*Mature students:* 8.3%
*Overseas students:* 12.2%
*Applications per place:* 8.7
*From state sector schools:* 76%
*From working class homes:* 14%

**Teaching quality assessments**
*1993–95 Rated Excellent:* business and
management; computer science; English;
history; law.
*From 1995 (top score 24):* **24** drama and
cinematics; economics; education;
philosophy; physics; politics; sociology.
**23** classics and ancient history; German;
media studies; molecular biosciences;
organismal biosciences. **22** mathematics.
**21** French; general engineering; history of
art; Italian; psychology.

## Overview

The most successful of the first wave of new universities, Warwick was derided by many in its early years for its close links with business and industry. Few are critical today. Tony Blair described the university as 'at the cutting edge of what has to happen in the future' and even brought Bill Clinton there on his last overseas engagement as American president. Both teaching and research are very highly rated, but the university's mission statement still stresses the extension of access to higher education, continuing education and community links.

There is a smaller proportion of independent school students than at most of the leading universities – less than a quarter – but this does not translate into large numbers of working-class undergraduates. The share of places going to students from the lowest social classes and the representation from areas sending few young people to higher education are both lower than the 'benchmarks' set by the funding council. But the mix helps to produce one of the lowest drop-out rates in Britain. Graduates have contributed more than £1 million to a scholarship scheme, which made 75 awards in 2001.

Warwick's teaching assessments have been outstanding, with economics and politics bringing the number of maximum scores to seven. The six subjects rated internationally outstanding for research – business, economics, English, theatre studies and statistics and applied mathematics – doubled the total for 1996. Nine out of ten academics entered for assessment were placed in the top two categories, preserving Warwick's place among the top five research universities. The overall standard of the 29 departments brought Warwick a top European award, while the science park, one of the first in Britain, is among the most successful.

While other leading universities were trying to cover the whole range of academic disciplines, Warwick pursued a selective policy. Without the expense of medicine, dentistry or veterinary science to bear, the university invested shrewdly in business, science and engineering. However, the temptation of medicine has proved too much to bear, and the university has gone into partnership with Leicester University to establish a new kind of course for graduates in biological sciences. The first students enrolled in 2000 and numbers are growing.

Another deviation from its academic norm has seen the university embracing the Government's two-year foundation degrees. One of the few leading universities to offer the vocational programmes, Warwick is offering one course for classroom assistants and another, in association with two local further education colleges, for community and voluntary workers.

Such is the demand for places on conventional degree courses, that many departments stick rigidly to offers averaging more than an A and two Bs at A level. Applications for courses beginning in 2002 increased by more than 15 per cent. Warwick has been building up its numbers in science and engineering, as other universities have struggled to fill their places. The business school has also been growing rapidly, with a new £15 million extension nearly completed. Computer science is also securing new,

upgraded facilities.

Some £335 million has been spent on the campus, which has often resembled a building site. However, students have welcomed larger union facilities, a number of academic buildings have been improved and the Arts Centre (the second largest in Britain) has been refurbished with a £33 million lottery grant. The 720-acre campus is three miles south of Coventry, where many students choose to live, and three times as far from Warwick. University accommodation is plentiful and the sports facilities both extensive and conveniently placed on campus.

## Accommodation

Number of places and costs refer to 2001–02

*University-provided places:* 5,121 (on campus); 1,650 (head leasing)

*Percentage catered:* 9% on campus include a dining scheme

*Costs for catered accommodation:* £73 (twin room) for 30 weeks; £83 (single room) for 30 weeks.

*Costs for self-catered accommodation:* £49.50 (standard); £75.00 (en-suite) a week.

*Policy for first-year students:* all first-year undergraduates are guaranteed campus accommodation provided an application is received before the start of the academic year (with the exception of those coming through Clearing).

*Policy for international students:* students designated for overseas fees have guaranteed campus accommodation in the first and final years (undergraduates), first year (postgraduates).

*Contact for further information:* accommodation@warwick.ac.uk

# University of the West of England, Bristol

**Times ranking:** 58 (2002 ranking: 60)

**Founded:** University status 1992, formerly Bristol Polytechnic

**Contact details**
*Address:* Frenchay Campus, Coldharbour Lane, Bristol BS16 1QY
*Tel:* 0117 344 3333
*Website:* www.uwe.ac.uk
*e-mail:* Admissions@uwe.ac.uk

**The Times rankings**
*Teaching assessment:* =27 (21.4)
*Research assessment:* =67 (2.8)
*Entry standards:* 58 (16.9)
*Student–staff ratio:* =80 (19.2)
*Library/IT spend/student:* =68 (£412)
*Facilities spend/student:* =64 (£145)
*Firsts and 2:1s:* 95 (41.9%)
*Work and further study:* =33 (95.3%)
*Expected completion rate:* =80 (81%)

**Students**
*Undergraduates:* 15,930 (3,520)
*Postgraduates:* 1,190 (1,720)
*Mature students:* 21.4%
*Overseas students:* 6%
*Applications per place:* 4.7
*From state sector schools:* 82%
*From working class homes:* 22%

**Teaching quality assessments**
*1993–95 Rated Excellent:* English; law.
*From 1995 (top score 24):* **24** biology and biomedical sciences; education.
**23** business and management; economics; sociology and social policy; town and country planning. **22** art and design; land and property management; media studies; nursing; psychology. **21** building; electrical and electronic engineering; health subjects; mathematics; modern languages; politics. **20** agriculture.

## Overview

West of England (UWE) boasts the best teaching quality record in the new universities and has always been regarded among the leaders in its peer group. Perfect scores for education and the joint assessment for biology and biomedical sciences are its best results, but every subject assessed since 1995 has been given at least 20 out of 24 points. Business and management, the university's biggest subject area with 3,400 students, and economics also scored well in 2001.

This record and a popular location are proving highly attractive to students. The demand for places has been rising steadily, but the university found itself in trouble with the funding council for missing its 'benchmarks' for extending access to under-represented groups in higher education. Almost one undergraduate in five attended a fee-paying school, a proportion exceeded by only one other new university. The share of places going to working-class students or those from areas without a history of higher education was also well below the national average for the subjects offered.

Given the intake, the drop-out rate of 18 per cent might have been lower. But this seems not to put off the thousands who flock to the region's largest university. More than half of the students come from the West Country and there are close links with local business and industry. A network of fifteen colleges stretches into Somerset and Wiltshire, offering UWE programmes. Hartpury College, near Gloucester, has become an associate faculty of the university, specialising in agriculture, equine studies and other land-based courses.

A tradition of vocational education regularly helps the university to a healthy graduate employment record. The entrance system credits vocational qualifications and practical experience equally with traditional academic results. Law received a commendation from the Legal Practice Board and the degree in Architecture and Planning won a similar accolade from the Royal Town Planning Institute for bringing together the two disciplines in one joint honours course giving dual professional qualifications. Industrial links are paying off in a variety of ways. Hewlett Packard, for example, has launched a scholarship scheme for up to 25 students studying Computing for Real-Time Systems, with up to £14,000 available to cover fees and living expenses for the four-year course.

Among the new universities, only Oxford Brookes entered a larger proportion of academics than UWE's 40 per cent in the 2001 Research Assessment Exercise. The results were an improvement on 1996, with accounting and finance rated nationally outstanding with much work of international standards. However, the scale of the entry also produced more low grades than the university would have wished.

There are four sites in Bristol itself, mainly around the north of the city, with regional centres in Bath, and Swindon concentrating on the growth area of nursing. Only Bower Ashton, which houses art, media and design, is in the south. The main campus at Frenchay, close to Bristol Parkway station but four miles out of the city centre, has by far the largest number of students and includes the Centre for Student Affairs, which brings together the various non-academic services. The St Matthias site (for psychology and humanities) and Glenside (for midwifery, nursing, physiotherapy and radiography) are more attractive but less lively. Education has moved from the Redland campus, near the city centre, to a £16 million headquarters at Frenchay.

Bristol is a hugely popular student centre: an attractive and lively city, but not cheap. University accommodation has become more plentiful in recent years, with almost 3,000 places available. Students complain that sports facilities are limited, but 21 acres have been acquired to provide pitches for all major sports.

## Accommodation

Number of places and costs refer to 2001–02

*University-provided places:* 3,000

*Percentage catered:* 0%

*Costs for catered accommodation:* n/a

*Costs for self-catered accommodation:* £4–£54 a week.

*Policy for first-year students:* applications are processed in the order of receipt. UWE guarantees accommodation for first years accepting an offer at UWE as their firm choice and who return their form by 1 July.

*Policy for international students:* all international students are offered accommodation. First years are given an additional month in which to apply, and second and third-year students are also offered accommodation during March/April.

*Contact for further information:* Sas@uwe.ac.uk

# University of Westminster

Times ranking: 69 (2002 ranking: 64)

**Founded:** Founded 1838, university status 1992, formerly Polytechnic of Central London

**Contact details**
*Address:* 309 Regent Street,
London W1B 2UW
*Tel:* 020 7911 5000
*Fax:* 020 7911 5858
*Website:* www.wmin.ac.uk
*e-mail:* admissions@wmin.ac.uk

**The Times rankings**
*Teaching assessment:* =70 (20.5)
*Research assessment:* =67 (2.8)
*Entry standards:* =76 (13.6)
*Student–staff ratio:* 9 (11.2)
*Library/IT spend/student:* 61 (£428)
*Facilities spend/student:* =74 (£132)
*Firsts and 2:1s:* 48 (56.0%)
*Work and further study:* 83 (91.7%)
*Expected completion rate:* 98 (74%)

**Students**
*Undergraduates:* 9,440 (5,980)
*Postgraduates:* 1,850 (4,030)
*Mature students:* 35.3%
*Overseas students:* 15.8%
*Applications per place:* 5.9
*From state sector schools:* 92%
*From working class homes:* 38%

**Teaching quality assessments**
*1993–95 Rated Excellent:* none.
*From 1995 (top score 24):* **24** psychology; tourism. **23** Chinese; French; health subjects; media studies; music; politics. **22** building; Middle Eastern and African studies; politics. **21** anatomy and physiology; art and design; electrical and electronic engineering; molecular biosciences; organismal biosciences. **20** business and management; civil engineering; German; linguistics; mathematics; town planning. **19** Italian; land management. **18** Iberian languages; Russian; sociology.

## Overview

Westminster spent much of the 1990s extending and upgrading its premises, and the task is still not complete. The university has turned its attention from what was Europe's largest university construction project – the £33 million transformation of the former Harrow College, in north London – to one of the three central sites, opposite Madame Tussauds. The large business school has acquired a 'cloistered environment' in a £9.5 million scheme which creates more space for teaching and research. The university is also seeking planning consent to redevelop its New Cavendish Street site, near the BT Tower. The greenfield Harrow campus now boasts a high-tech information resources centre with new facilities for the highly rated media studies courses. Computing and design are also based on a site designed for 7,500 students. The West End sites provide the perfect catchment area for part-time students, who account for almost half of the 21,000 places. Only the Open University has more. By no means all the students are Londoners, however: one in six come from abroad – among the highest proportions among the new universities. Westminster courses are also taught in nine overseas countries, from Oman to the United States, a characteristic which won the university a Queen's Award for Enterprise.

The historic headquarters building, near Broadcasting House, houses law, social sciences and languages. French and Chinese have scored particularly well in teaching assessments, and Westminster claims to offer the largest number of languages – 25 – in any British university. Science and health courses are concentrated on the Cavendish campus, near the BT Tower. The university's growing interest in health covers degrees from the British College of Naturopathy and Osteopathy and a range of courses in complementary medicine, including a BSc in acupuncture. There are degrees in herbal medicine, homeopathy and nutritional therapy, and a diploma in the traditional Chinese massage technique of Qigong.

A series of good teaching quality scores cemented Westminster's position among the leading new universities in *The Times* table. Psychology and tourism lead the way with maximum points, with Chinese, media studies, community care and primary health all on the next rung of the ladder. The university weaves work-related skills into its degree programmes.

No new university exceeded Westminster's haul of four subjects on grade 5 in the latest assessment exercise, although the decision to enter fewer than 30 per cent of academics limited both the funding rewards and the impact on the university's ranking. Asian studies, law, linguistics and media studies were all rated nationally outstanding with much work of international quality.

Almost four out of ten undergraduates are from working-class homes – a much higher proportion than the national average for the subjects offered. The university also matches the 'benchmark' set by the funding council for the admission of students from state schools and colleges, although the central London location reduces the share of places going to students from areas without a tradition of higher education. The drop-out rate, at more than one in five, could be lower, but is still less than the norm for the subjects offered.

Like those at all the London universities, Westminster's students complain of the high cost of living, particularly for accommodation. The university has added considerably to its residential stock in recent years, but there is no way round the capital's inflated housing market at some stage. The Harrow campus is lively socially, but those based on the other sites tend to be spread around the capital. Sports facilities are also dispersed, with playing fields and a boathouse in Chiswick, west London.

## Accommodation
Number of places and costs refer to 2001–02

*University-provided places:* 1,278

*Percentage catered:* 0%

*Costs for catered accommodation:* n/a

*Costs for self-catered accommodation:* £66.92–£79.94 (single room) a week.

*Policy for first-year students:* first years are prioritised. Students from within 25 miles of the university are not prioritised.

*Policy for international students:* first years whose applications are received by 1 May are guaranteed a place.

*Contact for further information:* housing@wmin.ac.uk

# University of Wolverhampton

**Times ranking:** 84 (2002 ranking: 87)

**Founded:** University status 1992, formerly Wolverhampton Polytechnic

**Contact details**
*Address:* Wulfruna Street,
Wolverhampton WV1 1SB
*Tel:* 01902 321000
*Website:* www.wlv.ac.uk
*e-mail:* admissions@wlv.ac.uk

**The Times rankings**
*Teaching assessment:* =74 (20.4)
*Research assessment:* =90 (2.0)
*Entry standards:* =85 (12.8)
*Student–staff ratio:* =63 (17.9)
*Library/IT spend/student:* 88 (£359)
*Facilities spend/student:* 27 (£195)
*Firsts and 2:1s:* 61 (51.4%)
*Work and further study:* 94 (89.3%)
*Expected completion rate:* =85 (79%)

**Students**
*Undergraduates:* 12,880 (5,700)
*Postgraduates:* 750 (2,150)
*Mature students:* 32.7%
*Overseas students:* 12.7%
*Applications per place:* 4.6
*From state sector schools:* 98%
*From working class homes:* 45%

**Teaching quality assessments**
*1993–95 Rated Excellent:* none.
*From 1995 (top score 24):* **24** philosophy.
**23** business and management; education; molecular biosciences; organismal biosciences; politics. **22** economics; health subjects; Russian. **21** American studies; art and design; linguistics; nursing; psychology; theology. **20** building; general engineering; Iberian languages; mathematics and statistics; sociology. **19** drama, dance and cinematics; French; media studies. **17** German.

## Overview

Wolverhampton is officially the most working class university in Britain, as well as being among the largest. The 47 per cent of undergraduates coming from the lowest socio-economic classes represents twice the proportion at some new universities and more than five times the figure at Oxford and Cambridge. The share of places is much larger than the 'benchmark' set by the funding council, reflecting the priority the university gives to extending access to higher education.

Almost a quarter of the students are from ethnic minorities, and more than a third live with their parents. With roots in the 19th-century mechanics institutes, Wolverhampton naturally leans towards vocational courses. The university pioneered the high street 'higher education shop' and big outreach programmes take courses into the workplace. More than half of the students come from the region, almost a quarter from areas without a tradition of higher education. The university is no longer confined to Wolverhampton, however. Four campuses, each with their own learning centres, are linked by a free bus service. Two are in Wolverhampton, but teacher training is based in Walsall. The original site adjoins the Wolves ground and boasts three pubs. The most significant development came with the opening of a purpose-built facility in Telford, which was given its own identity initially as the University in Shropshire. Sited appropriately in an Enterprise Zone, the campus provides a variety of courses for a county with no higher education institution of its own.

Wolverhampton has embarked on a £60 million infrastructure investment programme known as 'New Horizons'. A seven-year programme, the project includes the construction – already well underway – of a new flagship Millennium City Building to be completed and fully operational by August 2002. The new site will provide over 10,000 square metres of teaching space, incorporating a 300-seat lecture theatre, an area for informal study, an exhibition hall, refectory and provision for academic and administrative offices. In addition, it will be able to house 1,300 students comfortably, as well as being a base for 200 academic and support staff.

Future developments include plans for a Lottery-funded specialist Judo, Sports Science and Medicine Centre at the University's Walsall campus and a new technology for the Telford campus. The Compton campus will become the centre for postgraduate business courses and home of the Leadership Centre for school managers throughout the region.

Teaching assessments have improved, after a poor start, with philosophy achieving a perfect score and business and education only one point behind. Inspectors were critical of quality control on the many courses franchised to further education colleges, but procedures have since been tightened up. Research ratings are among the lowest in the university system, however, with fewer than one academic in five entered for assessment and no subjects in the top two of the seven categories.

Wolverhampton claims a number of firsts for its academic programme, pioneering Interactive Multimedia Communication degrees, as well as offering the only one in British sign language and one of the first in virtual reality design and manufacturing. It was the first university to be registered under the British Standard for the quality of its all-round provision, following up with a Charter Mark and then becoming an Investor in People. The Charter Mark has since been renewed for an unprecedented third time. The university was also the first to open a dedicated student employment bureau.

Social facilities vary considerably between sites, although they are close enough for students to come together for big events. Wolverhampton claims the fastest growing nightlife in the UK, although the basis of comparison is unclear, but there is no doubt that the cost of living is reasonable. A £21 million art gallery opened in 2000 and the cultural attractions of Birmingham are now only a metro tram-ride away.

## Accommodation
Number of places and costs refer to 2002–03

*University-provided places:* 2,067

*Percentage catered:* 0%

*Costs for catered accommodation:* n/a

*Costs for self-catered accommodation:* £42.50–£58.50 a week.

*Policy for first-year students:* no restrictions. First come, first served, but more than 90% get a place in hall.

*Policy for international students:* same as above, but most get a place.

*Contact for further information:* residences@wlv.ac.uk

# University of York

Times ranking: 8 (2002 ranking: 12)

**Founded:** Royal charter 1962

**Contact details**
*Address:* Heslington, York YO10 5DD
*Tel:* 01904 433533
*Website:* www.york.ac.uk
*e-mail:* admissions@york.ac.uk

**The Times rankings**
*Teaching assessment:* 2 (22.6)
*Research assessment:* =7 (5.8)
*Entry standards:* 10 (2.5.)
*Student–staff ratio:* 15 (13.0)
*Library/IT spend/student:* 37 (£520)
*Facilities spend/student:* =56 (£152)
*Firsts and 2:1s:* 22 (68.5%)
*Work and further study:* =14 (96.3%)
*Expected completion rate:* =6 (94%)

**Students**
*Undergraduates:* 5,560 (880)
*Postgraduates:* 1,370 (920)
*Mature students:* 6.3%
*Overseas students:* 7.5%
*Applications per place:* 8.3
*From state sector schools:* 80%
*From working class homes:* 15%

**Teaching quality assessments**
*1993–95 Rated Excellent:* architecture; computer science; English; history; music; social policy; social work.
*From 1995 (top score 24):* **24** economics; education; electrical and electronic engineering; molecular biosciences; organismal biosciences; philosophy; physics; politics; psychology. **23** sociology. **22** business; linguistics; mathematics and statistics; modern languages. **21** history of art; nursing.

## Overview

York is another university to have demonstrated in successive *Times* rankings and academic assessments that comparative youth is no bar to excellence. Only Cambridge has a better record for teaching quality. Almost half of the subjects assessed since 1995 – economics, education, electrical and electronic engineering, biosciences, philosophy, physics, politics and psychology – have achieved perfect scores, and none has slipped below 21 points out of 24. The university is increasingly recognised as a permanent fixture in the top rank of British higher education.

Like Warwick, the only one of its contemporaries to rate as highly in our table, York has chosen its subjects carefully and has no plans for dramatic expansion. There are still only 8,000 students, with no veterinary science, dentistry or law. However, the available subjects are offered in a variety of unusual combinations, many including a language component. Among the more recent additions have been nursing and midwifery, which grew out of the incorporation in 1996 of the former North Yorkshire College of Health Studies. From 2003 York will be offering a medical degree. A joint initiative with Hull, the Hull York Medical School will have a strong focus on learning in community settings.

There are ten applications to each place in most subjects, the total rising by 17 per cent for courses beginning in 2002, so entrance requirements are high. Although around eight out of ten undergraduates are state-educated, only 15 per cent come from working-class homes. However, the 6 per cent drop-out rate is among the lowest in Britain.

Unlike most universities, York concentrated on science and technology in expanding its entry during the 1990s, balancing an initial bias towards the arts and social sciences. The university won a Queen's Anniversary Prize for its work in computer science, which is rated internationally outstanding for research as well as excellent for teaching. Psychology and English were the other starred research departments in the latest assessments, which placed 84 per cent of the academics in the top two of seven categories.

Since 1990, York has been reviewing its courses every three years. External audits have also been complimentary, with surveys showing most students satisfied with their tuition. Every student has a 'supervisor' responsible for their academic and personal welfare. Existing courses include language and computer literacy training, and the programme will expand this year to include courses on personal effectiveness, financial management, active citizenship and introduction to accounting. The business community is involved at every level. Undergraduates can also take the 'York Award', comprising a range of courses, work placements and voluntary activities which aim to prepare students for the world of work.

The university is set in 200 acres of parkland, a mile outside the picturesque city centre. Modern buildings are clustered around an artificial lake. Students join one of seven colleges, which mix academic and social roles. Most departments have their headquarters in one of the colleges, but the student community is a deliberate mixture of disciplines, years and sexes. Nursing apart, only archaeology and history of art are located off campus, sharing a medieval building in the centre of the city.

Social life on campus is lively, despite the absence of a student union building, with colleges the main focus. A new retail centre, including a supermarket and bookshop, has recently opened. There are two newspapers, television and radio stations, as well as several magazines, to keep students abreast of campus issues. Sports facilities are good, and have been improved further with the opening of a new sports pavilion. Playing fields are on campus and the River Ouse fosters a strong rowing tradition. Cultural events abound in the city, which is also famous for a high concentration of pubs, and the club scene has improved in recent years.

## Accommodation
Number of places and costs refer to 2001–02

*University-provided places:* 3,772

*Percentage catered:* 0%

*Costs for catered accommodation:* n/a

*Costs for self-catered accommodation:* £48.51–£62.44 (single room) a week.

*Policy for first-year students:* first-year undergraduates are guaranteed university accommodation if an application is received by 8 September (UK residents) or 15 September (resident outside UK).

*Policy for international students:* overseas students (non-EU) are guaranteed accommodation for full duration of the course.

*Contact for further information:* accommodation@york.ac.uk
www.york.ac.uk/admin/accom

# University Cities

One glance at their glossy prospectuses shows that universities today are well aware that students look almost as carefully at their future surroundings as at their chosen courses. Those set in rolling countryside or a lively city flaunt their advantages. The lecture room and library are only part of the story, and students are not going to achieve peak performance if they are tied for three or four years to a place they do not like. These pages offer a brief guide to the main student centres. All have at least two universities.

Fashions change quickly among students, and a popular city can soon lose its attractions. London, for example, used to be a magnet for students, but some of the capital's universities have struggled to fill their places recently because of the high cost of living. Manchester, by contrast, with its full-time student community of 70,000 has become a particular draw while Newcastle is also challenging for the position of the students' favourite city.

The following pages profile:

| | | |
|---|---|---|
| Aberdeen | Belfast | Birmingham |
| Brighton | Bristol | Cambridge |
| Cardiff | Coventry | Dundee |
| Edinburgh | Glasgow | Leeds |
| Leicester | Liverpool | London |
| Manchester | Newcastle | Nottingham |
| Oxford | Sheffield | |

# Aberdeen

Population: 216,000
Student population: 20,000

Distance from city centre
University of Aberdeen: King's College about 1 mile (20 minute bus ride) north of the city, Foresterhill a 20-minute walk
The Robert Gordon University: five sites around the city

## Overview
Known as the Granite City, Aberdeen is Scotland's third largest city and home to Scotland's third oldest university, yet it is still compact enough to get around on foot. The city is close to the Grampian mountains and excellent beaches, as well as being a bustling social and commercial centre. The expansion of oil-related industries in the 1980s pushed up living costs, but the low local rate of unemployment means that part-time jobs are a real possibility for students. Social life tends to be focused on the students' unions, especially the older university's excellent facilities, to which all students have access.

## What to do
There are two cinemas showing all the usual latest releases. His Majesty's Theatre plays host to drama, ballet, opera and musicals whilst the Aberdeen Arts Centre and the Music Hall are the venues for other major musical events. The Exhibition and Conference Centre is often the most northerly stop on the circuit for many touring bands. The Lemon Tree and the Beach Ballroom cater for the student market. There is an enviable selection of eating places, pubs and clubs. The most recently completed indoor shopping centre is The Academy which offers a range of bars, cafés and specialist shopping. Sports enthusiasts are well-catered for with swimming pools, the largest bowling alley in Scotland, 11 golf courses and a Premier League football team. Aberdeen and Grampian Tourist Board is at 27 Albyn Place, Aberdeen, AB10 1YL.

## What to see
The City Art Gallery has an excellent collection of fine and applied art, in addition to silver and glass collections. The Arts Centre has a small gallery for contemporary arts and crafts. The Duthie Park Winter Gardens is Europe's largest indoor garden collection. Aberdeen Maritime Museum is housed in the 16th-century Provost Ross's House and the Marischal College Museum, the Zoology Museum at the University of Aberdeen and the Grampian Transport Museum and Satrosphere, the science discovery centre, are all worth a visit.

## Getting around
Local bus services are plentiful, but short distances mean that walking or cycling are reliable alternatives. Direct rail services link Aberdeen and London, including a sleeper service. The journey takes around 8 hours. Aberdeen is served by its own airport.

## Websites for more information
www.aberdeencity.gov.uk/
www.regionlink.com/grampian/aberdeen
www.agtb.org/

# Belfast

> **Population:** 300,000
> **Student population:** 37,000
>
> **Distance from city centre**
> **Queen's University, Belfast:** main campus half-mile south
> **University of Ulster:** only about 850 of the student population are based in Belfast, but many of those who study at Jordanstown (7 miles) live in the city.

## Overview

Belfast is the largest city in Northern Ireland, and is both the cultural and political capital. To those from outside the province wondering what life is like in the city, student union representatives have stressed the dangers of over-emphasising the effects of The Troubles, given that many students remain quite oblivious to goings on, wrapped as they are in the blanket of university life. Indeed, the peace process has even stimulated demand from the mainland. Belfast is better endowed than most student cities with theatres and cinemas. Student life tends to concentrate around the Queen's campus. One offshoot of this is that this area has the highest incidence of burglary and car theft in the city. But the area is popular and is home to a wealth of restaurants, theatres and shops. Student bars tend to be particularly lively on Thursday nights, after which many students go home for the weekend, leaving the campuses a little deserted This exodus is less of a problem now that the numbers of international students (including increasing numbers from the Republic of Ireland) have increased.

## What to do

There are five cinemas including a 10-screen Virgin and the Queen's Film Theatre. Theatre is provided at the Grand Opera House, the Lyric and the Civic Arts Theatre, whilst the Old Museum Arts Centre offers alternative productions. Major concerts are staged at the Ulster Hall and the Waterfront Hall; art exhibitions are held at the Ormeau Baths Gallery and the Ulster Museum on the Queen's University campus. There are plenty of clubs and pubs, and live music is part of the scene. Belfast Welcome Centre is at 47 Donegall Place, Belfast, BT1 5AD.

## What to see

Belfast Castle overlooks the city and its cellars have been transformed to offer trips back to Victorian times; attractions include an antique shop, craft shop, bar and bistro. The Georgian village of Hillsborough, Grey Abbey and Bangor, the local seaside resort, are all within easy reach. The Queen's International Arts Festival is in November.

## Getting around

There are reliable and reasonable bus and rail services; cycling is possible but the weather puts many off. Ferry services operate out of Belfast and Larne. Flights to London take about 1 hour from either the City Airport or the International Airport.

## Websites for more information

www.belfast.net/
www.belfastcity.gov.uk/
http://belfast.local.ie/

# Birmingham

**Population:** 1.000,000
**Student population:** 45,000

**Distance from city centre**
**Aston University:** campus a 10-min. walk
**Birmingham University:** campus 3 miles southwest
**University of Central England in Birmingham:** nine sites; the main site is at Perry Barr, 3 miles north

## Overview

Massive investment and bold cultural initiatives have transformed the cityscape and underpinned Birmingham's attempt to market itself as a major European city. Much still remains to be done but the brutalism of 1960s town planning is giving way to new skyscraper hotels, pedestrianised squares and rejuvenated historic areas. Among the most impressive developments are Centenary Square, the International Convention Centre and Brindleyplace, where many bars, restaurants and shops cluster around the renovated city-centre canals. The distances between the universities' sites mean that students from different institutions are more likely to meet up at city-centre pubs and nightclubs than at each others' students' unions. Town–gown tension is a problem in some areas, but the centre is much safer now than previously.

## What to do

Birmingham Royal Ballet is based at the Hippodrome, whilst Symphony Hall is the home of the City of Birmingham Symphony Orchestra. There are three theatres, five multiscreen cinemas and the Midlands Art Centre. The National Indoor Arena hosts many national sporting events and the National Exhibition Centre (NEC) stages major exhibitions and pop concerts. There is a great variety of clubs, pubs, music venues and restaurants, including over 49 different restaurants along the 'Balti Mile'. Premiership football is provided by Aston Villa, and Test and County cricket is played at Edgbaston. The City Plaza and Pallasades are big modern shopping malls but students may prefer the Victorian arcades like The Great Western, or the Rag Market. Birmingham Tourist Information Centre is at 130 Colmore Road, Birmingham, B3 3AP.

## What to see

The Birmingham Sealife Centre is the UK's first major city-centre aquarium. The City Museum and Art Gallery has a major collection of Victorian paintings, while contemporary art is shown at the Ikon Gallery. The Museum of the Jewellery Quarter chronicles the history of the trade in Birmingham. The science-based Discovery Centre opened in 2001.

## Getting around

There are plenty of ways of getting around the city – buses, trains and trams. There are some cycle ways but heavy traffic and busy roads are best avoided. Trains take 1 hr 45 mins to London. Birmingham International airport has flights direct to Europe and the USA.

## Websites for more information

www.birmingham.gov.uk
http://icbirmingham.ic24.com/

# Brighton

**Population:** 250,000
**Student population:** 24,000

**Distance from city centre**
**University of Brighton:** one site in Eastbourne and three in Brighton
**University of Sussex:** about 4 miles north

## Overview

Located just 50 miles south of London, the overwhelming majority of Brighton's students come from the London area, contributing to its reputation as 'London by the Sea'. The similarity to the capital city manifests itself not only in Brighton's variety and vitality, helped by large numbers of international students, but also in high prices and trendiness. Relaxed places, such as the North Laine, do exist, however. The variety of nightlife in the city centre means that Brighton's students' unions are less well used than those at other universities, but they do benefit from easy accessibility.

## What to do

There are 19 cinema screens in the city. Theatre is provided at the Theatre Royal, Komedia and the Gardner Arts Centre at the University of Sussex. The Brighton Centre plays host to the large pop and rock tours, whilst the Dome is home to the Brighton Philharmonic Orchestra and is an international centre for conferences and the arts. The Brighton Bears basketball team is based at the Brighton Centre and the football team, Brighton & Hove Albion, play at Withdean Stadium. With a reputation as the clubbing capital of the south coast, Brighton attracts big name DJs and specialist nights from all over the country. North Laine with its Saturday fleamarket and interesting shops is popular with students, while The Lanes provides trendy and expensive shops. Churchill Square has all the High Street favourites under one roof. The Marina with its factory outlet shopping village, restaurants, bars and leisure complex includes a health club and bowling alley. Brighton Visitor Information Centre is at 10 Bartholomew Square, Brighton BN1 1JS.

## What to see

There are ten museums including the state-of-the-art Brighton Museum and Art Gallery. The restored Royal Pavilion is a 'must see'. The Victorian Brighton Pier is packed with traditional seaside amusements, whilst the West Pier is undergoing a major restoration. The new-look Beachfront area between the two piers buzzes with bars, cafes, clubs, artists' and fishing quarters plus free events throughout the summer. England's largest arts extravaganza, the Brighton Festival, is in May.

## Getting around

Brighton is compact and easy to get around on foot. The bus services are plentiful, and there is a network of cycle lanes. Car parking is at a premium and there is a park-and-ride system. Trains to London take around 1 hour. London Gatwick Airport is 25 miles away.

## Websites for more information

www.visitbrighton.com
www.itchybrighton.co.uk
www.whatsonguide.co.uk

# Bristol

**Population:** 405,200
**Student population:** 36,000

**Distance from city centre**
**University of Bristol:** campus in Cotham area, close to the city centre
**University of the West of England at Bristol:** five campuses; the main purpose-built Frenchay Campus lies about 4 miles north

## Overview

Bristol is described by students as being large enough to be lively, but not so large as to be daunting. Bristol is a historic city, perched on hills overlooking the Severn estuary, with a dockland waterfront and acres of parks and gardens. It is the largest city in southwest England and Brunel's landmark Clifton suspension bridge affords an impressive approach to the city. Bristol is generally welcoming to students and offers a good deal of student-orientated entertainment. While many students from UWE and locals come to events in the University of Bristol Union, pubs in the town tend to be more segregated.

## What to do

The city is well provided with cinemas both large multiscreens and small independents plus an IMAX. The Bristol Old Vic is based at the Theatre Royal, whilst the Hippodrome is the venue for musicals, ballet and opera. The Colston Hall is host to a variety of comedy, rock, pop and orchestral concerts and exhibitions. The Arnolfini and the harbourside Watershed Media Centre also offer a lively programme of exhibitions, films and theatre.

Bristol has a good range of pubs and clubs. Broadmead, the Galleries and The Mall at Cribbs Causeway have all the high street names, whilst Park Street is useful for music and second-hand clothing. Clifton Village has many specialist shops but can be expensive. Sport is well catered for with two league football clubs – City and Rovers – and Somerset Cricket Club. Tennis, swimming, ice skating and golf are all available. Bristol Tourist Information Centre is at The Annexe, Wildscreen Walk, Harbourside, Bristol BS1 5DB.

## What to see

Bristol City Council boasts six museums with free admission. The Bristol Zoo Gardens are worth a visit, as are the new attractions at the Harbourside, such as @Bristol, consisting of Explore@Bristol, Wildwalk@Bristol and an IMAX cinema.

## Getting around

Travel by car and parking are difficult and expensive. Walking and cycling are preferable despite Bristol's hills. There is an extensive and reasonably priced bus network and the Studentlink bus service operates during the week. Trains to London take 1 hr 30 mins. GO flies out of the small airport at Bristol, and London Heathrow can be reached easily.

## Websites for more information

www.bristol-city.gov.uk/
www.about-bristol.co.uk/
www.digitalbristol.org/
www.visitbristol.co.uk
www.venue.co.uk

# Cambridge

**Population:** 118,211
**Student population:** 25,000

**Distance from city centre**
**Cambridge University:** ancient buildings form the city centre
**Anglia Polytechnic University:** campus 10-minute walk; its other campus is 40 miles away in Chelmsford

## Overview

One of Britain's most prestigious academic locations, Cambridge is a town-sized city easy to navigate on foot or bike. The city has also become the centre of the hi-tech 'Silicon Fen' industries. Despite the bustle created by throngs of students and tourists, the atmosphere in a small city of such beauty can feel cloistered or even stifling, especially to those from larger and livelier places. The gulf between new and old universities is nowhere wider than in Cambridge. Nonetheless, the two universities' students do mix, and those at Anglia enjoy access to a wide range of social events, which is fortunate because the university rather than the town is the main host. Town and gown relations are generally good.

## What to do

The Corn Exchange is the largest arts and entertainment venue and hosts a full range of events. The Junction is popular for bands, dance and experimental theatre whilst the ADC Theatre is owned by a student society and managed by the university. The Arts Picture House shows foreign and cult classics and hosts the two-week Cambridge Film Festival in July. Cambridge has a good array of pubs, but few clubs. The Cambridge Folk Festival is held each July and the Strawberry Fair in June. Shopping is located in the market place and the Grafton Centre. For sports enthusiasts there are two football teams based in the city – United and City – and the usual range of football, cricket, climbing and swimming are available, although many sport facilities are based within the university. Cambridge Tourist Information Centre is at The Old Library, Wheeler Street, Cambridge, CB2 3QB.

## What to see

The Fitzwilliam Museum offers free admission to its exhibitions of paintings and ceramics and the Kettles Yard Gallery is very popular with those who enjoy modern art and sculpture. An excellent way to see the sights of Cambridge, particularly the grounds of some of the oldest and most beautiful colleges, is to hire a punt, rowing boat or canoe and travel along The Backs at a leisurely pace or to go upriver to Grantchester.

## Getting around

Walking and cycling are the most popular modes of transport as much of the city is flat and easily accessible. Buses are fairly reliable but expensive; cars are not recommended in the centre. Trains to London take 50–70 mins. London Stansted airport is 30 mins away by train.

## Websites for more information

www.tourismcambridge.com
www.cambridge-news.co.uk/
www.gwydir.demon.co.uk/cambridgeuk/

# Cardiff

**Population:** 320,000
**Student population:** 25,000

**Distance from city centre**
**University of Glamorgan:** campus is 10 miles north
**Cardiff University:** buildings all round the city centre
**University of Wales, College of Medicine:** based at the University Hospital of Wales, 2 miles from the city centre
**Cardiff Institute:** four main teaching campuses situated in and around the city centre

## Overview

There is much to be proud of in this small but prosperous and attractive capital city. It is surrounded by a historic waterfront area on the one side and beautiful countryside on the other, with good public transport systems. Cardiff has all the cultural and commercial facilities one would expect in the home of the National Assembly for Wales. The university's buildings are dotted around the city's civic centre, a dignified and open area dominated by gleaming white buildings. Cardiff's students' union building is rated one of the best in the UK.

## What to do

The Chapter Arts Centre boasts two cinemas, three theatres, a visual arts centre plus café and bars. The Millennium Centre, which will be the new home for the Welsh National Opera, is due to be completed in 2004. Famous for rugby, the Millennium Stadium is currently the venue for major national and international football fixtures such as the FA Cup. Other sports catered for in the city include squash, ice skating, golf, swimming and football. The main shopping areas are Queen Street and the St David's Centre. The Edwardian arcades of the Capitol Centre offer a variety of unusual shops and cafés. The Atlantic Wharf entertainment complex offers a 12-screen cinema, bowling alley, nightclub, bars and restaurant. Cardiff Visitor Centre is at St David's House, 16 Wood Street, Cardiff CF10 1ES.

## What to see

The Cardiff Bay regeneration project reunites the city of Cardiff with its historic waterfront. Pierhead is the Visitor and Education Centre for the National Assembly, providing futuristic exhibitions with touch-screen technology. The National Museum and Art Gallery displays collections of paintings, silver and ceramics whilst the Museum of Welsh Life is an open-air museum set in 100 acres of parkland with over 30 reconstructions of Welsh buildings.The 11th-century Cardiff Castle is located in the city centre.

## Getting around

There is a reasonable and reliable bus service and cycling is popular. Trains to London take 2 hours. There are direct flights from Cardiff airport to a number of European destinations.

## Websites for more information

www.cardiff.gov.uk/
www.virtualcardiff.co.uk/
www.cardiffvisitor.info

# Coventry

**Population:** 300,000
**Student population:** 28,000

**Distance from city centre**
**Coventry University:** purpose-built campus in the city centre
**University of Warwick:** modern campus about 3 miles from the city centre

## Overview

Once a prosperous medieval town, Coventry's modern success is based on engineering and motor manufacture. It enjoys good communications and low prices, and is currently undergoing a major makeover with a number of new projects, notably the Phoenix Initiative. The city has good shopping centres and the town–gown relationship is generally relaxed.

The paths of students from the two universities rarely cross. Students at Warwick tend to stay on campus and prefer Kenilworth and Leamington Spa when looking for accommodation. Coventry University students make the most of the city-centre which complements their own sports centre and students' union.

## What to do

Cinema lovers are well catered for between the Odeon cineplex at The Skydome leisure complex, the Film Theatre, and the Showcase Cinema just outside Coventry. The Belgrade Theatre hosts musicals, pantomime and traditional theatre whilst the Warwick Arts Centre plays host to theatre, popular music, dance, classical concerts and opera. It is also home to the Mead Gallery with exhibitions of sculpture, paintings, art, craft and photography. The West Orchards Shopping Centre houses all the usual high street names, whilst out-of-town shopping is provided at the Central Six Retail Park. Coventry City Football Club is based here; Coventry Sports Centre offers three pools including a 50-metre Olympic-standard pool which is used by students at Coventry University. Speedway is also available in the city. Coventry Tourist Information Centre is at Bayley Lane, Coventry CV1 5RN.

## What to see

Coventry is home to the Museum of British Road Transport, the largest collection of British cars in the world. The Toy Museum and the Herbert Art Gallery and Museum with its Godiva City exhibition are also worth a visit. The Cathedral quarter links old and new Coventry and has been revived with a range of pubs, cafés and restaurants. Spon Street houses reconstructed medieval buildings, the Heritage Museum and a variety of pubs, bars and restaurants.

## Getting around

There is a good reliable bus service between the city and Warwick University. The area is good for cycling and walking. Trains to London take 75 mins, and Birmingham International airport is 20 mins by train.

## Websites for more information

www.coventry.gov.uk/
www.exponet.co.uk/peter/
www.coventry.org

# Dundee

Population: 165,000
Student population: 26,000

University of Dundee: main campus in city centre
University of Abertay Dundee: campus in city centre

## Overview

Called the 'City of Discovery', Dundee has been cleaned up and relaunched in recent years. Whilst not the loveliest of urban spaces, Dundee enjoys a cost of living estimated at 12 per cent lower than the UK average. Jute and jam may have disappeared, but the city is still home to DC Thomson, publishers of *The Beano* and *The Dandy*. It certainly benefits from its location on the Firth of Tay, with the Highlands within easy reach for outdoor pursuits. Regular train and bus services run between the city and Aberdeen, Glasgow, Edinburgh and on to London.

## What to do

The modern Dundee Contemporary Arts Centre is a popular venue for exhibitions, film and theatre. The Repertory Theatre, the Caird Hall, Marryat Hall complex and the Whitehall Theatre offer a range of venues for concerts and dance. The Odeon Multiplex and UGC Cinemas boast 15 screens between them. Shopping is centred on the Wellgate and the recently revamped Overgate Centres. Those looking for cheap and cheerful furniture will often find it at the Dens Road Market.

Dundee is home to two football teams. Golfers are spoiled for choice, and a running and cycling track is available at the Caird Park. Keen skiers have easy access to Scotland's slopes. The Olympia Leisure Centre has a range of leisure activities, including a climbing wall and leisure pool. Dundee Tourist Information Centre is at 21 Castle Street, Dundee DD1 3AA.

## What to see

Discovery Point is now home to Scott of the Antarctic's vessel, *Discovery*, originally designed and built in Dundee, as well as the 19th-century wooden frigate, *Unicorn*, used in the Napoleonic wars. The Verdant Works is a living museum depicting a working jute mill in the heart of Dundee; the McManus Galleries host an exhibition of history, art and natural history, whilst the Barrack Street Museum's natural history exhibition includes a 40-foot whale skeleton. The Queens Gallery on Nethergate has exhibitions of new artists and offers their work for sale. The Mills Observatory is the only full-time public observatory in the UK. 'Sensation' brings science to life with interactive exhibits.

## Getting around

There is a decent public transport network. The students' association at the University of Dundee runs a free nightbus for students within the city boundary. Trains to London take around 6 hrs 30 mins. Nearest major airports are at Aberdeen, Edinburgh and Glasgow.

## Websites for more information

www.angusanddundee.co.uk/intro.htm
www.dundeecity.gov.uk/
www.dundee.ac.uk/

# Edinburgh

**Population:** 500,000
**Student Population:** 30,000

**Distance from city centre**
**The University of Edinburgh:** Scattered around city centre, with science and engineering 2 miles south
**Heriot-Watt University:** Campus 7 miles west of the city centre
**Napier University:** 2 miles west of the city centre

## Overview

A visually spectacular and cosmopolitan capital, Edinburgh is one of the most sought-after cities by students. It is also the home of the Scottish Parliament. The compact city centre has an enviable range of pubs, bars and nightclubs, many with extended hours of opening. Students make up a good proportion of the population, and are generally welcomed. Shopping and entertainment costs are comparable with other major UK cities. Although students at Heriot-Watt tend to stay on their parkland campus, all three universities have access to each others' students' union facilities.

## What to do

Edinburgh offers 6 commercial cinemas and 3 independents. Theatres are plentiful: the Traverse for contemporary productions; the Royal Lyceum, the Playhouse and the King's and Festival Theatres for more traditional drama and music. Murrayfield Stadium is home to Scottish rugby and the city supports two football clubs – Hibs and Hearts. Princes Street is the main shopping street and boasts both national chains and Edinburgh institutions, such as Jenners. George Street, Rose Street, the Grassmarket, the Royal Mile and the Stockbridge area of the city have smaller and more unusual shops. The arrival of Harvey Nichols, created a new Bond Street style shopping area called The Walk. Edinburgh and Lothians Tourist Board is at 4 Rothesay Terrace, Edinburgh EH3 7RY.

## What to see

The city is home to a wealth of art galleries and museums, including the National Gallery of Scotland and the Royal Museum, as well as a zoo, botanical gardens, and the castle. The recently developed dockland area of Leith is alive with bars, restaurants and clubs. Ocean Terminal, a new shopping, leisure and culture complex is situated on the waterfront. Dynamic Earth, the geology and natural history exhibition, is worth a visit. Almost within the city centre is Holyrood Park with Arthur's Seat, the remnants of an extinct volcano, and Salisbury Crags. The Edinburgh Festival takes place every August.

## Getting around

Edinburgh's seven hills make cycling hard work but there is a reasonable public transport system with bus and cycle lanes. Driving is hampered by traffic congestion and an elaborate one-way system. Trains to London take 5 hrs. Edinburgh Airport is 6 miles west.

## Websites for more information

www.efr.hw.ac.uk/EDC/Edinburgh.html
www.edinburgh.org/
www.ebs.hw.ac.uk/visitors.htm

# Glasgow

**Population:** 611,440
**Student population:** 46,000

**Distance from city centre**
**University of Glasgow:** 3 miles from centre in the West End
**Glasgow Caledonian University:** situated in the city centre
**Strathclyde University:** main campus in the city centre

## Overview

Glasgow is Scotland's largest city, and one of Britain's liveliest. Glasgow has campaigned vigorously to change its 'mean city' image. Home of Charles Rennie MacIntosh and the Glasgow School of Art, it is Scotland's cultural capital, even if political power resides in Edinburgh. Scotland's opera, ballet and national orchestra are based in the city, which also boasts a profusion of art galleries, museums and theatres.

Students generally find the locals very friendly. The three universities are within easy reach of one another and many students live in the attractive West End, though the area's desirability has led to an increase in prices over recent years.

## What to do

Glasgow boasts a variety of theatres and performing/visual arts venues, for example the King's, Theatre Royal, Citizens, The Tron, The Arches and the CCA. Live music is very popular and venues range from the SECC to the Barrowlands. Glasgow is home to a great variety of classical music concerts, and has many cinemas, including four multiscreens and two independents. Glaswegians are famously fond of their pubs, and the city's club scene rivals those of London and Manchester. The Glasgow Science Centre features a Science Mall, IMAX cinema and the 127-metre-high Glasgow Tower.

A plethora of designer shops caters to the label-conscious, while the Buchanan Galleries, Princes Square and the traditional Barras street market offer variety for the cash-strapped student. The two leading football clubs based in the city are Rangers and Celtic, and other participative sports includes rugby and skiing on the city's two dry ski slopes. Glasgow Tourist Board .is at 11 George Square, Glasgow G2 1DY.

## What to see

Glasgow's medieval roots can be explored in the Cathedral and Provand's Lordship. There are 35 museums and art galleries including the famous Burrell Collection. The Trossachs and Loch Lomond are within easy reach for those interested in walking and climbing, and rail and ferry links make the nearby islands accessible.

## Getting around

There is a good cheap bus service and a reliable underground. Few regularly cycle because of the hills and heavy traffic. Trains to London take 6 hrs. National and international flights, including transatlantic, depart from Glasgow airport (8 mls) and Glasgow Prestwick (30 mls).

## Websites for more information

www.seeglasgow.com/
www.glasgow.gov.uk/

# Leeds

····················

Population: 725,000
Student population: 35,000

Distance from city centre
University of Leeds: compact redbrick campus a mile away
Leeds Metropolitan University: high-rise campus near the city centre; Beckett Park campus 3 miles away

## Overview

Leeds is a sophisticated commercial centre with more law and accountancy firms than anywhere outside London. Shopping in Leeds is unrivalled in the north of England and this Yorkshire city has a dazzling array of clubs which stay open late. The cost of living is generally low and the city itself is friendly and lively. The two universities huddle together in the city centre, and there is much interchange between their students' unions. Students who live out also tend to live in the same area, making a compact student enclave. Property rental prices are low, helped by the surplus accommodation in the city.

## What to do

Music lovers are well provided for with chamber music and jazz at the West Yorkshire Playhouse and folk and rock in Roundhay Park. The Playhouse, Grand Theatre and Civic Theatre exist alongside each other and the gas-lit Hyde Park Picture House offers a unique cinema experience. The City Art Gallery houses the new Henry Moore Centre for the Study of Sculpture. Clubs with live music include the Town and Country Club, the Music Factory, Joseph's Well and the Duchess. The recently developed Waterfront is now a dining quarter, and excellent shopping facilities exist in the Corn Exchange, Granary Wharf and the Victoria Quarter which is also home to Harvey Nichols, the fashionable department store. Leeds United plays at Elland Road and two international sporting venues – Yorkshire County Cricket Club and Leeds Rugby League Club – are both located in Headingly. Leeds also has the first city-centre boules court. Gateway Yorkshire Tourist Office is at PO Box 244, The Arcade, City Station, Leeds LS1 1PL.

## What to see

The Abbey House Museum focuses on childhood in Victorian Leeds and the history of nearby Kirkstall Abbey. The Royal Armouries is the purpose-built home for the Royal Armouries national collection of arms and armour, complete with live demonstrations. The Yorkshire Dales, North York Moors and the Vale of York on the city's doorstep allow ample opportunity for a peaceful escape.

## Getting around

A new Supertram network is under development. Buses provide a cheap and efficient method of transport. Cycling is possible, but not popular because of the hills and heavy traffic. Trains to London take 3 hrs. Leeds/Bradford airport is 8 miles north.

## Websites for more information

www.leeds.gov.uk/
www.leedsnet.com/
http://cgi.bbc.co.uk/leeds/

# Leicester

**Population:** 271,500
**Student population:** 39,000

**Distance from city centre**
**De Montfort University:** one campus in the city centre, another at Scraptoft
**Leicester University:** campus about one mile away

## Overview

Known as both the 'environment city' and a 'city full of surprises', Leicester is a compact and friendly place, rich in green spaces. Students find the city ideally sized and its central location means that it attracts students from all over England. The city is welcoming and friendly, and student social life tends to be spread evenly all over the city centre, with a few bars and clubs specifically for students. Both universities have good students' unions with reciprocal arrangements. Life in the city is inexpensive, and the fresh food market, which has the largest outdoor market in Europe, helps student finances to stretch that little bit further. Accommodation is still not too hard to find and is reasonably priced.

## What to do

Venues include the Haymarket Theatre, the Phoenix Arts Complex and De Montfort Hall, which hosts major concerts from pop to musicals. Leicester enjoys a number of annual festivals reflecting the city's cultural diversity, such as the Caribbean Carnival which is the second largest in Britain, and the Diwali Festival of Light which is the largest Diwali festival outside of India.

Shopping is mainly in the central Shires Centre and Haymarket shopping centre. Leicester has a selection of sports and leisure centres, including swimming, tennis, rugby, golf and squash, and nearby Rutland Water is very popular for watersports. Leicester Tourist Information Centre is at 7/9 Every Street, Town Hall Square, Leicester LE1 6AG.

## What to see

Tourist attractions include the New Walk Museum and the Jewry Wall Museum which has the largest free-standing Roman structure in the country. The National Space Centre is a recognition of the University of Leicester's involvement in space science. It includes the Challenger Learning Centre and combines leisure, education and research under one roof, as well as the largest planetarium in the UK outside London. The annual Comedy Festival is held in the city each February. Leicester City Football Club, Leicestershire County Cricket Club and the Leicester Tigers, one of the country's pre-eminent rugby union clubs, are all based at grounds in the city.

## Getting around

There is a good cheap bus service. As an environmentally friendly city, Leicester has miles of signed and green painted cycleways. Trains to London take 75 mins. The nearest airports are East Midlands and Birmingham.

## Websites for more information

www.leicester.gov.uk
www.discoverleicester.co.uk

# Liverpool

**Population:** 510,000
**Student population:** 36,000

**Distance from city centre**
**University of Liverpool:** modern campus in the city centre
**Liverpool John Moores University:** two main sites on opposite sides of the city centre

## Overview
Famous for its music scene, football clubs and comedians, Liverpool is currently enjoying a period of investment and development with the help of funding from Government and European sources. It aims to establish itself as a 'city of learning' and provides a friendly and economical base for students, with excellent opportunities for part-time work alongside study and one of the lowest costs of living in the UK. Both universities are centrally located and the compact city centre offers good shopping. Although the Kensington area is popular, students tend to live and socialise around the central Smithdown Road area, where cheap rents contribute to the generally low cost of living.

## What to do
The city has eight cinemas and numerous theatres including the Liverpool Empire and the Everyman, and the Philharmonic Hall for classical concerts. Liverpool has a reputation as a lively city after dark and new bars and clubs open weekly.

Home to both Liverpool and Everton football clubs, it also offers rugby union, golf, cricket and basketball. Watersports enthusiasts are catered for close to the Albert Docks and climbing is available at the Awesome Walls climbing centre. As well as the usual high-street stores, Cavern Walks caters for those who like designer gear. St John's Centre and Bold Street are popular with bargain hunters. Liverpool Tourist Information Centre is at Queen's Square, Liverpool L1 1RG.

## What to see
The National Museums and Galleries on Merseyside represents the eight museums and galleries of Liverpool including the Walker Art Gallery and HM Customs and Excise National Museum. The Tate Northern is famous for its modern art exhibitions and the Maritime Museum gives an account of Liverpool's seafaring history.

Aintree Race Course, home of the Grand National, now has a visitor centre complete with simulator ride. The Waterfront and the redeveloped Albert Dock with its shops and cafés and access to The Beatles Story are worth a visit.

## Getting around
An efficient bus service is supplemented by Merseyrail (the Metro). JMU operates a free shuttle bus between its sites. Cycling is possible but not popular. Trains to London take 3 hrs 30 mins. There are limited flights from Liverpool airport but good links with Manchester airport which has many more flights.

## Websites for more information
www.liverpool-wirral.co.uk/
www.liverpool.gov.uk/
http://icliverpool.ic24.com/

# London

## Overview

London is by far the largest city in the UK and it has universities located both in the centre of the city – University College London and Westminster University – and away from the centre – Kingston, Greenwich and Brunel. Check carefully the location of any London university that you are considering.

Whether you are interested in parks or pubs, theatres or cinemas, shopping or sightseeing, museums or art galleries, dancing non-stop throughout the weekend or eating every cuisine under the sun, London can meet your requirements. The city will also present you with a fairly hefty bill for most of the above, and for travel between them. That said, the diligent hunter will find bargains, but the temptation to spend is omnipresent.

Whatever bargains can be found elsewhere, accommodation will be a major expense for every student: even if rents away from the smart areas of the city centre are slightly less astronomical, travel to and from college can easily eat away any savings made although recent efforts by ULU (the students' union) mean most students can get 30 per cent off bus and tube fares. The capital city's hectic pace can overwhelm as easily as it excites, and loneliness can be a problem in a city where you might be living miles away from your college. Nevertheless, London is justly renowned as one of the most exciting cities in the world and, for those who can strike a balance between making the most of life and avoiding spending their way to bankruptcy, it is the ideal place to be a student.

London is such a large city with so many attractions that a description of particular activities is not given. There are many guidebooks to London.

## Getting around

London is well-served by an extensive bus, railway and underground network with special price deals available for students. In many areas the roads are very busy, making cycling a hazardous occupation. The main airports serving London are Heathrow, Gatwick, Stansted and Luton.

Websites for more information
www.london-daily.co.uk/
www.londontown.com/
www.uk-calling.co.uk/
www.timeout.com/london/
www.londonnet.co.uk/
http://cgi.bbc.co.uk/london
www.londoneye.com
www.londontheatre.co.uk/
www.tate.org.uk/modern/

# Manchester

**Population:** 405,803
**Student population:** 70,000

**Distance from city centre**
**University of Manchester:** campus just south of the city centre, south of the other two Manchester universities
**UMIST:** city-centre campus
**Manchester Metropolitan University:** city-centre campus plus sites in south Manchester, Crewe and Alsager
**University of Salford:** campus in Salford, one mile from the city centre

## Overview

Manchester is probably the most fashionable in Britain for prospective students, and to prove it, nearly 30,000 students come to the universities from outside the city. The city claims over 250 pubs, clubs and café bars in the centre, and many bands have originated on the Manchester scene – Oasis, Stone Roses, James, Happy Mondays and Simply Red to name a few. Issues of safety are the same here as in any large city and students tend to live in student-dominated enclaves like Fallowfield because of ease of access, cheapness and safety. The compact city centre holds three of Manchester's four universities.

## What to do

There are numerous cinemas including the multiscreens in addition to the Cornerhouse with its three screens, café and gallery. Manchester is home to the Royal Exchange Theatre Company, BBC Philharmonic Orchestra and the Hallé Orchestra. It also boasts one of the largest Chinatowns in Britain, 'Gay Village' in the city centre and 'Curry Mile' in Rusholme. The Lowry Centre, at Salford Quays, houses an arts centre and theatres. The Imperial War Museum, opened in May 2002, is also at Salford Quay

The 2002 Commonwealth Games, hosted by Manchester, testify to the city's excellent sporting facilities. These include the National Cycling Centre, a 20,000-capacity indoor arena, and Manchester Aquatics Centre. Home to Man United and Man City football teams and Lancashire Cricket Club, it also has the country's largest martial arts club, and is home to the English Wrestling Association and the British Mountaineering Council. Manchester Visitor Centre is at Town Hall Extension, Lloyd Street, Manchester M60 2LA.

## What to see

The Museum of Science and Industry gives a good insight into the city's technological achievements and Manchester City Art Galleries re-opened in May 2002 after a huge four-year refurbishment.

## Getting around

The city is well served by bus, train and tram and the lack of hills means that cycling is a viable alternative. Trains to London take 2 hrs 30 mins. Manchester airport is 10 miles south of the city and has a full range of international flights.

## Websites for more information

www.manchester.gov.uk/
www.manchesteronline.co.uk/index.html
www.destinationmanchester.com

# Newcastle

**Population** 280,000
**Student population** 40,000

**Distance from city centre**
**University of Newcastle:** campus in the city centre
**University of Northumbria at Newcastle:** 2 sites in the city centre, another 3 miles outside; 2 others in Longhirst (15 miles) and Carlisle (55 miles)

## Overview

Students enjoy living in Newcastle with its vibrant nightlife, excellent shopping facilities and one of the lowest costs of living in the north. Pubs in the city centre are cheap and welcoming to students at weekends. Newcastle is known as a very friendly city and is not as rough as it is often portrayed on the television. The addition of CCTV has made it a safer place after dark.

## What to do

There are three commercial cinemas, with the independent Tyneside Cinema showing cult and art films. Six theatres and five art galleries provide a range of cultural activities. The Hancock Museum is the place for natural history whilst the Discovery Museum is the largest museum complex in the region. The huge 10,000-seater Telewest Arena is a purpose-built centre playing host to major music tours, athletics and basketball. A range of smaller venues is complemented by the City Hall and the Riverside.

Newcastle offers several different shopping experiences and the famous Metro Centre is across the river in Gateshead. City shoppers can spend their time and money in Eldon Square or Monument Mall or can visit the area around the City Library where the really stylish shops are located. The Quayside area, with its many pubs, clubs, restaurants and hotels, is now linked to the Gateshead Quays by the new Millennium Bridge for pedestrians and cyclists. BALTIC, the Centre for Contemporary Art, opens in summer 2002, and the Regional Music Centre opens in 2004. Newcastle Tourist Information Centre is at 128 Grainger Street, Newcastle NE1 5AF.

## What to see

Many historic sites on Hadrian's Wall are within easy reach and the surrounding countryside of Northumbria is equally accessible. The Hoppings, a traditional fair, arrives on the Town Moor for ten days at the end of June. Life Interactive, a new attraction, is a virtual reality journey through life.

## Getting around

Newcastle's Metro connects the city centre with Gateshead, the airport and the railway station. The Sunderland extension opened in Spring 2002 There is also a good bus network. Trains to London take 3 hours. Newcastle airport is 6 miles north of the city. There is a daily ferry from the International ferry terminal at North Shields (7 miles) to the Continent.

## Websites for more information

www.newcastle.gov.uk
www.bbc.co.uk/tyne/student/index.shtml

# Nottingham

**Population:** 262,000
**Student population:** 33,000

**Distance from city centre**
**University of Nottingham:** campus about 4 miles from the city centre
**The Nottingham Trent University:** one city-centre campus; 2 other sites about 4 miles from the city centre

## Overview

Nottingham is probably still most famous for the legendary Robin Hood, whose redistribution of income policy would be welcome to most of the city's students. The modern-day crime figures suggest it is not quite as homely as it makes out, but Nottingham is safe enough for those who are sensible.

The distance between the two universities means that their students tend not to fraternise and live out in different areas. Lenton is favoured by students at the older university and Forest Fields by those at the newer. Accommodation takes some finding, but it is not exorbitantly priced.

What Nottingham lacks in rock venues it makes up for in clubs. The prices at some of these venues may keep students at arm's length, but there are plenty of student nights. Town–gown relations are generally good, and many students choose to settle here after graduation.

## What to do

Theatre is provided at the Theatre Royal and the Nottingham Playhouse and there is plenty of choice for cinemas, including the Savoy with its double seats. The Broadway Arts Cinema caters for more esoteric tastes. Nottingham offers a host of pubs – including the 'oldest pub in the world', The Trip to Jerusalem, dating back to 1189. The redeveloped canalside area has three bars and a comedy club. The Clinton Rooms, the Marcus Garvey Centre and Rock City cater for most musical tastes. The National Ice Centre has two Olympic-sized rinks, whilst the National Watersport Centre at Holme Pierrepoint offers white-water rafting in addition to rowing, canoeing and water skiing. Nottingham City Information Centre is at 1–4 Smithy Row, Nottingham NG1 2BY.

## What to see

The Galleries of Justice (to become the National Museum of Law) is an award-winning museum of the history of crime, punishment and British justice throughout the ages. The annual Goose Fair is a three-day event held each October on the Forest Recreation Ground. Around 400 caves lie under the city – many are open for tours.

## Getting around

Buses are reasonable and cycle lanes and fairly flat terrain make cycling popular with many. Trains to London take 1 hr 45 mins. The nearest airport is East Midlands.

## Websites for more information

www.nottinghamshiretourism.co.uk
www.thisisnottingham.co.uk/
www.usefulinfo.co.uk/nottingham/
tourism.htm

# Oxford
•••••••••••••••

**Population:** 141,600
**Student population:** 25,000

**Distance from city centre**
**Oxford University:** the colleges are an integral part of the city, with most of the undergraduate colleges being in or near to the city centre.
**Oxford Brookes University:** 2 campuses in Headington, 2 miles from the centre; another site at Wheatley, 6 miles east

## Overview
The city is beautiful, ancient and expensive, with prices nearly as high as in London. Expense is probably one reason why student social life tends to be concentrated in college bars and in the Brookes' students' union. Contact between the two universities is minimal, though probably greatest in the cosmopolitan Cowley Road area where many students look for non-collegiate and often overpriced accommodation.

## What to do
Oxford has four cinemas, plus the Phoenix and the Ultimate Picture Palace which cater for less mainstream tastes. The Oxford Playhouse hosts a varied programme of drama, music and comedy productions. The Apollo is a venue for rock, pop, opera and classical concerts. The numerous pubs include The Bear which dates back to 1242.

Oxford is well provided for museums and art galleries such as the Ashmolean and the Museum of the History of Science. Worth a visit is the Oxford Museum with its exhibits of ancient Oxford and the Oxford Story, which uses audiovisual presentations to take visitors back to the 13th century. The Museum of Modern Art exhibits 20th-century paintings, sculpture, photographs, films, video and performances.

Cornmarket Street and Queen Street are popular shopping areas, as are the covered Westgate and Clarendon Centres. The covered indoor market and the twice-weekly open market has a good supply of second-hand goods for bargain hunters. Book lovers are spoilt for choice.

The city has a range of swimming pools and leisure centres, an ice rink and an athletics track. Oxford Information Centre is at 15/16 Broad Street, Oxford OX1 3AS.

## What to see
Oxford has a wealth of historic buildings, most connected to the university and its colleges. The Botanic Garden, Christ Church Meadow, Port Meadow and the rivers Cherwell and Thames all provide an escape from city life. The Oxfordshire Visual Arts Festival occurs in May–June each year.

## Getting around
Most students use bikes, and cycle lanes and cycle parking are abundant. Local buses are inexpensive. Trains to London take 1 hour. The nearest airports are at Heathrow, Gatwick and Birmingham.

## Websites for more information
www.oxford.gov.uk/tourism
www.oxford-info.com/
www.dailyinfo.co.uk/

# Sheffield

| |
|---|
| **Population:** 530,000 |
| **Student population:** 45,000 |
| |
| **Distance from city centre** |
| **University of Sheffield:** campus about half a mile west of the city centre |
| **Sheffield Hallam University:** three sites, with one in the city centre; and two in the southwest of the city |

## Overview

Previously the capital of Britain's cutlery manufacturing industry, the rejuvenation of the city with new bars, cafés, restaurants and cinemas has put Sheffield back on the map. It has long been a popular city with students, a significant proportion of whom choose to settle here. Sheffield Hallam has a range of student accommodation in the Devonshire Quarter but students live throughout the city, not in isolated enclaves. Rents are generally reasonable and the cost of living lower than in many university towns.

## What to do

Sheffield has two main theatres, the Crucible and the Lyceum; the City Hall is an entertainment venue for popular and classical music, and comedy perfomances. Sheffield Arena seats 12,000 and hosts concerts, musicals, ice shows and exhibitions. Smaller venues, including the Leadmill and the Octagon Centre at the older university, host a variety of live bands. The Devonshire Quarter has bars, cafés and specialist shops aimed at the student market. Shopping in the city centre includes markets, the pedestrianised Fargate, Orchard Square and the Meadowhall shopping centre. Sheffield has a wide range of sporting facilities: two climbing centres; a ski village with outdoor ski slope and virtual snow; Ponds Forge provides an Olympic-standard swimming pool and the world's deepest diving pool. Ice hockey (Steelers) and basketball (Sharks) are both based at the Arena. There are two football teams, Sheffield Wednesday and Sheffield United, and Rugby league. Sheffield Visitor Information Centre is at 1 Tudor Square, Sheffield S1 2LA.

## What to see

The Millennium Galleries house major exhibitions from the V & A and the Tate. Magna, the new science adventure centre, celebrates the elements of earth, air, fire and water. Kelham Island Museum provides a fascinating insight into Sheffield's steel and cutlery industries. The Peak District National Park is on the doorstep and is ideal for hill walking and rock climbing. Chatsworth House is one of a number of nearby stately homes and castles.

## Getting around

Supertram serves both universities and the city centre, and buses are reliable but not cheap. Cycling is only for the fit or the determined as Sheffield is built on hills. Trains to London take 2 hrs 30 mins. The nearest airports are Manchester, Leeds/Bradford and East Midlands.

## Websites for more information

www.shef.ac.uk/city
www.sheffieldscene.co.uk/
www.sheffieldcity.co.uk/

# Higher Education Colleges

This listing gives contact details for higher education institutions not mentioned elsewhere within the book. All the institutions of the University of London which do not have their own entry are listed under the main entry for the University of London. All the institutions listed below offer degree course, some providing a wide range of courses while others are specialist colleges with a limited range of courses and a small intake. Those marked with a * are members of SCOP (the Standing Conference of Principals; www.scop.ac.uk).

## The Arts Institute at Bournemouth*
**address:** Wallisdown, Poole, Dorset BH12 5HH
**tel:** 01202 533011
**e-mail:** general@arts-inst-bournemouth.ac.uk
**website:** www.arts-inst-bournemouth.ac.uk

## Bath Spa University College*
**address:** Newton St Loe, Bath BA2 9BN
**tel:** 01225 875875
**e-mail:** enquiries@bathspa.ac.uk
**website:** www.bathspa.ac.uk

## Bishop Grosseteste College, Lincoln*
**address:** Newport, Lincoln LN1 3DY
**tel:** 01522 527347
**e-mail:** registry@bgc.ac.uk
**website:** www.bgc.ac.uk

## Bolton Institute
**address:** Deane Road, Bolton BL3 5AB
**tel:** 01204 900600
**e-mail:** mar1@bolton.ac.uk
**website:** www.bolton.ac.uk

## Buckinghamshire Chilterns University College*
**address:** Queen Alexandra Road, High Wycombe, Bucks HP11 2JZ
**tel:** 01494 522141
**e-mail:** marketing@bcuc.ac.uk
**website:** www.bcuc.ac.uk

## Canterbury Christ Church University College*
**address:** North Holmes Rd, Canterbury CT1 1QU
**tel:** 01227 767700
**e-mail:** admissions@cant.ac.uk
**website:** www.cant.ac.uk

## Central School of Speech and Drama*
**address:** Embassy Theatre, 64 Eton Avenue, London NW3 3HY
**tel:** 020 7722 8183
**e-mail:** enquiries@cssd.ac.uk
**website:** www.cssd.ac.uk

## Chester College of Higher Education*
**address:** Parkgate Road, Chester CH1 4BJ
**tel:** 01244 375444
**e-mail:** enquiries@chester.ac.uk
**website:** www.chester.ac.uk

**Conservatoire for Drama and Dance**
c/o London Contemporary Dance School
**address:** The Place, 17 Duke's Road,
London WC1H 9AB
**tel:** 020 7387 0145
**website:** www.theplace.org.uk
and
**Royal Academy of Dramatic Arts**
62-4 Gower Street, London WC1E 6ED
**tel:** 020 7908 4710
**website:** www.rada.org.uk

**Cumbria Institute of the Arts***
**address:** Brampton Road,
Carlisle CA3 9AY
**tel:** 01228 400300
**e-mail:** info@cumbria.ac.uk
**website:** www.cumbria.ac.uk

**Dartington College of Arts***
**address:** Totnes, Devon TQ9 6EJ
**tel:** 01803 862224
**e-mail:** registry@dartington.ac.uk
**website:** www.dartington.ac.uk

**Edge Hill College***
**address:** St Helens Road, Ormskirk,
Lancs L39 4QP
**tel:** 01695 584 274
**e-mail:** enquiries@edgehill.ac.uk
**website:** www.edgehill.ac.uk

**Edinburgh College of Art**
**address:** Lauriston Place,
Edinburgh EH3 9DF
**tel:** 0131 221 6000
**e-mail:** registration@eca.ac.uk
**website:** www.eca.ac.uk

**Falmouth College of Arts***
**address:** Woodlane, Falmouth,
Cornwall TR11 4RH
**tel:** 01326 211077

**e-mail:** admissions@falmouth.ac.uk
**website:** www.falmouth.ac.uk

**Glasgow School of Art**
**address:** 167 Renfrew Street,
Glasgow G3 6RQ
**tel:** 0141 353 4500
**e-mail:** info@gsa.ac.uk
**website:** www.gsa.ac.uk

**Harper Adams University College***
**address:** Edgmond, Newport,
Shropshire TF10 8NB
**tel:** 01952 820280
**e-mail:** info@harper-adams.ac.uk
**website:** www.harper-adams.ac.uk

**Kent Institute of Art and Design***
**address:** Oakwood Park, Maidstone,
Kent ME16 8AG
**tel:** 01622 757286
**address:** New Dover Road,
Canterbury CT1 3AN
**tel:** 01227 769371
**address:** Fort Pitt, Rochester ME1 1DZ
**tel:** 01634 830022
**e-mail:** info@kiad.ac.uk
**website:** www.kiad.ac.uk

**King Alfred's College, Winchester***
**address:** Sparkford Road, Winchester,
Hampshire SO22 4NR
**tel:** 01962 841515
**e-mail:** admissions@wkac.ac.uk
**website:** www.wkac.ac.uk

**Liverpool Hope University College***
**address:** Hope Park, Liverpool L16 9JD
**tel:** 0151 291 3295
**e-mail:** admission@hope.ac.uk
**website:** www.hope.ac.uk

**The London Institute***
address: 65 Davies Street,
London W1K 5DA
tel: 020 7514 6000
e-mail: prospectus@linst.ac.uk
website: www.linst.ac.uk

**Newman College of Higher Education**
address: Bartley Green,
Birmingham B32 3NT
tel: 0121 4761181
e-mail: registry@newman.ac.uk
website: www.newman.ac.uk

**North East Wales Institute**
address: Plas Coch, Mold Road,
Wrexham, N.Wales LL11 2AW
tel: 01978 290666
e-mail: enquiries@newi.ac.uk
website: www.newi.ac.uk

**Northern School of Contemporary Dance**
address: 98 Chapeltown Road,
Leeds LS7 4BH
tel: 0113 2193000
e-mail: admissions@nscd.ac.uk
website: www.nscd.ac.uk

**Norwich School of Art and Design***
address: St Georges Street,
Norwich NR3 1BB
tel: 01603 610561
e-mail: info@nsad.ac.uk
website: www.nsad.ac.uk

**Queen Margaret University College**
address: Clerwood Terrace,
Edinburgh EH12 8TS
tel: 0131 3173247
e-mail: admissions@qmuc.ac.uk
website: www.qmuc.ac.uk

**Ravensbourne College of Design and Communication***
address: Walden Road, Chislehurst,
Kent BR7 5SN
tel: 020 82894900
e-mail: info@rave.ac.uk
website: www.rave.ac.uk

**Rose Bruford College***
address: Lamorbey Park, Burnt Oak Lane,
Sidcup, Kent DA15 9DF
tel: 020 8300 3024
e-mail: enquiries@bruford.ac.uk
website: www.bruford.ac.uk

**Royal Agricultural College***
address: Stroud Road, Cirencester,
Gloucestershire GL7 6JS
tel: 01285 652531
e-mail: admissions@royagcol.ac.uk
website: www.royagcol.ac.uk

**Royal College of Art**
address: Kensington Gore, London
SW7 2EU
tel: 020 7590 4444
e-mail: admissions@rca.ac.uk
website: www.rca.ac.uk

**Royal College of Music**
address: Prince Consort Road, London
SW7 2BS
tel: 020 7589 3643
e-mail: info@rcm.ac.uk
website: www.rcm.ac.uk

**Royal College of Nursing Institute**
address: 20 Cavendish Square, London
W1G 0RN
tel: 020 7409 3333
e-mail: rcninstitute@rcn.org.uk
website: www.rcn.org.uk

**Royal Northern College of Music**
address: 124 Oxford Road,
Manchester M13 9RD
tel: 0161 907 5200
e-mail: info@rncm.ac.uk
website: www.rncm.ac.uk

**Royal Scottish Academy of Music and Drama**
address: 100 Renfrew Street, Glasgow
G2 3DB
tel: 0141 332 8901
e-mail: registry@rsamd.ac.uk
website: www.rsamd.ac.uk

**The College of St Mark and St John***
address: Derriford Road, Plymouth,
Devon PL6 8BH
tel: 01752 636890
e-mail: admissions@marjon.ac.uk
website: www.marjon.ac.uk

**St Martin's College***
address: Bowerham Road,
Lancaster LA1 3JD
tel: 01524 384384
e-mail: admissions@ucsm.ac.uk
website: www.ucsm.ac.uk

**St Mary's College***
address: Waldegrave Road, Twickenham,
Middlesex TW1 4SX
tel: 020 8240 4156
e-mail: enquiry@smuc.ac.uk
website: www.smuc.ac.uk

**St Mary's University College**
address: 191 Falls Road,
Belfast BT12 6FE
tel: 028 9032 7678
e-mail: admissions@stmarys-belfast.ac.uk
website: stmarys-belfast.ac.uk

**Southampton Institute***
address: East Park Terrace,
Southampton, SO14 0YN
tel: 023 8031 9000
e-mail: enquiries@solent.ac.uk
website: www.solent.ac.uk

**Stranmillis University College, Belfast***
address: Stranmillis Road,
Belfast BT9 5DY
tel: 028 9038 1271
e-mail: registry@stran.ac.uk
website: www.stran.ac.uk

**Surrey Institute of Art and Design, University College***
address: Falkner Road, Farnham,
Surrey GU9 7DS
tel: 01252 722441
e-mail: registry@surrart.ac.uk
website: www.surrart.ac.uk

**Swansea Institute of Higher Education**
address: Mount Pleasant,
Swansea SA1 6ED
tel: 01792 481085
e-mail: enquiry@sihe.ac.uk
website: www.sihe.ac.uk

**Trinity and All Saints College***
address: Brownberrie Lane, Horsforth,
Leeds LS18 5HD
tel: 0113 283 7100
e-mail: admissions@tasc.ac.uk
website: www.tasc.ac.uk

**Trinity College Carmarthen**
address: College Road,
Carmarthen, W. Wales SA31 3EP
tel: 01267 676767
e-mail: registry@trinity-cn.ac.uk
website: www.trinity-cm.ac.uk

**Trinity College of Music**
address: King Charles Court,
Old Royal Naval Court, Greenwich,
London SE10 9JF
tel: 020 8305 3888
e-mail: info@tcm.ac.uk
website: www.tcm.ac.uk

**University College Chichester***
address: Bishop Otter Campus, College
Lane, Chichester, W. Sussex PO19 4PE
tel: 01243 816000
e-mail: admissions@ucc.ac.uk
website: www.ucc.ac.uk

**University College Northampton***
address: Park Campus, Boughton Green
Road, Northampton NN2 7AL
tel: 01604 735500
e-mail: marketing@northampton.ac.uk
website: www.northampton.ac.uk

**University College Worcester***
address: Henwick Grove,
Worcester WR2 6AJ
tel: 01905 855111
e-mail: admissions@worc.ac.uk
website: www.worc.ac.uk

**University of the Highlands and Islands**
address: UHI Millennium Institute,
Caledonia House, 63 Academy Street,
Inverness IV1 1BB
tel: 01463 279000
e-mail: eo@uhi.ac.uk
website: www.uhi.ac.uk

**Welsh College of Music and Drama**
address: Castle Grounds, Cathays Park,
Cardiff CF10 3ER
tel: 029 2034 2854
e-mail: admissions@wcmd.ac.uk
website: www.wcmd.ac.uk

**Wimbledon School of Art***
address: Merton Hall Road, London
SW19 3QA
tel: 020 8408 5000
e-mail: info@wimbledon.ac.uk
website: www.wimbledon.ac.uk

**Writtle College***
address: Chelmsford, Essex CM1 3RR
tel: 01245 424 2000
website: www.writtle.ac.uk

**York St John College***
address: Lord Mayor's Walk, York
YO31 7EX
tel: 01904 716598
e-mail: admissions@yorksj.ac.uk
website: www.yorksj.ac.uk

# Glosssary and Websites

## Abbreviations

**EEA**
European Economic Area

**ELB**
Education and Library Board (Northern Ireland)

**EU**
European Union

**FTE**
Full-time Equivalent

**HE**
Higher Education

**LEA**
Local Education Authority

**NHS**
National Health Service

**PI**
Performance Indicator

**SSR**
Student:Staff Ratio

**TQA**
Teaching Quality Assessment (now Subject Reviews)

**UK**
United Kingdom

For university and city websites see their individual profiles.

## General

**DELNI**
Department for Employment and Learning, Northern Ireland
www.delni.gov.uk

**DfES**
Department for Education and Skills
www.dfes.gov.uk

**HEFCE**
Higher Education Funding Council for England
www.hefce.ac.uk

**HEFCW**
Higher Education Funding Council for Wales (part of Education and Learning Wales)
www.elwa.ac.uk

**HESA**
Higher Education Statistics Agency
www.hesa.ac.uk

**Mayfield University Consultants**
www.mayfield-uc.org.uk

**NUS**
National Union of Students
www.nusonline.co.uk

**OFSTED**
Office for Standards in Education
www.ofsted.gov.uk

**QAA**
Quality Assurance Agency for Higher Education
www.qaa.ac.uk

**RAE**
Research Assessment Exercise
www.rae.ac.uk

**SCOP**
Standing Conference of Principals
www.scop.ac.uk

**SHEFC**
Scottish Higher Education Funding
Council
www.shefc.ac.uk

**UniversitiesUK**
(formerly The Committee of Vice-
Chancellors and Principals)
www.universitiesuk.ac.uk

**Open Days**
www.opendays.com

**UCAS**
Universities and Colleges Admissions Service for the UK
www.ucas.ac.uk

**Uni4me**
www.uni4me.co.uk
**UKCourseFinder.com**
www.ukcoursefinder.co.uk

**University of Wolverhampton UK Sensitive
Maps**
**Universities & HE Colleges**
www.scit.wlv.ac.uk/ukinfo/uk.map.html

## *Applying to a University/University Profiles*

**BBC**
www.bbc.co.uk/schools/aimhigher

**ECCTIS**
UK Course Discover Database
www.ecctis.co.uk

**DfES**
www.dfes.gov.uk/aimhigher

**Foundation Degrees**
www.foundationdegree.org.uk

**HERO**
Higher Education & Research Opportunities in the United Kingdom
www.hero.ac.uk

**National Bureau for students with
disabilities**
www.skill.org.uk

**NISS**
National Information Services and
Systems
www.niss.ac.uk

## *Paying Your Way*

**University of Sussex Budgeting Guide for
Students**
www.sussex.ac.uk/Units/SEO

**CDL**
Career Development Loans
www.lifelonglearning.co.uk/cdl

**DfES**
Higher Education student support
www.dfes.gov.uk/studentsupport
www.dfes.gov.uk/studentsupport/student_
disabled.cfm

**Department of Health**
Financial support for health care students
www.doh.gov.uk/hcsmain.htm

**Endsleigh Insurance Services Ltd**
www.endsleigh.co.uk

**Mobiles Online**
www.mobiles.co.uk

**NAMSS**
National Association for Managers in Student Services
Student Finance and Benefits
www.support4learning.org.uk/money

**National Express**
Student Coachcard
www.gobycoach.com/

**Rail Travel**
www.nationalrail.co.uk
www.youngpersons-railcard.co.uk

**SAAS**
Student Awards Agency for Scotland
www.student-support-saas.gov.uk

**Scottish Executive**
Enterprise and Lifelong Learning Department
www.scotland.gov.uk/who/elld/
 support_he.asp

**ScholarshipSearch UK**
www.scholarship-search.org.uk

**SLC**
Student Loans Company
www.slc.co.uk

**Student Employment Offices**
(Full list of all Institutions providing a service)
www.jiscmail.ac.uk/files/NASES/
 listing.html

**studentmobiles.com**
www.studentmobiles.com

**SummerJobs.com**
www.summerjobs.com/

**Vacation Work Publications**
www.vacationwork.co.uk

## *Gap Year*

**CSV**
Community Service Volunteers
www.csv.org.uk

**Foreign and Commonwealth Office**
Know before you go
www.fco.gov.uk/knowbeforeyougo

**GAP Activity Projects**
www.gap.org.uk

**Gap Year Company Ltd**
www.gapyear.com/

**Lonely Planet online**
www.lonelyplanet.com/

**Millennium Volunteers**
www.mvonline.gov.uk

**Project Trust**
www.projecttrust.org.uk

**Raleigh International**
www.raleigh.org.uk

**Rough Guide Travel**
www.travel.roughguides.com

**Timebank (volunteering)**
www.timebank.org.uk

**Volunteering**
www.volunteering.org.uk

**Worldwide Volunteering for Young People**
www.worldwidevolunteering.org.uk

**Year in Industry**
www.yini.org.uk

**Year Out Group**
www.yearoutgroup.org

## *Coming from Overseas*

**ARELS**
The Association of Recognised English Language Services
www.arels.org.uk

**BASELT**
The British Association of State English Language Teaching
www.baselt.org.uk

**The British Council**
www.britcoun.org

**DfES**
Department for Education and Skills
(for non-UK EU students)
www.dfes.gov.uk/studentsupport/
   students_eu.cfm

**Education UK**
www.educationuk.org

**Embassy World**
www.embassyworld.com

**English in Britain**
Database of English language courses in
the UK
www.englishinbritain.co.uk

**FCO**
Foreign & Commonwealth Office
Visa Information
http://visa.fco.gov.uk

**UKCOSA**
The Council for International Education
www.ukcosa.org.uk

**UK NARIC**
National Academic Recognition
Information Centre for the UK
www.naric.org.uk

*Studying Abroad*

**ACU**
Association of Commonwealth
Universities
www.acu.ac.uk

**The European Choice**
www.dfes.gov.uk/echoice

**ERASMUS**
EU University Student Mobility
Programme
www.europa.eu.int/comm/education/
   erasmus.html

**FCO**
Foreign and Commonwealth Office
www.fco.gov.uk

**The Fulbright Commission**
www.fulbright.co.uk

**LEONARDO DA VINCI**
EU Vocational Training Action Programme
www.europa.eu.int/comm/education/
   leonardo.html
see also
European Training in the UK
www.leonardo.org.uk

**Maps in Minutes**
www.mapsinminutes.com

**SOCRATES**
EU Schools and HE Action Programme
www.europa.eu.int/comm/education/
   socrates.html
see also
UK Socrates-Erasmus Council
www.ukc.ac.uk/ERASMUS/erasmus/
   index.html

**Worldwise**
www.brookes.ac.uk/worldwise

*Work Experience and Graduate
Employment*

**AGCAS**
The Association of Graduate Careers
Advisory Services
www.agcas.org.uk

**Graduate Careers in Ireland**
www.gradireland.com

**Prospects Graduate Careers**
www.prospects.ac.uk/student/cidd

**STEP**
Shell Technology and Enterprise
Programme
www.step.org.uk

**Teacher Training Agency**
www.canteach.gov.uk

**Worktrain**
www.worktrain.gov.uk

# Index

THE TIMES

# HIGHER

### EDUCATION SUPPLEMENT

www.thes.co.uk

MARCH 1 2002  No.1,527  £1.30

EVE ARNOLD/MAGNUM

# V-cs mount campaign t...

...ernment's 50 ... target by 2010 may be ...d unless more is done to remove ...ved financial deterrents to the poor.

UUK's submission argues that although up-front tuition fees have been scrapped in Wales and Scotland, they have been wrongly highlighted as the main problem. The report says they are "the most progressive element of the current package of student finance". It says there is a "widespread misunderstanding" among poor students who are unaware that they are exempt from tuition charges.

The Department for Education and Skills, which is leading the review, is preparing to hand its student-support blueprint to Downing Street and the Treasury for consideration.

A consultation document is due to be issued in spring and a final report with recommendations is expected later in the year.

...titutions ...ent on cen... ...ching income.

Tony Bruce, policy director at UUK, said that a number of vice-chancellors at UUK were in favour of a "rapid move" to charging top-up and differential fees. He said, however, that the organisation's commitment to maintaining up-front tuition fees was determined more by a concern to protect universities' immediate income than by an enthusiasm to pave the way for top-up fees in the future. "Our members would be concerned that this income could disappear under a transition to a graduate tax or other deferred-payment system. We would be left at the mercy of public

## Trouble and strife: what it means to be a wife  26

### Zimbabwe
Students stand up to Mugabe terror  9

### Net losses
Pricing our rape of natural resources  25

### Pitch battle
Does sport breed violence in men?  17